Issues in
Business and Society
Third Edition

Issues in Business and Society
Third Edition

William T. Greenwood
University of Georgia

Houghton Mifflin Company
Boston   Atlanta   Dallas   Geneva, Illinois
Hopewell, New Jersey   Palo Alto   London

To Gladys and Nell

Contents

Preface

The number of business and society issues has been greater in the half decade of 1970–1975 than in either the 1960s or the 1950s. The feelings and actions of aggrieved individuals and groups have also increased in intensity. These conflicts have been in evidence in the 1970s within the physical, ecological, economic, industrial, technological, social, political, legal, ethical, and philosophical contexts of business.

As noted in the two earlier editions of this book, which covered the 1950s and the 1960s, many business-society conflicts are perennial and have been discussed in business periodicals for the past seventy-five years. The major business-society issues of the first half of the 1970s are presented in this edition. The most cogent position arguments have been retained from earlier editions, and others have been added to reflect more recent developments. The student may study these in-depth arguments and apply them to contemporary circumstances affecting the issues. Practical cases related to most issues are also provided at the end of each part of the book.

In this edition roughly 65 percent of the readings are new, with new topics expanding the book from eight to ten parts. Economic growth and the fear of an economic growth rate of zero as the result of environmental limitations on society are among the new issues discussed, as is the emphasis of fair employment practices on the rights of women and minority groups seeking equal pay and managerial opportunities. The interrelated problems of inflation, unemployment, and right-to-work laws are considered. New and evolving leadership theories and styles are compared with the more traditional authoritarian and participative styles.

The conflicts between business and its environment are treated within two major categories: those related to the ecological environment and those related to the social environment. The ecological environment is identified as providing the major limitations on economic and population growth in the world today. The social environment is especially important, in that the concept of social responsibility of business appears to have been institutionalized in the 1970s.

The intensity of protests by groups seeking representation before and within business has been virtually the hallmark of the 1970s.

The public expectations of these protest groups have approached the level of revolution. This edition analyzes the extent to which such revolution should take place and discusses in particular the new consumer movement, which has led to the consideration of national consumer protection laws. Perhaps most revolutionary of all has been the issue of representation of special interest and protest groups within business, especially on corporate boards of directors. This issue is treated in detail.

In summary, business-society issues and conflicts may have reached their zenith in the mid-1970s. As the concept of social responsibility has become institutionalized, business has developed more specific policies and programs to deal with these conflicts. For example, stiffer rules for business ethics have been considered in light of the revelation of unethical behavior on the part of some American business people. During this period attempts have been made to evaluate the social responsibility of business through social audits of the corporation. The social audit provides a systematic means of measuring the level at which business is meeting its social responsibilities. A ten-part social audit is included in this edition; its component parts correlate with the ten parts of the book.

A new turning point for the social responsibility concept may also have been reached in the mid-1970s. It is now contended that social responsibility is becoming a secondary priority as a matter of corporate concern with society. As problems of energy, inflation, and unemployment press upon the economy, social responsibility must be reevaluated and balanced against other responsibilities of business to society.

A comparative analysis of the evolution of business-society issues over the past three decades is provided in this edition. Some issues and conflicts, along with the social responsibility concept as a whole, appear to have gone full circle. As the problems of business and society are intensified by the current worldwide economic and resource problems, many issues will be treated differently, at least in the immediate future. This radical turnaround calls into question even the future of capitalism as a viable economic system; the last section of the book covers this topic.

The business-society issues considered in the third edition have contemporary significance for the study of business per se, business vis-à-vis society, business ethics, and business relations with government. The book is designed to be used either as a basic text or as a supplement to other books.

I would like to acknowledge the contributions of the writers of the articles and cases presented in this book and the cooperation of the periodicals in which the articles and cases were originally published. I am grateful for the suggestions and critiques offered by the book's reviewers: Edison E. Easton, Oregon State University; Edwin W. Tucker, University of Connecticut; James Gatza, Insurance Institute of America; and Edwin Timbers, George Washington University. I also wish to recognize the research assistance of Max Ledbetter and John Conlogue in pulling together the most significant contemporary business-society issues and cases. My thanks go also to Nancy Parks for the typing of the manuscript and to the University of Georgia for its support of this research endeavor.

William T. Greenwood
University of Georgia

Part One
Issues of Free Enterprise Capitalism

The number of issues and conflicts arising between business and society has increased dramatically over the past twenty-five years, especially in the seventies. The magnitude and significance of these issues require that management be better prepared to minimize and resolve conflicts to the benefit of both business and society. To achieve such balanced solutions business people should begin with a clear understanding of the free enterprise society in which they operate, the evolutionary nature of capitalism, and the interrelationships of business and society.

A. The Evolution of Capitalism

Capitalism and freedom take on different meanings depending upon the context and environment within which they are applied. Business people tend to equate freedom with free enterprise, seeing only their right to make business decisions and not the rights of others. Capitalism — or free enterprise — is the chosen economic system in the U.S. but it is a rapidly changing one due to the dynamic pressures of the private market and increasing social controls imposed by the government. In his article "Business Philosophy" [1] Robert E. Moore traces the evolutionary stages of capitalism and the various philosophies of business. The author contends that in "this era of dynamic capitalism" business has not yet developed a clear philosophy. If business is to inhibit society's enthusiasm for the ideas of socialism, and promote the value of the private market system, business people must become more aware of the inequities that exist between business and society in order to formulate a broad and flexible philosophy that is responsive to society's needs.

B. Economic Systems Problems

The magnitude of the problems faced by our capitalistic system is clear when examined from the perspective of the present. Widespread unemployment, inflation, and recession, if not an oncoming depression, pose problems not experienced in the past thirty-five years. And now we find that these problems are intensified by their international ramifications. In the article "The World Economy: A Bad Year for the Rich Countries" [2] Lawrence Mayer describes the interdependence of national economies in his examination of the attempts of countries to resolve their individual problems.

For perhaps the first time in history, the developed or "rich" countries have been deeply affected by the recent inflation-unemployment-recession spiral started by the quadrupling of oil prices. Balance-of-payments prospects for the future appear to reverse recent trends. Deficits are predicted for Canada and the United States, with major deficits predicted for France, Japan, Italy, and Britain.

The recession, and possible depression, trend of these national economies highlights the undesirability of traditional unilateral corrective economic efforts. Any traditional action, such as restricting imports or promoting exports, will tend to better an individual nation's position only at the expense of others. Such an effect takes on more importance in view of the foreign policy goals of the free-world countries, as cited in Mayer's article. The degree of interdependence of the free-world developed economies is now of such magnitude as to make their economic programs virtually one.

Not only do the trade-offs of the inflation-unemployment problem dictate delicately balanced national economic decisions, but any international moves by the rich countries must be maintained in an even more delicate balance because of the risk of worldwide recession or depression.

The power of the free-world developed economies has been overwhelmingly reduced or offset by the Organization of Petroleum Exporting Countries. This cartel is an oligopoly of energy power with no international antitrust laws to control its activity. Unless the developed nations can negotiate effectively with the oil cartel, or other sources of energy are found soon, the present fears of a worldwide recession or depression may not be reduced.

Not only does U.S. capitalism face increased social responsibilities to make the capitalistic system successful at home, but it also faces unique international responsibilities to offset almost immediate economic distress. Apparently the greatest fear faced today by business managers throughout the world is that each country will attempt to bail itself out of its economic woes by "going it alone." Therefore the scope of our economic system and business planning is now enlarged to include the worldwide effects of short- and long-range corporate planning. This new international responsibility for the first time will reach down to the grassroots level of individual and collective decisions of American business managers.

Not only have the responsibilities of corporate decision making become international in scope, even for the smaller business organization in America, but now those responsibilities include defining the long-run effects of problems of catastrophic proportions. In the article "How to Live With Economic Growth" [3] Henry C. Wallich evaluates and responds to the challenge of the alternatives to unbridled economic and population growth. In 1972 warnings were first issued in a study entitled "The Limits to Growth" by a team of systems analysts who had developed a computer model of the world economic system for projections into the future. The findings of this study warned that unless the world community takes immediate steps to arrest the present rate of population and economic growth, resource depletion, and pollution it faces catastrophe by the end of this century. Since the projections were supported by one of the most comprehensive analyses of the interrelationship of population, resources, food, pollution, and industrial output their warnings have been taken seriously. As a result, many people have projected that zero population and economic growth may be the major alternative we face in resolving these problems in both the immediate and distant future.

Unfortunately, as is so often the case, we appear to be left with two polar alternatives — either continued unbridled growth or zero growth. Wallich contends instead that we may resolve the problem better by some intermediary approach. He warns that the alternatives of zero population and economic growth have serious costs. First, we cannot project reliable expectations of zero population growth throughout the world in spite of the fact that we appear to be approaching it in the United States by the end of this century. Since population is perhaps the most important variable in the projection Wallich suggests that it may be more advisable to consider some more flexible goal in order to adjust to the varying rates of population growth in different parts of the world. In addition, the costs of zero economic growth are overwhelmingly uncertain. Zero rates of capital return coupled with the cost of continuing high levels of unemployment, and the lack of use for accumulated savings, could cause severe and unknown risks for the free enterprise system.

Professor Wallich recommends that instead of aiming for zero economic growth we can control the long-range effects of growth with a monitoring system based on the price system in the economy. He believes that by properly assigning costs to resources that may be depleted in the predictable future, to individual products and processes that cause pollution, and to resources that are already limited, such as land in the cities, we can both slow down the harmful results of growth and monitor those results for dangerous levels.

There should be a price for polluting and that price should be assigned to the process and not the product. This will provide an economic incentive to industries to shift to nonpolluting production processes, and will also assure that the costs will be borne by those actually creating the pollution. Professor Wallich contends that the price mechanism will also apply to predictable resource shortages, providing incentives for the substitution of other resources, for recycling, and for more extensive research and exploration to replace these resources. Unfortunately, prices today do not reflect future shortages and this is a major problem we face.

In addition to the assignment of costs for resource depletion and pollution there must also be more effective governmental policies to achieve these same goals. Unfortunately, in the past many governmental policies and programs, including public utility pricing, have had the opposite effect. That is, they have contributed more toward the rapid utilization and depletion of scarce resources. New governmental resource policies providing regulations, reserves, and discouragement for use of increasingly scarce resources, plus incentives toward more extensive research and development, may make major contributions to assist the price system in providing necessary and flexible controls.

One partial exception to this problem is the scarcity of urban land. The price system cannot be completely effective because of the lack of land substitutes as a response to the price mechanism. This situation would require public policies, regulations, and incentives to encourage the movement away from the cities to areas of less population concentration.

Since the release of the findings of the study "The Limits to Growth" the response and concern of both the citizens and government of the U.S. have been notable. But Professor Wallich sees the solution of zero growth as too extreme an alternative. Therefore he emphasizes that an intermediate approach is more desirable because it would continue to give us the benefits of economic growth and the quality of life sought in America along with the necessary adjustments and controls over population, resources, and pollution. What we do know is that some significant action must be taken, and taken soon. Wallich's proposal, combining the controlling effects of the price system with governmental policies, appears to offer a mean between the two extremes of unbridled economic growth and zero economic growth.

A   The Evolution of Capitalism

1   Business Philosophy

Robert E. Moore

Business history reveals that business has been a major factor in the development of our present civilization. Business is the "core" of modern society. Consequently, business philosophy (an explanation of the phenomena of business) should logically be considered of extreme importance in the realm of ideas and thoughts which shape and guide our civilization.

The various types of business or phases of capitalism in history are conspicuous for the ideas and thoughts of businessmen that reflected necessity, but the development of a formulated system of thought or a philosophy is not always evident. On the other hand, economic thought or the economist's explanation of business has been well formulated. However, economic thought in most instances is too far removed from the realities of business to suffice as a philosophy of business or to serve as a reliable guide to the businessman in conducting his affairs. The explanation of this divergence between business and economic thought is twofold: (1) Economists have been reluctant to extend their inquiry down to the level of actual business administration. (2) As an aid to logical thinking, economists are prone to deal with just a few of the multiple considerations involved in business.

The explanation of the phenomena of business, which is a part of the society, must of necessity begin with a general understanding of the individuals who compose society. The recognition of "individual differences" is the basic concept to which we owe our present advances in the field of psychology, psychiatry, and human relations. While the individual has many things in common with his fellow men, his peculiar needs must be taken into account at all stages of growth and development. Man is extremely heterogeneous, as opposed to the popular conception of homogeneity implied in the phrase "All men are created equal."

Each individual inherently has fundamental drives or instincts, such as self-preservation, desire for power, desire for possessions, sexual gratification, and others. Society forces the individual to sublimate these inherent drives in accordance with its own mores and needs. Professor Spranger of Halle, Germany, made an analysis of the various value systems arising in individuals as a result of this sublimation. He isolated six ideal types of men: theoretic, economic, political, religious, aesthetic, and social. These types constitute an interesting attempt to describe and classify the heterogeneous composition of society.

The principal characteristics that Spranger attributed to these six ideal types can be summarized as follows:

1. *Theoretical man* lives in a realm of thought. He is devoted to systematizing his ideas. He values knowledge and truth.
2. *Economic man* aims at security through his own efforts. Material things are his interest. He values utility and efficiency.
3. *Political man* seeks power. He is interested in obtaining control over his fellow men.
4. *Religious man* is interested in the supernatural. He desires to understand ultimate reality, his position in a universe governed by a deity.
5. *Aesthetic man* is creative in an artistic sense. Beauty is his ideal.
6. *Social man* loves his fellow men. He seeks the approbation of others in serving them.

It should be recognized that only rarely do we find an individual who could be clearly confined to just one of these classifications. The six values are present to some degree in each individual. However, each person tends to accent a value in relating himself to society. These values are a part of man's environmental nature and heredity. History serves to prove that this value system of which mankind is composed is roughly enduring. There seems to be a relative constancy in percentages of our society which can be broadly categorized into each of the six classifications.

Each of the groups comprising these ideal classifications makes an essential contribution toward the civilization and society upon which business is dependent and which it in turn supports and develops. The extreme heterogeneity, exemplified in Spranger's analysis, highlights the difficulty of tying the members of each group to a common system of thought and opinion. This general acceptance of such a common system is the phenomenon which permits a society to exist; for the degree of acceptance is a measure of the completeness of the social union, and the nature of the common thought and opinion determines its kind. A unit in society which illustrates to some extent an ideal oneness of thought and opinion is the family.

Recognizing the concept of the heterogeneity of man, and that a common system of thought or opinion is necessary to complete social union, it is not hard to see that business has had and will continue to have difficulty in relating itself to a total society. Beyond this, however, the businessman has had a rather narrow philosophy which has not been adaptable to change.

Because, in general, knowledge and thought precede action, there is a close connection between the businessman's philosophy of business and actual business practices. Consequently, the historic narrowness and inflexibility of the businessman's philosophy has indirectly resulted in one system of business or capitalism which is predominant at one time giving way to another. Business history classifies these stages of capitalism as follows: Pre-Business, Petty, Mercantile, Industrial, Financial, and National Capitalism.

By exploring the philosophies of the various stages of capitalism we can see wherein they lacked the universality to provide for the heterogeneity of society. Perhaps in some measure we may relate the conclusions drawn to our present system of national capitalism where the requirement for a more complete social union is the order of the day.

Pre-Business Capitalism (before 1100 A.D.)

The long period in the development of civilization which is classified as the pre-business capitalism phase is characterized by the evolution of the cooperative collective economy. The cooperative collective economy evolved to its highest point in manorialism and feudalism during the tenth century A.D.[1] This phase in history was not barren of progress in economic activity. Regular work was developed, work was divided somewhat according to the particular skills of the individuals, and the feudal lords developed administrative and supervisory techniques to control production and consumption. Rudimentary accounting was also developed during this period. However, there was no business because the necessary elements for business were not evident: (1) The guiding plan of social activity was based on social status obtained by birth rather than by each individual's skills, efforts, and contributions. (2) Production was primarily for consumption and there was little if any

---

[1] It should be noted that there had been a considerable development of private business capitalism in Ancient Times.

production for exchange. (3) There was no philosophy of advancing or progressing in material affairs.

We should note with interest this era of pre-business capitalism and collective economies, for it is a lesson in history that has present-day applications. Mankind since its inception struggled toward a collective economy and the security it provided. After many thousands of years of existence, the high point of feudalism was reached about 1100 A.D. only to give way to a new idea of social existence introduced by the petty capitalist. Petty capitalism arose because the philosophy of feudalism was too narrow and inflexible. It lacked the universality to appeal to the heterogeneity of man and his desire for progress. There was no place in the collective economy for the economic man, the group in society which emphasizes material progress and aims at security through effort directed toward economic advancement.

Today we again see the rise of collective economies under the banner of socialism — a type of social existence that has historically been rejected by mankind in spite of its long period of trial and development.

Petty Capitalism (1100 A.D.–1300 A.D.)

Petty capitalism was the first type of private business capitalism. The petty capitalist introduced business to society. The economic man, who had largely been dormant in the collective economy of pre-business capitalism, arose to create the beginnings of a revolutionary new social order. In order to appreciate the significance of this event, we have only to compare the advances made in civilization in the last 900 years[2] to those made in the countless thousands of years during the era of pre-business capitalism.

When the petty capitalist introduced business to society, he laid the cornerstone of our present civilization. Business freed mankind from the almost completely absorbing task of providing directly for his own basic needs. By producing goods for exchange as well as consumption, non-perishable capital could be accumulated. This accumulation of work and effort in the form of capital permitted man the leisure to contemplate, plan, and specialize in those areas in which he could make the greatest contribution to society.

The direct putting-out system of capitalism was a contribution of the petty capitalist. In earlier times the usecapital system had prevailed; under this system capital was used by the owner and in no other way could it yield a return. The direct putting-out system presented a way whereby the owner of capital puts out directly to the user a certain amount of capital goods or money in return for a promise to pay interest

---

[2] The developments of Ancient Times had then largely disappeared.

or dividends. It made capital dynamic. By this device a businessman, clergyman, artist, or widow could derive sustenance by putting-out capital to work and receiving income from it. The three principal methods of getting an income from capital by direct putting-out under the system of petty capitalism can be summarized as follows: (1) investing in a business partnership; (2) loaning goods or money; (3) selling goods on credit but at a charge.

It is difficult to determine to what extent the petty capitalist, embodied in shopkeepers, storekeepers, and traveling merchants, formulated his thoughts and ideas in relation to himself, business, and society. However, by assuming a rather close connection between business thought and business practices we can reconstruct in a general way his guiding principles or philosophy.

The petty capitalist had the idea that status in the material world should be obtained through the individual's skills and efforts. This concept was in direct opposition to the feudalistic concept of status by virtue of birth. The petty capitalist was an individualist. He believed in economic independence. He avoided control by other men except on an equal basis as within gilds. He offered apprenticeships to the able and industrious. Although the apprentice's wages were probably low, he had the opportunity to learn the trade and acquire a little capital with which he could become a partner or set up a shop of his own. Thus "opportunity knocked" for all who were willing and able. The petty capitalist's public policy can be summarized as democratic economic equality.

The petty capitalist recognized that his skill in the market place was the measure of his success. In order to fully utilize this skill, he confined his efforts primarily to the local market. He restricted the variety of goods and services offered to those with which he was intimately familiar so that his skill in exchange could be more effectively concentrated. He tried to buy his wares as cheaply as possible and sell them as dearly as possible.

To appreciate the atmosphere and the environment in which the petty capitalist conducted his affairs, it is well to consider the economic philosophy of the era. The economic doctrine of the church which culminated in the canon law was probably the first formulated body of economic thought. The canonist doctrine rested on theology or Christian ethics. It laid down certain principles of right and wrong in the economic sphere, and it was the work of canonists to apply these to specific transactions and to pronounce judgment on their permissibility. The two principal doctrines were those applying to "just price" and "usury."

The doctrine of "just price" was based on the fulfillment of the law of Christ, "Whatsoever ye would that men should do unto you, do ye also unto them." St. Thomas Aquinas, who summarized the doctrine of canon law, held that everything has one "just price," or what it is worth. He held that value was something objective, something inherent in the article which was outside the will of the individual purchaser. The marked difference between this point of view and the modern idea of "market value" is that "market value" includes a subjective measurement — what each individual cares to give for an article or service.

Aquinas contended that for every article, at any particular time, there was one "just price" that should not vary with momentary supply and demand, with individual caprice, or skill in the market. Included in his idea of "just price" was the desirability of trade. The distinction between licit and illicit trade depended on the motive of the trader. The exchange price should cover the "just price" paid by the merchant for the article together with such gain as would enable him to maintain his standard of living. If the price charged by the merchant for any article allowed him to improve his position, such trade was base. Clearly it was the desire for gain that impelled the merchant to trade.

There were two principal arguments by which theologians and lawyers of the time justified the prohibition of usury. The first was Aristotle's doctrine that money itself was barren, and that therefore fruit or payment cannot justly be demanded for the use of it. The second argument was more subtle and turned on the distinction in Roman law between consumptibles, such as corn, that are consumed or spent in use; and fungibles, such as a house, that are not consumed in use. Money, it was contended, belonged to the first class. To sell a thing, and then make a charge for the use of it, was unjust. The canonist argued that, when money passed into the hands of the borrower, it should be regarded as a sale of a fungible item in which payment of the price was deferred. No payment ought to be made for the loss of time in waiting for the price, because time was God's and ought not to be sold.

Let us not criticize too strongly this canonist economic thought. It consisted of logical reasoning based entirely on ethical considerations. The true nature of business and its role in society were not recognized. Rather, let us apply the lesson learned to present-day economic theories. Many of our present-day theories suffer from the same insufficient knowledge of business as did the canonist doctrine.

The petty capitalist did not suffer unduly because of the doctrine of canon law. The ways and means by which he evaded the penalties of the ecclesiastical courts are too numerous to be outlined here. Business progressed in spite of the doctrine of "just price," which if rigidly enforced would have curtailed all trade; for under that doctrine the merchant could not lose on one commodity of which there was a supply in excess of demand and hope to remain in business by charging a higher price for another commodity. As the benefit of trade began to be appreciated by society, the enforcement of the doctrine of "just price" and "usury" became more and more lenient even though canon law in its essential form lived on well into the sixteenth century.

When the petty capitalists were forced to give way to the mercantile capitalists, it was a result of their own philosophy of business. As noted earlier, the petty capitalist believed the future of business was in selling a restricted line of goods and services primarily in the local market. Business became static. The town economy, which the petty capitalist had helped to create, could not grow. The populace was being deprived of many desirable goods and services.

The petty capitalist's public policy of democratic economic equality presupposed an almost universal equality of man which history and psychology have proved false. The petty capitalist fought against control from outside, yet such control was a key to the improvement of business and society. During the period of petty capitalism a certain amount of over-competition resulted, which the petty capitalist gilds tried to prevent; however, it took the industrial capitalists to prove the unworkability of extreme individualism in a heterogeneous society.

Mercantile Capitalism (1300 A.D.–1800 A.D.)

Mercantile capitalism replaced petty capitalism because it offered more to society than the old system had provided. The mercantile capitalist, in the form of the sedentary merchant, perceived that if business was to grow the market must be extended. Goods must be brought in from a wider area and more goods must be sold to a vastly extended market. The mercantile capitalist believed that competition should exist primarily in the foreign market. This over-all concept was *a priori* to the theory of mercantilism that gave Europe its metropolitan economy. Accordingly the sedentary merchant adapted administrative techniques, policies, and practices that would enable him to fulfill this guiding principle of extending the market.

The mercantile capitalist introduced control to capitalism for good or evil. His central policy was to remain at home in the counting-house and take on the role of an administrator. He exerted control over his agents who carried his goods to the foreign market. In order to secure control over the type and quality of his merchandise, he tried to reduce the wholesale handicraftsmen to economic subordination. Perhaps he was the first businessman to realize the disruptive influence extreme individualism could have on society. At least he recognized that further progress in business at that time was possible only through some subordination of those engaged in economic activity to a better informed central control.

The sedentary merchant had a constant problem of risk. He met this problem by diversification and integration of functions. He commonly performed such diverse functions as importing, exporting, wholesaling, retailing, transportation, storage, banking and insurance.

The height of recognition for mercantile capitalism came when the basis of public wealth was seen to be private wealth, when the chief source of all wealth was thought to be foreign trade, and when the nation was held to the same limitations of policy as the merchant. Business thought and economic thought were united. Contrast this with the present governmental economic thought which is implied in many governmental activities: "The government can do anything that business fails to do that is socially and economically desirable, and it can do it better." Perhaps the politicians who advocate fiscal suicide under the guise of a planned and stabilized economy have never heard of mercantilism, or having heard are deaf to its logic.

Mercantile capitalism as a system in business lasted about six centuries. No other system of business capitalism has flourished so long. Its philosophy had a certain universality; it became part of man's thinking. The system was far from perfect, but each ideal group of that period from the theoretic man to social man apparently somehow made a workable adjustment to the society which mercantilism and mercantile capitalism helped develop and support.

The system of mercantile capitalism gave way to specialization from within and to the Industrial Revolution from without. As the volume of trade increased, the mercantile capitalist found it increasingly difficult to control and administer his diverse functions. He began to specialize in exporting or banking, allowing other merchants who also specialized to do the importing or provide transportation. The sedentary merchant generally did not have the technical ability for developing factory production techniques that were needed with the advent of the Industrial Revolution. Mercantile capitalism under mercantilist public policy also became overburdened with regulations designed primarily to protect business and guarantee a favorable balance of trade. This over-regulation began to prevent the essential flow of goods necessary to maintain a high level of economic activity.

When the system of mercantilism which embodied the sedentary merchant's business philosophy disappeared, the sedentary merchant disappeared with it. The petty capitalist, on the other hand, is with us today, even though petty capitalism disappeared as a dominant system of business about 1300 A.D.

Industrial Capitalism (1800 A.D.–1900 A.D.)

The industrial capitalist was a specialist. He used power machinery wherever possible, he drove his employees hard, and preferred paid workers rather than agents. The tendency toward specialization, however, was the fundamental characteristic of the industrial capitalist that differentiated him from the mercantile capitalist. The system of industrial capitalism gave the petty capitalists a new chance to seek dominance in the business world. Many petty capitalists, such as blacksmiths and craftsmen, had the technical ability for factory management and became successful industrial capitalists. For this reason, it is interesting to compare the similarity in the philosophies of the petty and industrial capitalists.

The industrial capitalist's guiding principle was to reduce costs — to reduce costs, and thus to reduce prices, providing more goods for all at cheaper and cheaper prices. He believed that as more goods were available at cheaper and cheaper prices, the general standard of living would be raised.

Classical economics added to the industrial capitalist's philosophy by providing for a business freedom to supplement the growing demand for social and political freedom furthered by the French Revolution. The political leaders in England recognized that complete freedom of trade would allow them to dominate the world market because of England's obvious margin in manufacturing facilities and techniques. Thus economic or business freedom was in fact incidental to the political and social freedom advocated in the doctrine of "laissez-faire." Although economic freedom was incidental to political and social freedom, it does not follow that social and political freedom can exist without economic freedom. "Laissez-faire" became a reality only after England proclaimed the desirability of business freedom. Today we face the same issue and it is phrased "opportunity or security." Let us not be fooled into believing that a true democratic system of government can be maintained if the ownership and control of business is not primarily in private hands.

The industrial capitalists, composed partly of petty capitalists, seized on the doctrine of "laissez-faire" as being akin to the previous doctrine of democratic economic equality. Industrial capitalism, in its brief period of approximately a hundred years, was to develop some of the essential weaknesses that forced petty capitalism to give way to mercantilism (i.e., over-competition and narrowness of distribution).

At first the industrial capitalists enjoyed profitable operations because their competitors were composed largely of businessmen using the old techniques. When the system of industrial capitalism advanced to the stage where competition arose between two firms having the same technical knowledge and equipment, the severity of competition led to bankruptcy or near bankruptcy. The industrial capitalist was commonly a poor financial manager. He capitalized his plant on a narrow base and plowed back earnings into more machinery and equipment and larger operations. Consequently, when he was faced with competition or the partial loss of the market due to depressed business conditions, he was hard pressed to survive.

The philosophy of industrial capitalism like classical economics overlooked the heterogeneity of man. Economic liberalism was based on the false premise that all men are economic men, and in a free society each individual would be able to satisfy his peculiar needs through his own efforts. Industrial capitalism failed in its complete lack of universality. It provided for only one segment of our total society — economic man.

The working class was exploited in the constant efforts to reduce costs, and the consumers were neglected in the emphasis on producers' goods. It might be said that, to the industrial capitalist, producers and sellers were persons, while workers and consumers were things.

Financial Capitalism (1890 A.D.–1933 A.D.)

Financial capitalism was a system of necessity. The industrial capitalists had become the victims of their extreme specialization and ruthless competition. Many industrial capitalists realized that further competition was not the answer to their financial distress, but it took the financial capitalists to restore order to the economic chaos that had been created during the brief period of economic liberalism.

Financial capitalism was so short-lived that it did not develop a formulated system of thought. However, in the ideas and thoughts that reflected necessity one may discern an arising neo-mercantilism or business economics. The beginnings of this unformulated philosophy can be deduced from the policies and practices of the investment bankers who took over the control of business to protect the interest of the investing capitalists.

The financial capitalist substituted diversification of products and multiple economic functions for specialization. He built up reserves to mitigate or prevent the bankruptcies that formerly resulted when demand or prices fell momentarily. Cut-throat competition was replaced by a new concept of cooperative competition. The growth of trade associations exemplified the financial capitalist's idea that policing and restraint should be accomplished from within. Although these economic ideas and policies were not formulated, they are still evident in business thinking today and may form a base for a new philosophy of business with the breadth and flexibility to meet the needs of our changing society.

Financial capitalism was in a position to perform a true social service. Cooperative competition allowed for rises in prices and wages, whereas the philosophy of the industrial capitalists, with its emphasis on reduced cost, made no such provision. The system of financial capitalism had a flexibility with which a workable balance between the principal elements in our economy could have been achieved. The financial capitalist, however, did not realize he was in control of a system. He did not recognize the inherent potential of this system to correct the social inequities that had been created during the era of industrial capitalism. If financial capitalism had been allowed for a longer period of time to operate effectively, this potential might have been recognized and exploited to the benefit of all.

Financial capitalists, however, were too preoccupied with the necessity of providing for the investing capitalists to develop the needed working balance between the three interest groups: the workers, the consumers, and the investors. The cry also arose that the financial capitalists through horizontal and vertical integrations were creating monopolies to the detriment of our economy. The petty capitalist found it harder and harder to get into the field and compete with big business. Of all the systems of capitalism that have existed, none have been so widely condemned as financial capitalism. "Industrial Absolutism" and "Money Trust" became popular everyday phrases describing the system.

The financial capitalists in the United States reached their greatest heights during the merger period, 1897–1903, and the recovery period, 1923–1929, following the postwar depression of 1920–1922. When excessive speculation resulted in the crash of 1929, and the subsequent depression of the 1930's, financial capitalism was through as the dominant system of business. Labor caught on to the old and outmoded idea of business "to get the most for the least" during the late 1920's and was instrumental in bringing on national capitalism in 1933, after the complete change in political administrations.

National Capitalism (1933 A.D.–   )

National capitalism took over control of business, not on behalf of the industrial capitalists as did financial capitalism, but on behalf of labor and the petty capitalists. Ownership of business is still primarily in private hands, but the government uses its power of regulation over capital and credit to control business according to its policies. The underlying purpose of national capitalism is of a social character — to remedy the inequities created under industrial and financial capitalism.

We should recognize that national capitalism and social democracy are very likely transitional business and political systems. At the end of the road there are two unwelcome alternatives, socialism and fascism. Socialism substitutes public ownership of business for private ownership. Fascism retains private ownership but establishes a tight political control over business. Each of the two alternatives has the undesirable but inevitable consequence of sacrificing personal liberty for autocracy.

Each of the ideal groups which roughly comprise our society has been continually struggling to adjust to the various systems of business that have existed in our civilization. The most extensive adjustment was made under the system of mercantile capitalism. When adjustment was not possible under an existing system, it was replaced by a new system that promised more to certain elements in our heterogeneous society. Each diverse group has also recognized that if business could not serve their desires, they could obtain a certain measure of relief through political action. This pressure from many diverse sources has forced our government to expand its sphere of influence over business and society. The ultimate end of the constantly expanding government participation and control is socialism or fascism.

Many of the measures taken by government in the past seventeen years have been clearly labeled "socialistic," even though they have filled a need of society. Unfortunately, this indiscriminate labeling has given the theory of socialism a certain respectability which is undeserved, for these so-called socialistic measures have been largely dependent on private business capitalism for their success.

The theory and philosophy of socialism have a universality of appeal that to this date has not been matched by the theory and philosophy of private business capitalism. The principal reason for this discrepancy is that the proponents of private business capitalism have been notably inarticulate. However, socialism in practice lacks the universality to provide for a total society. Socialism fails in that it needs economic contributions to exist and ultimately uses control or force to obtain them. Men are herded together according to the existing needs of the state, and any semblance of individualism is ruthlessly submerged. The increasing number of reports received in this country concerning the slave labor camps in Eastern Europe is testimony to the reality of a socialistic state. Socialism does not allow the six ideal groups in society to make a workable adjustment. Certainly the needs and contributions of the economic man are completely overlooked, as are others as well.

Obviously no business and political system can be universal enough to provide exactly for each individual in society. For example, an aesthetic man who finds no market for his "second rate" art creations cannot continue indefinitely in this chosen line of endeavor. He must adjust and find some other way to make his essential contribution toward society while retaining art as a hobby. Private business capitalism and social democracy have the inherent flexibility to allow these adjustments to be made so that a close social union may prevail. The challenge of business today is to formulate a philosophy of business around this inherent flexibility.

The modern businessman has not formulated a businessman's philosophy of national capitalism. He is largely conducting his business today with the ideas and thoughts of earlier business systems. Some of these earlier ideas are applicable to national capitalism but many are not. For example, the old and unworkable idea of "economic liberalism" that characterized industrial capitalism is still given a place of honor in the businessman's thinking today. A hope to return to "economic liberalism" was the underlying rallying point of business in the 1948 Presidential election. It is not too soon for business to separate these old ideas into two categories and to discard all those that have no present-day applicability.

The neo-mercantile thought that is discernible in some business policies and practices today may form the base for a new philosophy that recognizes and provides for the heterogeneity of man. The philosophy of national capitalism must be structured on the idea that each individual makes his contribution toward the civilization on which business depends, and business in turn must help to create the economic and social environment in which each individual can make necessary adjustments.

The need to formulate and articulate at least the tentative principles of business in this dynamic era of national capitalism stems from two primary considerations:

1. Business should have a guide for establishing business policies and practices that are in accord with the requirements of our total society. A broad and flexible business philosophy can give direction and emphasis to the concepts of "business statesmanship" and "business responsibility."

2. Our present society does not recognize that business is the vital "core" of our civilization. Business is still regarded by many as being predatory. The economic explanation of business is incomplete and in many instances lacks reality. Unfortunately, public action in regard to business is governed largely by public opinion and economic theory. Therefore, a businessman's explanation of business or of business economics must become part of the fabric of social thinking so that a working balance between the various forces in society can be achieved.

B Economic Systems Problems

2 The World Economy: A Bad Year for the Rich Countries

Lawrence A. Mayer

In terms of real economic growth, 1973 was one of the best years on record for the industrialized nations of the world. Their economies grew by more than 6 percent overall, because production hit high levels in a good many of these nations at the same time. The year's remarkable economic growth was accompanied, however, by accelerating inflation, fast-climbing interest rates, and international monetary strains. And, of course, toward the end of the year came the damaging effects of oppressive increases in the price of crude oil.

As a result, 1974 is proving to be an exceptionally unpleasant year for the richer nations of the world. We have the problems of 1973, and others besides, without the consolations of vigorous growth. It now appears that the overall growth rate for the developed world will not even reach 2 percent this year, the lowest in sixteen years. And 1975 may not be much better.

Signs of financial distress, public as well as private, are already evident. The city of Rome has suspended interest payments on its massive debts, and the creditworthiness of the Italian national government has been questioned. With interest rates high and stock prices low throughout the world, a great many companies are finding it exceedingly expensive to raise capital — in some cases, prohibitively so.

A number of individual banks have run into trouble. They include Franklin National in the U.S. and Herstatt in Germany, as well as lesser institutions in Italy, Britain, and elsewhere. In an unusual effort to maintain confidence in the international banking system, the central bankers of major countries have let word be spread that within their

Reprinted from the August 1974 issue of *Fortune Magazine,* pp. 158–163 and 230, by special permission; © 1974 Time Inc.

own countries they will assist banks threatened by the general liquidity squeeze.

Sign of a Cloudy Outlook

Not surprisingly, the piling up of so many economic troubles has brought more than the usual number of gloomy predictions about things to come. Various voices warn of catastrophic inflation or worldwide depression ahead — and sometimes both, the one followed by the other. Even some sober and hardheaded observers find the prospects deeply disturbing. It is a sign of a very cloudy economic outlook that so acute a financier as Britain's Jim Slater has been liquidating many of the assets of his company, Slater, Walker Securities, and putting the funds into short-term paper.

The cheerful view (comparatively cheerful, that is) foresees a marked reduction in the rate of inflation later this year — and an accompanying retreat in interest rates — without deep reductions in output and employment. On this view, the great surge in inflation starting last year resulted from an extraordinary concatenation of circumstances, including the run-up of food prices after poor harvests in 1972–73, the worldwide boom that pushed up the prices of raw materials, and the radically transformed situation in oil. This line of argument implies that the inflation will be largely self-correcting as more normal conditions begin to prevail.

If self-correction doesn't come about, however, a large dose of distasteful medicine may be needed to stop inflation. The old orthodoxy dictates deflation to slow the rise in prices and put credit on a firmer footing. But that course would bring on a lot of unemployment, and cause many companies to fail. In a time marked by widespread political and social instability, governments are even more reluctant than usual to impose such severe measures.

Besides intensifying inflation around the world, the quadrupling of oil prices has created grave problems in international trade and finance. Most advanced nations will be running deficits this year on their current accounts (mainly international trade in goods and services). Primarily because of the immense increase in payments for oil imports, the combined deficit of the advanced nations may run to $40 billion.

The Beggar-My-Neighbor Peril

The immensity of that deficit reflects the fact that the oil-producing nations are not in a position to use their added oil revenues to buy an equivalent amount of goods and services from the developed countries. Most of the oil-exporting countries are too small or too underdeveloped to be customers on that kind of scale. Meanwhile, poorer countries that have no oil are having to cut back on less essential imports in order to afford fuel, food, and fertilizer.

These circumstances place severe constraints on the ability of the industrialized nations to deal with their current-account deficits. Efforts by one country to improve its individual position by pushing exports or restricting imports will serve to worsen the position of other countries. The name of this game is "beggar-my-neighbor." (That phrase, frequently used in discussions of international economic relations these days, is the name of an old card game in which you try to capture all the cards.) Playing it could lead to economic downturns that would spread from country to country.

The developed countries have agreed not to take measures that would damage their trading partners. But before that argeement was formally signed, Italy, Denmark, and France had already taken actions that their neighbors did not like. And Britain's Labor government has decided to strive for "export-led growth" — although it is not clear who will take those additional exports, especially since the volume of world trade is expected to increase only about 5 percent this year, compared to 13 percent last year.

When trade deficits are so nearly universal among advanced countries, borrowing to cover a shortfall does less damage to international commerce than do drives to expand exports. But heavy borrowing will bring its own problems. Most of the funds would have to come from the recycling of money paid to oil-exporting countries, and this process involves some special financial complications (see "Oil, Trade, and the Dollar," FORTUNE, June, 1974). Oil-rich countries have wanted to lend at very short term, while governments of oil-importing countries need to borrow at medium or long term. This disparity has caused some big international banks to turn down short-term deposits from oil-exporting countries, or to lower interest rates on them.

The oil countries are putting additional strain on the system by depositing most of their funds in the twenty or so largest banks around the world; understandably, they are seeking safety. At the same time, the loans requested by money-short countries tend to be enormous. Lenders, of course, like to diversify their risks, so they are forming consortia to get the money together. About 100 institutions participated in a $1.2-billion loan to Italy last spring (the loan brought the total borrowed abroad by Italy in the last two years to $10.5 billion). As Arab money gets concentrated in a few big banks, these banks will have fewer other lenders to call on for funds in their effort to spread the risks on very large loans.

A Road to Depression

To help Italy and other national governments increase their borrowing capacity, the Group of Ten (the major financial powers) has agreed to let nations increase the value of their gold holdings, when used as collateral for loans. The official gold price remains at $42.22 an ounce, but gold can now be offered as collateral at a "market related" — i.e., negotiated — price, perhaps $100 to $125 an ounce. Even with the higher valuation, however, few nations have enough gold to cover their oil deficits for more than a year or two.

Some economists are concerned about the cumulative effects of heavy national borrowing over a span of years. William A. P. Manser, economic adviser to a London investment bank, has reached some dramatic conclusions about the possible consequences of piling up debt to buy oil. Assuming that oil-consuming nations get the loans they need, then at the end of five years they will have borrowed something like $250 billion. Manser calculates that it would take $25 billion a year just to service these debts.

As governments become conscious of the growing burden, Manser predicts, they will curb imports, push exports, and start down the every-nation-for-it-self road that can lead to a world depression. Like the American oil consultant Walter J. Levy, Manser believes the oil-consuming nations must somehow convince the oil producers that the only way to avert worldwide economic distress is to reduce the price of crude.

The industrialized world, then, must engage in a perilous balancing act. It must try to bring down the rate of inflation, and still hold down unemployment. It must pay its oil bills, and still prevent an international trade war. How these conflicting aims can be reconciled is not at all clear — nor is it clear that the governments involved, oil rich or oil poor, fully perceive the gravity of the dangers they all face.

The Diffusion of Power

The cartel set up by the Organization of Petroleum Exporting Countries has generated a massive shift in economic power. And the sudden improvement in the fortunes of O.P.E.C.'s members has certainly had more traumatic effects on other countries than did, for example, the gradual postwar emergence of Japan as an industrial power, or the economic growth in such "third world" nations as Brazil, Iran, Taiwan, and South Korea.

Producers of other raw materials, moreover, have noted the success of O.P.E.C.'s tactics. Jamaica has lifted export taxes on bauxite enough to yield it about $200 million this year, instead of $25 million. Among exporters of phosphate for fertilizers, Morocco, the largest, has already raised the price from $14 to $63 per ton.

In addition, producers of raw materials are having to seek price increases to counter the higher cost of the oil they use. This is one reason Chile and Peru are looking for a way to lift world copper prices. Malaysia has persuaded the International Tin Council, which represents both producing and consuming nations, to raise the guaranteed floor and ceiling prices of tin. As a result of all this, the world is witnessing a remarkable diffusion of economic power.

The various attempts by producers to get more control over pricing will contribute to world inflation while they last — but some of the attempts may not succeed for long. Among other things, artificially puffed-up prices discourage demand and encourage the use of substitute materials.

Prices of some commodities have already fallen quite a bit from recent lofty heights. From the end of 1971 to the peak reached early last May, total commodity prices tripled, as measured by the *Economist*'s index. But by mid-July they had dropped 12 percent. It seems very likely that some buyers who committed themselves for commodities in excess of real needs are now trying to unload. Such a development, coupled with improved food harvests this year, would mean that the broad-based commodity boom is over — for a while, at least. And that, of course, would be a big help in the fight against inflation.

Traveling Downward

Virtually every line of business has been affected by this year's combination of slowdown and inflation. This looks like a lean year even for international tourism, which for a long time seemed to be perpetually expanding. And the $28 billion or so that tourism now generates around the world is vital to the economies of a great many countries. The number of U.S. visitors to Europe this summer is down by at least 15 percent. The countries being hit the worst are among Europe's poorest — Portugal, Spain, Greece, and Italy.

For automobile manufacturers, general inflation and high gasoline prices are making 1974 a year of recession. Sales and production are down substantially for every major carmaker in the world. Both home-market and export sales are declining from the extremely high levels of 1973. Volkswagen, expecting its first loss since World War II, is furloughing some workers, while paying others a substantial bonus to quit for good. Even the Japanese auto industry, which more than doubled its output from 1968 to 1973 to become the second-largest producer in the world, is selling fewer cars than last year both at home and abroad.

Despite the downturn in autos, the steel industry has been doing surprisingly well. Total world production may exceed last year's record of 696 million metric tons. Some of the steel not being used by automakers has been picked up by appliance manufacturers, who are using it to replace plastics in their products. (There is a general shortage of plastics, and prices of those made from petroleum are up sharply.)

Energy producers will be supplying a strong base for the steel business for some time to come. Steel is going into coal mines, pipelines, supertankers, and nuclear power plants. In particular, immense quantities will be required for the oil and gas pipelines that are being built in the North Sea.

"I'd Rather Look Back"

If governments could moderate inflation without putting economic activity into a sharp downturn, a great new boom in capital investment might ensue — the result chiefly of the demand for energy and raw materials. But that prospect lies beyond the perplexities of 1974, a year that a lot of people would like to be done with. As one prominent European economist recently observed: "I would rather not look ahead at how 1974 will turn out — I'd rather look back on it."

If 1974 is a rather grim year for the developed world in general, things are a lot worse in some countries than in others. Here is how the situation looks in leading countries outside the U.S.:

Italy's economy is fragile. During most of the 1960's its growth rate was enviably robust, but beginning with a wave of strikes in late 1969, Italy frittered away a chance to become a first-rank economy. Over the years, weak and unstable governments became a drag on economic progress. They created a class of "golden bureaucrats" — civil servants with high pensions — and allowed an enormous number of other people to feed at the public trough.

The country was especially hard hit by the higher costs of oil and other commodities, since to a large extent its economy is based on the transformation of imported raw materials into manufactured goods for export. By last spring Italy was in such a state that Guido Carli, the forceful governor of its central bank, issued a stern warning: "Today's problem is not that of the quality of life in the factory, but that of the continuing life of the factory."

In May, the country moved to curb imports of consumer goods, including the expensive beef that Italians — to the horror of some economists — had grown very fond of. Stringent limits were also put on bank credit, and the country borrowed heavily abroad to help meet its external deficit. But all of this added up to just a stopgap program. And it didn't stop the gap very effectively — for example, the French were able to keep their beef flowing into Italy by supplying credit to Italian importers.

Last month, after much internal dissension, the political parties, trade unions, and big corporations got together, more or less, on an ambitious program to put Italy on the path to solvency. Tariffs were raised sharply. Taxes were increased on luxury goods, and efforts to tighten up the inefficient tax-collection process were promised. These and other measures should serve to reduce the budget deficit and cut excess imports. Capital stashed abroad is already on its way home — a cheering bit of news. There has been some relaxation of limits on bank credit for small enterpises, both to help them survive and to maintain employment.

Bruno Brovedani, chief economist of the Banca Nazionale del Lavoro, thinks that Italy's G.N.P. will increase about 4.5 percent in real terms for the year as a whole. But he expects the new program to cool off the economy toward the end of this year and into 1975.

The labor unions are already sponsoring sporadic strikes to protest some of the tough new policies, but those policies please Italian businessmen, by and large. Says Umberto Agnelli, the managing director of Fiat: "For the short term I'm pessimistic, for the medium and long term, I'm optimistic." In spite of Italy's problems, he believes that his country has "a very great strength."

Britain began the year with a coal strike, which made it necessary to put industry on a three-day week. The new Labor government, believing that inventories were severely drawn down during the strike, expected a mini-boom while restocking took place. The budget presented in March, therefore, was designed to be nearly neutral in economic effect, and the money supply was kept under tight rein. It turned out, however, that output during the strike had exceeded expectations, and so did the amounts of inventory left in the economy when the miners went back to work. Accordingly, the automatic recovery in production has been considerably weaker than was forecast. Now economic stimulation, rather than budget neutrality, seems to be required. And in fact, last month, Chancellor of the Exchequer Denis Healey proposed a number of mildly reflationary measures, including reductions in some taxes and an increase in the rate at which companies can raise their dividends.

Output held up surprisingly well during the three-day-week episode, in large part because of an unusual degree of cooperation between labor and management. Both sides made sacrifices to keep factories in operation. The whole episode suggests that the British economy has hidden reserves of productivity that are not normally brought into play.

Wage controls have just been lifted, but price restrictions remain in effect. In place of wage controls, the Labor government is trying to promote something it calls a "social contract," which it hopes will lead unions to ask for wage increases only as large as those justified by inflation. For its part, the government has already made considerable effort to win union cooperation — it has increased old-age pensions, imposed stiffer taxes on unearned income, provided subsidies on essential foods, and canceled a rise in rents.

Business confidence has been low for some time, and isn't being helped by a Labor suggestion that trade unions be given a share in the management of companies. In 1973 there was hope of breaking out of the long years of semistagnation, and indeed, the G.N.P. grew by 5.8 percent. But 1974 threatens to be a year of skimpy — perhaps negative — growth. The longer-term outlook is clouded, in part by fears among businessmen of what the Labor party may be cooking up.

Britain's exports are doing relatively well now but not nearly well enough to offset the increased costs of oil. Consequently the country is again in difficulty on its trade balance. One promising note for the balance of payments is that a good deal of oil money has been flowing into London — partly because Britain has traditionally been a banker to Middle Eastern countries.

France is making a fresh attack on some long-standing problems under the leadership of its new President, Valery Giscard d'Estaing. An economic expert, Giscard aims to give French workers a better deal; up to now, they have benefited less from national economic growth than workers in most of the other West European countries. Giscard has raised pensions, minimum wages, and family allowances. He is seeking guarantees of a year's pay for workers who lose jobs because of economic conditions.

The government plans to raise income taxes, principally of corporations and high-income individuals. Taxes on fuels also are going up. Consumer spending is being discouraged by tighter credit, and interest rates on savings accounts have been raised. Controls will be imposed on the use of heating oil.

All of these measures are intended to keep the budget in trim, while cutting France's bill for imported oil and freeing more goods for export. Meanwhile, an existing ceiling on increases in total bank credit is being more strictly enforced, and the central bank's discount rate has been pushed to 13 percent, the highest in the industrialized world. Giscard is trying to get the French inflation rate — now about 13 percent — down to 7 percent in 1975.

Another of Giscard's important moves involves a big deal with Iran. In the next decade, France is to help that country with a lot of advanced-technology projects, including nuclear power plants and a subway system for Teheran. This deal, valued at $4 billion, will partially offset France's oil bill. But the transaction blocks other countries from the possibility of meeting *their* oil deficits by selling to Iran. And in going to grand-scale barter, France is turning the economic clock back. Says one French economist: "For three centuries the path of progress has been to get away from barter to the use of money as an intermediary. Bartering is characteristic of the propensity of states to interfere in trade."

West Germany remains the strongest economy in Europe. With the Continent's stiffest monetary and fiscal policies, it has held the inflation rate to about 7 percent — even though wage increases have been running to 12 and even 14 percent. As a consequence, profit margins have been squeezed.

Restrictive governmental policies slowed the growth rate in the first half of the year, and growth for the year as a whole may be no more than 2.5 percent. Unemployment is rising, largely because industries such as autos, construction, and textiles are having a poor year, and the government — astonishingly for inflation-shy Germany — is contemplating a tax cut for 1975 as a tonic for the economy.

The big export industries — steel and machinery especially — continue to do amazingly well despite the revaluations of the mark. The conventional explanation for this sturdy performance cites the quality, reliability, and quick delivery of German goods. But Britain's three-day workweek earlier this year helped by bringing a switch of orders to West German manufacturers.

West Germany exports so much of its production that a good deal of the benefits from its gains in G.N.P. go abroad. Otto von Fieandt of the Paris-based firm of economic consultants, Eurofinance, calculates that the increase in the standard of living of West Germans last year lagged about 2 percentage points behind the increase in total G.N.P.

West Germany holds two important cards in the world oil game. First, its total exports exceed imports by a large margin, even counting in oil. This makes Germany a large potential lender to oil-deficit countries. The other card is an abundance of coal. Until recently a good many mines were uneconomic, but the new high price of oil has improved the artihmetic of coal.

Getting coal production to much higher levels will require large investments, however, and so will the development of coal-gasification technology. Germany produced gasoline out of coal in World War II, but the process is relatively expensive — gasoline from coal costs more than gasoline from crude oil, even today. Exactly how West Germany exploits its coal reserves will depend to a considerable degree on what energy-sharing policies emerge in the European Community — and what happens to oil prices.

Canada "is incredibly lucky," says Fred H. McNeil, president of the Bank of Montreal. "We are almost alone in the Western world in having no balance-of-payments problems due to oil. We have the things the world wants, and prices favor us — wood products, minerals, agricultural products. We have a virtually complete base in energy resources and materials for significant advance in manufacture . . . This is our time." A great many Canadians speak of their country's prospects in such expansive terms these days.

Last year Canada's real growth came to 7.1 percent, the best in seventeen years. The growth was spurred by an increased inclination of businessmen to export, as well as by some special tax concessions. Economic policies were less restrictive than in most other nations, because unemployment was relatively high, and the government was convinced that inflation in Canada is largely international in origin and therefore cannot be effectively dealt with by domestic restraints.

This year Canada will wind up with real growth of about 5 percent — one of the few major countries with a strong advance. Capital investment is again playing a big role, with increases of 13 percent in real spending on equipment and nearly 10 percent in nonresidential construction. Consumer durables and housing, which powered the Canadian economy for some years, are providing somewhat less impetus.

Prime Minister Pierre Elliott Trudeau's electoral victory gives him an opportunity to develop new policies toward the perennially sensitive subject of foreign capital. Nationalism is on the rise, but Canada plans to undertake extensive energy projects — and capital to help carry them out will certainly have to come from abroad. The major ventures are natural-gas pipelines, a huge hydroelectric project at James Bay, and development of Arctic gas fields. It will also take a lot of capital to exploit the Athabascan tar sands, which are estimated to contain 300 billion to 400 billion barrels of recoverable oil — nearly equivalent to the present petroleum reserves of all O.P.E.C. members.

Japan will not soon again attain the 10 percent rate of economic growth that it averaged over the past twenty years. Of all the major nations, Japan is the most dependent on imported oil. Accordingly, it has felt the impact of fuel prices sharply. Higher prices of other raw materials have also hurt. For these and other reasons, Japan's planners have reduced their goal for long-term growth to 6 or 7 percent. The short-term prospects are for quite modest growth: 2.5 percent or less for all of 1974, even with the pickup that is expected in the latter part of the year.

Prices have been going up faster in Japan than in other advanced nations. Wholesale prices of manufactured goods are up about 33 percent over a year ago, and consumer prices about 25 percent. One reason for the present rapid pace of inflation is that many Japanese workers won a basic wage increase of 32 percent last spring. While worker productivity has been doing remarkably well, it is not nearly high enough to offset wage increases of that magnitude, especially with industry not running at top speed.

Several industries have been hit hard by shortages and high prices — autos, textiles, appliances, and construction. Steeply climbing interest rates aren't helping. The discount rate has reached 9 percent, the highest by far in the modern history of Japan. Despite financial aid from the government, small businesses have been failing this year at a rate of about 800 a month. The industries doing best are those in which supply is short all over the world — steel, shipbuilding, petrochemicals, machinery, and paper.

Japanese exports continue to rise, but imports have been rising more — partly because of the large oil bills and the appreciation of the yen against other currencies. As a result, Japan's balance of payments has gone into deficit. The country has been losing reserves, and in the last few months the exchange rate of the yen has been edging down.

Despite Japan's economic troubles, labor is still in short supply, so people who are laid off can easily find jobs. Workers seem to be saving more, rather than spending all of their increased income. In short, the Japanese economic performance may now seem less miraculous than it once did, but there is still a lot of life in it.

3   How to Live with Economic Growth

Henry C. Wallich

The recent warnings about the risks of growth present a troubling dilemma. Are the risks so grave that we must stop growing in the near future? Should we ignore the risks, on the assumption that the ecologists have vastly exaggerated them? Given the stakes, the choice looks awesome. Fortunately, there is a way of avoiding the need to make the choice.

The prospects of running out of food, living space, or raw materials, of suffocating or collapsing by one computerized sequence or another, can be debated till doomsday, whenever that may be. Rather than accept an answer that may be wrong or inconclusive, we can guard against the harmful effects of economic growth by installing appropriate safety devices. If the critics of growth are right in thinking that ultimate

Reprinted from the October 1972 issue of *Fortune Magazine,* pp. 114–116 and 121–122, by special permission; © 1972 Time Inc.

limits are only a few generations away (to me this seems unlikely), these safety devices would slow the economic system in the near future and bring it to a halt in good time. If the critics are wrong, the devices will not impede growth, but will monitor the economy for adverse effects of growth.

The safety devices I have in mind take the form of an extended version of the price system. The price system can be made to function as an automatic pilot, or sensor for an emergency brake, that will stop growth when the costs become too high.

The Road to a Standstill

An enterprise grows so long as it can produce goods for less than it sells them for. It will have a positive return on capital and will continue to invest in plant and equipment. If costs rise to the point where expansion does not pay, the return on capital vanishes, investment stops, and the enterprise ceases to grow.

By generalizing this simple case, economists many years ago arrived at a model of the "stationary state." This is the economy that has ceased to grow, where the processes of production and consumption repeat themselves year after year without significant change. The stationary state is not the implausible construct of some lonely imagination. It is the logical end product of a process in which enterprises keep endowing each worker with a greater and greater volume of tools. The law of diminishing returns then sees to it that investment earnings gradually decline. When returns to capital have come to an end, a state of zero growth begins.

Who Pays for Degradation?

The faster costs increase, the faster returns on capital diminish. If an enterprise has to invest heavily in pollution-abating equipment, if it has to pay more for increasingly scarce raw materials and increasingly costly land, the point of zero return approaches rapidly. But if research and development succeed in pushing that point into the future, growth continues.

If, therefore, we are concerned about the dangers of growth, we should let these dangers find full expression in costs. This is the principle of internalizing the "externalities" — the pollution and other costs of growth that are now borne by the community. Degradation of air, water, or land rests lightly upon the company that does not have to pay for it. It rests lightly, too, upon the consumer of the company's products if he is not charged for the environmental costs.

Concern over such externalities has increased as the environment's capacity to diffuse them has diminished. Critics of the free-enterprise system have found externalities a welcome addition to their repertory of proofs that the market system is defective. They are right in demanding that these costs be taken into account in deciding what should be produced, and in what ways. But their indictment of the price system backfires, because further examination reveals that the best way of internalizing environmental costs is precisely to apply the price system.

The simple-minded reaction to the affront of pollution is to prohibit it. No need then to bother with internalizing environmental costs. The difficulty with this approach is that it sets up all the wrong motivations and is inefficient to boot. Confronted with edicts and regulations, polluters have every reason to prove that they cannot help what they are doing. Different polluters find that their costs of abatement differ unfairly and uneconomically. Perfection, moreover, is inordinately expensive. I doubt very much that many people would be willing to pay what it would cost to restore the waters around Manhattan to the condition in which Henry Hudson found them.

Licenses to Pollute

The price system sets up the right motivations. Let people pollute, but let them pay for it. Environmentalists' indignation about "licenses to pollute" is misplaced. The price of a license can be set at any level, and it can be set high enough to achieve any standard of cleanliness that is wanted. Given the cost, the polluter then has a full range of choices — pollute and pay, stop polluting by stopping production, invest in antipollution equipment, change his production process, his product, his location. Each polluter, in other words, can work out his own optimum response, depending on his circumstances. This freedom to optimize makes for equity and efficiency.

Setting the right level of tax or fee will present some difficulties, to be sure. For one thing, the response of the polluters to any particular level cannot be predicted with certainty. To the economist, the logical approach would be to set the permissible level of emissions, discharges, and other damage, and then auction off licenses to pollute to the highest bidders. Those who find pollution the cheapest of all available alternatives will pay what it takes to get the licenses they need. The rest will reform in some manner. But setting fixed prices on pollution, through a trial-and-error process, will accomplish the same results in time.

If the level of pollution is to be kept constant, standards of cleanliness will have to rise as the economy grows. The process of cleaning up is an unending race between the number of sources of pollution and the reduction in pollution per source. Since costs accelerate as 100 percent purity is approached, the outcome of this race has much to do with how far growth can go.

Business spokesmen often argue that subsidies of some sort, such as tax credits or easy financing for antipollution equipment, would be a more promising approach than taxation, And according to a respectable theorem of economics, a tax and a subsidy, both designed to encourage cutbacks of production that pollutes, will have equivalent effects on the level of output. (To the polluter who does not cut back, the loss of the subsidy is the same as a tax.) But in the long run the effects are not the same: a tax tends to drive companies out of the industry, a subsidy tends to attract them.

Subsidies of particular forms of pollution control, moreover, tend to restrict the scope of the polluters' search for alternative solutions. A tax credit for antipollution equipment, for instance, does nothing to encourage shifts to nonpolluting processes. Nor does it offer an incentive to keep the equipment operating once it has been installed. Since the costs of operation often are considerable, the results of a subsidy system might disappoint its advocates. On the other hand, tax credits for general R. and D. would not interfere with flexibility of business response.

Changing the Output Menu

For the sake of both fairness and efficiency, it is important to tax the pollution and not the product. This is the answer to the demand that the government intervene on a grand scale to revise the output menu. In the view of those who favor such intervention, one way to defuse the dangers of growth is to shift toward forms of output that throw off less pollution and make fewer demands on natural resources. From this viewpoint, big artifacts are worse than small. Fashion products are worse than indestructibles. Advertising that increases consumer demands is bad altogether. Work generating income and output is worse than leisure.

Such conclusions involve vast oversimplification. Big cars can be made to pollute less than small (and to be safer). Big objects made of plastic may require less use of scarce resources than smaller objects made of metal. Advertising may promote environmentally sound goods and services. Built-in obsolescence may encourage innovation.

Taxing pollution rather than products allows freedom for all this. In a very broad sense, however, pollution taxes will tend to shift the structure of output toward its low-pollution components.

Any method of internalizing external costs will require some intervention by the political process. Decisions have to be made about admissible levels of pollution and of resource use. The minority that is outvoted by the majority must accept something it does not want — for example, cars that are more expensive, or less efficienct, than the market would have produced if left to its own devices. The sweet free-market simplicity of voting with dollars will have been adulterated. But the environmental imperative will have been dealt with at the least possible cost.

The political process can serve to backstop internalization in still another way. To make people pay for the damage they do is the efficient way, but it is also sophisticated, and it will not always have adequate political support. To rally that support, some measure of direct intervention, through regulations, controls, and prohibitions, will probably be needed. These techniques, moreover, may have marginal advantages in cases where fine tuning of the constraints on pollution is called for. Pollution taxes should cut evenly across the board, the fewer exemptions the better, but evenness may entail some unfairness in special circumstances. Detailed regulation can provide relief from special-case hardship.

Virtues in Higher Prices

The reason we have only recently become aware of the need to internalize environmental damage is that until recently it was not necessary to regard air, water, and waste-disposal sites as scarce resources. Their use, or misuse, did not have to be paid for, and therefore did not enter into business cost calculations. On the other hand, scarce natural resources such as raw materials and fuels have always been internal to business cost calculations. Accordingly, one is tempted to assume that the price system can and will take care of the danger of "running out of natural resources," which plays such a prominent part in doomsday theology.

To deal with resource shortages, the price system can activate an impressive array of mechanisms. When some resource becomes more and more scarce, say copper ore, its price rises and the system responds. The working of lower-grade ores now becomes economically feasible. Seach for new ore bodies becomes profitable. So does recycling, as well as substitution of other metals, and the application of research to all these techniques. Where none of these alternatives avails, products containing copper will become more expensive and demand for them will decrease.

How well these processes work depends in large measure on how well the supply and the demand respond to price. It depends also on what economists call the elasticity of substitution — i.e., the extent to which a relative increase in the price of copper turns users to substitutes.

In a long view, the working of the adjustment processes also depends on how far the price system is able to look ahead. The threat of a coming shortage of a metal or mineral should be reflected in its price. The increase in price would activate response mechanisms and give them the long lead they sometimes need.

We know, of course, that the prices of most natural resources today do not reflect expectations of future shortages. The historical evidence, indeed, tells us that the cost of most natural resources has been declining in terms of the capital and labor required to make them available. Past predictions of shortages and steep price increases have so far proved erroneous. Numerous studies of future resource needs and availabilities envision no general shortages for the next fifty years.

It is unsurprising, therefore, that prices of raw materials today do not reflect future shortages. Nevertheless, we cannot be sure whether, given the prospect of shortages at some future time, the price system would in fact respond with sufficient foresight.

The Low Value of the Future

Various factors besides human fallibility suggest that it might not. To invest today in resources to be marketed many years later is a risky business. New technologies, new discoveries, shifts in demand may upset the estimates. A corporation holding potential output off the market in expectation of higher prices in the distant future would be exposed to risks of adverse taxation, expropriation, and other acts of God and man. Discounted at high interest rates, in any event, the present value of the future is not very high. All this offers a presumption, at least, that the price system may be slow in responding to threatened resource scarcities in the future.

This presumption may not be strong enough to call for large-scale government action to conserve resources across the board. A "raw-materials tax," such as that recently proposed by some British environmentalists, would be an assault on the economies of the developing countries, with minimal justification in the existing supply situation. But if the visible picture should change, a resource tax might serve to strengthen the price system for its job of conserving resources. It would contribute to internalizing the resource-depletion cost of growth, just as pollution taxes internalize the pollution cost.

For the time being, all that seems needed is to put an end to some government policies that are positively hostile to good resource management. The political bias is usually on the side of lower resource prices. In the field of public-utility regulation, this bias has been broadly appropriate because government action has been directed toward preventing the exploitation of monopoly. Cost is the proper basis for public control of utility rates. But government commits an elementary error when — as in the case of natural-gas regulation — it applies cost reasoning to a price that really reflects scarcity rather than monopoly. The natural-gas shortage is now demonstrating the consequences of not allowing the price system to do its job. And the recent decision of the Federal Power Commission to permit a little slack in the regulatory leash may be a sign of incipient wisdom.

The oil-depletion allowance, like capital-gains treatment for timber and certain minerals, occupies an ambiguous spot in the resource-conservation picture. If one anticipates a future shortage, it makes good sense to encourage the search for oil. But it does not make good sense to encourage heavy use of oil. What seems called for is a policy that encourages creation of reserves while discouraging use. Heavy current use seems appropriate only if one expects new sources of power to make oil obsolete before most of it is out of the ground, a fate more likely to befall coal than oil.

Examples of bad resource policy abound. The government encourages possible overuse by the way in which it sells or leases mineral rights. It discourages recycling of materials by maintaining special low freight rates for lumber and minerals. Its stockpile program, national security aspects aside, tends to reflect the needs of the moment more than those of the long-run future.

A constructive public policy toward R. and D., public and private, would be part of good resource management. In the field of natural resources even more than in the field of pollution, research is needed to aid the price system in promoting the right kinds of adjustments and substitutions. A well-meaning government will be subject to temptation to support research only in particular fields and for particular purposes. Given the unpredictable nature of much research, and the tendency for findings in widely different areas to interact, this temptation should be resisted.

Crowded Cities, Empty Spaces

The economics and politics of land represent a special aspect of the natural-resource problem. Land is broadly fixed in supply, assuming we do not plan to go underground or build a second floor over the U.S. Here again, the price system does not offer complete assurance of being able to take care of the situation.

As people move into an urban area, real-estate prices and rents go up. Those who do not want to pay the prices can move elsewhere. So can those who feel asphyxiated by the congestion. But there is something unsatisfactory about a system that imposes added costs upon a large number of people to satisfy the preference of one individual — in this case, a preference for city life, or for the higher pay available in cities. In most other market situations where the added demand of one person raises the price to all, the higher price calls forth a larger supply. In the case of city land, however, the supply does not increase as rents rise.

A good deal of evidence has accumulated that the price system, if not intrinsically inappropriate, is at least substantially inefficient in dealing with regional crowding. It appears that population movement responds to rising rents and rising congestion only with very long time lags. To some extent these costs of urban living are offset by higher pay. Discrimination, moreover, keeps some blacks who would like to move out of cities from doing so. Accordingly, a public policy with respect to urban crowding seems to be called for. It should involve nothing so repugnant as constraint on the freedom of people to move where they like. But the tax system, the credit system, and farm price supports could well be organized more effectively to induce larger numbers of people to live in the great empty spaces of this country.

Activating the Brakes

The measures I have proposed in the areas of environmental protection, natural-resource management, and land use will not produce an appreciable slowing in the rate of economic growth so long as the costs of growth remain moderate. But I could be wrong in believing that the costs of growth will not increase rapidly in years ahead. If pollution becomes very hard to control, if resources do run out and substitutes cannot be found, if the problems of congestion prove resistant to limited interventions, costs could climb to prohibitive levels. If they were internalized, high costs would activate the brakes that the price system builds into the economy. Investment would decline as its returns diminish. Growth would slow down and perhaps eventually come to a halt.

The declining rate of return would reduce the income of owners of capital. The distribution of income would become much more even. This is an important part of the slowing-down process. Without growth, it would be much more difficult for democratic societies to justify large inequalities of income. Opposition to inequality would no longer be moderated by the general upward movement of incomes, and the high degree of social mobility that growth makes possible.

Because the supply is fixed, ownership of land would present an exception to the rule of declining returns on capital. Rents would rise, and the value of land would rise enormously as interest rates fell. Public policy, through appropriate taxation, would have to extend the evening-up process to land ownership.

A growthless state, in the unlikely event it were reached, would leave many problems unsolved. We do not know how a society like ours would take to it. At present, Americans are not satisfied with the results of the stably rising prosperity over the last twenty-five years, as inflationary wage demands attest. How will people behave when their standards of consumption no longer increase? We do not know how the economy will function at a zero return on capital. Full employment can be maintained only if the government uses, for nongrowth expenditures, such savings as people still want to set aside — savings for which there will be little demand, since borrowed capital will provide no return. An economy based on free markets still seems possible, but the fate of private enterprise becomes obscure.

Any commentary on zero economic growth should add that attainment of a stationary state by the U.S. economy would not do much to solve the growth problems in the rest of the world. Growth-slowing processes will be at work elsewhere, of course, and ultimately there may be a worldwide cessation of economic growth; but that presupposes, above all, an end to population growth. While low birth-rate patterns already prevail in the industrial countries, the less developed countries have further to go in their population cycle. There are reasons to believe that they may complete the evolution to very low birth rates faster than the industrial countries did, but there is no assurance that this will prove to be so. For people concerned about the long-range consequences of continued growth, the core of the problem surely is the expanding population of the less developed countries.

As for the U.S., it has in a sense already completed the evolution to zero population growth. Births still exceed deaths, but this is a detail that reflects the age structure of the population. The total fertility rate has now fallen below the critical replacement level of 2.11 children per woman, which would bring about zero population growth in the first half of the next century.

Defeatist "Realism"

Anyone aware of the stir created by the zero-population-growth movement in the last few years might suppose that the virtual attainment of Z.P.G. in the U.S. would bring solutions to serious environmental problems within view. Unfortunately, this is not the case. Z.P.G. is not in itself an effective remedy for environmental problems. It does not end crowding, because a constant number of people can still dispose themselves in congested patterns. It does not help much with pollution or resource exhaustion, because the per capita income of a stationary population grows faster than that of an expanding population.

As must be abundantly clear by now, I am not an enthusiast for zero economic growth either. In a finite world, to be sure, growth cannot continue indefinitely. But advocates of zero economic growth would guard against the risks and penalties of growth by prematurely denying society the benefits of growth. At this chapter in the human story, it makes much more sense to accept the benefits but adopt protective measures. If they work properly, undesirable effects of growth will induce feedback that slows or halts the particular kinds of growth producing those effects.

This approach to the monitoring and control of growth, moreover, will tend to improve the allocation of resources and protect the environment, whether growth is affected or not. When factories have to pay for polluting waterways, they will do less polluting. Those who tell us that if we want growth we have to put up with its stinks, noises, eyesores, and poisons are sometimes credited with realism, but their attitude might better be called defeatist. There is no inherent reason why rising standards of consumption must be accompanied by declining quality of life.

Bibliography

Beckerman, W. "Case for Economic Growth." *Public Utility,* September 26, 1974, pp. 37–41.

Benoit, E. "Must Growth Stop?" *Columbia Journal of World Business,* May 1972, pp. 41–44.

Blau, J. "True Meaning of Capitalism." *Commercial and Financial Chronicle,* September 2, 1974, p. 4.

Freeman, O. L. "Demands of a Changing World." *Columbia Journal of World Business,* 9 (Summer 1974), 108–112.

Grayson, C. J., Jr. "Let's Get Back to the Competitive Market System." *Harvard Business Review,* 51 (November 1973), 103–112.

Leontief, W. "Structure of the World Economy: Outline of a Simple Input-Output Formulation." *American Economic Review,* December 1974, pp. 823–834.

_____."MIT Report: Is Doomsday Really That Close" (Study Sponsored by Club of Rome). *Business Week,* March 11, 1972, pp. 97–98.

Myers, J. G. "Energy Conservation and Economic Growth. *Conference Board Record,* 12 (February 1975), 27–32.

Schmidt, H. "Free Enterprise and the Public Interest." *Conference Board Record,* 10 (November, 1973), 30–32.

_____."World Economy: Special Report." *Business Week,* July 6, 1974, pp. 65–86ff.

_____."Worldwide Threat of Financial Instability." *Business Week,* December 21, 1974, pp. 54–55.

Part Two
Business, Government, and Society

A. Business Power and Antitrust

The debate between business and government has been significant among the changing issues between business and society. Rapid technological and demographic growth over the last fifty years have created economic problems requiring the attention of business and government alike. The problem of business growth and power has been dealt with for the past century by the Sherman Antitrust Act of 1890. Now, almost 100 years after the law was passed we find a contemporary movement of growing political pressure to toughen its enforcement and to break up large-scale corporations, as described in "Is John Sherman's Antitrust Obsolete?" [4]. Giant American corporations seem perennially unable to grow in a free competitive economy without creating and using size to influence the market. In defining their increasing size, these corporations argue the need for economies of scale for successful international competition, and the maintenance of a positive balance of payments for the economy. But this article reports that once again little empirical evidence supports their claims. So the controversy continues.

Today's major appeals for antitrust efforts are for new legislation and investigation with bigger budgets to implement these goals. The article considers alternatives of abolishing present laws, clarifying them, or replacing them with direct regulation and toughened enforcement. While there are some appeals for a new and more comprehensive approach to the problem, such as an Office of Antimonopoly Affairs or a Federal Competition Agency, it appears the most realistic alternative may be the strong and consistent enforcement of present legislation. The situation with antitrust is similar to other problems confronting business and government. The proposals for solutions range between two extremes, laissez faire corporate growth versus government regulations or strict legislative enforcement.

A more moderate solution to the conflicts between corporate freedom and the public interest is cited in "A Changing Balance of Power: New Partnership of Government and Business" [5]. The article quotes business leaders who recommend that a voluntary partnership of business with government and labor will serve to reconcile and coordinate the interests of the public and the interests of the company. The article predicts that a new relationship is developing between business and government that will strike a balance between the extremes of centralized government control and corporate irresponsibility.

Illustrations of the need for the voluntary reconciliation of the conflicts between business, society, and government are offered in two cases. In the U.S. Steel and the 1962 Price Increase case, we see a unique example of presidential influence and intervention into industry practices. When union requests for noninflationary wage-price guidelines were achieved through the participation of the federal government in discussions with the steel industry and labor, labor and government expected that business would not raise the price of steel. When business did not voluntarily comply with the terms of the negotiations President John Kennedy brought extraordinary pressure to bear upon the steel industry. The relationship of public interest to concomitant social responsibilities is further illustrated in the Prairie Eye-Opener case wherein a relatively small newspaper is confronted with demands for greater responsibility in its identification of advertising, and its affiliation with, and influence over, other communication media in the area.

In general, we are forced to conclude that managers must assume social responsibilities commensurate with the degree of power and influence they are capable of wielding, whether at the national, state, or local level. If managers do not assume this responsibility and if they misuse this power and influence, whether intentionally or unintentionally, we know from the lessons of history that society, through government, will seek redress through some type of intervention or regulation. If business is to maximize its freedom for decision making now and in the future, it must assume effective, socially responsible activities, especially in those areas where its influence and power may be felt.

B. Profits and Profit Sharing

Classical economic theory has emphasized profit maximization as the primary — if not exclusive — goal of business in the U.S. free enterprise system. Competition was understood by society to be a means of providing the optimal allocation of scarce resources in the production of goods and services; and profit was regarded as a reward for efficient risk taking by investors through management. Today, we find opposing theories that substitute "reasonable" and "satisfactory" for "maximum" when profit maximization is deemed inconsistent with the welfare and interest of society. However, in "What Is Wrong with Profit Maximization?" [6] Charles F. Phillips, Jr. argues that profit maximization is consistent with and essential to society's well-being. Without maximum profits, management cannot achieve efficient utilization of resources to insure a greater variety of goods of high quality and at lower cost to the consumer, with high returns to investors, management, and labor. For these reasons, Phillips voices the warning that social responsibility must not be a substitute for profit maximization, but that both goals may be achieved in the long run. He argues, "Only by performing the economic function well is a business firm socially responsible."

The voluntary sharing of profits by business as incentives to the work force has had a highly variable record of success. The question of sharing profits as a right of labor and the customer gives rise to the philosophical question of the source and extent of these rights. Traditionally, profits are the rewards for efficient risk taking. Therefore, any rightful claim to them should be related to the respective types and degrees of risks assumed. If profit rights are lost to any degree at the bargaining table, business can blame itself for not developing a thorough analysis of, and philosophical framework for, the nature of profits. In "The Ethics of Profit Sharing" [7] Benjamin L. Massee tells us that business and society have reduced significantly the risks taken by the individual employee by offering him or her a fixed wage with a relatively high degree of job security and a great variety of unemployment and fringe benefits. As a result, the risk taken by the employee seems to be much less than that taken by the investor. However, the question of whether or not profit sharing can become a right of labor will eventually be decided by the National Labor Relations Board as it adapts its decisions to what can and cannot be included under the items of wages, hours, and working conditions. The significant point is that in the future, if the risks are found to be high for the worker, the NLRB may make profits subject to collective bargaining. Presently, profits are shared at the discretion of management.

The three concepts of freedom, capitalism, and society have taken on new meanings and emphases. Freedom is not absolute, either for those involved in business or any other individual or group in a democratic society. Contrary to the view held by particular groups, the determination of the operative limits of freedom are influenced by our total society rather than by any particular interest group. Capitalism is not a static system but one that has gone through and will continue to go through evolutionary changes. The causes of these changes and the role of business will be of paramount significance now and in the future. The concepts of business and society require analysis in depth and in breadth. To be complete this analysis must identify the roles of the federal, state, and local governments, and particular interest and power groups in our democratic society, as well as the basic prerogatives of the individual.

Our free enterprise society is no longer a topic for debate reserved to legislative halls and academic classrooms. It is of direct concern to the individual business firm, regardless of size or location, and to its managers. The articles and cases presented in Part Two emphasize the new meanings and dimensions of each of these concepts and their interrelationships. They also raise questions business people must face concerning their firms, their freedom, and their profits in a democratically determined society.

A   Business Power and Antitrust

4   Is John Sherman's Antitrust Obsolete?

Business Week

The head of the major U.S. corporation spoke feelingly: "I would be very glad if we knew exactly where we stand, if we could be free from danger, trouble, and criticism." His plea could have been made yesterday, by executives at IBM, Xerox, GTE, General Motors, AT&T, Exxon, Standard Brands, Chrysler, or dozens of other large companies that have recently stood in the dock, accused of violating the nation's antitrust laws.

It was, in fact, said back in 1912 by Elbert H. Gary, chairman of U.S. Steel Corp. He was giving a Congressional committee his views on the need for updating the country's first antitrust law, the Sherman Act, to which Ohio Senator John Sherman gave his name in 1890. Echoing the sentiments of many executives, Gary complained bitterly of the restraints imposed by the antitrust law on his company's ability to compete in world markets. Business had grown too big and complex, Gary maintained, to be shoehorned into laws drawn from Adam Smith's economic model of many small companies competing in local markets.

Two years later Congress gave Gary an unwelcome answer to his plea. It passed an even more restrictive antitrust measure, the Clayton Act, and set up the Federal Trade Commission to police business practices and methods of competition even more closely.

Today business faces much the same danger, trouble, and criticism that disturbed Gary, and is raising much the same complaints against antitrust. The International Telephone & Telegraph Corp.

Reprinted from the March 23, 1974 issue of *Business Week*, pp. 47–56, by special permission. Copyright © 1974 by McGraw-Hill, Inc.

scandal and corporate participation in Watergate has stirred up deep public distrust of national institutions, including business. In response, as in Gary's day, the antitrust wind is rising, blown up currently by the oil crisis and fanned by consumerists, such as Ralph Nader, who argue that antitrust weapons have been used like peashooters against dinosaurs. Business almost certainly faces even tougher antitrust enforcement and possibly even a new antitrust law aimed at breaking up the corporate giants in the country's basic industries.

This prospect points up the underlying question businessmen ask about antitrust: Are laws framed more than three-quarters of a century ago appropriate legal weapons in a market system grown increasingly large, complex, and multinational? In raising this basic issue, businessmen can point to a far-reaching, intricate web of laws and rules that has made the government the regulator, watchdog, and even partner of business. Wage and price controls, health and safety regulations, and disclosure laws, are all a far cry from the economy of Sherman's or Gary's day.

Businessmen complain of the unsettling vagueness of the antitrust laws, which permits antitrusters to attack many long-standing business practices in their effort to root out restraints of trade and monopoly. The FTC, for example, is now suing Kellogg, General Foods, General Mills, and Quaker Oats, alleging that such procedures as having route men arrange their breakfast cereals on supermarket shelves are anticompetitive. The Justice Dept. has a similar suit against tire makers Goodyear and Firestone.

Executives of International Business Machines Corp., caught by both government and private antitrust suits attacking pricing and promotion policies, privately declare that they are baffled over what they can legally do. Bertram C. Dedman, vice-president and general counsel for INA Corp., echoes a widely held view: "We never really know precisely what antitrust means. It's frequently strictly a matter of opinion."

Enormous economic stakes are involved in antitrust enforcement. Such current cases as those against IBM, Xerox Corp., and other giants involve billions of dollars' worth of capital investment and stockholder interests. Executives fear that such suits give broad power to courts not schooled in business, economics, or industrial technology. This power was dramatically illustrated last fall when U.S. District Judge A. Sherman Christensen announced a $352-million judgment against IBM and then confessed error, sending IBM's stock into wild gyrations.

Many businessmen wonder whether their companies are often targets of antitrust prosecution simply because they are big and successful. Philadelphia lawyer Edward D. Slevin sums up this attitude: "If the free market is pushed to its fullest extent, somebody wins. But the Justice Dept. seems to say: 'Now that you've won, you've cornered the market. We're going to break you up and start over.'"

All this, say many executives, makes it increasingly difficult for American business to compete internationally. Douglas Grymes, president of Koppers Co., argues that "big corporations are the only ones that can compete with big corporations in world markets." He says that the antitrust laws seem to equate bigness itself with monopoly and thus hinder American corporations from reaching the size necessary for world competition.

Tougher Enforcement Likely

Despite all these deeply felt concerns, the antitrust laws are likely to become even tougher and more restrictive. Starting with the Sherman Act, antitrust has been a product more of politics than of economics. Today's rising populist sentiment has led to demands for tighter antitrust enforcement. Only a decade ago historian Richard Hofstadter wrote, "The antitrust movement is one of the faded passions of American reform." Today it is the darling of reform. As James T. Halverson, director of the FTC's Bureau of Competition, sums up: "The political atmosphere is very favorable to antitrust right now."

The many signs of stepped-up antitrust activity in the last one or two years make an impressively lengthy list. They include:

New investigations

Last week three federal agencies — Justice, the FTC, and the SEC — as well as some congressmen, revealed that they are turning to a little-used section of the Clayton Act to investigate the complex of interlocking directorships among major oil companies.

New legislation

The industrial reorganization bill that Senator Philip A. Hart (D-Mich.) introduced in Congress last year would provide a new legal basis for breaking up leading companies in the nation's most basic industries: autos, iron and steel, nonferrous metals, chemicals and drugs, electrical machinery and equipment, electronic computing and communications equipment, and energy. It is given no immediate chance to pass, but its ideas could find their way into future legislation. Another bill introduced by Senator John V. Tunney (D-Calif.), already approved by the Senate and taking a back seat to impeachment considerations in the House, would increase the current maximum criminal antitrust fine from $50,000 to $500,000 for corporations and $100,000 for executives. It would also require the Justice Dept. to explain publicly its reasons for accepting a consent decree instead of preparing a case and actually going to trial.

Bigger enforcement budgets

The Administration is seeking large increases, by usually puny antitrust standards, in the fiscal 1975 budgets of both the Justice Dept. and the FTC for their antitrust departments. If Congress approves, Justice's Antitrust Div. will pick up 83 additional staff slots, more than half lawyers and economists. At the last big increase, fiscal 1970, the division got only 20. The FTC is due for an additional $3-million, or a 20% increase in its present antitrust budget.

Growing muscle at FTC

After a long hibernation, the FTC is stepping out as a feisty agency with a new esprit, a highly professional staff, and a taste for going after bigness. It filed the monopoly suits against Xerox Corp. and the four biggest cereal makers. It has a special unit with an extra $1-million appropriation to litigate its case to break up the eight leading oil companies. And it got important new powers from Congress last year, including the right to demand otherwise unavailable product-line sales and profit figures from companies without first clearing with the Office of Management & Budget.

Reorganizing justice

If the Justice Dept.'s monopoly case against IBM, filed more than five years ago, is successful, it would give new spirit to the Antitrust Div., which at least until recently has been demoralized by the successive shocks of ITT and Watergate. Even so, the division reorganized and beefed up its economics staff last fall to enable it to undertake investigations and prosecutions with a sharper eye to the economic impact of its actions.

More and tougher antitrust enforcement is foreshadowed by more subtle changes in mood and belief as well as by these specific developments. One such change is a growing recognition that the government itself creates monopoly power. Several weeks ago Columbia Law School called together many of the nation's leading industrial economists and antitrust lawyers for a conference on industrial concentration. The participants examined what business concentration means both for the economy and for antitrust policy. About the only thing generally agreed on was that governmental attempts to regulate an industry often result in preserving the monopoly power of those being regulated. In line with this belief, insiders say that the Antitrust Div. will step up its policy of intervening in other government proceedings to shape regulatory policy consistent with antitrust principles. Last January, for example, the division formally intervened in FCC proceedings in an attempt to deny renewal of the broadcasting license of Cowles Communications, Inc., in Des Moines, and those of Pulitzer Publishing Co. and

Newhouse Broadcasting Corp. in St. Louis. All these companies also own newspapers.

Another change has been the dramatic multiplication of private antitrust suits — those brought by one company against another. These include the 40-odd private business suits against IBM, ITT's suit to split up General Telephone & Electronics Corp., and the large class actions against plumbing and wallboard manufacturers. In fiscal 1973 the government filed 45 antitrust suits. By comparison, businessmen and other private parties filed 1,152, making the business community itself a significant factor in antitrust enforcement. . . .

All this is leading to an antitrust Congress. Victor H. Kramer, director of Washington's Institute for Public Interest Representation and a leading antitrust lawyer, expects that "more supporters of an effective antimonopoly program are going to be elected to the 94th Congress than to any previous Congress in many years."

The Alternatives

But as antitrust action steps up, so do the conflicts over the direction antitrust policy should take. The populists contend that antitrust enforcement in the past has been spineless. Businessmen complain that current policy paralyzes corporations because they are uncertain what practices are lawful and that they are being punished for being successfully competitive. Who is right?

The conflicts lead many businessmen to push for an updating of the antitrust laws. Richard L. Kattel, president of Atlanta's Citizens & Southern National Bank, which has been sparring with the Justice Dept. over the bank's expansion plans, feels that the antitrust laws "need complete revamping."

Major revamping, though, will not come because there is no general agreement on what form it should take. Most of the Columbia conference participants believe that the economic evidence for a change in policy is scanty and inconclusive. Suggestions ranged from doing nothing to pushing the tough Hart bill through Congress.

In approaching antitrust policy, there are alternatives:

1. Abolish the laws altogether A very few economists, such as Yale Brozen of the University of Chicago, talk as though antitrust laws are largely unnecessary. But as Robert L. Werner, executive vice-president and general counsel of RCA Corp., told a Conference Board antitrust seminar earlier this month: "There should be little disagreement by industry over the basic validity of the doctrine of antitrust. Certainly no businessman would seriously suggest that we scuttle that doctrine and return to a pre-Shermanite jungle." The courts have ruled that such practices as fixing prices, dividing markets, boycotting, some mergers, and predatory pricing designed to destroy competitors unlawfully impose restraints on the market.

2. Clarify the laws by specifying precisely what business practices are unlawful If various practices can be identified and prohibited through case-by-case litigation, why not draft a detailed code of conduct?

But the very difficulty of identifying such practices when business conditions are constantly changing led to the broad wording of the Sherman Act originally. No one has ever produced an all-inclusive list of anticompetitive conduct. No one can possibly delineate all the circumstances that amount to price fixing and other illegal practices. If publication of future prices by members of at trade association is unlawful, as the Supreme Court held in 1921, is dissemination of past inventory figures and prices equally unlawful? (No, said the Court in 1925. . . .) Moreover, as Thomas M. Scanlon, chairman of the American Bar Assn.'s 8,500-member antitrust section points out: "There's uncertainty in any kind of litigation. Laws intended to bring more certainty often bring less."

3. Replace antitrust laws with direct regulations U.S. Steel's Gary favored and Koppers' Grymes favors a business-government partnership with this approval. Its advocates agree with John Kenneth Galbraith that antitrust is a "charade," that it has not and cannot produce a competitive economy in the face of the technological imperatives of large corporations. University of Chicago's George J. Stigler concludes that antitrust has not been "a major force" on the economy to date. "The government has won most of its 1,800 cases," he points out, "and there has been no important secular decline in concentration." On the other hand, many economists and lawyers would argue that Stigler has drawn the wrong conclusion. As Almarin Phillips, professor of economics and law at the Wharton School of Finance & Commerce, puts it: "The success of antitrust can only be measured by the hundreds of mergers and price-fixing situations that never happened."

Moreover, in the view of an increasing number of observers, regulation that is designed to mitigate the effects of "natural" monopolies, such as telephone service, often winds up fostering them instead. Civil Aeronautics Board regulations, for example, have compelled higher airline rates than prevail on federally nonregulated intrastate flights. Wesley James Liebler, recently named director of policy planning at the FTC, says: "What the airline industry needs is a little competition. In the long run we should get rid of the CAB and let in some free competition." Liebler also wants to abolish fixed commission rates for stockbrokers.

Much of the energy of regulatory commissions seems to be devoted to anticompetitive ends. The Federal Communications Commission promulgated rules several years ago designed to stifle the growth of pay-cable television. Sports events, for example, may not be broadcast on pay-cable TV if similar events have been shown on commercial television any time during the previous five years.

Walter Adams, a Michigan State University economist, notes that regulatory commissions can exclude competitors through licensing power, maintain price supports by regulating rates, create concentration through merger surveillance, and harass the weak by supervising practices that the strong do not like. To combat this kind of government behavior, the Antitrust Div. itself has, for the past several years, been intervening or attempting to intervene in such agencies as the ICC, CAB, and SEC to force decisions that spur competition in industry.

In support of their position, reformers make a further point: Large corporations have the political muscle to force the government to support their anticompetitive goals. Adams charges that the government has established an industrywide cartel for the oil companies through publishing monthly estimates of demand; through establishing quotas for each state pursuant to the Interstate Oil Compact, which Congress approved at behest of the oil companies; and through "prorationing devices" that dictate how much each well can produce. It is illegal to ship excess production in interstate commerce. Tariffs and import quotas protect only the producers, Adams says.

What all this amounts to is maintenance of shared monopoly power with the active cooperation of government. Only when the power of large companies is reduced, argue the populists, will the government be able to guide a competitive economy rather than serve as a prop for large interests. This was one of the original arguments for the Sherman Act in the 1880s.

4. Move toward tougher enforcement Populist critics of antitrust, such as Nader and Senator Hart, agree with Galbraith that antitrust has been all too ineffectual, but they move in the opposite policy direction. Since they believe that government regulation usually entrenches the power of big firms and concentrated industries, they favor a get-tough antitrust approach. They argue for two related tactics: extending existing law through the courts to curtail many practices of large firms in concentrated industries and getting Congressional legislation such as the Hart bill to attack the structure of these industries.

The Hart bill would permit the prosecution of companies because of their size alone. The history of antitrust has largely been to define and prosecute practices that courts would rule were restraints of trade, such as price fixing by agreement among competitors. But with increasing fervor, "structuralists" argue that size itself can be harmful.

Historical Deficiencies

Before the Civil War, Americans felt uncomfortable with corporate bigness. The image of the yeoman farmer and the small, fiercely competitive businessman largely reflected economic reality. But the growth of railroads, with their "pools" carving up markets, changed all that. By 1871, Charles Francis Adams, grandson and great-grandson of presidents, was writing that corporations "have declared war, negotiated peace, reduced courts, legislatures, and sovereign states to an unqualified obedience to their will."

Populist politics, such as the formation of the Grange movement, picked up steam, but at the same time, in 1882, the first big trust, Standard Oil of Ohio, was born, followed by the Whiskey Trust, the Sugar Trust, the Lead Trust, and the Cotton Oil Trust. Senator Sherman warned that without federal action the country would confront "a trust for every production and a master to fix the price for every necessity of life." The upshot was his Sherman Act.

But federal prosecutions were limited, aimed mostly at fledgling labor unions, and the Sherman Act failed to curb bigness. Corporate mergers speeded up. U.S. Steel, Standard Oil (New Jersey), American Tobacco, American Can, International Harvester, and United Shoe Machinery were all put together at this time. As a result, antitrusters increased pressure for even tougher laws and an independent agency, which could develop industrial expertise, to enforce them.

These efforts came to fruition in 1914, with the passage of the Clayton and Federal Trade Commission Acts. The Clayton Act specifically banned anticompetitive mergers, while the FTC Act set up an agency to police "unfair competition" in the marketplace but not to regulate prices and output.

Like the Sherman Act, the Clayton Act proved ineffectual for many years, largely because of the way courts interpreted the law. As recently as 1948 the Court permitted U.S. Steel to acquire one of its own customers.

Partly in response to this decision, Congress passed the Celler-Kefauver Act in 1950, amending the Clayton Act to prohibit mergers through acquisition of assets or stock as well as those that would tend to foreclose competition in any market in the country. This effectively closed the door on many mergers. But the merger wave of the late 1960s comprised so-called conglomerate get-togethers of companies in different, often unrelated, industries. The case intended to settle this issue — ITT — never got to the Supreme Court because it was settled by a consent decree.

Mergers became the target of antitrusters because they mean the disappearance of independent competitors and lead to concentrations of industrial power. And, argue antitrusters, a few large companies may "share" monopoly power simply by dominating a given market. But unless collusion among competitors can be proved, there is no way under conventional enforcement to prosecute them.

Conflicting Views

To remedy this supposed defect, Senator Hart's new law would create a presumption of monopoly power whenever:

A company's average rate of return is greater than 15% of its net worth for each of five consecutive years.

There has been no substantial price competition for three consecutive years among two or more corporations within an industry.

Four or fewer companies account for half or more of an industry's sales in a single year.

Clearly, these criteria create a net that would sweep up hundreds of large corporations. Hart's staff estimates, for example, that a quarter to a third of all U.S. manufacturing concerns meet the third condition.

A company that met any of these criteria would not automatically have to divest. Its defense before the special agency and court the bill would create could be either that its position rests on legally acquired patents or that divesting would deprive it of "substantial economies." (At present economies are not a defense.)

Howard O'Leary, chief counsel to Hart's antitrust subcommittee, argues that without "some mandate" from Congress, the Justice Dept. would be unlikely to embark "on an antitrust crusade." The bill would provide that mandate.

Senator Hart asserts that statistics can be misleading. He cites concentration ratios which according to economists show competition in the oil industry. But, says Hart, "Look at the evidence of joint ventures, banking interlocks, vertical integration, joint ownership of facilities, joint production, absence of real price competition, and lockstep decision-making, and one must wonder."

Economist Walter Adams agrees. He points out that between 1956 and 1968, 20 major oil companies were involved in 226 mergers and thereby gained control over a variety of substitute fuels, such as coal and atomic energy. The oil companies also moved into allied businesses, such as fertilizers, plastics, and chemicals, through vertical integration. Adams believes that a new law is necessary to fragment the power of the companies in the oil and other industries.

The only businessmen to come forward so far in support of at least the thrust of what Senator Hart is trying to do, says O'Leary, are some in communications and data processing. Through a series of hearings the subcommittee hopes, says O'Leary, "to persuade politicians and to some extent the public that it is feasible to come up with more firms than now exist, that the market won't crash, and that jobs won't be lost."

Most other businessmen see little good in the Hart bill. Carl H. Madden, chief economist for the U.S. Chamber of Commerce, brands its basic thrust as "faulty." He told Senate hearings last spring that the bill would thwart competition, not aid it, "by changing the legally permitted goal and cutting back the prizes."

Legal experts have many other objections. Richard Posner, of the University of Chicago Law School, feels that the Hart bill is symptomatic of "antitrust off on a tangent." Antitrust chief Thomas E. Kauper is not "satisfied with the economic evidence favoring broad deconcentration statutes." Kellogg Co. vice-president and corporate counsel J. Robert O'Brien says: "There is no reason whatever to assume that a 'concentrated' industry will necessarily be any less competitive than a fractionated industry. A course of antitrust enforcement that seeks to break up companies and restructure industries by looking at little more than concentration levels is misguided, to say the least."

Many have pointed out that among the defects in Hart's approach is the difficulty of measuring and the ease of manipulating rates of return. Further, even Ralph Nader, a supporter of the bill, says that deconcentrating an industry "is a 15-year job, at least."

Other Tactics

Antitrusters are not holding their breath waiting for legislation. In a series of cases initiated during the past five years, they are using existing laws prohibiting monopolization and unfair methods of competition to check alleged anticompetitive conditions in concentrated industries.

The FTC's suit against Xerox and the Justice Dept.'s against IBM represent marked change from the past. The government has brought very few cases against single companies for alleged monopoly, partly because of limited prosecution budgets, partly because of political pressure from business, and partly because officials thought them unnecessary. These two recent suits single out a variety of practices — pricing policies, for example, and such things as announcing products embodying new technology far in advance of actual availability — that are alleged ways the two companies exercise monopoly power. The antitrust subcommittee's O'Leary says, "The IBM case is potentially very significant, if it is won and a remedy can be found. It is the first such case in 25 years."

The Justice Dept. also brought suit last August against Goodyear and Firestone, charging them with monopolizing the replacement tire market through a combination of practices, including acquisitions, periods of uneconomically low prices designed to drive out competitive products, service station tie-ins, and reciprocity deals. The two companies are charged with acting independently to maintain their dominant positions; they are not charged wtih collusion.

Perhaps the most innovative case is the FTC's suit against the four leading breakfast food makers, charging them with a variety of unfair methods of competition. The Commission is not claiming any conspiracy among the companies. It is trying to prove, instead, that a lengthy list of long-standing industry practices are anticompetitive and permit the companies, whose market shares have gone from 68% in 1940 to 90% today, to "share" monopoly power in their respective industries. If successful, this suit would strengthen the commission's ability to use its statute . . . to go after many heavily concentrated industries.

The FTC's current prosecution against the eight major oil companies also attempts to break new ground. The key allegation is that the majors have been "pursuing a common course" in using control of crude oil and shipping facilities to stall the development of independent refineries. This includes eliminating retail competition by keeping prices low at the refinery and marketing end and high at the production end of the business. The FTC also charges the companies with such practices as using barter and exchange agreements to keep crude oil in their own hands and reluctance to sell to independent marketers. Unlike the cereal suits, the FTC charges that some of the oil practices are collusive.

Can We Compete?

In the face of government attack, some businessmen wonder whether such antitrust action aimed at cutting down corporate size might not handicap U.S. companies in keeping pace with the growing number of multinational corporations around the world. Koppers Co.'s Grymes, who argues for permitting mergers, would prefer to see the government "adopt a whole new philosophy of life." He would like to see 26 steel companies, for example, merged into five or six. "Let them get together, produce together, sell together," he says. He concedes that to make up for the absence of competition, the government would have to levy an excess-profits tax or put limitations on investments. He vigorously opposes the Hart bill.

So does J. Fred Weston, a professor at the University of California at Los Angeles' Graduate School of Management, and for similar reasons. "The world market requires increasingly large firms," he argues. "If we hold on to the 18th Century idea of a nation of small shopkeepers and small farms, we will become a small nation." Unlike Grymes, Weston would not encourage mergers. Rather, he is against "fighting a rear-guard battle to prevent deconcentration based on invalid premises." Corporate size, he insists, should be judged in relation to the world market. "If there are firms of increasing size abroad and there are economies of scale, U.S. firms have to be able to compete."

Supporters of deconcentration policy do not quarrel with the premise that U.S. companies must be able to compete, but they do argue that existing levels of concentration in many industries are more than adequate. They believe that size alone is not a guarantee of economies of scale or of efficiencies. And they point to industrial studies indicating that economies of scale relate primarily to plant size but not necessarily to the numbers of plants that any one manufacturer controls.

Frederic M. Scherer, the FTC's incoming economics bureau chief, believes that economic studies show that many industries are more concentrated than efficiency requires. Nader argues that the best evidence is "clinical, not statistical." He says that studies of industries that have become less concentrated would show consumer gains without loss of efficiency. The arrival of a new supermarket chain in the Washington metropolitan area several years ago, he says, forced prices down, and he cites the aluminum industry after Aluminum Co. of America had to face competition. It was still able to compete.

Moreover, the fact that a company can be efficient does not mean that it will be. On the contrary, absence of competition may make the company fat and lazy — capable of efficiency but acting inefficiently because it is not spurred by the need to compete.

In the 1950 Congressional hearings on monopoly power, Benjamin Fairless, president of U.S. Steel, admitted that his company had less efficient production processes than its competitors, including much smaller foreign companies. Studies have demonstrated that American steel producers lagged woefully in innovation. Between 1940 and 1955, 13 major inventions came from abroad, yet American steel boasted the largest companies in the world.

The basic oxygen process, which Avery C. Adams, chairman and president of Jones & Laughlin Steel Corp., described in 1959 as "the only major technological breakthrough at the ingot level in the steel industry since before the turn of the century," was perfected by a tiny Austrian steel company in 1950. It was introduced into the U.S. in 1954 by McLouth Steel Corp., which then had less than 1% of American ingot capacity. Jones & Laughlin waited until 1957, and U.S. Steel and Bethlehem Steel Corp. waited until 1964 to adopt the process, resulting in lost profits to the steel industry, according to one study, of some $216-million after taxes by 1960 alone.

As for ability to compete abroad, there is practically no evidence that the Justice Dept. has impaired the competitive posture of U.S. companies in world markets. In the past few years the Justice, Commerce, and Treasury Depts., as well as Congressional committees, have practically pleaded for businessmen to come forward with examples of how Americans have been hurt, with minimal results. The Antitrust Div.'s recent release of business review letters from 1968 through 1972 indicates not a single turndown of joint export ventures.

David H. Baker, director of the Commerce Dept.'s Office of Export Development, made an intense search for examples of antitrust harm. A large food company wanted to enter a joint venture with another big U.S. outfit to bid on a plant an Eastern European government planned to build. The Justice Dept. indicated that it might refuse to approve the deal, and the food company pulled out. A small U.S. company then bid for the contract on its own and won.

A New Approach

Some experts believe that the government cannot deal with business complaints adequately unless it develops a comprehensive approach to competition generally. Victor Kramer suggests the creation of an "office of antimonopoly affairs" within the Executive Office of the President. The function of this office, Kramer says, would be to implement a new executive order he would like to see promulgated, directing all federal agencies to act to promote a "free competitive enterprise system." It would require the federal departments and bureaus to prepare antitrust impact statements whenever they suggest action that would "significantly affect competition in the private sector."

Professor Neil H. Jacoby, of UCLA's Graduate School of Management, agrees with the general thrust of Kramer's suggestion. Jacoby, who believes that oligopoly is here to stay, proposes the creation of a Federal Competition Agency, either as an independent commission or within the White House. He would have it submit a "competition impact report" for "all proposed federal legislation."

Kramer concludes that his policy would have compelled the State Dept. to evaluate publicly the competitive impact of the voluntary steel import agreements with Japan and European nations. The Pentagon would have been called on to explain how the public benefits from the awarding of nonbid contracts. The Internal Revenue Service and the White House, he believes, would have to consider the competitive effects of proposed changes in tax laws.

This broadened approach to competition could come closer to resolving the conflicts between the tendency of companies to exert control over their markets and the public requirement that monopoly be held in check. Short of this, the evidence suggests that antitrust is the best we have.

5 A Changing Balance of Power: New Partnership of Government and Business

Business Week

A new pattern is emerging in the relationship between business and government in the U.S. Its concrete manifestations can be spotted all over the map:

In the area of wages and prices, the federal government seeks to get business and labor to stay within "noninflationary wage-price guideposts."

In race relations, business and government join in efforts to create more and better employment opportunities for Negroes.

In foreign trade, investment, and lending, "voluntary" programs by U.S. business and banking are helping government to eliminate the deficit in the nation's balance of payments.

In the war against poverty, government is drawing on the help of business to upgrade the knowledge and skills of the poor.

In science and technology, government depends on private industry to advance national interests in areas as wide-ranging as economic development, military power, and exploration of outer space.

In matters of taxation and public expenditure, government and business are working more closely to shape fiscal policy in ways to promote full employment and more rapid economic growth.

Dilemma for business

Caught up in the swirl of these rapidly changing business-government relations, businessmen are facing some tough decisions. The central problem is whether big business should accept "voluntarily" a new and closer relationship with big government — or whether they should oppose any such "partnership" lest it transform the traditional free enterprise system beyond recognition and obliterate what they consider to be their economic freedom.

Some leading business executives are moving toward the conclusion that the dangers to their own freedom, and to society's, will be reduced rather than increased if a new balance — involving elements of both cooperation and conflict — can be worked out between business and government. These men are already working to achieve such a balance of business and government functions and responsibilities.

Ending a "cold war"

Some put it in terms of ending what has been an almost traditional conflict between business and government in the U.S. One of these is Lammot du Pont Copeland, president of E. I. du Pont de Nemours & Co.

"It would be in the national interest, as well as our own interest," says Copeland, "to put an end to what at times has seemed like a cold war between business and government." He suggests a "conscious, determined effort on both sides to improve the relationship."

The University of Michigan's Kenneth E. Boulding describes the "cold war between business and government," which he traces back as far as 1880, as the most crucial problem facing the U.S. "I think we have now got to the point," he says, "where failure to come to some kind of resolution of this ancient conflict is our most serious handicap."

Pervasive

Whatever the attitudes of the two sides may be, the actual overlaps between business and government interests today are multiple; they embrace not only the areas already mentioned but also housing and urban redevelopment, communications, transportation, banking, power, farming, and other regulated or subsidized industries.

So pervasive are these overlaps that some observers feel the very nature of the U.S. economic system has already been changed from what used to be called capitalism to something that needs a new name.

Many names have been proposed for the present system: the mixed economy, the managed economy, the pluralistic economy, the garrison state, the welfare state. Whatever the system is called, however, it has become increasingly clear to businessmen that the role of government in their affairs has "changed drastically in our lifetimes," as Logan T. Johnston, president of Armco Steel Corp., puts it. "Government," says Johnston, "is now a partner of business — some even think the dominant partner. Whether or not business wants such a partner is academic. The partner is there.

"Whether or not this partner's advice is sought does not matter. He will offer it. If need be, he will enforce his views."

Here to stay

This state of affairs deeply distresses — even infuriates — a great many businessmen. Many, as Johnston notes, "blame their partner for the majority of their problems — including their ulcers." And many ardently wish their government partner would just go away and let them run their businesses in peace.

"Yet," says Logan Johnston, "businessmen who are frank with themselves in their moments of introspection know that this partner is not going away, at least in the foreseeable future."

Whether they like it or not, practical businessmen know that the huge and changing role of government in the U.S. economy presents them with a critical managerial problem.

How Businessmen See the Basic Issue

The issue has uncovered differences within the U.S. business community that are both intellectual and emotional.

On one side, many businessmen strongly resist the contention that they should run their businesses in such a way as to serve not only their private interests but also "the public interest." Many condemn this notion that private business should seek to fulfill "social responsibilities" as — in the words of Professor Milton Friedman, an adviser of Barry Goldwater in the 1964 Presidential campaign — "a fundamentally subversive doctrine."

Friedman asks: "If businessmen do have a social responsibility other than making maximum profits for stockholders, how are they to know what it is? Can they decide how great a burden they are justified in placing on themselves or their stockholders to serve that social interest? Is it tolerable that these public functions of taxation, expenditure, and control be exercised by the people who happen at the moment to be in charge of particular enterprises, chosen for their posts by strictly private groups?"

He warns that if businessmen once begin behaving like civil servants, then sooner or later they will become nothing but civil servants — elected or appointed like many others.

The doctrine of "social responsibilities," traditionally minded businessmen fear, may lead to a highly centralized and controlled economy in which their freedom and independence as businessmen — or citizens — will be lost.

George Champion, chairman of the Chase Manhattan Bank, recently launched a heavy attack against the government's setting of guidelines for business behind "the facade of friendliness and partnership between business and government."

"In my judgment," said Champion, "the new trend toward government-by-guideline is one of the most insidious and dangerous on the national scene today, and one which businessmen should work to reverse with all the energy and dedication they can muster. The guideline approach represents a giant step away from self-reliance and personal responsibility, and toward federal domination of our national economy."

Balance of interests

On the other side of this emotional — and ideological — debate are businessmen who believe that, with corporations as big and important as they are today, there is simply no way for corporate executives to avoid affecting the public interest.

Hence, they contend that, if U.S. business leaders want to retain their private freedom and autonomy to make decisions, they must take cognizance of the effect of their actions on the public interest — with which their own basic corporate interests are inevitably bound up.

Some proponents of this view, in fact, assert that the most critical job facing the head of a major corporation today is to determine how best to coordinate a company's interest with the public interest.

One who holds the view that a businessman can take account of the public interest in his business decisions "and still be successful" is Thomas J. Watson, Jr., chairman of International Business Machines Corp. Watson says: "I would be the first to admit that it's a good deal easier to state this proposition than to put it into practice."

Yet he feels sure that one of the most important problems American management must face in the years ahead is "how we can strike a balance between what is sound business practice in the management of our large corporations and what is good for the national interest."

Profits and the public

Businessmen who take the position that corporations should seek to serve public as well as private interests do not think this means sacrificing profits — at least not in the long term. On the contrary, they insist that efforts to improve corporate earnings are wholly consistent with national interests.

Profits, these men contend, are both rewards for past efficiency and innovations, and incentives for future business achievement. They are a means of financing growth and of efficiently allocating human and material resources to uses that the public — the buying public — favors.

Thus, these businessmen refuse to concede that they are any less hardheaded or profit-oriented than their fellows. Indeed, they consider themselves more realistic in facing up to the hard facts of how to operate successfully in today's economy — an economy in which government has a big role to play and the public not only demands "socially responsible" behavior from business, but can enforce its demands politically if it grows dissatisfied with business action and policies.

Clash over Steel—And a Fresh Start

The critical issue in this debate is how to define the "public interest," a concept that many businessmen regard as foggy. One skeptic says: "On the most difficult issues, 'socially responsible' behavior is not obviously revealed to all or deductible from the Ten Commandments. It has to be enunciated by someone. In practice this usually means the President.

"I think the real issue is not whether individuals should do what is right," says this man, "but whether the President should tell them what is right, as distinct from what is legal, and whether individuals have any responsibility to do what he says."

But Joseph L. Block, chairman of Inland Steel Co., declares that those who deride the "public interest" as a "nonexistent will-of-the-wisp, a self-serving device used by politicians to cloak ulterior objectives," are speaking "utter nonsense." Block contends that they are denying not only the need for private businessmen to consider the public interest but even the right of government itself to define the public interest.

"Surely," says Block, "the greater good of the nation as a whole should be of paramount importance to everyone." He maintains that "while no one has an omniscient power to define 'public interest' accurately at any given time, and certainly not all of the time, it surely behooves all of us — and most particularly government — to endeavor to do so."

Moment of truth

Block and his fellow executives at Inland Steel faced a moment of truth on this issue in April, 1962; it came during the confrontation between the Kennedy Administration and the steel industry over the hike in steel prices following labor negotiations with the United Steelworkers.

The refusal of eighth-ranking Inland Steel — strategically located in Chicago in the heart of a major industrial market — to go along with the steel price hike was probably the critical factor that forced other steel companies to rescind their across-the-board price increase.

The often-told story involved telephone calls by Under Secretary of Commerce Edward Gudeman to Inland's vice-chairman, Philip D. Block, Jr. (Joseph Block was in Japan), and to others in Chicago.

The upshot was that Inland held the price line, though the White House never specifically asked this. The White House did, however, threaten the steel industry with antitrust action, and it genuinely frightened businessmen by what they regarded as "police state" tactics.

Turning point

Though the Kennedy Administration nominally won the steel battle, the confrontation was regarded as a fiasco by both sides. It left deep scars on relations between business and government, scars that President Kennedy — and Roger M. Blough, chairman of U.S. Steel Corp. — never succeeded in healing, despite efforts on both sides.

Yet that battle was a turning point in efforts to put the business-government "partnership" on a healthier basis.

Johnson's moves

After President Kennedy's assassination, Lyndon B. Johnson quickly moved to establish closer and friendlier relations between Washington and the business community — and to "draw a veil" over the steel battle of 1962. He consulted not only with liberal businessmen who had been sympathetic to Kennedy but with conservatives as well, many of whom had strongly opposed the Kennedy Administration as "anti-business."

A combination of circumstances, in fact — the steel episode, a reported insulting remark of the late President's about businessmen, the "intellectual" tone of the Kennedy Administration, its reformist leanings — had united to awaken in these business circles the kind of intense hostility toward the Kennedy Administration that had marked the conservative business thinking during Franklin D. Roosevelt's New Deal.

President Johnson was determined to allay this hostility. Shaken by the assassination, many business leaders were, on their side, eager to repair relations with Washington.

Era of good feeling

As Johnson pressed his program to gain business cooperation, many businessmen felt that he had succeeded remarkably in dispelling the once bitter atmosphere. Said one who had known Kennedy and liked him personally — David Rockefeller, president of the Chase Manhattan Bank: "Johnson has established much better relations with business. Kennedy wasn't terribly interested. Johnson has talked to more businessmen, and has shown his sincerity. He's put his relations with the business community on good strong footing."

These efforts bore political fruit. Johnson got the influential support of some top businessmen — led by Henry Ford II, of Ford Motor Co. and Stuart T. Saunders of the Pennsylvania RR — for his big tax cut (proposed at a time when the federal budget was running heavily in deficit).

Johnson even succeeded in attracting a sizable amount of big business support for his political campaign in 1964. The Republican candidate, Senator Goldwater, complained during the campaign about "the Eastern establishment" of businessmen and financiers who were supporting Johnson.

Johnson's cultivation of the business community was not aimed solely at getting votes or campaign contributions. Rather, it was intended to restructure business-government relations as a means of dealing with a number of crucial national problems.

Johnson's Moves: Policy and Practice

Soon after winning his landslide victory over Goldwater, Johnson sought to define his concept of separate and joint business-government responsibilities. He did this in an address before the Business Council — a body of predominantly conservative chiefs of major corporations. The Business Council in 1961 had brawled with the Kennedy Administration and cut itself off from official government connections.

President's aims

The President told the Business Council that government and business must "operate in partnership," not as antagonists, to solve many problems. He listed four as paramount:

Accelerating the rate of economic growth.

Maintaining price stability.

Strengthening the U.S. balance of payments.

Finding ways to reduce high rates of unemployment among teenagers and to assure "adequate economic opportunities for all our people" — obviously including Negroes.

Role of government

In attacking all those problems, said Johnson, business and government had distinct roles. One of government's main jobs was to produce a tax system that would not overburden businessmen or consumers, and would maintain incentives for productive effort.

The big 1964 tax cut — totaling $14 billion — had clearly produced a major effect in accelerating growth and reducing unemployment. Johnson emphasized that the U.S. government would seek, through both fiscal and monetary policy, to create conditions of stable economic growth in which individual businesses could prosper.

The government's role should not be confined, said Johnson, to creating enough total money demand to keep the economy functioning at a high level. Government should also shape expenditure programs to improve human and natural resources and make "social investments . . . to support private enterprise."

But the government, Johnson told the bussinessmen, should avoid trespassing on the proper area of private business; it should leave a "clear field" wherever competitive enterprise is the most efficient way of getting a job done.

. . . and business

The major responsibilities of business, according to the President, were to produce high-quality goods, to innovate, to cut production costs, to sell vigorously at home and abroad, to offer workers both job security and incentives, and to invest in growth. For its own sake as well as the economy's, business should try to plan investments carefully and avoid hectic inventory building and dumping.

Solving some national economic problems, the President added, would require joint efforts by business and government. These included steps to cope with the nation's international balance-of-payments problem in such a way as to permit economic expansion to continue at home.

Prime rate story

On Nov. 23, 1964, shortly before the President went before the Business Council, the Federal Reserve had raised the discount rate from 3½% to 4%. This was done to guard against any rush of money out of the country in response to a hike to 7% of the British bank rate in an effort to protect the pound sterling.

President Johnson pleaded with U.S. bankers not to put up their interest rates to domestic borrowers just because the Fed had raised the discount rate; this, he said, might slow economic expansion. He was "sure," said the President, that bankers must realize their own long-term interests were inseparable from the nation's prosperity. And he warned that, if the economy slid into a recession, it might force him to increase government spending and increase the size of the deficit.

Soon afterward, three banks outside New York did boost their prime rate by ¼% to 4¾%. But they put the rate down as the President continued his jawbone campaign — and the New York banks held their prime rate at 4½%. An overwhelming majority of bankers — including even those friendly to the White House — grumbled that this was undue meddling in their business. But their public protests were muted.

Those guideposts

Johnson has not interpreted his "era of good feeling" to mean that he should not try to guide or influence the lending, investing, price, or wage decisions of business.

On one of the most inflammatory issues — the "noninflammatory" wage-price guideposts that were first spelled out by President Kennedy's Council of Economic Advisers in 1962 and that were at stake in the Kennedy-steel confrontation that April — Johnson has continued to call for business and labor cooperation.

But his own criticisms have been muted when the guidelines — which would hold wage settlements to national productivity gains of 3.2% — were violated, as in the 1964 automobile and 1965 aluminum settlements.

Voluntary gains

As the balance-of-payments problem persisted, President Johnson issued a strong call to U.S. bankers to participate in a "voluntary" program to curb the growth of lending abroad, and to industrialists heavily involved in foreign operations to handle their affairs in such a way as to reduce the U.S. payments deficit.

The small number of highly visible — and vulnerable — big banks heavily engaged in international lending (nine banks do 83% of all lending abroad) saw no alternative but to cooperate. Somewhat more surprising has been the degree of cooperation by the heads of a large majority of 600 major industrial companies.

What business did

Says Albert L. Nickerson, chairman of Socony Mobil Oil Co., the key business executive working with Commerce Secretary John T. Connor, on the voluntary balance-of-payments program: "We all felt that if top management of each company reviewed its specific programs for new plant, working capital, and cash balances overseas, some reductions and postponements could be made with only a slight adverse effect on long-range profitability."

Neither from the nation's viewpoint nor that of business, said Nickerson, could companies be asked to forego market opportunities that would repay costs of expansion for many years to come, or to skimp on projects for modernization, new technology, or increased scale that would yield real efficiencies.

But he said top management was finding there are ways of economizing on cash that serve both corporate and national interests.

Partnership, but No "Establishment"

The Presidential pleas for business cooperation — and the willingness of business to cooperate — are founded on a fundamental but usually unstated assumption: That the free market does not necessarily provide satisfactory — or prompt — answers to many of the crucial economic and social problems facing the nation, including not only economic growth, price stability, and balance-of-payments equilibrium but also such vital — and interrelated — political issues as unemployment, poverty, and race relations.

Increasingly, executives of large corporations are coming to see that, if they are to keep their own company's sales and profits growing, and to operate in a healthy political and social environment, it is essential to work for the stability and development of the system as a whole.

Common interests

Thus, in many important respects, executives see their corporate interests bound up with those of other groups:

With the interests of political leaders who are pressed to produce full employment, stable prices, and balance-of-payments equilibrium.

With labor leaders, who must strive to gain job security and rising incomes for the rank and file.

With other manufacturers and businesses, who want strong and rising demand for their own products or services, and are themselves customers of every major industry.

With financial institutions — banks, life insurance companies, pension funds, savings and loan associations — which want to be sure that savings continue to flow to them and that their investments will produce stable and rising returns.

Even with foreign governments and business institutions, whose political and economic decisions can mean life or death to a U.S. corporation.

In this interdependent financial and industrial system, the nation's business leaders begin to see more clearly a need to concert their aims with those of other important policy-makers, whether in business, banking, government, politics, labor, education, or other institutions.

Control—but where?

Indeed, many observers now contend that the U.S. corporate world — along with American society generally — is now controlled by some kind of interlocking directorate among business, government, and other national leaders — an "establishment" like the one that is thought to control Britain.

However, the pictures drawn of this alleged U.S. establishment vary greatly. The late C. Wright Mills of Columbia University called it a "power elite," which he saw as a conservative or reactionary force. Leaders of the civil rights movement refer to it as "the white power structure." Former President Eisenhower, in his farewell speech, warned about a "military-industrial complex," a group that was forcing the nation's economy toward excessive dependence on government defense spending.

Richard H. Rovere has suggested that this "American establishment" covers a political spectrum from slightly left to slightly right of center. It would thus apparently include such diverse personalities as the lawyer, banker, and public servant John J. McCloy; the Harvard professor, economist, and sometime ambassador to India, J. Kenneth Galbraith; and the head of the AFL-CIO, George Meany.

Religion seems to be a critical element to some observers. Professor E. Digby Baltzell of the University of Pennsylvania calls it "the Protestant establishment." But William F. Buckley, Jr., and the editors of the right-wing *National Review* see it as a kind of liberal-big business conspiracy — a version that was apparently the basis of Senator Goldwater's "Eastern establishment."

Even a subcommittee of the U.S. Congress — the Celler subcommittee of the House Banking Committee — this year used such terms as "power elite" and "business establishment" to describe the men who allegedly are most influential in controlling U.S. economic life, and who sit on many corporate boards of directors.

No central group

These differences in descriptions of the nature, composition, and role of the "U.S. establishment" strongly suggest that there is no such thing — at least not in any simple or literal sense.

The pluralistic U.S. society has many centers of power — in industry, government, politics, the foundations, the press, banking, labor, the intelligentsia — none of which has anything approaching absolute control. There are regional and local as well as national "establishments" — or power groups. Alliances among them are shifting and uncertain.

Both the nature of the political democracy and the still important forces of competition in the economy curb the power of any single group — or of any existing coalition of groups.

Historic Roots of the Partnership Goal

Yet there are, of course, unmistakable signs that the entire U.S. system has become more centralized with the growth of big business, big government, and big labor. This trend has gone on for a long time — at least since the 1880s — with the rise of the large corporations.

Early political reform movements, such as Populism and Progressivism, failed in their aim to halt the growth of huge corporations, just as the early industrial empire builders foresaw.

James B. Dill, the lawyer who brought Andrew Carnegie and J. P. Morgan together to form the U.S. Steel Corp., once told the muckraker Lincoln Steffens: "Trusts are natural, inevitable growths out of our social and economic conditions. You cannot stop them by force, with laws. They will sweep down like glaciers upon your police, courts, and states and wash them into flowing rivers. I am clearing the way for them."

Psychic split

Despite the Sherman Antitrust Act of 1890 — and continued popular concern over bigness in the decades that followed — it became clear that technological advance and the growth of a national market were making huge corporations inevitable. These in turn gave rise to huge labor and governmental institutions, in part meant to curb or oppose corporate power.

There was a major split in the American psyche over whether it favored conflict or cooperation among these powerful institutions. Businessmen themselves were split. So were liberals, some decrying "the curse of bigness" and some favoring socialism — which represented an acceptance of bigness but a turning away from competition toward state control.

Mark Hanna's way

In 1912, Herbert Croly — a brilliant editor of *Architectural Record* (now a McGraw-Hill publication) who was soon to found the liberal journal, *The New Republic* — saw a third alternative in the career of the great Republican political boss, Mark Hanna. Croly saw Hanna's life as an effort to coordinate business and government interests for the public welfare. Hanna envisioned a kind of business-government partnership that would be cooperative, not compulsory.

"Of course," wrote Croly, "as a politician he could not help representing business because business was a part of himself — because business was in his eyes not simply moneymaking, but the most necessary kind of social labor."

Mark Hanna, said Croly, saw no evil in what he was trying to do. Rather, he sought to keep alive "the traditional association between business and politics, between private and public interest, which was gradually being shattered by the actual and irresistible development of American business and political life." Hanna, in Croly's view, saw an essential harmony between business interests and those of the whole American community, and sought to develop it.

Central issue

But how could this be done? How avoid the danger that this harmony would be at the expense of the "common people" — the workers and farmers — and possibly at the expense of freedom itself?

This had been the central issue in U.S. politics from the beginning — from the classic debates between Alexander Hamilton, the proponent of a strong central government founded on the combination of business and government interests, and Thomas Jefferson, the advocate of a weak government and of extreme individualism.

Hamilton's opponents had accused him of being the enemy of liberty. But in fact, Croly declared in a book, *The Promise of American Life* — which had a major impact on the "New Nationalism" of Theodore Roosevelt — Hamilton wished, "like the Englishman he was, to protect and encourage liberty, just as far as such encouragement was compatible with good order."

Hamilton realized, Croly said, that genuine liberty "could be protected only by an energetic and clear-sighted central government, and it could be fertilized only by the efficient national organization of American activities."

Croly was somewhat ahead of his time in worrying about ways to concert business and government activities for national aims. World War I naturally focused the attention and energies of both on the same national cause. In the 1920s, business had no reason to complain of government, partly because the Republican Administrations were regarded as business' own creatures, partly because the role of government was of slight importance in that period of prosperity.

Depression impact

The end of that era came with a bang in 1929. President Hoover sought to rally business support for government efforts to steady the economy and spur recovery — but the real problem was to determine exactly what government could or should do.

Looking back later in his Memoirs, Hoover insisted that "no President before had ever believed there was a governmental responsibility in such cases. No matter what the urgings on previous occasions, Presidents steadfastly had maintained that the federal government was apart from such eruptions; they had always been left to blow themselves out."

Any such idea of governmental laissez-faire ended dramatically with the New Deal. President Franklin D. Roosevelt began to intervene all through the business sphere, with his long list of "alphabetical" agencies, starting with NRA.

Both because of traditional business opposition to governmental intervention and because Roosevelt excoriated businessmen as "economic royalists" and virtually accused them of responsibility for Depression miseries, bitter hatred developed between business and government.

Pause and revival

That conflict was adjourned by the exigencies of World War II, and the postwar boom obviated any need for business and government to go to the mat again during the Truman years. With the coming of Eisenhower, businessmen felt that at last they again had an Administration sympathetic to their interests.

The old issue was reopened, however, with the end of the "postwar era" in the recessions of 1957–58 and 1960, followed by the election of John F. Kennedy. It soon turned out that amid the harassments of slumps, unemployment, balance-of-payments problems, and slow growth, the long-standing issue of government-business relations in the U.S. needed a better solution.

New start

Today some business leaders are sensing a fresh relevance in the Alexander Hamilton-Herbert Croly-Theodore Roosevelt philosophy. For this is a period in which government seeks the cooperation of business to achieve many ends, ranging from stable economic growth to advancement of Negroes and low-skilled workers. And these are ends difficult or impossible to achieve through legislation alone — and ends that Americans do not wish to achieve by radical change in the political-economic system.

To gain such objectives, some business leaders are turning away from their traditional version of the "Jeffersonian" creed, with its anti-government bias, its commitment to laissez-faire, its emphasis on "rugged individualism." They are wondering whether such doctrines have become inappropriate to the efficient operation of a modern industrialized society — and even to individual liberty and progress.

Constitutional amendments and civil rights laws may be insufficient, without conscious business cooperation, to promote the advancement of those left behind in U.S. economic and social development.

Can Corporations Act for Social Ends?

These trends have brought a new focus to the business-government relationship.

Over a century ago a prophetic Virginia statesman, Benjamin Watkins Leigh, declared: "Power and property may be separated for a time by force or fraud — but divorced, never. For so soon as the pang of separation is felt . . . property will purchase power, or power will take over property. And either way, there must be an end to free government."

Business leaders today — and government and intellectual leaders as well — are searching for ways of forming a fruitful and healthy relationship between power and property — one in which neither side corrupts or abuses the other, and in which neither oversteps the appropriate limits of its own role. This is an incredibly complex and crucial problem — or series of problems, since it continuously presents itself in different guises.

Classic case

One already classic episode in the evolution of the problem affected U.S. Steel Corp. and its Tennessee Coal & Iron Div. in Birmingham, Ala., in 1963.

During that spring, Birmingham was gripped by racial tensions and violence. Under the urging of the U.S. Dept. of Justice, a group of Birmingham's leading citizens — industrialists, bankers, lawyers — formed a committee to work out some kind of settlement of the racial conflicts.

But this Community Affairs Committee had met only twice when four Negro girls were killed on Sept. 15 by a bomb planted in their Sunday school.

Pressures — from the federal government, civil rights groups, liberal newspapers, even from some Southern moderates — quickly built up for U.S. Steel to use its power to improve the racial situation in Birmingham. A young Birmingham lawyer, Charles Morgan, talking to the Young Men's Business Club, rhetorically asked, "Who is guilty?" — and replied that the "good people" of the city, its business, professional, and religious leaders, were as guilty as the perpetrators of violence.

"Birmingham," said Morgan, "is a city in which the major industry, operated from Pittsburgh, never tried to solve the problem."

Limits of power

Responding to these pressures and criticisms, U.S. Steel's chairman, Roger Blough, set forth his view of the limits of corporate powers and duties.

Blough declared that Arthur V. Wiebel, president of the TC&I Div., had been "working since 1946 developing understanding and strengthening communications between the races in Birmingham." Blough said that "as individuals we can exercise what little influence we may have as citizens, but for a corporation to attempt to exert any kind of economic compulsion to achieve a particular end in the social area seems to be quite beyond what a corporation can do . . ."

Indeed, such resort to economic compulsion by a private corporation would be "repugnant to our American constitutional concepts," said Blough, though U.S. Steel should and did provide equal opportunities in its own plants. It is the job of government, not business, he asserted, to seek to compel social reforms.

Controversial

Whether U.S. Steel — or any corporation — does have the power to change community behavior, and if it does, whether using it to promote better community racial relations would be a misuse of power, remain controversial issues.

Some Alabama businessmen thought TC&I would have been hit by a severe strike if it had gone further than it did; as one said, "the rank and file of the unions are rabid segregationists." But a leading Birmingham lawyer argued: "TC&I wouldn't have had a strike; not if everybody, the banks, other mills and power companies came in with them."

On whether the power should be used, if it exists, many businessmen feel that Blough correctly drew the important distinction between rights and responsibilities of individual company officials acting as citizens, and those of corporations.

Contrary view

Others — such as Rodman C. Rockefeller, 33-year-old vice-president of the International Basic Economy Corp. — feel this distinction is artificial and no longer meaningful. Today, Rockefeller argues, corporations are more than an extension of the property rights of their owners; they are "free participants in our society."

Rockefeller outlined his views in an address this spring at Dartmouth College — the institution whose dispute with the State of New Hampshire over the inviolability of its corporate charter established the basic freedoms of U.S. corporations in 1819.

Society, in recognizing the corporation's right to private property and tolerating the private ownership and use of the means of production, Rodman Rockefeller declared, expects the corporation in return to produce "the minimum socially and economically needed good."

"Other people's money"

Other thoughtful men feel that corporate officials have no right to take such crucial moral or social matters into their own hands, or to use "other people's money" to achieve social ends. Some even doubt whether this would provide better answers to critical social questions than simply aiming to achieve the corporation's economic and financial objectives.

"For example," asks one skeptic, "would racial discrimination be greater or less if all employers operated in a coldly profit-maximizing way than if they operated in conformity with the moral standards of their own communities?"

A New Structure—and New Leadership

In the American society today, no longer is there a simple division between power (meaning political authority) and property (meaning business interests). The concept of property itself has been drastically modified by the rise of the great corporation and the wide diffusion of ownership and control of the means of production, both through financial institutions and through the political process.

Many institutions — labor unions, racial and religious groups, the press, scientists and intellectuals, as well as political parties and their leaders — have some degree of power to influence the course of American life. The business corporation clearly does not bestride U. S. society like a top-hatted Wall Street banker in a cartoon in *Pravda* or *Izvestia*. Yet few would deny it has a crucial role to play.

The ancient cold war between business and government is breaking up — on both sides. The new partnership is still in process of evolution. There is always the possibility — some would say probability — that it will collapse under fresh political, economic, or social pressures. Certainly, the U. S. business community, which is far from unified, does not feel itself committed to any one party's, or to one man's, concept of the Great Society.

Yet there are reasons for thinking that the kind of restructuring of business-government power relations that is going on in the U. S. represents a genuine change in the workings of the system.

Worldwide

For one thing, what is going on in the U. S. is only a manifestation of changes at work in all modern industrial societies throughout the world. As Duke University's Calvin B. Hoover puts it:

> The experience of all modern industrialized societies demonstrates that some sort of the new "mix" of the responsibilities and functions of the state, of economic organizations, and of individuals essentially different from that of capitalism of the past is inevitable.

Every Western democracy is striving to discover for itself the means of achieving a better balance between private and public responsibilities in solving key problems. There are parallels between the President's Council of Economic Advisers and his Advisory Committee on Labor-Management Relations, and the new Dept. of Economic Affairs and the National Economic Development Council in Britain, or the Economic and Social Council in France.

The U.S. way

No two nations are tackling these problems in quite the same way. The U. S. government still plays a less controlling role in industry than do governments in other countries. U. S. industry, says Thomas J. Watson, Jr. — whose IBM Corp. operates in many countries — is still "less fettered than in any other country, by a long, long shot."

This, he thinks, is a major reason why U. S. industry is so strong and innovative. U. S. industrial success, as he sees it, is closely related to "the speed of the decision process."

The willingness of private business voluntarily to work with government is, in Watson's view and that of a growing number of other business leaders, a way to retain their present degree of freedom and to avoid what they fear will be inefficient or wrongheaded government controls.

Formidable

The technical and operating problems facing businessmen who would measure up to the needs of the time are formidable. They may range from fiscal and monetary policy to urban renewal to race relations to problems of national defense and the uses of outer space — and, of course, a knowledge of how to run their own businesses successfully in a period of explosive technological change.

The education of tomorrow's business leaders will have to offer better preparation for such a wide range of problems than the education — and experiences — afforded the present generation of business leaders.

Models

Some business leaders of today, however, do provide models of how to serve the interests of private business and the broad society. One such man is Robert A. Lovett — banker, World War I Navy hero, World War II public official, Secretary of Defense under President Truman, and a leading candidate for inclusion in the mythical "U. S. establishment."

Says Lovett: "The corporation should not seek to replace public authority. Yet the corporation is endowed with the public interest — a bit. It is created by the state, and it must be responsible . . ."

Democracy, Lovett adds, requires that freedom be coupled with restraint. There is no simple formula for this, he concedes, but says: "I can't believe that there is not enough wisdom or wit in this country so that we can handle our problems within a context of freedom."

There is growing support within the U. S. business community for such views.

The Hard Choice that Faces Business

It is becoming clear that what U. S. business faces today is a set of choices on the role it is to play in relation to the broad society. Business cannot avoid the necessity of choice, because the modern corporation has become the towering institution of today's society — and the problems of society have become its problems as well.

The society is demanding the achievement of a great many national objectives — national security (which inescapably involves the corporation), maximum employment, racial equality, rising living standards (especially for groups left behind in the growth race), improved education, better medical care, a healthier urban environment, the safeguarding of natural resources.

Two roads

In attempting to achieve those ends, which involve overlapping business and government functions and responsibilities, there are two basic choices:

To increase the role of government and, where business is concerned, to make greater use of coercion or fiat to bring about the kind of business behavior desired.

To seek to develop more fruitful, voluntary cooperation between business and government.

Either approach has obvious dangers.

The first may involve excessive centralization of power in the government, posing genuine threats to the freedom and efficiency of business, and to society itself.

The second may be too loose and uncertain, and can scarcely avoid the problem of sanctions against "chiselers," or simply hard-pressed businesses that are not able to measure up to the standards of "social responsibility" assumed by large and prosperous corporations.

No "either-or"

But the choice is not a simple either-or decision.

Indeed, the success or failure of the voluntary approach in particular areas will largely determine whether the coercive role of government is to be closely limited or greatly expanded.

And how far government intervenes in the economy or in social relations will depend heavily on its ability to create conditions making for a healthy and growing over-all economy.

There are reasons to hope that thanks to progress in the understanding and use of fiscal and monetary policy by government, the detailed decisions on production, distribution, employment, location of industry, and such matters can on the whole be handled by business on its own.

Yet specific problems have emerged — and others will continue to develop — that require business and government cooperation, or legislative solution.

Today, some of these issues involve collective bargaining and strike threats in key industries, the nation's balance of payments, race relations, unemployment, poverty, urban decay. What specifically the critical issues of the future will be no one can know for sure.

Cautions

Just as they do today, viewpoints in the future are bound to differ on the gravity or nature of particular problems and on how to deal with them. These viewpoints will be colored in part by the interests of the parties that are involved and by their ideologies — including interests and ideologies of government officials and their academic or other allies, as well as those of business.

That means it will be vitally important to guard, on the one hand, against the notion that "the public interest" is always best defined and understood by public officials. The power of the state, as Calvin B. Hoover warns, "cannot automatically be assumed to be wielded in the public interest."

On a host of matters, businessmen must be free to make their own decisions, or society will suffer. They should not — as one of them recently told the President — be treated "like children."

At the same time, some businessmen point out, it cannot automatically be assumed that whatever the President, or other government policymakers, propose is damaging to business interests. Frederick R. Kappel, chairman of American Telephone & Telegraph Co., in thinking back over the forces that prompted the growth of his own giant corporation, has stressed that one of the most essential factors — besides technical innovation and entrepreneurial drive — was "the public consensus, the political decision . . ."

Leadership and economics

The U. S. system puts heavy responsibility on the federal government, and the President in particular; and the American people have come to expect Presidents to exert leadership whenever and wherever national problems are serious — whether in matters of national defense, foreign affairs, race relations, or economic affairs.

The last is a relatively new area for Presidential leadership. But it emerged as a crucial area with the development of full-scale modern industrialism and came to crisis with the Great Depression — which the American people are determined never to let happen again.

Economics has persisted as an area of Presidential concern in a society in which some critical problems can better be solved by high-level decision makers, in government and business, rather than being left to the "marketplace" — or to accident or fate. Wherever possible, however, it makes good sense to let competition in the marketplace and consumers' choices determine economic activity.

How tension helps

One of the great advantages of a free society is that, though one respects one's political chief, one must not necessarily do what he says. Businessmen have a different perspective from government, and society's ends — "the public interest" — may often be best promoted by a tension between business and government. Tensions and conflicts may be as constructive for the broad society as within any single organization.

But they may sometimes become destructive. The endless problem, within an organization or society as a whole, is to find a balance — to permit tensions, but set limits on conflict lest it become ruinous.

Role for business

The problems of avoiding excessive power for the business corporation are as worthy of concern as is limiting the power of government. There are inherent restrictions, however, for the corporation is not the only significant or powerful institution today. Labor unions in many respects provide a useful check on the power of both business and government. So do farm groups, universities, foundations, professional organizations, racial and religious groups, even the family.

The corporation may unavoidably be involved in moral issues, but it cannot presume to replace the churches, or the conscience of the individual. Nor can the corporation be mother and father to its employees. A free society is a pluralistic society — one in which no one institution (or one political party) can be all-powerful and controlling.

Yet businessmen today are increasingly coming to understand that they do have considerable power and that they can play — as heads of huge organizations — a major role in shaping the fortunes of a free society.

B   Profits and Profit Sharing

6   What Is Wrong with Profit Maximization?

Charles F. Phillips, Jr.

Corporate management must face up to a predicament that has crucial economic and social implications. On the one hand, many argue that business must assume social responsibilities, in addition to its historic economic and legal obligations, by becoming involved even more deeply in such activities as corporate giving, support of higher education, political participation, and representation in community affairs. In discussing the changing role of business in our economy, David Rockefeller, President of the Chase Manhattan Bank, argues:

> In *social* terms, the old concept that the owner of a business had a right to use his property as he pleased to maximize profits has evolved into the belief that ownership carries certain binding social obligations. Today's manager serves as trustee not only for the owners but for the workers and indeed for our entire society. . . . Corporations have developed a sensitive awareness of their responsibility for maintaining an equitable balance among the claims of stockholders, employees, customers and the public at large.[1]

On the other hand, an equally vocal group contends that management should adhere to its traditional economic function of producing

From *Business Horizons,* Winter 1963, pp. 73–80. Copyright 1963 by the Foundation for the School of Business at Indiana University. Reprinted by permission.

[1] David Rockefeller, "The Changing Role of Business in Our Society," in an address before the American Philosophical Society, Philadelphia, Nov. 8, 1962.

goods and services at maximum profit. In the words of Milton Friedman, the University of Chicago's well-known economist:

> Few trends could so thoroughly undermine the very foundations of our free society as the acceptance by corporate officials of a social responsibility other than to make as much money for their stockholders as possible. This is a fundamentally subversive doctrine.[2]

Professor Friedman believes, moreover, that even business contributions to support charitable activities represent "an inappropriate use of corporate funds in a free-enterprise society."

The choice of a course involves far more than mere intellectual exercise. As challenging as that may be, management faces the grave prospect of undergoing a significant modification of its traditional role unless it faces decisively the issues raised by the present controversy. As a result of indecision, a solution may be forced upon management — perhaps against its best interests.

The Thesis

In the past few years, some businessmen have tended more frequently to soft-pedal profit maximization and to emphasize the modern corporation's growing list of social obligations. But the phrase "social responsibility," rarely defined, remains a hazy concept. Sometimes it implies only a shift in emphasis, perhaps for public relations purposes, without modification of business goals or values. At other times, however, the implication is that corporations should step beyond their traditional economic and legal functions *even at the sacrifice of long-run profit*. This view of social responsibility is, to use Joseph W. McGuire's phrase, "a crude blend of long-run profit making and altruism."[3]

In the writer's opinion, both business and our private enterprise system would suffer if profit maximization were sought irresponsibly, but they would also suffer if uncritical philanthropy were introduced in the guise of social responsibility. Profit maximization must remain as the basic goal of business firms. In turn, the profit maximization approach can guide management in the area of social responsibility. Businessmen must be socially responsible insofar as social responsibility leads to higher profits, but they must possess a fine sense of double-entry bookkeeping! Argues Henry Ford II, Chairman of the Board of the Ford Motor Company:

---

[2] Milton Friedman, *Capitalism and Freedom*, The University of Chicago Press, Chicago, 1962, p. 133.
[3] Joseph W. McGuire, *Business and Society*, McGraw-Hill Book Company, Inc., New York, 1963, p. 144.

Once "business is business" meant dog-eat-dog, the devil take the hindmost, the law of the jungle. Today we need that phrase "business is business" just to remind us that business is *not* first and foremost a social institution, a charitable agency, a cultural gathering, a community service, a public spirited citizen. It is an action organization geared to produce economic results in competition with other business.[4]

Why is it felt that management should be responsible to society as a whole rather than to its stockholders? What are the long-run implications of social responsibility? What is a socially responsible enterprise in a market economy? Finally, is the quandary regarding social responsibility and profit maximization real or illusory?

Social Responsibility: Origins

The traditional justification for a private enterprise economy rests on the assumption that rigorous competition will prevail. One of the basic tenets of competitive theory, as developed by Adam Smith and other classical economists, is that business firms will seek to maximize profits. By so doing, business will allocate society's scarce resources in the best possible manner, and serve the best interests of both their stockholders and the general public. A competitive market system thus reconciles private interests with the public good.

In 1932 Adolf A. Berle, Jr., and Gardiner C. Means questioned the relevance of these assumptions for modern capitalism and, in so doing, started a continuing debate over corporate responsibilities.[5] The authors noted that the ownership of corporate stock was becoming dispersed among society's members, while control of corporate capital assets was becoming concentrated in the hands of a relatively few salaried managers. The first trend tends to reduce the effectiveness of stockholder control and the second to increase the economic power of management.

Few today disagree with the conclusions of the Berle and Means study; statistics on the dispersion of ownership and the concentration of control of corporate assets are familiar. More important for present purposes are the problems raised by these developments.

The first arises from the fact that in our modern economy stockholders own property without effective control while management

---

[4] Henry Ford II, "What America Expects of Industry," in an address before the Michigan State Chamber of Commerce, Oct. 2, 1962.

[5] Adolf A. Berle, Jr., and Gardiner C. Means, *The Modern Corporation and Private Property*, The Macmillan Co., New York, 1932. See also Adolf A. Berle, Jr., *Power without Property*, Harcourt, Brace and Company, Inc., New York, 1959.

has power without substantial ownership. The classical economists assumed that ownership and management were synonymous; profits were the reward for successfully exercising this ownership-management function. The separation of ownership and control, therefore, raises a question: to whom is management responsible? To use Berle's phrase, the stockholder has become a "passive receptive" who cannot manage and who is thus functionless. But management has no legitimate claim on profits because it lacks ultimate ownership. On the matter of corporate control, Edward S. Mason writes:

> What Mr. Berle and most of the rest of us are afraid of is that this powerful corporate machine, which so successfully grinds out the goods we want, seems to be running without any discernible controls. The young lad mastering the technique of his bicycle may legitimately shout with pride, 'Look, Ma, no hands,' but is this the appropriate motto for a corporate society?[6]

The second problem is raised by corporate size. Economists generally believe that competition among large enterprises is different from competition among small decision-making units. This belief is reflected in the popular feeling that competition has declined in the United States and that prices are administered or institutionally determined. Management, the argument goes, has the freedom (within limits) to set prices and to determine the rate of technological change and economic growth. Competition, many feel, is not the strict disciplinarian it was once thought to be and, as a result, the goals of management have changed. Management is far more interested in the corporation as an institution and in its continued existence than in immediate, or even long-run, profits.

Because the irresponsible use of this immense power is unthinkable, management must become socially responsible; it has been suggested that management has no choice. The accumulation of power by any group in a democratic society has always been suspect. The tremendous economic power of Big Business, unless used justly, will be further restricted by Big Labor and Big Government. (Both of the latter have also been subjects of debate.) To maintain a private enterprise economy, so the argument goes, business must assume new social responsibilities.

Social Responsibility: Its Implication

If social responsibility becomes the dominant force in business decision making, three significant implications should be understood. In the first place, the idea of a corporate conscience assumes that

---

[6] In Edward S. Mason (ed.), *The Corporation in Modern Society*, Harvard University Press, Cambridge, 1959, pp. 3–4.

management has the option of being socially responsible or not. While such an assumption may be vehemently denied by business leaders, the fact remains that vigorous competition and social statesmanship are logically incompatible. In the words of Theodore Levitt:

> . . . only businessmen who are free from the rigid demands of competition are free to practice the prerogatives of business statesmanship. Statesmanship is a luxury of some degree of monopoly. Any business that habitually practices statesmanship must be presumed to have achieved the felicity of not having to keep its nose continuously to the competitive grindstone. If it can purposefully hold prices down or freely raise them, if it can have extravagant employee welfare plans, make handouts to every solicitor for a supposedly good cause, make its headquarters a crystal palace of ankle-deep rugs and solid-gold water coolers — if it can do these, one may begin to question whether the industry is entirely competitive.[7]

Levitt may be pushing the argument to the extreme, but his point is valid; a business firm cannot have the best of two worlds. The first implication of social responsibility, then, is that competition in our economy has become so "imperfect" that the market is a poor regulator of corporate behavior.

In the second place, conscience requires that value judgments be made. Two questions immediately arise: does business know what is good for society and, even if it does, should business force its value judgments on society? One may properly question whether any interest group in the economy knows what society really wants or should want; clearly a consensus does not exist. Argues Ben W. Lewis:

> Economic decisions must be right as society measures right rather than good as benevolent individuals construe goodness. An economy is a mechanism designed to pick up and discharge the wishes of society in the management of its resources; it is not an instrument for the rendering of gracious music by kindly disposed improvisers.[8]

In the third place, the acceptance of social responsibility may make it impossible for business to carry out its major function of economizing, that is, to be efficient in the use of the nation's scarce and limited resources. Responsibility or conscientiousness has nothing to do

---

[7] Theodore Levitt, "The Mythological Potency of 'Peoples' Capitalism,'" in *The Corporation: Its Modern Character and Responsibilities*, The Ohio State University, Columbus, 1960, pp. 15–16. See also, by the same author, "The Dangers of Social Responsibility," *Harvard Business Review*, XXXVI (Sept.–Oct. 1958).

[8] Ben W. Lewis, "Economics by Admonition," *American Economic Review*, XLIX (May 1959), 395.

with economizing. Should society at large come to accept the idea of a corporate conscience, business may find it exceedingly difficult to make sound economic decisions with respect to prices, wages, and investment. Such decisions are often unpleasant — for example, the decision to move a plant from one community to another. Again, Professor Lewis' words are well worth considering:

> Ponder the plight of the management of a giant firm producing a basic commodity, employing thousands of workers at good wages, making splendid profits, and presently facing a crippling strike unless it accedes to a demand for a wage increase. The increase can easily be passed along in higher prices. Workers want higher wages and no interruption in employment; consumers want continued output at an increasing rate and so do stockholders. The public does not want further inflation, and large numbers of small firms do not want further increases in wages. The White House, which wants high production, full employment, healthy wages, abundant profits, and low prices, now admonishes industrial statesmen to recognize their public responsibility and to adopt measures appropriate to the maintenance of equity, full employment, stability, and progress. The management — as allocator, distributor, stabilizer, trustee, conservator, prophet, and chaplain, as well as manager — consults its conscience. The diagnosis of the attending psychiatrist will be "multiple schizophrenia." The management's personality will not be split. It will be shredded and powdered![9]

One can sympathize with United States Steel's Roger Blough when, in the face of overwhelming governmental displeasure, he attempted to defend his company's 1962 price increase to the nation in terms of profits and investment needs. But it would be difficult to imagine his defense in terms of social responsibility: to maintain equity among the company's interested groups, higher wages were voluntarily granted to workers and increased prices to suppliers, which, in turn, necessitated higher steel prices to provide greater profits for stockholders' dividends and for new investment to satisfy consumer demand (all beneficial to society at large). Or consider the following reply by an executive of one of the country's largest corporations when asked by a stockholder to defend his firm's annual educational gifts: "We in the . . . Company believe in being good corporate citizens. We think the principle of corporate giving is well established. It is encouraged by our tax laws; it has been upheld in our courts; and the public has come to expect it of corporations."

Is not this the crux of the issue faced by management? Since bigness is frequently suspect and the level of existing profits as well as

---

[9] "Economics by Admonition," p. 396.

the need for higher profits often questioned, corporate actions are frequently defended in terms of responsibility. But such a defense will subject management's conscience to countless pressures, and the public will come to expect contributions, even when the corporation cannot expect either direct or indirect benefits. "A competitive establishment cannot be selfless in any genuine fashion. Selflessness, however, is what socially responsible behavior implies," writes Levitt.

If these implications are correct, management's attempt to justify both its size and its power in terms of social responsibility may end in gigantic failure. The corporation is an economic institution, not a welfare organization, and its real justification is profit maximization for the benefit of its stockholders. By stepping into the social arena where there are few, if any, acceptable standards of efficiency in the use of society's resources, business may invite restrictions on its freedom.

Social responsibility is a function of government, civic organizations, and business leaders as individuals. Public officials are responsible to the public at large, but "it is highly repugnant that a corporate manager, not publicly elected and hence not subject to popular recall, should have a special responsibility for what the managerialists call the process of government. At least a socialistic government can be defeated at the polls." [10] Benevolent management rule is not, I am confident, the intent of those advocating social responsibility.

The Case For Profit Maximization

Eugene V. Rostow has succinctly stated the case for profit maximization:

> The law books have always said that the board of directors owes a singleminded duty of unswerving loyalty to the stockholders, and only to the stockholders. The economist has demonstrated with all the apparent precision of plane geometry and the calculus that the quest for maximum revenue in a competitive market leads to a system of prices, and an allocation of resources and rewards, superior to any alternative, in its contributions to the economic welfare of the community as a whole. . . . If, as is widely thought, the essence of corporate statesmanship is to seek less than maximum profits, post war experience is eloquent evidence that such statesmanship leads to serious malfunctioning of the economy as a whole.[11]

In short, according to Rostow, social responsibility will "sabotage the market mechanism and systematically distort the allocation of

---

[10] "Have Corporations a Higher Duty than Profits?" *Fortune*, LXII (August 1960), 148.
[11] Eugene V. Rostow in *The Corporation in Modern Society*, p. 63.

resources," thereby making "the task of monetary and fiscal authority in controlling general fluctuations of trade more expensive and more difficult," and perhaps making "it impossible to sustain high levels of employment save at the cost of considerable price inflation."

In everyday phraseology, profit assumes that management is responsible for running an efficient business organization, that is, performing its economic function. *In so doing, the organization is being socially responsible.* In making a decision, whether that decision concerns prices, investment, plant location, or an educational contribution, some criteria must be used as guides. Profit maximization is a criterion; social responsibility, emphasizing equity, is not.

> The corporate conscience is irrelevant to the corporate purpose. Conscience is not something you introduce as a piece of organizational decor, performing simply a decorative function. If it is allowed to influence the mechanism of economic decision-making, conscience automatically assumes a central role. Nothing could be worse. The stronger the conscience the harder it will be to make a businesslike decision and get the economic job done.[12]

Further, the primary of philosophy adopted by management — whether social responsibility or profit maximization — determines the decisions made. Should Firm X continue to operate in Community Y, where it is the largest employer, or should it move to Community Z where its profit potential is greater? Should corporations sponsor higher quality television programs at the risk of smaller audiences in an attempt to get the industry out of the "vast wasteland," or should program content be aimed at capturing the largest possible audience? Clearly, social responsibility and profit maximization are two entirely different concepts involving different goals and values.

It might be argued that the traditional or orthodox justification for profit maximization is no longer suited to the needs of modern capitalism. One of the basic assumptions of those advocating corporate social responsibility is that the market mechanism no longer functions as effectively as was once thought and that corporations consequently have some degree of market power or choice over such variables as prices and the rate of technological innovation. My own opinion is that competition, whether in the price or nonprice dimension, exists in sufficient strength to limit the long-run area of choice open to the managements of most American corporations.

Let there be no misunderstanding. Competition is far from "perfect" and public policy could and should promote, to achieve maximum efficiency and personal freedom, a stronger pro-competitive

---

[12] "The Mythological Potency of 'Peoples' Capitalism,'" p. 15.

policy (by eliminating trade barriers and fair trade laws, to name only two examples). Yet in most industries, the existing degree of competition is sufficient (in economic terms "workable") to protect the consumer interest. The danger in accepting the philosophy of social responsibility is that management will forget its economic function and will attempt to assume the functions that have traditionally been assigned to the market mechanism. (Just as dangerous are attempts by either government or labor to assume managerial functions.[13]) Concludes Ford:

> I have deep faith in the stimulating power of competition and in the capacity of the free market to allocate resources and to bring us optimum growth and progress, if we will only let it work. And we will let it work if we can bring ourselves to accept a few very simple ideas about business: that business is a tool, and that the sharper its cutting edges are the stronger its motivating power, the better job it will be able to do for all of us.[14]

It has been suggested that a compromise is necessary to solve the issue of social responsibility. Thus, Richard Eells argues that "the root of the conflict over social responsibilities lies in the irreconcilability of two equally untenable theories of the corporation," namely, the "traditional corporation," which intends to maximize profits, and the "metrocorporation," which assumes limitless social obligations. He puts forward the "well-tempered corporation," a compromise between these two extremes, which regards profits as primary but also considers its social obligations in the decision-making process.[15]

The editors of *Fortune* find it difficult to distinguish between the "well-tempered corporation" and the "metrocorporation." In their words:

> . . . it is impossible to attach a definite meaning to the expression "profits are secondary" or even to "profits are primary but coordinate with other functions." If profits are secondary, then they can *always* be sacrificed for the sake of fulfilling obligations that are primary; but since profits are an indispensable condition of the corporation's existence, this is tantamount to saying that the corporation can sacrifice its existence and at the same time fulfill its obligations to the community. Again, to say that profits are a primary function, coordinate with other functions, amounts to saying that these other functions are also

---

13 Charles F. Phillips, Jr., and Harmon H. Haymes, " 'Psychological' Price Control: Meddling or Masterstroke?" *Business Horizons,* V (Summer 1962), 99–106.

14 Henry Ford, "What America Expects of Industry."

15 Richard Eells, "Social Responsibility: Can Business Survive the Challenge?" *Business Horizons,* II (Winter 1959), 37.

primary and hence of equal importance. So what does the corporation do in the event of a conflict?[16]

The management of a modern corporation may be a "self-perpetuating oligarchy" (Berle's phrase), but that management making inadequate profits will not survive for long. Moreover, social responsibility is a fair-weather concept; management cannot even think in terms of philanthropy unless profits are adequate.

Social Responsibility in a Market Economy

The basic proposition, as every businessman knows only too well, is that profits are the indispensable element in a successful business enterprise. The role of profits may not be recognized or understood by as many of our citizens as would be desirable, but to duck the issue by hiding behind the cloak of "social responsibility" does not seem to be the answer. Management must operate at maximum economic efficiency to get rid of the evil connotations attached to the word "profit." The corporation that is efficient, that constantly strives to improve old products and introduce new ones, and that seeks to satisfy consumer demand in the most efficient manner and at the lowest possible price is the one with the strongest case for maximum profit.

Yet conscience is an integral part of management's everyday decision making and profit maximization functions. Responsible behavior requires scrupulous adherence to the spirit of the law as well as to its letter, avoidance of any misrepresentative advertising, and bargaining with labor in good faith. This point has been well stated by Frederick R. Kappel, Board Chairman of the American Telephone & Telegraph Company:

> . . . the purpose of business is not simply to provide the opportunity for making a fast buck. . . . The fast-buck philosophy not only stands in the way of a good job, it also robs the individual of the feeling of accomplishment that he needs in his personal life. I don't mean that one needs to be a "do-gooder" in the sense in which that phrase is often used. But *the person of character* will approach business life with the idea that he has obligations to fulfill. He will set his ethical sights high and hold himself strictly to account. He will act on the principle that good management, sound business practice, and balanced judgment are ideals well worth his best striving.[17]

Similarly, profit maximization does not imply that business

---

16 "Have Corporations a Higher Duty than Profits?" p. 109.
17 Frederick R. Kappel in an address at the commencement exercises of Michigan State University, June 9, 1963 (emphasis added).

leaders can be indifferent to the country's social system. Management has an interest in trying to maintain and aid the development of a social system in which firms can operate with maximum freedom, profitability, and longevity. However, *business should seek society's good in ways that are also good for business.* Philanthropic acts often have economic justification: gifts to a local school construction program may improve the company's labor force; matching employees' gifts to their universities or other philanthropies may increase both the stability and the effort of its labor force; and community gifts of many kinds may improve community relations in ways that admittedly are difficult to measure. For these reasons, insurance companies conduct safety education, banks employ agricultural specialists, and railroads promote area development.

Therefore, a contribution to a charitable organization should be made because it benefits the corporation and not because it is the thing to do or because it is expected. The executive who was quoted earlier concerning his company's policy of contributing money to educational institutions was asked to defend the policy again a year later. This time, however, his answer was quite different: "When we finally commit ourselves to an expenditure, we feel that within the limits of human fallibility we have done our best to be able to say: 'This expenditure, this investment, will be profitable and remunerative for the company and, through it, for the shareholders.' We devote exactly the same attention to our contributions for philanthropy and education." No longer is the emphasis upon responsibility; it is upon profits.

Would it not be ironic for management to lose the struggle for public recognition of the role of adequate profits, for which it has fought so long, just at a time when it appears that the chances of success may be at hand? It has been a long time since an administration has actively advocated and sought a tax cut to stimulate economic growth. And it has been an even longer time since a Democratic president has publicly argued that increased business profits are one means of achieving this goal. Many obstacles remain before words become deeds, but this hardly seems to be the time for a basic shift in management's philosophy.

What is wrong with profit maximization as management's basic decision-making goal? Nothing, if properly understood. The choice between profit maximization and social responsibility is not an either-or proposition. As long as profit maximization is the dominant factor in corporate decision making, guiding management in the area of social responsibility, no problem exists. But if business adopts a dominant philosophy of social responsibility, our free, competitive, private enterprise system cannot survive.

A business firm is not a chartable or philanthropic organization. It is an economizing institution and its basic function is to economize; only by performing its economic function well is a business firm socially responsible. Nor is a business firm an instrument through which its management seeks to replace the functioning of the market with its value judgments as to what is good or bad for society. Business operates within a legal framework and is subject to market control. If the market does not adequately control business decisions, then the public can be expected to demand government control. Market control is the essence of a democratic, private enterprise system.

Many will disagree with the view being expressed. Some, such as McGuire, have termed profit maximization the "traditional" approach, one that does not permit business "to adapt to a changing world." Nothing could be further from the truth; business has changed and will continue to change. Certainly the public expects more from business today than it did fifty years ago and assumes that businessmen will be men of character with a high sense of what is right and wrong. But as executives of corporations, business leaders' major responsibility is to manage as efficiently as possible the allocation of that portion of society's resources that come within the corporation's control. Is this not, after all, the only economic, legal, and social justification for a business enterprise in a free society?

7   The Ethics of Profit Sharing

Benjamin L. Masse

In response to certain remarks of the writer on the moral aspects of profit sharing ("War or Peace in Detroit," *America,* March 1, 1958, pp 626–629), a number of readers have written in to express a dissent. A few contended that I had aided and abetted a sinister plan to subvert the American system of private enterprise. Most of the corre-

Reprinted with permission from *America,* 106 West 56th Street, New York, New York, May 31, 1958, pp. 285–287.

spondents, however, suggested that my approach had been too conservative. They argued that in the light of Catholic social teaching there was much more to be said in defense of a union demand for profit sharing than I had given the reader reason to believe. Obviously, a more extended treatment of this question is indicated.

In the article which stirred up this discussion, I stated that, so far as remuneration went, an employer who paid his workers a fair wage had fully discharged his obligation in justice to them. I wrote that such workers "cannot demand a share in profits as a strict right," or, as a consequence, resort to economic force to support a demand for profit sharing. In taking this stand I leaned heavily on the late Pope Pius XI, who upheld the justice of the wage contract against those who insisted that it must be replaced by a partnership contract. Though the Pope did commend profit sharing, as well as labor's sharing in management and ownership, he presented these modifications of the wage contract only as something "advisable." I therefore concluded that, although workers could submit a profit-sharing proposal to their employer, the employer was under no moral obligation to grant it, or even to consider it.

I gladly concede that this highly condensed statement of the case gives not only an inadequate but also a misleading impression of Catholic writing on the morality of profit sharing. It is, indeed, an easy task to cite writers who contradict it. Here are a few of them.

In Commutative Justice

In the final revised edition of his well-known *Distributive Justice,* the late Msgr. John A. Ryan raises the question whether workers who are receiving just wages have any claim upon profits (p. 294ff.) By profits in this context, Monsignor Ryan seems to mean the residue remaining after the payment of all costs of production, including dividends. He says that where the employer carries on his business in competitive conditions, workers who are already receiving just wages — what he calls the "equitable minimum"— have no strict right to any additional compensation out of the rare "surplus profits" which may develop. However, in companies that are monopolies or quasi-monopolies, all who work for the business have a right to share in its "surplus profits." In such companies, he writes, "the surplus profits should all be distributed among those who perform any function in the industry, from the president of the company down to the office boy."

The distribution of such profits, he adds, "should be in proportion to their respective salaries and wages"— a standard which reflects, presumably, the contribution of each employer to the success of the enterprise. Monsignor Ryan could find "no conclusive reason" for forbidding workers to use their economic power to gain a share in surplus profits.

Does not this division of the corporate income do violence to the rights of stockholders? No, answers the monsignor. So far as their contribution to the success of the enterprise goes, he could see no difference between bondholders and stockholders. Aside from providing capital, neither contributes in any way to the productive process. "Why," he asks, "should the non-working stockholders receive any part of the surplus to the production of which they have contributed neither time nor thought nor labor?" Therefore, he concludes:

> If matters are so arranged that they are certain to receive the prevailing rate of interest each year, and if a sufficient reserve is set aside to protect them against losses, they are receiving all that seems to be fair and all that is necessary to induce men to invest their money in a concern of this sort (p. 337).

In the first edition of *Distributive Justice,* Monsignor Ryan had been somewhat more generous to the stockholders. In *commutative* justice, which governs the claims of workers and owners on corporative income based on their contributions to the common enterprise, he allowed stockholders a dividend of one per cent above the prevailing rate of interest. In *social* justice, which governs the distribution of corporate income in the interest of the general welfare, he conceded them an additional four per cent return from the surplus profits.

Prof. J. Messner of the University of Vienna is another distinguished writer who holds that workers have a right in commutative justice to a share in profits, but he argues the case differently. In a capitalistic economy, he explains in *Social Ethics,* the employer is supposed to assume the risks of fluctuations due to market circumstances. In practice, however, the employer tries so far as possible to shift this risk to his employes by cutting their wages and laying them off. "The worker," he concludes, "is therefore in the right when he endeavors to gain a share in surplus profits" (p. 765). Professor Messner observes, however, that when the profit position of the firm is favorable, workers as a rule strive to compensate for past losses by demands for higher future wages.

In Social Justice

Like Monsignor Ryan, the Rev. Raymond J. Miller, C.Ss.R., in his commentary on *Quadragesimo Anno, Forty Years After: Pius XI and the Social Order,* distinguishes between small businesses, employing "less than 100 workers," and "the hundred-million and billion-dollar giants, which do the greater part of the business of the nation." The small employer, he holds, is entitled to whatever profit he can make.

The stockholder in the big corporation, on the other hand, since he renders no service beyond providing capital, is entitled in commutative justice only to a fair return on his investment. Who, then, asks Father Miller, owns the undistributed profits —"that portion of the income of a business which remains after all the creditors and all the stockholders of the business have been paid off"?

At this point Father Miller parts company with Monsignor Ryan. The stockholders own these "surplus profits" he says, morally as well as legally. They are not free, however, to use them as suits their fancy, since they have the obligation "of allocating or distributing them in the way that will best serve the common good." That workers who have been paid just wages have no claim in commutative justice to surplus profits is clear, Father Miller believes, from Pius XI's defense of the justice of the wage contract. "It is of the essence of the wage contract," he argues, "that the workers give up any rights they might have to the profits in return for a fixed wage."

Granted this analysis of the problem, the only basis for a union demand for profit sharing lies in social justice. Father Miller holds that such a demand can be justified because "the common good will be served if both the capitalists and the workers get a share of the profits." To charges that union demands for profit sharing are an invasion of management rights, Father Miller replies that the same Pope who taught that the capitalist owns the profits and should have the "leading voice" in distributing them for the common good taught also that it would be advisable to give workers a share not only in profits but in management as well.

In a doctoral dissertation submitted to the Faculty of the School of Sacred Theology at Catholic University, *Distribution of Profits in the Modern Corporation,* the Rev. George F. Bardes likewise holds that stockholders in the big corporation have a claim in commutative justice "to no more than an interest rate somewhat higher than the pure and simple creditor." The profits remaining after the payment of fair dividends should be retained in the business or distributed as the needs of the enterprise and the general welfare of society suggest. Where surplus profits are foreseen, writes Father Bardes, who is a priest of the Archdiocese of New York, they "are aptly presented for discussion at a bargaining table." And he adds: "The worker is free to bargain at this time for a change from a pure wage-earning status to one of modified partnership whereby he may become a sharer in profits, ownership and management." Father Bardes holds that such a demand for a form of modified partnership "may be the subject of a strike."

From this sampling of the literature on the subject, it will be clear that there is a case for profit sharing on the grounds of both commutative and social justice. How strong is that case?

The Ethics of Profit Sharing

Conclusion

With all respect for the memory of John A. Ryan, whose friendship I cherished, *I do not see how workers have any claim in commutative justice to "surplus profits."* If we assume that all contractual obligations have been met and that the customers have not been overcharged, then these profits belong to the owners of the corporation, and they belong to them morally as well as legally. As Father Miller rightly says, by contracting for a fixed wage, the workers forgo any further claim on the corporation's income. Even if one grants that the status of the stockholder in big corporations is coming more and more to resemble the status of bondholders, and that they are amply compensated for the risks involved in this type of ownership by a somewhat higher return on their investment than bondholders receive, workers would still not acquire on that score any title in commutative justice to surplus profits.

As for Professor Messner, his argument is based on the assumption that the workers have not in the past received a just wage. In this case, he says, they rightly claim a share in future surplus profits. But such a claim resembles more a demand for compensation due and not paid than a demand for a share of profits in the strict sense.

With those who seek to find in social justice a basis for worker participation in profits, I am more in sympathy. I have no difficulty in accepting the proposition that the stockholders of a corporation fortunate enough to have excess profits — in practice, the board of directors — have an obligation to use these earnings to promote the general welfare. I am also persuaded that in many cases this could most effectively be accomplished by sharing the profits with the workers, as is being done now by an impressive and growing number of U. S. companies. My problem here arises in conceding to workers the right to force stockholders, by the threat and use of economic force, not only to discharge *their* obligation in social justice, but to determine as well *how* they are to do it. This right, it seems to me, resides in the community, whose well-being is the object of social justice, and can in practice be legitimately exercised only by the supreme authority in the community, namely, the state.

With Father Miller I agree that a union may raise the question of excess profits at the bargaining table and try as best it can to convince the company that the common good would be fostered by sharing them with the employes. But I cannot see that it has a moral right — a right based on the natural law — to insist that the owners live up to their obligation of using surplus profits to promote the general welfare, or that they discharge it by sharing profits rather than in some other way. I must conclude, therefore, that workers would violate the rights of private property were they to employ economic force to oblige their employer to practice profit sharing. I am not sure that Father Miller would dissent from this conclusion.

What chiefly influences me to take this stand is the parallel between worker demands for profit sharing and worker demands for sharing in management. When a decade ago some Catholics argued that workers had a natural right to share in management, the Holy See felt obliged to issue a warning. While reiterating the teaching of Pius XI that some modification of the wage contract through profit sharing and sharing in management and ownership was advisable and to be commended, the present Holy Father warned against any exaggeration that would infringe on the rights of owners. In an address to the Ninth Congress of the International Union of Catholic Employer Associations on May 7, 1949, the Pope rejected the opinion that all employes of a business enterprise have a right to share in its ownership or profits on the ground that the enterprise is a society wherein relationships are governed by the norms of distributive justice. However much he favored liberalizing employer-employe relationships, he insisted that "the owner of the means of production, whoever he be — individual owner, workers' association or corporation — must always . . . retain control of his economic decisions."

Advisable, not Mandatory

A little more than a year later, on June 3, 1950, in a talk prepared for an audience of Catholic social scientists, the Holy Father returned to the question of co-management. Discussing the threat to personal responsibility in business inherent in some postwar proposals for reform, the Pope wrote:

> A similar danger is likewise present when it is claimed that the wage-earners in a given industry have the right to economic joint-management. . . .
> As a matter of fact, neither the nature of the labor contract nor the nature of the business enterprise in themselves admit necessarily of a right of this sort.

The Pope is obviously talking here of a natural right, and he is talking in the context of Pius XI's treatment of the alleged moral inadequacy of the wage contract. Like his predecessor, he hails the "usefulnesss" of what has been achieved by giving workers some share in ownership, or profits, or management; but if he isn't making it clear at the same time that workers have no strict right to these features of partnership, I am at a loss to say what he is talking about. In other words, I agree with what Canon Brys, chaplain of the Belgian Christian Labor Movement, wrote about the Holy Father's June 3, 1950 address in the September,

1950 issue of the information bulletin of the International Christian Social Union:

> The Holy Father has no intention of disapproving or discouraging what is being done to make the worker participate in the property, management or profits of the enterprise. But he does not want us to go beyond a *certain limit,* nor will he admit *as rights* certain claims that have nothing to do with the sphere of natural right.

With due regard, then, for the opinions of others, and not without some diffidence, I incline to the belief (1) that those who in the name of the owners control our big corporations have a duty to use surplus profits to promote the common good; (2) that one highly desirable way of doing this is to share the profits with all the corporation's employes; (3) that workers receiving a just wage have no strict right to share in profits, either in commutative or social justice; and (4) that while workers may raise the question of profit sharing at the bargaining table, they cannot demand profit sharing in the sense that they may strike to bring the employer around to their way of thinking.

The last proposition assumes, obviously, that the objective sought through strike action must, if it is to be a just cause, have a foundation of some kind in justice. It must be based on something more, that is, than convenience, propriety, desirability or equity.

That this is a large assumption I willingly grant. Even those, however, who refuse to restrict the right to strike in this way would probably concede that where justice is not involved, "the accompanying circumstances more readily tend to make the strike illegitimate."

A similar warning seems appropriate to strikes for objectives due in social justice. As one highly regarded moralist informed this writer: "It may well be that one could seldom verify the condition of proportionate reason if the sole object of the strike were to obtain a share in profits." (So far as the negotiations in the auto industry go, the issue, fortunately, is not likely to arise in these difficult terms. In the improbable event that a strike should follow a breakdown in bargaining, its sole object will almost certainly not be profit sharing.)

Finally, it should be noted that workers may acquire a legal right to demand profit sharing. This could happen if the Government broadened the matter of collective bargaining, which is now restricted to wages, hours and conditions of employment, to include profit sharing. In that event workers would also have a moral right to demand and strike for profit sharing.

Cases

Prairie Eye-Opener

Frank Whittaker spent a week in Brownridge, Alberta on business. During this time he read the daily edition of the *Prairie Eye-Opener* published in Sagitawa, a major city about fifty miles from Brownridge. This had been the first time he had had the opportunity of reading the *Prairie Eye-Opener* for several consecutive days and he was somewhat disturbed by some of its articles. In particular, there was a series on automobiles during this week which seemed more like advertising than news, though the articles carried no indication of being ads. Each one was given about seven or eight column inches. Typical headlines were:

"Dual Lights Plymouth Standard"

"Dodge Tail Fins Reduce Steering Effort"

"1958 Ford Features Complete Styling Change"

"Wider Look Featured in 1958 Studebaker"

"New Type Engine Featured in GM Trucks."

Mr. Whittaker felt an obligation to write the publisher of the *Prairie Eye-Opener* and make the observation that the paper was offering as news what was, he felt, advertising. He believed that a newspaper had a responsibility to the public to present news. Advertising and editorial opinion, he felt, should be clearly marked and should be kept separate, though these were properly an important part of any paper.

Mr. Whittaker wondered if he should writer a letter, what good it might do, and what form it should take.

Exhibit 1

1958 Ford Features Complete Styling Change

The 1958 Ford car featuring major styling changes will go on display at four Sagitawa dealers Thursday. Dealers showing the new Ford are: Sagitawa Motors, Ottawa Avenue and Main Street, Dominion Motors, 2739 Manitoba Avenue, Prairie Motors, 720 Church Street, and Alberta Motors, 6929 Center Avenue.

In making the announcement, P. G. Wiley, General Manager, Ford-Edsel Division, Ford Motor Company of Canada, Limited, pointed out that historically auto companies have made basic changes in their cars over three years. "But in the 1958 models, Ford has actually created basic design and engineering changes just a year after the new 1957 model," he said.

Different lengths Demonstrating the change are 20 models on two separate wheel bases, the Fairlane and Fairlane 500 with overall lengths of 207 inches and the Custom, Custom 300 and station wagon covering 202 inches.

New 332 and 352 cubic inch displacement engines are the result of more than 25 years sales and Ford engineering leadership in the V-8 engines. They combine new highs of efficiency, durability and economy with the added time and convenience of quick service accessibility.

Also new will be air suspension, optional for Ford Fairlane, Fairlane 500's and station wagons with V-8 engines and automatic transmissions.

Replace springs Air domes made of specially strengthened rubber, reinforced with steel sleeves, replace springs on each wheel. Air pressure inside the domes is supplied by a compressor and air storage tank and varies according to the weight of the passengers and luggage to keep the car at a constant height and optimum springing for a "boulevard" ride.

The external appearance of the new car features Ford's sculptured-in-metal treatment in which styling lines are moulded into the sheet metal.

The distinctive Ford '58 styling is emphasized in the massive, wrap around one-piece bumper with anodized aluminum grille, dual headlights and power flow hood.

New sheet metal treatment incorporates reducing front fenders, new roof with seven front rear flutes or grooves and trunk lid and rear quarter panel innovations.

Ford also introduced the newest and most modern overhead valve V-8 engines. The "332" has a torque rating at 340–360 foot pounds at 4600 r.p.m. and horsepower ranging from 240 with two-barrel carburetor to 265 with four-barrel carburetor. The "352" engine is rated at 395 foot pounds at 2800 r.p.m. and horsepower at 300.

The economical six is available for most models and the 292 V-8 engine is standard on some series.

The new engines feature completely machined, wide-type combustion chambers, larger cooler running valves, new carburetion and exhaust porting and direct flow intake for peak performance at all engine speeds.

Each engine is electronically mass balanced while running at operating speed under its own power.

Brownridge, Alta.
November 8, 1957

Mr. David Dale, Publisher
The Prairie Eye-Opener
Sagitawa, Alberta

Dear Mr. Dale:

You may recall that we met one day when I was visiting the office of Charles Ormsby, your production manager.

During the past week I have been visiting Brownridge. I have had the opportunity to read the Eye-Opener nightly. I am writing you because it seems to me that some of your "news" articles do a dis-service not only to the public but to yourselves.

I refer specifically to the series of announcements re: new 1958-model cars, e.g., Friday night's paper carries articles titled "New Type Engine Featured in GM Trucks" and "American Motors Offers 'All-New' 1958 Model." These are advertisements and should be so labelled. Too often newspapers headline announcements which are merely ads, but the very fact that they are not so labelled provides, perhaps, better readership. Your articles indicate a blatant misuse of the trust and responsibility you bear towards the public to give *news*. I believe that such misuse invites public control. Please don't.

Sincerely,
Frank Whittaker

cc: C. Ormsby
(written by hand)

Putnam, Alberta,
December 3, 1957

Mr. David Dale, Publisher,
The Prairie Eye-Opener
Sagitawa, Alberta.

Dear Mr. Dale,

On November 8th, I wrote you from Brownridge concerning certain advertisements which purported to be news. Perhaps this letter never reached you, so I am enclosing a copy.

Sincerely,
Frank Whittaker

Encl.

Office of the Publisher
The Prairie Eye-Opener
Sagitawa, Alberta
December 4, 1957

Mr. Frank Whittaker
Putnam, Alberta

Dear Sir:

In the absence of Mr. Dale from the city, I am acknowledging your letter of December 3. You will no doubt be hearing from Mr. Dale on his return to the office some time next week.

Very truly yours,
Harriet Goodyear
Secretary to Mr. Dale

Office of the Publisher
The Prairie Eye-Opener
Sagitawa, Alberta
December 9, 1957

Mr. Frank Whittaker
Putnam, Alberta

Dear Mr. Whittaker:

I decided to ignore your letter of November 8.

Yours very truly,
David Dale

Putnam, Alberta
19th December, 1957

Mr. Gordon Parker
COCO-TV
Sagitawa, Alberta

Dear Gordon:

When I was in Brownridge in November I had the opportunity of reading the Prairie Eye-Opener over a period of two weeks. I became somewhat perturbed by the distortion in the newspaper. I wrote David Dale by hand concerning a series of articles about the new automobiles. These purported to be news, but were unquestionably advertisements. A copy of my letter is enclosed, enclosure # 1.

I did not hear from Mr. Dale for three weeks and therefore sent a follow up letter to which I received a response from his secretary per enclosure # 2. I then received a note from Mr. Dale per enclosure # 3.

I had shown my original letter to Scotty Ingram[1] who expressed an interest in this problem. Upon my return to Brownridge I showed him the complete correspondence and he suggested that this might be a proper subject for debate on TV.

This can, of course, be a hot potato, but I should like to make an offer to you that I will debate this matter with Mr. Dale on your station for a period of 15 or 30 minutes.

In actual fact, I doubt if Mr. Dale would accept such an offer but I should like to be able to make it. I find this situation shocking. Mr. Dale is in a position of public responsibility.

I should appreciate it if you would keep this matter confidential for the moment. Then, if you should be good enough to grant me TV time, I can make the offer directly to him.

Sincerely,
Frank

F. Whittaker
Encls.

---

[1] A television executive.

COCO-TV
Sagitawa, Alberta
December 30, 1957

Mr. Frank Whittaker
Putnam, Alberta

Dear Frank:

It was very nice to hear from you again. I read your enclosures with interest and must say that I was amazed at Mr. Dale's reply to your letter.

I am sure that he would not accept your suggestion and I do not feel that we are in a position to make the offer since the Prairie Eye-Opener is a substantial part owner of the television station.

The only suggestion might be to discuss it with one or two appropriate people in Toronto next week. If I find an opportunity to put across your point of view effectively, I may do this. Otherwise, I haven't and won't mention it to anyone.

Sincerely,
Gordon Parker

U.S. Steel and the 1962 Price Increase

On March 31, 1962, congratulations were extended to the steelworkers and to the steel industry for their "early and responsible settlement," well in advance of the June 30 deadline, and the earliest settlement in the quarter-century relationship between the industry and the union. This early settlement contrasted with the 1959 negotiations, which included a 116-day strike. President Kennedy in a telephone message to David J. McDonald, President of the United Steelworkers, said:

> When I appealed to the union and to the industry to commence negotiations early in order to avert an inventory buildup — with consequences detrimental to the nation at large as well as to the industry and its employees — I did so with firm confidence that the steelworkers union and the industry would measure up to their responsibility to serve the national interest.
>
> You have done so through free collective bargaining, without the pressure of a deadline or under the threat of a strike. This is indeed industrial statesmanship of the highest order.
>
> The settlement you have announced is both forward looking and responsible. It is obviously noninflationary and should provide a solid base for continued price stability.

An industry statement said the new benefits would increase employment cost by about 2½ per cent during the first year. That compares with an average annual increase of 3½ to 3¾ per cent under the contract negotiated in 1960, and with 8 per cent a year in the period between 1940 and 1960. R. Conrad Cooper of U. S. Steel, chief industry negotiator, said that the settlement cost did not fall wholly "within the limits of anticipated gains in productive efficiency." The industry statement estimated the cost of the settlement exceeded by about fifty per cent its productivity gain. Cooper added that the accord represented real progress in the development of voluntary collective bargaining in the steel industry.

Steps in the Negotiation

The 1960 steel contract provided for several wage increases, the last of which was scheduled for October 1, 1961. Prior to that date, executives of major steel companies were hinting at a general rise in steel prices to coincide with that wage increase. On September 6, 1961, President Kennedy wrote the heads of twelve steel companies expressing his concern with stability of steel prices. Mr. Kennedy wrote: "The steel industry, by absorbing increases in employment costs since 1958 has demonstrated a will to halt the price-wage spiral in steel. If the industry were now to forego a price increase, it would enter collective bargaining negotiations next spring with a record of three-and-a-half years of price stability. It would clearly then be the turn of the labor representatives to limit wage demands to a level consistent with continued price stability. The moral position of the steel industry next spring and its claim to the support of public opinion will be strengthened by the exercise of price restraint now." He eventually received replies from all twelve companies. The reply from Roger Blough for U. S. Steel denied that the cause of inflation would be found in the levels of steel prices and profits. Blough's letter noted that the President's letter "does raise questions of such serious import, including the future of freedom of marketing, that I feel impelled to include a word on that score also, for whatever value it may be." He wrote of "the admittedly hazardous task which your economic advisers have undertaken in forecasting steel industry profits at varying rates of operation. . . . Moreover, it might reasonably appear to some — as frankly, it does to me — that they seem to be assuming the role of informal price setters for steel — psychological or otherwise."

In January, 1962, President Kennedy urged an early agreement to avoid the upsetting uncertainty of a possible strike, and especially the speculation which precedes the strike deadline, such as heavy buying by steel users. At his news conference on January 15, Mr. Kennedy said that Secretary of Labor, Arthur J. Goldberg, would be available "for whatever good offices he may perform." In reply to a question at the conference, the President stressed his desire for a settlement which would not force an increase in steel prices, i.e., the cost of the wage increase should not exceed the savings resulting from increased productivity. The President's economic report to the Congress released the following week went so far as to urge that average productivity gains for the general economy be used as guidelines for wage settlements. The report of the Council of Economic Advisers recommended that the overall increase in output per man-hour of 2½ to 3 per cent a year be taken as the measuring rod for higher wages and fringe benefits in any industry. If efficiency of a specific industry has been going up faster, this would call for price reductions. (On January 27, 1962, *The New York Times* estimated that if the Council's productivity gauge were to be applied, a package settlement of about 10 cents an hour "would meet the test of equity this year.")

One of the strongest statements about the role of government in collective bargaining was Secretary Goldberg's "definitive" statement of the Kennedy Administration's labor-management philosophy to the Executive Club of Chicago, on February 23. Goldberg said that in the past, when government officials assisted in collective bargaining, their only aim had been to achieve a settlement. But today, in the light of the nation's commitments at home and abroad, government and private mediators must increasingly provide guidelines to the parties in labor disputes. Such guidelines should insure "right settlements" that take into account the public interest as well as the interests of the parties. Goldberg said he did not mean that government should impose the terms of a settlement, but he claimed that "everyone expects the government to assert and define the national interest."

Anonymous steel industry sources took exception to the Goldberg position. "The moment the government goes beyond being a policeman or offering its service as mediator, it has an impact on the outcome of collective bargaining and converts it from an economic to a political process. From a broad philosophical standpoint, most businessmen feel that in a competitive system you serve the national interest in pursuing your private interest. Government exertion of its influence prevents the system from operating as it should. From a practical standpoint, labor represents more votes than businessmen, so businessmen feel that any settlement that is a political settlement is likely to be more pro-labor than pro-management."

George Meany, President of the American Federation of Labor and Congress of Industrial Organizations, also brusquely rejected Secretary Goldberg's "definitive" statement. Mr. Meany said: "I don't agree with it. The government's role is mediation, conciliation or anything else it can do to help industrial peace. When he says the role of the government is to assert the national interest, he is infringing on the rights of free people and free society, and I don't agree with him whatsoever. This is a step in the direction of saying the federal government should tell either or both sides what to do, and I don't agree with that."

Support for Secretary Goldberg came from Joseph L. Block, chairman of Inland Steel, who was at the speaker's table when Goldberg spoke. (Block is a member of President Kennedy's twenty-one man Advisory Committee on Labor-Management Policy.) "I heartily endorse Mr. Goldberg's concept. It is the government's function to elucidate the national objectives, to point out what the national needs are. Those guidelines should be taken into account in collective bargaining. A contest of strength where the stronger side wins doesn't prove a thing. Each side has to represent its own interest, but neither side must be unmindful of the needs of the nation. Who else can point out those needs but the government?"

A. A. Berle, Jr. also supported the Goldberg view and the work of the Council of Economic Advisors, contending that there is an unwritten "social contract" holding both sides to certain responsibilities as well as granting both the privileges that make this power possible, and that under this social contract the government can — and perhaps must — intervene when economic power in private hands threatens the economic community of the United States. Berle sees the "emerging relationship" as this: "When the wage and price levels markedly affect, or threaten to upset, the economy of the country, the government claims power to step in on behalf of the 'public interest.'" The difficulty is in telling what the words 'public interest' mean. Berle sees the Council of Economic Advisors as the future key agency here, for "its views on acceptable wage and price levels are, and should be, extremely important."

The council can advise the President — and through his authority advise both big labor and big corporations — about where the peril points are. It can advise the President when the government should intervene to modify private decisions based on power, either of labor to tie up plants by strike, or of management to set prices by administration. It can and indeed does keep a close check on these allegedly private decisions, taken in company offices or union headquarters. It could communicate to either or both when it sees a peril point approaching. And it can advise the President when intervention is needed in the "public interest" — that is, when employment, production and purchasing power under free competitive enterprise are likely to be weakened, when inflation becomes a danger, when economic stability generally is likely to be threatened.[1]

U. S. Steel's annual report, released March 20, 1962, pointed to its holding of the price line in 1961. Mr. Blough's statement to stockholders said that in 1961 "the inexorable influences of the market place in our competitive free enterprise system continued to dictate the course of U. S. Steel's pricing actions." No reference to pricing plans for 1962 appeared in the report, but Blough indicated deep concern about competition and slack demand. Robert C. Tyson, chairman of U. S. Steel's finance committee, called "unsatisfactory" the idea that productivity is a criterion for setting wages. "The notion appears to be that if an enterprise or industry learns how to produce more efficiently, then it can pay more to its employees without raising its product's prices. If we can do this, it is proper to force us to do so." Mr. Tyson said this theory is unsatisfactory because if more money is paid to those with jobs, there is less available for rehiring those workers without jobs. Unemployment becomes chronic and the incentives for creating new jobs are stultified. Productivity, he went on, is useful as a method of describing economic facts, rather than as a measure for determining wage rates. It indicates only that a price increase or widespread unemployment must result if the average wage level rises faster than productivity. "No increase in employment costs in excess of the nation's long-term rate of productivity increase can be regarded as noninflationary." (At this stage in negotiations, the industry was holding out for employment cost increases not exceeding two per cent annually, coinciding with the annual productivity increase as figured by the companies for recent years.)

Steel Prices Go Up—and Come Down Again

U. S. Steel signed the labor contract agreed upon at the end of March on April 5. This contract provided for costs (not in direct wages but in other benefits) which were subsequently estimated at 10.6 cents

---

[1] A. A. Berle, Jr., "Unwritten Constitution for Our Economy," *The New York Times Magazine,* April 29, 1962.

an hour, or a total of $159,000,000 a year for the industry, with some 520,000 workers. On April 10, the company announced an average increase of $6 a ton in the price of steel, accompanying the announcement with a statement signed by Leslie B. Worthington, president, explaining this increase:

Since our last over-all adjustment in the summer of 1958, the level of steel prices has not been increased but, if anything, has declined somewhat. This situation, in the fact of steadily mounting production costs which have included four increases in steel-worker wages and benefits prior to the end of last year, has been due to the competitive pressures from domestic producers and from imports of foreign-made steel as well as from other materials which are used as substitutes for steel.

The severity of these competitive pressures has not diminished; and to their influence may be attributed the fact that the partial catch-up adjustment announced today is substantially less than the cost increases which have already occurred since 1958, without taking into consideration the additional costs which will result from the new labor agreements which become effective next July 1.

Nevertheless, taking into account all the competitive factors affecting the market for steel, we have reluctantly concluded that a modest price adjustment can no longer be avoided in the light of the production cost increases that have made it necessary.

In the three years since the end of 1958, United States Steel has spent $1,185,000,000 for modernization and replacement of facilities and for the development of new sources of raw materials. Internally, there were only two sources from which this money could come: depreciation and reinvested profit. Depreciation in these years amounted to $610,000,000; and reinvested profit, $187,000,000 — or, together, only about two-thirds of the total sum required. So after using all the income available from operations, we had to make up the difference of $388,000,000 out of borrowings from the public. In fact, during the period 1959–1961, we have actually borrowed a total of $800,000,000 to provide for present and future needs. And this must be repaid out of profits that have not yet been earned, and will not be earned for some years to come.

During these three years, moreover, United States Steel's profits have dropped to the lowest level since 1952; while reinvested profit — which is all the profit there is to be plowed back in the business after payment of dividends — has declined from $115,000,000 in 1958 to less than $3,000,000 last year. Yet the dividend rate has not been increased in more than five years, although there have been seven general increases in employment costs during this interval.

In all, we have experienced a net increase of about 6 per cent in our costs over this period despite cost reductions which have been effected through the use of new, more efficient facilities, improved techniques and better raw materials. Compared with this net increase of 6 per cent, the price increase of 3½ per cent announced today clearly falls considerably short of the amount needed to restore even the cost-price relationship in the low production year of 1958.

In reaching this conclusion, we have given full consideration, of course, to the fact that any price increase which comes, as this does, at a time when foreign-made steels are already underselling ours in a number of product lines, will add — temporarily, at least — to the competitive difficulties which we are now experiencing. But the present price level cannot be maintained any longer when our problems are viewed in long-range perspective. For the long pull a strong, profitable company is the only insurance that formidable competition can be met and that the necessary lower costs to meet that competition will be assured.

Only through profits can a company improve its competitive potential through better equipment and through expanded research. On this latter phase we are constantly developing lighter, stronger steels which — ton for ton — will do more work and go much farther than the steels that were previously available on the market. They thus give the customer considerably more value per dollar of cost. As more and more of these new steels come from our laboratories, therefore, our ability to compete should steadily improve. But the development of new steels can only be supported by profits or the hope for profits.

The financial resources supporting continuous research and resultant new products as well as those supporting new equipment, are therefore vital in this competitive situation — vital not alone to the company and its employees, but to our international balance of payments, the value of our dollar, and to the strength and security of the nation as well.[2]

President Kennedy was informed of U. S. Steel's price increase at a meeting requested by Roger Blough at 5:45 P.M. on April 10. Mr. Kennedy spoke at his news conference the next day in "a tone of cold anger," reading a long indictment of the steel company's actions:

The simultaneous and identical actions of United States Steel and other leading steel corporations increasing steel prices by some $6 a ton constitute a wholly unjustifiable and irresponsible defiance of the public interest.

In this serious hour in our nation's history when we are confronted with grave crises in Berlin and Southeast Asia, when we

---

2 *The New York Times*, April 11, 1962.

are devoting our energies to economic recovery and stability, when we are asking Reservists to leave their homes and families months on end and servicemen to risk their lives — and four were killed in the last two days in Vietnam — and asking union members to hold down their wage requests, at a time when restraint and sacrifice are being asked of every citizen, the American people will find it hard, as I do, to accept a situation in which a tiny handful of steel executives, whose pursuit of private power and profit exceeds their sense of public responsibility, can show such utter contempt for the interest of 185,000,000 Americans.

If this rise in the cost of steel is imitated by the rest of the industry, instead of rescinded, it would increase the cost of homes, autos, appliances and most other items for every American family. It would increase the cost of machinery and tools to every American businessman and farmer. It would seriously handicap our efforts to prevent an inflationary spiral from eating up the pensions of our older citizens and our new gains in purchasing power. It would add, Defense Secretary McNamara informed me this morning, an estimated $1,000,000,000 to the cost of our defenses at a time when every dollar is needed for national security and other purposes.

It will make it more difficult for American goods to compete in foreign markets, more difficult to withstand competition from foreign imports and thus more difficult to improve our balance-of-payments position and stem the flow of gold. And it is necessary to stem it for our national security if we're going to pay for our security commitments abroad.

And it would surely handicap our efforts to induce other industries and unions to adopt responsible price and wage policies.

The facts of the matter are that there is no justification for an increase in steel prices.

The recent settlement between the industry and the union, which does not even take place until July 1, was widely acknowledged to be noninflationary, and the whole purpose and effect of this Administration's role, which both parties understood, was to achieve an agreement which would make unnecessary any increases in prices.

Steel output per man is rising so fast that labor costs per ton of steel can actually be expected to decline in the next twelve months. And, in fact, the Acting Commissioner of the Bureau of Labor Statistics informed me this morning that, and I quote, "employment costs per unit of steel output in 1961 were essentially the same as they were in 1958." The cost of major raw materials — steel scrap and coal — has also been declining.

And for an industry which has been generally operating at less than two-thirds of capacity, its profit rate has been normal and can be expected to rise sharply this year in view of the reduction in idle capacity. Their lot has been easier than that of 100,000 steelworkers thrown out of work in the last three years.

The industry's cash dividends have exceeded $600,000,000 in each of the last five years; and earnings in the first quarter of this year were estimated in the Feb. 28 Wall Street Journal to be among the highest in history.

In short, at a time when they could be exploring how more efficiency and better prices could be obtained, reducing prices in this industry in recognition of lower costs, their unusually good labor contract, their foreign competition and their increase in production and profits which are coming this year, a few gigantic corporations have decided to increase prices in ruthless disregard of their public responsibility.

Price and wage decisions in this country, except for a very limited restriction in the case of monopolies and national emergency strikes, are and ought to be freely and privately made. But the American people have a right to expect, in return for that freedom, a higher sense of business responsibility for the welfare of their country than has been shown in the last two days.

Sometime ago I asked each American to consider what he would do for his country, and I asked the steel companies. In the last twenty-four hours we had their answer.

Question: Is the position of the Administration that it believed it had the assurance of the steel industry at the time of the recent labor agreement that it would not increase prices?

Answer: We did not ask either side to give us any assurance, because there is a very proper limitation to the power of the Government in this free economy.

All we did in our meetings was to emphasize how important it was that . . . there be price stability . . . and to persuade the union to begin to bargain early and to make an agreement which would not affect prices. . . .

We never at any time asked for a commitment in regard to the terms — of the agreement from either Mr. McDonald or Mr. Blough, because, in our opinion, that is — would be passing over the line of propriety. . . .[3]

A great many actions were taken by governmental agencies during the 72 hours between U. S. steel's announcement of its increase on the afternoon of April 10 and its rescinding of this increase at 5:28 P.M. on April 13. In addition to the governmental actions, three companies made no move to increase prices in line with U. S. Steel's announcement — Inland, Armco, and Kaiser. After consulting with Joseph L. Block, who was vacationing in Japan, the directors of Inland issued the following statement on the morning of the 13th:

---

[3] *The New York Times,* April 12, 1962.

Inland Steel Co. today announced that it will not make any adjustment in existing prices of its steel mill products at this time. The company has long recognized the need for improvement in steel industry profits in relation to capital invested. It believes this condition, which does exist today, will ultimately have to be corrected. Nevertheless, in full recognition of the national interest and competitive factors, the company feels that it is untimely to make an upward adjustment.

The following week, after the prices had come back down, the joint Senate-House Republican Leadership issued a statement summarizing nine governmental actions used by the White House, and deploring their use:

1. The Federal Trade Commission publicly suggested the possibility of collusion, announced an immediate investigation and talked of $2,000 a day penalties.
2. The Justice Department spoke threateningly of antitrust violations and ordered an immediate investigation.
3. Treasury Department officials indicated they were at once reconsidering the planned increase in depreciation rates for steel.
4. The Internal Revenue Service was reported making a menacing move toward U. S. Steel's incentive benefits plan for its executives.
5. The Senate Antitrust and Monopoly subcommittee began subpoenaing records from twelve steel companies, returnable May 14.
6. The House Antitrust subcommittee announced an immediate investigation, with hearings opening May 2.
7. The Justice Department announced it was ordering a grand jury investigation.
8. The Department of Defense, seemingly ignoring laws requiring competitive bidding, publicly announced it was shifting steel purchases to companies that had not increased prices, and other Government agencies were directed to do likewise.
9. The F.B.I. began routing newspaper men out of bed at 3:00 A.M. on Thursday, April 12, in line with President Kennedy's press conference assertion that "we are investigating" a statement attributed to a steel company official in the newspapers.

Taken cumulatively these nine actions amount to a display of naked political power never seen before in this nation.

Taken singly these nine actions are punitive, heavy-handed and frightening.

We condone nothing in the actions of the steel companies except their right to make an economic judgment without massive retaliation by the Federal Government.

Temporarily President Kennedy may have won a political victory, but at the cost of doing violence to the fundamental precepts of a free society.

This nation must realize that we have passed within the shadow of police state methods. We hope that we never again step into those dark regions whatever the controversy of the moment, be it economic or political.[4]

James Reston, writing of the steel-price dispute, concludes that the reason for all the friction lies in a little known fact:

This is that the Kennedy Administration is dissatisfied with the labor-management collective bargaining process and has set out to change it. The process, as the Administration sees it, is now having a profound effect on the nation's economic growth, on its ability to achieve full employment, to compete against foreign goods, to sustain the heavy burden of arms and foreign aid, and is therefore too serious a business to be left to labor and management alone.

The President is insisting not only that paralyzing labor-management disagreements, but even labor-management agreements at the cost of higher noncompetitive prices, are not in the national interest and that something, therefore, must be done to strengthen the public's voice in the collective bargaining process. That the Administration does not quite know yet what that "something" should be is clear enough from its savage lurch into the U.S. Steel price dispute.

The movement now is toward a series of experiments in tripartite discussions, with the Government taking a more active part in asserting the national interest. As the President sees it, this is merely the common sense of the new industrial, scientific and commercial revolution of the world. But as Roger Blough sees it, the President is moving toward the substitution of a managed for a free economy. This is why feelings have been running so high on both sides.[5]

What Comes Next?

The new wage contract went into effect on July 1 with no change in steel prices. Both Kennedy and Blough were at considerable pains to explain their actions further and to demonstrate, after a further private meeting on April 17, that both sides were seeking much the same things. President Kennedy told the U. S. Chamber of Commerce, on April 30, that his administration was seeking "an economic climate

---

[4] *The New York Times,* April 20, 1962.
[5] James Reston, "Why Not A Summit Meeting on Wages and Prices?", *The New York Times,* April 18, 1962.

in which an expanding concept of business and labor responsibility, an increasing awareness of world commerce and the free forces of domestic competition, will keep the price level stable and keep the government out of price-setting." He acknowledged that "many of you" wanted much more liberal tax allowances than the administration was planning to grant for writing off the costs of modernizing plant and equipment, but explained that greater allowances would cut the government's revenue too much, and would hamper efforts to balance the federal budget. It was reported that the reception of the President's talk was cool, in contrast to the talk of Richard Wagner, outgoing president of the Chamber, who was interrupted by applause several times. Mr. Wagner said that business earnings are inadequate "because too much is siphoned off" for government spending and for excessive wages. "Business leadership must make certain that both business and labor remain free to make their decisions without government intervention." Departing from his prepared address, Mr. Wagner said he was "very much comforted" by the President's attention to tax write-offs, but suggested that the loss-of-revenue argument was not convincing.

When Roger Blough faced his stockholders on May 7, he was greeted by a round of applause after his initial comment: "It has been sort of a warm spring." The next wave of applause was triggered by the comment that "I do not believe the public interest can ever be served by hostility between government and business." He said that government and business had to gain a better grasp of each other's needs in the national interest, an interest that could never be served by direct or indirect peacetime price controls. After the unsuccessful effort to raise prices, the most important need was to build "a better understanding of the economic problems and of the profit needs of the entire business community." Mr. Blough said he was encouraged by President Kennedy's Chamber of Commerce address, since Kennedy had said that if business did not earn a fair profit, the government could not earn sufficient revenues to cover its outlays. U. S. Steel's own profits had slipped from $304,000,000 in 1960 to $190,000,000 in 1961. Later, in answer to a stockholder's question, Blough added, "In Washington we have had some very interesting indications that this whole incident has acted as a catalyst to thinking" on the profit-squeeze plight of industry.

When U. S. Steel released its report of better first quarter 1962 earnings, Chairman Blough had said at a news conference that at the moment the company did not contemplate any price changes in the future. He did add that the company would do everything possible to improve earnings, but that the government could help by revising depreciation regulations. He made it clear that the company's capital spending plans were definitely under a "damper" because it could not raise prices. The following day, April 25, when Inland Steel reported its first quarter earnings, which were also up, Chairman Joseph L. Block welcomed limited government intervention to protect economic stability. Mr. Block did assail direct price-setting and said that this and other administrations had used the steel industry as "a whipping boy." When asked whether Kennedy had overstepped his bounds in his blitz against a steel price increase, Mr. Block said:

> I think any president is well within his rights in pointing out the national interest with regards to costs and prices or anything that affects the welfare of the people. The methods used, however, are subject to individual criticism. I for one, don't think that F.B.I. men and subpoenas and grand juries should be part of these methods.

Block also revealed that his concern intended, if financial and market conditions allowed, to go ahead with an expansion program previously set.

The day after Chairman Blough had spoken to U. S. Steel's stockholders, President Kennedy addressed the convention of the United Automobile Workers, and called on labor to exercise restraint and responsibility in its bargaining demands:

> This Administration has not undertaken and will not undertake to fix prices and wages in this economy. We have no intention of intervening in every labor dispute. We are neither able nor willing to substitute our judgment for the judgment of those who sit at the local bargaining tables across the country.
>
> We can suggest guidelines for the economy but we cannot fix a single pattern for every class and every industry. We can and must under the responsibilities given to us by the Constitution, and by statute and by necessity, point out the national interest and, where applicable, we can and must and will enforce the law on restraints of trade and national emergencies.
>
> But we possess and seek no powers of compulsion, and must rely primarily on the voluntary efforts of labor and management to make sure that their sense of public responsibility, their recognition of this dangerous and hazardous world, full of challenge and opportunity, that in this kind of world fulfilling our role that the national interest is preserved. . . .
>
> This country has the world's highest real wages and living standard simply because our output per man-hour is the highest in the world. No financial slight of hand can raise real wages and profits faster than productivity without defeating their own purpose through inflation.
>
> And I need not tell the members of this union, with its constructive history and policies, that unjustified wage demands which require price increases and then other demands and then other price increases are equally as contrary to the national interest as unjustified profit demands which require price increases. But when productivity has been raised by the skills of

better management, the efficiency of labor and the modernization financed by investors, all three groups can reap the rewards of that productivity and still pass lower prices on to the consumer.

When the American Iron and Steel Institute met late in May, Chairman Blough again spoke in conciliatory terms about the need for better government-business relations. The next day, on May 24, Allison R. Maxwell, Jr., President of Pittsburgh Steel, gave a sometimes bitter speech about the "route to socialism" which "drew a standing ovation from some 1000 steel industry executives and technical personnel." This response suggests that there was more resentment smoldering in the steel industry. Mr. Maxwell, like Mr. Blough, called for cooperation with government, despite the "effrontery" of some administration comments questioning the patriotism of steel leaders. He said he was disturbed when U. S. Steel and others were treated as "transgressors." "We may decry specific power tactics, but these are merely symptoms of an issue far more dangerous. It would be an error to dismiss these actions as merely anti-business, when the real issue is that 'Big Government' is anti-individual rights. The obvious direction of all its policies is toward a form of socialism in which the pretense of private property is retained, while in fact prices, wages, production and distribution are dictated by bureaucrats."

As July 1 approached, the steel companies were continuing to stress the squeeze on capital fund sources, due to continued rising-cost pressure on profits, and to cash-generating depreciation charges that fall short of equipment replacement costs. Although the industry was pursuing cost-reduction programs and expanding research activities, much hope was expressed about a reform of "woefully inadequate" depreciation laws. Some authorities have suggested that capital expansion funds could be raised through new sales of stock or debt issues. Most steel men contend, however, that a low profit potential is hardly an inducement for further investments. Avery C. Adams, Chairman of Jones and Loughlin, said, "If the Kennedy Administration really wants to assure us that this is a pro-business administration, the most electrifying statement would be that the administration would work for giving our country the best depreciation policies in the world, instead of the worst." The contention is that with shorter depreciation periods, the cash set aside for depreciation, or the wear and tear of old equipment, would tend to match more closely the capital outlays considered necessary for replacing, expanding, and modernizing industrial plants. This would encourage more capital spending.

Industry insiders still expect a price rise eventually, barring the "miracle" of a national business boom rich enough to ease the cost squeeze that has narrowed steel profits. Steel is reported to have begun a major selling campaign to convince President Kennedy's key aides of the case for a price rise. Stress has been laid on the fact that steel profits have "backslid" while taxes, wages and other major cost ingredients have been advancing. Steel, it is emphasized, needs profits to modernize and expand plant and equipment for a growing economy in world competition. Often quoted is Labor Secretary Goldberg's estimate that some $90 billion of U. S. industrial plant and equipment is obsolete today. But whether President Kennedy will see it steel's way next time is the industry's major headache. A humorous sign in one steel vice president's office says in large letters: "I miss Ike." In much smaller printing it adds: "I even miss Harry."

Bibliography

————. "Bill Barody's Job: The Industry Views into Government Plans." *Industry World,* July 8, 1974, pp. 10–11.

"Business and Government — The Odd Couple." *Business Horizons,* 17 (February 1974), 48–50.

Ewing, D. W. "Who Wants Corporate Democracy?" *Harvard Business Review,* 49 (September 1971), 12–14.

————. "Government Intervention." *Business Week,* September 14, 1974, pp. 102–103.

"How Well Does Industry Communicate with Congress?" *Industrial World,* May 14, 1973, pp. 42–43.

Lawrence, F. G. "Common Threat Mandates Industry-Government-Labor Alliance." *Industrial World,* December 10, 1973, 484.

Linowes, D. F. "Profit Motive, Social Problems Will Dovetail." *Industry Week,* March 23, 1970, pp. 12–13.

Moskowitz, D. B. "Constitutionalizing the Corporation." *Business Week,* October 26, 1974, p. 109.

Perry, G. L. "Wages, Productivity, and Profits." *Conference Board Record,* 8 (March 1971), 41–43.

————. "Profit Sharing Plans Run into Trouble." *Business Week,* December 7, 1974, pp. 106ff.

Winkler, J. "Two Faces of Capitalism." *Director,* October 1974, pp. 91–93.

Part Three
Business and the
Individual

The conflicts that arise between business and groups in our society can usually be traced to the basic rights of the individual. Many conflicts fall into the categories of human relations, leadership, and conformity. Philosophically, the basic issue involves the fundamental ends versus the means of work accomplished by persons in our society. Should business consider individual employees as means to the economic-productive ends of our economy, or should business reorganize for and around the employees, with goals for their satisfaction primary to the efficient accomplishment of work? The dilemma posed by these two points of view is far from reconciled, but significant efforts have been made toward its resolution. In general, management has been condemned for a purely scientific approach to business that has ignored the sociological, psychological, esthetic, and physical value needs of individual employees.

A. Fair Employment Practices

New governmental guidelines have recently been defined for achieving "fair" employment practices, as described in "Guidelines for Complying With Equal Employment Practices" [8]. This article reports guidelines established by the U. S. Department of the Treasury for banks with more than fifty employees. Under the umbrella of Affirmative Action Programs, the guidelines place emphasis on the more effective use of minorities compared to their past and present underemployment. Bank policies must be defined and disseminated. Policy formulation and implementation responsibilities must be specifically designated and problem areas defined. Attention must be directed toward specifics in goal setting for affirmative action for all levels and units of banks. Practical action-oriented programs must be instituted and audit and reporting systems implemented. Support of local and community action programs must be demonstrated. In short, banks are now "audited" on the performance of their social functions in achieving fair employment practices through the Affirmative Action Program.

The reform of employment practices to extend opportunities to black and other minority groups may create difficulties for many firms. These difficulties are specifically noted in the article, "Where Civil Rights Law Is Going Wrong." [9] The author points out that many business people are concerned that reverse discrimination will preclude opportunities to the well-qualified candidate who is not a member of a minority group. With the Civil Rights Act of 1964 guaranteeing equality of opportunity between the sexes, businesses are also being forced to reappraise their hiring practices as more women are demanding access to jobs traditionally reserved for men.

Many problems that fall within the domain of equality of job opportunities may take time and experience to resolve, and business faces a difficult job of alleviating these new pressures and conflicts. Managers must adopt new attitudes that are appropriate to present-day social reform. Patience, understanding, and education alone will not serve to change ingrained attitudes. New attitudes develop as a result of close association and shared experiences with black and other minority groups. One concern of management, reflecting its attitudinal bias, is that aggressive recruitment of minority employees will result in reverse discrimination; yet, those expressing that concern do not often propose alternatives for achieving some semblance of equity and justice to offset past discrimination in jobs and education. While management is certainly a target of criticism and pressure, the pervasiveness and long history of discrimination requires that justice be served immediately. In effect, management must now adapt to changes that are rapidly, and belatedly, imposed on our society's mores.

The most recent nationwide efforts to bring about fair employment practices have been made by women. Emphasis has especially been placed on creating opportunities for women in the managerial ranks of business organizations. This is well detailed in the article "Will Women Ever Be Accepted As Managers?" [10] as presented in a conference at the Stanford Graduate School of Business in 1974 on "Women in Management."

The major impetus to business to respond to the women's movement could be attributed to court settlements of over $43 million that have been paid out over the past ten years under the Equal Pay Act. Civil action suits brought by the Equal Employment Opportunities Commission have been the major factor in these settlements. Business now must face tests of *"bona fide* occupational requirements" versus any arbitrary or subjective judgment by management in setting selection criteria for minority employees. Women are now asking and demanding full participation at *every* level of management in U.S. corporations.

Concerned people are also attacking the socialization process that has traditionally cast women in roles subordinate to men in American society. As steps toward correcting that attitude, women's groups have asked businesses to change this stereotype in their advertising, and have asked schools to encourage girls to seek management careers.

Sex discrimination now faces costly court cases that should immediately change past policies and practices of American business. Legislation, judicial processing, and court settlements should reduce sex discrimination in business in an extraordinarily short time period.

In the Seabrook Manufacturing Company case the inconsistency of management decisions resulting from the lack of clear-cut personnel policies affects employee specifications required for the job. Management can, through the tools of job evaluation, merit rating systems, and job specifications, clearly delineate those factors most common to employee-company conflicts and thereby help to resolve internal personnel problems.

Where management's arbitrary decisions result in discrimination based on race, color, or creed, the records show that social opposition will be forthcoming eventually. The Well-Run Oil Company case illustrates the degree to which pressure may be exerted in the form of economic boycott as retaliatory action against management's hiring decisions involving race or color of applicants. If these grievances and conflicts are to be reconciled, management must establish a basic framework of principles, objectives, and policies that will be compatible with prevailing social mores.

Although the Seabrook Manufacturing and Well-Run Oil Company cases occurred at an earlier time, the situations reflect problems that still exist and illustrate the controversy between "arbitrary" and "essential" characteristics in job specifications.

B. Leadership Style Conflicts

The conflicts between conformity and individualism underlie all philosophies of organization and human relations. If authority in industrial organizations creates perennial conflicts between individuals, work groups, and the total social system and business, the question will necessarily be raised whether or not the individual has been relegated to the role of an "organization person." On the one hand, business asks greater employee adaptation to organizational needs and goals. On the other hand, society discourages any business requirements that may create "organization people." It appears that the extremes of conformity or individualism must be avoided. Unacceptable forms and degrees of nonconformity create intolerable conflicts both in the achievement of organizational goals and in the working harmony of the organization itself. However, excessive managerial domination over employees through overt or subtle pressures to conform to organizational practices often stifle initiative and adversely affect work performance necessary to achieve economic goals.

The analysis and formulation of business leadership philosophy has been essential to the achievement of economic-production-work goals and human relations goals. Our democratic heritage, the participation needs and values of individuals within democratic organizations, and the maximum development and utilization of human potential have served as goals for an ideal leadership theory. The process of maximizing individual human potential meets the dual objectives of effective resource utilization in our economy and the enhancement of human dignity in the development of employees as individual personalities. But the problem is not so easily resolved by defining ideal objectves. For example, participative management as an ideal of democratic leadership within business organizations has been promoted and argued for several decades.

Robert C. Albrook presents analysis of participative management in the selection "Participative Management: Time For A Second Look" [11]. A review of this leadership style reveals that it does not have universal application, but instead is essentially situational. It is generally known that this leadership theory has emphasized the communication and motivation skills of managers in dealing with their subordinates. But this "second look" includes other factors such as the delegation of responsibility for decision making, the formulation of goals and performance standards, and the definition and application of managerial controls. When we define the responsibility aspects of these decisions and problems, we can more realistically analyze the application of participative management. We now know that participative management is certainly not just a process of "keeping people happy," or allowing them to participate solely on the basis of their whims or inclinations.

A shift of perspective on participation and leadership style is presented in "After X and Y Comes Z." Focusing on the differences between the participating employee and the manager's leadership style, J. M. Colin assesses the need for adaptation to change. Colin assumes chronic change as an organizational forecast and describes the employee of this future as an "adaptive achiever." Theory Z is based on the hypothesis that innovation and motivation are inseparable, and that these must be present in future employees, for their successful adaptation to Theory Z organizations will require both a spirit of inquiry and an orientation toward acceptance, status, and achievement. Therefore leadership styles of the future will also require the selection and development of this type of employee participants. The human relations, leadership, and conformity problems will not be easily reconciled. In fact, it is important to realize that these problems will be perennial. We must adapt the varying types and degrees of leadership and human relations to the legitimate needs of the organization, the individual, the work group, and society.

The Ball Wholesale Drug Company case examines the effects of different types of leadership upon an existing organization. There are problems involved in making a transition from two distinctive styles of leadership. The goals, accepted practices, and philosophies of both subordinates and leaders in this case emphasize the effects of different types of leadership. While theories of "ideal" types of leadership are constantly debated, a leadership style must always meet the pragmatic test of effective operation, given a particular environmental structure of personnel and organizational goals.

A   Fair Employment Practices

8   Guidelines for Complying with Equal Employment Practices
Banking

Federal depositaries and issuers of U.S. Savings Bonds and Notes, commercial banks, savings banks, and savings and loan associations who, as issuing and paying agents for U.S. Savings Bonds and Notes, are included and affected by Executive Order 11246, as amended. All banks and savings and loan associations are subject to the regulations of the U.S. Department of the Treasury, and because of the provision made in such regulations, must provide equal employment opportunities in accordance with Executive Order 11246, as amended.

All banks and savings and loan associations having 50 or more employees are required to develop and maintain a written affirmative action compliance program. While there is no requirement for any initial filing of such programs, they must be available for review and examination by the Department of the Treasury. The purpose of the program is to provide a positive guide for the officials of the various banks and savings and loan associations in all personnel activities and to better enable analysis and evaluation of the minority employment utilization. The Affirmative Action Program must contain, but not necessarily be limited to, the following information:

> An analysis of all major job categories at the facility, with explanations if minorities are currently being underutilized in any one or more job categories (job "category" herein meaning

one or a group of jobs having similar content, wage rates, and opportunities). "Underutilization" is defined as having fewer minorities in a particular job category than would reasonably be expected by their availability. . . .

Development or reaffirmation of bank policy of nondiscrimination in all personnel actions.

Formal internal and external dissemination of bank policy.

Establishment of responsibilities for implementation of the bank's affirmative action program.

Identification of problem areas by division, department location, and job classification.

Direct special attention to the following three categories in analysis and goal setting: Management; professionals; and technicians. (Based upon the Government's experience with compliance reviews under the Executive Order programs and the bank/contractor reporting system over the past three years, minority group persons are most likely to be underutilized in the three categories as defined by the Employer's Information Report, EEO-1).

Establishment of goals and objectives by division, department, location, and job classification; including timetables for completion.

Development and execution of practical action oriented programs designed to eliminate problems and further designed to attain established goals and objectives.

Design and implementation of internal audit and reporting systems to measure effectiveness of total program.

Active support of local and national community action programs.

Eleven-Point Program

Here are 11 suggestions for action covering the above items:

1. The bank policy statement should indicate the chief executive officer's attitude on the subject matter, assign over-all responsibility, and provide for a reporting or monitoring procedure:
Specific items to be mentioned should include, but are not limited to: Recruit, hire, and promote all job classifications without regard to race, color, religion, national origin, or sex; base decisions

on employment solely upon an individual's qualifications for the position being filled (beginning job leading to uppermobility, for example, support position behind a teller line); make promotion decisions only on the individual's qualifications and his seniority, as related to the requirements of the position for which he is being considered; insure that all other personnel actions such as compensation, benefits, transfers, dismissals, company sponsored training, education, tuition assistance, social, and recreation programs, will be administered without regard to race, color, religion, national origin, or sex; the bank should periodically conduct analysis of all personnel actions to insure equal opportunity.

2. Formal internal and external dissemination of bank policy:

Internal Dissemination: Include in bank policy manual; publicize in available media such as bank newspaper, magazine, annual report, and other media; conduct special meetings with executive, management, and supervisory personnel to explain intent of policy and individual responsibility for effective implementation, making clear the chief executive officer's attitude; schedule special meetings with all employees to discuss policy and explain individual employee responsibilities; discuss policy thoroughly in both employee orientation and management training programs; publish articles covering EEO programs, progress reports, promotions of minority employees, etc., in bank publications, if any; post policy on bank bulletin boards; when employees are featured in bank advertising, both minority and nonminority employees should be pictured.

External Dissemination: Inform all recruiting sources from which you recruit verbally and in writing of bank policy, stipulating that these sources actively recruit and refer minorities for all positions listed; notify minority organizations, community agencies, community leaders, secondary schools and colleges, of bank policy, preferably in writing; when employees are pictured in bank or help wanted advertising, both minorities and nonminorities should be shown.

3. Establishment of responsibility for implementation of affirmative action program:

An executive of the bank should be designated as director or manager of its Equal Opportunity Program. Depending upon the size and geographical alignment of the bank, this may be his sole responsibility. He should be given the necessary top management support and adequate staff to execute his assignment. His responsibilities should include, but not necessarily be limited to: Developing policy statement, affirmative action program, internal and external communication techniques; assisting in the identification of problem areas; assisting line management in arriving at solutions to problems; designing and implementing audit and reporting systems that will measure effectiveness of the bank's programs; indicating need for remedial action, and determining the degree to which bank goals and timetables have been attained; serving as liasion between the bank and enforcement agencies, minority organizations, and community action groups; keeping management informed of latest developments in the entire equal opportunity area.

The appropriate level or line of authority should include, but not be limited to, the following: Assisting in the identification of problem areas and establishment of goals and objectives by division, department, and location; active involvement with local minority organizations and community action groups; periodic audit of hiring and promotion patterns to insure that goals and objectives are met; regular discussions with managers, supervisors and employees to be certain bank policies are being followed; review of the qualifications of all employees to insure that minorities are given full opportunities for transfers and promotions; career counseling for all employees; periodic audit to insure that each location is in compliance in areas such as posters are properly displayed, all facilities are, in fact, desegregated, both in policy and in use, and minority employees are afforded a full opportunity and are encouraged to participate in all bank sponsored educational, training, recreational, and social activities; the appraisal of all supervisors that their work performance is being evaluated on the basis of their equal employment opportunity efforts and results, as well as other criteria.

4. Identification of problem areas by divisions, department, location, and job classification:

Make an in-depth analysis of the following, paying particular attention to all job categories: Racial composition of work force; racial composition of applicant flow; total selection process including position descriptions, man specifications (the minimum qualifications required of the applicant who is to fit a particular job), application forms, interview procedures, test validity, referral procedures, final selection process, and test administration; transfer and promotion practices; facilities, bank sponsored recreation and social events, and special programs such as educational assistance; all bank training programs, formal and informal; pay particular attention to attitude of work force toward minority group employees; technical phases of compliance, such as posters and retention of applications.

5. Establishment of bank goals and timetables by division, department, location with respect to percent of population and job classification; including target completion date:

Establish goals and objectives covering problem areas identified in preceding section.

Involve personnel relations staff department and division heads, and local and branch managers in the goal setting process.

Goals should be significant, measurable and attainable, if not attained, explain why not.

Goals should be specific both for planned results and timetables for completion.

Goals may not be rigid required quotas, but must be targets reasonably attainable by means of applying every good faith effort to make all aspects of the entire affirmative action program work.

6. *Development and execution of action oriented programs designed to eliminate problems and further designed to attain established goals and objectives:*

Conduct detailed analysis of position descriptions to insure that they accurately reflect position functions.

Validate man specifications by division, department, location, and job classification using job performance criteria.

Approved position descriptions and man specifications should be made available to all members of management involved in the recruiting, screening, selection, and promotion process. Copies should also be distributed to all recruiting sources.

Evaluate total selection process to insure freedom from bias and attainment of goals and objectives: All personnel involved in the recruiting, screening, selection, promotion, disciplinary, and related processes should be carefully selected and trained to insure elimination of bias in all personnel actions; validate all selection criteria.

(The following key points are included in the Department of Labor Order covering the Validation of Employment Tests and Other Selection Techniques by contractors and subcontractors, including banks, subject to the provisions of Executive Order 11246.)

Each bank regularly using tests to select among candidates for hire, transfer or promotion to jobs must have available for inspection, within a reasonable time, evidence that tests are valid for their intended purpose. Such evidence should be examined during compliance reviews for indications of possible discrimination, such as instances of higher rejection rates for minority candidates than nonminority candidates.

Evidence of a test's validity should consist of empirical data demonstrating that the test is predictive of or significantly correlated with important elements of work behavior to the job(s) for which candidates are being evaluated.

Empirical evidence in support of a test's validity must be based on studies employing generally accepted procedures for determining criteria-related validity, such as those described in the American Psychological Association's *Standards for Education and Psychological Tests and Manuals.*

When a concurrent validity study is conducted, the sample should be, so far as technically feasible, representative of the minority groups currently included in the candidate population.

Tests must be administered and scored under controlled and standardized conditions, with proper safeguards employed to protect the security of test scores and insure that scores do not enter into any judgments of individual adequacy that are to be used as criterion measures.

The work behavior or other criteria of employee adequacy must be fully described. Whatever criteria are used should represent major or critical work behaviors as revealed by careful job analyses.

Presentations of the results of a validation study must include graphical and statistical representations of the relationships between the test(s) and the criteria, permitting judgments of the test(s) utility in making predictions of future work behavior.

Data must be generated and results reported separately for minority and nonminority groups wherever technically feasible.

7. *Suggested techniques to increase the flow of minority applicants follows:*

Certain organizations such as the Urban League, Job Corps, Equal Opportunity Program, Inc., Concentrated Employment Programs, Neighborhood Youth Corps, secondary schools, colleges, and "city" colleges with high minority enrollment, the state employment service, specialized employment agencies, Aspira, LULAC, SER, the G.I. Forum, and the Commonwealth of Puerto Rico are normally prepared to refer qualified minority applicants. In addition, community leaders should be added to recruiting sources.

Formal briefing sessions should be held, preferably on bank premises, with representatives from these recruiting sources. Plant tours, presentations by minority employees, clear and concise explanations of current and future job openings, position descriptions, man specifications, explanations of the bank's selection process, and recruiting literature, if available, should be an integral part of the briefings. Formal arrangements should be made for referral of applicants, follow-up with sources, and feedback on disposition of applicants.

Minority employees should be actively encouraged to refer applicants.

A special effort should be made to include minorities on the personnel relations staff.

Minority employees should be made available within reason for participation in career days, youth motivation programs, and related activities in their communities.

Active participation in "job fairs" is desirable.

Active recruiting programs should be carried out within your normal recruiting area at secondary schools, junior colleges, and colleges with minority enrollments.

Special employment programs should be undertaken whenever possible. Some possible programs are: Technical and nontechnical co-op programs with the predominantly Negro colleges and other colleges with minority enrollment; after school and/or work-study jobs for minority youths; summer jobs for underprivileged youth; summer work-study programs for faculty members of the predominantly minority schools and colleges; motivation, training, and employment programs for the hard-core unemployed.

When recruiting brochures pictorially present work situations, the minority members of the work force should be included.

Help wanted advertising should be expanded to include the minority news media on a regular basis.

8. Assure that minority employees are given equal opportunity for promotion.

This can be achieved by:

An inventory of current minority employees to determine academic, skill, and experience level of individuals.

Initiating necessary remedial, job training, and work-study programs.

Developing and implementing formal employee evaluation programs.

Being certain "man specifications" have been validated on job performance related criteria.

When apparently qualified minorities are passed over for upgrading, require supervisory personnel to submit written justification to the director of the bank's EEO coordinator.

Establishing formal career counseling program to include attitude development, educational aid, job rotation, buddy system, etc.

9. Make certain facilities and bank-sponsored social and recreation activities are desegregated. Actively encourage minority employees to participate.

10. Design and implement internal audit and reporting systems to measure effectiveness of total program by:

Monitoring records of referrals, placements, transfers, promotions, and terminations at all levels to insure non-discriminatory policy is carried out.

Requiring formal reports from unit managers on a schedule

basis as to degree to which corporate (headquarters) or unit goals are attained and timetables met.

Reviewing report results with pertinent levels of management and with chief executive officers.

Advising top management of program effectiveness and submit recommendations to improve unsatisfactory performance.

11. Actively support to the extent practicable local and national community action programs:

Appoint key members of management to serve on Merit Employment Councils, Community Relations Boards and similar organizations dealing with promotion of EEO.

Encourage minority employees to actively participate in National Alliance of Businessmen Programs for Youth Motivation.

Support Vocational Guidance Institutes, Vestibule Training Programs, and similar activities. Such support might include funding, participation, and utilization by staff.

Assist secondary schools and colleges with significant minority enrollment in programs designed to enable graduates of these institutions to compete in the open employment market on a more equitable basis.

Publicize achievements of minority employees in local and minority news media.

Support programs developed by the National Alliance of Businessmen, the Urban Coalition, and similar organizations. Such support might include funding, participation, and utilization.

Appendix

Office of Federal Contract Compliance Order No. 4 specifies the following nine factors as its definition of "underutilization":

1. The minority population of the labor area surrounding the facility;
2. The size of the minority unemployment force in the labor area surrounding the facility;
3. The percentage of minority work force as compared with the total work force in the immediate labor area;
4. The general availability of minorities having requisite skills in the immediate labor area;
5. The availability of minorities having requisite skills in an area in which the contractor can reasonably recruit;
6. The availability of promotable minority employees within the contractor's organization;
7. The anticipated expansion, contraction, and turnover of and in the work force;

8. The existence of training institutions capable of training minorities in the requisite skills; and

9. The degree of training which the contractor is reasonably able to undertake as a means of making all job classes available to minorities.

9 Where Civil Rights Law Is Going Wrong

Nation's Business

Few businessmen in America today even suspect that an agency of the federal government would:

Send out teams of investigators with authority to go through your company's files without telling you exactly why.

Write out tests for every job in your organization and pressure you to use them as a basis for hiring.

Deny you the right to put your son in a training program in your own company.

Encourage your employees to lodge complaints of discrimination in your company, but refuse to tell you who your accusers are.

Required you to exhibit "proper" social attitudes as defined by a board of government appointees.

Receive unsworn complaints about you and then threaten to make them public if you refuse to do what the agency wants you to.

Tell you to hire a man instead of a woman as your personal secretary.

Reprinted with permission from *Nation's Business*, November 1965, pp. 60–62, 64, 66, 68, 70, 73.

Force you to hire persons who are not qualified for a job and make you educate them.

Make you put young women in expensive executive training programs, even though experience shows many will quit.

Require you to give back pay to anyone the agency thinks has been denied advancement in your firm in the past because of his or her race, sex, color, religion or national origin.

Further require you to put some persons in the positions they would have been in today if discrimination had not occurred and to give extra money to the rest of your employees to soften the impact on them.

Preposterous?

These are just some of the suggestions being seriously considered by a U.S. government agency which is gathering momentum since being set up four months ago and already has indicated that it intends to step beyond the letter of the law to achieve its purposes.

Called the Equal Employment Opportunity Commission (EEOC), it is a creature of Title VII of the Civil Rights Act of 1964 which forbids discrimination in employment because of race, color, religion, sex or national origin.

Distortion Feared

Few Americans oppose the basic objectives of the Act. Certainly reasonable citizens today want their fellow citizens to have equal opportunity, whatever their race, creed, color or sex. But there are unmistakable signs that implementation may now be distorted through bias or economic ignorance of those charged with administering it.

The commission is supposed to receive complaints and oversee compliance with the law. It consists of five commissioners and a staff plucked from the ranks of unions, civil rights groups and the Peace Corps.

While the group is still organizing and deciding how to carry out its charge, there are strong movements in Congress to give it even more sweeping power.

There is, for example, a bill sponsored by Rep. Augustus F. Hawkins (D., Calif.), officially called the Equal Employment Opportunity Act of 1965 (H. R. 10065). The bill, which was rushed through the Education and Labor Committee, would transform the commission from an agency designed mainly for conciliation into one that would act largely as prosecutor, judge and jury.

The Hawkins bill would allow the commission, which now can

seek its aims only through the courts, to issue "cease and desist" orders to employers, unions and employment agencies.

The Hawkins bill, which counts the activist Student Non-Violent Coordinating Committee among its chief supporters, also would — for all practical purposes — eliminate state fair employment practices commissions and substitute federal control.

The powers outlined at the beginning of this article were among recommendations made in August during a two-day White House Conference on the new commission. And most of these recommendations can be implemented under the current law.

The conference started with a general session in the State Department's auditorium and then broke into seven "workshops." The 300 conferees included many sociologists, civil rights proponents and representatives of unions, women's organizations and state fair employment commissions.

Dissent Stifled

There was also a group representing employment agencies and employers. A few from this group spoke out indignantly at suggestions being made. But many sat silent fearing accusations of bigotry from a confused public or in a few cases even retaliation by the federal government when government contracts are let.

Government officials have put pressure on many large employers to hire more Negroes, even though a number of business firms have been making special efforts to seek out qualified employees and even quietly giving preference to Negro applicants over whites.

News of the White House conference has now spread, and businessmen are beginning to voice their dismay. *Nation's Business* has talked confidentially with dozens of executives. Many requested that their names and firms not be mentioned.

A typical reaction came from E. J. Shroedter, assistant industrial relations director of Evinrude Motors, Milwaukee.

The reports of the White House conference workshop panels are "disturbing," he said. "In many instances it will disrupt the basic philosophies upon which hiring, promotion and other practices have been established.

"Certainly, no one is advocating that discrimination against minority groups continue, nor should practices that foster discrimination be retained. However, the reverse should not happen either. Preference and greater considerations should not be given to less competent applicants regardless of race or color, because this would be discrimination in reverse."

Danger in Numbers

The vice president of a major phone company commented on one important phase of the conference this way:

> I would strongly urge that the EEOC not automatically assume a pattern [of discrimination] exists because of statistical evidence indicating a high proportion of minority employees in specific jobs. They must carefully ascertain the facts and recognize that "pockets" of minority employees may not only exist, but may also be inevitable, due to the qualifications of the individuals. They certainly should not reason that numbers per se indicate discrimination.

Some conference participants urged a complete merger of seniority lists according to dates of entrance in firms. This would put everyone, no matter what his duties or qualifications, on one big list.

"Such a rule would be onerous to follow," argues a steel executive, "and, in the case of hundreds of applications filed with a large operation in a day or a week, would create countless problems in filing and processing."

It was further suggested at the workshops that something be done to soften any impact that realigned seniority lists might have on members of the majority group, since they were not directly responsible for any discrimination.

"This type of relief," says the Commission's official report on the workshops, "might be the use of the back-pay provision which would cause the employer to bear the burden of the readjustment."

The president of a Midwest manufacturing firm argues that this approach would result in "nothing short of chaos." He suggests that instead of expending effort "correcting" the past, the commission concentrate on building for the future.

"The notion that back pay might be paid employees discriminated against in the past is highly objectionable," says a railroad vice president. "It assumes that they can be identified and that the extent of the discrimination can be defined in monetary terms. It would penalize employers as the result of the unsound presumption that they are responsible for every instance of past discrimination.

"The elimination of present and future discrimination is a more than adequate task for the commission — and is clearly the assignment given it by the law."

Thomas J. Hogan, executive vice president of Eastern Express, Inc., of Terre Haute, Ind., fears the commission will order "some careless general merger" of seniority lists which would place unqualified drivers on city and road units.

One workshop at the White House conference took up the

problems of complaint procedures and the relationship between federal, state and local regulations regarding discrimination in employment.

Representatives from some civil rights groups at the workshop expressed "serious and severe distrust" of the Federal Bureau of Investigation and of the ability of present federal and state agencies to protect persons complaining about discrimination. They suggested that EEOC commissioners file charges without naming the complaining parties.

"My blood curdled when I read suggestions that the employer be denied rights that are granted to criminals in the matter of discovery according to the rules of the court," said Claire T. Grimes, executive secretary of the Hollywood, Calif., Chamber of Commerce.

"Why must a complaining witness be completely protected in an accusation against an employer who is contributing to the advancement of society, whereas a criminal in a dope arrest — even though the evidence is found on him — cannot be convicted unless he is informed as to who the informer is? This is a double standard of the worst order and makes me indignant beyond all comprehension that such absurdities can be proposed."

A New York corporation lawyer says he can't believe the power of the federal government is "so weak and inadequate that it is unable to protect an individual who files a complaint with a governmental agency." Withholding the name of the charging party from the accused employer, he adds, would deprive the employer of the opportunity to develop his defense.

The burden of proof should be borne by the accuser, another businessman insists. Requiring an employer to furnish all the proof that he is innocent of any charge would place him at a severe disadvantage, he says, because of the adverse publicity usually connected with cases of this type.

Harassment Made Easy

"Ignoring the legal principle of the accused being confronted by his accuser," another maintains, "makes it both attractive and safe to fabricate trial cases or otherwise harass the employer."

One executive said the commission should reject the suggestion to take information in any form, sworn or unsworn. Instead, he said it should follow the National Labor Relations Board safeguards of requiring sworn complaints with criminal penalities for perjury.

"I read the workshop report without getting the idea that EEOC was going to do anything special to protect the employer," says Frank C. McAlister, director of personnel and labor relations of the Indiana State Chamber of Commerce. "I feel the employer should have some protection from harassment and unfounded charges that could be filed promiscuously against him."

Another businessman takes issue with the suggestion made at the workshop that a state agency should be allowed to discuss a case with the commission prior to the state's decision on it.

"It would, in effect, deprive an employer of his fundamental right to an unbiased appeal," he says. "In essence the state agency's decision would be the commission's decision." Still another claims that the commission's duty to act as a conciliator would be destroyed if it adopted a workshop suggestion that investigators' reports be made available in future cases.

"If statements and comments of an employer could possibly be used against him in subsequent litigation," he says," "he would have no other course open than to take a legalistic and cautious approach at the very inception of an investigation by the federal agency."

Regarding a proposal that any failures in conciliation be made public routinely, George T. Heaberg III, employment manager of Smith Kline & French Laboratories, argues: "Even though failure to conciliate is due to reasons other than discrimination on the part of the employer, we believe publicity in several of these cases would very likely damage the employer's reputation as an equal opportunity employer. Therefore, we question the advisability of unnecessarily risking damage to the employer's reputation."

Coercion Charged

The vice president of a large manufacturing firm calls the proposal "a blatant attempt to coerce an employer into accepting any solution the commission might suggest regardless of its merit." It verges on compulsory mediation, he adds, and is obviously contrary to the spirit and intent of the law.

"It implies," says an Oregon executive, "that the employer is automatically resisting conciliation if he stands on his convictions."

The civil rights law generally provides that states with satisfactory fair employment practice laws have jurisdiction for 60 days before cases go to the federal authorities.

Theoretically, businessmen complain, a single company could find itself involved with the new commission, the NLRB, the Community Relations Service, the Justice Department, the President's Committee on Equal Employment Opportunity and the Labor Department in addition to numerous state and local fair employment commissions.

"The area of jurisdiction between individual states and the federal government needs to be cleared up very quickly," says M. E. Berthiaume, manager of industrial relations for the Arrow Co., Troy, N.Y. "This is particularly important for a company that does business in many different states.

"For example, we have had a civil rights commission in New

York State for a good many years and are familiar with its method of operation and can appreciate that there will be no areas of conflict between the federal government and the state. However, in Alabama, where we also have plants, the area of agreemnt between federal and state is not so clear and it tends to leave an employer under difficulties as to how to operate under the law.

"It is, therefore, important that this area be cleared up completely before an employer is held liable for any error on his part."

Workshop No. 3 concerned discrimination because of sex. The word "sex" was put into the civil rights legislation to delay passage of the bill. Once it was in, congressmen were afraid to speak out against including the word for fear of ruffling the hair-dos of half of their constituents. So the commission is faced with the problem of determining what is meant by discrimination because of sex.

Hire Male Bunnies?

Title VII says the only time you can't hire people of either sex is when there is a "bona fide occupational qualification," an oft-used term reduced by commission staffers to "BFOQ." The search for a definition of BFOQ took up a good part of workshop No. 3.

Some refer to this as "the bunny problem." What, they ask, do you do when a knobby-kneed male waiter shows up at a Playboy club seeking a job as a bunny? Or a woman wants to be an attendant in a men's Turkish bath? Or a man has an urge to clerk in a woman's corset shop?

Suggestions were made at the workshop that only the narrowest interpretation be given to BFOQ.

"The burden is on the employers," said one commission staffer. "If they can't think of any reason not to hire women for jobs traditionally held by men, then they better do it."

Commission Chairman Franklin D. Roosevelt, Jr. said his agency "should be alert to distinguish those situations where it is merely a convenient extension of tradition and those where sex appears to have a stronger tie to the requirements of the job or other basic values."

One speaker at the workshop said women and men should be allowed any job except where only one sex could reasonably be expected to do the work or where "national mores" would require selection of one sex over the other — as in the case, for example, of a washroom attendant or a fashion model.

The workshop suggested that most jobs are interchangeable between sexes and that, for example, weight lifting would be no problem, assuming adequate mechanical handling equipment.

But an electric executive says:

"Unfortunately, I envision accelerated physical, if not emotional, failure and increased claims for compensation. What assurance does the employer have that — in exchange for accepting any instabilities of women, interruptions for child bearing, earlier retirement and the ever present possibility that a woman will quit to let her husband be the breadwinner — he will get undivided attention to the job, loyalty and a fair return on his investment?"

Another suggests that the commission force only new plants to provide facilities for women.

A widespread hope among businessmen who are aware of commission plans is that the commission will use panels of experts, including responsible representatives of industry, to advise it in establishing bona fide occupational qualifications and in setting a course where federal law conflicts with state laws.

Commission staffers also believe business should not favor men as candidates for executive training programs.

Industry representatives point out that women are a greater risk in such situations because when they marry, they usually leave a company.

This is not a valid defense, commission representatives counter. They said no BFOQ could be based upon "such broad propositions as an assumed or actual increased cost of employing women due to higher turnover, higher sick leave or other alleged generally high cost of employment."

The director of industrial relations for a large manufacturer argues: "The suggestion that the commission be empowered to extend state labor laws to both sexes where the law relates only to one is on its face unconstitutional. Obviously, no federal regulatory agent has any authority to alter, amend or vary a state statute."

On record-keeping and reporting, it was recommended that employers be made to keep secret records on each employee, indicating his race, sex, religion, national origin and source of referral.

Industry men at the conference argued that this could conflict with state or local laws prohibiting such records and that trained investigators do not need such written records to determine validity of a complaint.

Records Foster Bias

"We are color-blind rather than color-conscious in our record-keeping and other personnel operations," comments S. Lester Block, labor attorney for R. H. Macy & Co., Inc. "I believe that recorded information on an employee's race would be a disservice to employees and could actually abet discriminatory practices.

"Further, the proposal that a record indicating the employee's race should be 'kept only under circumstances where it would not be available to those responsible for personnel decisions' is unrealistic and unworkable.

"It is significant that states having long experience with fair employment practice regulations, such as New York and California, have frowned upon racial indications on employment records."

John E. Stark, vice president of industrial relations, Westinghouse Air Brake Co., says, "The completing of forms is becoming a major task. As time goes by, employers are required to complete increasingly more forms, particularly governmental. We would like to see some controls established to exert a diminishing effect on this practice."

Title VII gives the commission access to any records required by it or any state or local fair employment practice agency and makes it unlawful to interfere with agents of the commission.

The commission's attitude toward unions seems to differ from that toward industry. The commission staff proposed that unions be exempted from the record-keeping requirement except in hiring halls and apprentice programs.

Employer representatives pointed out that Title VII of the Civil Rights Act specifically covers labor unions as well as them. Certainly unions have been criticized widely for discrimination in employment policies.

Lunacy in Apprenticeship

It was suggested in workshop No. 5 on apprenticeships and the general upgrading of skills, that the commission consider Title VII violated if members of minority groups are not selected in apprentice programs.

M. E. Lantz, manager of industrial relations for Perfect Circle Corp., Hagerstown, Ind., contends that hiring as apprentices minority group members who do not have the capacity to advance beyond the trainee stage would be "sheer lunacy."

There's also concern over the prospective problem of an owner-father who has spent, say 25 years building up a business to pass on to his son and then is denied the privilege of hiring him as an apprentice.

"According to present interpretations of the equal opportunity law he could hire his son only if he were at the top of the eligibility list," one executive says, "I am not convinced this is reasonable or, frankly, the American way of doing business."

Workshop No. 6 of the conference concerned hiring, promotions and dismissals. Preferential treatment for nonwhites was put forth as a way to correct past inequalities in hiring.

"Title VII forbids preferential treatment of any type," the commission said in its report on this workshop. But it added that, "After much discussion it was determined that the question was not whether we are meeting the letter of the law, as pertains to Title VII, but whether we are meeting the spirit of the law in going an extra step to provide sufficient means to enable Negroes to obtain jobs on a basis equal with whites."

A West Coast labor relations executive argues that industry already has adequate means to assure merit employment practices "without a government agency — insulated as it often is from an understanding of a free, competitive economy — entering the arena."

Representatives of industry and private employment agencies today complain of the lack of qualified Negroes to fill many present job vacancies.

"We have run into government competition for qualified Negro personnel on several occasions where Negro applicants in whom we have shown an interest have taken government jobs," says Donald S. Frost, vice president of Bristol-Myers Co. "In one particular instance a Negro research scientist left the company to take a government position. It is our feeling that if government is trying to encourage industry to train and hire Negro employees, the various agencies should be instructed not to compete actively against industry in this area."

Negro Employers Lose

"From the viewpoint of a Negro employer," says A. T. Spaulding, president of North Carolina Mutual Life Insurance Co., "I am convinced that I have more difficult problems now, because of the loss of trained manpower to white employers. Segregation no longer is a protective tariff for the Negro employer."

Another issue in the race discrimination question involves job descriptions and job qualifications.

Several White House conferees called on industry to train "occupational analysts" to perform job audits, rewrite job specifications and insure that personnel tests are geared to find the right kind of employee. Sometimes, it was said, job specifications are designed to find an employee who can perform a job without training even though it might take only a little training for an unskilled person to do the same job.

Some civil rights advocates argue that testing is discriminatory per se and that it has been the chief device by which many minority group workers have been denied equal opportunity in the job market.

Some say that tests, instead of being abandoned should be redesigned to meet "realistic requirements" for jobs putting the accent more on the ability of a person to learn rather than on his technical knowledge.

They contend also that some tests are discriminatory because they contain cultural questions which many nonwhites do not have the background to answer.

"Complete elimination of tests would be terrible," maintains Sherry D'George, owner of a personnel agency in Altoona, Pa. "It would leave us with no way of evaluating an applicant.

"As for the suggestion that the federal government step in and decide what quesitons should be on tests, we'd then be like the Soviet Union. It would be a catastrophe. The government would be in complete control, telling us whom to hire and whom to fire."

Employers Defend Tests

Many employers insist that the use of tests is extremely important in hiring, not as a tool of racial discrimination but as a means for determining skills, abilities, interests and attitudes.

"Testing programs should not be discarded just because some firm abuses them," argues an Indiana industrialist. "The idea of different 'acceptable minimums' for 'culturally deprived groups' is in itself discriminatory and has no place in our society."

The commission should not attempt to force employers to lower hiring standards that employers have determined are pertinent to the job, businessmen argue.

"Industry should strive to cooperate with local school systems to insure that students are trained properly in skills which industry needs," the commission says. "Industry should be more willing to accept persons for employment who lack required skills but have the ability and desire to learn. . . .

"It is the responsibility of industry and the unions to provide the climate in which equal opportunity to train for employment and to compete for employment exists for all. It is especially incumbent on industry to make known to the schools and the unemployed the needs of industry. It is not enough to obey the technical letter of the law. We must go a step beyond in order to assure equal employment opportunity."

Some businessmen will question whether industry should be forced to train people if the job market can produce the applicants needed.

Most businessmen believe that promotions and dismissals should be a function of management rather than subjects for unwarranted scrutiny by the commsision.

Management is charged with the responsibility of operating an efficient and profitable organization; every employee's job future depends on this.

"In today's labor market there is an acute shortage of qualified and technically competent people," notes one business executive, "and

I can't believe that management would destroy its chance for survival by denying promotion to minority groups."

One of the workshops of the White House conference was entitled "Affirmative Action." Civil rights lawyer Herman Edelsberg, chairman of the panel, defined affirmative action as activity beyond the letter of the law.

Among affirmative actions suggested for employers were:

Voluntary group deeds to create a "climate of welcome for previously disadvantaged minorities."

Aggressive recruiting to counteract any minority group feelings of defeatism or timidity.

Display of commission posters and distribution of information on equal job opportunities.

Contributions to the Negro College Fund.

Spending "idle funds in the development of integrated suburban housing."

Business Role Limited

Influencing community attitudes can be accomplished only in part by employers, most businessmen believe. "Patience, understanding and education will do more to move the citizenry than any corporate action which to many people has implications of being politically motivated," declares one executive.

"Aggressive recruiting of minority employees for promotion is segregation in reverse which will lead to dissension within groups where a climate of welcome may once have existed," points out another.

Many businessmen express the fear that the vaguely worded Title VII will be administered according to prejudices of members of the commission. They compare the commission in this respect with the National Labor Relations Board.

James B. O'Shaughnessy, of the Labor Relations Committee of the Illinois State Chamber of Commerce, urges the immediate appointment of a citizens advisory committee to the commission. Composed of business and union representatives, it could act unofficially, suggesting procedures and approving or disapproving rules as made.

"Employers need to know the new ground rules — the procedural regulations under which they will have to operate," emphasizes Howard E. Eades, vice president of research and personnel for W. T. Grant Co., New York.

Rep. Glenn Andrews (R., Ala.), member of the full Committee on Education and Labor, cautions:

"When an individual risks his own capital and employs people, his capital, and his alone, is at stake and it is not a matter of public concern that he fail or not fail. The prerogative should be entirely his and whoever he hires is an important part of his success or failure. The proprietor of a business is entitled to full responsibility for his business venture.

"It is wrong that a public fair employment commission sit with him on his executive board and direct his employment. They are not a stockholder in his enterprise simply because he might have borrowed from a national bank or government directly, or may manufacture a product and paint it with a lacquer which has traveled once across a state line.

"Most responsible Americans, and absolutely including the decent and responsible citizens of my state and region, believe in fair employment practices. We may be a long way from that goal — in New York as well as in Alabama — but attempts at compulsion which reach into the private lives and businesses of our citizens harvest more rancor and resentment than equality of employment opportunity."

10 Will Women Ever Be Accepted as Managers?

Concerned Business Student Report

In recent years increasing numbers of women have been seeking professional degrees at graduate schools. Yet many people believe that even after acquiring the degree and entering corporate training programs, women are still not given the same opportunities as men to utilize their talents and skills in business. The problem of assuring greater female participation at all levels of management was the topic of a one-day

Reprinted with permission from *Concerned Business Student Report,* May–June 1974, pp. 2 and 7.

conference "Women in Management" held April 18 by the Graduate School of Business at Stanford.

Fully integrating women into the firm is fast becoming a political and economic necessity for corporations as more and more women take their grievances to various federal agencies and the courts for reconciliation. In a speech before the Stanford conference, Harvard Law School Teaching Fellow Colquitt L. Meacham indicated that settlements such as that paid by AT&T to women and minority men are apt to become more common. Under the Equal Pay Act, business has paid out $43 million to more than 100,000 employees over the past 10 years. Meacham credits these settlements largely to the civil actions brought by the Equal Employment Opportunities Commission (EEOC) under enforcement powers granted to the Commission in 1972. She outlined several of the key issues recently tested in the courts: special tests and educational requirements were held to be in violation of the law except where they can be specifically related to successful job performance; "Bona fide occupational requirement" has been narrowly interpreted by the courts and the EEOC to thwart discriminatory practices, such as justifying discrimination on the basis of customer preference; and denying women job security, seniority, disability compensation, health and life insurance and normal leave allowances because of pregnancy is being disallowed. The Supreme Court has held that mandatory leave for pregnant teachers in Ohio and Virginia violated the due process clauses of the Fifth and Fourteenth Amendments.

Treating women differently from men generally serves to create institutional barriers to women. According to Professor Cynthia Fuchs Epstein of Queens College, another speaker at the conference, "Women have typically not been treated to the same reward structure that men have." Not all rewards in the business world are economic; in every industry certain jobs carry more esteem and are the informal if not formal prerequisites to top management positions. "Even where women are given higher level administrative jobs, these are positions which are not on a track to management, but rather are on ancillary routes," Epstein stated. "Inclusion of women [in top management] can occur only when they expect and are given full participation in the formal and informal structures of their occupations and at every level, including the top one." Their exclusion from the informal learning opportunities vital to success in any field deters women from achieving the success enjoyed by their male counterparts. She added that, "Those who are not admitted or admissable to inner circles cannot become as competent. They are cut off from what is perhaps the most crucial learning of their trade. . . . Top surgeons learn their special skills not in medical school, but only if they are selected to be residents with the finest physicians in their specialty. Top lawyers start in apprenticeship to the senior partners in the large firms."

Labor economist Myra J. Strober of Stanford further emphasized this problem in her speech, indicating that any effective programs to bring women into middle and upper level management jobs must originate in the president's office. Because of their traditional exclusion from responsible positions women "have been socialized to believe that management, like fatherhood, is for men," Strober said. She proposes a set of short- and long-run strategies "to solve the problem of underrepresentation of women in management." In the short run, corporations should encourage women to become managers and change the ways they search out and groom management talent. In the long run "people's perceptions about women and their role in business and society" must change, Strober noted, and called for business to eliminate sexual stereotypes from product advertising, influence schools to alter sexual stereotypes and encourage girls and women to consider management careers and to support or set up child-care systems to bring more women into the labor market. Some attitudes are so strongly held that they create nearly insurmountable obstacles to full management participation. "Men and women have learned to relate to one another as actual or potential sexual partners or in frequently encountered work or social situations such as doctor-nurse, boss-secretary, or wife-husband's friend. Most men find it difficult to dismiss the 'potential sexual partner' model from their minds when they are asked to deal with women as equals," said Strober. She also observed that the stereotype about women holding lower prestige jobs gets in the way for some men who feel that loss of male exclusiveness in the management field lowers the prestige of being a manager.

The changes necessary to rid society and the business world of sex discrimination patterns are so major they will undoubtedly create sizable employee anxiety and resistance to change. In her remarks before the April 18 meeting, Francine E. Gordon, an assistant professor of organization at the Stanford Business School, compared the problems encountered with affirmative action to those found when introducing computers for the first time. Both are major changes and the fate of the company might be dependent on the success of the conversion. One big difference, she said, is that where a corporate conversion to computers would get priority attention and involvement of top management, affirmative action programs are typically identified with the personnel department, where they are "isolated from the routine work of the organization." Most efforts begin and end with top management statements expressing general commitment to the principle of affirmative action. Gordon outlined a nine-step affirmative action plan which stressed the need for setting goals that are as specific as possible and then enforcing the process with performance measures for individual managers that relate to the reward structure.

B   Leadership Style Conflicts

11   Participative Management: Time for a Second Look

Robert C. Albrook

The management of change has become a central preoccupation of U.S. business. When the directors have approved the record capital budget and congratulated themselves on "progress," when the banquet speaker has used his last superlative to describe the "world of tomorrow," the talk turns, inevitably, to the question: "Who will make it all work?" Some people resist change. Some hold the keys to it. Some admit the need for new ways but don't know how to begin. The question becomes what kind of management can ease the inevitable pains, unlock the talent, energy, and knowledge where they're needed, help valuable men to contribute to and shape change rather than be flattened by it.

The recipe is elusive, and increasingly business has turned to the academic world for help, particulary to the behavioral scientists — the psychologists, sociologists, and anthropologists whose studies have now become the showpieces of the better business schools. A number of major corporations, such as General Electric, Texas Instruments, and Standard Oil (N.J.), have brought social scientists onto their staffs. Some companies collaborate closely with university-based scholars and are contributing importantly to advanced theoretical work, just as industry's physicists, chemists, and engineers have become significant contributors of new knowledge in their respective realms. Hundreds of companies, large and small, have tried one or another formulation of basic behavioral theory, such as the many schemes for sharing cost savings with employees and actively soliciting their ideas for improved efficiency.

Reprinted from the May 1967 issue of *Fortune Magazine*, pp. 166–170, 197, 198, and 200, by special permission; © 1967 Time Inc.

For forty years the quantity and quality of academic expertise in this field have been steadily improving, and there has lately been a new burst of ideas which suggest that the researchers in the business schools and other centers of learning are really getting down to cases. The newest concepts already represent a considerable spin-off from the appealingly simple notions on which the behavioral pioneers first concentrated. The essential message these outriders had for business was this: recognize the social needs of employees in their work, as well as their need for money; they will respond with a deeper commitment and better performance, help to shape the organization's changing goals and make them their own. For blue-collar workers this meant such steps as organizing work around tasks large enough to have meaning and inviting workers' ideas; for middle and upper management it meant more participation in decision making, wider sharing of authority and responsibility, more open and more candid communication, up, down, and sideways.

The new work suggests that neither the basic philosophy nor all of the early prescriptions of this management style were scientifically sound or universally workable. The word from the behavioral scientists is becoming more specific and "scientific," less simple and moralistic. At Harvard, M.I.T., the University of Michigan, Chicago, U.C.L.A., Stanford, and elsewhere they are mounting bigger, longer, and more rigorous studies of the human factors in management than ever before undertaken.

One conclusion is that the "participative" or "group" approach doesn't seem to work with all people and in all situations. Research has shown that satisfied, happy workers are sometimes more productive — and sometimes merely happy. Some managers and workers are able to take only limited responsibility, however much the company tries to give them. Some people will recognize the need to delegate but "can't let go." In a profit squeeze the only way to get costs under control fast enough often seems to be with centralized, "get tough" management.

Few, if any, behaviorists espouse a general return to authoritarian management. Instead, they are seeking a more thorough, systematic way to apply participative principles on a sustained schedule that will give the theory a better chance to work. Others are insisting that management must be tailor-made, suited to the work or the people, rather than packaged in a standard mixture. Some people aren't and never will be suited for "democracy" on the job, according to one viewpoint, while others insist that new kinds of psychological training can fit most executives for the rugged give-and-take of successful group management.

As more variables are brought into their concepts, and as they look increasingly at the specifics of a management situation, the behaviorists are also being drawn toward collaboration with the systems designers and the theorists of data processing. Born in reaction to the cold scientism of the earlier "scientific management" experts with their stopwatches and measuring tapes, the "human relations" or behavioral school of today may be getting ready at last to bury that hatchet in a joint search for a broadly useful "general theory" of management.

Why Executives Don't Practice What They Preach

Before any general theory can be evolved, a great deal more has to be known about the difficulty of putting theory into practice — i.e., of transforming a simple managerial attitude into an effective managerial style. "There are plenty of executives," observes Stanley Seashore a social psychologist at the University of Michigan's Institute for Social Research, "who'll decide one morning they're going to be more participative and by the afternoon have concluded it doesn't work."

What's often lacking is an understanding of how deeply and specifically management style affects corporate operations. The executive who seeks a more effective approach needs a map of the whole terrain of management activity. Rensis Likert, director of the Michigan Institute, has developed a chart to assist managers in gaining a deeper understanding of the way they operate. A simplified version is on pages 148–149.[1] By answering the questions in the left-hand column of the chart (e.g., "Are subordinates' ideas sought and used?"), an executive sketches a profile of the way his company is run and whether it leans to the "authoritative" or the "participative." Hundreds of businessmen have used the chart, under Likert's direction, and many have discovered a good deal they didn't realize about the way they were handling people.

---

[1] The chart on pages 148–149 is adapted from a technique developed by Rensis Likert, director of the Institute for Social Research at the University of Michigan, to help businessmen analyze the management style used by their companies. Anyone — executive or employee — can use it to diagnose his own company or division. Check the appropriate answers, using the guide marks to shade your emphasis. After the first question, for example, if your answer is "almost none," put the check in the first or second notch of the "none" box. Regard each answer as a sort of rating on a continuous scale from the left to the right of the chart. When you have answered each question, draw a line from the top to the bottom of the chart through the check marks. The result will be a profile of your management. To determine which way management style has been shifting, repeat the process for the situation as it was three, five, or ten years ago. Finally sketch the profile you think would help your company or division to improve its performance. Likert has tried the chart on a number of business executives. Most of them rated their own companies about in the middle — embracing features of System 2 and 3. But nearly all of them also believe that companies do best when they have profiles well to the right of the chart, and worst with profiles well to the left.

Diagnose Your Management

	System 1 Exploitive Authoritative	System 2 Benevolent Authoritative	System 3 Consultative	System 4 Participative group
Leadership				
How much confidence is shown in subordinates?	None	Condescending	Substantial	Complete
How free do they feel to talk to superiors about job?	Not at all	Not very	Rather free	Fully free
Are subordinates' ideas sought and used, if worthy?	Seldom	Sometimes	Usually	Always
Motivation				
Is predominant use made of 1 fear, 2 threats, 3 punishment, 4 rewards, 5 involvement?	1, 2, 3, occasionally 4	4, some 3	4, some 3 and 5	5, 4, based on group set goals
Where is responsibility felt for achieving organization's goals?	Mostly at top	Top and middle	Fairly general	At all levels
Communication				
How much communication is aimed at achieving organization's objectives?	Very little	Little	Quite a bit	A great deal
What is the direction of information flow?	Downward	Mostly downward	Down and up	Down, up, and sideways
How is downward communication accepted?	With suspicion	Possibly with suspicion	With caution	With an open mind
How accurate is upward communication?	Often wrong	Censored for the boss	Limited accuracy	Accurate
How well do superiors know problems faced by subordinates?	Know little	Some knowledge	Quite well	Very well

	Question				
Decisions	At what level are decisions formally made?	Mostly at top	Policy at top, some delegation	Broad policy at top, more delegation	Throughout but well integrated
	What is the origin of technical and professional knowledge used in decision making?	Top management	Upper and middle	To a certain extent throughout	To a great extent throughout
	Are subordinates involved in decisions related to their work?	Not at all	Occasionally consulted	Generally consulted	Fully involved
	What does decision-making process contribute to motivation?	Nothing, often weakens it	Relatively little	Some contribution	Substantial contribution
Goals	How are organizational goals established?	Orders issued	Orders, some comment invited	After discussion, by orders	By group action (except in crisis)
	How much covert resistance to goals is present?	Strong resistance	Moderate resistance	Some resistance at times	Little or none
Control	How concentrated are review and control functions?	Highly at top	Relatively highly at top	Moderate delegation to lower levels	Quite widely shared
	Is there an informal organization resisting the formal one?	Yes	Usually	Sometimes	No—same goal as formal
	What are cost, productivity, and other control data used for?	Policing, punishment	Reward and punishment	Reward, some self-guidance	Self-guidance, problem solving

Adapted with permission from *The Human Organization: Its Management and Value* by Rensis Likert, published in April 1967 by McGraw-Hill.

Likert leads his subjects in deliberate steps to a conclusion that most of them do not practice what they say they believe. First, the executive is asked to think of the most successful company (or division of a company) he knows intimately. He then checks off on the chart his answers as they apply to that company. When the executive has finished this exercise, he has nearly always traced the profile of a strongly "participative" management system, well to the right on Likert's chart. He is next asked to repeat the procedure for the least successful company (or division) he knows well. Again, the profiles are nearly always the same, but this time they portray a strongly "authoritative" system, far to the left on the chart.

Then comes the point of the exercise. The executive is asked to describe his own company or division. Almost always, the resulting profile is that of a company somewhere in the middle, a blend of the "benevolent authoritative" and the "consultative" — well to the left of what the executive had previously identified as the most successful style. To check out the reliability of this self-analysis, Likert sometimes asks employees in the same company or division to draw its profile, too. They tend to rate as slightly more "authoritative" than the boss does.

Likert believes that the predominant management style in U.S. industry today falls about in the middle of his chart, even though most managers seem to know from personal observation of other organizations that a more participative approach works better. What accounts for their consistent failure to emulate what they consider successful? Reaching for a general explanation, Likert asks his subjects one final question: "In your experience, what happens when the senior officer becomes concerned about earnings and takes steps to cut costs, increase productivity, and improve profit?" Most reply that the company's management profile shifts left, toward the authoritarian style. General orders to economize — and promptly — often result in quick, across-the-board budget cuts. Some programs with high potential are sacrificed along with obvious losers. Carefully laid, logical plans go down the drain. Some people are laid off — usually the least essential ones. But the best people in the organization sooner or later rebel at arbitrary decisions, and many of them leave.

At the outset, the arbitrary cost cutting produces a fairly prompt improvement in earnings, of course. But there is an unrecognized trade-off in the subsequent loss of human capital, which shows up still later in loss of business. In due course, management has to "swing right" again, rebuilding its human assets at great expense in order to restore good performance. Yet the manager who puts his firm through this dreary cycle, Likert observes, is often rewarded with a bonus at the outset, when things still look good. Indeed, he may be sent off to work his magic in another division!

Likert acknowledges that there are emergencies when sharp and sudden belt-tightening is inescapable. The trouble, he says, it that it is frequently at the expense of human assets and relationships that have taken years to build. Often it would make more sense to sell off inventory or dispose of a plant. But such possibilities are overlooked because human assets do not show up in the traditional balance sheet the way physical assets do. A company can, of course, lose $100,000 worth of talent and look better on its statement than if it sells off $10,000 worth of inventory at half price.

A dollars-and-cents way of listing the value of a good engineering staff, an experienced shop crew, or an executive group with effective, established working relations might indeed steady the hand of a hard-pressed president whose banker is on the phone. Likert believes he is now on the trail of a way to assign such values — values that should be at least as realistic as the often arbitrary and outdated figures given for real estate and plant. It will take some doing to get the notion accepted by bankers and accountants, however sophisticated his method turns out to be. But today's executives are hardly unaware that their long payrolls of expensive scientific and managerial talent represent an asset as well as an expense. Indeed, it is an asset that is often bankable. A merely more regular, explicit recognition of human assets in cost-cutting decisions would help to ensure that human assets get at least an even break with plant and inventory in time of trouble.

Likert and his institute colleagues are negotiating with several corporations to enlist them in a systematic five-year study, in effect a controlled experiment, that should put a firmer footing under tentative conclusions and hypotheses. This study will test Likert's belief that across-the-board participative management, carefully developed, sustained through thick and thin, and supported by a balance sheet that somehow reckons the human factor, will show better long-run results than the cyclical swing between authoritarian and participative styles reflected in the typical middle-ground profile on his chart.

Conversion in a Pajama Factory

Already there's enough evidence in industry experience to suggest that participative management gets in trouble when it is adopted too fast. In some cases, an authoritarian management has abruptly ordered junior executives or employees to start taking on more responsibility not recognizing that the directive itself reasserted the fact of continuing centralized control. Sometimes, of course, a hard shove may be necessary, as in the recent experience of Harwood Manufacturing Corp. of Marion, Virginia, which has employed participative practices widely for many years. When it acquired a rival pajama maker, Weldon Manufacturing Co., the latter's long-held authoritarian traditions were hard to crack. With patient but firm prodding by outside consultants, who acknowledge an initial element of "coercion," the switch in style was finally accomplished.

Ideally, in the view of Likert and others, a move of this kind should begin with the patient education of top executives, followed by the development of the needed skills in internal communication, group leadership, and the other requisites of the new system. Given time, this will produce better employee attitudes and begin to harness personal motivation to corporate goals. Still later, there will be improved productivity, less waste, lower turnover and absence rates, fewer grievances and slowdowns, improved product quality, and, finally better customer relations.

The transformation may take several years. A checkup too early in the game might prove that participative management, even when thoroughly understood and embraced at the top, doesn't produce better results. By the same token, a management that is retreating from the new style in a typical cost squeeze may still be nominally participative, yet may already have thrown way the fruits of the system. Some research findings do indicate that participation isn't producing the hoped-for results. In Likert's view, these were spot checks, made without regard to which way the company was tending and where it was in the cycle of change.

A growing number of behaviorists, however, have begun to question whether the participative style is an ideal toward which all management should strive. If they once believed it was, more as a matter of faith in their long struggle against the "scientific" manager's machine-like view of man than as a finding from any new science of their own, they now are ready to take a second look at the proposition.

It seems plain enough that a research scientist generally benefits from a good deal of freedom and autonomy, and that top executives, confronted every day by new problems that no routine can anticipate, operate better with maximum consultation and uninhibited contributions from every member of the team. If the vice president for finance can't talk candidly with the vice president for production about financing the new plant, a lot of time can be wasted. In sales, group effort — instead of the usual competition — can be highly productive. But in the accounting department, things must go by the book. "Creative accounting" sounds more like a formula for jail than for the old behaviorists' dream of personal self-fulfillment on the job. And so with quality control in the chemical plant. An inspired adjustment here and there isn't welcome, thank you; just follow the specifications.

In the production department, automation has washed out a lot of the old problem of man as a prisoner of the assembly line, the kind of problem that first brought the "human relations" experts into the factories in the 1920's and 1930's. If a shop is full of computer-controlled machine tools busily reproducing themselves, the boy with the broom who sweeps away the shavings may be the only one who can put a personal flourish into his work. The creativity is all upstairs in the engineering and programming departments. But then, so are most of the people.

"Look what's happened in the last twenty years," says Harold J. Leavitt, a social psychologist who recently moved to Stanford after some years at Carnegie Tech. "Originally the concern of the human-relations people was with the blue-collar worker. Then the focus began to shift to foremen and to middle management. Now it's concentrated in special areas like research and development and in top management. Why? Because the 'group' style works best where nobody knows exactly and all the time what they're supposed to be doing, where there's a continuous need to change and adapt."

Democracy Works Better in Plastics

One conclusion that has been drawn from this is that management style has to be custom-designed to fit the particular characteristics of each industry. The participative approach will work best in those industries that are in the vanguard of change. A Harvard Business School study has compared high-performance companies in three related, but subtly different, fields: plastics, packaged food, and standard containers. The plastics company faced the greatest uncertainties and change in research, new products, and market developments. The food company's business was somewhat more stable, while the container company encountered little or no requirement for innovation. The three achieved good results using markedly different management styles. The plastics firm provided for wide dispersal of responsibility for major decisions, the food company for moderate decentralization of authority, and the container company operated with fairly centralized control.

Less successful enterprises in each of the three industries were also examined, and their managements were compared with those of the high-performance companies. From this part of the study, Harvard researchers Paul Lawrence and Jay Lorsch drew another conclusion: not only may each industry have its own appropriate management style, but so may the individual operations within the same company. The companies that do best are those which allow for variations among their departments and know how to take these variations into account in coordinating the whole corporate effort.

Both the sales and the research departments in a fast-moving plastics company, for example, may adopt a style that encourages employees to participate actively in departmental decision making. But in special ways the two operations still need to differ. The research worker, for example, thinks in long-range terms, focusing on results expected in two or three years. The sales executive has his sights set on results next week or next month. This different sense of time may make it hard for the two departments to understand each other. But if top management recognizes the reasons and the need for such differences, each department will do its own job better, and they can be better coordinated. On the other hand, if top management ignores the differences and insists, for example, on rigidly uniform budgeting and planning timetables, there will be a loss of effectiveness.

It seems an obvious point that sales must be allowed to operate like sales, accounting like accounting, and production like production. But as Lawrence comments, "The mark of a good idea in this field is that as soon as it is articulated, it does seem obvious. People forget that, five minutes before, it wasn't. One curse of the behavioral scientist is that anything he comes up with is going to seem that way, because anything that's good *is* obvious."

People, Too, Have Their Styles

Other behavioral scientists take the view that management style should be determined not so much by the nature of the particular business operation involved, but by the personality traits of the people themselves. There may be some tendency for certain kinds of jobs to attract certain kinds of people. But in nearly any shop or office a wide range of personality types may be observed. There is, for example, the outgoing, socially oriented scientist as well as the supposedly more typical introverted recluse. There are mature, confident managers, and there are those who somehow fill the job despite nagging self-doubt and a consuming need for reassurance.

For a long time, personality tests seem to offer a way to steer people into the psychologically right kind of work. Whether such testing for placement is worth while is now a matter of some dispute. In any case, the whole question of individual differences is often reduced to little more than an office guessing game. Will Sue cooperate with Jane? Can Dorothy stand working for Jim? Will Harry take suggestions?

The participative approach to management may be based upon a greatly oversimplified notion about people, in the view of psychologist Clare Graves of Union College in Schenectady, New York. On the basis of limited samplings, he tentatively concludes that as many as half the people in the northeastern U.S., and a larger proportion nationwide are not and many never will be the eager-beaver workers on whom the late Douglas McGregor of M.I.T. based his "Theory Y." Only some variation of old-style authoritarian management will meet their psychological needs, Graves contends.

Graves believes he has identified seven fairly distinct personality types, although he acknowledges that many people are not "purebreds" who would fit his abstractions perfectly and that new and higher personality forms may still be evolving. At the bottom of his well-ordered hierarchy he places the childlike "autistic" personality, which requires "close care and nurturing." Next up the scale are the "animistic" type, which must be dealt with by sheer force or enticement; the "ordered" personality that responds best to a moralistic management; and the "materialistic" individual who calls for pragmatic, hard bargaining. None of these are suited for the participative kind of management.

At the top of Graves' personality ladder are the "sociometric," the "cognitive," and the "apprehending" types of people. They are motivated, respectively, by a need for "belonging," for "information," and for an "understanding" of the total situation in which they are involved. For each of these levels some form of participative management will work. However, those at the very top, the unemotional "apprehending" individuals, must be allowed pretty much to set their own terms for work. Management can trust such people to contribute usefully only according to their own cool perception of what is needed. They will seldom take the trouble to fight authority when they disagree with it, but merely withdraw, do a passable but not excellent job, and wait for management to see things their way. In that sense these highest-level people are probably not ideal participators.

Graves believes most adults are stuck at one level throughout their lifetimes or move up a single notch, at best. He finds, incidentally, that there can be bright or dull, mature or immature behavior at nearly all levels. The stages simply represent psychological growth toward a larger and larger awareness of the individual's relationship to society.

If a company has a mixture of personality types, as most do, it must somehow sort them out. One way would be to place participative-type managers in charge of some groups, and authoritarian managers in charge of others. Employees would then be encouraged to transfer into sections where the management style best suits them. This would hardly simplify corporate life. But companies pushing the group approach might at least avoid substituting harmful new rigidities — "participate, or else!" — for the old ones.

The Anthropological View

Behaviorists who have been studying management problems from an anthropological viewpoint naturally stress cultural rather than individual differences. Manning Nash, of the University of Chicago's business school, for example, observes that the American emphasis on egalitarianism and performance has always tempered management style in the U.S. "No matter what your role is, if you don't perform, no one in this country will defer to you," he says. "Americans won't act unless they respect you. You couldn't have an American Charge of the Light Brigade." But try to export that attitude to a country with a more autocratic social tradition, and, in the words of Stanley Davis of Harvard, "it won't be bought and may not be workable."

Within the U.S. there are many cultural differences that might provide guides to managerial style if they could be successfully analyzed. Recent research by Lawrence and Arthur N. Turner at the Harvard Business School hints at important differences between blue-collar workers in cities and those in smaller towns, although religious and other factors fog the results. Town workers seem to seek "a relatively large amount of variety, autonomy interaction, skill and responsibility" in their work, whereas city workers "find more simple tasks less stress-producing and more satisfying."

In managerial areas where democratic techniques *are* likely to work, the problem is how to give managers skill and practice in participation. The National Education Association's National Training Laboratories twenty years ago pioneered a way of doing this called "sensitivity training" (see "Two Weeks in a T-Group," *Fortune,* August, 1961). Small groups of men, commonly drawn from the executive ranks, sit down with a professional trainer but without agenda or rule book and "see what happens." The "vacuum" draws out first one and then another participant, in a way that tends to expose in fairly short order how he comes across to others.

The technique has had many critics, few more vocal than William Gomberg of the University of Pennsylvania's Wharton School. Renewing his assault recently, he called the "training" groups, "titillating therapy, management development's most fashionable fad." When people from the same company are in the group, he argues, the whole exercise is an invasion of privacy, an abuse of the therapeutic technique to help the company, not the individual. For top executives in such groups, Gomberg and others contend, the technique offers mainly a catharis for their loneliness or insecurity.

"Psyching Out the Boss"

Undoubtedly the T-group can be abused, intentionally or otherwise. But today's sensitivity trainers are trying to make sure the experience leads to useful results for both the individual and his firm. They realize that early groups, made up of total strangers gathered at some remote "cultural island," often gave the executive little notion of how to apply his new knowledge back on the job. To bring more realism to the exercise, the National Training Laboratories began ten years ago to make up groups of executives and managers from the same company, but not men who had working relationships with one another. These "cousin labs" have led, in turn, to some training of actual management "families," a boss and his subordinates. At the West Coast headquarters of the T-group movement, the business school at U.C.L.A., some now call such training "task-group therapy."

Many businessmen insist T-groups have helped them. Forty-three presidents and chairmen and hundreds of lesser executives are National Training Laboratories alumni. U.C.L.A. is beseiged by applicants, and many are turned away.

Sensitivity training is supposed to help most in business situations where there is a great deal of uncertainty, as there is in the training sessions themselves. In such situations in the corporate setting there is sometimes a tendency for executives to withdraw, to defer action, to play a kind of game with other people in the organization to see who will climb out on a limb first. A chief ploy is "psyching out the boss," which means trying to anticipate the way the winds of ultimate decision will blow and to set course accordingly.

The aim of sensitivity training is to stop all this, to get the executive's nerve up so that he faces facts, or, in the words of U.C.L.A.'s James V. Clark to "lay bare the stress and strain faster and get a resolution of the problem." In that limited sense, such therapy could well serve any style of management. In Clark's view, this kind of training, early in the game, might save many a company a costly detour on the road to company-wide "democracy." He cites the experience of Non-Linear systems, Inc., of Del Mar, California, a manufacturer of such electronic gear as digital voltmeters and data-logging equipment and an important supplier to aerospace contractors. The company is headed by Andrew Kay, a leading champion of the participative style. At the lower levels, Kay's application of participative concepts worked well. He gave workers responsibility for "the whole black box," instead of for pieces of his complex finished products. Because it was still a box, with some definite boundaries, the workers seized the new opportunity without fear or hesitation. The psychological magic of meaningful work, as opposed to the hopelessly specialized chore, took hold. Productivity rose.

Vice Presidents in Midair

But at the executive level, Kay moved too quickly, failing to prepare his executives for broad and undefined responsibilities — or failing to choose men better suited for the challenge. One vice president was put in charge of "innovation." Suspended in midair, without the support of departments of functional groups and lacking even so much as a job description, most of the V.P.'s became passive and incapable of making decisions. "They lost touch with reality — including the reality of the market," recalls Clark. When the industry suffered a general slump and new competition entered the field, Non-Linear wasn't ready. Sales dropped 16 percent according to Kay. In time he realized he was surrounded with dependent men, untrained to participate in the fashion he had peremptorily commanded. He trimmed his executive group and expects to set a new sales record this year.

Sheldon Davis of TRW Systems in Redondo Beach, California, blames the behavioral scientists themselves for breakdowns like Non-Linear's. Too often, he argues, "their messages come out sounding soft and easy, as if what we are trying to do is build happy teams of employees who feel 'good' about things, rather than saying we're trying to build effective organizations with groups that function well and that can zero in quickly on their problems and deal with them rationally."

To Davis, participation should mean, "tough, open exchange," focused on the problem, not the organizational chart. Old-style managers who simply dictate a solution are wrong, he argues, and so are those new-style managers who think the idea is simply to go along with a subordinate's proposals if they're earnestly offered. Neither approach taps the full potential of the executive group. When problems are faced squarely, Davis believes, the boss — who should remain boss — gets the best solution because all relevant factors are thoroughly considered. And because everyone has contributed to the solution and feels responsible for it, it is also the solution most likely to be carried out.

One of the most useful new developments in the behavioral study of management is a fresh emphasis on collaboration with technology. In the early days of the human-relations movement in industry, technology was often regarded as "the enemy," the source of the personal and social problems that the psychologists were trying to treat. But from the beginning, some social scientists wanted to move right in and help fashion machines and industrial processes so as to reduce or eliminate their supposedly anti-human effects. Today this concept is more than mere talk. The idea is to develop so-called "socio-technical" systems that permit man and technology *together* to produce the best performance.

Some early experimentation in the British coal mines, by London's Tavistock Institute, as well as scattered work in this country and in Scandinavia, have already demonstrated practical results from such a collaboration. Tavistock found that an attempt to apply specialized factory-style technology to coal mining had isolated the miners from one another. They missed the sense of group support and self-direction that had helped them cope with uncertainty and danger deep in the coal faces. Productivity suffered. In this case, Tavistock's solution was to redesign the new system so that men could still work in groups.

In the U.S. a manufacturer of small household appliances installed some highly sophisticated new technical processes that put the company well in the front of its field. But the engineers had broken down the jobs to such an extent that workers were getting no satisfaction out of their performance and productivity declined. Costs went up and, in the end, some of the new machinery had to be scrapped.

Some technologists seem more than ready to welcome a partnership with the human-relations expert. Louis Davis, a professor of engineering, has joined the U.C.L.A. business-school faculty to lead a six-man socio-technical research group that includes several behaviorists. Among them is Eric Trist, a highly respected psychologist from the Tavistock Institute. Davis hopes today's collaboration will lead in time to a new breed of experts knowledgeable in both the engineering and the social disciplines.

"It's Time We Stopped Building Rival Dictionaries"

The importance of time, the nature of the task, the differences within a large organization, the nature of the people, the cultural setting, the psychological preparation of management, the relationship to technology — all these and other variables are making the search for effective managerial style more and more complex. But the growing recognition of these complexities has drained the human-relations movement of much of its antagonism toward the "superrationalism" of management science. Humanists must be more systematic and rational if they are to make some useful sense of the scattered and half-tested concepts they have thus far developed, and put their new theories to a real test.

A number of behaviorists believe it is well past time to bury the hatchet and collaborate in earnest with the mathematicians and economists. Some business schools and commercial consulting groups are already realigning their staffs to encourage such work. It won't be easy. Most "systems" thinkers are preoccupied with bringing all the relevant knowledge to bear on a management problem in a systematic way, seeking the theoretically "best" solution. Most behaviorists have tended to assume that the solution which is *most likely to be carried out* is the best one, hence their focus on involving lots of people in the decision making so that they will follow through. Where the "experts" who shape decisions are also in charge of getting the job done, the two approaches sometimes blend, in practice. But in many organizations, it is a long road from creative and imaginative decision to actual performance. A general theory of management must show how to build systematic expertise into a style that is also well suited to people.

The rapprochement among management theorists has a distinguished herald, Fritz J. Roethlisberger of Harvard Business School, one of the human-relations pioneers who first disclosed the potential of the "small group" in industrial experiments forty years ago. He laughs quickly at any suggestion that a unified approach will come easily. "But after all, we are all looking at the same thing," he says. "It's time we stopped building rival dictionaries and learned to make some sentences that really say something."

12 After X and Y Comes Z

J. M. Colin

Both theories X and Y[1] have had their respective place in time. It is now time for a new approach which goes beyond the precepts and constraints of these two time proven theories.

Theory Z is in order, if the firm is to be prepared for the future. The key to the future will be the ability to "adapt to chronic change." The theory Z developed in this article purports to do just that; it is based on the following hypothesis:

Innovation and Motivation are inseparable. One cannot exist without the other. However, it is entirely possible that the direction taken by them can be detrimental to the overall good of the firm — unless channeled properly toward coordinated company/employee goal(s).

The Operational Environment Required for Theory Z

Motivation and innovation depend on the existence of a certain climate within the firm. This climate must consist of the following key or "select" concepts:

Reprinted with permission from *Personnel Journal*, January 1971, pp. 56–59.
[1] D. McGregor, *The Human Side of Enterprise*, McGraw-Hill Book Company, New York, 1966.

1. *There must be stress on high productive norms.* This would be true of manufacturing, staff, research, or the executive levels of the organization.
2. *Careful selection* is paramount for success. Selection does not end with the hiring, but continues to follow the every move of the individual within the organization. This exposes him to all aspects of firm life which will benefit and enhance his ultimate development and contribution.
3. *Specialization opportunities* must exist after careful selection has placed the individual in his proper location and strata. Placement does not preclude the possibility or desirability of moving people into other disciplines as they rise within the corporate structure. Rather, it gives them a firm foundation on which "to hang their hats" during early developmental stages of their careers.
4. *Maslow's* five levels of needs must be satisfied.[2]
   a. Physiological
   b. Safety and security
   c. Social
   d. Ego
   e. Self-actualization
5. *Mutual trust* must exist throughout the firm. Back-biting and "politicking," while possibly never completely eliminated, must be minimized to the extent where they are literally nonexistent.
6. *Identification* both with the job, project and the firm must be possible for the individual.
7. *Interaction* of ideas and concepts with his peers and supervisor must make it possible for the individual to fully explore and develop his potential.
8. *The opportunity for the individual to undertake "tough" assignments* that "stretch and challenge" should present the potential for success or failure and the corresponding rewards.
9. *Recognition* is essential to fulfill both the ego satisfaction and self-actualization principles put forth by Maslow.
10. *Opportunity to develop* — already identified in detail in points 3 and 8.
11. *Success* — the potential to succeed, but also providing the opportunity to fail. However, there must be security for the individual to stretch and "reach for the stars" as Thomas Watson Sr. (late) of IBM wished of his employees. The type of security mentioned here is the *security to fail* without elimination from the firm. This does not violate point number 8 above,

---

[2] A. Maslow, *Motivation and Personality*, Harper and Row, Publishers Incorporated, New York, 1964.

in that failure here is in the pursuit of excellence and not the result of incompetence.

The above discussion adequately describes the vital environment necessary for the employees to innovate and be motivated. It remains to determine what type of individual(s) will prosper in these surroundings. Fundamentally, there are four personality types of interest:

A. The security oriented individual. Here "security" means the more conventional view of job security and the middle of the road approach, i.e., the mediocre nonachievement worker.
B. The acceptance oriented individual. This person is out to win group acceptance. Recognition and acceptance are foremost in his life.
C. Status oriented individual. Here is the power-directed person, the authoritarian leader much discussed as the "Theory X" man.
D. Achievement oriented individual. This person represents the ultimate criterion proposed by proponents of "Theory Y."

It is worth discussing the acceptance oriented individual. In many cases the stress on acceptance merely is a reflection of a lack of maturity on the part of the individual. This can be the result of youthfulness or unpleasant associations during the early work career. The acceptance oriented person can be converted into the truly productive worker by presenting him the proper environment to self-develop. Opportunity can move him from one who is inner directed to a more outer directed personality. If this person can be brought out of his "shell," he can be extremely productive and useful to himself and the organization as either a more status- or alternatively, achievement-oriented personage.

Perhaps it is now time to examine the future of motivation/innovation. Traditionally, there has been considered to be a duality of goals for the individual and the firm:

1. Efficiency: The least cost, least time, etc. way of achieving the completion of a task. This approach is best illustrated through the work of Frederick L. Taylor, the disciples of "Scientific Management" and is recognized as the Theory X approach to management.[3]
2. Human satisfaction: Here the individual needs and desires are considered. This work represents the Theory Y approach to management forwarded by McGregor, earlier by Mayo[4] — and

---

[3] Daniel Bell, *Work and Its Discontents,* Beacon Press, Boston, 1956.
[4] Milton Derber, *Research in Labor Problems in the United States,* Random House, New York, 1967, p. 49.

even as an earlier example, the work of Robert Owen in the 18th Century.[5]

Unfortunately, the above approaches will not function properly now or will they be effective in the future. The future motivational approaches will have to recognize that the whole organizational concept must change and, in fact, a whole new structure forwarded. This structure must recognize that the whole future of the firm will depend on *its ability to survive in the face of chronic change.*

The Theory Z Organization

The whole organizational concept is in direct conflict and totally inconsistent with traditional methods of motivation/innovation and bureaucratic organization structures as we know them today. The new organization will have as its foundations:

1. The spirit of inquiry
2. Achievement
3. Inner direction
4. Motivational drives of a new form:
   a. The desire for autonomy by the individual.
   b. The desire for creative tasks for the individual to perform.
   c. Real motivation is the product of self-direction.

While the above represents the basic foundation for new organizations and approaches to motivation and innovation, there are several important "principles" that will be present or develop through Theory Z approaches:

1. *The growth of professionalism* will evidence itself in loyalty to the scientific method rather than to the firm. This has been developing over the past twenty years and is becoming a more important influence in the management of firms. The first "rumblings" were heard from some of the atomic scientists in their revolution concerning the development of the original hydrogen bomb. Certainly, it is gaining force from such organizations as the AICPA (American Institute of Certified Public Accountants), and the AMA (American Medical Association) and various engineering societies.
2. *Higher levels of education* will bring more demands from the individual for increased measures of autonomy and freedom from organizational constraints. The more knowledgeable the individual becomes, the less constrained he will be by his environment. This does not say that he will necessarily be more

---

[5] Robert L. Heilbroner, *The Wordly Philosophers,* Simon and Schuster, New York, 1961, p. 96.

"intelligent" than his predecessor workers; rather, education coupled with experience will make him "smarter" and less easily duped or controlled through restricted information or propaganda.

3. *Full communications* will be absolutely necessary as a result of higher levels of education discussed above (point 2).

4. *Project organization* will become the rule rather than the exception for the organizational structure. More frequent team approaches will be found for the solution to complex problems. These projects will draw from across every discipline within the firm. Being temporary in nature, the project management will be transient and fluid, so fluid that the project leader on one effort may well be a "worker" in several others before (and if) he is a project leader again. The principle here will be that the project leader will come from the discipline that is most critical to the fulfillment of the project goal — it might be accounting, engineering, research, or, for that matter, mechanical maintenance. Perhaps the most inconsistent possibilities, at least in light of today's management practices, will be the sight of people from higher strata of the firm working for a project leader from a lesser rank and organization, who from the most critical skill requirement for this particular project, qualifies as the project leader.

5. *The matrix organizational* structure will be found to best fit the conditions and situations discussed in point 4 above, since the company outlined is definitely project-oriented rather than task-oriented along traditional lines of thinking. This type of organization will be necessary to fully respond to the challenge of survival in an ever-evolving technological environment.

6. *Tasks will become increasingly complex.* In this sense, they will be "unprogrammable," at least in the context of current management thought. Because of this increased complexity, planned approaches to determining the objectives and strategies for the firm will become absolutely primary if the firm is to survive. Control over these complex projects will require responses in "real time" to prevent the misapplication of the resources of the firm down a road that has become uncontrolled or out of step with the present thinking of management or needs of the market.

As far as the over-all organization is concerned, there will be a need for even more democratic organizations to exist.[6] Basically, this will come about through emphasis on increased education. The aura of cooperation definitely will be required for the organization to fully

---

[6] W. G. Bennis, *Changing Organization,* McGraw-Hill Book Company, New York, 1966.

succeed. The "matrix" organization concept requires cooperation if revolving leadership is to yield a maximizing result for the firm. Of the "foundations" mentioned earlier, the "spirit of inquiry" is perhaps the single most important point. The firm must inculcate its employees with the desire to explore the unknown and find new vistas where the firm may fit, "survive" and adapt to the very-changing business environment. For the firm to fully succeed, it will have to attack value problems, value levels, and merge them into a cohesive structure.

1. Individual: Align the individual's values to those of the firm. This can only be accomplished if the individual identifies with the ideals of the firm and can project into a role within the "system."
2. System: Here the individual attempts to identify with the organization for the reinforcement or maintenance purposes described by Maslow in the need for social acceptance and belonging.
3. Universal frame of reference: Here the individual attempts to determine which alternative is more important to him, etc. This benchmark is referred to by both Ayres and Veblin throughout their various works.[7, 8]

If any conclusions can be drawn from the foregoing, they would be:

The primary yardstick for future success of the organization firm will be the ability to change/adapt in the face of chronic change.

In addition, even the most viable, vigorous and productive firm cannot legislate value premises. A prime example of this is the controversy between the automobile industry and government with respect to motorist safety. The government has legislated safety features into automobiles. However, it appears that no matter how much safety feature legislation exists, the general public *cannot* be legislated into employing the features. An examination of the various seat belt utilization figures at the National Safety Council more than adequately supports this thesis.

It is, therefore, of utmost importance to the firm to clearly differentiate between *value levels* and *value premises* and determine which of these are subject to modification. The firm which fails to make the distinction will be the one which falls from the ranks of industry in a dynamic society.

The person best suited to this environment will be some combination of status-oriented and achievement-oriented individual. He might well be characterized as the "adaptive achiever."

---

[7] C. E. Ayres, *The Theory of Economic Progress*, Schocken Books, New York, 1965.
[8] Ben B. Seligman, *Main Currents in Modern Economies*, Free Press of Glencoe, New York, 1963, pp. 142, 144–145.

Cases

Seabrook Manufacturing Company

"All we need now is a strong man to complete the side show!" exclaimed Joe Larson, purchasing manager of the Seabrook Manufacturing Co., as he entered the office of Dale Wolff, personnel representative for the purchasing department.

"What do you mean, Joe?" asked Dale.

"You know that we have a lot of visitors and suppliers through here, and that old bag isn't doing much to doll up the area. These secretaries have a good deal to do with the impressions people get of our outfit, and they should be at least presentable! We spend thousands of dollars for carpeting and pictures and now this!"

"Who are you talking about?"

"I don't know what her name is, but you know damn well who I'm talking about! The Blimp! Take care of it, will you?"

The purchasing department of Seabrook Manufacturing Co. occupied the major portion of the third floor of the headquarters building of the company. The main working force was located in a large open area at several rows of desks. Executives of the division, all of whom were under the general control of Mr. Larson, were located in private offices that extended along the outer edge of the general working area. The secretary for each executive was situated at a desk directly in front of the office of the executive for whom she worked, but was separated

---

From *Human Elements of Administration: Cases, Readings, Simulation Exercises* by Harry R. Knudson, Jr. Copyright © 1963 by Holt, Rinehart and Winston, Inc. Reprinted by permission of Holt, Rinehart and Winston.

from the rest of the workers by a wide aisle. This aisle was the main passage used by visitors and personnel from other divisions of the company to get from the reception lobby to the executives' offices. The secretaries' desks were finished with a walnut stain as contrasted with the lighter-colored finishes used on other desks in the open area, and the space between secretaries' desks was significantly greater than the space between other desks on the floor.

Mary Lampson, the secretary in question, had just been promoted to her new position as Jack Henderson's secretary and had moved to her new location while Mr. Larson had been away on a business trip. After his former secretary had submitted her resignation, Jack Henderson had selected Mary Lampson as his new secretary after reviewing the personnel files and talking with several individuals currently employed in the department whom Dale Wolff had recommended as candidates for the position.

Mary Lampson was forty-eight years old, and had been with the Seabrook Manufacturing Company for seventeen years, ten in the Purchasing Department. She had started work at Seabrook shortly after her husband had died. Prior to her assignment as Mr. Henderson's secretary, she had performed secretarial duties for several units in the department, but had always been located in the open area with the general employees of the division. She had two grown sons who had completed college and had moved to other parts of the country, and one other son, twenty years old, who was a sophomore at Eastern State University. Her record at Seabrook was unblemished. She had created favorable impressions wherever she had worked, and her former supervisors were unanimous in their praise of her abilities.

Mary Lampson was 5′ 4″ tall and weighed 225 pounds. Although her weight had been a continuing problem for her, she was very pleased with her recent progress on a weight control program, and had lost sixty pounds in the last two years by following her doctor's orders very closely. She was enthusiastic about her new job, for she could use the increase in salary to help put her youngest son through college, and, as she put it, "keep the creditors a little farther from my door."

While not knowing quite how to "take care of it," Dale Wolff decided that his first step should be to talk with Jack Henderson, Mary's boss.

After Mr. Wolff related his conversation with Mr. Larson, Jack Henderson replied: "What a hell of a way to run a railroad! You do what you want to, Dale, but things are in pretty miserable shape when looks are more important than ability. I'm certainly not going to mention this to Mary!"

The Well-Run Oil Company

Robert Jackson, President of The Well-Run Oil Company of Philadelphia, was faced with a decision to make concerning the hiring of additional Negro employees in his company.

During the previous month, Jackson had been meeting with a group of four Negro ministers who, according to their spokesman, represented the combined Negro church population in the Philadelphia area. The first meeting found the ministers politely urging Jackson to hire more Negroes for positions of "greater responsibility" in the company. In reply, Jackson balked at what he regarded to be an "intrusion on management's rights," contending that the Well-Run management reserved the "right to make any employment policy it saw fit." "After all," Jackson continued, "we're in business to make a profit and not to solve the city's social problems." The ministers restated their request, after which Jackson concluded the meeting by saying, "I understand your problems, but frankly, it's not ours to solve."

Three weeks passed without further action being taken. Then the ministers returned with a more specific request. They asked that, "Well-Run hire twenty-eight Negro employees; twenty-two additional office workers, four permanent truck drivers, and two motor products salesmen within one month." And, "if Well-Run failed to comply," the ministers told Jackson, "we have no other choice but to call a city-wide Negro boycott of company products until there has been a change in company policy."

Jackson was amazed at their request. He resented what he termed, "a complete disregard for the free enterprise system." On the other hand, he realized that the ministers "meant business"; consequently, he attempted to remain courteous and objective about the matter. In doing so, he carefully pointed out to them that the company already had hundreds of Negro employees working in a nearby refinery, some of whom were in responsible supervisory jobs. In addition, he mentioned that the company had recently decided to include three Negro

Reprinted with permission of Professor Larry E. Greiner, Harvard University. Copyright © 1961 by the University of Kansas.

colleges in its yearly talent search. To this, the ministers replied, "we aren't interested in the number of Negroes working in the refinery. Negroes have always held jobs like that. You hired three Negro clerks a year ago, but none since. Three in an office of fifteen-hundred isn't much, is it? And even though you plan to include Negroes in your talent search, you haven't actually hired any." Not wishing to prolong the discussion, Jackson adjourned the meeting, saying that he'd take their advice under consideration.

Immediately afterwards, Jackson began to think about the decision he would have to make. In doing so, he came across this comment in a recent issue of *The Reporter*[1] magazine:

> When four hundred ministers in one city advise their congregations not to buy something, a lot of whatever that something may be goes unbought and the company that makes it is quickly made aware of the fact. For a month and a half, starting March 19th, the congregations of four hundred Negro churches in Philadelphia have not bought Sunoco gas or oil for their cars or trucks or Sun fuel oil to heat their homes. Last January for exactly one week they were not buying Gulf gas or oil. Last October for two weeks they were not drinking Pepsi-Cola. And last summer for two months they were not eating any cakes or pies made by Tasty Baking Company.
>
> . . . With the Tasty Baking Company, the second firm they visited and the first one where they encountered opposition, the ministers asked the company to hire two Negro driver-salesmen, two Negro clerical workers, and three or four Negro girls in the icing department, where the workers had traditionally been all-white. They were not interested in the fact that the Tasty Baking Company already had hundreds of Negro employees. What they are interested in is placing Negro workers in positions of dignity and responsibility. Their aim is to change the public image of Negro workers. The Tasty Baking Company did not have any Negroes driving trucks or working in its office.
>
> When Mr. Pass, the personnel manager of the company, and Mr. Kaiser, the president, pointed out that they had no need, just then, for more driver-salesmen or clerical workers, the ministers said politely but firmly that they still hoped these people could be hired within two weeks. If not, the four hundred ministers they represented would have to advise their congregations on the Sunday following not to buy any Tasty cakes or pies until they were hired.
>
> Mr. Kaiser understandably felt pushed and resistant. The Negro driver-salesmen and clerks and icers were not hired within two weeks, and the ministers did tell their congregations

[1] Lees, Hannah, "The Not Buying of Philadelphia's Negroes," *The Reporter* (May 11, 1961), p. 33.

The Well-Run Oil Company

not to buy any Tasty cakes or pies until further notice. Printed advertisements to this effect mysteriously appeared in bars, beauty parlors, and barbershops. Nobody knows how many thousand dollars' worth of sales the Tasty Baking Company lost during those summer months, but there are 700,000 Negroes in Philadelphia and a large proportion have some connection with those four hundred churches. When the boycott was officially called off two months later from four hundred pulpits, the Tasty Baking Company had in its employ two Negro driver-salesmen, two Negro clerical workers, and some half-dozen Negro icers.

Ball Wholesale Drug Company

Early in 1954 the Third Area office of the Ball Wholesale Drug Company advertised for an Assistant Chief Accountant. Sales volume in the area had expanded considerably over the past year and Mr. Paul Donovan, Area Manager, had secured the agreement of the home office to make this addition to his staff. Mr. Donovan had felt for some time that the accounting department needed improvement. He had been criticized by the home office for the lateness of various weekly reports and for the seeming inability of his area to submit monthly data to the home office on time.

As a result of the advertisement and referrals from several employment agencies, fourteen applicants were interviewed and tested over the next month. The field was narrowed down to two men on the basis of the interviews and test results. One of the applicants was Henry

Prepared by Robert J. Agnew for the School of Business Administration, University of Pittsburgh, and reprinted with his permission.

League, a man who had had three years' experience in accounting in an area related to the kind of work done by the accounting department at Ball. He had an extremely pleasing personality and made a good appearance. Mr. Fred Wright, Jr., the Chief Accountant, recommended the hiring of Mr. League.

Paul Donovan, however, preferred Russell Phillips, a man with even more outstanding aptitude who had scored at the very top in all of the tests. Mr. Phillips was extremely tall, seemed rather shy and unsure of himself, and, although dressed neatly at the time of his interviews, did not present as impressive an appearance as Henry League. Mr. Donovan and Mr. Wright had several discussions on the subject of which man to hire. Wright felt that, since the position would involve the supervision of six girls in the bookkeeping department, Mr. League should be chosen. He argued that League, despite his slightly lower test results, would make a better supervisor because of his more outgoing personality and more forceful manner.

Mr. Donovan was more concerned with the speed and accuracy of the accounting department and he felt that the position required an accountant of great ability. In his opinion, the supervisory aspects of the job were only secondary. He advised the hiring of the less dynamic and personable Mr. Phillips in consideration of his superior accounting aptitude, better test performance and equal experience.

Wright was persuaded, somewhat reluctantly, to offer the position to Mr. Phillips who accepted and assumed his duties on the first day of the next month.

There was an almost immediate improvement in the performance of the Accounting Department. After only two weeks of Phillips' tenure, fewer errors were being committed and allowed to reach the home office. Within only a few months the deadline dates for the weekly and monthly reports began to be met and within six months the "on time" performance of Mr. Donovan's area became the best in the Central Region.

Mr. Donovan also sensed an improvement in the morale of the bookkeeping office. The girls seemed to be less tense. Mr. Donovan attributed this to their no longer being under such pressure to meet deadlines. Overtime work in the department was reduced almost to the vanishing point and employees of that department were able to join other members of the office force in coffee breaks. The section members became, for the first time in years, really a part of the office society.

In his first semiannual review of Phillips, Mr. Wright gave him excellent ratings and recommended a salary increase. Mr. Donovan agreed with enthusiasm and the raise was approved by the New York office. Privately, Mr. Wright commented repeatedly to Mr. Donovan on the fact that Phillips was doing an excellent job and indicated complete satisfaction with the choice of Phillips over Mr. League. Wright confessed that he was somewhat puzzled by the fact that the performance of the department as a whole had improved so remarkably. He reported that Phillips appeared to be doing very little real "supervising" of the girls in terms of organizing their work, arranging coverage for the office telephones during coffee breaks, assigning definite responsibilities to the girls, etc. The work, however, was getting done and Wright told Mr. Donovan that he hesitated to interfere. He did report that Phillips had not followed through on several suggestions for system improvements that Wright himself had made and which he felt would serve to reduce some of the confusion he could see in the department.

Mr. Donovan agreed with Mr. Wright that Phillips did not appear to be "on top of the job" but felt that the greatly improved accuracy and outstanding "on time" record more than compensated for the minor deficiencies of Mr. Phillips as an organizer.

In thinking about this situation after one of his talks with Wright, Mr. Donovan came to the realization that there had been some marked changes in Russell Phillips. It seemed to him that most of the girls in the department had taken an almost personal interest in Phillips' appearance. His manner of dress had become much neater and his bearing and self-assurance had improved.

Mr. Donovan overheard a conversation one morning in the bookkeeping section where he had gone to check on a delinquent account. Two of the girls were chiding Phillips about his choice in neckties. "You shouldn't wear that tie with your brown suit, Russell. It makes you look like the janitor," one of the girls had said. "Yes," said the other, "you have the dignity of the Department to uphold." The three of them had laughed but Mr. Donovan noticed that Phillips had returned from his lunch wearing a different necktie. Donovan had laughed at the incident at the time, but could not help but feel that much of the improvement in Phillips' appearance had resulted from the personal attention of the girls in his office.

Some months later the Third Area Accounting Department won an annual award given by the home office to the Area scoring highest in a contest, which included an examination of all the records and accounts kept in each area office from the point of view of accuracy and current status, as well as "on time" performance on the weekly and monthly reports.

The Third Area had never before won this award. Mr. Donovan provided a dinner party at company expense for the entire Accounting Department and their escorts. Mr. Wright and his wife joined Mr. and Mrs. Donovan at the head of the table while Mr. Phillips and a young lady from the order department whom he had invited presided at the other end.

Mr. Donovan was struck by the easy air of camaraderie which prevailed at the dinner and the ease with which Phillips conducted himself. He remarked to Wright that Phillips had "come a long way in a little over a year and a half." The party was made even gayer when Russell Phillips and June Larson, the young lady from the order department, chose the occasion to announce their engagement.

Several months after his marriage, Mr. Phillips requested an interview with Mr. Donovan. Donovan was prepared to grant Phillips an increase in salary but was not prepared for Phillips' announcement that he was leaving the company.

In the interview Donovan learned that Mrs. Phillips who had originally come from the West Coast, had expressed to her husband a keen desire to return, and convinced him that they should move to California. Mr. Donovan expressed his disappointment but recognized that this was not a bargaining tactic. The Ball Company had recently absorbed a smaller drug wholesale firm in California. Mr. Donovan was able to arrange a transfer to California for Phillips, whom he regarded as a valuable employee worth keeping in the Company. The Accounting Department held a farewell party for Mr. and Mrs. Phillips and Mr. Donovan and his wife were honored guests.

The problem of replacing Phillips had been considered before his departure. Mr. Wright reported that Mr. League, his original choice for the position, had taken other employment as an accountant but at a lower salary than that offered by Ball. It was agreed that Wright would approach Mr. League and that the position would be offered to him rather than to go through the time consuming routine of interviewing a new lot of applicants. In his interview, League again impressed Mr. Wright very favorably but Mr. Donovan still held a few reservations. He was not able to point to any specific fault and ascribed his impression to his previous preference for Phillips. However, in view of League's excellent performance on the tests some two years before and his support by Wright Mr. Donovan did not make an issue of the hiring and the position was accepted by Mr. Henry League.

The excellent performance of the accounting department continued and Mr. Donovan and Mr. Wright agreed that they had been extremely fortunate in securing so able a replacement. Mr. Wright felt that, if anything, there had been an improvement in the operation of the bookkeeping function directly under Mr. League's control. He indicated his belief that discipline had improved and that there was less time wasted under Mr. League than there had been under the more informal supervision of Mr. Phillips. Wright also indicated that Mr. League was much more willing to adopt suggestions and had improved and simplified various aspects of the work flow.

Mr. Donovan received a friendly letter from Mr. Phillips a month or two after his arrival in California expressing enthusiasm for his new position and also thanking Mr. Donovan for having arranged the transfer. Donovan learned from the New York office that Phillips had made a very favorable impression upon his superiors in the California office.

About six months after Mr. League had taken over, errors and incomplete reports began to appear. The "on time" performance of the accounting department became less than perfect. Mr. Donovan was chided by the home office for this fall from grace, but agreed with Mr. Wright that Mr. League was in no way to blame. The poorer performance was blamed on an increase in the work load and an additional girl was hired for the bookkeeping section.

However, the record of the department failed to improve. Mr. Wright was still unwilling to hold Mr. League responsible for the poor performance, even when the record of the department fell to the level it had been before the hiring of Phillips. Mr. Wright indicated that he felt that Mr. League perhaps needed more time to get his feet on the ground in the job and that they owed him that time because Ball had hired him away from his former position.

Mr. Donovan agreed that they had a certain responsibility to Mr. League but became increasingly concerned about the poor performance and the criticisms directed at his area by the home office. Overtime in the department and particularly in the bookkeeping section became the rule, rather than the exception. The New York office, in no uncertain terms, ordered Mr. Donovan to reduce this item of cost.

Later in the same week in which the order relating to the reduction of overtime arrived, Mr. Donovan received a letter from Mr. Phillips. Mr. Phillips expressed his satisfaction with the California position and with the company. He did not like the location, however, and stated that the climate had proved detrimental to the health of his wife. He also said that an old sinus condition of his own had been aggravated and that he would like to move. His wife's parents had died and she no longer felt the attraction to the area which had taken them there in the first place. His letter concluded:

> I know that my old job in Prenticeburg has been filled and I do not expect the company to make another place for me. I would like to ask you, however, to keep your ears open around town for any opening you think I might be able to fill. Both you and Mr. Wright are familiar with my record and abilities and I would much appreciate your doing what you can for me in this connection.

Bibliography

"AT&T Makes Reparation." *Economist,* January 27, 1973, p. 42.

Berlew, D. E. "Leadership and Organizational Excitement." *California Management Review,* 17 (Winter 1974), 21–30.

"Clack Woman on Three Boards." *Business Week,* May 29, 1971, p. 22.

Fryberger, L. B. "Maternity Leave Policies under Title III." *Labor Law Journal,* 26 (March 1975), 163–173.

Hanan, M. "Making Way for a New Organization Man." *Harvard Business Review,* 49 (March 1972), 128–130.

Jacobson, C. J. "ERA: Ratifying Equality (27th Amendment)." *American Federationist,* January 1975, pp. 9–13.

————."Management and Operations Auditing." *CPA Journal,* November 1974, pp. 69–72.

"Protection against Religious and Ethnic Discrimination." *Monthly Labor Review,* 96 (April 1973), 81.

Schwartz, Eleanor Brantley, and James J. Rago, Jr. "Beyond Tokenism: Women as True Corporate Peers." *Business Horizons,* 16 (December 1973), 69–76.

"Symposium: Workers' Participation in Management — an International Comparison." *Industrial Relations,* 9 (February 1970), 117–214.

Thorp, C. D. "Racial Discrimination and Seniority." *Labor Law Journal,* 23 (July 1972), 398–413.

Wearing, A. J. and D. W. Bishop. "Fiedler Contingency Model and the Functioning of Military Squads." *Academy of Management Journal,* September 1974, pp. 450–459.

Weinwurm, G. F. "Creative Challenge of Individualism." *California Management Review,* 13 (Winter 1970), 89–96.

————."Women Are Equal — Official." *Personnel Management,* December 1974, p. 5.

Part Four
Labor-Management
Relationships

Of the many business-society relationships, the one that has been most publicized is that between business, as a dominant institution in society, and labor, as represented by organized labor unions. Among the vast array of issues that fall within this realm are the controversies over the collective bargaining process, nationwide bargaining issues, and the organizing activities of unions.

A. Management Rights and Collective Bargaining

The general success of labor-management relations depends for the most part on the collective bargaining process. Society recognizes the desirability and necessity of maximum freedom in collective bargaining agreements for both labor and management. In spite of this necessity, the feasibility and long-run success of the process has been seriously questioned. In "Crisis in Collective Bargaining" [13] Benjamin L. Masse notes that European critics are disillusioned with the American process and feel that it has not responded effectively to technological changes and increased foreign competition. They argue that collective bargaining contributes to continuing inflation because management appears to defer to unions in their demands for higher wages, which are then passed on to the consumer in the form of higher prices. In spite of these problems, both labor and management insist that collective bargaining remain as free as possible, and that government remain aloof, especially from any form of compulsory arbitration.

Another major criticism of collective bargaining is its emphasis upon the adversary rather than cooperative aspect of the process, since both parties are opposed to each other and seek to maximize their own goals exclusively at the bargaining table. The question, therefore, of whether or not the process can be made more "cooperative" is a major challenge. Ideas for summit meetings, federal coordinators, or regional groups working for some form of cooperation appear to exist only in the literature today, rather than in actual practice.

Management traditionally has exercised its rights in attempts to increase productivity, growth, and profits. But management cannot exercise these rights with total freedom. The other side of this issue has been stated by Neil Chamberlain in "What is Management's Right to Manage?" [14] If, as Chamberlain contends, management's rights relate only to the control of property delegated to it by the stockholders, it actually has no rights over personnel other than those negotiated in individual and union employment contracts. This point of view would identify the source of management's rights as the constitutionally protected right of private property plus the legislative provision for, and recognition of, collective and individual labor contract agreements.

Individual managerial rights are generally limited by managerial job definitions and company policies. In addition, there is a most significant change that has occurred in business during this century. This change started with the original concept that employees were subject to the general authority of management in all areas of work activity. Today the employee is subject to management's authority insofar as it affects the specific items contained in his or her job description. This can complicate business problems in the future when we envision the need for achieving employment stabilization through work changes resulting from automation. Such changes will necessitate retraining and transferring employees. With these impediments to the adaptation of business to a changing society and economy, the question of management's rights becomes a paramount issue of society as well as of business and labor.

Management versus employee rights, and their priority in business operations, are examined in two cases. The Ralph Bennett case dramatically presents the need for defining clearly, for both parties, the responsibilities of a job. The failure to communicate job rights and responsibilities fully creates a stand-off situation for a new manager in a foreign environment, leading to his consideration of resignation as the only way out. Similarly, in The Insubordinate Operator case, employee and job rights and responsibilities appear to conflict in a situation where an employee ignores or disobeys management orders while meeting crisis responsibilities successfully. These cases illustrate the day-to-day complexity of reconciling management with employee rights and the need for a fundamental understanding of the theory and philosophy of each.

B. Unemployment and Right-to-Work Laws

Unemployment and inflation are the two major problems faced by U.S. society today. While the two problems "in theory" used to operate in an inverse relationship with each other, in recent years both have been increasing upward and attempts to resolve them have been unsuccessful. Business contributes to inflation through price increases, and then faces conflicting responsibilities in meeting full employment goals. While this goal is an implicit one for business, it nevertheless is a real one, especially in terms of the attitudes and feelings of the American worker.

Maintaining full employment is a responsibility that even the federal government has been unable to meet in idealistic terms. In the past, a goal of 3 percent unemployment equaling "full employment" has been changed to 4, 5 and 6 percent and we now realize that rates of 7 or 8 percent or more may exist for the coming years. As a result, actions taken toward resolving full employment problems will be the responsibility of all groups, especially business and the federal government. The problem is so extensive that new approaches are being raised as indicated in the article "First Aid for Recession's Victims" [15] by Lawrence Mayer. With both inflation and unemployment rates extraordinarily high, the government is now taking direct measures to alleviate unemployment. The government has relied most upon increasing unemployment benefits, in terms of length of benefits and extension of them to cover workers heretofore not included. Congress has provided $3 billion in extra unemployment benefit funds to achieve these goals. Congress also passed a $125 million public works program aimed chiefly at the problems in the construction industry. Unfortunately, even with this type of help, unemployment will not be significantly reduced. Congress is considering other aid in the form of public works, but since these tend to take such a long period of time for effective implementation, they do not meet the immediate needs of the current recession-inflation-unemployment crisis. Instead Mr. Mayer recommends that a more promising solution might lie in the area of public employment.

Public employment would provide temporary jobs for unemployed people, particularly useful work needed by local communities. Mayer contends that the double payoff of reducing unemployment and meeting specific community needs makes it significantly attractive. This type of program would fulfill a variety of criteria, such as usefulness of the work, temporary nature of the work, and wage levels below the current market wage. Congress passed a public employment bill providing $875 million for the year 1975 for this purpose. The average pay is expected to be $9,000. Congress expects to increase the program to $1.6 billion in order to create 180,000 more jobs. Even if these efforts are successful, and a total of 270,000 jobs are created, this would amount to less than 5% of the present unemployed. Nevertheless, it would provide double benefits in terms of helping both the unemployed and the community. Since these projects are labor intensive, they also create more jobs than other types of employment opportunities.

Since this public employment type of aid would not reach anywhere near the magnitude of the present unemployed, Mayer also raises questions of whether or not governmental help might be injected into the private sector. The ability of the government to subsidize jobs in private industry in an equitable fashion for all competing firms is a serious problem, as well as the ability of medium- and small-size firms to handle governmental aid with its complexity of red tape and government regulations. Mayer specifically recommends two examples: first, the rehabilitation of slum housing, and second, the improvement of railway roadbeds. In both instances these needs will not apparently be met unless some outside aid is forthcoming. Also, since the benefits from these projects would have widespread effects for society, they appear to justify consideration. In conclusion, Mr. Mayer tells us that in the past thirty-five years neither the president nor the Congress has faced up to the problems of a potential depression. And so we have not developed ways of thinking that would provide alternatives to such an impending catastrophe. He suggests that public employment would be especially useful in providing a choice between the present extremes of too much unemployment or too much inflation.

Unemployment, inflation, and recession are all affected by the collective bargaining process, with management and labor pursuing their respective goals. Although collective bargaining became the law of the land in 1935, recognition of unions, and of employees seeking to form unions, is still being contested in many states. In spite of the law protecting the right of the individual employee to bargain collectively with his or her potential or actual employer, there have been numerous managers, companies, and business and industry associations that have systematically fought the unionization of employees. These battles contributed to the inclusion of Section 14(b) in the Taft-Hartley Act of 1947 which delegated to the states the right to pass so-called right-to-work laws. These laws gave to the individual employee the right to join or not to join, and also the right to leave a union. Ever since this law was passed, the labor unions have sought its repeal.

In seeking repeal of Section 14(b) of the Taft-Hartley Act, the labor unions have attempted to return control of labor policy to the federal government. This controversy is presented in "The Battle Over 14(b)" [16]. Since approximately half of the states have passed right-to-work laws, unions are concerned about the problems caused by these laws. In particular, unions claim that most attitude polls have revealed that workers definitely prefer union shops, which prevent an individual from leaving the union. Unions also maintain that, as in our democratic form of government, the minority must go along with the majority decisions of union workers. They contend that the ability to leave the union arbitrarily serves to encourage free riders who do not want to pay for, or participate in, the strikes that have led to increased wages and benefits, or to participate in union programs protecting their rights. Union leaders argue that many states have used the right-to-work laws as a means of attracting industries out of heavily unionized states into states where union influence might be minimized or precluded.

Pro-retention arguments for the right-to-work laws appeal first to the constitutional guarantee for the freedom of association, emphasizing the right of each worker to freedom of choice in joining or not joining a union versus compulsory membership and union dues. They contend that union leaders, rather than workers, would benefit most. Other arguments maintain that those interested in union membership are free to exercise their rights, while others are also free to avoid corrupt unions. Arguments about wage benefits with and without the law, and movement of industry to the south because of the law, seem debatable, or resolved mostly with half truths.

When we review the extensive arguments for and against the repeal of Section 14(b), we find ourselves reduced to the fundamental issue of collective bargaining. That is, collective bargaining was created to offset the serious and overwhelming imbalance of power between the individual employee as he or she bargained with employers. Given the massive resources in the hands of the manager, the individual employee, unless holding unique technical and professional skills, has little bargaining power. The argument that corrupt and dictatorial tactics on the part of labor union leaders jeopardize business could be offset by recourse to the Landrum-Griffin legislation, which provides for the prosecution of labor leaders misusing the power of their office. For these and other reasons, we must carefully consider the means available for maintaining some equality of bargaining power between labor and management.

In conclusion, there are two important questions to consider. If the corrupt practices of labor leaders can be checked by the Landrum-Griffin bill, what methods — other than collective bargaining via organized trade unions — are available to strike a balance of power between individual employees and managers? And if the individual employee is free to leave the union and deny it his or her active and financial support, will the labor union survive as an effective instrument in providing some equality of bargaining power with management now and in the future?

A Management Rights and Collective Bargaining

13 Crisis in Collective Bargaining
Benjamin L. Masse

After the war European industrialists and trade-union leaders streamed across the Atlantic to learn the secret of our industrial relations. They are not coming to these shores any more. Whatever the reason may be, people from advanced industrial countries, as Solomon Barkin, research director of the Textile Workers, noted in the November *Fortune,* have ceased to regard collective bargaining, American style, as the answer to modern labor-management relationships.

What has gone wrong with our 25-year-old national policy that survived the shock of war and looked so promising in the late 1940's? Why has a feeling of frustration spread widely through the AFL-CIO? Why do the meetings of management men rumble with dissatisfaction over the course of industrial relations? Why did such a knowledgeable man as Victor Borella, who keeps industrial relations at Manhattan's Rockefeller Center humming smoothly, write recently that "we find our nation's labor-management set-up is not only an unhappy but an unfortunate stance to meet the truly great challenges of our time"?

As a curious, and concerned, reporter digs around for answers to those questions, several themes keep recurring. They are, though not necessarily in order of importance, the Cold War, inflation, foreign competition and automation. In one or the other of these, or in some combination of them, must be sought the causes of the growing doubts about collective bargaining.

Reprinted with permission from *America,* 106 West 56th Street, New York, New York, January 14, 1961, pp. 469–471.

In a typically thoughtful address at Roosevelt University last August 17, Senator [John] Kennedy's popular choice for Secretary of Labor, Arthur J. Goldberg, bore down heavily on the disruptive effects of the Cold War and automation:

> We live in an age of revolutionary technological change and in an age of extraordinary internal tension.
>
> Traditional practices, which have served us so well, and which would continue to do so if we were really at peace, must be adapted to a period where our whole way of life is being challenged. Traditional practices, which served us so well, must be adapted to an age when our industrial society is being transformed by technological advance.

In the *Fortune* article referred to above, Mr. Barkin, though approaching the problem somewhat differently, arrives at conclusions strikingly similar to Mr. Goldberg's. "The machinery of industrial relations is at dead center," he writes, "bogged down in costly and irritating parochial bickering." Neither labor nor management, he says, is dealing in a creative, dynamic way with the growing threat of foreign competition. Unions tend to meet the danger by fighting stubbornly for the security of a declining labor force. Equally traditional in their approach, employers strive to cope with the threat by slashing payrolls. The clash between these short-term, self-interest approaches, Mr. Bakin believes, "is at the heart of the current high tension in industrial relations."

Mr. Barkin argues, furthermore, that traditional methods of collective bargaining are proving no more adequate to cope with inflation and the forces of industrial change than they are with foreign competition. Probably every responsible union leader in the country would echo his lament on inflation:

> Union leaders have been perplexed as to how to proceed responsibly in wage negotiations in order to minimize the possibility of price increases. They have had no guarantee that, if they adopted wage restraint, management would make a parallel commitment for price restraint.

The Textile leader, one of the most stimulating intellectuals in the labor movement, sadly concludes that collective bargaining as we have known it cannot deal with the great issue — in which the public is so keenly interested — because management "has refused to discuss price and production policy with union representatives."

The crisis in collective bargaining was given an exhaustive airing last summer at a conference sponsored by the Fund for the Republic's Trade Union Project. This informal seminar assumes special importance because among the thirty participants who assembled during the week of July 17 at Santa Barbara, Cal., were men prominent in industry, labor, government and education. The following paragraph from the summary of the discussions — which Paul Jacobs, director of the project, kindly made available to the writer — emphasizes the importance the seminar attached to technological change:

> Thus, it is fair to say that the entire conference agreed that a rethinking of traditional collective bargaining practices was required. The world market, the Cold War, union structure, these and other factors were mentioned as affecting, and being affected by, this crisis. But the central factor which occupied the conference discussion was that of technological change. The rate and range of this process in recent years was seen as creating problems which were so serious and extensive as to require the United States to go beyond its old, familiar way of doing things.

Industry views of the strains in industrial relations tend to place the emphasis elsewhere. Fairly typical were the advertisements which the steel companies published during the long strike in 1959. Over and over again, these statements, stressing the dangers of inflation and foreign competition, proclaimed the need for wage restraint on the union's part and a willingness to accept changes in working rules dictated by considerations of efficiency. The wage and work-rule issues also preoccupied the rail transportation industry in its protracted struggle last year with the railroad brotherhoods. (There was a complete breakdown of collective bargaining on the rules issue and this problem, at the instigation of the White House, has now been handed over for study to a special Presidential panel.)

To many management men, the Cold War, automation, foreign competition and the rest are not so much causes of the crisis in industrial relations as occasions which have revealed ingrown weaknesses in our system.

On the one hand, they explain, unions have come to believe that workers are entitled to an annual increase in wages and fringe benefits. On the other, they have curbed management's freedom to effect the changes in production methods that would make higher wages economically possible. So long as demand was strong and foreign competition negligible, management found it expedient to acquiesce in most union demands. Now that foreign firms have become aggressive and the American public will no longer stand for inflationary price increases, management has been obliged to reassert its rights to direct the business as it thinks best. This means that it must be solicitous, not only for employees, but for the company's stockholders, suppliers and customers as well.

Very much to the point, according to management men, was the sermon which the National City Bank of New York preached to its audience in its *Monthly Letter* for December. In the context of an economy faced with intensified competitive pressures and a balance-of-payments problem, the bank exhorted:

In exercising their power in collective bargaining, union leaders as well as managements must face up to the fact that prices can no longer be raised each time that big wage raises are negotiated. They must recognize that they defeat their own cause when they demand pay increases that outrun gains in efficiency and wipe out profitable return on new investment.

Prescriptions for handling the crisis in collective bargaining reflect the different evaluation put on it by management and labor. If the machinery is breaking down because inflation, foreign competition, technological change and the pressures of the Cold War have overburdened it, then one kind of medicine is indicated. Another kind entirely might be called for if the pressures of the times have not caused the breakdown but only revealed old defects in the machinery.

Management believes that whatever is wrong with collective bargaining would soon be righted if (1) unions stopped challenging and impeding its function of managing, and (2) union "monopolies" were prohibited by law. What the government should do is attack labor's monopoly power by outlawing all types of union security, as right-to-work legislation does, and by subjecting unions to the nation's antitrust laws. Presumably if this were done, most unions would no longer be in a position to challenge management control.

These are the key reforms in management's programs. In addition to them the National Association of Manufacturers feels that the atmosphere surrounding collective bargaining would be much improved if secret ballots were required for strikes and if union political activities were even more restricted than they are by the Taft-Hartley Act.

As for labor, which regards the industry solution as no solution at all, it has officially endorsed the proposition, first advanced by Arthur J. Goldberg, that the problems besetting industrial relations are too far-reaching for resolution at the bargaining table. By its very nature, Mr. Goldberg contends, the bargaining table emphasizes the adversary rather than the cooperative aspect of industrial relations. It is, consequently, a poor mechanism for discussing questions that go beyond individual companies and unions. Such questions should first be discussed, he says, by a small group of top men in labor and industry in circumstances free of the pressures of bargaining. Accordingly, he suggested a union-employer "summit meeting" under the aegis, but not the domination, of the White House.

After some hesitation President Eisenhower, at the insistence of AFL-CIO President George Meany, accepted the idea. Early last year he asked the NAM and the AFL-CIO to sit down together and chart an ascent to the summit. Although some meetings have been held, there has been as yet no report of any progress.

This silence may be significant. Generally speaking, management has no desire to go to the summit. That was obvious enough even before Ford and General Motors rejected an invitation from Walter Reuther, head of the United Auto Workers, to discuss matters of common interest on an industry level. Since Mr. Reuther sent his invitation under the patronage, so to speak, of President Eisenhower — in a speech in Detroit on October 17 the President had urged such a meeting — the intensity of management opposition to the summit idea can easily be imagined.

On the other hand, the AFL-CIO has little confidence in joint meetings with the NAM. When the idea of a summit meeting was first broached, President Meany warned that it would accomplish nothing unless industry was represented by the heads of companies actually engaged in bargaining with AFL-CIO unions.

The Fund for the Republic conferees split over remedies for the collective-bargaining crisis. One group was so impressed by the complexity of today's problems that it despaired of any exclusively labor-management approach to them. In dealing with issues like inflation, foreign economic policy and the rate of technological change, collective bargaining, they insisted, is only one of many factors involved — and a subordinate one at that. This group called, therefore, for a national, coordinated approach in which the Federal Government would have a substantial role. They recommended the creation in the Executive Branch of a council composed of government officials and leaders of management and labor that would thresh out problems too big for the bargaining table and seek to reach agreements on broad policies.

Another group felt that traditional methods of collective bargaining were not so inadequate that they could not be adapted to the changing times. They conceded that some place had to be made today for public representation in labor-management affairs, but they believed that this could be provided for without involving the government. It was suggested, for instance, that the role of arbitrators might be enlarged, so they could act more creatively and energetically than is now the case, or that labor-management meetings on a regional or industry level be held in which the public would be represented.

All the conferees agreed that in any event both labor and management had to abandon some of their cherished positions, and that a new spirit of cooperation for the common good was urgently required.

In an account of this kind, dealing with such a vast field, there must be room for a minority report or two.

Some management and labor men wonder what all the wringing of hands is about. They don't perceive any crisis in industrial relations.

The management men who feel this way are likely to be found in big business circles, where the most recent negotiations in autos, steel and electrical manufacturing have been a source of considerable satisfaction. On the other side, the old AFL unions, though still bitter over some provisions of the Taft-Hartley and Landrum-Griffin Acts, seem not to be conscious of any crisis in their affairs. Inventions and new processes have caused some jurisdictional troubles, but then these are an old story in the building trades unions. As for the Teamsters, the only crisis they know about is the one involving Jimmy Hoffa. Over the past few years, this scandal-scarred union has greatly prospered.

On the question of a summit meeting, a few industry people have publicly supported the proposal. Presumably they are as aware as their colleagues that a meeting of this kind would lend prestige to the labor movement and help to offset the damaging effects of the McClellan committee hearings. They probably suspect that Arthur Goldberg's original proposal was partly motivated by a desire "to get labor off the hook." Even so, they say, the proposal itself is sound and statesmanlike. Mr. Goldberg didn't start the Cold War. He didn't create the inflationary pressures of what is, in fact, a semi-war economy. He is certainly not responsible for the swift pace of technological change and the unemployment it is causing. No one suggests that he fostered foreign competition or invented the balance-of-payments squeeze. These are all real life problems; and when Mr. Goldberg, pondering them and noting the growing polarization of hostile management-labor attitudes, calls upon both sides to attack them in a cooperative, public-minded spirit, what is wrong with the proposal?

But, as I say, this is a minority sentiment in industrial circles. That is why some observers doubt that a summit meeting will be held, or if it is held — under White House pressure — that any good will come of it. They fear that all it may do is dramatize the gulf which has come to exist between management and labor thinking on the great issues of the day.

As this survey was being completed, news arrived that President George Romney and Vice President Edward Cushman of American Motors have suggested a variant of the summit approach. They want a clergy committee representing Protestants, Catholics and Jews to invite top industry and labor leaders to meet with them in some secluded spot and there together, without a formal program, talk out their problems. The formula is not new, and it certainly promises no miracles. If, however, labor-management relations continue to deteriorate, it may offer an acceptable alternative to some head-cracking by a tough and impatient government.

14 What is Management's Right to Manage?

Neil Chamberlain

The recent unpleasantness between the Ford Motor Co. and the United Automobile Workers about the speed of assembly lines provided the latest of a series of dramatic conflicts over the issue of managerial prerogatives in the automobile industry. Control over assembly-line speeds was also in dispute in the prolonged Chrysler strike of 1939, when Herman L. Weckler, Vice President in charge of operations, stated: "Management cannot abdicate its responsibility for any aspect of this business, whether it relates to labor, to engineering, to production or to selling. It cannot consent to sovietize the plants." And the General Motors shutdown in the winter of 1945–46 brought the pronouncement from H. W. Anderson, Vice President in charge of personnel, that the "functions of management cannot be delegated to anyone not responsible for the continuing of the business. They will not be surrendered to the union."

While the issue has thus been dramatized in the automobile industry, there are few companies in the U.S. in which it has not been raised at some time during the course of collective-bargaining negotiations. Indeed, the nature of the managerial prerogative in relation to the union was one of the points on which the President's postwar labor-management conference broke down, with union and management committee members rendering separate and diametrically opposed reports. Ira Mosher, then president of the National Association of Manufacturers, subsequently asserted. "Labor wouldn't even agree to an effort to define the functions of management, although we made a real effort to get that issue settled. We drew up a list of some thirty-odd specific acts, such as the determination of prices, accounting procedure, and so forth, which it seemed clear to us must be reserved to management. Labor refused to accept a single one, and we were told . . . the reason . . . was that at some future time labor may want to bring any one of these functions into the realm of collective bargaining." Mosher's statement points attention to one reason why the conflict remains unresolved. If

Reprinted from the July 1949 issue of *Fortune Magazine*, pp. 68–70, by special permission; © 1949 Time Inc.

the "right to manage" can be defined *only* by a listing of "specific acts, such as the determination of prices," no general principle is available to serve as the standard for inclusion or exclusion of such specific acts. Does any principle of management rights exist to provide the needed standards?

There seems ample reason for believing that in the minds of many managers the right of management is virtually synonymous with their right to make business decisions. Weckler's concern for "responsibility" and Anderson's for "the continuing of the business" are in line with this view. If this is to be regarded as a principle, however, what can be said of management's willingness to bargain on wages, hours, layoffs, promotions, and the host of other matters that go into the modern collective-bargaining agreement? Consider wages, for example. Is not the size of the wage bill a business decision of first importance? Prior to the advent of the union in an industrial enterprise, is not one of management's chief problems — in charting the continuing success of the business — that of bringing its cost and price structures into line, with wages an important element of costs? Does the introduction of collective bargaining make this any less a business decision? Why is managerial prerogative not raised as a barrier to negotiation on the subject of wages? Is the size of the wage bill of different order of significance from the speed of assembly lines? What principle bars negotiation of rates of operation and permits bargaining on wages, if both are managerial decisions?

The answer appears to be that no principle is involved, but rather that the process of inclusion and exclusion suggested by Mosher is at work. Wages have become accepted as "legitimate" matters of collective bargaining, while production speeds have not. In 1851 the New York *Journal of Commerce* editorialized that it would not yield "the control of our business to the dictation of a self-constituted power outside of the office" in the matters of hours and apprenticeship. Today both of these subjects are commonly to be found in collective agreements. In 1945 Inland Steel and other companies fought the union's demand for a voice in a company pension plan. Today welfare programs, including pensions, have become rather widely accepted as a bargaining matter. Today Henry Ford II asserts, in his recent conflict with the U.A.W.: "I want to make it quite clear that this company now *and always* will hold to its right — fairly and firmly guaranteed under our contract — to establish work standards which will assure efficient operation without impairing in any way the health or safety of our employees." Are Ford's strong words to be taken as evidence only of *present* exclusion, or is he gifted with prophetic vision that this subject, unlike others before it, will *never* find acceptance as a "legitimate" matter for collective agreement?

At the root of the problem of management's right to manage is simply the increasing insubstantiality of management's ability to maintain it. It has been said that the right emerges from the laws of private property, in which management as the actual or representative owner has the privilege of determining the use to be made of its property. It was Justice McReynolds, dissenting in the Jones & Laughlin case, who objected to the National Labor Relations Act on the ground that "a private owner is deprived of power to manage his own property by freely selecting those to whom his manufacturing operations are to be entrusted." But it is sometimes overlooked that the property basis of management involves no duty on the part of others to *be* managed.

That is to say, the trouble with property ownership as a conferer of authority is that it gives command only over *things*. This involves no special difficulties in a society of small property holders and individual proprietorships, for control over things is all that is needed to produce for, and sell in, the market. But when business enterprise assumes a corporate form and requires the cooperation of large numbers of people performing specialized functions, control over things ceases to be sufficient.

Except for authoritarian relationships (for example, in the military services at home, and in totalitarian societies generally abroad), people can be managed and directed only with their own consent. While property rights carry with them a power of disposition of goods, they do not carry an equal power to use those goods *if* the cooperation of others is necessary to that use. Cooperation, without which the property right is reduced to a power of disposition, cannot be commanded. It can only be won by consent. The property rights of the stockholders, exercised for them by management, can be made meaningful only with the cooperation of all those who are actually needed to operate the business, including the workers.

But there is no legal compulsion upon the workers to cooperate. There is no legal statement of the terms on which cooperation must take place. The definition of those terms is left directly to the parties involved, and there is nothing in the law to stop the union from demanding as the price of the cooperation of its members a voice in some matter previously independently determined by management. Since property rights do not give command over others, management *may* find it essential to share its authority as a means of inducing cooperation, in order to maintain the value of a going business. Over a period of time it becomes customary to share authority, in order to win cooperation, in certain recognized areas of business decisions — wages, for example, or hours; perhaps someday the speed of assembly lines.

Thus the management and direction of others do not flow out of legal rights but must be granted by those very people who are managed and directed. And the price of the grant may be, in the words of the editorial writer for the New York *Journal of Commerce* in 1851, that management — and the owners — yields their independence in certain matters of business operation. *What* matters? Potentially none would seem to be excluded — whatever matters are deemed important to those whose cooperation is being sought.

What then is the managerial prerogative? The answer may come more easily if management is viewed as a function rather than as a group of people — the function of making and effectuating business decisions. This function is to be found at all levels of organization in an enterprise. It may be remembered, for example, that in recent years a drive has been under way to instill in foremen the feeling of being part of management. Any definition of the managerial prerogative would presumably, then, have to include within its scope the foremen as well as the president.

A good working definition of the management prerogative is, perhaps, that it is the power to make decisions and see to their effectuation within whatever framework of discretion may exist. If the framework changes, so does the prerogative. The limits of the foremen's prerogatives are thus set for him by the decisions of higher management, within which his authority must be exercised. The extent of top management's prerogatives is defined by national and state legislation and by the decisions of the board of directors if the board functions de facto as well as de jure. But the power to make a decision is not the same as the power to carry it out. The power to decide the speed of assembly lines is not the same as the power to secure the operation of assembly lines at that speed. To translate decision into accomplishment requires the assent of those whose cooperation is essential.

In winning that assent it may be necessary to reach some agreement with the union that represents the employees. The decision becomes a collective decision, and establishes the framework within which the management prerogative at lower levels of organization must be exercised. It may thus be the case that the *management* prerogative (of determining the speeds of operation, for example) can be exercised *only* through union participation, if management is regarded as a function. Or to put the case another way, the management prerogative — in the sense of power to carry out decisions made — *may* in some instances be preserved only if the union joins in making the decision.

Looked at in this fashion, it becomes evident that *collective bargaining is in fact one method of management.* It is a process for making business decisions that can be carried out. It is no guarantee of good decisions or of proper effectuation — any more than any method of management can provide such a guarantee. But it may be, in specific instances, a more appropriate method of management than some other.

This view does not, of course, lead to the conclusion that

management should necessarily accede to the union's demand for a voice in particular aspects of the managerial function. The Ford Motor Co. may have been well advised in making the stand that it did. Possibly it may not have been well advised. The exclusion of certain subjects from the process of collective agreement or the inclusion of other subjects within its terms must be justified on the basis of all the relevant facts. The only question involving any principle of the management prerogative, however, is whether the union's participation in the decision-making process is essential or conducive to the effectuation of the decision. Strike or threat of strike, if the union is not included in the making of a business decision, is not the only test. There is no necessary assurance that union participation in the matter of rates of operation will in fact secure compliance with the decision even though it is a collective one. If the union is torn with factionalism or controlled by a minority so that employee-union cohesion is weak and there is danger that joint no less than unilateral decisions will be disregarded or subverted, strong ground may be found for declining to share the management prerogative with the union.

There is thus perhaps some salutary effect in management's resistance to the union's expanding role in the making of business decisions. It may bring weight upon the unions to perfect their organizations so as to *improve* their business performance; and it may thus provide conviction to those now skeptical that sharing managerial authority with a union carries the advantage of inducing compliance with decisions once reached. No benefit would seem to inhere, however, in a doctrinaire conviction that certain areas of control must be preserved inviolate of union influence. On any particular subject, good management may someday if not now suggest an opposite conclusion.

This conception of the relationship between collective bargaining and the management prerogative suggests a further conclusion. For years schools of business administration have been preoccupied with teaching students improved methods of business management. Professional managers have likewise encouraged continued investigation of efficient business procedures. If it becomes evident that collective bargaining is in fact a method of management, there would seem to be some point in approaching it similarly, with the intent of improving it as a decision-making process in industry. The fact that conflict of interests is present in the process makes the problem difficult, but it is no secret that conflicts arise now within the so-called "family of management" and procedures must be found for resolving them. Techniques of management will not, of course, provide solutions in themselves, but they assist in arriving at decisions when needed. If collective bargaining *is* management — one form of it — business interests might well be persuaded that its improved practice will help rather than hinder business

performance, and unions might be led to believe that increased participation will be facilitated by paying attention to the procedures they
employ. The study of collective bargaining *as one method for making
business decisions* might lead to conclusions for its greater effectiveness,
which would benefit all concerned. In such an analysis unions would
have to be viewed not as something falling outside of the structure and
process of management but actually included within its terms.

B Unemployment and Right-to-Work Laws

15 First Aid for Recession's Victims

Lawrence A. Mayer

That grim recession-time quandary — how to alleviate unemployment without stoking inflation — has confronted the country before, but never so painfully as in the current travail. Unemployment has climbed to heights that modern societies consider intolerable, while inflation is still moving along at a gallop. Blue-ribbon corporations — General Electric, General Foods, Kodak, Monsanto, Xerox, to name a few — have been laying off. So have state and local governments — a dramatic break in a long expansionary trend. The unemployment rate for white-collar workers is the highest since the government began reporting white-collar unemployment on a monthly basis, back in 1958.

Even in times when the economy is booming, a few million Americans are counted as being unemployed, but only a minority of them are people who have actually been laid off. In December, 1968, for example, 62 percent of the unemployed had quit their jobs, or had reentered the labor force after being out of it for a while, or were looking for their first jobs. Now, however, the pattern is the reverse: well over half of the unemployed (54 percent as of December) are people who have been laid off.

Despite the high rate of unemployment, to be sure, a majority of the jobless are not the principal breadwinners of families. Roughly a quarter are teenagers. About a third are adult women. Still, the unemployment rate among married men was 3.7 percent in December, the highest it had been in a dozen years. (Six years ago that rate

Reprinted from the February 1975 issue of *Fortune Magazine*, pp. 74–77, 158, and 160, by special permission; © 1975 Time Inc.

reached a low of 1.4 percent.) The actual number of male household heads out of work was 1.9 million, 31 percent of all the unemployed. When female heads of families are added in, the proportion comes to 39 percent.

A $3-Billion Cushion

With unemployment and inflation at high rates simultaneously, it makes sense to try to alleviate unemployment by direct measures, so as to reduce pressures for general deflation. And the Administration and Congress have been doing that. So far, the government is relying on unemployment insurance as the primary means of helping the unemployed. Congress has appropriated funds both to increase the length of time people can collect insurance and to cover workers who were not eligible before. In most states, recipients of unemployment insurance get approximately one-half their weekly wage, up to a stipulated maximum. The average weekly payment comes to $65 (tax-free). The maximums vary widely from one state to another — from $67 a week in Michigan (where laid-off auto workers draw supplementary benefits from the companies) to $104 a week in Connecticut.

All together, Congress has provided $3 billion in extra unemployment-benefit funds. After deducting the increased overhead expenses of putting more people on the insurance rolls, $750 million is available to keep those who are presently eligible on the rolls for an extra thirteen weeks, in addition to the standard thirty-nine weeks. Another $2 billion will go to pay twenty-six weeks of benefits to unemployed people not previously covered by unemployment insurance — agricultural workers, household help, employees of state and local governments. In all, the measure extends coverage to 12 million additional people. (Still left out are youngsters looking for their first jobs, reentrants into the labor force, and those who had not held a job for a specified minimum of time.)

Congress has also passed a $125-million public-works program, chiefly to put some unemployed construction workers on payrolls. These funds are available to states that are suffering from the closing of bases and other military cutbacks. This program will almost certainly be enlarged by the new Congress, perhaps to the tune of an additional $375 million or so (though the federal agency that may handle it, the Economic Development Administration of the Department of Commerce, already has $250 million in unspent funds available).

It is doubtful, though, that even if they were considerably larger, new appropriations for public works would affect the current unemployment. With public works, it typically takes a considerable span of time to move from the start of planning through numerous stamps of approval to actual construction. Start the process during a recession, and you're likely to get the lift in employment after the recovery is well underway. Public works, in other words, should be undertaken on their merits as public works, not as a means of combating unemployment during recessions.

A Double Payoff

A more promising means of alleviating unemployment is public employment — programs designed to put people to work on local-government projects. The idea is to create temporary jobs to tide unemployed people over until they can find permanent jobs in the labor market. There is something very attractive about the concept. On the one hand, there are people who are looking for work. On the other hand, there is useful work that for one reason or another would not otherwise be done — perhaps because the labor costs are too high or other public needs are more insistent. If the jobs and the jobless can be satisfactorily matched up, the community receives a double payoff.

Certain principles should be followed, it seems fairly obvious. The jobs should be useful — sheer make-work is not clearly better than undisguised dole. Work whose effects last a while is to be preferred to work whose effects are transient — e.g., street repairs, if needed, should take preference over street cleaning. The jobs should be temporary, so people will return to private-sector jobs as soon as opportunities reopen there. For the same reason, temporary public jobs should pay wages below what the same skills normally command in the market — the jobs are meant to provide short-term sustenance, not careers. It is obviously a good thing, though, for workers with minimum skills to get work training that enhances their job prospects for the future.

In its closing days, the last Congress passed a public-employment bill, which the President later signed. It reasonably fills the criteria on temporariness, though it might be considered somewhat generous on pay. Congress appropriated an initial $875 million, to provide for perhaps 90,000 jobs before the first half of 1975 is ended. The average pay is expected to be $9,000 (including fringes), with a ceiling of $10,000. This ceiling is almost equal to the average pay prevailing in the U.S. today. (State and local authorities will be permitted to pay more, but at their own expense.) The new Congress, it appears, will fill out the program by appropriating another $1.6 billion or so to create perhaps 180,000 more jobs later this year.

To get a job under the new program a person must be unemployed for at least thirty days, except in areas of exceptionally severe unemployment. Preference is to be given to people who have exhausted their unemployment insurance. The program will be run by the Secretary of Labor through his existing authority under CETA — the Comprehensive Employment and Training Act, proposed by President Nixon and enacted late in 1973. CETA was the first piece of "special" revenue-sharing legislation, as opposed to "general" revenue sharing. The purpose was to put into a single jurisdiction the hodgepodge of manpower programs already in existence, as well as to establish local offices that could distribute the money according to local needs.

CETA's funds are already quite considerable. Before it got the new program, it had $3 billion at its disposal — $1 billion to provide 170,000 public-service jobs for "disadvantaged" workers and $2 billion for job training. Since localities have been slow in gearing up for those 170,000 jobs, Congress has stipulated that if a municipality doesn't use the special new allocations reasonably soon, the funds can be shifted elsewhere in the same state. Congress has also waived some previous impediments to rapid spending for new jobs and given the localities a freer hand in using money. Accordingly, some members of Congress think the new program will get under way a lot faster than the regular CETA program. Getting under way quickly is extremely important. Past anti-recession programs sometimes got going too late, and so added fuel to a subsequent boom instead of helping the recovery.

Assuming that the new Congress does appropriate the additional $1.6 billion (it may appropriate more), the public-employment program will create a total of about 270,000 jobs. That would amount to less than 5 percent of the present number of unemployed. The program proposed by President Ford last fall would have created somewhat more jobs, but at lower pay — about $7,000 per job. The job counts for all these programs are actually "job slots." Since some people will return to regular jobs during the life of the programs, more than one person may fill a slot in a given year.

The critical difference between what Ford proposed and what Congress provided has to do with termination. The Ford program was mainly built on projects that would last only six months, while the congressional measure is built on individual jobs that can last a year or more. The Ford program was designed to wane automatically as unemployment declined; Congress will vote its program more funds or less funds in late 1975 as its judgment dictates. If the program is continued while the unemployment rate drops below, say, 5.5 percent, that may bring a debate about what level of unemployment is tolerable, and perhaps about what the term "full employment" means.

A Case for the Broom Pusher

What will the new public employees do? President Ford proposed "projects to improve, beautify, and enhance the cities, our towns, and our countryside." An Administration document later explained that he had in mind such undertakings as conservation, maintenance or restoration of natural resources, and efforts to combat pollution and improve environmental quality. Unemployed people might, for example, be put to work cleaning up and fixing up parks, playgrounds, and other public facilities. Municipalities heavily burdened with welfare and payroll costs tend to skimp on such amenity work, but looked at from a broad social viewpoint, it can be done inexpensively if the people doing it would otherwise be unemployed.

Short-term public-service projects would mainly be labor-intensive, and it is generally assumed that this is a good thing, since labor-intensive work provides the most jobs for the funds available. Such projects, to be sure, may not be economical in a strict sense of that word. Argues economist Lester C. Thurow, of M.I.T.: "I would be willing to bet that if we were to compare the costs of a $4,000-a-year broom pusher with a $15,000-a-year sanitation man operating a $30,000 street sweeper, we would find the second combination the cheaper." Thurow may well be right about that for permanent jobs, but the point may not apply to temporary public employment during a recession. Recessions are inherently "wasteful" anyway, and in such times concentration on creation of jobs per se may on balance tend to minimize social waste.

A more forceful objection might come from some labor unions, especially unions of government workers, on the grounds that concentration on low-wage work could undercut prevailing wage rates. But it would be awkward for unions to oppose new jobs in a time of high unemployment, and they will have hardly any case at all if the jobs are truly temporary. The national leadership of the A.F.L.-C.I.O., in fact, has been advocating large public-employment programs.

Some other negative thoughts about public employment as a temporary remedy for unemployment should be mentioned. Some municipalities may be tempted to create jobs just because federal money is available, without seriously trying to give the new employees useful work to do. Other municipalities may find it embarrassing to hire new people, even with federal funds, when the local budget situation requires layoffs of regular civil-service employees. Or they may be reluctant to take on the moderate capital costs associated with public-employment projects. Even labor-intensive work will require some equipment — tools, trucks, cleaning supplies, etc. — and local governments in tight budget binds may look upon any additional costs as a burden.

An important factor that may undermine a public-employment program of any duration is the likelihood of "displacement." That's the term manpower experts use to describe the process by which the funding of extra local jobs by the national government ends up as funding for regular jobs in regular state and local budgets. Washington has developed a great sensitivity to the displacement problem. For example, both President Ford and Congress placed limits on how quickly a local administration might use federal job-creating funds to refill positions that it had recently vacated. The President's proposal set a minimum wait of thirty days; Congress said fifteen days.

An End to Wine and Roses

State and local governments currently have a strengthened incentive to try to get away with displacement: the recession is severely squeezing their budgets after a long period of payroll expansion. Practically all the increase in government employment in the U.S. since 1966 has occurred at the state and local levels — a total of 3.5 million people. This expansion burdened state and local budgets and led many governments to introduce or increase income and sales taxes. Enhanced revenues produced by the long and strong business expansion of the 1960's, plus the injection of extra federal funds through general revenue sharing, also provided money to meet the swelling expenses.

Now, as the governor of New York recently told his legislature, "the times of plenty, the days of wine and roses, are over." Aside from pension funds — which are fenced off by law — state and local budgets have as a whole gone into deficit. The deficit will probably amount to $10 billion in 1975. This fiscal pinch seems bound to increase the temptation to use federal job-creation funds to help meet regular payroll costs.

The scope and usefulness of federal job-creation efforts might be greatly increased if they could somehow reach into the private sector. The question of whether to subsidize jobs in private industry has arisen from time to time, but most people who have thought seriously about the idea seem to come out on the negative side. Congressman William Steiger of Wisconsin, an outstanding young Republican legislator, doesn't see how the government can subsidize an employer and fail to do the same for his competitors. Andrew Biemiller, the chief congressional lobbyist for the A.F.L.-C.I.O., worries about the same point. Paul O'Neill, who was made deputy director of the Office of Management and Budget last December, argues that there is no satisfactory way of separating the federally subsidized hires from those the employer might have put on his payroll anyway.

Carl Madden, chief economist of the U.S. Chamber of Commerce, says that in the experience of the chamber's typically small and medium-sized business membership, job subsidies "get you into a thicket of red tape and government regulation. Moreover, you can get into the question of whether you are a government contractor — a relationship which brings in new regulations. Our businessmen feel it costs more to get tangled up in such programs than it is worth. They would rather not be involved."

Still, it might be worthwhile to put a great deal of effort, imagination, and ingenuity into devising ways of subsidizing job creation in the private sector for certain kinds of work — socially useful work that otherwise would not get done. Two examples are rehabilitation of slum housing and improvement of railway roadbeds.

A Need for Unusual Arrangements

Large numbers of Americans live in deteriorated slum buildings that owners could not afford to rehabilitate if they wanted to. The costs are so high that it would be impossible to recover them through increases in rents. So bad housing gets worse, often to the point where the owner abandons it entirely.

Improvement of housing conditions for the ill-housed is a well-recognized objective of public policy. And to the extent that unemployed people could be mustered to do the work, rehabilitation of slum housing seems a promising venture in cost-benefit terms. Some unusual arrangements would be required, however. Even with public housing, rehabilitation under a job-creation program would raise questions about how union labor fits in. While some of the work certainly could be done by people without special building-trades skills, extensive rehabilitation would require the services of carpenters, masons, plumbers, and electricians, who normally get very high wages. Unemployed craftsmen could not expect to get their regular pay on job-creation projects. Would they be willing to work for much less? Would the building-trades unions go along? The answers are far from clear.

With privately owned housing, matters would be further complicated by questions of who gets what share of the benefits and who pays what share of the costs. How much of the rehabilitation costs would the owner have to pay? To what extent would he be free to increase rents on the improved housing? Again, the answers are not immediately clear. But answers could be found.

Thirty-five Years of Not Thinking

There is perhaps an even better case for job-creation projects to improve railway trackage. With conservation in the use of petroleum an important objective of national policy, it makes sense to encourage rail transport, which is more economical than road transport in terms of energy use. Yet even in the midst of a grave, long-term energy bind, railway roadbeds continue to deteriorate. Some railroads are caught in a trap from which it seems impossible to escape by their own efforts: they are so broke they cannot afford maintenance work, but lack of maintenance causes slowdowns and delays, which cost them business and worsen their financial difficulties. With track and roadbed improvements that enable freight to move faster and passengers more comfortably, high energy costs might bring a significant shift in favor of rail transport and improvement in the finances of some ailing railroads.

Mustering the unemployed to help out would involve some problems of arrangements. What supervisory role would the railroads have? What share of the costs would they be required to pay? Who would provide the equipment and on what terms? Again, answers are not obvious but are probably attainable.

So far, neither the Administration nor Congress appears to be thinking about such possibilities. Robert Nathan, a Washington-based economic consultant who is close to the leadership of the Democratic party, provides a possible explanation for the deficiency of imagination. "For thirty-five years we have not had a depression," he says, "and we are not oriented to thinking about how to make useful work." But we should start thinking, for an effective program of getting otherwise jobless people doing socially useful work offers a measure of escape from that terrible recurrent choice between too much unemployment or too much inflation.

16   The Battle Over 14(b)

Pro-Repeal Clair M. Cook

Should section 14(b) of the Taft-Hartley Act be repealed? My answer is a firm Yes. However, before I present specific reasons for my answer, let me sketch a bit of the background of the issue.

Copyright © 1965 by the Christian Century Foundation. Reprinted by permission from the July 28, 1965 issue of *The Christian Century*, pp. 937–940.

Many strikes by labor unions in the past 150 years have grown out of the refusal of members to work alongside nonunionists. In 1890 the newly formed American Federation of Labor put it succinctly: "It is inconsistent for union men to work with nonunion men." This is one of the American labor movement's strongest traditions. As Andrew J. Biemiller, legislative director for the A.F.L.-C.I.O., said in testimony on June 23 before the Senate labor subcommittee in hearings on the repeal of 14(b): "A worker who refuses to join the union weakens it, and to that extent weakens the collective effort to win the terms that all should enjoy. That is why union workers feel so deeply about this matter of union security."

"Closed" and "union" shops

Until about 1900 the term "union shop" simply meant a workplace where all employees were union members. The National Association of Manufacturers in its 1903 "Declaration of Labor Principles" proclaimed its "unalterable antagonism to the closed shop" — one of the earliest uses of that phrase. Remarked Samuel Gompers in 1907: "Those who are hostile to labor cunningly employ the term 'closed shop' for a union shop because of the general antipathy which is ordinarily felt toward anything being closed, and with the specious plea that the so-called open shop must necessarily be the opportunity for freedom."

But nothing could prevent usage of the term and so "closed shop" now refers to a work situation in which an employer may hire only persons who are already union members. This practice is expressly forbidden by the National Labor Relations act of 1947, commonly called the Taft-Hartley act. "Union shop," on the other hand, has come to mean a situation in which union membership is required as a condition of continued employment — an employer may hire anyone, but the new employee must join the union within (usually) 30 days if he wishes to remain on the job. This requirement is a part of the union contract and therefore bears the signatures of both management and labor as a joint decision arrived at through collective bargaining.

A source of conflict

Just as "closed shop" was a phrase "cunningly" advanced by antiunionists, so "right to work" is an expression which has won advocates on the strength of its misleading phraseology. Banning the right to bargain collectively for the union shop form of security does not bestow any "right" to work; only an employer, in making a job offer, can extend that right, and a union shop clause in a contract does not limit his freedom to do so.

Far more accurate is "compulsory open shop," a phrase which

I coined in an article in *The Christian Century* (January 1, 1958) and which has gained some currency in labor circles. A "right to work" law compels employer and union to permit any worker to remain outside the union, while at the same time requiring that he be given all wage increases and other benefits won by the union. Thus "right to work" laws encourage "free riders" to evade responsibility. For this reason leading churchmen of all faiths have condemned such laws.

The question before us here and before Congress, however, is not whether the open shop should be compulsory; neither is it a question of requiring a union shop, for, contrary to what the defenders of 14(b) contend, its repeal would not make the union shop mandatory. In fact, repeal would accomplish precisely what the National Council of Churches' General Board advocated some eight years ago: "Union membership as a basis of continued employment should be neither required nor forbidden by law: the decision should be left to agreement by management and labor through the process of collective bargaining." As Secretary of Labor Willard Wirtz declared in his June 22 Senate testimony: "The issue underlying the question of whether Section 14(b) should be repealed is not, therefore, whether there is to be a 'right to work.' It is whether there is to be a *right to decide.*"

Now for the reasons which in my opinion dictate the wisdom of repeal.

First, 14(b) is internally inconsistent both with the purposes of the law of which it is a part and with our total national legislative policy. The U. S. Supreme Court itself has noted that this section allows the states "to carry out policies inconsistent with the Taft-Hartley Act itself." The act in other respects decrees a uniform labor policy for the entire nation, recognizing the need for national controls in a time when business and manufacture are nationwide even for a single company. While outlawing the closed shop and preferential hiring of union members, Taft-Hartley specifically authorizes contracts requiring workers to join the union within 30 days after being hired (the requirement has been cut to seven days in building and construction trades). It states that the union cannot refuse membership to a worker thus hired so long as he pays "uniform" dues and initiation fees ("excessive" fees are forbidden), and it requires only payment, not attendance at meetings or any other duties. If the union members wish, they may request an election supervised by the National Labor Relations Board in order to determine by majority vote whether a union shop arrangement is to be retained. Thus the federal law both allows for the union shop and establishes sufficient controls to regulate it.

But 14(b) negates all this. It enables the states to ignore Congress' specific sanction of union shop contracts — the built-in restrictions notwithstanding — if they have a more restrictive statute of their own. In effect the federal government says to the states, "We have a national set of standards, but we will allow you to break them if you decide you want to be tougher on unions."

This odd provision is not, however, a two-way street. New York and California have laws explicitly permitting the closed shop — but here national law supersedes and invalidates state law. As the Supreme Court has noted, "There is thus conflict between state and federal law; but it is a conflict sanctioned by Congress." In no other area does the federal government preempt an area for regulation and then permit the states to override national policy. Section 14(b) should be repealed in order to restore the basic control of national labor relations policy to the federal level of government.

To strengthen democracy

Second, retention of 14(b) is inconsistent with Congress' 1951 amendments to the Railway Labor act. The basic act (1926) preceded by several years the federal government's first general labor regulations of the 1930s, and railway labor relations have always been conducted under the act's own separate formulas. Though the 1951 amendments took the union security provisions of the Taft-Hartley act as their model, they uniformly authorized the union shop without provision for state restrictions. Thus even the 19 states forbidding the union shop have a union shop in the railroad industry. Here federal law takes precedence. As Secretary Wirtz has pointed out, in this action Congress "expressed its policy on this point in clear and firm language." It should be consistent and do the same in regard to the basic national labor law in other industries.

Third, repeal of 14(b) will strengthen, not undermine, democracy in the workplace. The 1947 act stipulated that in states permitting a union shop contract, approval must be voted by the workers for such a contract to become effective. Some legislators thought that opponents of the union shop agreement might be right in claiming that it did not reflect the true wishes of the workers and was only a tool by which union officers could build membership. Between 1947 and 1951, 46,119 polls to determine worker sentiment were held among *all* workers in bargaining units, not merely among union members. Out of the 5.5 million voters, fewer than one worker in ten voted against the union shop; 97 per cent of the elections resulted in ratification. Congress in 1951 saw the pointlessness of this expensive procedure and eliminated the requirement. As Secretary Wirtz notes: "There is no violation of freedom in a minority's having to accept a majority's fair judgment fairly arrived at."

To reduce conflict

Finally, repeal of 14(b) would reduce conflict both in internal industrial relations and among the states. It is noteworthy that the opponents of repeal and the proponents of "right to work" laws are seldom workers themselves. The cry of "freedom for the worker" is most often raised by employers. For example, heading the list of 34 signatories in the Citizens Committee to Preserve Taft-Hartley full-page advertisement in the May 4 *Washington Post* was A. D. Davis, president of Winn-Dixie Stores, Inc. — a company which has been found guilty by the N.L.R.B. on four charges of unfair labor practices. (The sixth circuit court of appeals on February 27 sustained the N.L.R.B. findings — among them, a refusal to bargain.) Too often support for "right to work" and for 14(b) has been a convenient cover for attacks on unionism itself.

Within the workplace, the requirement that the union's services be extended to workers who refuse to join it inevitably causes conflict, diversion of energies and even lower production. Frequently employers prefer a union shop for this very reason, but as long as 14(b) stands, *their* freedom to achieve better harmony through collective bargaining is curtailed.

States which have adopted "right to work" laws have used them to try to lure companies away from the more industrialized areas. And some companies have been receptive. General Electric president Ralph Cordiner told a group in Richmond, Virginia, on October 11, 1956: "We believe that we should go to states that have right-to-work laws. That's where we feel we should invest our shareholders' money." And G.E. vice-president Lemuel Boulware informed the Phoenix chamber of commerce on May 21, 1958: "A very important factor in G.E.'s decision favoring Arizona . . . was the fact that you do have a right-to-work law." The nation cannot afford the kind of low wage competition between states which 14(b) encourages.

Perhaps the best summary of the argument for repeal of 14(b) is to be found in the conclusion of the House report issued June 22 by the committee on education and labor and titled "Repeal of Right-to-Work Provisions." In recommending repeal the committee declared:

> The Federal labor code has been carefully constructed over a long period of years pursuant to the sound principle that the Nation constitutes an economical and integrated whole. Experience with the impact of these State laws in this area of union security has satisfied the committee that there is no longer any justification for permitting this single statutory departure from the principle of Federal supremacy. In the committee's judgment, the time has come for removing this issue from the political arena and returning it to the bargaining table where it belongs.

With this I concur. And I have no doubt that the Senate committee and the majority of both houses of Congress will also concur. Then sometime before Labor Day or soon after, President Johnson will sign the repealer he has requested and "right-to-work," with its long history of controversy, will become a dead issue. The industrial health of the nation should be considerably improved as a result.

Pro-Retention William Jones Fannin

This is the year in which we decide whether the principle of civil rights is to be applied consistently in our nation. Just last year Congress enacted legislation to guarantee the rights of individuals of any race, color or creed in reference to public establishments, employment and schools. Currently before Congress are two more bills pertaining to civil rights. One would eliminate the requirement, still existing in several southern states, that an individual pay a poll tax to vote in state elections. Contrastingly, the other would establish a national labor policy in favor of agreements requiring an individual to pay union dues in order to work. This paradox is before Congress because labor union officials have listed repeal of section 14(b) of the Taft-Hartley act (National Labor Relations act) as their number one legislative goal.

The repeal bill would remove the following provision of the Taft-Hartley act:

> Nothing in this Act shall be construed as authorizing the execution or application of agreements requiring membership in a labor organization as a condition of employment in any State or Territory in which such execution or application is prohibited by State or Territorial Law.

This part of the act affirms the right of a state to protect its citizens by a law making illegal the requirement that a worker be compelled to join a union in order to continue his employment.

To understand the significance of the effort to repeal 14(b), one must understand the terms "closed shop" and "union shop." A closed shop is one which requires that a man be a union member before he can be hired. The only difference between a closed shop and a union shop is that in regard to the latter a worker is permitted a grace period — usually 30 days — before he must join a union. The Taft-Hartley act makes closed shops, but not union shops, illegal.

Section 14(b) of the act, on the other hand, provides that a state may make the union shop illegal — may outlaw compulsory unionism by a right-to-work law. Thus a right-to-work law declares illegal any agreement which makes membership or nonmembership in a labor union a condition of employment. Repeal of section 14(b) would nullify the right of a state to pass laws to protect workers from being compelled to pay union dues.

The First amendment to the U.S. Constitution guarantees freedom of association. Congress cited this fundamental right in the policy declaration of the Taft-Hartley act, stating that the act's purpose is to be achieved "by protecting the exercise by workers of full freedom of association." Repeal of section 14(b) would violate this basic American principle of freedom of association. No one should be required against his will to pay dues to a private organization whether it be church, civic club, chamber of commerce or the A.F.L.-C.I.O. If this section of the Taft-Hartley act is repealed, ours will be the only country in the free world which sanctions compulsory union dues.

The effort to repeal 14(b) is a salient example of special interest legislation which can be harmful to the public. If the proposed repeal is successful, union treasuries will receive millions of dollars from workers forced to pay dues. Labor officials, not union members and other workers, are the ones who would benefit from repeal; though their unions would experience a tremendous increase in membership, they would not have to worry about losing members for lack of satisfaction.

Section 14(b) is designed to protect the individual worker, whether union or nonunion. To dispel the claims of union officials that right-to-work laws are detrimental to the employee, let us analyze the status of a union member who happens to be employed in a state having such a law.

First, the union member laboring in a right-to-work state need not fear that his employer will discriminate against him because he belongs to a union. Section 9(a)(3) of the Taft-Hartley act specifies that it is an unfair labor practice for an employer to discriminate against union members in either hiring or firing practices. Thus the union member is protected against discrimination in a right-to-work state just as in other states.

Second — and more importantly — the union member in a right-to-work state is *free to choose* whether to belong to the union. This is important because he may not want to belong if the union is not providing a service or if its officials are corrupt or espouse beliefs contrary to his own. In a right-to-work state he can resign his membership but still keep his job.

The National Labor Relations act protects the workers' right to organize in a right-to-work state. If a majority of the employees of a company so vote, the union can enter into negotiations with the employer for higher wages, better working conditions, fringe benefits — in other words, it can fulfill the very purpose for which unions were created. The only aspect of bargaining which right-to-work laws prohibit is compulsory membership agreements. Such agreements are for the benefit of labor officials rather than that of the workers. Protection of an individual is not unusual in legal contracts. The courts limit the freedom of contract whenever there is coercion or duress or where they find that an agreement is contrary to the public interest.

The chief argument of advocates of repeal is that all workers should be union members if they are to receive the benefits of collective bargaining. This is known as the "free rider" argument. It assumes that it is better for a worker to be forced to join the union than for the union to be deprived of his dues. It should be remembered, however, that a substantial portion of union dues is spent on civic, political and promotional activity having no relation to the service of collective bargaining — a fact which seriously weakens the "free rider" argument.

In the battle of statistics, union officials claim that the southern states which have right-to-work laws are among the lowest worker income states. Their opponents often answer that wages in southern states have increased at a faster rate than in union shop states. Both statements are half-truths. Owing to economic factors, southern states had lower wages than northern states long before right-to-work laws were enacted. As for wages increasing at a faster pace in the south than in union shop states, this is a consequence not of right-to-work laws but of the recentness of industrialization in the south.

Secretary of Labor Willard Wirtz acknowledged the fallibility of statistics before the special subcommittee on labor on May 24 while testifying in favor of the administration bill to repeal section 14(b):

> I could give the committee, if I felt confidence in it, a whole stack of studies which purport to show, translated into economic results, the effect of having right-to-work laws or not having right-to-work laws. I have no confidence in them. What it comes to is this: If you take a percentage impression or picture of what has happened in the last 18 years, the right-to-work states show gains, large percentage gains, economically during that period, because they start from a lower base.

Advocates of repeal also charge that right-to-work laws are to blame for an increasing movement of industry from north to south. It is true that some industries have moved to the south — but for reasons having to do with climate, water, transportation and power. No one has claimed that industry has been stolen from industrial states such as Minnesota by the right-to-work states of North Dakota, South Dakota and Kansas, or from California by Arizona, Nevada, Utah. It is both erroneous and unfair to generalize on the basis of developments in some but not all of the right-to-work states.

For the benefit of better labor-management relations, union officials should heed the words of a former labor union attorney, Supreme Court Justice Arthur Goldberg, when as secretary of labor he told the American Federation of Government Employees in 1962:

> We want to preserve the merit system for entry and retention in the federal service. I had my share of winning the union shops for unions in private industry, but I know you will agree with me that the union shop and the closed shop are inappropriate to the federal government. . . .
>
> In your own organization you have to win acceptance not by an automatic device which brings a new employee into your organization, but you have to win acceptance by your own con-

duct, your own action, your own wisdom, your own achievements.

Let me say to you from my experience representing the trade union movement that this is not a handicap necessarily.

Very often even the union that has won the union shop will frankly admit that people who come in through that route do not always participate in the same knowing way as people who come in through the methods of education and voluntarism.

Voluntary unionism is in the best interest of the worker because it does not force him to support a union which is corrupt or which espouses political and social beliefs with which he does not agree; in the best interest of the public because it helps to safeguard the concept of freedom of association as set forth in the Constitution; and in the best interest of the union because it makes for a healthier, more responsible and efficient oganization.

Cases

Ralph Bennet

Ralph Bennet arrived in the Near East in October, 1955 to work in the personnel department of a large oil company. He had formerly been employed in the States by several large manufacturing companies. In his most recent job he served in the capacity of training supervisor. Prior to leaving the States, arrangements had been made for his wife and two children to join him before Christmas. Arrangements were also made for picking up, crating and shipping his household effects the latter part of November. The lease on his apartment had been terminated and arrangements made to vacate the apartment by the end of November.

Ralph and his family had approached the new job with great enthusiasm. He regarded it as a real challenge and considered it an opportunity to make an important contribution to life. He visualized helping native workers improve their lot, both within the company and the community. The pay was better than he had ever received before and he was told that there was ample opportunity for advancement. His wife had never been out of the States before. She realized that living standards would differ from those to which she had been accustomed. Even so, she was quite anxious to go and tended to regard the whole affair as an adventure. This attitude was shared by the two children.

Shortly after his arrival Ralph was notified that the company was contemplating transferring him to one of its districts as the training supervisor. Because of a lack of housing in this district the company indicated that it would not pick up and ship his household effects until such time as field housing could be assigned. It was requested that his family not join him until adequate housing was available. Thus, their arrival might be delayed for as long as nine months, perhaps even one year.

Ralph was naturally distressed by this turn of events, especially since it had been understood clearly at the time of his employment that he could bring his family and their effects to the Near East shortly after his arrival. He therefore notified the company that if it did not fulfill the terms of his employment he would resign. Within a few days the company granted his request. The Bennet family arrived before Christmas and their household goods were picked up on December 24 and placed in storage until a final destination could be assigned.

In January, 1956, the company decided to locate Ralph at headquarters. Its offices in the States were given notice to ship his furniture. His job assignment was to assist all district field training supervisors in production training. This meant that he would spend considerable time in the field helping the various district supervisors with their programs. His time at headquarters would be spent working up course materials and preparing training aids.

About the middle of May, Fred Ackerman, a field training supervisor at District A, told Ralph that he was being recommended as his vacation replacement for the months of July and August. In the subsequent weeks Fred and Ralph discussed the work which was to be done during Fred's absence. Arrangements were also made for Ralph to use Fred's house and car. Ralph discussed all these matters with his headquarters supervisor who indicated that upon receipt of the district's request he would give a favorable answer. On or about June 1, Fred notified Ralph that the district superintendent had agreed to the plan and that an official request for his services was to be sent.

At about the same time, the headquarters personnel manager discussed with Ralph the possibility of being permanently assigned to District B. The subject was to be reviewed with the production department to obtain housing clearance. The training job at this camp had been vacant for almost a year. It was the job the company had initially wanted him to take, but housing had not been available. Ralph was willing to accept this "permanent" job, especially since it meant a promotion to the next higher grade. His supervisor informed him that the attempt to obtain for him a permanent transfer had complicated the temporary assignment. Ralph was informed, however, that there was to be a meeting in the field during the week of June 11 at which time his status would be decided. It was stated that he should know what was going to happen by June 15.

While waiting word on his future assignment Ralph learned

that the company was considering transferring Richard Clueman, the training supervisor at District D, to take over a vacancy in the headquarters office. Ralph also learned, unofficially, that the district superintendent had stated that he would not release Clueman unless an adequate replacement could be obtained. Ralph immediately saw the possibility that he might be considered as Clueman's replacement. He became upset when he learned via the grapevine that he was being considered for this job. He felt that he should have been consulted during these discussions. A few days later he heard from an "informed but unofficial source" that headquarters had not only talked about him as a replacement but had, in fact, nominated him for the job and had received an official acceptance from District D.

In presenting the job to Ralph, the personnel manager apologized for the switch and then explained the reasons "why." He reviewed the background of the change and said, "We'd like to have you go to District D as Clueman's replacement. It's a great opportunity because not only will you be promoted but you'll get more and better experience. Your new assignment means supervision over one of our special craft schools in addition to your other training work. It's a nice area too — not nearly as hot as some of the other districts. Besides, there's no housing problem, since you can have Clueman's house. It's very adequate."

Ralph replied, "I've moved around a lot and I'm accustomed to making my own decisions about where and when I go. Besides, I'm not so sure I want to work for the district superintendent. From what I hear he's a rough character and a lot of fellows have trouble working for him. I'm supposed to be a training supervisor and morale's my business; yet I'd have a rough go of it with such a boss."

The personnel manager replied that he knew the superintendent well and, while he wasn't all peaches and cream, he was really a nice guy who wouldn't give Ralph any trouble. Also, he said that the morale problem was greatly exaggerated.

Ralph finally closed the discussion by requesting permission to visit the district and see the situation firsthand. He was particularly interested in meeting and talking with the district superintendent. His request was granted and the following day he left by plane.

In discussing the job with the district superintendent Ralph was surprised to find the job referred to as a developmental assignment holding the same rating as he now held. The explanation given was that it was hoped the present job rating would be upgraded and that when this did occur the individual on the job would be promoted. The superintendent thought this job change might come along "any time now." Ralph replied that he thought it wiser to have the rating changed before he took the job. The matters of the job level were left open and the superintendent said he would radio headquarters shortly as to their decision about the assignment. While Ralph was waiting to hear whether the district still wanted him and whether the job would be upgraded, he discussed his problem with an associate.

In talking about this situation Ralph reflected the feeling that his refusal to accept the transfer quickly had been resented. He indicated he was not sorry he had come to the Near East but added that if a similar situation had occurred in the States he would "probably be with another company by now." He expressed anxiety about how his wife might come to feel about the company and the work environment. He said that all this experience had taken some edge off his enthusiasm and that if the company behaved toward other employees in this way, its human relations in general must be bad. He expressed the opinion that the company disliked anyone to question a decision made by a department manager. He felt that the company had not outgrown its old concepts sufficiently to recognize that employees need to be consulted when their future is involved.

He also pointed out that he was not sure what his alternatives were. The other jobs had by then been filled. He guessed he could stay on doing coordination work at headquarters (the job he had held since January), but he was not sure where this job would lead. He was convinced that management had not considered the possibility that he might not accept the job in District D, were it offered, regardless of whether a promotion were involved.

The Insubordinate Operator

As the fuel-transfer operation entered its critical stage, a hush fell over the work group. All eyes focused on Joe Brown in the operator's position. His actions during the next few tension-packed minutes would determine the success or failure of the operation.

Joe was considered one of the company's most qualified operators. In his early thirties, he had two years of engineering school behind him. He was ambitious, intelligent, and trained to the minute in his trade, which, with an improving technology, was becoming daily more complex, varied, and difficult. He seemed to glory in these moments of tension and excitement when he pitted his training, knowledge, and judgment against the vagaries of the pipeline system.

Problems seemed endemic to the pipeline system. Since they seldom repeated themselves, the operator was constantly forced to search through his repertoire of responses to find solutions. Twisting dials and opening and closing valves in instant response to gauge readings, the operator resembled a matador meeting each new tactic of the bull. These few moments were certainly the "moment of truth."

With the tension mounting Joe's supervisor, Mark Redding, now shifted his position to a point just behind Joe. This gave him a good view of the instrument panel on which Joe's attention was glued. The six other crew members had also gathered around the panel.

Five years ago, when he had been promoted to supervisor, Redding had been a top operator himself. Sometimes he wistfully recalled the thrill of overcoming challenges such as Joe was meeting tonight. He also regretted the fact that his other duties took so much of his time that he had not been able to keep fully abreast of changes in the details of operating.

Redding was definitely worried about tonight's operation. This operation would be especially tricky because of new equipment which had recently been incorporated into the system. A mistake could cost the company $75,000 in lost time and fuel.

Reprinted by the courtesy of Dr. A. Ranger Curran, Youngstown State University.

Redding's attention was suddenly directed to the pressure gauge, which was fluctuating violently. He noted Joe's dial and valve handle settings. These didn't seem correct.

"What in hell is going on?" he shouted.

"Don't worry about anything, it's going OK," Joe answered.

Redding watched the pressure gauge for the next few seconds. It didn't seem to be responding as it should. After what seemed to him an eternity, he spoke sharply and with authority . . .

"Switch to the backup pump!"

"Don't be crazy. That would really screw things up at this point. Sit down and relax . . ."

Joe's reply was made without ever taking his eyes from the panel. His hands continued to play on the board like a maestro conducting an orchestra.

The reply had brought a gasp of disbelief from the work crew but they were too involved in following the operation's progress to really meditate on it. That might be the subject of discussion later tonight, but right now the game was still on.

Three minutes passed. The gauges had all steadied down by this time, and Joe began to relax.

"It's all OK now, chief," he said, turning to Redding.

Redding nodded and then walked away.

The next morning Redding reported to his boss. He described the incident and requested that Joe be fired for insubordination.

Bibliography

"Collective Bargaining: Bent but Not Broken." *Industry Week,* May 11, 1970, pp. 11–12.

Einzig, P. "Inflation Is Unethical." *Commercial and Financial,* January 25, 1973, p. 336.

Faltermayer, E. "Better Way To Deal with Unemployment." *Fortune,* June 1973, pp. 146–149.

"Insensitive Bargaining Keeps Inflation Alive." *Industry Week,* June 14, 1971, pp. 63–64.

Lawrence, F. S. "More Unemployment vs. More Inflation." *Industry Week,* January 20, 1975, pp. 38–39.

"Revolt against Full Employment." *Fortune,* July 1974, p. 2.

Samuelson, Paul A. "The Businessman's Shrinking Prerogatives." *Management Review,* March 1972, pp. 55–57.

Skotzko, E. "Right-to-Work Fracas." *Monthly Labor Review,* January 1974, pp. 74–75.

"Stoking Up a Drive for Right-to-Work." *Business Week,* March 14, 1970, pp. 28–29.

"Troubling Dip in Efficiency." *Time,* June 3, 1974, pp. 68–71.

"Through the Minefields of Inflation." *Fortune,* May 1974, p. 49.

"Why Inflation Is So Hard To Cure." *Business Week,* June 1, 1974, pp. 80–81.

"William F. Buckley, Jr., Talks about Compulsory Unionism." *Nation's Business,* 59 (June 1971), 32–34.

Part Five
Business Environmental Problems

Since the beginning of the seventies environmental problems have been a paramount issue for the U.S. Widespread concern with pollution, the shortage of scarce resources, and the recent energy crisis command a high priority in the nation. While the problems of our physical environment have become critical, problems of our social environment have also increased in importance.

A. The Physical Ecology

In the article "Toward an Economics of Ecology" [17] Hazel Henderson reports that today even economists are challenging traditional economic theories. She advises that neither developed nor developing countries can maintain viable economies while pollution continues unabated. The conflict between economic growth and environmental conservation is reflected in the approaches to the problem taken by each side: the ecologist views economics as a subsystem of ecology, and the economist views ecology as a substystem of economics. The economic assumptions and analyses no longer appear valid. Economics is not value free, as economists attempt to be in their analyses. What is needed, therefore, is not just economic analysis, but rather economic synthesis. Such a synthesis can be best achieved from an ecological perspective of the problems of the nation and the universe.

The concept of profit, for example, may require a new definition that will include debit entries for the social and environmental costs of increased production. Instead of growth economics we may have to take recourse in an ecological equilibrium in economics or a steady-state or stationary-state economy.

New perspectives question the ability of corporate social responsibility to meet ecological needs in the solution of these problems. At the same time many corporate leaders contend that excessive restrictions by ecologists under the guise of socially responsible actions may bring ruin to the U.S. corporation in its attempts to compete in world markets. On the other hand, if managers continue to act exclusively to maximize profits, they may produce suboptimal solutions to both national and world economic and ecological problems.

Business corporations also face the question of how to handle the new social costs of environmental problems. It appears that these costs will probably be shared, but not necessarily equitably at all points in time. Costs may be passed on to the consumer in higher prices, may be partly borne by the producer with less profits, and partly borne by the taxpayer in society. But the fact remains that ecological problems must be resolved, and socially responsible actions and programs by U.S. industry must be achieved in both the short and long run.

In the article "Corporate Responsibility and the Environment" [18] Phillip Blumberg tells us that the concept of corporate social responsibility has gone through a radical transition. It has been cited in business literature throughout the twentieth century, linked with the concept of stewardship of large corporations. Individual companies have declared their dedication to social responsibility, and while it has been debated as a proper objective of business, in recent years it has become not only a proper action but a duty. An analysis of the many business-society issues in conflict over the past twenty-five years reveals that business survival demands socially responsible actions; that for whatever reason, such accountability is "good business." As such, it may become a means to an end, or for the idealistic person, an altruistic objective. But the degree of altruism may well be contested in considering, for example, the amounts corporations have made as gifts to society, in light of legal approval for contributions up to 5 percent of net earnings after taxes. In actual practice we find that the overall nationwide average contribution of corporations is less than 1 percent of net profits.

Both the frequency and the intensity of the needs of society, caused by the interactions of business with society, have increased. As a result it appears that corporate social responsibility may well become mandatory. We find, for example, that between 10 and 20 percent of expenditure plans for new plant and equipment cover costs to meet environmental control regulations. This involuntary type of expenditure and effort are certainly socially responsible, but not the voluntary kind we have known in the past.

Politicalization of the corporation appears as the ultimate concern in the eyes of Mr. Blumberg. If the trend toward involuntary social requirements for business increases, the widespread effect of public interest groups may well politicize the corporations in this realm of activity. For example, stockholders are being asked to act as individuals rather than representatives of the investors in the corporation in the war of public opinion on social issues between business and society. The Securities and Exchange Commission is considering changes in proxy voting in corporations that could increase the level of public involvement in making proposals to board meetings.

New issues are raised for the immediate future such as whether or not our present economic system will meet environmental needs purely through market demands, whether or not industry-wide standards can be voluntarily developed and imposed, who will pay the cost of environmental programs and standards, and how business will organize to go about approaching these problems. The ultimate concern is whether or not all of this will lead to governmental determination of all social priorities. We do know that national social goals were defined for the U.S. for the sixties by a President's Committee on National Goals, and revised in a statement of these goals for the seventies. It therefore might even be naive of us to raise the question of whether government could or should determine social priorities, since it already does. We should rather ask to what extent these priorities might be imposed as regulations for the business person, rather than used as guidelines for him or her in socially responsible activities.

Many business-society issues are so pervasive that only an industry-wide approach provides an economically feasible way of attacking them. We also see the necessity for business leadership at all levels of government and industry, if many of these problems are to be resolved by participation of the private sector of economic life in our free enterprise system. It therefore becomes incumbent upon the business person to define environmental problems in systems-, government-, or industry-level terms. He or she should therefore consider that the scope of present problems demands a collective approach rather than an individual or no approach at all. Corporate leadership understands that unless they can work together to resolve these problems the government will probably take over with programs of its own.

The Mason Chemical Company case examines the realities of urban pollution problems. Management is particularly concerned with its public relations image and its role in industrial pollution. Management is also vitally concerned with the possibility of governmental action to enforce pollution control. As the company plans a major modernization and expansion program, it must consider the additional cost of pollution control. In this case, policymakers are faced with the alternatives of reducing pollution — perhaps at great cost to the firm — or moving to another location, which will reduce the number of job opportunities and tax base of the local community. Obviously, those making the decision must perceive and evaluate the problem in terms of all alternatives and their effects upon the company and all segments of the local community.

B. The Social Environment

In the article "How Business Tackles Social Problems" [19] we find some outstanding examples of the extent to which business has participated in the resolution of social problems. *Business Week* magazine established awards for business citizenship for U.S. corporations making the most outstanding contributions to society. Winners have included the following: Dow Chemical Company, Hallmark Card Company, Colorado Economic Development Association, International Business Machines, and Reverend Leon H. Sullivan, a board member of General Motors. In addition to the awards *Business Week* identified nine commandments a company should follow in dealing with social problems. The guidelines deal with matters of commitment, expectations, and involvement and are provided especially for those organizations interested in becoming more involved in social problems.

Contrary to this interest in social programs, others have said for many years that business cannot become a social agency and also maintain its survival and profit objectives. In William Ahfeld's article "Pragmatic Limits on Business Involvement" [20] we see the other side of the issue, and perhaps a warning against extreme involvement in social programs to the detriment of the organization. Since social responsibility is now in vogue, it can readily become excessive without the identification of some pragmatic limitations on business involvement. The pragmatic limitations include first, a concern that these activities are inappropriate to the inherent structure and principles of business. Mr. Ahfeld contends that the organizational structure of business is not the same as that of a welfare system, but rather is designed for the most efficient allocation of resources. Business is also without the means to determine the proper expenditures for the great variety of social needs. And, if social goals are sought to the eventual detriment of the economic goals of the total economy, the society and its social programs will suffer from declining resource support. Can the "social individual'" and "economic individual" be reconciled in every business organization? Or, will the economic individual be the primary concern of business, with a secondary consideration for social goals?

The second limitation identified by Mr. Ahfeld is that individual business attempts to meet social needs are likely to be fragmented, uncoordinated, and therefore inefficient. Should not business do the job that it can do best, that of the efficient production and distribution of goods and services? The needs of many individuals and groups are so complex that they would not receive efficient resolution without a system-wide approach. How would this be achieved by individual business firms?

Another pragmatic limitation is that business has no scorecard or means of effectively measuring and determining which programs to become involved in, and to what degree. The concepts of social accounting or social auditing have been suggested, but apparently none have been completely developed or widely applied. The final question raised is whether or not individual business firms can determine the perfect balance between social and economic goals at any given point in time.

Pragmatic limiting guidelines are just as necessary as calls for involvement in social programs. Just as there is amost an infinite variety of social needs and intensities of these needs, the very complexity of them requires that some evaluation be made as to the appropriateness or legitimacy of business involvement in particular programs, and the extent of their involvement in time and dollar costs. Since such a variety of external restrictions are being placed on business through society and government, it is not only the right, but also the responsibility, of business to delineate the legitimate limits of its involvement.

A   The Physical Ecology

17   Toward an Economics of Ecology

Hazel Henderson

The social manifestations of what has come to be known as the "movement for corporate responsibility" and the widespread questioning of narrowly defined economic values are rapidly becoming a worldwide phenomenon. In the United States increasing numbers of social and environmental questions are finding their way into corporate proxies, while the annual meeting activists as well as the advocates of consumer and environmental protection are negotiating directly with corporations for the redress of dozens of old and newly perceived grievances.

While U.S. corporate managers are beginning to complain that these activities will ruin their competitive position in world markets, similar activists in other nations are busy trying to place the same kind of restraints on their own industries. For example, Sweden's liberal tradition of state-supported citizen activism now embraces the often corporate-targeted forays of environmental groups, while none other than Prince Philip champions the environmental cause in Great Britain.

In state-controlled economies the goals are remarkably similar, although the form of implementation may be different. In the U.S.S.R., Leonid Brezhnev noted in a recent speech, "As we take steps to speed up scientific and technical progress, we must see to it that it should combine with a rational treatment of natural resources and should not

Reprinted with permission from pp. 31–40 of the May–June 1972 issue of the *Columbia Journal of World Business*. Copyright © 1972 by the Trustees of Columbia University in the City of New York.

cause dangerous air and water pollution or exhaust the soil." [1] Giving teeth to Brezhnev's words, the Central Committee of the Communist Party decreed deadlines for the installation of water pollution controls in the two pulp mills discharging waste into Lake Baikal, the world's largest fresh water lake. In the People's Republic of China the Communist Party's picturesque rhetoric, labeling polluters "counter-revolutionary revisionists," was buttressed with sweeping new anti-pollution laws. Ralph Nader has held his first meeting with French consumers in Paris to discuss the deficiencies of French automobiles.

Some multinational companies have already been affected. Royal Dutch/Shell has been stalled in its attempt to build a supertanker terminal in Wales. Gulf Oil has been ordered to close its new ethylene plant in Rotterdam, whose town council has also delayed construction of a new steel mill, jointly proposed by West Germany's Hoesch and Holland's Hoogovens firms, until it can pass pollution control certification. At the same time, the European Common Market, the Council of Europe, the Intergovernmental Maritime Consultative Organization, the World Health Organization and NATO are among the international groups now trying to coordinate pollution-control efforts. For multinational companies such coordination may be preferable to more piecemeal national legislation and the continued "bootlegging" of pollution by nations willing to opt for "economic development" even at the price of depreciation of their "environmental capital."

Challenge to Traditional Economics

All of these activities, as well as the U.N. Conference on the Human Environment to be held in Stockholm in June augur a decade of unprecedented challenges to traditional economic theories, as well as heightening tensions over the disposition of the planet's remaining resources. The speedup of technological advance and its disruption of old production patterns, combined with the concomitant lag in response time of nation states, corporations and other institutions, threaten to exacerbate these worldwide clashes between narrowly-defined goals of economic development and environmental preservation.

Participants in a meeting on Development and Environment held in Founex, Switzerland in preparation for the U.N. Conference in Stockholm, noted that pollution by industrialized nations is already adversely affecting the developing regions. Moreover, as environmental concern grows, the developing nations may find themselves in the position of having to share the costs of pollution control and at the same

---

[1] Leonid Brezhnev, *Report of the Soviet Union by the Central Committee of the Communist Party,* 24th Party Congress (quoted in *Information Letter #1* of the U.N. Conference on the Human Environment).

time deal with "neo-protectionism" as industrialized nations set up barriers to imported products not meeting their new environmental criteria.

The report from Founex states that "concern for the environment must not and need not detract from the commitment of the world community . . . to the overriding task of development of the developing regions of the world." It continues by stressing that poverty is the most important aspect of the environment for the majority of mankind. However, it also views environmental considerations as providing new dimensions to the concept of development. "In the past, there has been a tendency to equate the development goal with the more narrowly conceived objective of economic growth as measured by the rise in gross national product. It is usually recognized today that high rates of economic growth do not guarantee the easing of urgent social and human problems. Indeed, in many countries high growth rates have been accompanied by increasing unemployment, rising disparities in income — both between groups and between regions, and the deterioration of social and cultural conditions. A new emphasis is thus being placed on the attainment of social and cultural goals as part of the development process." [2]

This growing consciousness that the policy of maximum growth, by private or state-directed means, often produces unacceptable and unanticipated social and environmental costs naturally leads to deeper questioning of underlying economic tenets. This, in turn, leads to closer examination of the major economic institution of our time, the corporation. Many believe it has become a political force within both capitalist and mixed economies, and, in its multinational form, is the only institution capable of challenging the former hegemony of the nation-state system.

In the United States, the corporate-responsibility activists believe that large corporations shape the national culture via advertising, and manipulate political power through lobbying, electoral compaign contributions and influence over regulatory agency policy and personnel. These activists do not believe in the existence of a "corporate conscience," as their tactics clearly show. Rather, they see the corporation as a mindless, amoeba-like system, programmed by its structure and goals to behave in a largely pre-determined fashion. In fact, their analysis is remarkably similar to that of economist Milton Friedman: that in a private-property, free-enterprise system, management is still basically the agent of the stockholders and has no authority to make decisions of a social nature. The activists believe that only massive pub-

---

[2] Final Draft of the Report on Development and Environment by the Panel of Experts convened by the Secretary-General of the U.N. Conference on the Human Environment, Founex, Switzerland, June 1971.

lic pressure and direct petitioning of the stockholders themselves, can bring about a reformulation of the corporate mandate.

Neil Jacoby of the University of California, on the other hand, believes that "Americans have recently demanded social improvements beyond the capacity of this or any other society to produce." [3] He maintains that a social problem may be defined as a gap between society's expectations of social conditions and the present social realities. The pervasive influence of American advertising has raised these expectations domestically, while American movies and TV have propagated similar rising expectations among most of the world's peoples, and drawn attention to the inequitable overconsumption of world resources by the industrialized nations.

The fear of overconsumption was evident at a recent meeting in Prague of the United Nations Economic Commission for Europe. Experts from both Eastern and Western nations agreed that "consumption" must no longer count as the determining indicator of living "standards." Henceforth, human well-being and quality of life — not gross national product — should be the measurements of standard of living. [4]

Also visible is the more subtle clash between the traditional, quantitative value assumptions justifying industrial growth still commonly shared by proponents of capitalism, communism and socialism and the much more radical, qualitative concepts shared by those embracing the ecological viewpoint. To put it in a nutshell: economists see ecology as a sub-set of economics, while ecologists see economics as a sub-set of ecology. Or to put it even another way: economists favor analysis while ecologists prefer synthesis.

Economists, of whatever political persuasion, tend to view the new ecological questions as a set of minor variables which sooner or later must be accommodated in their models. Naturally, out of this viewpoint grows the conviction that it is not necessary to change the basic model but merely to incorporate the sudden explosion of new variables and factors in their effects. Economists have had considerable experience in the handling of new variables, and historically have been forced to embrace those such as the activities of governments, the vagaries of rising nationalism, changing patterns in international trade and payments, the growing power of labor unions, the recent rise of consumerism and the movements for racial and social equality. As each of these variables became more dominant it diminished the usefulness of existing theoretical models of economic behavior. However, the

---

[3] Neil H. Jacoby, "What is a Social Problem?" *The Center Magazine,* July–August 1971.
[4] David Leff, "A Meeting in Prague," *Environment,* November 1971.

new ecological variables are so far-reaching that they will force a major restructuring of current economic assumptions.

A New Definition of "Profit"

One of the first concepts needing redefinition is that of "profit." Economists will have to face the difficult question of whether what capitalist countries call "profit" and state-controlled economies call "economic expansion" has not, in the past, been won at the expense of an equal but unrecorded debit entry in some social or environmental ledger. A graphic telescoping of this issue is visible in Japan's rapid economic expansion and its accompanying environmental chaos. In fact, Maurice Strong, Secretary General of the U.N. Conference on the Human Environment, reported recently that Japanese business leaders are now planning to divert to other countries much more of their new industry, particularly the high-labor, high-pollution and high-energy-consuming industries. This situation may become more common as other polluted industrial nations attempt to export their most environmentally damaging operations. It will be a double-edged sword for poorer host countries, many of which are anxious to avoid being targets of low-cost labor practices or further environmental exploitation.

As more stringent and expensive environmental control criteria are factored into foreign assistance and technology transfer programs, these additional costs will further erode the over-all amounts of donor-country assistance. Offsetting this are possibilities that greater assistance might be forthcoming for more environmentally neutral programs in the social sectors of developing nations, such as education, nutrition and public health, many of which have been ignored because in current economic parlance, they produced a "lower return on investment" than technical projects.

A new definition of "profit" might reformulate its present narrow assessments, as well as traditional inputs into such indicators as gross national product. It might also lead to refinement of other social and political indicators of national well-being. Even economist Simon Kuznets, developer of the methodologies used to compute gross national product, never conceived of his tool as the ubiquitous indicator of national well-being that it has become. Many economists agree with Herman Daly of Louisiana State University that a policy of maximizing GNP is practically equivalent to a policy of maximizing depletion and pollution! By stressing consumption and obsolescence, he believes, we are stressing "throughput" or flow of wealth rather than maximizing and conserving the *stock* of wealth and its durability, such as occurs in the models existing in nature, which are closed-loop systems of material cycles powered by the sun.

Reformulation of GNP might have led to a very different set of proposals than those geared to stimulating automobile consumption in the New Economic Program of President Nixon. From an ecological viewpoint, an economy is grievously distorted if it must be given an adrenalin shot to boost production and consumption of automobiles, which have already produced an incredible backwash of social and environmental diseconomies. The "automobilization" of the United States has already led to decaying inner cities, 50,000 traffic fatalities annually, an overburdened legal system, some 60% of all U.S. air pollution, and the sacrifice of millions of square miles of arable land to a highway system that is the most costly public works project undertaken by any culture since the building of the Pyramids and the Great Wall of China.

New Measurements for "Growth"?

With new analytical tools, governments might reassess some of the social and environmental diseconomies of their national "growth." One approach is to quantify, where possible, these diseconomies — the "bads" as Ezra Mishan of the London School of Economics calls them — and subtract them from a given gross national product, leaving a net national product. These data, conveniently dubbed "externalities," are often quantifiable, although they remain uncollected because no institutional support for such tasks is forthcoming in cultures biased by traditional economic, growth-maximizing theories. Economist Allen V. Kneese of Resources for the Future, a Washington-based research institute, believes that new account must be taken of the fundamental laws in physics of conservation of mass, while philosopher Bertrand de Jouvenal of France states pragmatically, "We would deem foolish the management of a business enterprise which counted against its receipts merely its operating costs, and gave no attention to the maintenance of its plant: this, however, is just how our global economic system is being managed." [5]

In his new book *Alienation and Economics,*[6] Alvin Weisskopf traces the creeping myopia of economics as it became split off from the broad philosophical and political enquiry into the narrowly-conceived reductionist discipline that we know today. He suggests that real security is in another dimension: not economic scarcity but existential scarcity, of life, time and energy, which are the ultimately scarce resources because of man's finitude, aging and mortality. Recognition of man's needs — love, self-actualization, order, beauty, etc. — can never be satisfied by purely economic activity. Another recent book, *Power in*

---

[5] *Ibid.*

[6] Alvin Weisskopf, *Alienation and Economics,* E. P. Dutton & Company, New York, 1971.

Economies, edited by Professor K. W. Rothschild of Linz, Austria,[7] examines an additional shortcoming of economic theories, namely, that they pay too little attention to the variables introduced by the exercise of power, including corporate lobbying power, government and union power, and all other forces which are too often omitted as "extra-market factors" in economic models.

Indeed, the whole concept of "development" now requires re-examination, as does that of economic growth itself. Ever since Malthus stated some 150 years ago that food supply would eventually force a reduction of population, we have debated this issue. Now, in addition to Malthus' correct identification of food supply, ecologists bring new inhibiting factors into consideration of exponential growth. They include depletion of natural resources, pollution, and in the opinion of many, capital investment itself, which leads to ever faster depletion of resources and increase of pollution. Jay Forrester states flatly in his book, *World Dynamics,*[8] that it is not a question of whether growth will cease, but rather whether the coming transition to equilibrium will occur traumatically, or will be guided by human intervention, which may yet head off some of the most tragic outcomes. Indeed, Forrester believes that, with all our discontents, we are now living in the planet's "Golden Age" and that we must begin to reduce our more unrealistic expectations.

The "Steady State Society"

How will the world's economists respond to all this talk of zero population growth and the "steady state society"? The readjustment will be hardest for Americans, who have been conditioned by the myths of the frontier and Horatio Alger to "hitch their wagon to a star." Now they may have to learn to hitch their star to a wagon. Already some of the euphoria of the 1950s over imminent abundance is being reassessed, along with the escapist promise that an ever bigger pie to share would lead to greater equality, while conveniently sidestepping the question of redistribution.

Some economists, such as Kenneth Boulding, J. Kenneth Galbraith, Barbara Ward and Ezra Mishan are in the vanguard in wrestling with concepts of economic equilibrium within a closed planetary system. One resulting tool, developed by Mishan, which may prove increasingly relevant is that of "amenity rights." These he claims, should share equal status in law and custom with property rights, with which they often conflict. Another stimulating concept is advanced by ecol-

---

[7] K. W. Rothschild, Ed., *Power in Economics,* Penguin Books, Middlesex, England, 1971.

[8] Jay Forrester, *World Dynamics,* Wright–Allen Press, Cambridge, Massachusetts, 1971.

ogist-engineer Howard T. Odum in his new book *Environment, Power, and Society.*[9] Odum suggests that money is no longer an adequate metaphor to describe accurately our various resource allocations and human transactions. The money metaphor needs to be augmented by a system of energy accounting and simulation. This would provide descriptions of how underlying energy/matter exchanges operate and how hidden energy subsidies or outflows obscure or prevent accurate accounting of all the real costs, benefits and trade-offs in human activities.

Some of the most intellectually stimulating sets of concepts put forth in support of the equilibrium economy are embodied in Jay Forrester's planetary models and their gloomy scenarios in his *World Dynamics.* Among the shattering implications to current economic assumptions are: (1) There may be no realistic hope that presently under-developed nations will ever reach the standards of living enjoyed by industrialized nations; (2) Industrialization may be a more fundamentally disturbing force in world ecology than population growth (a thesis supported by biologist Barry Commoner in his book *The Closing Circle*[10]); (3) A society with a high level of industrialization may be non-sustainable and self-extinguishing; (4) From the perspective of a hundred years hence, the present efforts of underdeveloped countries may be unwise, because they may now be closer to the ultimate equilibrium with the environment and in better condition for surviving the forthcoming worldwide pressures than industrialized nations (a conclusion shared by Odum on the basis of his energy simulations).

Forrester fears that within the next century man will have to cope with four possibilities: suppression of modern industrial growth because of natural resource shortages; decline in world population due to pollution; limitation on births imposed by food shortage; or population collapse from war, disease, and social stresses caused by physical and psychological crowding. It is ironic that Forrester's dire predictions and his heretical deductions concerning the necessity of limiting capital investment should have been instigated by the Club of Rome with the support of many prominent industrialists, such as Aurelio Peccei, vice chairman of Italy's Olivetti and Company and a grant from the Volks-wagen Foundation.

If there is any merit to all of this new ferment over the ecological implications of industrialization, then we are faced with a strange paradox. Far from accepting the current view that environmentalists are those harboring widely unrealistic expectations from their respective national economies, we may have to countenance the opposite view:

---

[9] Howard T. Odum, *Environment, Power, and Society,* Wiley Interscience, New York, 1971.
[10] Barry Commoner, *The Closing Circle,* Alfred A. Knopf, New York, 1971.

that industrialization, whether under the aegis of private businessmen or state commissars, aided and abetted by traditional economic theories of unlimited growth, may be the institutional force whose expectation trajectory has soared out of line with the reality curve of the earth's available resources! And to exacerbate matters, corporations have used the power of advertising to sell to millions of people a euphoric set of expectations, while leaders of state-controlled economies have used their mass media to similarly propagandize their proletariat on the glories of industrial growth.

At the same time, many analysts of the world economic scene are predicting the replacement of the nation-state system with a system of world order based on the multinational corporation. Richard Eells of Columbia University states, "In the next ten to fifteen years nation states will slowly yield various attributes of their sovereignty to the multi-national and transnational corporations." He adds, "The survival of the multi-national corporation in the future will depend heavily upon the manning of its top posts with people who understand the dynamics of world politics and can envisage the optimum role for a global corporation in a hazardous environment." [11] The implicit value assumption in this statement is clearly posited from the viewpoint of the corporation and traditional economics. An ecologist, on the other hand, would claim that it is the corporation itself that constitutes the environmental hazard.

In similar vein, José R. Bejarano, group vice president of Xerox Corporation, stated recently at the National Foreign Trade Convention, "The multinational corporation today is a force that can serve global needs of mankind far better than the medieval concepts of nation states. Technology transfer, a new era with basic supra-national scope, provides an opportunity for pioneer supra-national thought and action." To solve the problem of development, he believes "that the world corporation, to be effective, must reach across . . . imaginary lines on a map to synergize crude natural resources of undeveloped regions with capital, technology and markets of the rest of the world." [12]

Views diametrically opposed to those of Eells and Bejarano were set forth by 33 prominent British scientists in a recent manifesto, "Blueprint for Survival." In addition, some 2,000 scientists, from 22 nations presented a report to U.N. Secretary General U Thant delineating the "planet's almost unmanageable problems." They called for "a moratorium on technological innovations, the effects of which we cannot tell," including new weapons, pesticides, nuclear power projects and all ecologically unresearched projects such as the damming of large rivers and undersea mining. They urged a decrease in the consumption

---

[11] Richard Eells, "The Optimum Role for Transnational Corporations," *Center Report,* October 1971.
[12] *New York Times,* December 5, 1971.

levels by "privileged classes" in all nations.[13] This juxtaposition of views casts doubt on the proposition that the multinational corporation committed to industrial development, represents a superior system to that of the nation state. In fact, ecologists view it as a disastrous model for any emerging world ecological order, simply bceause it is so effective in the purposes to which it is dedicated.

How Will This Change the Corporation?

If the ecologists' views have validity — for instance, the view that the exponential growth curves in such areas as power consumption will collapse and that some new economic equilibrium, based on redistribution and less consumption, is in the making — how will this change the corporation? First, added constraints will make themselves felt as more costs now externalized become internalized and added to the market price of products. This will alter market and production patterns as it more rationally assigns to the consumer, rather than the taxpayer, the full social and environmental costs of production. For instance, if rates for electricity include full environmental costs, the aluminum industry, based on low-cost electricity, would also change. One outcome could be the disappearance of the throw-away aluminum can; another might be wholesale replacement of aluminum in hundreds of products. Other obvious consequences would be the increasing cost of high energy-and-matter-input goods and their gradual replacement by lower energy-and-matter-input goods, and the continued growth of services in the public and private sectors that is already visible in the "post-industrial" nations.

All this may be initially inflationary while readjustments and reallocations of resources are occurring, and may cause many U.S. products to face even stiffer competition in world markets. This is contested, however, by James B. Quinn of The Amos Tuck School of Business Administration. He believes that the new environmental costs will eventually be sold as "value added" in products; that the new pollution-control processes will result in raw materials savings; that while foreign competition may initially cause some disruption, this problem may be offset by the rising ecological awareness in other nations, by added exports from a growing domestic pollution-control industry and by other factors.

Constraints have already been felt by the corporation which relocates its operations in a country providing cheaper labor and a blank check to pollute. Labor unions in advanced economies are busy going "multinational," and the U.N. Conference on the Environment has received sheaves of draft proposals for international pollution monitoring

---

[13] *Information Letter #1*, U.N. Conference on the Human Environment.

and regulation. Of course, some companies will look for and find many short-term advantages in poorer nations. Samuel Pisar, Paris-based international lawyer and author of *Coexistence and Commerce,*[14] told a group of multinational corporate executives about a U.S. company which had consulted him as to whether they should move their entire operation to a more "favorable" European country, in spite of the shift in employment it would cause between home and abroad. Pisar replied politely, "Gentlemen, I am your lawyer, not your priest."

With these new constraints, future benefits will probably lie in three general areas: (1) Better energy-conversion ratios. For example, we will no longer be able to afford the thermal inefficiencies of the internal combustion engine or the current generation of light-water nuclear fission reactors. It is becoming clear that adding pollution control equipment, such as precipitators, cooling towers, or catalytic mufflers on cars, may, on a total energy basis, leave us with a trade-off. Only by developing inherently more efficient energy-conversion systems, such as fuel cells or nuclear fusion, can we hope to achieve actual economy of resources and environmental benefit. (2) Better resource management and rehabilitation. Production loops must be closed by recycling, but probably not in the current U.S. mode of recycling bottles and cans. This does not constitute a valid feedback loop for the container industry. It permits companies to continue externalizing the heavy costs of collection. A recent energy analysis of relative values of returnable container versus recycling of throw-aways indicates that throw-away bottles consume 3.11 times the energy of returnables.[15] A more likely model of recycling is the recently reported practice in the People's Republic of China of resoldering and resealing burnt-out light bulbs for a new lease of life. (3) Better market research into those areas where individual consumer choice is inoperative until it is "aggregated." This could provide more flexible, speedy corporate response to social change and indicate where unmet and potentially profitable public needs exist. The public-sector needs for clean air, clean water, mass transit or medical services might well become coherently aggregated with corporate support for the political activities of citizens groups and other potential consumers now working to underpin them with government expenditures. New methods of multi-stage public-sector marketing must be learned.

Only grass-roots coalitions of potential consumers can create enough genuine political steam to capitalize new economic activities. Yet many companies, still blind to these new market opportunities, con-

---

[14] Samuel Pisar, *Coexistence and Commerce,* McGraw-Hill, New York, 1971.
[15] Bruce M. Hannon, "Bottles, Cans, Energy," *Environment,* March 1972.

tinue to lobby and oppose demands for clean air or mass transit, while identifying with past vested interests in old, rapidly saturating markets. Companies interested in developing new markets must first contact citizen organizations pushing for new priorities in public spending and assess which new needs they are best equipped to serve. Then they must determine the citizens' expectations for the performance of these new public-sector goods and services and involve the groups in setting the design criteria and functional goals to be optimized.

The size and shape of the total market must be measured by extensive polling and interviewing. Additional monitoring of "little" magazines and underground media would help to flag new modes of consciousness that will change life styles and expectations. Sophisticated new methods for social choice, employing computers, cable TV and electronic voting, now in the experimental stage, have already proved capable of increasing citizens' motivation and participation in articulating public issues, assessing options and formulating community goals. The same methods have been used to analyze and profile the resulting feedback.[16]

Finally, the corporate marketing men can join with these potential groups of consumers in lobbying efforts to pass the legislation or bond issues necessary to create the public-sector markets for these big-ticket items. This was the way the pollution-control market developed after consumer demand had been expressed through the political system; the fledgling firms in the field put their marketing dollars together to back a trade association program of providing speakers and film strips to inform civic groups of the technology available. They thereby raised enthusiasm for appropriations and this often led to discreet but positive pressure on the recalcitrant companies to purchase needed equipment.

"Market failure research" is in essence the art of finding "social indicators" of subjective states of satisfaction with the over-all quality of life. These data could provide supplements to narrow economic models of markets. For example, an "amenities index" could quantify levels of satisfaction about such things as national parks, local recreation facilities, schools and hospitals. Indices could also be developed to measure performance of such federal agencies as the U.S. Federal Trade Commission in policing business practices, the Food and Drug Administration in protecting consumers, or the Federal Communications Commission in protecting citizens' rights in broadcasting.

If corporations are to adapt to the prospective changes of the Seventies, they will need to restructure themselves along more participatory lines; to increase their sensitivity to new motivational forces (of

---

[16] Hazel Henderson, "The Computer in Social Planning: A Chance for the Little Guy to be Heard," *The MBA*, December 1971.

which ecology is one) identified by behavioral scientists such as Maslow, Argyris, Herzberg, and others. Their work has already undermined yet another outworn theoretical model: *"homo economicus."*

New Life Styles and Consumption Patterns

If the ecological view of the future is valid, there will be continuing changes in life styles and consumption patterns in the advanced nations. External freedoms will become more circumscribed as population densities increase. More satiated consumers will continue to search for greater psychological freedom. Leisure activities dependent on high energy inputs, such as snowmobiling and hot-rodding, will give way to more environmentally neutral and self-actualizing activities such as hiking, biking, painting, ceramics and handicrafts. Tourism will increase, with mixed blessings for developing nations as they trade their scenic "capital" to the hotel developers and suffer the kind of deterioration now being faced by Hawaii. The need to "ephemeralize" modes of living will become more urgent. Retraining of the senses to maximize pleasurable physical sensation and the joys of meditation could bring Western values more into convergence with those of Eastern cultures. Cities in post-industrial economies may gradually re-orient themselves away from production, consumption and marketing and move toward the patterns of the festival cities of the ancient cultures of pre-Columbian Central America. Communication might become the more important side of the coin of human interaction relative to the high energy transportation patterns of the present.

This does not mean a wholesale return to nature or a rejection of technology. Current population levels in industrialized nations already preclude such a course. Truly committed environmentalists are not Luddites. They are merely experimenting with low-consumption, low-reproduction life styles to see how well they can cope when the crunch comes. Even a cursory examination of their "survival manuals." such as the *Whole Earth Catalog* and *Radical Software* makes this clear. Rather they are seeking an end to gross, wasteful, "meat-axe" technology which they insist has characterized our industrial age. They seek a second-generation technology, more refined, miniaturized and organically modeled along biological analogies. Buckminster Fuller calls this process of doing more with less "ephemeralization" and futurist-economist Carl Madden describes it as "negentropic" industrial activity.

In such a new social climate, the concept of prior societal assessment of technology is becoming more widely accepted. Two new international organizations have been founded recently to carry out such assessments; the International Institute of Applied Systems Analysis under the auspices of the United States, the Soviet Union, East and West Germany, Britain, France, Italy and Poland, and the International

Institute for the Management of Technology sponsored jointly by Austria, France, Britain, the Netherlands, Italy and West Germany. Meanwhile the Club of Rome is currently expanding with its new Geneva-based Decision-Making Testing Laboratory, which will provide the Club's World Dynamics models to world decision-makers and so widen their process of validation.

The thought is gaining acceptance that the application of technology should be slowed sufficiently to prevent "future shock." As Geoffrey Vickers of Britain suggests, we need to develop calculations and indicators of optimal rates of change by measuring subjective human response and discomfiture, and, in addition, possibly include its manifestations in violence or emotional illness.

Information technology can be used not only to manipulate people's buying habits or to intimidate them politically by government surveillance and data banks, but also for electronic town meetings, instantaneous polling and eventually voting in referenda and in modeling public problems and issues, as the very hardware of participatory democracy. Of special interest is the move in "post-industrial" economies toward developing a "counter-technology" more consonant with the values of the "counter-culture" groups, using computers and mass communications, such as TV, not in their centralized and monolithic modes as heretofore, but to rewire the individual citizen back into the central nervous system of the body politic. Similarly, more computer power can be devoted to quantifying world resources and developing from these data optimum population levels as targets for future achievement.

"The Ultimate Perspective"

The basic quarrel that ecologists have with economists is that their theories no longer fit the observable phenomena in the real world and their analytical tools are no longer adequate. Such a critique can be applied to many disciplines, but in the case of economics these inadequate concepts are hitched to the most powerful political forces in the modern world: industrialization and the continued march of unbridled technology. While unexamined economic assumptions fuel the engine of rapid technological change, there has been no concomitant pragmatism within economics itself which might have provided the impetus for its reform. Instead, dissident economists, hemmed in by the traditional notion that economics was a "value-free" scientific discipline, have been forced further into arid abstractions. Consequently their dissent is too often siphoned off into the sterile nineteenth century dialectics of Marxism versus Socialism and Laissez-Faire Capitalism; the endless reassessments of old dogmas.

Meanwhile broad avenues of fruitful enquiry go untrod: charting the diseconomies of a host of industrial activities; devising "social auditing criteria for corporation accounting; measuring the effects of power in the market; devising social indicators of human well being and three-dimensional models of costs, benefits and trade-offs so as to include social and environmental criteria. Consequently today's economics is becoming useless as a tool for managing national economies or world resources. It must incorporate more hard data from the physical sciences as well as develop the philosophical overviews necessary to integrate itself with anthropology, biology, psychology and the major systems of ethical and moral values.

The direction of the ecologists' inquiries is based on many past insights, including John Stuart Mill's concept of the "stationary state economy" and his keen awareness of the political nature of all economic distribution. Keynes also drew attention to the spiritual limitations of economic goals and activities. The newly perceived ecological threat appears to Maurice Strong as "the basic issue confronting the world, for it requires man to face the question of his own survival and be enlightened enough to understand the profound changes that must take place in his own values and priorities."

And so too, must industrialists and economists face the humbling question "Can man evolve and adapt his value system to the requirements of an interdependent world society which must operate in equilibrium on a finite planet?" If the goal of evolution is survival, the goal must also be the regulation of all sub-systems for the optimal functioning and maintenance of the macro-system. Barbara Ward and Kenneth Boulding call it the "space-ship economy." Jay Forrester adds his reminder that the narrow short-term goals of sub-systems are generally in conflict with long-term goals of optimizing the macro-system. Biologist Garrett Hardin calls it "the Tragedy of the Commons." Theologian Reinhold Niebuhr summed it all up in his concept of God as simply "the ultimate perspective."

18 Corporate Responsibility and the Environment

Phillip I. Blumberg

At the outset, it is desirable to review briefly what is meant by corporate responsibility. This concept is a philosophy of business enunciated by leaders of major American enterprise as far back as Owen D. Young of General Electric in the 1920's, Frank Abrams of Standard Oil (N.J.) in the 1950's, and innumerable others in the years since — a philosophy that business must serve its employees, customers, suppliers, and the American society generally, as well as its shareholders; that business is too important a factor in society to confine its objectives simply to making as much money as possible for its shareholders.[2] In General Motors' contest with Campaign GM at its 1970 Annual Meeting,[3] even General Motors' management sought to defend its stewardship by expressing its dedication to the principles of corporate responsibility.[4]

Corporate social responsibility, as expressed in this fashion, has been evidenced by highly welcomed business support for charities, for education, for the arts, for employment of minority groups, for efforts to deal with poverty, race relations, and urban problems, and for other social objectives commanding an overwhelming consensus of public approval.

Corporate participation in the solution of such problems has become a commonplace. In part, this has developed in response to the

---

Reprinted with permission from *The Conference Board Record,* April 1971, pp. 42–47. © The Conference Board 1971.
[1] "In some ways, state ownership . . . may actually exacerbate . . . the situation." Marshall I. Goldman, "The Convergence of Environmental Disruption," *Science,* October 2, 1970, p. 37.
[2] Professor Heyne points out "that businessmen have been among the most strident proclaimers of the new social gospel, that they have been major contributors to the literature and philosophy of social responsibility, and that with near unanimity they have announced their willingness to bear this burden." Paul T. Hayne, *Private Keepers of the Public Interest,* McGraw-Hill, New York, 1968, p. 108.
[3] See Egerton, p. 48.
[4] General Motors Corp., *GM's Record of Progress in Automative Safety, Air Pollution Control, Mass Transit, Plant Safety, Social Welfare* (1970).

urgent social problems of the times, and in part, it is a consequence of the affirmation in lofty moral terms of business leaders themselves that such participation is not only a proper objective, but the social duty, of business. Business has led the public to expect that it will play a constructive role in the solution of the impelling social problems of the day, and management has recognized that it is "good business" to respond to this expectation. This is a dynamic process intensified by the urgency of the underlying social problems, which I have elsewhere described as the process of public acceptance-expectation-demand.[5]

Notwithstanding the pressures of public expectation and demand, corporations participating in the social sphere — as distinct from the environmental field — are still operating under circumstances in which there is considerable freedom of choice. Corporate action in this area, although profoundly influenced by the social climate, essentially reflects a deliberate management election from a number of realistic alternatives. It reflects management's evaluation, in the normal course of running its business, of appropriate means for fulfilling its corporate objectives in the light of the realities of the times.

Such corporate conduct in the social sphere, carried out because it is "good business," is for practical purposes no longer subject to criticism. Professors Milton Friedman and Henry Manne, while contending stoutly that the sole and overriding objective for management is to maximize profits for shareholders, simultaneously concede that corporate action in the social sphere when performed as a result of hardheaded business judgment in order to advance business objectives is, of course, permissible — indeed, desirable;[6] their criticism is essentially confined to the point that use of terms such as "altruism" or "social responsibility" to describe such corporate conduct is misleading or even "subversive." Even the old debate over whether corporate management may properly select objects of charitable bounty using corporate funds belonging to shareholders, rather than distributing the funds in question to shareholders who could then decide for themselves on charitable contributions to institutions of their own selection, seems to have come to an end. Because of the corporate tax deduction, the amount available for philanthropy is doubled if performed on the corporate level and even Professor Friedman, who in the past castigated corporate charitable contributions, has recently announced acquiescence to such corporate conduct.[7]

---

[5] Phillip I. Blumberg, "Corporate Responsibility and the Social Crisis," *Boston University Law Review,* 50 (1970), 157.
[6] Milton Friedman, "The Social Responsibility of Business Is to Increase Its Profits," *N.Y. Times,* Sept. 13, 1970; Henry Manne, "The Myth of Corporate Responsibility" (Address, Annual Meeting of American Bar Association, Aug. 11, 1970), *Business Lawyer,* 26 (1970), 536–37.
[7] Friedman, *supra.*

The continuing debate on corporate responsibility in the social sphere is thus confined to the theoretical level and revolves around the rhetoric. There is little profit in such debate. The critical element is the fact of the response, not the label. Does it really matter whether the corporate response to the social crisis is derived from a sense of moral obligation, or a concern with long-term profit potential, or a view as to enlightened self-interest, or a concern as to "corporate image," or a desire to "insure" against confrontation with minority groups, or from recognition of a duty to be a corporate "good citizen," or from a number of the foregoing considerations? [8] In the end, the corporate conduct rests on management's concept of what is "good business" in the light of the expectations and demands — private and governmental — of the times. This undoubtedly is what Professor Peter Drucker had in mind when he suggested that corporate social responsibility was a term that served no useful purpose and should be discarded.[9]

A final comment is necessary on the response of American business with respect to corporate responsibility in the social sphere where relative freedom of management decision still exists. The amounts spent in the area — highly desirable though they may be — are small. Under Section 170 of the Internal Revenue Code, corporations may deduct up to 5% of net taxable income for charitable, scientific, educational, and similar contributions. In 1968 total expenditures in this area were estimated at $925,000,000, or only 1.06% of pre-tax net income.[10] By the fall of 1970 it was estimated that such expenditures had risen slightly to approximately one billion dollars per year.[11]

To the extent that corporate operations are conducted in a competitive market, the expenditures for social responsibility in any area where management freedom of decision still exists must essentially be borne by shareholders. Therefore, it is no surprise that in very few cases in the social sphere is there any indication that business is yet prepared to expend up to the tax-deductible limit of 5% of pre-tax income or, indeed, any amount which would have impact on that supreme index of its performance — its earnings per share.[12]

---

[8] See McKinsey & Company's survey as to motivation factors of 201 companies with urban affairs programs: Cohn, "Is Business Meeting the Challenge of Urban Affairs?" *Harvard Business Review*, March–April 1970, p. 70.

Wolfgang Friedmann, "Corporate Power, Government by Private Groups and Law," *Columbia Law Review*, 57 (1957), 155, 161–62.

[9] Peter F. Drucker, *The Age of Discontinuity*, Harper & Row, New York, 1969, pp. 205–07.

[10] Council for Financial Aid to Education, 1968 Survey of Corporation Support for Higher Education.

[11] *Wall Street Journal*, October 7, 1970.

[12] According to a recent survey of 78 corporations: "Among the larger firms [whose executives were willing to reveal the aggregate amount of

Thus, in the nonenvironmental area, the remaining question is not business recognition of corporate social responsibility, but whether the public acceptance-expectation-demand process will increase in intensity so that the voluntary nature of business response will be progressively restricted and the funds allocated to this area as a result of public demand (funds which will then for practical purposes be involuntary social costs of doing business) increase to a level nearer the tax-deductible ceiling. The role businessmen themselves play in this process of acknowledgment and acceptance of such social costs may well have significant influence on the future place of business in the society. It is recognition of this factor that has led such business leaders as David Rockefeller, Henry Ford II and others to emphasize the need for business leadership in this area.[13]

Corporate Action in the Environmental Area

When we turn from the traditional areas of corporate social responsibility to the field of the environment, the question arises whether such a development may not have occurred already and whether the public acceptance-expectation-demand process has not already reached such a level of intensity that business has lost much of its freedom of choice.

The dynamics of the intensification of public expectation and demand in the environmental field have been marked by at least three new major elements not included in the factors which have led in the past to the development of corporate responsibility in the social sphere. This marks out the area as novel and helps explain why public pressures for corrective action have reached such overwhelming proportions.

In the first place, the consequences of environmental abuse are faced directly by all members of the community, and the public is

---

their contributions to all recipients] annual contributions range from 1 to 1.5% of pre-tax earnings; a few go as high as 2% and in one instance as high as 6% of pre-tax earnings." Fry Consultants, Incorporated, *Social Responsibilities* (1970), p. 4.

But see Dayton Hudson Corporation, *Contributions for Community Improvement* (1969): "The Board of Directors of Dayton Hudson Corporation believes that it is in the shareholders' interest to utilize 5% of our pre-tax profits for the improvement of the urban areas in which we operate. If business does not assist in the crucial work of solving society's problems, society will not continue to grant business its traditional opportunity for profitable growth."

[13] Henry Ford II has recently stated: "It seems clear that neither business in general nor the auto business in particular will survive in its present form," and added, "if business doesn't catch up with consumer expectations, Government will step in — even if there is little that Government can do." *Wall Street Journal,* November 16, 1970.

accordingly aroused to an extent never experienced in the more traditional areas of social responsibility. The problem presented by environmental abuse affecting the community as a whole is radically different from the concern that an individual not directly affected by a social problem may feel for those who are affected and for the impact that such social problems affecting others may have on the community as a whole. Thus, the considerations presented by smog in a community which affects every resident directly, and from which he cannot escape, are plainly different from the considerations involved in the evaluation by a middle-class white of his response to such community problems as employment opportunities for disadvantaged minority groups. The entire community, not a limited group, is the victim of the problem.

Second, in the environmental area, business is being called upon to help solve problems which it has itself created. There is no question as to the responsibility of the plant which is causing air or water pollution in the community. That business is not sharing a common concern with other groups in the community in the solution of problems facing the community. It is being forced to defend itself against the consequences of its own direct impact on the community and its environment. Its own conduct is at issue.

Third, there is increasing recognition by management leaders [14] and others [15] of the need for governmental guidance and regulation. It is apparent that the public demands vigorous response with an intensity not previously experienced, that competitive factors may impede or retard the degree of business response, and that the problem has become too big for business to solve on its own. In 1970 Dr. Lee A. DuBridge, then President Nixon's advisor, described the role of government to be the imposition of regulations to protect responsible companies from the less enlightened.[16] On the other hand, some are still calling for business

---

[14] *E.g., Mobil Oil World,* December 1970, p. 4: "Now that it [Federal Environmental Protection Agency] is in operation Mobil's environmental control experts look forward to having even clearer guidelines for pollution control from the federal government. That can only be good for the public, and for Mobil"; Ford Motor Corp., Third Quarter Report 1970; B. R. Dorsey, president, Gulf Oil Corp., *Finance,* November 1970, p. 18; Combustion Engineering, Inc., *Progress,* Number 3 (1970), p. 9; Continental Oil Co., Third Quarter Report 1970, p. 2.

[15] *E.g.,* George Cabot Lodge, "Why an Outmoded Ideology Thwarts the New Business Conscience," *Fortune,* October 1970, pp. 106, 150; Neil Jacoby, "The Environmental Crisis." *Center,* November 1970, pp. 37, 43–45; Paul Samuelson, *N.Y. Times,* December 26, 1970, §4 p. 17.

[16] Dr. Lee A. DuBridge, "Toward a Better Environment" (Address at dedication of Union Oil Co. refinery, June 29, 1970): "Regulations are necessary to protect conscientious companies from being at a competitive disadvantage compared to those who are less careful about pollution."

mobilization on an industry-wide basis for solution of environmental problems in order to head off otherwise inevitable governmental action.[17]

Thus, in the environmental area, corporations are faced with a challenge which is clearly different from the questions presented in the traditional areas of social responsibility. In the environmental area, corporate management is not concerned with the role of business as a participant on a relatively limited level in programs for social or community improvement. The questions for discussion are not such items as whether corporate funds might properly be expended for conventional philanthropic objectives by shareholders than by corporate managers, or whether banks and department stores are well advised to expend corporate funds to help sustain the inner cities with which their businesses are inextricably interrelated.[18] The questions in the environmental field relate to harder decisions of more formidable import. In summary, management faces a crisis in which business is vulnerable because the problem is one which it has created itself, where the objective of the struggle is to anticipate or shape the pattern of inevitable legislation, where the stakes are so high that the motivation is essentially one of self-preservation, and in consequence, where the corporate response may no longer be fairly regarded as voluntary.

Because business response no longer reflects relative freedom of choice, business has, for the first time, been obligated to make major expenditures in an area of corporate responsibility. Pollution control costs have emerged as a substantial item in the capital budget, unlike efforts in other social areas which have never had any real impact on earnings per share. It has been estimated that industry is spending from $1.5 to $3 billion a year on air and water pollution abatement.[19] For example, air and water pollution abatement equipment in the new Union Oil Company of California refinery near Chicago cost $37,000,000, or 18½% of the total cost of $200,000,000; Sun Oil Company similarly

---

[17] William C. Stolk, president, American Can Co., "Business Involvement in Social Problems: Tokenism or Leadership," in *Business and Social Progress,* Clarence C. Walton, contrib. ed., Praeger, New York, 1970, p. 71.

[18] William S. Renchard, chairman, Chemical Bank New York Trust Company, made it plain that his bank's well-publicized policy of making nonprofit loans for anti-pollution purposes in New York City was not altruistic. He pointed out: "We can't move the bank out of the city. It has to stay here." Combustion Engineering, Inc., *Progress,* Number 3 (1970), p. 6.

[19] An April 1969 survey by McGraw-Hill estimated investment expenditures of almost $1.5 billion for air and water pollution control in 1969; W. Chartener, "Changing Economic and Political Goals and Their Impact on Investments" (Address at the New School, January 31, 1970).

A more recent estimate is that more than 3 billion dollars per year is being spent on air and water pollution abatement. W. Stolk, *op. cit.*

advises that environmental control equipment will account for at least 10% of the cost of its new Puerto Rico refinery.[20] Bethlehem Steel Corporation states that 11% of its capital budget is now represented by pollution control facilities.[21]

Union Carbide Corporation reports that with pollution abatement costs running at approximately 3 to 4% of its capital budget, increased operating costs — without regard to such items as the cost of servicing the increased debt involved in the increased capital cost, or the increased depreciation charges — were reducing net income after taxes by 8¢ per share, and that this figure would increase at the rate of 2¢ per share per year.[22]

In view of the essentially involuntary nature of business response, the term "corporate social responsibility" hardly seems applicable to problems in the environmental field, whether or not it may have usefulness elsewhere. The battle which business must fight relates so much to the vitals of the enterprise that questions of "enlightened self-interest," or concern with long-range profit-making potential, or good public relations — the typical justifications for corporate social responsibility in the area of voluntary activity — are hardly appropriate to represent the hard decisions and substantial expenditures which business is being forced to make to satisfy the public demand for environmental protection.

The "Politicalization" of the Corporation

These hard decisions must be considered against a changing corporate background. As the problems of American society have grown more complex, as concern with its fundamental values has become more widespread, particularly among younger people, as the size and economic influence of the largest 500 industrial corporations have increased to the point where in 1968 they represented almost 64% of total industrial sales and 74.4% of total industrial profits,[23] an increasing politicalization of the large public American corporation seems to be taking place. Such developments as Campaign GM, the Council for Economic Priorities, angry confrontations at the annual meetings of shareholders of American Telephone, Bank of America, Boeing Aircraft, Chase Manhattan Bank, Dow Chemical, Gulf Oil, International Business Machines, Honeywell, Union Carbide, and others, the public

---

[20] Union Oil Co. of California, Third Quarter 1970 Interim Report; *Sun Shareholder Quarterly* (May 1970).

[21] Bethlehem Steel Corp., Statement on Environmental Quality (1970), p. 7.

[22] Union Carbide Corp., *Presentation Before the New York Society of Security Analysts,* March 19, 1970, p. 26.

[23] *Fortune,* May 15, 1969, p. 166.

concern of companies such as Polaroid about continuing to do business in South Africa, the demand of the Episcopal Church that General Motors cease manufacturing in South Africa, the demand of the United Church of Christ that Gulf Oil terminate its concession in Angola, and of the United Presbyterian Church that Gulf Oil exclude investments in all colonial areas [24] — all illustrate this trend. It is marked in appeals to the corporation's shareholders — not as shareholders, but as persons whose fundametal interests as citizens transcend their relatively minor interest as shareholders — as well as appeals to consumers and to the public. It is a war waged for control of public opinion. The annual shareholder meeting at this moment is merely the forum for attracting the public eye and ear.

However, it does not seem realistic to suppose that the process will stop there. The Securities and Exchange Commission is under increasing pressure to broaden the availability of the proxy solicitation machinery for utilization by "public interest" groups for these purposes, and is presently reviewing its proxy solicitation rules.[25] If SEC Rule 14a-8 is liberalized, as seems likely, and (1) the management proxy solicitation is required to include an extended range of proposals by shareholders, (2) is required to allocate a reasonable amount of space to the reasons advanced for such proposals in place of the present indefensible 100-word limitation, and (3) perhaps even to list shareholder nominees for the board as recently proposed by Campaign GM,[26] the corporate proxy solicitation process financed by corporate funds may well provide a forum for increased politicalization of the corporation, which may ultimately lead to significant changes in American corporate life. Already, it is apparent that nonprofit institutions, such as universities and churches, will provide a substantial base to mount such efforts. Church sponsored resolutions have already been presented for consideration at the 1971 annual meetings of General Motors, American Metal Climax, Inc., and Kennecott Copper Corp.[27]

---

[24] *Business Week,* Feburary 27, 1971, p. 39; *Wall Street Journal,* February 22, 1971; *N.Y. Times,* February 2, 1971; *United Church Herald,* December 1970, p. 47.

[25] Statement of Chairman Hamer H. Budge, *N.Y. Times,* November 7, 1970, p. 37.

[26] Campaign GM Round II, Proxy Statement dated November 19, 1970.

[27] See note 24; *N.Y. Times,* February 11, 1971.

At the General Motors 1970 Annual Meeting, 11 institutions of higher learning supported one or both proposals of Campaign GM; five others abstained. *Chronicle of Higher Education,* June 1, 1970, p. 2.

A number of church agencies as well as trust funds of New York City, Boston and San Francisco supported Campaign GM. *Project on Corporate Response,* Campaign GM Scorecard.

The executive council of the United Church of Christ has recently recommended that not less than 10% of unrestricted funds be placed in

Indeed, whether or not these efforts will be successful in the proxy contest itself is not critical. The critical element is that corporations will face increasing efforts in this area and that the public opinion, mobilized and intensified by such efforts, will likely force management to accept in substantial measure the objectives of such campaigns. Management may win all the proxy battles and still lose the war.

Finally, as recent articles by Professor David L. Ratner and Professor Melvin A. Eisenberg illustrate,[28] the corporate voting and proxy solicitation processes themselves may undergo fundamental changes and further contribute to the foregoing result.

New Questions Posed by the Environmental Problem

What are some of the hard questions presented to American corporations by environmental problems? Without in any way intending to propose an all-inclusive list, some of the major issues would appear to include the following:

1. Will competitive factors in the marketplace prevent individual businesses from dealing effectively with the pollution factors inherent in their operations so long as pollution abatement is a matter in which management has some significant freedom of decision?

2. To what extent will such competitive factors be reduced or eliminated as a result of the continuing intensification of public demand, or through the voluntary establishment of industry-wide standards by trade associations or similar organizations? Will such collective efforts present problems under the antitrust laws?

3. To what extent are industry-wide governmental standards, controls, and enforcement necessary or desirable?

4. Who is to pay the bill for pollution abatement?
    (a) To what extent are governmental financial incentives, such

---

"high risk and low return investments" with "maximum social impact." United Church of Christ, "Investing Church Funds for Maximum Social Impact," Report of Committee on Financial Investments, October 26, 1970, pp. 3, 51.

See statement of Senator Metcalf calling on universities to influence the racial, environmental, safety, and pricing policies of the corporations in which they own stock. *N.Y. Times*, December 28, 1970, p. 27.

[28] David L. Ratner, "The Government of Business Corporations: Critical Reflections on the Rule of 'One Share, One Vote' ", *Cornell Law Review*, 56 (1970), 1.

Melvin A. Eisenberg, "Access to the Corporate Proxy Machinery," *Harvard Law Review*, 83 (1970), 1489.

as tax credits, accelerated depreciation deductions, subsidies and the like, necessary or desirable? In other words, to what extent should taxpayers generally pay the bill?

(b) To what extent will the costs involved in pollution abatement be borne by consumers through higher prices?

(c) To what extent will such costs be absorbed internally, affect previously accepted profit margins, reduce earnings, and therefore be borne by shareholders?

5. Will environmental concern lead to governmental determination of social priorities? Will utility commissions, for example, be forced to choose between power and pollution? Will other agencies be forced to face similar decisions in other industries? In brief, will environmental concern lead to a degree of governmental economic planning not previously seen in American life?

6. Will environmental concern lead to a continuing politicalization of the American corporation through increased use of the existing proxy solicitation machinery by "public interest" groups, or through confrontations at shareholder meetings?

7. Will environmental concern lead to fundamental changes in the proxy solicitation machinery itself through changes in SEC Rule 14a-8, or through such changes in organic corporation law as involved in Professor Ratner's recent suggestion of the substitution of "one man, one vote" in place of "one share, one vote," or in the proposal for the addition of "consumer," "supplier," and "dealer" directors to the General Motors Board contained in the Campaign GM Round II Proxy Statement?

As the American society moves to solve its environmental problems, some of the answers to the foregoing questions will in time become apparent. One possibility is clear. The urgency of the problem may well lead to solutions which could have a profound influence on the future shape of American corporate life.

B   The Social Environment

19   How Business Tackles Social Problems

Business Week

The U.S. corporation's involvement in social projects is attaining maturity. When the *Business Week* Awards for Business Citizenship were established three years ago, the entire activity was so new for business that the emphasis in the entries and in the judging was on the pioneering nature of the projects undertaken by corporations. Businessmen no longer are bemused by the novel activities in which they find themselves engaged; they now concentrate their energies (and their contest entries) on performing their social tasks well.

So the winners of this year's awards are notable less for the pioneering nature of their projects than for the excellence of their execution. The winners are Dow Chemical Co., of Midland, Mich., and Hallmark Cards, Inc., of Kansas City, Mo., for improving the physical environment; International Business Machines Corp., of Armonk, N.Y., and the Colorado Economic Development Assn., of Denver, for developing human resources; and the Reverend Leon Sullivan, of Philadelphia, for exceptional leadership.

Dow incorporates antipollution systems in its operations to reduce ecological damage. Hallmark, with private capital, has embarked on a major residential-commercial development of a rundown central city area. IBM operates a manufacturing plant in Brooklyn's black ghetto to provide jobs and executive training. CEDA expedites loans to minority entrepreneurs and follows through with managerial support. The Reverend Sullivan works for black employment and other

Reprinted from the May 20, 1972 issue of *Business Week*, pp. 96–104, by special permission. Copyright © 1972 by McGraw-Hill, Inc.

interests in areas ranging from job training to a General Motors Corp. directorship.

The New Role

None of the award winners is doing anything spectacularly different from a fair number of other companies and individuals. All of the winners are doing it spectacularly better.

The relative rarity of these exceptional results speaks volumes for the dedication, perseverance, money, and intelligence required to achieve success in corporate social service. More significantly, the hundreds of similar attempts testify to the widespread acceptance of the principle underlying them. In 1972, corporate social responsibility is no longer unique, startling, or, in most cases, controversial. Social responsibility has become part of the business of business.

The evidence that businessmen have accepted a new role is all around. A shoe company runs a daycare center for children of its employees, a bank issues an admittedly risky $5.4-million loan to enable a Chicano organization to construct low-cost housing, a mining company landscapes areas scarred by its operations, a controls manufacturer conducts an educational program on drug abuse, scores of companies provide seed money to minority suppliers.

In this swelling chorus of good works by business, the winners of the business citizenship awards are in the first row. The reasons are reported in the following Special Report.

For Improving the Physical Environment

Lifting the face of Kansas City

More than 15 years ago, Joyce C. Hall, founder and board chairman of Hallmark Cards, Inc., looked around at the run-down neighborhood around his headquarters building in Kansas City, Mo., and declared: "Something should be done with this area."

These days, something is being done. Hallmark is now completing the first buildings of its $200-million, 85-acre major office-residential development, called Crown Center. Carefully planned and designed by top-flight professionals, Crown Center is a dramatic urban project that will have a far-reaching impact on Kansas City's downtown. It also represents a rare act of faith by a large corporation in the future of the city.

When fully completed in 1983, Crown Center will add some 50 new buildings to the Kansas City skyline. These will include office buildings containing 1-million sq. ft. of space, a 750-room hotel, two motor inns, several movie theaters, a legitimate theater, shops, underground parking space for 7,000 cars, and — making the Center more than simply a day time commercial project — some 2,400 residential apartments. As befits a design-conscious company, Hallmark has made sure that the project was planned and designed as a single development, spaciously landscaped and admirably set into the hilly terrain. Nathan Stark, chairman of the Crown Center Redevelopment Corp., says: "What we're going to get here is a real mix of people. We're building a life-style that people like and want."

Genesis Crown Center is situated about 12 blocks from Kansas City's present downtown in an area of warehouses, clumps of retailers, small eating places, and honky-tonk bars. Once Hall decided to do something about it, he realized that only a large-scale project would stand a chance of reversing the decline. Over the next few years, he began buying up parcels of land, running market studies, and bringing in architects and land planners. Groundbreaking finally took place in 1968. Near completion are a 2,500-car underground garage, plus five 7-story office buildings designed by Edward Larrabee Barnes, who is also the coordinating architect for the project.

Crown Center is being financed privately, and no federal urban renewal is involved. But Hallmark did take advantage of Missouri's own land redevelopment laws, which offer the project significant tax abatements on the buildings.

After the announcement that Crown Center would be built, property owners in the neighborhood were slow to accept its reality. But steel and cement began to convince them, and now values are on their way up. There are other economic stirrings. Banks are moving into the neighborhod. Crown Center helped bring plans to a head for a $36-million medical complex on a site just east of the project. Businessmen who were considering a move to the suburbs are reconsidering. Says Stark: "The attraction of moving an office to the suburbs is diminishing."

Impact Although Crown Center officials insist that their project is not competitive with the older downtown, it is luring away some companies. For example, Waddell & Reed, Inc., a mutual fund management company, has moved into Crown Center from downtown. But Stark argues that the long-range impact of Crown Center will help downtown. "Kansas City population is projected to be in excess of 2-million people by 1985," he says. "For such a large city, we've got to have a really solid and thriving downtown core, and in order to have that, we must have people living around it."

People not associated with Crown Center agree. Joseph Shaughnessy, an architect and councilman-at-large, lives in an area called Westport, to the south of the center. "It has lots of old-town character," he says. "I see it developing as a low-density residential area. Crown Center has already had a big impact on Westport."

Crown Center should also have a healthy impact on the area to the north, locally called the "corridor," that separates it from the old downtown. Largely commercial, the corridor has remained static over the years.

Harold Oppenheimer, chairman of Oppenheimer Industries, Inc., thought to be the corridor's largest landholder, is "highly enthusiastic" about Crown Center. "It is changing the thinking of the whole community," he explains. "There is virtually no residential slum between the Center and the business district.

Crown Center is not the only large-scale construction project under way in Kansas City these days. A $212-million airport, 20 minutes from the central business district, will open this year. And a $64-million sports complex, consisting of twin stadiums, is nearing completion. But Crown Center offers the best chance to bring true urbanity to the central city.

For Improving the Physical Environment

Where pollution control pays off

To hear most businessmen tell it, purging pollution is a costly task that will eat up capital investment funds and erode profits. Out in Midland, Mich., this attitude is greeted with polite smiles. For Dow Chemical Co., *mirabile dictu,* is managing to offset completely the costs of its ambitious pollution-control program.

In Dow's view, pollution is a wasted resource — valuable material dumped into the air and water or fed into costly treatment plants. The company is out to eliminate pollution at the source, by changing production processes and by recycling waste streams for further processing. So far, Dow has recovered enough valuable chemicals and boosted its process efficiencies so much that its abatement program is more than paying its own way.

Last year Dow invested $20-million in pollution control equipment; at a 9% depreciation rate the annualized capital cost came to $1.8-million. In addition, Dow spent $10.5-million to run abatement equipment, thus raising its environmental cleanup tab to $12.3-million. "We recovered at least that much," says Chet Otis, director of Dow's two and a half-year-old ecology council.

Retrieving chemicals Two examples underscore Dow's approach. At Midland, Dow is erecting 28 cooling towers, which will reduce by half the heat load added to the Tittabawassee, a small river that snakes through Dow's huge chemical complex. Though the towers cost $7.2-million, they will more than pay for themselves by enabling Dow to reduce corrosion and cut its water intake from the river by 100-million gal. daily. Technicians also surveyed all 4,552 air vents at

Midland, then equipped each with additional filters, condensers, and charcoal absorption devices that stem pollution and recover chemicals.

In all, Dow's Midland division has saved chemicals worth more than $6-million in the last three years. And since 1969 it has trimmed the amount of waste flowing to its treatment plants by 35% — a further saving. Perhaps more important, Dow is one of the first chemical companies to have built "zero discharge" plants that completely recycle waste.

"Dow has shown great sensitivity to environmental needs," says Spenser Havlick, conservationist at the University of Michigan. Adds Howard Brown, of the Manufacturing Chemists' Assn., "In water treatment, Dow is outstanding in the industry."

Dow's approach stems from the company's unusual circumstances in Midland. Started there in 1897, the sprawling complex now produces one of the industry's most diverse arrays of chemicals: some 500 product families ranging from consumer goods, such as Saran Wrap, to tongue-twisting industrial chemicals like Isopropylidenediphenol. Yet unlike the large complexes on the Houston Ship Channel or the Gulf Coast, Midland has only the tiny Tittabawassee to assimilate pollutants. By the 1960s, Dow had devoted 400 acres to pollution control, and Dow men joked that "the outhouse was getting bigger than the house." They soon realized that the problems of a big plant on a small river would never be solved by treatment plants alone — not without putting Midland at a competitive disadvantage vis-a-vis Texas-based producers.

Competition's spur In short, Dow simply had to find ways to offset abatement costs, and that meant critical examination of every process. Since Dow was already one of the most efficient chemical companies, the task was a little like using the squeal of the pig. Dow set up its high-level ecology council, with 24 sub-councils to cover every product line. Ground rules were simple: Decentralize pollution responsibility to achieve building-to-building accountability, and delay capital spending until pollution problems were identified and solutions designed. In addition, Dow set up a special laboratory to study waste prevention, established a panel to test new industrial products for environmental hazards, and required all researchers to assess the environmental impact of their products.

For all its efforts, Dow is not yet out of the ranks of corporate polluters. The company will not eliminate serious air pollution from its power plants in Midland until a nuclear plant is completed in the mid-1970s. And Dow has been indicted for discharging mercury from a chlorine plant in Canada. Dow has since cut the discharge sharply, and is phasing out the mercury process entirely.

For now, Dow is clearly on the right track, and its experience offers encouraging evidence that well-managed companies can abate pollution at minimum cost — or perhaps even earn a buck in the process. Says Dow Chairman Carl A. Gerstacker, "There's a profit opportunity in pollution prevention that we have only just begun to realize."

For Exceptional Leadership

A new kind of corporate director

At his first few General Motors board meetings, says the Reverend Leon H. Sullivan, everybody was wary: "I was looking at them, and they were looking at me." That was last year, after the Reverend Sullivan had become the first black director of the world's largest corporation. Today, the time for two-way appraisal is over, and Sullivan now is quick to praise his fellow board members. "I have been impressed by the developing commitment of the men on the board to human values," he says. "They listen and are responsive to my talking."

As a Baptist minister, Sullivan has a talent for talking, and he admits to doing quite a lot of it. But his talk generally has a purpose. Over the past year, he has exposed the GM board to an ebullience, drive, and persuasiveness that have made him probably the country's leading worker for black economic progress.

It is a role that has not always gained him popularity or the ear of important businessmen. Back in the 1950s, when he was leading boycotts against Philadelphia companies to force them to hire blacks, businessmen "thought I had horns," he recalls. But gradually, the key concept behind his efforts to help blacks began to emerge. That concept — self-help — is one with which most businessmen agree.

Contagious idea The institution that best embodies this approach, and represents Sullivan's most significant contribution to black economic improvement, is the Opportunities Industrialization Center, which he founded in Philadelphia in 1964. From that city, OICs spread widely. They are operating in 105 cities today, compared with 90 a year ago.

OICs combine intensive job training with strong doses of self-confidence and self-reliance. Typically, the trainees start with so-called "feeder" courses covering some basic skills, such as writing and arithmetic, and even consumer education and minority history. No set period of time is required for these courses and the emphasis is on individual needs. From these courses, the trainee moves into the skills program. He can choose from some 20 vocational skills.

Nationally, OICs aim at training some 27,000 people a year, and Sullivan takes pride in pointing out these include whites as well as blacks. They have placed an average of 70% of their graduates in jobs.

In Philadelphia, for example, OICs have placed just under 12,000 people in jobs since 1964. These graduates have a combined payroll, OIC estimates, of some $70-million a year.

Sullivan complains that the OICs are still operating "on a shoe-string." His budget this year will run about $40-million, some $32-million in grants from such organizations as the Dept. of Health, Education and Welfare and the Office of Economic Opportunity, the rest from private companies. Even so, Sullivan points out, OICs have 50,000 people on waiting lists for training.

To drum up support and other help, Sullivan a few years ago put together a 25-man national industrial advisory council. Today, it is headed by former Chase Manhattan Bank Chairman George Champion. Sullivan singles him out for praise as well as such men as Thomas McCabe, former head of Scott Paper Co., Paul Austin of Coca-Cola, and Virgil Day of General Electric.

Sharp aim In addition to the OICs, Sullivan, with the help of his church in Philadelphia, found time to launch several businesses, two manufacturing enterprises, a shopping center called Progress Plaza.

This was the background Sullivan brought to GM, when former chairman James M. Roche sought him out for board membership in January, 1971.

Once on the board, Sullivan developed a set of goals to upgrade GM's efforts to help blacks. Today he calls these efforts, "on target." Some achievements:

Dealerships A year ago, GM had a dozen or so black dealers, many of whom were in financial trouble. Today, reports Sullivan, "We have 18 black dealerships with three more upcoming in the next few months." Sullivan says he and his OIC people have met with all of GM's zone managers. He hopes that GM will eventually open a black dealership in each of the zones. He persuaded GM to open a "model dealership" in Philadelphia, where he can keep on top of how blacks are trained.

Training Sullivan points out that few blacks had attended the GM Institute. This year 100 blacks will be graduated from it, and that number will rise to 250 next year. Further, the institute now has 17 black teachers. Sullivan helped recruit 25 men now receiving training there in all phases of dealer operation.

Upgrading GM now has around 2,000 blacks in "salaried" jobs, according to Sullivan.

Black business GM has deposited some $5-million in black banks around the country and has placed $250-million in reinsurance business with black insurance companies. The corporation is also helping many black enterprises to develop products for sale to GM.

Sullivan is pleased with GM Chairman Richard C. Gerstenberg for making a film to be shown throughout GM strongly condemning discrimination within the company. "He is a new kind of industrial leader that I didn't expect to find at the world's largest industrial corporation."

It is clear, too, that GM is finding Sullivan a new kind of director.

For Developing Human Resources

Aid for minority businesses

In a business society, encouraging minority group members to become businessmen seems like a logical way to help them achieve an equal status in the community. Give them low-interest loans to start their own companies and you give them a running start toward success.

That's the theory. In practice, it has not always worked out that way. Minority businessmen tend to present loan proposals unacceptable to banks under the most relaxed credit rules. Banks tend to misunderstand the minority entrepreneur's needs. Where loans are granted, inexperience frequently leads to business failure, making the banks even warier of future loans. Despite increasing pressure on the Small Business Administration to step up its loan program to minority businessmen and despite widespread efforts in the private sector, the campaign to aid minority business has produced mostly disappointment.

An exception In Denver, there is a conspicuous exception. The Colorado Economic Development Assn. has helped to get financial aid totaling more than $15-million for more than 500 minority businessmen, a record unapproached by any similar group in the country. Its loans have a default rate of less than 10%, compared with an SBA rate of 15%, and the SBA figure is for loans to both minority and nonminority businessmen. The CEDA has backed a $2,000 janitorial service and a multimillion-dollar real estate project. On its list are a rifle range, a trucking firm, and a lavishly assorted selection of other businesses — all run by minority entrepreneurs, all successful by the criteria applied to the "majority" business world.

The organization scores as high on the social scale as on the financial one. Directed by a Chicago accountant, Edward Lucero, CEDA has steered clear of antagonisms both within the Mexican American community and between Chicano and black groups. CEDA conducts feasibility studies for the Chicano who wants to open a corner *bodega* (grocery) and also for Rudolfo (Corky) Gonzales, who plans a cooperative *mercado* (market) as part of his anti-gringo Crusade for Justice. Lucero's top assistants are black, CEDA routinely packages loan proposals for black entrepreneurs, and the local NAACP calls on CEDA when it can use technical assistance.

Along the way, CEDA has eased relations between Denver's minority and majority groups, if only because now they have done business together. It cannot be coincidence that the Chamber of Commerce's No. 1 project is low-income housing for minorities.

Low profile The only scale on which CEDA rests lightly is the one that weighs public commotion. The organization cultivates so low a profile that no one is even sure how it started — whether it was first proposed by Lucero, a former Colorado National Bank trust officer, Office of Economic Opportunity official, and Touche Ross & Co. employee, or by Bruce M. Rockwell, president of Colorado National. Neither man claims credit, and no one else remembers.

In any case, CEDA opened shop in April, 1969, with $35,000 from the Colorado National Bank and Denver's First National Bank and $25,000 from the SBA. Its current working capital of $215,000 comes from four banks, the SBA, the Economic Development Administration, the Ford Foundation, and clients' fees. Judged by the funding levels of similar groups, each CEDA dollar does the work of six or seven.

The secret appears to lie in the prosaic word, "professionalism." Before the applicant so much as roughs out his loan application, he is urged to attend Lucero's course on business problems at the University of Colorado — and 95% do. Five weeks of immersion in accounting, marketing, advertising, taxes, and related matters generally convinced half the students that business is not for them. Inevitably, the survivors return to CEDA with a better idea of what lies before them.

Teamwork From there on in, a client relationship prevails. Community involvement is important to many social projects, CEDA believes, but not here. No outsider has a voice in decisionmaking, both entrepreneur and bank official can count on strict confidentiality, and CEDA helps plan the business and package the loan proposal. If the loan is granted, CEDA provides managerial aid during the early difficult period — a reassuring arrangement for both inexperienced entrepreneur and gun-shy banker.

It seems reassuring also to government officials eager to improve their record in promoting minority enterprise. SBA recently formed its first Chicano MESBIC (Minority Enterprise Small Business Investment Corp.), La Raza Investment Corp. of Phoenix — to be managed from Denver by CEDA.

For Developing Human Resources
It kept the faith in a ghetto

The Bedford-Stuyvesant neighborhood of Brooklyn is the nation's largest ghetto, with an unemployment rate of 17% and — in sheer numbers — probably the largest concentration of "hard-core unemployed" in the U. S. In April, 1968, International Business Machines Corp. decided to locate a plant there for three purposes: to manufacture and recondition connector cables for computers, to create jobs and opportunities for a population so clearly in need of them, and — by its example — to attract other large companies to Bedford-Stuyvesant in the hope of achieving a significant impact on the community economy.

So far, IBM has failed signally in its third aim. The rehabilitated warehouse in which 400 employees (95% black or Puerto Rican) produce cables and other IBM supplies remains a lonely industrial outpost amid the urban decay. But it has succeeded solidly in its first two aims. After a financially disastrous beginning, the Bed-Stuy facility became profitable in early 1970, and it is now competitive with the other six facilities in the company's Systems Manufacturing Div. It has also created jobs for far more residents than the employees currently on the payroll. Increasing numbers of IBM-trained workers have found jobs with other companies or moved into jobs at other IBM facilities. Black manager Hal Leiteau (who heads a supervisory staff that is 75% black or Puerto Rican) notes wryly that other IBM plants compete for his aides. Despite the disadvantages inherent in a plant operating on seven floors with an inexperienced work force, IBM's Bed-Stuy facility has proved that workers branded as unemployable can be hired, trained, and upgraded productively and profitably.

As a fringe benefit, neighborhood businesses profit from the company policy of buying supplies within the community — $250,000 worth in 1971.

Some variations None of this came easy. The plant's original daily absenteeism rate was 12%. It is now 6%. Unfavorable turnover (a category that excludes such happy circumstances as leaving for a better job) originally reached 18%. The 1971 rate was 6%, and the projection for 1972 is 3%. This is disappointing compared with IBM's companywide rate of less than 1%, but sensational contrasted to neighboring Bed-Stuy rates, which run as high as 50% a year.

So what did IBM do right? The company says only that it followed the practices in effect in all its plants, intensifying and modifying some in ways appropriate to the community. The modifications worked like this:

All IBM plants offer a variety of educational programs, such as in-plant job training, tuition refund programs, and courses on company premises after working hours. But at Bed-Stuy, education staffers sought out prospective students rather than waiting for applications.

All IBM facilities have medical departments. But the Bed-Stuy department is exceptionally large relative to the plant's size. And its staff, aware of the shortage of neighborhood doctors and a man's natural reluctance to sit around clinic waiting rooms, frequently provides medication instead of directing the sick worker to his own doctor.

Above all, management recognized early that workers unaccustomed to the discipline of a work environment were unlikely to accept dead-end jobs. The Bed-Stuy facility has added at least one new product line every year, each requiring more skill than its predecessor.

Proud employees The increased costs of training, met without government subsidy, are well worth it, Leiteau says. The new products not only open up avenues for promotion and higher pay, but give workers the stimulation and flexibility that will keep them on the job. "Management has got to abandon the idea that you bring in a guy and say, 'Here's a job flicking chickens,' or whatever it is, and then you forget about him," Leiteau says.

Business Week's Manual for Social Action[1]

It is a rare executive these days who does not talk about the social responsibility of corporations and what part it plays in his company's operations. But ask him how to run a corporate responsibility program and you are likely to get a series of throat-clearings and generalities.

The trouble is, a management reacts to the condition in which its own corporation must exist. Sometimes you cannot even get top executives to agree on what society expects of them. Surveying businessmen across the country over a period of months, *Business Week* has come up with its own manual for corporate social performance:

Don't argue over goals Henry Ford II last week told Ford Motor Co. shareholders: "I believe that the social responsibility of the corporation today is fundamentally the same as it has always been: to earn profits for shareholders by serving consumer wants with maximum efficiency. This is not the whole of the matter, but it is the heart of the matter."

General Electric Co. Chairman Fred J. Borch, addressing himself to the country's social concerns, has taken a different view: "It has become increasingly apparent that a company that walks with the giant strides of GE is going to have to walk on two strong legs. One leg cannot be shorter or weaker than the other without our progress being impeded."

The Bank of America, which has been through boycotts, and

---

bombing of its branches, skips the metaphors and says simply: "The corporation, by virtue of its own enlightened self-interest, the conscience of its officers, and expectations of the public, has a role to play in solving contemporary ills. Profits are and must continue to be the central concern of any responsible enterprise. . . . But in the long pull, nobody can expect to make profits — or have any meaningful use for profits — if our entire society is wracked by tensions."

Be sure the top man is committed The pragmatic truth that the chief executive makes or breaks a company's corporate responsibility effort turns out to be the most critical point of all. One or two speeches by the chairman on the topic is not enough. Assigning the company public relations department to the task, without the accompanying influence only a top man can give, will insure a token effort. To create an "urban affairs" department with no clout is a sure prescription for failure. It is only when the word gets out that "the chief" is serious that the employees will get serious.

"Whatever a company does or does not do," says Albert F. Watters, vice-president of corporate affairs at Allied Chemical Corp., "can be linked to the length and breadth of the shadow of the top man."

California's First Western Bank & Trust Co. is an example. Says Stafford R. Grady, president and chairman: "Our branch managers know that things like hiring minorities are expected. If I hear they are not following through, I ask why. The word travels fast that the old man is behind something, and they'd better go along with it. It's incredible how much persuasive power I have if I want to argue."

Don't expect clear cost figures The costs of corporate responsibility are so obscure that most top executives figure that if expenditures are not made now, the costs will be much higher over the long term. "Superficial number counting won't do it," says David Hertz, a McKinsey & Co. partner. "We really don't know what we are measuring against. It is difficult enough to audit the effectiveness of a management in straightforward profit making."

First Western's Grady contends that "in the long run, you just get compensated in some way." He speaks from experience. He refused to close the bank's Watts branch, the only bank in the Los Angeles ghetto, when all other business fled after the riot — even though "banks don't make money by cashing welfare checks and handling the food stamp program." But now the branch is making money. "You take your licks, but sooner or later, doing a service in the community will give you a profitable branch."

Forget about structure "Once you institutionalize social action, you frustrate the effort and the people involved," says Fletcher L. Byrom, chairman of Koppers Co., Inc. "When you make an organization chart for something like this, you tend to set the structure in concrete and you can't adapt."

Byrom's theory is shared by most corporate chief executives when social responsibility is considered in its total concept. But there are components of it which come under federal, state, and local law such as pollution abatement, minority hiring, occupational health and safety. So, for these, you need some in-house unit to compute the reports that government agencies demand and to insure that the company is in compliance with the laws.

Allied Chemical, for example, has set up an Environmental Services Dept. with jurisdiction over air and water pollution control, occupational health, safety and loss prevention, and product safety. Headed by a general manager who reports directly to Frederick L. Bissinger, the company's president and chief operating officer, the department has four technical specialists, each in charge of one of the four categories. They work with Allied divisions and plants in each of the areas, monitoring progress and providing counsel and technical assistance.

Less easy to organize is a management's decision to "do something" about social problems. By nature, such efforts are less formal even though they may have the trappings and titles of more conventional functions. Bank of America, for example, has created what it calls a "new portfolio" within its top operating group, the 11-member managing committee, to deal with four areas it feels merit "intensified bank action" — housing, minorities, environment, and social unrest. One of the bank's executive vice-presidents, G. Robert Truex, Jr., has the full-time assignment to run what is called the Social Policy Committee. He reports to BOA President and Chief Executive A. W. Clausen.

Truex operates, says the BOA, "in a manner comparable to the executive officer responsible for any other of the major policy functions within the bank, such as loans, branch administration, international banking, or money policy." Thus Truex, instead of worrying about a change in the interest rate, has duties which include negotiating with leaders of a student-organized boycott — a task that was one of his first after taking his new job last February.

Be concerned about credibility The familiar plaint by executives that the public does not understand or appreciate the problems business faces in meeting social demands will not sell in today's era of activism. Just as the Securities & Exchange Commission is requiring fuller disclosure on financial matters, society is doing the same thing on corporate responsibility. In the process, both business and its critics are learning something. As in any bargaining situation, you cannot get an agreement unless you communicate.

In a six-page "citizenship" section of its 1971 annual report,

Allied Chemical exhibited a candor seldom found in such documents. "As you might expect," Allied told its shareholders, "we have heard some cheers for our pollution control work well done. And we have felt some brickbats over the jobs still undone." The ensuing description of what the company had done took on a credibility because of this admission that more remained to be done.

General Motors Corp. earlier this year held a seminar on its efforts to curb auto pollution, aid minorities and improve auto safety for representatives of its large institutional investors including universities and foundations. Then GM went a step further. It printed the proceedings of the sessions in a 75-page booklet and distributed it to shareholders.

Get all employees involved There was a time when an employee felt he had satisfied top management's commitment to social responsibility when he contributed to the United Fund. Today, in most corporations, this is just the first step. Managements are now encouraging employees to volunteer for work in the community, and in many instances on company time. In some companies, this involvement may take the form of a paid sabbatical. In others, it may be a half-day a week where an employee works with a local social agency or ghetto group.

Last year, when Koppers hired a graduate of the University of Pittsburgh's graduate school of social work, he checked the various community social agencies to see which ones needed volunteer workers. He then catalogued the needs of the various organizations and compiled an audio-visual presentation for employees. Now, some 100 Koppers employees from clerk-typists to middle managers are working with local groups.

Not only is the commitment to social problems widespread throughout the company because of the informal program, but Koppers' management views it as a morale booster. Says Arthur W. Cowles, vice-president for human resources: "Jobs have a way of verticalizing, tending to move into routine performance areas somewhat demeaning to human existence. We are trying to enlarge employee dimensions. It's a form of job enrichment."

Get the directors involved Winning the endorsement of the board of directors for a company's corporate responsibility effort is not only necessary, it is essential. A tactic used by such companies as GM and Mead Corp. is to create a public policy committee composed of outside directors. At Mead, for example, three outside directors are members of a Social Involvement Committee along with three members drawn from junior management. This way, the directors get a first-hand report on how the company is responding to social needs and the employees have a direct communication link with the board.

Koppers has added a different twist. Last March, Byrom set up two committees of four outside directors each. One is the environment committee, the other is the human resources committee. The plan is to have the committees sit for a briefing with Koppers employees at least twice a year. Ideally, the directors will force the management and the employees to come up with answers on corporate responsibility and will be in a position to judge whether or not enough is being done. "There is also the chance," says Byrom, "that our people will be spurred to do a better job if they know they'll have to face the directors and report on what they have accomplished and are planning."

Give seed money along with advice Aid to minority-owned business is one of the biggest areas of today's corporate service. It can range from depositing funds in minority-run banks to sponsorship of MESBICs (Minority Enterprise Small Business Companies). Often, it involves basic business consulting and financial assistance, such as the help Eaton Corp. gave a black-owned Cleveland company, the American Dream Soap Co.

One of the problems was a lack of capital. Eaton paid the company's rent for a year. The struggling soap maker's fortunes improved enough in the second year so that it could pay the rent. But then it needed more volume. Eaton sent one of its salesmen to the company, and with his help, American Dream increased volume and broke even the second year.

Eaton, like other Cleveland companies, has also counseled black businessmen on how to bid for contracts. Many of the aspiring entrepreneurs had no cost figures available or experience in such transactions. They were underbidding and winding up losing money. "We used people in our industrial engineering and marketing department to help people to bid. Then we helped open some doors where they could go and bid," says the Eaton spokesman.

Don't make the program a maverick When the corporate conscience was awakened on the social responsibility issue, most managements immediately put a high priority on responding to the need. But the new function, despite attempts to fold it into the regular organization, remained outside the mainstream. Now, however, it is gradually being melded into a company's activities.

One company where this is happening is Coca-Cola Co. Today Coca-Cola does not regard its expenditure of $1.5-million on housing, education, and health services for migrant field workers in Florida as part of its corporate responsibility program. The migrant labor project is only two years old and was ordered by Chairman J. Paul Austin after reports of squalid living conditions among migrant workers led to a personal investigation by J. Lucian Smith, then president of Coca-Cola's food division. At the time, it was widely cited as an example of corporate responsibility.

"These are things we have to do as an employer," says William Pruitt, Coca-Cola's assistant vice-president. That remark illustrates how the concepts of corporate responsibility have changed and developed over the past few years.

20 Pragmatic Limits on Business Involvement

William J. Ahfeld

Social responsibility is in vogue. Theodore Levitt observes: "Pronouncements issue forth so abundantly from the corporations it's hard for one to get a decent play in the press. Everybody is in on the act, and nearly all of them actually mean what they say!"

My basic point is there are some pragmatic limitations on business involvement in social probems. Recognizing these practical boundaries will surely help public relations people do a more effective job — and permit business to develop a clearer rationale — rather than pretending such limits do not exist.

On my list the first need is to clean up the rationale. To illustrate one reason why, let me quote Alfred C. Neal, president of the Committee for Economic Development. He warns:

> . . . when corporate executives can't rationalize something well enough to delegate it, to make it part of the ongoing, workaday business of the company, not a great deal is going to happen.

And as a result he complains:

Reprinted with permission from *Public Relations Journal,* May 1971, pp. 6–9.

Those levels of company management that hold the responsibility for actually managing the work — who operate where the action is — have not really become involved in the search for solutions to social ills.

I agree with Mr. Neal. To get real action some hard-nosed questions *have* to be asked and answered with something more compelling than the rhetoric borrowed from philanthropy or the viewpoint of the long, longer, and longest range. Hear the farsighted Henry Ford II:

> There is no longer anything to reconcile — if there ever was — between social conscience and the profit motive. . . . It seems clear to me that improving the quality of society — investing in better employees and customers for tomorrow — is nothing more than another step in the evolutionary process of taking a more farsighted view of return on investment.

Non-Economic Factors

Ah, but how farsighted? How much pressure on earnings can a "socially conscious" company accept and stay solvent? At what point might there be a disclosure problem — i.e., a legal requirement to disclose to stockholders the extent to which operations are being affected by non-economic considerations? (A non-economic consideration would be one with a high opportunity cost and a low or non-competitive return relative to other investment.)

I doubt, also, that the rationale for philanthropy really applies to business involvement in social problems:

First, the corporate contribution program is ordinarily an option of top management limited to specific areas which can be cut back readily when profits are under pressure.

Second, donations usually do not affect the operations of the company since they do not require managers to crank non-economic considerations into *their* "regular" business decisions; e.g., hiring, product mix, plant locations, capital expenditures, etc.

Third, amounts are normally small, averaging less than one per cent of pre-tax earnings, according to a recent study by C. W. Shaner & Company.

Of the arguments used to support business involvement in social problems, one of the oldest is the idea that business *must* siphon off part of its profits as a kind of premium on an insurance policy. By paying out so much to help cure social ills, business insures a healthy environment in which businessmen can continue to make profits over the long pull.

Another and related argument is that *action* on social problems is something the public expects. Business is supposed to do it as a response to this expectation, which is now greater than ever, and in fear of the pressure of public opinion. If a company does not, it gets a bad reputation; loses sales and investor confidence; and could conceivably have its corporate charter revoked by the state in response to irate voters.

Positive Consequences

On the other hand, if business discharges its social responsibility well and faithfully — if it digs in and helps supply answers to social issues — the gain is a measure of *"goodwill,"* — a good image. As a positive consequence people will love the company, want to do business with it, buy its stock and help it as bad times occur.

I haven't done these arguments strict justice by presenting them in shorthand terms. Certainly they have some validity and, doctored up with the latest "in" phrases used in the *Harvard Business Review,* they can even be useful. But they leave me uneasy and unsatisfied as a philosophy for business involvement in social problems.

There should be a firmer foundation — and, as observed earlier, we need to recognize some pragmatic limitations. Without this understanding of the parameters, business could barge in on social problems with programs and actions that might be well-intentioned but ineffective, at best, and even counter-productive, as the worst consequence. Idealism can be as dangerous as ideology in meeting the problems of the human condition.

When a company takes action on a social problem there is an associated cost. It's logical to conclude that this cost must be covered at the expense of one or more of the company's stake-holders — either in a reduced dividend for shareowners; less in employees' wages or hours or higher prices for customers. Just how socially responsible is a contribution to inflation or unemployment, or a shifting of the burden to shareowners and/or wage earners?

When the public is unwilling to pay the price of social improvement, you have a much narrower choice in covering the cost of involvement. For example, General Motors developed a used-car pollution control kit and test marketed the device in the Phoenix area.

In a two-month campaign in which GM spent $50,000 to promote the kits, owners of only 528 of an eligible 334,000 pre-'68 cars decided to shell out the $20 needed to install the kit. GM estimated it cost them almost $100 for every sale made. Despite intensive promotion and much public concern over air pollution, the response was dismal.

On the other hand, it's true that business is uniquely equipped to handle those social probems the public assigns to it with an accompanying indication they are willing to pay. When there is an economic justification, business can put its capability in problem solving to work and be effective.

The problem in developing a better rationale for business involvement in social problems may be that fundamentally it is more of an individual's job than an institution's. Basically, involvement relates to an individual manager's awareness of the world around him, and his ethical recognition of responsibility to this total "surround" in which he lives and works.

Business, after all, is made up of people — people who invest, who manage and are managed. So, what we are really talking about is the responsibility of a group of individuals within a business organization.

Pragmatic Limitations

Some of the pragmatic limitations I see to business involvement in social problems include these:

1. The inherent principles and structure of business are inappropriate to solve social problems.
2. Actions taken by business are likely to be fragmented, uncoordinated and thus inefficient in terms of defining "social problems" and tackling them with any logical sense of priorities.
3. There is no scorecard. Unlike government, business hasn't got a constituency to respond to its efforts. There is no way for society to say "yes, that's good" or "no, that's not the problem."

The first limitation is structure. Business is not built to deal with social questions as, for example, our welfare system is. Business is founded on economic principles. Managers are trained to think and act — and be measured — on the basis of practical considerations that provide tangible, *economic* returns.

To a business manager the efficient allocation of resources is related to market forces of supply and demand and a competitive return on capital. There is no way for him to contemplate expenditures to benefit society in an idealistic sense unless failure to do so would lead to a loss of corporate security or opportunity that exceeded the cost.

Furthermore, the more business becomes concerned with social problems, the less it may be dedicated to the pursuit of profits. The more this happens, the less likely society will have the benefit of the most efficient use of resources which, paradoxically, produces the wherewithal that *can* be applied to the well being of people.

David P. Eastburn, president of the Federal Reserve Bank of Philadelphia, points up this basic conflict in a comparison between what he terms "social man" and "economic man." It's clear this "economic man" dwells in the business world and "social man" represents all those critics of business out there in society.

In drawing his comparison, Mr. Eastburn makes the point that "economic man" believes "self-interest in a market economy is expressed largely in monetary terms; that monetary rewards are directed by competition to the efficient and enterprising; and that the puritan ethic of hard work and self-discipline is still a major guidepost to the good life."

On the other hand, "social man" sees the good life reached by quite a different route: "He stresses people rather than things; human rather than monetary values; and freedom not to pursue one's self-interest but to realize one's true individuality by involvement in a cooperative way in solving society's problems."

Within the business structure and the category of "economic man," there is a *need* to be primarily concerned, in my judgment, with doing what business does best. When this happens it creates the *means* for people to meet economic needs. And the fact that business has met those needs very well has, ironically, made it possible for "social man" to gain a sympathetic hearing for *his* concerns about the quality of life. After all, you can talk about the "quality of life" *if* you've already accomplished the quantity of goods.

Wherewithal for Freedom

Essentially, what business has done is to provide *enough* wherewithal for a *new freedom*. By and large, this has made it possible for many people to seek higher goals, including the solution to social problems and improvement in the quality of life.

But, to repeat my conviction, business will do best by staying at the economic job it knows how to do and not by trying to run a welfare system with the principles governing a competitive economy. The principles involved are not necessarily incompatible — they are just different.

My second limitation was that whatever business elects to do about social problems cannot help but be fragmentary, on-and-off with the swing of business conditions and largely uncoordinated with the priorities established by various other private companies. With the magnitude of our set of social problems we might as well send Christmas baskets.

There are in existence now a number of wishful, vague and often splintered efforts that wouldn't be productive — in an overall sense — even if they were successful. Furthermore, if expectations are built up far beyond attainability it won't be long before the result will be castigation of business for its failure to solve social problems.

My third pragmatic limitation was the fact that the responsibility of business to become involved — and to what degree — is not measured as is the duty to investors. Businessmen haven't got a scorecard on *performance* as managers relating to social problems that is in any sense comparable to the grades they get in share of market return on net assets, earnings per share, or price/earnings ratios.

Social Accounting

There is a good deal of research — and much talk — about the development of social accounting, or a new kind of balance sheet that would fold in social as well as economic responsibility. But until this concept emerges from the present fog, let me just suggest that no one knows what a perfect balance between social and economic responsibility is for any one firm for any particular point in time.

Without a way for people to respond to business efforts on social problems, there is no democratic measure of effectiveness. And to presume that businessmen have the necessary skills to set priorities and develop programs to cure society's illnesses is like expecting a pre-med student to diagnose and prescribe for sick people.

Michael Harrington, a business critic, puts its more bluntly. He says:

> . . . whatever other qualifications they may have, businessmen are not competent to design a new civilization . . . [and] *have no democratic right to do so.*

The businessman's friend, Ted Levitt, is really worried. He says:

> The corporation *could* eventually invest itself with all-embracing duties, obligations, and finally powers — ministering to the whole man and molding him and society in the image of the corporation's narrow ambitions and its essentially unsocial needs.

I believe a company must meet its obligations to society. It must recognize that its operations touch the lives of many people who may not be employees, customers or shareowners and it should take specific actions and frame policies that are responsive to society within the company's interests, economic capabilities and pragmatic limitations.

One way to determine what action to take on problems in our society is through a grid. A series of 22 questions can help determine both the positive and adverse consequences of the company's action or inaction.

The most important question is whether or not the company contributes directly to the problem in some manner. Next, whether there is some immediacy; and finally, a set of questions to pinpoint both the plus or minus effect any action or inaction would have on those people identified as most important to company success.

The scale used, the questions and the grid are not fully developed. They represent one approach to gain perspective on what social problems the company has any business being concerned with — and which problems the company should do something about for *realistic* reasons.

For example, let us say the social problems of greatest concern to the company include:

Pollution

Consumerism

Woodlands and Timber Use

Equal Employment

Community Welfare and Leadership

Housing

Student Discontent

Urban Poverty and Welfare

The questions asked are:

Is this an issue or a problem which we either create or contribute to in the manufacturing process, in the product itself, or in a direct business or employment practice?
Is this an immediate problem area? If action is initiated or maintained, will we gain more investors? Will we be able to make economic gains or, at least, prevent economic loss?
Avoid conflict with government restrictions and/or regulations?
Have better community relations?
Have better employee relations?
Receive favorable press?
Gain recruiting benefits?
If initial action or further action is not taken will we possibly lose investors or suffer from stockholder criticism?
Suffer an economic loss?
Enhance the possibilities of further governmental restrictions?
Strain employee relations?
Be vulnerable to community criticism and/or strain existing community relations?
Suffer unfavorable press?
Suffer recruiting problems?
Is it feasible to initiate positive action?
Is there a need for an additional policy and/or mechanism to be established to solve the problem?

Is the public unaware of our role in fighting this problem?

Is it important that the overall general public find out what we are doing toward the problem's solution? Are other industries involved in solving this problem?

Could we feasibly become a leader or forerunner in expressing concern?

Answers can be based on a scale of 0 to 10.

0	5	10
No	Doubtful	Perhaps	Yes	Definitely

Our president, James W. McSwiney, has addressed himself to the problem of social responsibility for Mead.

The heart of the matter, he said, is — "Can we help solve such problems as pollution, jobs for the disadvantaged, urban decay, poverty and better education, and still make the grades we have to make in order to respond to the investor?"

In Mr. McSwiney's judgment, the court of public opinion has already decided. The answer is "yes!" What we are now doing is attempting to write some new rules of the road — how to proceed on a reasonably equitable basis in a competitive enterprise system.

While it's true that the primary business of business is to provide opportunities for people to meet their economic needs — that objective can no longer be an exclusive preoccupation. Managers have to keep in focus what is going on in the streets, in the schools, in Congress, in ghettoes, in cities and farms.

Managers need to understand that the company *must* be more concerned about the way it does business — avoiding further pollution — finding ways to protect the environment from the very technology and affluence we have helped create.

We must select resources with greater care, conserve and utilize them with maximum efficiency. And not just the land and buildings and machines and minerals, but people. We cannot afford human waste — such as that created by illogical and obsolete barriers to human progress in racism or in outmoded attitudes toward women.

While there *are* pragmatic limits that *must* be recognized — the choice is not going to be either/or — between the pursuit of profits and involvement in social problems. The two are becoming increasingly interwoven. Yet, it would be unrealistic to expect business to assume so much social responsibility that the result would be a number of firms going broke with halos around their heads.

The major social responsibility of any business firm, in my judgment, will continue to be to operate profitably and utilize efficiently the resources at its disposal. Although vitally important, other activities that relate to the use of corporate resources to solve problems will realistically be second to this purpose.

Finally, the most pragmatic limitation I can think of is the fact that we have yet to define and set down among the principles governing business some new "rules of the road" which can be applied to business decisions and a competitive enterprise system. Such rules would help business relate to social problems and to link its involvement logically to the principal business assignment: to create value through efficient use of resources.

Case

Mason Chemicals, Inc.

Early in February, 1965, U. S. Secretary of Health, Education, and Welfare Anthony Celebrezze, called for a public conference to consider the problem of water pollution in the Chicago area. The conference, called under legislative authority granted in 1948 and amended in 1956, was to convene March 2 at McCormick Place, Chicago, and run for four days.

A few days before Secretary Celebrezze's action, the U.S. Public Health Service had issued a special report stating that dangerous amounts of sewage and industrial wastes were being discharged into Lake Michigan and the Calumet River system in Indiana and Illinois. Public Health Service officials, whose concern in the matter was based on the fact that the pollution moves across state boundaries, said that the Grand Calumet River and Indiana Harbor Canal are grossly polluted, and that the southern end of Lake Michigan was becoming seriously affected by pollutants.

Lake Michigan provides the water supply for nearly five million people in Chicago, its suburbs, and the Indiana cities of Gary, Hammond, Whiting, and East Chicago. The lake also is a source of water for industrial processes and cooling purposes in dozens of major industrial plants in the area, and is used for swimming, boating, water

This material was prepared by Professor Richard W. Barsness utilizing public sources and a student report by Charles Henning. Northwestern University cases are prepared to stimulate class discussions. No judgments about the described events are intended nor should any be implied from their use here. Reprinted with permission of the author.

skiing, and fishing. The rivers and canals in the area are used primarily for shipping, but also somewhat for recreational boating.

Among the business firms called to appear at the anti-pollution conference was Mason Chemicals, Inc., a medium-sized producer of heavy industrial chemicals. Its diversified line of specialty chemicals includes those used in petroleum refining, metal processing and coating, and the production of such diverse products as iron and steel, automotive and refrigeration equipment, and insulation and building materials. Over 80% of the company's production occurs at its large plant in East Chicago, Indiana, and most of its sales are made to other industrial firms located in Indiana, Illinois, Wisconsin, Ohio and Michigan.

The firm's sales for the past five years have averaged about $120 million, and in fiscal 1965 the company had sales of $146,700,000, and a net operating profit of $17,764,000. Sales and operating profits for 1965 were both about 6% higher than in 1964. Other income (from investments, real estate, patent royalties, etc.) totaled $1,931,000. As a result of certain business deductions and special tax credits, Mason Chemicals paid only $6,919,000 in Federal and state income taxes on its total income of $19,695,000.

With a net income of $12,776,000, the company paid $4,373,000 in common share dividends (no preferred stock is outstanding), and added $8,403,000 to its retained earnings. The addition of this sum brought its retained earnings to a total of $50,834,000 at the end of fiscal 1965. The stockholders' equity in the company at the end of 1965 was approximately $90 million.

Property, plant, and equipment were valued at a cost of $120 million, less accumulated depreciation of $65 million. Annual depreciation charges have averaged about $6 million. In recent years new capital expenditures by Mason Chemicals for plant and equipment have varied greatly, but have averaged about $8 million per year. Long-term debt at the end of 1965 stood at $25 million, and is being reduced at a rate of from $3,500,000 to $4 million per year.

Federal Concern over Water Pollution

The Public Health Service report issued in February, 1965, declared that large quantities of municipal sewage and industrial wastes, "treated to varying degrees," are discharged into the area's waters. As a result, the streams are discolored, often smelly, and marked by floating debris and oil. "Along the shores of Lake Michigan, in Indiana and the southern shore in Illinois, the waters are discolored by suspended and dissolved waste materials, in sharp contrast to the pleasing appearance of the rest of Lake Michigan," the agency said.

United States Steel Corporation, Youngstown Sheet and Tube

Co., and Inland Steel Co., were cited by the report as the largest sources of waste in the river and canal, and three petroleum refineries (Cities Service Petroleum Co., Sinclair Refining Co., and Mobil Oil Co.) were listed as "lesser but still major sources of waste."

The principal sources of waste discharged directly into Lake Michigan were identified by the Public Health Service as Union Carbide Chemicals Co., American Oil Co., American Maize-Products Co., United States Steel Corporation, and Mason Chemicals, Inc.

Communities in the area, however, were equally at fault, the agency said. It cited ineffective disinfection in municipal waste disposal systems, the prevalence of combined storm-sanitary sewage systems that discharge untreated sewage during and after heavy rains, and the increasing number of small treatment plants that discharge into ditches and small streams.

The public conference called by Secretary Celebrezze involved sewage and industrial wastes from about 35 municipalities and 40 plants. Under Federal law, the participants in a water pollution conference are expected to draw up a program to improve their local situation. If this fails, then the Secretary of Health, Education, and Welfare may convene a hearing at which sworn testimony is given, following which the hearing board makes recommendations and the Secretary orders specific action. If local governments and plants still do not cooperate, then the Secretary has authority to take the matter to court.

Use of this three-step enforcement machinery, with its emphasis on giving the contributors to water pollution ample opportunity to remedy the situation voluntarily, has accelerated considerably in recent years. And Federal action seems likely to continue to grow since public concern over both air and water pollution has risen sharply in the past three years, and President Johnson has committed his Administration to work toward effective remedies. The Chicago area conference represented probably the most complex water pollution problem tackled thus far by the conference approach, and much depended, of course, on the attitude and degree of cooperation shown by the participating municipalities and companies.

Background of Mason Chemicals and the Problem of Water Pollution

The history of Mason Chemicals, Inc. in the matter of waste disposal is fairly typical of other firms in the industrial region at the south end of Lake Michigan. Prior to 1940, there were no sewage treatment facilities of any nature in this plant. The entire effluent was discharged into Lake Michigan, which the plant had access to by means of some large private sewers. In 1940, sanitary sewage facilities were made available to the plant by the East Chicago, Indiana Sanitary Board.

At that time, sanitary sewage was separated from the cooling waters that were being returned to Lake Michigan.

In 1944 an extensive six-month survey and study of all industrial wastes was initiated by the company for the following purposes:

1. to classify the pollution load of industrial wastes on the basis of individual sources
2. to determine the basic characteristics and magnitude of waste from each source
3. to determine seasonal fluctuations affecting each waste
4. to develop methods to reduce and control the strength of these wastes

On the basis of the findings obtained in this survey, Mason Chemicals, Inc. embarked on a waste abatement program which was completed in 1950. Through this program the daily plant sewer loadings to Lake Michigan were reduced from 61,148 pounds of BOD (biochemical oxygen demand, a measure of pollution) to 3,200 pounds. This was accomplished by the isolation of all waste-bearing waters, the re-use of process waters, the recovery of all solids possible, and the reduction of considerable volatile organic matter. To accomplish this reduction in pollution the company spent approximately $8 million.

In 1952 Mason Chemicals began a modernization and expansion program, the most important feature of which was the shift from a batch operation process to continuous process production of most chemicals. This change resulted in more waste waters than could be handled by the existing waste abatement program. In order to cope with the larger volume of waste waters and provide a "permanent" type system for controlling pollution, Mason Chemicals built a lagoon treatment system.

Chemical production capacity at the East Chicago plant has increased 38% since 1952, and the pollution load is currently 6,076 pounds of BOD per day. Presently some twelve million gallons of water are pumped from the lake each day and about ten million gallons are returned as cooling water. The two million gallons retained by the plant are treated in its waste abatement facilities before being discharged into the lake again. The water returned to Lake Michigan is chlorinated, and is sampled on a frequent basis seven days a week. A complete analysis is made each day of the samples taken. Capital expenditures by Mason Chemicals, Inc. for industrial waste control from 1940 through 1962 totaled approximately $14,327,000. The operating cost of the waste abatement program currently is about $1,225,000 annually.

Up to the early 1960s, the anti-pollution controls placed on firms such as Mason Chemicals were relatively lax. Only occasionally did either state or Federal authorities take action to reduce water pollution. Such action typically was in the form of setting minimum standards of waste abatement to be achieved by individual firms by a certain date, with court action to be brought against those failing to comply. A shortcoming of this approach, however, was the fact that any *relative* improvement in the quality of each gallon of industrial water returned to Lake Michigan often was more than nullified by the fact that increased production required more and more water, hence increasing the *absolute* total of pollutants.

Although Mason Chemicals, Inc. did not find it a hardship to meet such standards as government imposed in the past, the company realized early in 1965 that the "good old days" were all but past regarding water pollution, and that the firm would have to devote serious attention to shaping new policies to meet new conditions. One aspect of the new situation, of course, was the Federal Government's call for a public conference on water pollution in the Chicago area, and the increasing likelihood of extensive Federal activity in the future. A second aspect of the problem for the company was how to handle the growing volume of complaints by East Chicago residents about both the company's role in water pollution of the lake, and the objectionable odors which originate in its waste treatment facilities and pervade a considerable portion of the city.

If Mason Chemicals were forced to meet the water standards which some Federal officials apparently had in mind for Lake Michigan, the company knew that it would be faced with a difficult problem both technically and financially. The cost could easily run in the neighborhood of $25 million, and depending upon the time limit involved, such a requirement would have a profound effect on the future course of the company's business. In particular, management at Mason Chemicals had been giving serious consideration to a series of steps to modernize and expand production facilities at the East Chicago plant, and whatever position the company took in the proceedings at the Federal antipollution conference would have to be made in this light.

Mason Chemicals' Planned Expansion

The firm's desire to modernize and expand had its origin in the prosperity of the early 1960s. Sales, profits, and tax considerations were favorable, and the prolonged period of prosperity was accompanied by an expanding demand for heavy industrial chemicals, especially in the Midwest, where steel producers, auto manufacturers, and other major industrial chemical users were experiencing rapid growth.

As a well-established firm with excellent access to this market, Mason Chemicals believed it would be desirable to modernize and expand the productive capacity of its East Chicago plant by about 30% over the next five years, providing suitable financing could be arranged.

A variety of considerations precluded the issuance of additional common stock, thus any new capital investment would have to be financed by retained earnings and long-term borrowing. Depending upon the specific facilities to be included in such an expansion program, the cost was estimated at between $70 million and $85 million. These figures, when contrasted with the cost of previous major expansions in the company's history, emphasized the steady inflation which had occurred in the absolute dollar cost of expansion, but more troublesome than this observation was the fact that the cost of such major expansion would not fall evenly over the whole five-year period. The principal burden of the necessary capital expenditures would come in a twenty-month period during the third and fourth years.

Furthermore to achieve the desired increase in the capacity of the East Chicago plant, it would be necessary to utilize virtually all remaining vacant land at the site. As far as efficiency in production was concerned, this made good sense, but it presented two unattractive prospects with respect to waste abatement. First, it would prevent any additional land from being devoted to waste treatment facilities; second, it would increase the demand on existing waste treatment facilities by at least 30%, and Mason Chemicals was already being criticized by the Federal Government and local residents for the inadequacy of its waste abatement program.

The only available alternatives for boosting the capacity of the present space devoted to waste abatement were: (1) to deepen the existing settling lagoons (an expensive process which promised diminishing returns in terms of keeping pace with the increased quantity of pollutants accompanying any plant expansion); (2) the development of some entirely new technology to cope with the company's particular pollution problems. The latter certainly was not inconceivable, but even if successful, the time and money required for a technological breakthrough were quite unpredictable.

Thus the spatial demands and cost of more extensive waste treatment facilities seemed directly opposed to the spatial and financial requirements of plant modernization and expansion. And along this line, Mason Chemicals was troubled by some information concerning its strongest competitor in the heavy industrial chemical market in the Midwest.

This competitor also was known to be considering expansion to strengthen its position in the growing market, and while it had some financial problems of its own to contend with, it did not face any spatial problems, since its plant site in neighboring Hammond, Indiana, contained a substantial quantity of unused acreage. Furthermore, in reference to the forthcoming Federal anti-pollution conference, at which this firm also was to appear, one of the firm's vice-presidents said in a newspaper interview that the Public Health Service had "grossly misinterpreted the facts" about water pollution in the area, and that the company had no intention of disclosing the amounts and types of materials in its industrial wastes, since such information would aid its competitors.

Mason Chemicals recognized that to some extent their competitor was correct in suggesting that information about industrial wastes could be of assistance to a competitive firm. Set against this, however, was the fact that government officials and the public generally were likely to regard this viewpoint simply as a corporate refusal to admit guilt in the matter of water pollution, and a rejection of any responsibility to help correct the situation.

As the date for the Federal anti-pollution conference neared, the management of Mason Chemicals recognized that they faced two problems of differing magnitudes which called for some decisive action on the part of the company. The lesser of these was the problem of community relations involving the objections being raised by some residents of East Chicago. These complaints were regarded by the company as somewhat contradictory, since they criticized the company both for its contribution to water pollution in Lake Michigan, and for the strong odors which emanated from the company's efforts to treat waste in its lagoon system. Nonetheless, they could not be lightly dismissed.

The greater problem facing management concerned the position the company should take at the forthcoming anti-pollution conference. The considerations here were: what water quality standards should the company support as a satisfactory compromise between its own interests and the public interest; how much information should the company make public regarding its past and present waste abatement program; how could the firm reconcile its desire to modernize and expand its East Chicago plant with its future policy in regard to waste abatement; and finally, what type of public relations effort, if any, should accompany the decisions which the company reached in these matters?

Bibliography

Berstein, J. "Capitalism and Consumerism: Boon to Corporate Advertising." *Public Relations Journal,* 30 (November 1974), 24ff.

Boyd, T. D. "Involvement Corps Matches Corporate Employees to Social Needs." *Management Review,* June 1974, pp. 20–24.

Buehlen, O. M., and Y. K. Shetty. "Motivations for Corporate Social Action." *Academy of Management Journal,* December 1974, pp. 767–771.

Cravens, D. W., and G. E. Hills. "Consumerism: A Perspective for Business." *Business Horizons,* 13 (August 1970), 21–28.

Gordon, T. J. "America's Social Crisis: Future Perspectives." *Conference Board Record,* 8 (July 1971), 33–35.

Hill, R. "Should Firms Try To Solve Social Problems?" *International Management,* 27 (April 1972), 50–51ff.

"Is Business Cooling on City Problems?" *Business Week,* May 30, 1970, pp. 31–32.

Lerbinger, O. "Long View of the Environment." *Public Relations Journal,* 29 (May 1973), 20ff.

Mulford, R. H. "Environmental Quality — A Challenge to Business." *Michigan Business Review,* 23 (July 1971), 7–11ff.

Revelt, J. "Power of New Congressmen Bodes Well for Consumerists." *Advertising Age,* January 27, 1975, pp. 1ff.

Sawyer, G. C. "Social Issues and Social Change: Impact on Strategic Decisions." *Michigan State University Business Topics,* 21 (Summer 1973), 15–20.

Part Six
Representation for
Protest Groups

Issues in business and society have grown almost exponentially in the decade of the seventies. Not only have the issues expanded, but the numbers of protest groups represented, and the intensity of the feelings and the actions taken by these groups have also increased. For these reasons, business people must now systematically consider these protests, and receive and interpret the content and intent of their messages. Because many of the protests are of varying legitimacy, it is incumbent upon management to identify and assess them in terms of appropriate organizational responses.

A. Revolution in Rising Expectations

The new wave of activity constitutes a revolution in both protests and actions. In the first selection Henry Ford II evaluates these in "The Revolution In Public Expectations" [21]. He identifies the protests of the consumer and also that of the employee seeking improved working conditions, greater opportunities for individual self-fulfillment, and a higher quality of life. The recent changes in protest group expectations are of an explosive nature that puts additional pressure on management in its attempts to reconcile the needs of business and society. Mr. Ford cites the apparent clash between society and the stockholder, but maintains that it is not necessarily a means-or-ends conflict. He suggests instead a third alternative in which business would formulate policies as responses to changes in these protests. He would interpret these changes in protests as value changes on the part of society, and he recognizes that these new values may present profit opportunities for business, rather than barriers. Ford would identify these protests as market incentive opportunities or opportunities to governmental regulation or legislation that would further constrain business freedom. He especially emphasizes a large organization's need to change and to meet the changing needs of the individual and society. While the comments of Mr. Ford are particularly applicable to the year in which they were written, 1970, they also represent the prevailing mood of the seventies, and especially identify the extreme to which public protests may go.

The revolution in public expectation in recent years has raised a question of the extent to which change is legitimate or needed. George Kozmetsky makes an assessment of the amount of revolution in "How Much Revolution Does American Business Need?" [22]. As a rough rule-of-thumb, he suggests that the revolution is legitimate in proportion to its relevance. He does identify excessive limits such as destructive protest actions including violent means. Mr. Kozmetsky recommends a response by restructuring the nature of the capitalistic system. He suggests that capitalism undergo a second industrial revolution in which innovative management takes the place of the professional management of the past industrial revolution. He recommends a shift, or revolution, in goals for business from the purely economic to the humanistic. He calls this creative capitalism, and suggests that we will have to use technology and intellectual resources plus increasing amounts of information for decision making in the maximum development of each individual's talents and potential. In the new capitalism, profits are to be identified as a business constraint, as opposed to their normal consideration as the primary objective of business.

Both Mr. Ford and Mr. Kozmetsky recognize the need for adaptation and change in the system, its organization, and its management. Both emphasize positive orientations toward the resolution of these problems by which businesses would use its innovative managerial talents to turn problems into opportunities. What is most significant is the realization that there is a radically different type of protest with which to contend, and that it can no longer be handled by public relations, or arbitrarily by individual managers. Therefore, business must be prepared to approach revolutionary protest systematically. Corporate policies appear as a starting point, and will be considered later in this work.

It is ironic to note that while business has been beset with an array of pressures for solving the social ills in society it seems also to have failed in meeting the needs of its primary social group, the consumer. This seems incredible indeed when for the past decade business has been increasingly concerned with the new "marketing concept" in which the consumer is paramount in all of the plans and actions of the business organization. If these activities of business are overwhelmingly determined by the wants and needs of the consumers, how then could the consumer become one of the major protest groups in American society? The article "Consumerism and Marketing Management" [23] considers the status of "consumerism," which has been the label of this movement over the past decade. Results of a survey of students, unemployed women, and businessmen indicated a major consensus among all three groups on a number of aspects of consumerism. First, they agreed that the issue of consumerism in the 1970s is *very* important, and that it will most likely increase in importance in the future. They also agreed that 75 percent of the issues treated in the survey — consumer information, health and safety, repair and servicing, pricing issues, product quality, and consumer representation in government — should all be considered within the domain of consumerism. The survey somewhat surprisingly showed that the three groups also agreed that corrective actions should be moderate or even nonexistent rather than strong.

It appears that consumerism has also become institutionalized, as evidenced by the number of governmental bodies recently created to represent the consumer, and the prospect in the near future of a federal Consumer Protection Agency.

Implications of the survey findings, especially for marketing managers, include actions, programs, and organizational changes for both companies and industries. *Caveat emptor* is once again decreed dead, and replaced by an emphasis on the implementation of the marketing concept, early actions to avoid increased governmental regulations, and company programs directed toward the long-term interests of the company. The authors present examples of actions such as designation of corporate responsibility officers — departmental or organizational positions dealing with consumer problems — or committees created for the same purpose. The article recommends that problems common to an industry will be best resolved at the industry level, and at lesser costs than for individual organizations. The authors describe arbitration boards as an example of resolving irreconcilable differences between the consumer and individual companies. As would be expected, they cite Better Business Bureaus, but they also include the criticism that the BBBs are primarily used to protect business rather than the consumer, therefore calling for a reevaluation of their function and purpose.

For the business person the issue of consumerism is one that will continue to increase in scope and complexity. If this favored public of U.S. business is to become an increasing foe, what then can we say of the other publics, and the justification of their protests? The history of consumerism over the past decade should serve as a warning to business managers. Social issues are here to stay, and management must consider organizational responsibility assignments and action programs at both company and industry levels to deal with these issues in ways that are both enlightened and advantageous for business.

B. Representation On Boards Of Directors

One of the appeals of the protest groups has been for participation in the decision-making process for an organization as a whole at the top level of management through representation on the board of directors. In the selection "Who Belongs On Corporate Boards" [24] Phillip Blumberg identifies the many special interests and public appeals for directors' positions on the board. With large company power has come a higher degree of public responsibility, but also an apparent lack of accountability of the corporation to society in any direct way. Blumberg suggests that perhaps in the next 15 years the possibility exists for participation on boards of directors like that known in Germany today as codetermination. While it does not appear that employees or members of special interest groups will serve on boards in the immediate future, Blumberg does expect some type of change to allow for the presentation of their protests or their representation at boards of directors' meetings.

The corporation is a public institution presently incorporated by the states. However, the pervasive power of our major corporations could eventually cause the federal chartering or incorporation of these institutions. It is important to note that many special interest groups such as blacks, women, nonbusiness interests, and foreign interests are not able to present their legitimate complaints for consideration by boards on decisions significantly affecting these groups. It appears that the board is responsible only to itself by its control of proxy votes. Even if protest-interest groups were represented on the board, the likelihood is overwhelming that their votes would not constitute a majority. We are faced with the dilemma of lack of adequate representation of legitimate special interest groups on boards of directors.

While Mr. Blumberg does not feel that changes will be made in the near future, he does believe that problems like environmental crises will become matters of primary importance to boards, whether such issues are represented by the specific interest groups as members of a board or not.

Harold Koontz takes the position against representation on the board by special interest groups in "The Corporate Board and Special Interests" [25]. He questions the adequacy of the socially responsible actions of the corporation today, but raises a larger question of whether or not representation by special interest groups on boards of directors would be in the best interests of both the corporation and society. Professor Koontz identifies the role of the board of directors as a managerial one. He then questions that the board could actually manage the corporation if it is composed of a highly divisive group of people with conflicting interests. He feels that the overriding interests of these members would not produce the checks and balances necessary for effective management of the corporation.

While social problems are increasing and special interest groups are articulating legitimate concerns, Professor Koontz feels that the primary responsibility of the corporation is to its market function. He does recognize that this can also become excessive, as General Motors has admitted that they may have been too concerned with the business of business. On the other hand, he does not feel that the corporation will be effectively managed in the interests of either society or the stockholder by a board operating in an atmosphere of dissension.

As a means of dealing with this problem Professor Koontz would recommend that corporations develop more balanced boards, choosing more outside directors. These would include people with other than business experience who would possess expertise in problems affecting the total environment of the corporation. He would also expect a trend toward a greater focus on socially responsible actions of the board in economic, social, and technological areas. In addition, Koontz recommends that boards be kept up-to-date on special interest needs through regular presentations.

A number of outstanding U.S. corporations have already included members of minority groups such as blacks and women on their boards of directors. Whether this will be adopted by other major corporations and becomes a trend remains to be seen. But it appears inescapable that the appeal for representation will persist and that corporations will have to seek some effective resolution of the issue. It seems wise for corporations that are the targets of revolutionary protest groups or groups with legitimate appeals to insure the presentation, if not representation, of such appeals at board meetings. Corporations should have the final choice of members for the board, but unless they give adequate consideration to external interests businesses may well be pushing themselves toward further governmental determination of this representation in the form of regulations or legislation. As a specific example the Securities and Exchange Commission is already considering requirements for proxy voting on boards. If it should become possible through the SEC for these special interest groups to obtain representation then business will have lost its cause without ever making an adequate effort to propose its own resolution.

The Drew Olympic Motors case analyzes the conflict of needs in the form of corporate goals. The board of directors of the corporation is faced with three alternative strategies for the future. One would lead it toward a higher priced segment of its line, reduce its market share, and increase its prices, but the product would not meet forseeable federal pollution standards. Another alternative would increase its market share and meet exhaust emission standards, but would reduce the present management by one-third. The third alternative would entail a new design meeting emission standards with a significantly higher price, but would result in a reduction of the labor force by 40 percent. Since the company is explicitly committed to accountability to its stockholders, customers, employees, executives, and to society as a whole, it is faced with the complex decision of balancing these conflicting goals. Since the fulfillment of all goals is an unattainable ideal, the solution must reside in some equitable sharing of these goals via tradeoffs and compromises.

A Revolution in Rising Expectations

21 The Revolution in Public Expectations

Henry Ford II

We are living in truly revolutionary times and it is difficult to imagine the magnitude, much less the nature, of the changes that will take place during the next three decades.

In my judgment the most important of these changes, for business, will be those involving the relationship between business firms and the society they serve. As customers, as employes and as citizens, people are expecting many more things and much different things from business than they ever expected in the past.

The revolution in expectations has already come far enough to suggest how much farther it may go. It has already had a profound and varied impact on business costs and operations. At Ford Motor Company, for example, we are now spending half a billion dollars a year in the United States and Canada to keep up with government standards and catch up with public expectations with respect to automotive safety and air pollution.

And that's just the beginning. Leaving safety regulations aside, concern over polluted air has led to proposals in Congress and in several state legislatures to ban the internal combustion engine altogether, and surveys show that many people think this would be a good idea. Several state governments are suing the auto manufacturers to force them to install and pay for emission control devices on all cars built before these devices became standard equipment. However these particular

Reprinted with permission from *Public Relations Journal*, October 1970, pp. 16–18.

efforts turn out, it is abundantly clear that the auto industry needs to develop virtually emission-free vehicles as quickly as possible.

Another set of changes in public expectations is usually described under the heading of consumerism. For the auto industry, consumerism means, first of all, a rising tide of customer impatience with the cost and inconvenience of auto repairs and services. Dissatisfied service customers are finding a sympathetic hearing in Congress, in state legislatures and in regulatory agencies. Recently, they have found another ally — the auto insurance companies, many of which are losing money in spite of rapidly rising premiums. Again, the lesson is clear. The auto companies will have to find ways of making faster progress in reducing the need for and the cost of auto repairs and services.

Employment policies and practices are also affected by changing expectations. Our company, along with many others, has accepted a responsibility to modify employment practices in such a way as to help solve the national race crisis and help bring Negroes and other minorities into the mainstream of the economy. We are not only employing minorities in growing numbers, but are also implementing specific plans and programs to promote them as rapidly as posssible and to help them to become successful dealers and suppliers as well as successful employes.

In the past, management has taken it for granted that there would always be an adequate supply of people willing to perform a hard day's factory work in return for a good day's wages. Now we are beginning to wonder. More and more employes and potential employes are deciding that they would rather accept less pay for easier and pleasanter work. The costs of absenteeism and turnover are rising steeply, and it is increasingly difficult to maintain plant discipline.

The list of ways in which business costs and operations are affected by changing public expectations is almost endless. We are asked, among other things, to help control inflation, reduce the balance of payments deficit, contribute to the economic growth of the under-developed countries, subsidize the revival of public transit and get rid of junked cars.

There is, I believe, one basic reason why everyone expects more from us than ever before. We are the victims, primarily, of our own success. As the saying goes, "Man does not live by bread alone" — but he has to have the bread before he begins to think of other things. Modern industry has provided the bread in abundance, and so has made it possible for masses of people to think about what else life could offer.

As employes, people are wondering if they have given up too much of their time, their freedom and their dignity for the sake of the paycheck. As consumers, people are realizing that affluence can be a burden. Their cars and appliances break down, their plumbing leaks, their lawns get weedy, and getting things fixed is troublesome, expensive or even impossible. As citizens, people can see that their material possessions have been purchased at a high cost in environmental pollution — dirty air, dirty water, ugly landscape.

Modern industrial society is based on the assumption that it is both possible and desirable to go on forever providing more and more goods for more and more people. Today, that assumption is being seriously challenged. The industrial nations have come far enough down the road to affluence to recognize that more goods do not necessarily mean more happiness. They are also recognizing that more goods eventually mean more junk, and that the junk in the air, in the water and on the land could eventually make the earth unfit for human habitation.

In short, the terms of the contract between industry and society are changing. Industry has succeeded by specializing in serving one narrow segment of society's needs. We have bought labor and material and sold goods, and we have assumed that our obligations were limited to the terms of the bargain. Now we are being asked to serve a wider range of human values and to accept an obligation to members of the public with whom we have no commercial transactions. We are being asked to contribute more to the quality of life than mere quantities of goods.

Of course, these changes have been building for a long time. They are reflected in many restrictions on business activities already imposed by legislatures, regulatory agencies and the courts. Now the changes in people's values are pressing in on us more heavily than ever — and the danger of losing our business freedom is greater than ever. How much freedom business will retain in the closing decades of this century depends on the quality of management's response to the changing expectations of the public.

Whether inside business or outside, and whether friendly to business or hostile, most people think about these changes by dividing the responsibilities of business into two competing categories. On the one hand, there is the traditional responsibility of business to make a profit for the stockholders. On the other hand, there are the new responsibilities of business to the society at large. From this point of view, the question is, how much will business neglect one responsibility in order to serve the other.

Although some businessmen argue that business has learned to put social responsibility before profit, many people are convinced that business will never sacrifice enough profit to meet its social responsibilities adequately. Sometimes businessmen, myself included, have tried to reconcile their two responsibilities by arguing that business must sacrifice profit in the short run in order to help build a healthy and grateful society that will permit higher profit in the long run. But hardly anyone disputes the proposition that service to society requires at least a short run sacrifice of business profit.

Public Expectations Exploding

This point of view may have been tenable in the past. As long as public expectations with respect to the social responsibilities of business were relatively narrow and modest, business could pass muster by sacrificing only a little of its short-run earnings.

Now that public expectations are exploding in all directions, we can no longer regard profit and service to society as separate and competing goals, even in the short run. The company that sacrifices more and more short-run profit to keep up with constantly rising public expectations will soon find itself with no long-run to worry about. On the other hand, the company that seeks to conserve its profit by minimizing its response to changing expectations will soon find itself in conflict with all the publics on which its profits depend.

There is, however, a third alternative, and that is to stop thinking about the pursuit of profit and the pursuit of social values as separate and competing business goals.

They are not the same sort of things at all. One is a means and one is an end, and which is which depends on where you stand. From the standpoint of business, profit is the end and public service is the means. Business earns profit by serving public needs — but profit, not service, is the goal of business. From the standpoint of society and its members, on the other hand, service is the end and profit is the means. Society gets many of its tasks done by providing profitable market opportunities — but service, not profit, is the goal of society. Whichever way you look at it, the important thing is to stop thinking that the way to increase one is to reduce the other.

What this implies for business policy is that management should stop thinking about changing public expectations as new costs which may have to be accepted, but certainly have to be minimized. Instead, we should start thinking about changes in public values as opportunities to profit by serving new demands. We have to ask ourselves, what do people want that they didn't want before, and how can we get a competitive edge by offering them more of what they really want? We have to think more like entrepreneurs and innovators, and less like administrators and problem solvers.

What this approach implies for government policy is that the most effective way to encourage business to serve new public needs is to rely, when possible, on market incentives. When the marketplace does not automatically translate a public need into a market demand, then government action may be required to change market conditions.

The reduction of motor vehicle emissions is an excellent example. Prior to the establishment of government emission standards, there was no market for emission control features. Although many people wanted cleaner air, individual customers would not have been willing to pay the extra cost of a low emission car because the benefits would have been imperceptible unless all customers were required to pay this cost.

When the need for abatement of air pollution was recognized, the government established realistic emission standards. By doing so, the government created a market and the auto industry has moved quickly to supply it. Within a few years, hydrocarbon emissions from new cars have been reduced by more than 80 percent and carbon monoxide emissions have been cut by two-thirds. Orderly tightening of emission control standards, in step with technical advances, will lead to even greater reductions in the future.

Business is always alert to market changes caused by shifts in consumer preferences. Now we face a new phenomenon — market changes caused by legislation and regulation. In the years ahead, we shall have to be as alert to these developments as we always have been to consumer desires. Whether the will of the people is expressed directly in the market, or indirectly through government, our responsibility is to earn profits by anticipating and supplying what people want.

Changes in the values and expectations of the public are now having an impact on automobile design that goes well beyond the addition of safety and emission control features. In the past, the American auto companies have responded to public taste by placing a heavy emphasis on styling changes and by offering steadily bigger, more luxurious, more complicated, more powerful and more costly cars.

In recent years, however, it has become apparent that these qualities have lost their appeal to a growing segment of car buyers. While many people continue to prefer big, powerful, complex cars and are willing to pay more for them, many others are more interested in simple cars designed for maneuverability, durability, low maintenance and repair costs and error-free assembly. The market for cars with these qualities is large, growing and profitable. By contrast with the public's interest in cleaner air, the public interest in reliable, economical, trouble-free cars is automatically translated into market demand and therefore requires no special government action.

Challenges Faced

We at Ford are doing everything in our power to stay ahead of our competitors in this segment of the market. The Maverick, which was introduced a year and a half ago, was the first step. Since then, we have brought three additional small car lines to the North American market. Last April, we began to import the sporty but economical Capri from

Europe. More recently, we introduced the new compact Comet and the sub-compact Pinto — the smallest and lightest car produced in North America. The Pinto is the best and toughest small economy car we know how to make, and we're not going to change it until we learn how to make it better — not just better-looking.

Space will not permit an extended discussion of the challenges we face in adjusting many other aspects of our business operations to fit the changing values and expectations of our publics, but I would like to make a few brief comments.

There is much truth in the charge that large organizations — whether they are corporations or universities, or government agencies — have a built-in tendency to become impersonal, inflexible and unresponsive to the needs of individuals. The evidence is piling up, however, that people are less and less willing to tolerate the frustrations that normally arise out of their relationships with large organizations.

With growing affluence, people want more out of life than just money and goods. They want freedom and dignity and leisure. They want to be treated less impersonally, more equitably, more considerately. If those of us who manage large organizations want to get more out of the people who work for us and with us, we will have to give them more of what they want. We will have to improve our relations with people across-the-board. We will have to listen to them, pay attention to their hopes and grievances and respond promptly and fairly. We will need to be less impersonal, more flexible and more humane.

Among other things, we will certainly have to provide genuinely equal promotional opportunities not only for Negroes and other minorities but also for women, young people, and people without college degrees — all of whom are too often discriminated against in one way or another. In the future, management will have to put more emphasis on what individuals *actually* can do, and less emphasis on such formal criteria as education, experience, age and sex which are intended to predict what they *probably* can do.

All of this adds up to one simple proposition: If management wants to get the most out of people, it will have to treat them as individuals. Twenty-four years ago, in one of my first public speeches, I said that if business could learn to manage people as intelligently as it managed money and facilities American industry would enter a new era. We still have a long way to go in that direction and we have to hurry, because the people we manage are getting more and more impatient.

The changes my generation has lived through are nothing compared to the changes that will come during the closing years of this century. The company that looks upon those changes as problems to solve and as costs to cut will be overwhelmed by them.

The successful companies in the last third of the 20th Century will be the ones that look at changes in the environment as opportunities to get a jump on the competition. The successful companies will be those that anticipate what their customers, their dealers, their employes and their many other publics will want in the future, instead of giving them what they wanted in the past. The successful companies will be managed by men who regard themselves as entrepreneurs, and not merely as good administrators.

The challenge to public relations inherent in these developments is self-evident. Business can continue to play a vital role in American life only to the extent that public expectations and business performance can be brought into and kept in reasonable correspondence. To keep public expectations and business performance in step requires effective two-way communication. The basic responsibility of public relations is to communicate and interpret public expectations to management, and to communicate and interpret business performance to the public. The task is the same as it always has been, but the responsibility is heavier and the standards must be higher than ever.

22   How Much Revolution Does American Business Need?

George Kozmetsky

The amount of revolution which American business needs is directly proportional to the relevance of the revolution itself. Abraham Lincoln stated the revolutionary rights of Americans as follows:

> This country, with its institutions, belongs to the people who inhabit it. Whenever they shall grow weary of the existing

Reprinted with permission from *The Conference Board Record,* March 1971, pp. 17–20. © The Conference Board 1971.

government, they can exercise their constitutional right of amending it, or their revolutionary right to dismember or overthrow it.[1]

Today each of us is aware to varying degrees of the crises in our nation relating to Cambodia, Vietnam, the Middle East, SDS, the South, the Dow-Jones Index, the drug scene, pollution, crime, unemployment, and the earth environment. It is abundantly clear that these crises, singly or collectively, have not yet reached the proportions, in Lincoln's terms, wherein most of our fellow Americans "grow weary of the existing government." There is confidence in most of society's "revolutionary tactics" provided they are within the framework of our constitution — and despite the increasing minority who have adopted violent tactics outside the structure of law and order.

Historically we can distinguish at least three distinct types of revolutions. The *predominantly self-fulfilling* revolution is concerned with changes that are accidental and unpremeditated; the French and Russian revolutions exemplify this type. Prevailing discontent spurred the revolutions that overturned the monarchies. The *predominantly plan-fulfilling* revolution is concerned with premeditated and longer-range plans for the restructuring of the government or its various institutions. An example is the Chinese Communist revolution, which began to train cadres and utilized them to topple the power structure. The *predominantly evolutionary* process is constructive and, above all, concerned with human rights and values, such as dignity and justice. The process appears to be inevitable and prevailingly peaceful. It involves people in the choosing of the direction in which the change proceeds, and in the establishment of the particular goals required (and the priorities for the attainment of these goals). This type of revolution does not require extended bloodshed nor undue violence. I believe appropriate examples might be found in Mexico and, more particularly, Chile.

An ever-increasing number of American businessmen, especially of our generation, have found in the past decade that they were constructively involved in the second industrial revolution — a predominantly evolutionary process that is yet to be recognized by most of the academic community or a majority of progressive college students. These businessmen found that they had to envision socio-political problems beyond the traditional.

They were made aware, moreover, that many social and economic problems could not be solved merely by taking positive political actions. The higher expectations of every class of Americans were, in fact, more cultural than socio-economic. These problems also went beyond those resulting from traditional cost-price-profit pressures, wage

---

[1] From his First Inaugural Address, March 4, 1861.

demands, or appropriate government regulations. At the same time, many business leaders noted that in a number of respects their own actions as human beings — as thinking and positively acting individuals — seemed of more importance than their exalted institutional titles of President, Chairman of the Board, Chief Administrative Officer, or Vice President.

The Vanguard Managers

And who are those evolving and learning American business-men? They are not the generally recognized elite — although some may be of it. They are the college graduates of the past two decades. Many are from the comfortable middle class, though some have come from the extremes of wealth and poverty. They had been educated to think for themselves in the age before Aquarius. They are innovative managers rather than "professionals" of the new industrial state.

Such men have wrought many useful changes within their companies, dispelling the images of rigid and insensitive bureaucracy and the classic organization man. By the same token, they have evolved methods of sharing their companies' equity growth not only with their outside investors but, more importantly, with the creatively contributing employees at all levels of their organization. Equally important, many of their creative employees have gone on to establish additional corporations that reflect these more democratic business practices. Their ever-increasing number throughout our country forms the vanguard of America's technological entrepreneurs; they will play an increasingly important role in American business tomorrow.

The pity is that these practices and philosophies have yet to be made known generally. Our innovative business leaders have had to spend the better part of their lives doing, rather than engaging in rhetoric or writing. Nor can they stop innovating within their companies. The skyrocketing demands of our society impose on them the need to broaden their innovations rapidly and beyond the limits of their companies and their industries, if they are truly to become tomorrow's leaders for creative change.

Daniel Yankelovich, in his recent series on American business and the revolution in values of our youth, defined business' need for new theory and language as follows:

> It would be fatally easy for a confrontation between students and business to degenerate into a false battle between the semantics of Marxism and capitalism. Both sets of semantics are outmoded and neither theory in its pure historical form applies to present realities. Only misunderstanding can result from such a shadow contest. We must bypass ideology and bring to bear a nondoctrinaire, problem-solving approach on each separate

issue, resisting the temptation to generalize. Business needs a new language and theory to explain itself and its social role. It also needs new types of executives at high levels in the corporation who have a bridge-building function to perform. The job of these new executives should be to understand the world of business at firsthand, and they should be capable of building a bridge between the two worlds. Business would be wise to take this new public seriously.[2]

Capitalist philosophy has gone through several phases in the United States. The business historian, Professor Norman De Gras, delineated these phases in terms of "financial capitalism" — to cover the period of U.S. business growth from the 1860's to the 1930's — and "national capitalism" — to cover the period from the 1930's on. At the outset the first period relied on private capital from outside the United States and, in later times, on internal private financial institutions in the United States. The shortcomings of "financial capitalism" led to the Depression. The second period relied upon Federal sources for financing or government guarantees and the extensive use of private management. In fact, the major concentration of this second period has been the dramatic partnership between the Federal Government and private enterprise to prevent the scourge of depressions. The successes of this partnership have made our nation economically affluent and thrust it out among the foremost of world political powers.

Success at a national level, as at a personal level, too often sows the seeds of unforeseen problems. Today it is clear that national capitalism has been deficient in at least two respects. The first is that it has resulted in the United States' creating and consuming from 40 to 60% of the total world wealth, with only 6% of the total world population. The second is that national capitalism has, by its very success, dulled our ability to react to the problems of underprivileged classes, urban crises, pollution, crime, lost youth, an emerging new left; and it has given us an insufficient regard for our rural areas and their problems in making the transition into tomorrow's industrial society. In short, then, the deficiences of national capitalism have created the need for "creative capitalism," based on innovative private management.

The Task of Creative Capitalism

Today there is a relative decline in mass-production jobs. The routine requirements of the past two-thirds of this century are rapidly being replaced by machines. To date much of our educational system has been, and still is, geared to educate and develop people for a predominantly mass-production society.

The task that the last third of the 20th century industrial state

---

[2] Daniel Yankelovich, "Business' Response to the New Values," *Bell Telephone Magazine,* November–December 1969, pp. 5–6.

imposes on our business system is developing people's capacities for nonroutine jobs under creative capitalism. Particularly since World War II we have seen the rise of what we could call technological industry, which is concerned with nonroutinized kinds of problems and demands that require a new order of solution. These are problems of space exploitation, building megalopolises, control of the environment, water pollution, marine sciences, crime, and transportation. These areas can become the 21st century industries of America, rather than the disaster areas of today.

There are, however, two underlying requirements for all these nonroutine pursuits. First, they demand large quantities of technical and intellectual resources: individual scientists, social and physical; engineers and other professionals; and service personnel and technicians as aides to the professionals. Second, they require the information necessary to solve the nonroutine problems. The key requirement, however, is for managers with the ability to identify and formulate the problems and to manage the technical and intellectual resources.

The task for management is not merely to select the gifted person for training but to develop all levels of skills to meet the requirements of society. It is essential to fully cultivate each individual's talents.

The problem for business managers is to evolve innovations which result in intelligent actions that will renew a democratic society. Rhetoric alone will not work; nor is it possible for any one of our 20th century institutions to solve these problems alone. The 1950's and 1960's saw the development of a new complex that was instrumental in solving many of our defense, space, and nuclear energy problems — the Federal Government, working with universities and private enterprises. The 1970's and 1980's could well see the rise of a broader set of complexes which would include not only the Federal Government but also local governmental entities; not only universities but also graduate centers; not only private enterprises, as represented by urban home offices and plants, but also regional plants situated in the rural areas. In many respects, I believe, creative capitalism can well be institutionalized on these broader-based complexes.

Creative capitalism must advance our society beyond the need for imperialism or the exploitation of people. Creative capitalism's success depends on its creation of wealth in a manner that truly establishes the community of humanity as the goal of our society. Wealth produced under creative capitalism must be distributed in a manner which makes it possible to increase the standard of living of all peoples in the world.

Revolutionary Goals

What, then, should be expected from the business managers who are evolutionary revolutionists? The era of transition to our nonroutine industry can learn significant lessons from the 1960's. The first lesson is that one must have pride-in-self. Many youths do not have pride-in-self. That is why they have a tendency to move toward demoralization — emotional and physical. They are, in truth, escaping from self. On the other hand, the Negro, through "black power," and "black is beautiful," is on the first rung of pride-in-self. Professional people attain pride-in-self through educational avenues and their accomplishments within their social or cultural institutions.

Second, when a human being has pride-in-self his need to participate in "man's inhumanity to man" naturally diminishes. Black power and white supremacy questions would, I think, become less significant.

Third, as the transition progresses from pride-in-self and one turns towards man's humanity to man, the whole rate of positive and meaningful advance accelerates exponentially. As each man clearly sees his role in the new era of social stability, I would expect, minority lines as well as intellectual and religious lines will disappear. Then the true community of humanity becomes apparent, and remains as a lasting heritage of the coming generations.

Finally, man is, in every aspect, human and imperfect. No simple or complex perfection is possible either in personal actions or in the institutions which man forms. Therefore the dedication of self to man's humanity to man requires, above all, a patience of high order to mitigate the inhumanity which results from emotionally irresponsible personal or professional behavior.

The insurrectionists of the 1970's are dedicated to achieving utopia through the destruction of today's institutions. They often exploit the lesser flaws of present and past institutions without due regard to their benefits — nor to the results of their irresponsible destruction of these institutions. Their amplification of minor flaws is no better than any other instance of man's inhumanity to man — inhumanity under any guise is still barbarism. Barbarism under any condition and in any society is not an answer. Violence and retaliation are not modern solutions; they are decadent answers from the past.

Responsible actions cannot be performed in silence nor in violence. Man's humanity to man as a goal of society is not the creation of destruction or apathy. Confidence in self demands a quiet confrontation with those who are involved in violence or silence. An active confrontation calls for a halt to wanton destruction of self, property, and society. Peaceful actions are demanded if one truly believes in and is prepared to seek man's humanity to humanity. For, in fact, quiet nonviolence demands a vast majority. Only with such a majority can a society proceed toward its true goals. Nonparticipation, silence, merely looking on will not diminish the threat of man's inhumanity to man. But enough people supporting nonviolence could make possible the choice of peaceful means for change. Nonviolence can provide more meaningful change for right rather than change based on appeasement derived from violence or temper tantrums.

The Capital for Change

Let us focus for a moment on tomorrow's business leadership. Technology and science have forced those of yesterday's leaders who want to be tomorrow's leaders to change. The creation of wealth demands responsible leadership for the community of humanity. Creative, positive leadership and innovative management cannot be put off.

One axiom is evident: no change is possible without capital; that is, monies. The evolutionary process equally demands innovation in the manner of distributing wealth. There is no single theory by which one can allocate the wealth or determine by priority the multiproblems associated with the techno-socio-cultural needs of our society. On the other hand, to continue one-day teach-ins, protests, or violent confrontations with single or confused objectives in mind can do no more than prolong man's inhumanity to man.

Businessmen have been our major creators of wealth. Their objective must be to move toward increasing the standards of living of all peoples in the world, as well as increasing the meaningful leisure time of all peoples. Private enterprise and creative capitalism in their evolutionary process demand that profits become constraints rather than, as in the past, the primary objective.

23 Consumerism and Marketing Management

Norman Kangun
Keith K. Cox
James Higginbotham
John Burton

Despite predictions that today's consumer movement would subside as its predecessor had subsided, consumerism continues to grow in both scope and support as society proceeds through the 1970s. An earlier wave of the consumer movement, stimulated by Upton Sinclair's exposé of the meat packing industry, created action and attention for a while and then diminished. However, the current consumerism movement appears to be becoming increasingly institutionalized, as evidenced by the formation at all levels in government of new agencies to represent and protect the consumer interest. Some examples are the Office of Consumer Affairs, now located in the Department of Health, Education, and Welfare, and the Consumer Product Safety Commission. The creation of a federal Consumer Protection Agency is likely in the near future, while state and local government agencies set up to protect consumer interests continue to expand. Other countries are also struggling with adequate representation of consumer rights.[1]

Previous studies on consumerism focused on the deficiencies of the market system, the specific causes of consumerism, the semantic problem that exists between businessmen and their critics, and general attitudes on the part of consumers about specific marketing activities.[2] The focus of the study reported here is on (1) the meaning of con-

Reprinted from "Consumerism and Marketing Management," by Norman Kangun, Keith Cox, James Higginbotham, and John Burton in *The Journal of Marketing,* 39 (April 1975), 3–10 published by the American Marketing Association.

[1] See, for example, Hans B. Thorelli, "Consumer Information Policy in Sweden — What Can Be Learned?" *Journal of Marketing,* 35 (January 1971), 50–55.

[2] See Andrew Shonfield, *Modern Capitalism: The Changing Balance of Public and Private Power,* Oxford University Press, New York, 1965; Philip Kotler, "What Consumerism Means for Marketers," *Harvard Business Review,* 50 (May–June 1973), 48–57; Raymond A. Bauer and Stephen A. Greyser, "The Dialogue that Never Happens," *Harvard Business Review,* 46 (January–February 1969), 122–128; and Hiram C. Barksdale and William R. Darden, "Consumer Attitudes toward Marketing and Consumerism," *Journal of Marketing,* 36 October 1972), 28–35.

sumerism, (2) the importance of certain consumer issues, (3) the choice of corrective actions as they relate to specific consumer problems, and (4) the perceived importance of the consumer movement today and in the future. The results of this study suggest some implications for the actions marketing management can take to meet the challenge of consumerism.

Research Methodology

A convenience sample of 367 respondents living in the metropolitan area of a large southwestern city was surveyed in 1973. The sample was composed of 241 students drawn from marketing classes at a major state university in that city, 55 nonemployed adult women, and 71 businessmen. The completed questionnaires from nonemployed women and businessmen were collected from neighborhood civic clubs and professional business organizations in the area.

Table 1 presents a description of the demographic characteristics of the subsamples. The students were considerably younger and their income substantially lower than the other two groups. The students'

Table 1 Characteristics of Sample Respondents

Demographic Characteristics	Students (N = 241)	Nonemployed Women (N = 55)	Businessmen (N = 71)
Age			
Under 25	66.4%	5.5%	—%
25–34	30.7	49.1	38.0
35–44	2.5	38.2	45.1
45 and over	.4	7.2	16.9
Total Annual Income (Household)			
Under $10,000	38.6	3.6	1.4
$10,000–$14,999	27.8	16.4	8.5
$15,000–$24,999	19.1	47.3	54.9
$25,000 and over	11.2	29.1	33.8
No response	3.3	3.6	1.4
Number in Family			
1	15.4	1.8	5.7
2	30.7	16.4	18.3
3	20.3	14.6	18.3
4	18.3	29.1	31.0
5	6.2	23.6	21.1
6 or more	6.6	14.5	5.6
No answer	2.5	—	—
Political Philosophy			
Liberal	20.8	18.2	9.9
Moderate	68.1	56.3	60.5
Conservative	7.4	20.0	29.6
No response	3.7	5.5	—

political philosophy as self-reported was slightly more liberal than that reported by the nonemployed women. The businessmen were the most conservative, but perhaps not as conservative as might have been predicted. Both the nonemployed women and business groups indicated higher income levels than the general household levels in the United States.[3]

The division of respondents into student, nonemployed women, and businessmen groups will enable us to measure the extent to which different perceptions about consumerism exist among these groups. When perceptions among these segments are homogeneous, fertile ground exists for cooperative endeavors. Where beliefs differ among various groups, conflict and debate are likely to make the advancement of consumerism interests more difficult to attain.

The Meaning of Consumerism

The term *consumerism* is of recent vintage, as illustrated by its absence from many dictionaries.[4] In the marketing literature, there appears to be no generally accepted operational definition of consumerism. For example, Buskirk and Rothe define consumerism as "the organized efforts of consumers seeking redress, restitution and remedy for dissatisfaction they have accumulated in the acquisition of their standard of living." [5] This definition, like most, is highly ambiguous because it does not distinguish the issues included within the domain of consumerism.

Table 2 summarizes the perceptions of the students, nonemployed women, and businessmen about whether the issues of information, health and safety, repair and servicing, pricing, pollution in the environment, marketing concentration, product quality, and consumer representation in government definitely should be included as components of a definition of consumerism. The majority of respondents in each of the three groups "definitely agree" that all of the issues listed in the table, with the exception of "pollution in the environment" and "market concentration," should be considered within the domain of consumerism. Differences do exist among the three groups in the exact proportion of respondents who believed the issues listed above should be included in consumerism. Over 80% of the nonemployed women

---

[3] See Monroe Friedman, "The 1966 Consumer Protest as Seen by Its Leaders," *Journal of Consumer Affairs,* 5 (Summer 1971), 1–23.

[4] An example is the *Random House Dictionary,* Random House, New York, 1967.

[5] Richard Buskirk and James Rothe, "Consumerism — An Interpretation," *Journal of Marketing,* 34 (October 1970), 62.

Table 2 Consumers Who Definitely Agree Issue Should Be Included under Consumerism

Issues	Students (N = 241)	Nonemployed Women (N = 55)	Businessmen (N = 71)
Information (such as more informative advertising, clearly written warranties, etc.)	82.2%	89.1%	95.8%
Health and Safety (such as testing and evaluation of drugs, stronger auto bumpers, etc.)	80.1	92.7	83.1
Repair and Servicing (such as improved servicing of appliances and automobiles)	70.1	85.5	71.8
Pricing Issues (such as the high price of food, insurance, hospital care)	59.3	81.8	63.4
Pollution in the Environment (such as dirty air, water, excessive billboards)	61.8	47.3	36.6
Market Concentration (such as lack of competition in the marketplace)	26.1	45.5	42.3
Product Quality (such as frequent obsolescence, product breakdowns)	72.2	89.1	78.9
Consumer Representation in Government (such as a lack of consumer representation in government agencies)	58.5	69.1	52.1

definitely agreed that information, health and safety, product quality, repair and servicing, and pricing issues should be considered under the domain of consumerism. Agreement within the student and businessmen groups exceeded 80% on only two issues — information, health and safety. As might be expected as a result of their greater involvement in family shopping activities, more women than either businessmen or students associated pricing with consumerism.

Further, more students placed the pollution problem under the domain of consumerism than either the women or businessmen. This may be a function of the concern about ecological issues raised on college campuses during the 1970s.

In summary, there appears to be a broad consensus among all three groups that the four issues — information, health and safety, repairs and servicing, and product quality — definitely belong under the domain of consumerism. Pricing issues were associated with consumerism by over 80% of the women and by approximately 60% of the students and businessmen. A majority in all of the groups definitely agreed that consumer representation in government should be included as part of consumerism. On the issue of pollution in the environment, large differences existed among the students, nonemployed women, and businessmen as to whether this should be included under consumerism. According to a majority in all three groups, market concentration does not belong under consumerism. Therefore, this issue will be eliminated from further analysis.

Importance of Specific Issues to Consumers

Although a majority of respondents may indicate that an issue belongs under consumerism, this tells us little about how important the respondent perceives the issue to be. Accordingly, respondents were asked to rate each of the seven issues listed in Table 3 in terms of its importance to them. The proportion of businessmen who rated each issue extremely or very important was substantially lower than the proportion of students or women for all issues except repair and servicing. All issues except consumer representation in government were rated important by over 75% of the students and nonemployed women, which seems to suggest a strong consensus for future action in these areas of interest. Although businessmen rated the importance of pollution lower than the other two groups, it is interesting that 65% *did* rate the issue important because only 37% of the businessmen definitely agreed that this issue should be considered part of consumerism. There was a considerable lack of consensus both within and between groups as to the importance of consumer representation in government. The businessmen generally preferred less rather than more governmental involvement, but this issue may pose additional threats to their existing business policies and practices.

Table 3 Consumers Who Rated Specific Issues Extremely/Very Important

Specific Issues	Students (N = 241)	Nonemployed Women (N = 55)	Businessmen (N = 71)
Information	84.7%	85.5%	76.1%
Health and Safety	85.9	90.9	75.1
Repair and Servicing	87.5	90.9	85.9
Pricing Issues	80.9	81.8	64.8
Pollution in the Environment	78.9	76.4	64.8
Product Quality	85.5	85.4	76.1
Consumer Representation in Government	60.2	58.2	39.4

Choice of Corrective Actions

There are no easy or simple solutions to the vast array of problems that consumers confront in the marketplace. The remedies available to consumers in dealing with such problems are limited. They range from taking no action, taking moderate action (i.e., complaining to the retailer or writing the manufacturer), or taking strong action (i.e., selective buying routines, boycotts, or legal action).

To ascertain the remedies that consumers might seek, four situations were created. Respondents were presented with a list of possible actions and asked to select from that list those actions they would most likely take in each situation. The four situations are described below:

Situation 1: A color-tuning component in your television set was malfunctioning. The retailer from whom the set was bought was called in to fix the set. Two months later, the new color-tuning device would not work. The dealer refused to repair the set without an additional service charge and a charge for the cost of another color-tuning device.

Situation 2: You bought a brand name refrigerator at a leading department store on installment credit. The refrigerator was delivered to your home three weeks later, but you noticed that the contract called for interest to be paid from the date on which you signed the contract. In effect, you were paying interest for three weeks without the merchandise in your possession.

Situation 3: The retail cost of meat items has increased 25% over the last two months. Operating on a fixed budget for food, you find it difficult to buy meat items for your family and stay within your budget constraints. Because of the importance of meat as a source of protein, you are reluctant to substitute nonmeat items for meat.

Situation 4: You bought a doll for your daughter's birthday. Soon afterwards, the head became disengaged from the doll, revealing a sharp metal nail which was used as a fastener for the head and the body. Fortunately, the doll was taken from the child before she sustained an injury.

As Table 4 shows, in all of the situations except rising meat prices, the vast majority of respondents in each group preferred either moderate action or no action at all. This finding is not surprising for a number of reasons. Consumers may believe that most consumer problems can be solved without resorting to strong action, which is likely to be costly to them in terms of time and money. To the extent that many consumer problems involve relatively small amounts of money for the individual, strong action usually is not economically feasible. Many consumers are not aware of the legal remedies available to them in dealing with consumer problems. Finally, some consumers may hold

Table 4 Corrective Action Chosen in Four Situations

Situations	Students (N = 241)	Nonemployed Women (N = 55)	Businessmen (N = 71)
Television Malfunction			
No action[a]	9.7%	2.2%	10.0%
Moderate action[b]	84.5	94.2	84.0
Strong action[c]	5.8	3.6	6.0
Illegal Interest Charges			
No action	22.2	8.4	18.3
Moderate action	67.7	89.8	78.2
Strong action	10.1	1.8	3.5
Rising Meat Prices			
No action	47.9	46.8	71.5
Moderate action	6.6	13.2	10.2
Strong action	46.5	40.0	18.3
Doll Safety Hazard			
No action	20.0	11.8	19.9
Moderate action	73.3	83.6	80.1
Strong action	6.7	4.6	—

[a] *No action* encompasses the following behaviors: (a) probably take no action because it is unlikely to get results, or (b) probably take no action because of the time and expense involved.

[b] *Moderate action* includes the following: (a) write or call the manufacturer, (b) complain directly to the dealer, or (c) call the Better Business Bureau or a local consumer protection agency.

[c] *Strong action* includes the following: (a) take legal action, that is, initiate a class action suit or go to a small claims court, or (b) take economic measures, e.g., participate in a boycott.

fatalistic outlooks and believe little can be done to alleviate the excesses that occur in the marketplace.

By contrast, the situation involving rising meat prices seemed to provoke more students and women to choose stronger actions. With real incomes declining as a result of rising prices, this budget squeeze creates frustration, which gives rise to stronger actions against the visible and vulnerable supermarket. A substantial minority of the women and students preferred stronger action as a means of making their feelings known.

The businessmen appeared to be much more reluctant to use strong action such as boycotts in coping with rising meat prices. As businessmen, they may be more sympathetic to the problems of retailers. Thus, they probably are unwilling to support the concept of economic boycotts.

In summary, there was a strong tendency in all situations except the meat problem to "work within the system" by taking no action or some form of moderate action such as contacting the manufacturer, retailer, or Better Business Bureau. This tendency for no action or moderate action was consistently high among the student, nonemployed women, and businessmen groups.

The Importance of Consumerism Today and in the Future

After analyzing what the respondents perceived to be issues under consumerism, their personal judgment as to the importance of these issues, and their choices of corrective action to four consumer situations, the researchers asked all of the respondents to give their opinions as to the importance of consumerism today and in the future. The answers to these two questions give insight into consumers' viewpoints as to whether consumerism is a temporary or permanent phenomenon. Table 5 shows that approximately 85% of the students and nonemployed women believed that consumerism was extremely or very important today. Perhaps more surprising is the fact that 70% of the businessmen shared this view. Given these figures, the importance of consumerism today seems to permeate all three groups of consumers.

But, is the present consumerism movement likely to recede in importance over time? Table 5 indicates that a large majority of respondents in all three groups believed the importance of consumerism would be *greater* in the future. About four-fifths of the students and women expressed this belief, while two-thirds of the businessmen concurred.

Problems associated with affluence, such as increased product complexity and rising consumer expectations, are likely to continue. Thus, the belief in the increased importance of consumerism in the future by all three groups may be well founded.

Implications for Marketing Management

The data uncovered in this survey seem to indicate that: (1) consumerism, like marketing, is perceived to encompass a wide variety of issues and is broadening its domain; (2) consumers perceive the

Table 5 Present and Future Importance of Consumerism

Statements	Students (N = 241)	Nonemployed Women (N = 55)	Businessmen (N = 71)
How important do you believe Consumerism is today?			
Believe to be extremely/ very important	84.2%	85.4%	70.4%
In the future, do you believe that Consumerism will be more or less important than it is today?			
Believe to be much more/ slightly more important.	83.8	78.2	66.2

specific consumerism issues to be important; and (3) consumerism is here to stay and will grow in strength in the future. For many marketing managers, *caveat emptor* is an inappropriate philosophy today. Because the pressures to attend to consumer problems are likely to remain, the obligations of marketers, particuarly consumer goods marketers, will change drastically. Further, it behooves marketing managers to be sensitive to the demands of consumers since marketing is at the interface between the company and its external environment.

Two frameworks for evaluating possible alternative courses of action for marketing management are (1) company action and (2) industry-wide action.

Company action

Implementation of the marketing concept implies that a firm is responding to consumer wants and needs. Profit and sales opportunities exist for those who can develop and communicate broad consumer programs that satisfy consumer needs. For example, Giant Foods — a supermarket chain based in Washington, D.C. — has pioneered in the development of a comprehensive, consumer-oriented program. Under the guidance of Esther Peterson, former head of the federal Office of Consumer Affairs, Giant Foods was among the first in the industry to institute unit-pricing and open-dating programs — long before government pressures were placed on the industry to adopt such programs.[6] The company also has been instrumental in promoting nutritional labels and has spent substantial amounts of money to educate the public.

A second reason for individual firms to react to the challenges posed by consumerism is to minimize government action. From the firm's perspective, government regulation is, at best, a mixed blessing. Government agencies can define and make explicit acceptable and unacceptable norms of conduct whether they are related to sales practices, advertising, packaging, labeling, or the like. These agencies also can be insensitive, inept, and burdensome. If individual firms want to minimize governmental controls on consumer issues, they must address many consumer problems. What can firms do to improve their repair and servicing capacities? Can product warranties be written to tell consumers precisely what the manufacturer's liability is and not simply to limit the producer's liability? Can package sizes be simplified and standardized to allow consumers to choose more economically if they wish to do so? Can simpler designs and more reliable products be developed? Can additional product information be provided? How can firms minimize the safety and health hazards of products such as toys, flammable products, and appliances? Can the organizational structures of large retail

---

[6] Esther Peterson, "Consumerism as a Retailer's Asset," *Harvard Business Review,* 51 (May–June 1974), 91–101.

establishments be altered to permit greater contact with customers and easier ways of dealing with problems?

Finally, it is in the long-term best interest of the firm to develop programs that are responsive to consumer problems. If consumer frustrations are not dealt with, the firm may suffer as a result of reduced sales and lower profits.

Consumerism requires a greater awareness by marketing managers and businesspeople of happenings in the marketplace. A number of companies are responding to these challenges by modifying their organizational structures to be more responsive to consumer problems. In one survey of 157 companies, of which 109 were consumer goods companies, 29 have created one or more organizational positions or departments to deal with consumer problems.[7] With respect to such departments, some companies indicated that they had established a separate office of consumer affairs or a customer relations department. A second study reported the results of a questionnaire sent to the presidents of 400 of the nation's largest corporations that resulted in 96 responses. It revealed that 54 of these firms had a "corporate responsibility officer" whose task was, among other things, to report to the corporation's many publics how well the company was fulfilling its societal obligations.[8] Another 34 firms utilized a committee arrangement for this purpose.

By itself, the creation of an organizational position or department with the word *consumer* in the title does not mean a great deal. In some companies, such positions may be established as a public relations gambit. To be effective in dealing with consumer problems, a firm must understand the real problems, not just their superficial symptoms. For instance, the Whirlpool "cool line" provides customers with immediate personal contact with the firm should they experience problems with their appliances. In addition to handling problems promptly, the "cool line" tackles the impersonality problem that often afflicts large organizations.

If the organization is to address fundamental consumer problems, it must identify these problems and establish priorities among them. Such a goal requires the development of information systems that are oriented toward obtaining information about various aspects of consumer discontent. What is needed is a research group with a broad, on-going mission aimed at identifying basic consumer problems, detecting changes in attitudes and life styles, and developing new measures for determining the seriousness of these problems. Firms need

---

[7] Frederick E. Webster, Jr., "Does Business Misunderstand Consumerism?" *Harvard Business Review,* 50 (September–October 1973), 89–97.

[8] Henry Eilbert and I. Robert Parket, "The Corporate Responsibility Officer: A New Position on the Organizational Chart," *Business Horizons,* 16 (February 1973), 45–51.

to be able to anticipate consumer problems and convert them into profitable opportunities.[9]

After consumer problems have been identified, the firm must develop and implement programs to deal with these problems. The development of such programs requires innovative thinking as well as a leadership group that looks favorably on change.[10]

Industrywide action

A second way of dealing with consumer problems is industry-wide action. There are many reasons for marketers to turn to trade associations and other business groups to deal with consumer problems. First, many problems are common to a particular industry. Consider the educational problems associated with nutritional labeling or the informational problems associated with maintaining up-to-date credit records. It makes sense for members of the industry to grapple with these problems jointly. Second, and perhaps more important, consumer programs initiated by an individual company will involve costs; unless emulated by competition, these costs can threaten the competitive position of that company. Thus, where uncertainty exists about competitors' actions, the incentive to act independently is diminished. Consequently, industrywide action in dealing with consumer problems is attractive because it can be undertaken by firms without threatening their competitive postures.

The potential for industrywide action is great. Trade associations are in a good position to develop educational materials and then work through dealers to improve both the quality and flow of information about products to consumers. Witness the efforts of the National Commission on Egg Nutrition to educate consumers about the importance of protein in one's diet. Further, an arbitration board, to which injured consumers can turn as a last resort, is often best handled through business associations. The cost of supporting the board is shared and, because it represents all or most of the membership in a given industry, its power to get members to adhere to its rulings is enhanced. As an illustration, the moving and storage industry (i.e., the largest firms in that industry) has set up an arbitration board to act as a court of last resort should a consumer fail to resolve a complaint with his

---

[9] For an extension of this idea, see Philip Kotler, *Marketing Management: Analysis, Planning, and Control,* 2nd ed., Prentice-Hall, Englewood Cliffs, N.J., 1972, pp. 58–62; and Daniel Yankelovich, "The Changing Social Environment," *Marketing News,* March 1971, reprinted in *Readings in Marketing Research Process,* Keith Cox and Ben Enis, eds. Goodyear, Pacific Palisades, Calif., 1972.

[10] For a more extensive discussion of company initiatives regarding consumer problems, see David A. Aaker and George S. Day, "Corporate Responses to Consumerism Pressures," *Harvard Business Review,* 49 (November–December 1972), 114–124.

mover. Similarly, the advertising industry has created the National Advertising Review Board, whose function is to monitor advertisements and to investigate complaints about advertising. If an advertiser is found to be in violation of board standards and refuses to change or withdraw his ad, that action is published and the case is turned over to the Federal Trade Commission (FTC). In the Schick case, the board came out looking tougher than the FTC, which showed a reluctance to act. In this case, the board found the Schick comparative ad campaign for its Flexamatic electric shaver to be "false in some respects and misleading in its overall implications" regarding the closeness of its shave when tested against competitive shavers.[11]

The traditional role of the Better Business Bureau is perhaps the best example of industrywide action taken by firms to deal with consumers. However, many critics today hold that the Better Business Bureau is set up primarily to protect the businessman. Perhaps business should reevaluate the function and purpose of the Better Business Bureau in terms of today's consumer problems.

Today, the question for business is not *whether* to undertake efforts to identify and correct consumer problems but *how* to make such efforts effective, particularly if firms are to survive the joint pressures exerted by consumerists and government. Consumer education, the establishment of product standards in terms of quality, and the development of programs for handling consumer complaints are all areas where industrywide efforts may be productive.

Conclusion

Those consumerism issues for which there is a broad acceptance of needs and the cost of implementing solutions is not too great are logical places for many firms to voluntarily take actions. It appears from the survey results that company actions in the areas of product information, health and safety standards, repair and servicing warranties, and product quality may be very beneficial in terms of long-run company goals. On the other hand, consumerism issues for which broad consensus does not exist and the costs would be high are not likely to be addressed voluntarily by a business firm. The pollution issue appears to be an area where government action may be necessary and desirable. In any case, business should act to protect consumers from abuses in the marketplace. If businesses do not respond, government forces will undoubtedly act.

---

[11] For a more detailed report on the Schick case, see "Competitors Hail NARB for Schick Shaver Ruling," *Advertising Age*, January 7, 1974, pp. 1, 6; and Stanley E. Cohen, "NARB's Schick Ruling Highlights Secrecy of FTC's Regulations Role," *Advertising Age*, January 7, 1974, p. 16.

B   Representation on Boards of Directors

24 Who Belongs on Corporate Boards?
Phillip I. Blumberg

One of the recurring proposals of those campaigning for reform of the corporation has been the change of the composition of the board of directors by inclusion of "special interest" or "public" directors. Such proposals have been the subject of shareholder resolutions in a number of so-called "public interest proxy contests." These proposals possess a common objective: to transform the large corporation into a "public" institution, in which the public, or the groups affected by the corporation, participate significantly in corporate decision-making.

These efforts to broaden the composition of the board of directors are best understood against their larger backdrop. They are inspired by certain features of the modern corporation and present-day society.

The first of these features is the simple fact of sheer corporate power. Recognition of the power and role of the large corporation in American society inevitably leads to an examination of how so paramount an institution is governed.

The second feature is the worldwide social and environmental crisis. We are living in a world undergoing profound and accelerating changes in attitudes, values, and institutions. Such things as the struggle for racial and social justice, and concern with the physical impact of industrial technology upon the quality of life and upon life itself, inevitably lead to a reexamination of previously accepted institutions. The large corporation is one of these. In particular, acceptance of the con-

Reprinted with permission from *Business and Society Review/Innovation,* Spring 1973, pp. 40–47.

cept of corporate social responsibility, however imprecise the concept may be, has given rise to a reconsideration of the fundamental aims of the corporation. This necessarily has meant a close look at the structure of the board of directors.

Third is the lack of accountability by the management of the large, publicly-held corporation. Because of the separation of ownership and control resulting from the widespread distribution of shares, stockholders in the large corporation generally no longer have an effective, independent voice in selecting the board — or in other matters submitted for their consideration. With rare exceptions, board members have become a self-perpetuating group, accountable only to themselves, or perhaps to the chief executive officer who was responsible for their selection (who himself is accountable to no one). Management's ability to rule unchallenged by takeover bids by outsiders is reasonably assured so long as it achieves minimally acceptable earnings per share.

Fourth, corporations lack legitimacy. No longer is the corporation an enterprise that significantly affects only its own managers. It affects wide segments of society. "Private" has become "public." However, the social and economic groups whose lives and fortunes are profoundly influenced by the corporation have no part in its direction. Government regulation of corporate conduct in certain areas is regarded by reformers as a limited and inadequate response to this problem. Reformers want the affected social and economic groups to participate in corporate decision-making. They demand changes in the board because it is unrepresentative. Even if the board were not self-perpetuating and stockholders possessed real power of selection, the problem of the legitimacy of a board reflecting solely stockholder interests would remain, although the problem of accountability might be resolved.

Fifth, the view that the interests of vitally affected groups are not receiving adequate consideration in corporate decision-making represents a rejection of the concept of managerialism. This concept is the view that the directors act as trustees not only for stockholders, but for employees, consumers, the community, and other groups as well, and that the function of the board is to mediate among the legitimate claims of these conflicting groups. This view not only has little resemblance to reality, but runs directly contrary to the established legal principle that the board owes single-minded loyalty to the interests of stockholders.

Alternative Approaches to Reform

At the outset, it should be recognized that there is serious concern with the role and importance of the corporate board of directors. There is serious doubt as to whether the board really determines corporate policy and effectively supervises management, or whether it functions as a prisoner of the corporate bureaucracy. Of course, if the corporate bureaucracy or technostructure ultimately exercises corporate power, representation on the board may be much less meaningful than anticipated. Further, there is the question of how effective directors can be so long as they are part time, not well compensated, and not assisted by an adequate staff. Proposals for reform of the board must be evaluated against this background.

Reform proposals may be divided into two classes: (1) efforts to broaden the perspectives of the board, and (2) more sweeping proposals to change the structure of the board through the addition of "special interest" or "public" representatives.

There has been increasing support for the movement to broaden the board's perspectives through the addition of individuals with different backgrounds and experience, who would bring fresh perspectives and values to board decision-making. This may be termed the "window-out" aspect of this type of proposal: the provision for a fresh look at corporate social problems from a different vantage point. In addition, many advocate the "window-in" aspect: additional public disclosure of corporate performance to ventilate the decision-making process and to improve channels of communication.

The individuals who might provide a fresh view on corporate problems include people drawn from certain long-neglected groups:

1. *Blacks.* Black members of the board of directors are becoming part of the accepted pattern of American corporate life. Approximately 70 major American corporations, as well as the New York and American Stock Exchanges, have elected blacks to their boards.
2. *Women.* Some 20 major American corporations have women directors at present. General Motors recently added a woman to its board, an act that no doubt will accelerate this process.
3. *Nonbusiness persons.* Dayton-Hudson and First Pennsylvania Co. are among the corporations that have placed nonbusiness persons on their boards.
4. *Foreign nationals.* American multinational corporations are beginning to add foreign nationals to their boards in order to operate more effectively abroad.

The selection of such new directors by the board itself has certain obvious strengths and weaknesses in terms of the reformers' aim of introducing new factors into corporate decision-making. Selection by the board assures new members of a harmonious reception and full inclusion in board deliberations. On the other hand, if the new members lack independence and firmness, their selection has limited importance. Obviously, the addition of one or two black or female directors does not change the allocation of power within the corporation.

Although at present such additions to the board may be just symbolic gestures, they have considerable significance in their own right because of their influence on public attitudes. They also symbolize the board's dedication to nondiscriminatory principles in the operation, as well as recognition of the aspirations of deprived groups for fuller participation in the decision-making process.

The second and more far-reaching class of reform proposals seeks to transform the corporation into a public institution through representation on the board of either (a) special interests affected by the corporation, or (b) "public" or government members representing the community as a whole. Both special-interest and public representation have more profound objectives than simply broadening the perspectives of the board. They aim to change the allocation of *power* within the corporation, to assure the public — or particular groups — of a role in the decisions that affect them, and to render the corporation both accountable and legitimate.

The essence of special interest representation is that such representatives primarily serve the interests of the group selecting them, rather than the interests of the institution they help to govern. In such representation's most stringent form, the representative receives instructions from his interest group, reports back to it, and may be recalled if his performance fails to satisfy it.

There have been recent shareholder proxy proposals for many types of special interest representatives: employees, consumers, women, minority groups, dealers, suppliers, environmentalists, persons experienced in conversion from military to nonmilitary production, public interest advocates, and even investment bankers. Many of these proposals are clearly intended solely as symbolic gestures, or as efforts to broaden board perspectives without (at least for the moment) undertaking a campaign to redistribute corporate power. None has attracted significant support thus far; indeed, some can hardly be taken seriously. Let us take a closer look at the special interest groups covered by some of these proposals:

1. Employee directors

The idea of employee representation on the board is unquestionably the most serious of the proposals for special interest representation. It springs from the belief that of all the groups affected by the corporation, including stockholders, it is employees upon whom the corporation has the greatest impact. This proposal is reinforced by the experience of Germany — where industry has prospered during two decades of employee representation on corporate boards — and the increasing acceptance in Europe generally of the principle of employee representation. In recent years, employee representation on the board has been recognized in Norway, Sweden, France, and the Netherlands, and is a part of the Draft Statute for the European Company in the European Economic Community.

The crucial limitation to employee representation is that it simply does not reflect a serious objective of the American trade union movement or of American workers generally. At present, it is a theoretical solution advanced by intellectuals; it has no grass roots support. Professor Robert Dahl has pointed out that "workers and trade unions may be the greatest barriers at present to any profound reconstruction of econmic enterprise in this country." So long as such attitudes persist, employee representation will remain an academic question.

Another problem with employee representation is the inescapable fact that American trade unions do not represent American empolyees as a whole. In a labor force of 83 million, only 20 million are union members.

From the standpoint of corporate behavior, the question must be asked whether employee directors would be more likely than other directors to be concerned with the impact of the corporation on the consumer, the community, the environment, or, indeed, on other workers. Is the "special interest" director any more apt to be concerned with the "public" interest?

There is also the question whether the advantages of employee representation outweigh the disharmony and lack of unity it may bring to the board. Conflict on the board makes effective functioning difficult. When such conflicts have arisen among competing stockholder groups, independent directors often have demonstrated an unwillingness to be in the middle, and have resigned. Finally, employee representation transfers to the board level the contest between labor and management. It is far from clear that it is desirable to have labor negotiations conducted in the board room.

2. Consumer, supplier, or dealer directors

There is little or no support for proposals to include these representatives; such proposals are purely theoretical or symbolic. Furthermore, there are serious practical problems in determining the constituency to select such directors: Who would be entitled to vote? How would votes be allocated between, say, major and incidental suppliers? What procedures would ensure the conduct of a contested campaign?

The case for adding consumer directors to the board receives little support from the history of consumer-owned enterprises in this country, such as the mutual insurance companies owned by policyholders, or the mutual savings banks owned by depositors. These companies invariably possess self-perpetuating boards, and have shown no greater concern for consumers than their stockholder-owned competitors. If possible, they have even less public accountability because of the absence of the stock market as a measure of performance — and there is no takeover bid as a possible discipline.

3. Stockholder directors

A special interest group which has *not* been the subject of representation proposals paradoxically appears to be the only group that may realistically hope to achieve such recognition in the foreseeable future — the stockholders themselves. As I have pointed out, the theory that stockholders elect the board is a fiction. Through control of the proxy solicitation machinery, the board in fact selects itself; the stockholder vote merely ratifies that self-selection. The board represents itself, not the stockholders.

In contrast to individual stockholders, financial institutions possess the power (were they prepared to act in concert) to exercise the traditional prerogatives of owners and elect their representatives to the board. These institutions — mutual funds, investment trusts, bank trust departments, pension and welfare funds — have substantial concentrated holding in many public corporations. According to a New York Stock Exchange study, 28.3 percent of the equity shares of listed corporations were held by financial institutions and pension funds; the total exceeds 40 percent with the inclusion of nonbank trusts, foreign institutions, investment partnerships, and unregistered mutual funds.

Although financial institutions clearly possess the potential power of ownership, it is as yet unexercised, as the Institutional Investor Study Report of the SEC concluded. Nor is there any sign that such institutions are now, or in the future will be, ready to act in concert. The knowledge that exercise of management controls over companies in the institution's portfolio has little advantage, and serious disadvantages, is likely to prevent such a development. Designating directors on the boards of such portfolio companies would not only limit the flexibility of the funds in disposing of their shares, but would make them highly vulnerable to charges of interlocking directorates and to increased regulatory controls. Concern wtih the possibility of further government controls obviously has increased since the critical Patman subcommittee report on the shareholdings of banks and trust companies in their fiduciary capacities.

A more likely possibility is pressure by funds for the election of prominent public figures to corporate boards, to represent not the funds as such but public stockholders generally. This could constitute a form of special interest representation for stockholders. The aims of such "stockholder" directors presumably would be generally in concord with the aims of the incumbent management, but such directors, not dependent on management favor for their selection, could function as genuinely independent directors.

A fundamental problem would remain, however. While stockholder representation in this form would restore a measure of corporate accountability and introduce "public" influence into the private corporation, it would not restore corporate legitimacy. The stockholder in the large public corporation is a temporary investor, not an "owner" in the traditional sense. Stockholder representation, furthermore, does not provide any recognition for the other interests in a society vitally affected by the corporation.

4. Public and government directors

A more sweeping approach to the problem calls for directors who would represent the public, not merely particular "special" interests. Thirty years ago Mr. Justice Douglas suggested the addition of "public" or "professional" directors to the board. Robert Townsend recently revived the proposal, changed its emphasis by charging public directors with a quasi-trusteeship to represent not simply the investing public but the community at large, and added supporting features for funding and staff assistance.

A basic problem with the public or professional director is the matter of selection. Who is to be the appointing authority? If the board does the appointing, the public director becomes simply a variation on the efforts of a board to broaden its perspectives by including individuals with different values among its membership; he or she will hardly mark a substantial change in the board's composition. So long as the public or professional director lacks a constituency with public influence, the impact on corporate policy will be limited.

The New York Stock Exchange has successfully pressed for the election of at least two "outside" directors to the boards of listed corporations. Even if the Exchange were to go further and require as a condition to listing that corporations elect to their board persons chosen from a panel nominated by the Exchange (or some independent agency which it designated), this would hardly satisfy reformers. An Exchange-designated panel inevitably would be composed of establishment figures, orthodox in their views, from within "the club," as it were. They would display essentially the same set of values and attitudes currently dominating corporate boards; their presence would not make significant difference in corporate goals or behavior.

The remaining alternative for structural reform is the addition of "government" directors to represent the public interest. This hardly seems a satisfactory solution. The thought of a government representative in every board room stirs little enthusiasm among either corporate management or reformers. Lack of confidence in the government — and in the type of person likely to be selected — and concern about further increase in centralized government power, explain the lack of enthusiasm. The appointees of President Nixon, for example, are hardly likely to be regarded as allies by social reform groups seeking to change the direction of corporate policy.

This country's limited experience with government-appointed directors in such companies as the Union Pacific Railroad, the Illinois Central Railroad, and the Prudential Life Insurance Co. inspires little confidence that such representatives will help produce decisions that better reflect the public interest. The more recent introduction of government directors into newer ventures, such as the Communications Satellite Corp. (COMSAT), so far has given no reason for a different conclusion.

Nor does the European experience with government directors support the proposal. Neither the British nor the French experience with government directors on the boards of nationalized companies, nor the more recent Swedish experience with government directors on the boards of some private companies, has demonstrated a greater degree of public accountability or increased sensitivity to the needs of the community at large.

Problems with Special Interest Directors

The proposals for special interest representation on the board present serious problems. The first of these general problems is the lack of American experience with such solutions. While the European experience may give us some insight, European models cannot be expected to function in the same manner in the different political, economic, historical, and cultural setting of the United States.

Second, it is doubtful how effective special interest directors could be. The imposition of a minority of such directors upon the board may accomplish little in the face of the hostility of the majority of the board. If decisions are made in caucus prior to the board meeting, reducing it to an empty formality; if there is an inadequate flow of information; if there is limited cooperation from management — the special interest director will be unable to function effectively. This has happened in Germany under partial codetermination. Minority representation has built-in limitations. Mr. Townsend's proposal that the public director receive corporate funds to support an independent staff of his own would provide a partial answer. But the question remains whether support from the board as a whole is not essential for the effective functioning of any director.

Third, to whom would the special interest director owe primary loyalty? Under traditional corporation law, the director owes undivided loyalty to the corporation and to the stockholders; further, such loyalty runs to all stockholders, not merely to those who elected him or her. The special interest director representing the interests of a particular group would face a fundamental conflict of interest.

British nationalized industries have sought to sidestep this problem by requiring primary loyalty to the corporation. Labor directors installed on the boards of nationalized firms have been required to resign all formal affiliation with the trade union movement. Labor directors come to boards as persons with a trade union perspective, but not as representatives of the trade union movement. (The same pattern is found in Norway.) The labor director, at this point, is no longer representing a "special interest"; he or she instead serves the function of broadening the perspectives of the board.

Special interest representatives are bound to face a conflict of interest, unless their addition to the board is accompanied by far-reaching corporate changes. If the present purely economic objectives of the corporation were broadened so that the advancement of stockholder interests were no longer the primary goal, then of course the obligation of undivided loyalty to stockholders would disappear. New fiduciary standards for directors would have to be fashioned, which would reflect the changed composition of the board and the revised objectives of the corporation — and almost inevitably the new criteria would have to recognize the paramount loyalty of special interest directors to their constituencies.

The Board as Political Battleground

However, this development would transform the board into a political institution, a microcosm of the community. *All* the directors would become, in effect, special interest representatives (whether for an outside group or simply for the shareholders), working to satisfy their particular constituency. The problem of conflict of interest for the individual board members would be replaced by the problem of *conflict among* all the directors. It is extremely doubtful that such a board could manage a corporation effectively. Board decisions would involve shifting alliances between the constituent groups, with log-rolling deals (for the exchange of support for respective proposals), all of which would lead to a condition aptly described by Beardsley Ruml decades ago as "gangsterism." In France, for example, the tripartite structure of nationalized corporations (with government, employee, and consumer directors) has been strongly criticized by Professors Friedman and Garner as resulting "in a constant tug of war between the different . . . interests instead of providing a balanced administration in the public interest." The board, in short, could be reduced to a battleground of competing interests.

Last, special interest representation presents the fundamental problem of assuring adequate representation on the board for all the groups in society affected by the corporation. Even if so awesomely difficult an objective were somehow achieved, with appropriate degrees of recognition for all interests, the adverse consequences of transforming the board into an arena of conflicting forces would remain.

It is apparent that some of the problems presented by special interest representation on the board arise because of the *unitary* board system with which we are familiar. It is worth asking whether a change in the structure of the board might sidestep some of these problems.

It is perhaps no accident that codetermination has taken root in Germany, and been adopted in the European Company Draft Statute, as part of a corporate structure that features a *dual* board. Under the German system, faithfully followed in the Draft Statute, employees are represented only on the upper, or supervisory, board, which has important but limited functions. It does not manage. It does not set policy. It is not concerned with day-to-day operations. It has two major roles: it elects the members of the lower or managing board, and it receives reports from the managing board and supervises it. It is the managing board that conducts the business of the corporation.

The insulation of the employee directors from the conduct of the business and the determination of policy significantly reduces the lack of harmony or unity that would imperil the functioning of the unitary American or English board. Moreover, as a political matter, it makes the introduction of employee directors more palatable to management and stockholders.

Apparently, there have been no formal efforts to introduce the dual board into the United States. Nevertheless, some movement in this direction has occurred in practice. A number of major American corporations have sought to reorganize senior management through creation of a collegium of officials at the highest level. Organizing the office of the chairman, or of the president, to include not only that officer but also a limited number of directors, working full time and without other duties or titles, amounts to the introduction of a new dual structure; the reorganized office bears some resemblance to the German managing board.

One should not make too much of the development of these offices. It is still in the early stages and the ultimate nature of the dualism it creates is not clear. It could, however, lead in time to some variation of the dual board system.

The growing influence of the executive committee points in the same direction. In those corporations where an active executive committee meets at least monthly, and a relatively inactive board meets quarterly, confining its actions to ratifying the acts of the executive committee, an important functional change has taken place. In such corporations, too, there is a resemblance to the dual board system.

Both trends, the collegium of senior officials and the expanded use of the executive committee, could conceivably reduce some of the difficulties of special interest representation.

Employee Directors: A Possibility

Until the proposal for employee representation is adopted and vigorously pursued by American trade unions, it is a purely academic idea. Nevertheless, there are three powerful forces at work which could, in time, make employee representation a reality.

The first factor is the changing attitudes of workers. The attitudes of both blue- and white-collar employees toward their work are a matter of growing concern. Job alienation, increased absenteeism, increased labor turnover, declining productivity, low morale, resistance to dull and repetitive work, and hostility to the production line — all are familiar features of the current scene and have made business aware of the importance of increasing job satisfaction. Lordstown has become part of our vocabulary.

Added to the underlying dissatisfaction with work is the growing phenomenon of employee dissent. Underground newspapers highly critical of employer policies, leafletting on company premises, boycotts by employees protesting company attitudes, and "whistle blowing," the unauthorized disclosure of "antisocial" company conduct, all illustrate the current ferment. Traditional employer-employee relationships are clearly being affected by the profound and accelerating change in American society in values, attitudes, and "consciousness."

In response to these manifestations, the fundamental relationship of the employer to the employee is undergoing reexamination. It is recognized that one of the most effective ways of reducing worker alienation is human fulfillment through participation in decision-making.

Increasing employer-employee consultation on the grass roots level as to job organization, work allocation, and production may well involve greater employee participation in lower-level management decisions. In turn, this could lead ultimately to pressure for employee representation on the board itself. However, there is serious question whether board representation is as useful or important in achieving the values that flow from worker participation as are opportunities on the plant level.

The second factor is the developing interest in federal incorporation of major corporations. The increasing abdication of control by various states over the internal conduct of corporate affairs, and growing concern with the role of the large corporation in society, makes enactment of a federal incorporation statute within the next 15 years quite possible.

The open question is the content of such a statute. We have little idea of what to expect. Clearly, however, consideration of so fundamental a departure as a federal incorporation statute would inevitably involve a serious inquiry into possible areas of corporate reform. Proposals for employee representation on the board, and for public or government directors, would be given high priority on such an agenda.

The third factor is the strength of the movement for employee directors outside the United States. The world grows smaller and smaller and the experience of other nations increasingly significant to us. The widespread acceptance in Europe of employee representation is bound to influence American business attitudes. In addition, the multi-national experience of many large American corporations will make a great deal of difference. Firsthand experience with employee representation in practice can only increase understanding of the proposal.

In summary, there is no sign at present that fundamental change in the American corporate structure to embrace any form of special interest representation (whether in a single or neodual board system) is apt to become a serious possibility in the near future. Nevertheless, public concern with the objectives and responsibilities of the large corporation in a period of social and environmental crisis, combined with the factors described above, may in time create a climate in which proposals of this nature could become a matter of realistic concern.

25   The Corporate Board and Special Interests

Harold Koontz

One of the interesting and unsettling signs of our time is the developing movement toward forcing special interest representation on the boards of directors of large companies. Privately owned businesses have come under fire from a variety of special interest groups — racial minorities, consumer groups, students, ecologists, and others — and

From *Business Horizons,* October 1971, pp. 75–82. Copyright 1971 by the Foundation for the School of Business at Indiana University. Reprinted by permission.

government agencies, both legislative and administrative, have recently accelerated regulatory approaches instituted by the New Deal nearly forty years ago. It is understandable, therefore, that the composition and effectiveness of corporate boards of directors would be matters of major concern. To the public and members of legislative bodies, the board is naturally perceived as standing at the pinnacle of our corporations. This is not surprising because legally and managerially it is, or at least should be.

Because of the belief, as erroneous as it may be in most cases, that business and other enterprises lack adequate social responsibility, it is natural for a feeling to arise that the problem is with boards of directors. Many believe that representation of special interest groups on governing boards would help correct this deficiency. We have seen a mounting pressure for special interest representation in university councils, public school boards, government legislative bodies, and in high places of federal, state, and local governments. It is understandable that, with business enterprises, the earliest pressures would be exerted on such highly visible quasipublic enterprises as large banks, the automobile companies, and public utilities.

The basic question is whether this trend is so real that it cannot be ignored, whether special interest representation on the board is in the best interest of our companies and our society, or whether there are better and more acceptable ways to deal with the problem and assure that the modern large corporation will be attuned to current significant social trends and demands. In my opinion, representation of special interest groups on a corporate board is neither appropriate nor necessary and, in fact, can even have negative repercussions.

The Role of the Board

It is well understood that, by law, corporations must be "managed" by a board of directors. This requirement is buttressed by a long tradition in all kinds of societies that the final managerial responsibility in important enterprises of all kinds should not be entrusted to a single individual but should be exercised by a group.

It is obvious that a board cannot, in a complete sense, manage a corporation. However, in my judgment, the public is not in a mood to allow any board of an enterprise of great public interest to be a passive auditor or observer with the function of only seeing that it is well-managed. Therefore, it becomes important that boards exercise the kind of managing that will ensure that the long-run interests of the corporation and its shareholders are served.

This means that its role is more than trusteeship — the safeguarding and husbanding of the company's assets in the long-term interests of the shareholders. It must specifically include responsibilities for determining enterprise objectives, assuring effective operating management, securing long-range business stability and growth in a changing environment, making certain that major plans are designed to meet objectives, and assuring as far as possible that objectives are achieved and plans succeed.[1]

Lord Cole, former chairman of Unilever, has stated that the task of a board is "to allocate the resources within the control of the company in such a way as to give the company's customers the maximum satisfaction, as measured in price that they will pay for the company's products, at the minimum of expense to the company as measured in the costs it has to incure to produce these products." [2] In other words, Lord Cole concludes it is the board's job to see that a company conducts its business to make the maximum continuing profit through proper allocation of resources.

One must bear in mind that the board is a company's true top management and that all managers at all levels in any kind of enterprise have the same basic task. This it to design and maintain an environment for the effective and efficient performance of individuals working in groups in contributing to achievement of enterprise objectives. In the setting of enterprise objectives and the means of accomplishing them, all managers, and especially the board of directors in its top management role, have the common-sense need, in their own and their enterprise's interest, to be responsive to the external environment — whether economic, technological, political, social, or ethical. A business is primarily an economic enterprise and, while its main task is not to solve social problems, its own self-interest demands that it be fully aware of and responsive to its entire external environment.

It is the moral and logical obligation of all managers to manage so as to achieve the most in terms of enterprise purpose with the resources at their command, or to accomplish purposes with the minimum of human and material resources. In business, this happens to be called "profit." But a moment's reflection will show that a "surplus" goal is appropriate for a chief of police, a university administrator, or a head of a government agency. In a real sense, this was the goal Lord Cole was referring to in his statement concerning the task of a board of directors.

The board in particular has also a special additional function of "legitimation" to the community. This point is well-made by a prominent sociologist in his study of boards of directors. His position is essentially that the most effective board, and one most likely to be most

---

[1] These functions and responsibilities are discussed in Harold Koontz, *The Board of Directors and Effective Management,* McGraw-Hill Book Company, New York, 1967, Chapter II.

[2] "The Future of the Board," *The Director,* XX (February 1968), 234–37.

effective in respect to the administrative leadership, is one closely in tune to its total environment. In this way, the board can assure community acceptance and support for the enterprise.[3]

Recent Concerns with Boards

A number of recent events have attracted more than ordinary public interest and concern to corporate boards. Exactly how great their effect will be, no one can yet say. However, these events have given fuel to many legislators and various interest groups who thrive on increasing government intervention and who often fail to understand that our system of free competitive private enterprise — not really very free any more — has been largely responsible for the economic and cultural progress of the United States.

The recent explosion of urgent social problems related to racial minorities, unemployment, ecology, education, an unpopular war, drug addiction, and growing crime have served to focus extraordinary public attention on the deficiencies of our system and culture. This convergence of problems has given rise to a belief that business should somehow "do something" and certainly "do more."

The Nader book, his safety campaign, and the Congressional hearings in 1966, coupled with some unfortunate behavior by the automotive industry and by the world-wide recognition of the smog problem have had an impact on corporate boards and top management quite beyond the auto industry. People have unduly blamed the automotive industry and have often unreasonably held boards and top managers responsible for these problems. People overlook the fact that, in a market economy, it is the task of companies to serve the market. While it may be wrong for buyers to purchase cars with expensive automatic transmissions, high horsepower, and air conditioning, rather than demanding safety and smog control devices and construction, the fact is they have.

The only appropriate criticism to be aimed at the automotive industry is that their responsible top managers did not perceive earlier the growing social concerns and had not prepared for the present climate through more intensive research and development. It has been indeed a case where, as Frederick Donner, former chairman of General Motors, conceded: "We have got a tradition in General Motors of maybe too much sticking with our business problems." [4]

---

[3] Mayer N. Zald, "The Power and Functions of Boards of Directors: a Theoretical Synthesis," *American Journal of Sociology,* LXXV (July 1969), 97–111.

[4] Dan Cordtz, "The Face in the Mirror at General Motors," *Fortune,* LXXIV (August 1966), 117 ff.

Unfortunately, too, the image of corporate boards has been somewhat tarnished by several cases involving lack of full disclosure of information and insider stock trading. In such incidents as the BarChris Construction Corporation and Texas Gulf Sulphur cases, legal action has caused executives and board members to be subjected to financial penalties or recoveries and the management system of the nation to adverse publicity. The responsibility and effectiveness of corporate boards has understandably come in for considerable criticism.

Perhaps no greater impact on public interest and distrust of corporate boards has occurred than with the recent bankruptcy of the Penn Central Railroad. The country's largest railroad had a prestigious and experienced board of directors, but was found to be a case where, at least in the opinion of the press and the public, the directors did not direct. One must appreciate that it is difficult for the public to understand how an apparently profitable very large company could have so many financial and performance deficiencies that could and did so completely escape its boards of directors for so long.

Trends in Board Practice

Increasing public and management concern with boards of directors has been evidenced by a number of trends in board practice and by certain questions that can be raised about board composition.

Outside directors

There has been a perceptible trend in this country and in other nations, such as Great Britain and Australia, toward increasing the number of outside, or nonemployee, board members. Studies of the National Industrial Conference Board from 1938 through 1966 have verified this trend in the United States. In 1938, boards were evenly split between those with a majority of outsiders and those with a majority of employee directors. But about 53 percent of the manufacturing companies had a majority of outsiders by 1953; 57 percent by 1958; 61 percent by 1961; and 63 percent in 1966. Among nonmanufacturing companies, the number of those with a majority of outside directors has long been high, being 85 percent in both 1959 and 1966. In banking and insurance companies, where boards tend to be large, the percentage of outside members has also long been high, with only some 15 percent of the directors being officer employees.[5]

---

[5] The results of studies made in 1938, 1953, 1958, 1961, and 1967 are summarized in J. Bacon, *Corporate Directorship Practices* (Business Policy Study No. 125; National Industrial Conference Board, New York, 1967), p. 6.

Perhaps the trend toward outside representation on corporate boards is best indicated by the action of the New York Stock Exchange, which adopted the rule in 1966 that all newly listed companies should have at least two outside directors on its board. While already listed companies were not required to do so, such long-standing inside boards as Standard Oil Company of New Jersey and Bethlehem Steel Corporation hastened to add outside members to their ranks.

The point should be made that one cannot accurately measure inside or outside influence by a numerical count of directors; presumably, however, the more outsiders on boards, the more influence they will have. The real point is how the board actually operates — whether it is another management committee advising the chief executive officer or whether it is a truly plural executive with outsiders bringing fresh and independent views. In either case, there has been clear evidence of internal and external pressures toward boards more representative of shareholders' interests generally and less dependent on executive officers.

Qualifications of directors

There is evidence that more attention is being paid to the needs for directors with certain qualifications. One sees this concern expressed in many studies of boards of directors and certain editorial comments. There has been considerable agreement that the effective board member will possess intelligence, judgment, and ability to analyze problems; will come to rational solutions; be willing to identify himself with the company and its stockholder interests; have the ability to speak out independently on board matters; and be an individual of high integrity who thoroughly understands the ethics of his company and community.

Specifically, companies generally appear to look for persons with business experience, knowledge, and capability; ability to contribute to board balance (complement the abilities and weaknesses, primarily of knowledge and experience, of other board members); and success in his principal occupation or profession. Other desirable qualifications include stature in the community; maturity, but young enough to be counted on for a reasonably long period of service; interest in the company; and willingness to spend the requisite time.

What companies actually do is interesting. Studies of both manufacturing and nonmanufacturing companies of the occupations of outside directors show that a predominant number are selected from the following occupations: bankers, retired corporate officers, chairmen and presidents from other companies, prominent businessmen, attorneys, brokers, and investment and financial counselors. Among larger manufacturing companies, only some 4 percent of all directors were educators; in nonmanufacturing companies, less than 2 percent were educators; and among banks only one-fourth of 1 percent were educators.[6]

Surveys of studies, books, and responsible comments on board qualifications indicate a complete unanimity of opinion that *no director should be selected to represent some faction or special interest group,* other than, of course, large shareholder groups. To be sure, it must be recognized that these studies are mostly made by experienced directors or reflect actual experience.

The business experience syndrome

In setting qualifications for directors and, even more especially, in actually selecting directors, top level business experience is heavily emphasized. Often, in addition, this experience is thought of as best when closely related to the industry of the business corporation concerned.

This view is understandable because of the desire to have people who can contribute to solution of a given business' problems. But such a background can lead to several questionable results: inbreeding of thinking and attitudes, picking business cronies, and naming people with views and values similar to other directors. It can tend to perpetuate Frederick Donner's perceptive remark of "too much sticking to our business problems." [7] Without intending to imply support for selecting pleaders of special interests as directors, one can raise the question of whether even the highest caliber, experienced, and well-meaning business executive can and will "read" adequately the total external environment and its future impact on a company.

The rising focus on responsibility

The literature in and around business, whether studies, books, or editorial comments, has increasingly reflected a rising focus on the social responsibility of our business corporations. Much of this reflects a lack of appreciation of the role of business in a relatively free enterprise society. It is based on a lack of understanding to the extent to which better managed companies are actually now responsive to the external social as well as to the economic and technological environment.

But some is appropriately aimed at the tunnel vision or myopia of many people who are responsible for the leadership of our business

---

[6] J. Bacon, *Corporate Directorship Practices,* pp. 15, 22.

[7] It is interesting that Mrs. Virginia H. Knauer, Special Assistant to the President for Consumer Affairs, has formulated "Knauer's Theory," which states that responsiveness of the firm is directly proportionate to distance on the organization chart from consumers to the board chairman. See *New York Times,* Sept. 18, 1970, p. 47.

enterprises. In any case, the public interest and concern is here and growing. No responsible business can ignore it.

Codetermination

One long experience in the introduction of special interest groups on boards of directors is the case of codetermination. This is a term applied to the practice (which originated, among capitalist countries, in Germany over a century ago) of legally requiring labor representatives on many boards of directors. In Germany, larger companies are required to have one-third of the supervisory board (the top level board that is empowered only to elect the executive board members, approve certain issues, and disapprove certain operating decisions) elected from among the workers. In coal and steel companies, workers elect half the directors on the supervisory board and one of three directors on the executive board, which really operates a company, reporting in certain specific and limited ways to and subject to veto in certain specific matters by the supervisory board.

Codetermination has not been adopted widely in capitalist countries, although it does exist to some extent in a few European countries, principally for certain national interest industries. But worker representation on boards is common in socialist countries. In Egypt, for example, company boards are comprised normally of nine members — four elected by the workers and five appointed by the government. The appointed directors are commonly insiders and are usually comprised of the top management of the state-owned companies.

To date, experience with codetermination has indicated two major results. In the first place, workers on the board normally concern themselves only with matters of direct interest to their constituents, namely pay, fringe benefits, working conditions, and grievances. In the second place, it is common for the management and shareholder members of the boards to meet informally before regular board meetings to caucus and make preliminary decisions on business matters before the main board meets. These results are hardly surprising to anyone with experience in group decision making where special and narrow interest representatives are involved.

Minority representation

While no complete statistics are available, a few major American corporations have recently placed racial minority members on boards of directors. They include such prominent businesses as the General Motors Corporation, Pan American World Airways, Standard Oil Company of Ohio, and Columbia Broadcasting Company, all of whom have Negro directors. However, while race may have been a factor in these appointments, all have been prominent and apparently well-qualified board members.

The lack of members of racial minorities, particularly of the black race, on the boards of larger companies has not gone unnoticed. A black writer has proposed a plan whereby over the next twenty years 10 percent of the largest 500 industrials, 10 percent of the largest banks, and 10 percent of the 500 next largest industrials would be transferred by government arranged and financially assisted transfer to black capitalists and managers.[8] While this proposal has overtones of complete impracticability and certainly smacks of socializing a portion of American industry for the benefit of one minority group, the very fact that it comes from a well-educated and apparently responsible black must give white America pause.

Special Interest Representation

The case for

In reviewing the thinking on the question of special interest representation on corporate boards, there appear to be a number of major considerations in favor of doing so.

First, the distinctive concerns of special interest groups will be constantly considered in the formulation of a corporation's strategy and policy.

Second, the corporation will indicate to the public in general that it is in fact concerned with and giving attention to major social problems.

Third, special interest group representation will meet pressures of the groups, soothe the temper of the times, and placate the various legislators and other public figures who are highly critical of large businesses.

Fourth, such special interests as banking, law, marketing, and engineering have long been represented on boards. In view of the corporation's need for profitable survival in a *total* external environment, it might be good practice if such special interests as racial minorities, ecologists, and consumers are also represented.

The case against

The following arguments appear to be the case against inserting representatives of the various special interest groups on company boards of directors.

First, appointment of special interest representatives is inconsistent with the fundamental role of the director — to represent the interest

---

[8] Richard F. America, Jr., "What Do You People Want," *Harvard Business Review,* XLVII (March–April, 1969), 103–12. It is worth noting that America is a graduate of the Harvard Business School and has been with the Stanford Research Institute since 1965, where he is a development economist in the urban and regional economics group.

of all the shareholders for continuing growth, stability, and profits. While certain specialized talents and experience are now represented on the typical board, the effective board should not have these talents for their specializations alone; they should be coupled with an ability and willingness to take a total corporate view of board level problems.

Thus, the fourth argument in favor of special interest groups overlooks the fact that representatives from these would almost certainly see themselves only as acting for and on behalf of these special interests. Certainly inclusion of worker members on boards overseas has proved this.

Also, it cannot be forgotten that, for the outside director, his objectivity is clearly thought to be basic to his function. He is on the board primarily to provide an objective view to offset the possibility of parochialism and excessive reliance on history that can sometimes characterize employee directors.

Second, there would be considerable danger of continual factionalism on the board. Studies of group behavior by sociologists and social psychologists have shown that dangerous, if not destructive, factionalism and coalitions result in such cases, particularly if the perceptions of organizational goals of special groups are different from those of the corporation, as they are likely to be. While differences of opinion among board members are highly desirable, factionalism based upon fundamentally distinct differences in goals and policies can hardly be constructive.

Third, it is also possible that special interest representatives on a board will suffer disillusionment and even be self-defeating. If the majority of the board, even for good reason, does not agree with the position of a special interest group representative, he and his constituents may well feel that they have been misled and used only for "window-dressing," with predictable results. If the special interest group representative takes a balanced position on a board matter and does not appear to be actively representing his constituents' interests, he will likely be regarded as having "sold out" or as an "Uncle Tom." Should this occur, as seems probable, the result may be more negative to the corporation than if he had not been put on the board in the first place.

Probabilities Ahead

In my opinion, we can see trends that will influence the character of boards and their operation. Certain pressures are certain to build up. For example, there will unquestionably be continually greater pressure for increasing evidence of social responsiveness by business firms. Not only must businesses actually be more responsive to their entire external environment while still continuing their economic mission in society, but the public must be given evidence of an objective nature (contrasted to public relations ballyhoo) that they are in fact responsive and responsible.

In addition, the pressure for more demonstrably effective boards of directors will continue to mount. The day is passing where at least large public company boards can be clubby groups of superficial observers of company top management action and the passing business scene. The pressure for more effective outside representation on corporate boards will continue, supported by the belief that boards will actually operate with the objectivity and perspicacity expected of such representation.

We can also expect increased regulation of private business to assure — and probably overassure — the interests of consumers and environmentalists as perceived by legislators and various special interest groups. Unfortunately, some of this may end up as thwarting the legitimate and desirable interests of our private enterprise market economy.

I do not anticipate in the foreseeable future any legislation, such as the German-type codetermination, requiring elected labor representatives on boards. Even though precedent appears to favor this as a first step toward special interest group representation, growing public concern over labor union power, plus the labor union's desire to remain independent of business for bargaining purposes, would appear to make legislation of this kind unlikely.

What Should Companies Do?

A company, I believe, should not embark on a program of appointing representatives of special interest groups on a corporate board of directors. While I would not advise against having a member of such a group on a board if he is otherwise fully qualified, I do not think he should be appointed just because he represents a special interest.

A company should embark, however, on a program of leavening pure business or executive experience on the board; this means appointment of more persons who have distinguished themselves in other ways than high level business experience. These are persons who not only have the ability to act responsibly as a director on behalf of the long-range interests of the total corporation, but whose experience, training, and outlook would force appropriate consideration of all environmental factors in current policy decisions. It is important that a board avoid what I have referred to previously as the excessive business experience syndrome.

A company should also engage in a program of regular briefings to the board, by inside or preferably by outside specialists, on forecasts of environmental factors which may affect the company's business. We have long done this with economic forecasts, and a growing number of companies are briefing boards on technological expectancies. The view of the probable environment in which a company will operate should be as carefully and expertly extended to social, political, and ethical factors.

Finally, a company should develop a far more effective program than anyone has yet done to convince the general public that it does act responsibly and is responsive to our entire social environment. While solving major social problems is not its primary purpose, it nonetheless recognizes it does not stand aloof from them, and that good social citizenship and good business are and can be consistent.

Most people are not aware of the extent of responsiveness and responsbility of the large majority of American business firms. I am mindful that it is not easy to convey these facts to the public. But judging by the inadequate efforts our business corporations undertake to convince university students of these facts and attitudes, I am impressed that very little that could be done is in fact being done.

It could be a harmful mistake if our large public corporations yielded to pressure for special interest group representation in order to solve the problem of being more responsive to the entire business environment. The problem does exist, more often than is realized, but boards should look in other directions for dealing with it.

Case

Drew Olympic Motors

In June of 1971 the board of Drew Olympic Motors faced a major decision which would have a lasting effect on the firm. Without substantial changes in product line, Drew Olympic could expect a deteriorating competitive position and possible ultimate bankruptcy. The board was considering several courses of action which could maintain the firm's profitable existence, and was attempting to determine which alternative best fit the objectives of the company as they saw them.

The present firm of Drew Olympic Motors was formed by the merger of several small automobile manufacturers in the 1950's, the oldest of which, the Drew Motor Carriage Co., had been established by David Drew in 1907. Since the merger Drew Olympic has been able to establish a stable and profitable position for itself in the automobile industry. At the present time the firm's board of directors is faced with the necessity of deciding which of three mutually exclusive alternative courses of action should be followed. Each of the alternatives will have substantial and differing effects on the future of Drew Olympic Motors.

During the 1960's and early 1970's, Drew Olympic was able to acquire and maintain a relatively stable 15 percent share of the automobile market, concentrating its efforts on the production of reliable and moderately innovative cars in the low and intermediate price ranges. In addition to the popularity of its cars, a portion of Drew Olympic's success was undoubtedly the result of its efficient and loyal dealer organization and its exceptionally harmonious labor relations.

Reprinted by the courtesy of Professor Conrad Doenges, University of Texas.

Drew Olympic's competitive success was reflected in its common stock. Both earnings per share and dividends have exhibited a moderate but stable growth rate over the past ten years. At the present time earnings per share and dividends per share are $4 and $2, respectively. In recent years, Drew Olympic's common stock has been regarded as of "blue chip" quality. Stockholder studies made in the current year show that a majority of the shares are held by mutual funds and small investors who are interested in a combination of stable income and moderate (or better) growth, and by pension funds.

Drew Olympic's record within the auto industry, as well as the performance of its stock in the market, have generated considerable interest both within and without the industry. A recent issue of a major business and financial periodical featured an in-depth study of the company and carried a portrait of Kurt Konrad, chairman of the company's board of directors, on its cover. The article included an interview with Mr. Konrad, an excerpt of which follows:

Question: Mr. Konrad, we've already established the extent of your firm's success technically, competitively, and in the stock market. But as you know, there is increasing public interest in the social role of industry. In particular, the public seems increasingly concerned about the responsibilties of the auto industry to consumers and to the quality of our environment. Do such concerns have any influence on policy decisions at Drew Olympic?

Kurt Konrad: It would be easy to answer your question with optimistic and self-serving platitudes. Truthfully, such concerns are considered, but to be completely honest with you, I must outline the philosophy behind our policy decisions, a philosophy that represents the consensus of both our board and our senior management people.

As we see it, we must attempt to attain a number of objectives in any major decision. First of all, we are concerned with the welfare of our stockholders, primarily in terms of maximizing their wealth over the long run. Specifically, this means that we strive for stable and increasing earnings and dividends. We believe that such a course will maximize the market price of our stock. Closely related is our objective of maintaining and increasing our 15 percent market share. By the nature of our business, this is necessary if we are to continue to be successful; equally important, this market share is essential to the strength and profitability of our dealer organization, to which we owe a great deal.

In addition to these objectives, there are several others we strive to attain. We have a responsibility to our customers, in terms of quality and price of our products. We have, in recent years, been able to offer increasingly safe and reliable cars and, at the same time, to hold our annual price increases at the lowest level in the industry.

Similarly, we have a responsibility to our employees and the communities in which they live. Obviously, this translates into wage rates and working conditions and harmonious labor relations. But it also means maintaining a high level of employment, since we are the major employer in each of the areas in which our plants are located.

In addition, we are very much aware of our responsibility to society as a whole. This responsibility is exercised in many ways. In terms of two areas of concern, safety and pollution, we consistently exceed federal standards for safety and exhaust emissions. In fact, an independent testing agency has rated our cars as both the safest and least polluting on the road. Naturally, we spend substantial sums for research in these and related fields. I should add that our concern for society is not limited to these two areas but extends into a number of others also.

Finally, I would be remiss if I did not add that we have a responsibility to all our executives. So long as their performance is as excellent as it has been, they must be rewarded, not only in terms of salaries and bonuses, but also in terms of both job security and opportunity for advancement.

In summary, we have established multiple goals for our company. The welfare of our stockholders is first, but only the first among equals. In addition, we consider, in every major decision, its effect on our market share, on our employees, on our customers, on society, and on our executives. Fortunately, we have never been forced to sacrifice any one of these for the sake of another.

Question: Mr. Konrad, that sounds very impressive. But I find it hard to believe that any one group of men can be aware of all the significant aspects that must be considered if such a wide range of objectives are to be satisfied. How do you do it?

Kurt Konrad: I can understand your disbelief. Let me point out that both management and shareholders are represented on our board. In addition, we often invite representatives of consumer organizations and the union to meet with us. But I think that most of the credit for our capability of evaluating the effects of a policy decision in terms of a number of objectives should go to our corporate research and planning staff. This group was first formed in 1960; in the intervening years it has developed an almost uncanny ability to forecast, not only technical developments, but also social and economic developments of significance to the company. Their track record is truly amazing, and we owe much of the success of our company to their ability.

At the June 1971 board meetings, Chairman Konrad presented the other directors with an outline of the problems faced and the alternative solutions possible. Several lengthy board meetings were held, at which neither modifications in the analysis were made nor additional feasible alternatives were discovered. The situation facing the board remained the same as that described in the following summary:

> A series of studies have been made over the course of the past year by Drew Olympic's research and planning department and by independent consulting firms. All these studies have arrived at the same conclusion: because of changes in the product market and in competitive products, Drew Olympic can not continue to compete successfully unless it changes its product line drastically. Failure to adjust to these changing conditions will lead to bankruptcy within the next five to seven years.

In response to this requirement for change, the research and planning department identified three alternative courses of action and forecast the effects of each. Each of the plans is feasible for the company, but the three are mutually exclusive. Only one plan can be followed. Characteristics of the plans and the results of their acceptance have been summarized as follows:

Plan A

Drew Olympic would concentrate its efforts in what is now the higher priced segment of its line. Market share would certainly be reduced from the present 15 percent to a maximum of 10 percent. At the same time, it would be necessary to increase retail prices by an estimated 10 percent. In other respects, the change would not have undesirable results: care produced would exhaust emissions at least 10 percent below all foreseeable federal standards, employment would remain unchanged, and the number of executive positions would remain unchanged. Most desirable is the fact that both earnings and dividends would double (to $8 and $4 per share, respectively) over the next four years.

Plan B

Drew Olympic would concentrate its efforts on its least expensive models, eliminating frequent changes and building a mass-market, utility car. Market share was expected to increase initially to 20 percent and could reach 30 percent over the next four years, in part because prices would remain unchanged from their present levels. The exhaust emissions of cars produced under this plan should meet all foreseeable federal requirements. Stockholders could expect that earnings and dividends would be maintained at their present levels of $4 and $2 per share, respectively. Unfortunately, approximately one-third of the present management — including two vice presidents — would be no longer needed. On the other hand, factory employment would increase by 20 percent, an increase sufficient to reduce the present 7 percent unemployment rate in factory communities to an all-time low of 2 percent.

Plan C

Drew Olympic would eliminate its present lines and concentrate on a new design incorporating a revolutionary new power plant and exhaust system. The new design would result in a car with exhaust emissions no greater than 50 percent of foreseeable federal standards. The new cars would require a price increase of at least 35 percent initially, with 10 to 15 percent annual price increases probable because of the necessity for continued research and development. Even so, market share would remain at 15 percent because of public interest in the reduction of pollution. The new design would require a substantial and continuing investment in sophisticated new equipment. Automation and new techniques would require the employment of a number of new executives, as well as promotions and expanded responsibilities for many present executives. However, the factory labor force would be cut by at least 40 percent, raising unemployment in factory communities to the 18 percent level. Finally, investment needs would require the elimination of dividends, and increases in costs and expenses would prevent earnings per share from rising above $2 in the next five years.

Bearing in mind the objectives established by the board, which plan should Drew Olympic follow?

Bibliography

"Activists Adopt New Tactics, Goals." *Industry Week,* April 30, 1973, pp. 28ff.

"Arthur Goldberg on Public Directors," *Business and Society Review/ Innovation,* 5 (Spring 1973), 35–39.

Berstein, J. "Capitalism and Consumerism: Boon to Corporate Advertising." *Public Relations Journal* 30 (November 1974), 24ff.

"Business Brief: Workers on the Board." *Economist,* March 24, 1973, pp. 66–67.

Clutterback, D. "How Effective Are Worker Directors?" *Industrial Management,* February 1974, pp. 14–16.

"Companies Feel the Wrath of the Clergy." *Business Week,* March 18, 1972, p. 85.

"Corporate Critics Gain New Allies." *Business Week,* February 13, 1971, p. 29.

Cravens, D. W., and G. E. Hills. "Consumerism: A Perspective for Business." *Business Horizons,* 13 (August 1970), 21–28.

"How Bosses Feel about Women's Lib." *Business Week,* September 5, 1970, pp. 18–19.

McGuire, Joseph, and John Parrish. "Status Report on a Profound Revolution." *California Management Review* 13 (Summer 1971), 79–86.

Revelt, J. "Power of New Congressmen Bodes Well for Consumerists." *Advertising Age,* January 27, 1975, pp. 1ff.

"Social Activists Stir Up the Annual Meeting." *Business Week,* April 1, 1972, pp. 48–49.

"The Board: It's Obsolete Unless Overhauled." *Business Week,* May 22, 1971, pp. 50–58.

Vanderwicken, P. "Change Invades the Boardroom." *Fortune,* May 1972, pp. 156–159.

"Voice of Labor Will Be Heard in the Boardrooms." *Chemical Week,* March 7, 1973, pp. 19–20.

"When Workers Become Directors." *Business Week,* September 15, 1973, p. 188.

Part Seven
Social Responsibility for the Professional Manager

A. The Social Responsibility Concept

In the fifties and sixties controversies raged over the question of the social responsibility of the business person. The concept was heatedly debated, and both accepted and rejected throughout this period. The article "How Social Responsibility Became Institutionalized" [26] describes a further development of the concept in the form of numerous social action programs established by U.S. business. For example, in recent years legislation has taken over the social responsibility function in handling pollution problems. Also, the Equal Employment Opportunity Commission has forced extensive compliance with antidiscrimination laws through a variety of law suits. As a result companies have pulled back their more public relations-oriented projects and have focused instead upon internalized social action, concentrating on those things that they can do extremely well and those that are basic to the operations of the company. For example, Western Electric has been effective in developing minority suppliers, Sears, Roebuck has provided counseling for minority business people, and the Borden Company has established a minority affairs council. *Business Week's* Business Citizenship Awards for the past number of years have identified leaders in socially responsible programs, and a U.S. Chamber of Commerce spokesperson has stated that "sensitivity to social problems has become institutionalized, at least on the first two levels of management." Additional activities such as programs for resolving ecological problems, urban renewal programs, and more extensive and effective programs for minorities appear to have refuted arguments against the social responsibility concept.

But while the social responsibility concept *appears* to have been institutionalized for the business person, it is still contested by able opponents and arguments. In the article "The Hazards of Corporate Responsibility" [27], Gilbert Burck identifies the problems created by the social responsibility doctrine and its applications. It is a debate that leaves the U.S. business person confused and defensive. The classical school of economics has Milton Friedman as its spokesperson, but he is opposed by Paul Samuelson in this same field. The functions and goals of business are the efficient utilization of scarce resources in the production and distribution of goods in a free market economy. But supporters of Ralph Nader appeal for extreme social responsibility programs, and others ask that business shift from profit-maximizing goals to profit-optimizing goals. Some individuals contend that business can perform the social responsibility functions better than government, and others that business *and* government will inevitably complement each other in these efforts.

The cost of social programs established by business is anything but clear, but it appears that ultimately those costs will be borne by the consumer. Some people advocate the social audit as a means of measuring social contributions, but the widespread application of such an instrument is yet to be achieved. The greatest hazard in economic terms may well be that the costs of such activities may threaten rising productivity and aggravate the problems of inflation and unemployment. Under difficult economic conditions it appears that social responsibility programs may fall to the bottom of the priority list, while in times of prosperity, with high levels of "ability to pay", corporations will find this goal pressed toward the top of the hierarchy. But Friedman contends that even in prosperity only monopolists have funds to spend on social responsibility.

Whether business's social responsibilities should exceed those defined by law is in continual debate. The dynamics of national social goals and the economic and political environments will most likely not allow for any fixed or static guidelines. These dynamics, applied to an endless variety of industries, size of firms, and relative states of growth and prosperity necessitate the use of general rather than particular goals.

We also find the institutionalization of the social responsibility concept in statements of corporate philosophy and policies. Implementation of this concept will most likely be made within the goals of long-run profit maximization. Therefore, the present question concerning the social responsibility concept appears to relate to the degree of its application and its measured costs and benefits to both society and the corporation.

A milestone has been reached in the institutionalization of the social responsibility concept. Rather than taking recourse in semantical debates on the issue, business faces threats of impending legislation, regulation, and the effective force of protest groups to find explicit answers to explicit problems. This means that business must systematically approach these problems rather than attempting to avoid them as it has done too often in the past. The Viking Air Compressor case offers one example of such an approach. This company hired a new MBA and assigned him the task of proposing to the board of directors the best criteria to use in deciding how to make corporate gifts to charitable organizations. He was to make recommendations to management on the participation of company employees in public service activities, propose future strategies for the company in the employment of minority groups, and serve as secretary to a new committee composed of board members. His primary tasks were identified as the "proposal of new policy guidelines" to the board for an oncoming meeting, guidelines for the corporations' attitude toward public service of employees, and the development of criteria for corporate philanthropic giving. The young MBA reported in some detail specific guidelines in four basic areas of activity, but was rebuffed by the chairman of the board for his "wooly-minded" theoretical thinking.

Formulating programs and guidelines for social responsibilities is indeed complex, even within an organization that systematically attempts such a program. How far can, and should, managers in business go in specifically determining socially responsible actions, and limits on these actions? What does constitute a valid systematic approach to an evaluation of these problems, with recommendations for their resolution? Once again, the social responsibility concept appears institutionalized, but its implementation will involve problems before it can be adequately developed.

Given the economic function of, and the mandate for, maximum allocation of resources by society, business desires to operate in a free enterprise system with profits serving as both incentive and goal. The achievement of this goal will be conditioned by responses in the marketplace and by social controls in society. Another consideration of the dominant values of our society reveals maximum freedom for all individuals and groups as a corollary goal for business. Maintaining the highest degree of freedom normally requires checks and balances among power groups in society. If the acceptance of social responsibilities on the part of the business person would be detrimental to these checks and balances, as cited by some writers, business as an institution would be forced to re-evaluate these responsibilities. But until this situation exists in fact, management faces the problem of recognizing and adapting to the current values emphasized by society.

While many businesses are justifiably accused of a lack of social concern, critics also suggest that a preoccupation with social concerns may be detrimental to the success of the firm. For example, in an article entitled "Should You Buy Stocks for Your Children?" which appeared in the April 21, 1968 issue of *Parade,* investment analysts warned readers against investing in companies whose concern for profits was preempted by social concerns. These companies, the authors suggested, tended to show a "slow" profit.

Social responsibilities must be delicately balanced in the light of a company's survival. In the Grafton case, a business faced with the economic necessity of changing its location is confronted with the virtual collapse of the community that depends upon it for the majority of its jobs, economic support, and long-term municipal bonded debt. This case dramatically portrays the rather frequent situation in which groups in society are almost totally dependent for their survival on one business firm's decisions.

B. The Professional Responsibilities of Management

Management must recognize the effects of the specialization and division of labor in our economy resulting in increased types and levels of interdependence between individuals, groups, and institutions. This interdependence leads to concomitant social responsibilities, since it places business in a dominant position of power. The existence and use of this power is an issue of concern in the daily press, particularly in its manifestations of monopoly or oligopoly. In addition, business possesses social power both in the local community and in the organization. In the article, "Can Business Afford to Ignore Social Responsibilities?" [28] Keith Davis points out that if business uses its power in an irresponsible and arbitrary fashion, other forces and groups will meet the responsibilities due consumers and employees. He then raises the question: Could these power conflicts be minimized if professional managers formulated and met their social responsibilities at lower organizational levels in industry and society? This would be especially important if business acted before these issues reached proportions requiring countermeasures by government or organized labor.

One of the responsibilities business people may have as a power group is that of establishing certain professional criteria. They already have access to an increasingly standardized body of management knowledge, which is the first criterion of any profession. But there is some debate over the need for other criteria that identify a profession — licensing by examination and the codification and enforcement of a code of ethics.

Licensing by examination is a very remote possibility, for it would tend to deter entrepreneurs, and it would be impossible to define a "qualified" manager. But "certification" on a voluntary basis by tests might be substituted for licensing.

The question of an enforced code of ethics appears to have both advantages and disadvantages. Howard R. Bowen contends in "Business Management: A Profession?" [29] that enforcement of such a code of ethics by professional groups in the economic realm could evolve into oligopolistic, if not monopolistic, practices. And we have but to look at the "classical" professions today to realize that social goals are not effectively sought, nor are professional members widely prosecuted under the codes. But this should not undercut the potential benefits of meaningfully stated and positively oriented codes of business and management ethics. These might, for example, take the form of business-society goals similar to the national goals presented in Part Eight.

A The Social Responsibility Concept

26 How Social Responsibility Became Institutionalized

Business Week

"Corporations are bored and disgusted with 'good works.' They don't want to be good guys because they are doing a nifty thing in Bedford-Stuyvesant." The speaker is Owen Kugel, director of the U.S. Chamber of Commerce's Urban Strategy Center, and he is probably in touch with more corporate urban affairs and community affairs directors than anyone else in the country. Their mood, he reports, is "gruesome, especially those who built careers on those little deals and projects."

If Kugel, who lives with this every day, is perhaps overstating things a little, it is obvious that something has changed in the attitude of business toward social goals that were considered unimpeachable only a few years ago. In part, what Kugel sees as disenchantment is merely one reaction to the increasing institutionalization of social action. When *Business Week* inaugurated its awards for Business Citizenship four years ago, the environmental protection movement was just starting and enforcement of employment statutes was uneven.

Since then, a flood of federal, state, and local laws has put much of industry's antipollution efforts beyond voluntary action. Everyone must meet an increasingly high standard.

Similarly, the Equal Employment Opportunity Commission (EEOC) has galvanized companies with a wave of lawsuits to force compliance with antidiscrimination laws. "At some point," says William H. Brown III, EEOC's chairman, the commission's court record "on substantive issues" will persuade companies to meet the legal requirements without going to court.

The emphasis on the law may be why much of the steam has gone out of the National Alliance of Businessmen, a nationwide voluntary effort to stimulate hiring of minority employees. The NAB has been plugging along at something under a quarter-million "hires" a year, which officials concede does not even keep up with the growth of the minority labor force. And the organization's operating budget has been cut 20%, forcing it to drop support of offices in 60 cities. Fewer than half of those have continued on local funding.

Aside from the leveling effect of law enforcement, an increasing sophistication has called worthy social-action efforts into question. What once seemed bold now seems routine — or worse. Says Carl Holman, president of the National Urban Coalition: "We no longer like the phony deals — a bank staking a black man to a clothing store in a dying neighborhood. They're willing to write off the loss. But why not get that man into a shopping center?"

A good many companies seem to have gotten the message and pulled back from some of the more public relations-oriented projects that were peripheral to their businesses. Instead, they have in essence internalized social action by concentrating on things they can do well in the context of normal operations. As with Western Electric, for example . . . , more and more companies are formalizing programs that develop lists of minority suppliers that can bid on business competitively. Levi Strauss has such a program, and so does Honeywell and Indiana Standard, both of which are considered models for industry in that area. Sears, Roebuck & Co. has been testing a program for several years. In all cases, the effort includes a good deal of counseling and patient advice to the minority businessman on exactly how to cost out a product and how to bid.

Dozens of companies have actively searched for minority banks in which to deposit money. They not only add needed funds to banks struggling for deposits, but they do it within the normal parameters of business operation.

What seems to have happened, says the U.S. Chamber's Kugel, is that the experience of the past few years has meant that "sensitivity to social problems has become institutionalized, at least on the first two levels of management." Chief executives have accepted the need to take certain actions and have tried to make those actions a part of regular operations.

At Borden, Inc., for example, Chairman and President Augustine R. Marusi two years ago established a Minority Affairs Council, with representatives from nearly every staff and line department in the company. The ultimate function of the council, says Thomas K. Hammall, Borden's director of civic affairs, was to make sure that Borden's social policy was "multi-dimensional." Every area of operations that conceivably could contribute has been rung in, including management development in the form of a draft for an MBA program for minority employees and a women's testing and assessment center at Columbus (Ohio) headquarters.

In addition, Marusi gave orders a year and a half ago that henceforward Borden would add another input to its site planning: "In the future, all investment proposals for new or expanded installations must contain a report that addresses itself to minority socioeconomic issues, i.e., how communities within which a site is viable act with regard to equal employment opportunities (including construction trades) and open housing. A condition for joining a community or expanding Borden's operations within it will be that it qualifies in every sense." Marusi's rationale: "Communities that have major racial prejudices and/or problems do not represent good investments for the future."

A couple of sites, says Hammall, have passed the test, and a couple of others are now being scrutinized.

Borden's kind of deep involvement in the day-to-day administration of social aims is becoming increasingly common. And while Borden is still in the planning stage for much of its program, some corporations have carried the process so far beyond the law's basic requirements that they stand out for that reason alone. This is why Owens-Illinois, Inc., and Polaroid Corp. have won *Business Week*'s Business Citizenship Awards for 1972.

This year, also, *Business Week* felt that it was time to take stock of how other companies that pioneered in their time and were similarly recognized have fared over the years. The following report on past award winners is by and large encouraging. Nearly all the people and the companies are still committed. In some respects, of course, they would do things differently if they had it to do all over again. But even mistakes are valuable if someone else can learn from them.

Three Success Stories

Several of the award winners have had a comparatively smooth time of it. Without claiming perfection, they say that they have either achieved the results they set out to attain or that success is virtually assured.

In part, this is because the goals — while far from modest — are not quite so ambitious as, say, to attempt to remake the rotting core of a whole city. More important is the quality of the commitment, to the project and its goals. "I'm convinced," says Walter A. Haas, Jr., chairman of Levi Strauss & Co., "that to be successful in social programs is not dependent on the amount of money you spend, but the attitude and concern of management."

Haas's own company, where managers are held accountable for social policy decisions just as they are for production goals, received one of the first *Business Week* awards for business citizenship nearly four years ago. The company still enjoys a golden reputation for enlightened social action. And it still routinely allocates 3% of its net profits to community projects ranging from an intensive care unit for the East Tennessee Children's Hospital ($7,000), to a program to explore ways of getting government and foundation money for Alabama's dirt-poor Green County ($20,000). The company has plants in both places, and like most of Levi's social programs, both projects are run by "community relations teams." These are made up of local employees and have been set up at many of Levi's nearly 40 plants in the U.S.

The plants were fully integrated long before the Equal Employment Opportunity Commission got busy. Its 33% minority employment statistic is impressive. Nearly 14% of the company's managers and officials last year were women, double the proportion of the year before, and 10.1% were classified as minority employees.

Levi has also set up a minority purchasing program, now six months old, under which the company will buy $1.7 million worth of goods and services from minority suppliers over the next two years. A letter announcing plans for a $1-million computer center in San Jose, Calif., required general contractors to "obtain bids from competent minority businesses for each subcontract." Three such subcontractors have won $144,000 in contracts. Says Walter Haas, "We'll pay competitive rates, but not a premium. Businessmen must keep their business hat on."

Coca-Cola Co. has also made great strides in dealing with its minority workers. Nine months after receiving a *Business Week* award for its attempt to improve conditions among migrant workers in its Minute Maid orange groves, Coke signed the first — and so far the only — contract in Florida with Cesar Chavez' United Farm Workers.

The contract did away with the infamous crew chief system of hiring, raised wages, instituted fringe benefits, and gave the workers some say in setting piece-work rates. But there is general agreement that Coke's goals, announced long before the contract, have been substantially achieved.

For instance, Coke's plan to develop permanent employees has worked out pretty much as planned. Some 300 are on hourly wages year-round. And when 350 fruit pickers on piece-work rates are not picking, they are switched to maintenance duties in the groves at hourly wages.

Coke is also getting rid of the squalid labor camps. Most of the fulltime employees have been able to buy their own homes with Coke's help. And near Frostproof, Fla., which lacks suitable existing housing, the company has built 85 houses in a planned development. All but eight have been sold to farm workers at a small loss.

In all, the company has plowed some $3-million into its program. And it thinks it has come out ahead, not only in benefits to its work force, but in increased productivity.

Productivity is also the watchword at Fairchild Camera & Instrument Corp.'s pioneering semiconductor plant on the Navajo reservation at Shiprock, N. M. This is due largely to the efforts of plant manager Paul W. Driscoll, who received a *Business Week* award for exceptional leadership in 1971. Driscoll built Shiprock from a small — and troubled — facility in the mid 1960s, nursed it through the 1969–70 recession into a successful plant employing 1,000.

Driscoll himself is pleased with the way things are going. "The people had the basics to perform the task we wanted done," he says, "and there was sensitivity in our top management."

If there is any disappointment, it is in the pace at which the Navajos have been able to move into management levels. Driscoll's goal was to push them ahead at Shiprock and then into Fairchild operations elsewhere.

Two years ago, Driscoll fully expected a Navajo to take over his job as plant manager someday, but that hasn't yet happened. Driscoll left Shiprock in May for greater responsibilities in Fairchild's international operations, probably in the Far East. His replacement is another white man, Mercer E. Curtis, Jr. "Paul," Says Curtis, "is going to be tough to follow."

The Ferment in Ecology

Of all the areas of endeavor covered by the *Business Week* awards, achievements in improving the physical environment are most likely to look routine when reexamined even a year later. That is because the whole environmental movement is so volatile: Attitudes, legal doctrine, and technology are moving so rapidly that it is easy to forget how bold the first steps seemed.

Five years ago, at its big, new molybdenum mine at Henderson, Colo., American Metal Climax, Inc., launched what was then a unique ecological experiment. The goal was to reduce the environmental impact of the mine. This involved tunneling through a mountain and building a 13-mi. railroad so that the mill and tailing pond could be built away from public view. The mine has become a motherlode of expertise that a dozen companies have tapped.

The Henderson site is still, of course, far from perfect. For one thing, no one has come up with the technology to get rid of the ugly tailing pond. And in ecologically disturbed areas, the fragile tundra vegetation has not returned to cover the scars as fast as had been expected. "As a pioneer in the area of relating environmental concerns and environmental information to land-use decision-making, you do not expect a project to represent the ultimate in environmental planning," says Roger Hansen, executive director of the Rocky Mountain Center on Environment. "The Henderson project paved the way for others."

Paving the way is nothing new to giant Weyerhaeuser Co., which won a *Business Week* award in 1971 for its sustained efforts to control pollution in the pulp and paper industry. Now, the big Tacoma (Wash.) company is pushing for better coordination with regulatory agencies. Says President George H. Weyerhaeuser: "In the matter of pollution control, the major block to investment has not been the stringency of regulation per se, but continuous changing of the rules, accentuated by conflict between regulatory agencies."

The problem, as Weyerhaeuser identified it, was that the company had wound up as broker among overlapping environmental jurisdictions. For example, in the endless negotiations over its Longview (Wash.) facility, the company dealt with four agencies.

Weyerhaeuser wanted out of the coordinating role. What evolved was a "team concept" for joint planning by the company and all the concerned agencies, probably the first in the country. The parties at least agree on the facts concerning plant operation and waste volumes, and on joint plans for satisfying requirements.

In the case of the Longview plant, Weyerhaeuser was unable to get what it wanted, a "one-stop" permit for construction and operation. But the team approach looks promising. "If it works out," says George Weyerhaeuser, "it may provide a breakthrough not just on a state level but nationally."

Dow Chemical Co., which won an award last year for an abatement program that managed to pay for itself, is successfully continuing its ambitious efforts. "Dirty processes are inefficient processes," says Chet Otis, director of Dow's ecology council. "We're keeping the pressure on our people to solve pollution problems in the process itself."

The approach still pays off — both environmentally and economically. In 1972, Dow completed 400 abatement projects at a capital cost of $17-million. But the expenditure is producing an annual saving of $4-million in recovered chemicals, higher product yields, and lower raw materials costs.

But Otis admits that by 1974, Dow "may be scratching to break even" on pollution control. "As we get closer to zero discharge — 100% pollution control — costs soar and it's harder to offset them," he says. Zero discharge is the controversial goal of the 1972 Federal Water Pollution Control Act, and by next year, five of Dow's 25 U.S. plants will have achieved it, which is probably the best water pollution control record in the nation. "But in some plants," says Otis, "we don't know how to."

Like Dow Chemical, Aaron Teller stresses the recycling of waste streams back into production processes. The former dean of engineering at New York's Cooper Union won a *Business Week* award in 1971 for advocating this environmental concept. Now, he says, "the real problem emerging is not pollution control but resource preservation."

But Teller has had only moderate success in translating his ideas into business. His engineering company, Teller Environmental Systems, has grown, of course. In three years, its staff expanded from three to 16, and its annual engineering fees and royalties increased from $50,000 to $1.5-million, which represents perhaps $15-million in actual systems installations in such manufacturing industries as fertilizer, and secondary aluminum smelting.

Now, Teller finds himself at something of a crossroads. He needs help in developing marketing techniques, in financial and profit-center controls, and in some branches of engineering. So he has been searching for a merger partner and hints that he may finally have found one.

Frustration in Urban Renewal

Many companies, trying to be good corporate citizens of their troubled cities, have taken on the endless frustrations of restoring blighted neighborhoods.

Consider William Wendel, president of Carborundum Co. As boss of the only national company in Niagara Falls, N.Y., Wendel decided in 1964 to do something about rehabilitating the blowsy old city that adjoins the great waterfall. With enormous energy, Wendel organized agencies to accomplish an ambitious urban renewal program, stimulate housing, and lay the groundwork for metropolitan government on the Niagara Frontier.

The early housing goals — about 1,000 new or rehabilitated units — were subsequently trimmed. But 400 units are either built or under construction. And the Wendel-led Society for the Promotion, Unification & Redevelopment of Niagara, has pushed through some projects in public administration.

But a number of big projects have faltered, most visibly the redevelopment of the city's rotting downtown. So far, Rainbow Center consists of the new 10-story Carborundum headquarters and the adjoining Carborundum ceramics museum. A convention hall and hotel will be finished next year, along with some open plazas. But 75 acres of the urban renewal area remain unspoken for.

Even worse, the effort to develop regional government was defeated last November, when the voters rejected a referendum to establish an elected county executive.

Wendel, who puts about 10 hours a month into his civic work, says that his involvement has been both "good and frustrating." He notes: "I'm still as heavily involved as ever."

Campbell Soup Co. has found its efforts in city-saving even more frustrating, since it must deal with Camden, N.J. Camden has the second-highest crime rate in the nation, and parts of it look like Dresden after the fire storm.

Campbell has put a lot of effort into Camden, and top management has been deeply involved, including President Harold A. Shaub. Says Osborne Boyd, executive director of the Greater Camden Movement: "Every morning, Shaub drives around town. Then he calls, wondering why this or that isn't being done. He gets into the nitty-gritty."

But despite years of commitment and a good many millions of dollars in special projects and aid for housing development, progress is painfully slow. Still, Campbell can show 464 homes rehabilitated in North Camden, as well as construction of 93 low-income townhouses, and 104 high-rise apartments. Last week, the Housing & Urban Development Dept. released additional money for more rehabilitation.

Campbell is by no means pessimistic, pointing to the $26-million of construction contracts awarded or completed last year. Says Shaub: "Sooner or later, that amount of money must begin to show."

Another award winner — Hallmark Cards, Inc. — is considerably happier because its renewal scheme in Kansas City, Mo., is considerably further along. Joyce Hall, Hallmark's formidable chairman, set out to transform the drab neighborhood in which his headquarters are located, and he has substantially done it.

Crown Center, designed to complement the central business district, boasts, in addition to the Hallmark building, a 730-room hotel, five low office buildings, landscaped terraces, a central square complete with fountain, underground parking, and a two-story bank. Slated for completion this fall are a tri-level retail complex housing 160 shops and a $2-million audio-visual communications center. The final target project, apartment housing, has just been started, and the first occupancy is due in 1975. By the time the whole project is completed in 1984, it will consist of 50 buildings, including apartments and condominiums for 8,000 residents and a daytime population of 50,000.

But the happiest of the city stories among the *Business Week* award winners is Rouse Co.'s Columbia, Md., a brand-new city set down in the countryside between Washington and Baltimore. Columbia, which received its award for the sensitivity and sophistication with which its environmental planning was done, is a roaring success.

Columbia has had its flurries of publicity about drugs among teenagers, racial conflict, and environmental fights. But much of its plan seems to work: the general design of the villages, the "downtown" shopping mall, and the orderly growth. Columbia now has a fully integrated population of about 35,000 in 10,000 pleasant housing units. It offers more than 10,000 jobs, including 2,300 at General Electric's appliance plant and 800 at Bendix research facility. All in all, the town is about one-third of the way toward its goal of 110,000 population in an eminently livable community.

If any part of the plans has not panned out, it is internal transportation. Despite bus lines, bikeways, and walk-ways, nothing appears to be able to separate the American suburbanite from his car.

The developers stand to make a handsome profit in four or five years. And, says Padraic Kennedy, manager of the Columbia Assn., which represents the residents: "Most people here feel that this is a terrific place and that Rouse has done a terrific job."

A Fair Shake for Minorities

If there is any place that business confronts its responsibilities toward minorities most directly, it is in the economic areas: jobs, job-training, and the development of minority business. And probably the best-known man in all three is the Rev. Leon Sullivan of Philadelphia, who won a *Business Week* award last year for his singular influence and effectiveness.

Sullivan is the founder of the Opportunities Industrialization Center, a self-help job-training organization that spread to 100 cities and now has a national board. But because of repeated federal fund cutbacks, OIC is not growing, and industry and community financial support remain low. Sullivan is pinning his hopes on an ambitious OIC assistance bill now in the Senate.

Aside from OIC, Sullivan is probably best known as a director of General Motors Corp., probably the only GM board member many people have ever heard of. Sullivan joined GM's board in 1970, and took on himself the responsibility for promoting greater minority participation in all phases of the company. His assessment: "I am encouraged." Black dealers increased from six to more than 20 since he joined the board, and 24 more are in a special training program. His goal: 100 dealers by 1975.

Sullivan is also pleased with the GM Institute, whose black enrollment has risen from fewer than 40 to 350 men and women out of 2,000 students. "My goal," he says, "is to have at least 20% within several years."

Sullivan is not so happy with the number of blacks in salaried jobs. There are now 5,000 at GM, but Sullivan would like to see double that number. As for black suppliers, "there were very few of any consequence when I started. Today there are 400, doing $18-million worth of business."

If Sullivan provides the overview on minority employment, two other award winners provide specific object lessons. Last year, International Business Machines Corp. was singled out for its pioneering cable plant in Brooklyn's Bedford-Stuyvesant district, home of probably the largest concentration of hard-core unemployed in the U.S. Despite a general impression that this kind of ghetto enterprise is a passing thing, the IBM plant is very stable.

The plant still has 400 employees, and the proportion of black or Puerto Rican supervisors is up to 80%. Absenteeism is still an acceptable 6%.

In the opinion of plant manager Hal Leiteau, the plant would have become competitive quicker if IBM had started with a higher opinion of the employees' trainability and gone to more complex products more quickly. "There's opportunity in coming into an area like this," he says. "Business should focus on it, not on the good works."

Ghetto job training doesn't sound like so much fun when you talk to the people at Western Electric Co. "I would have to say," states J. G. Blake, Western Electric's manager of community relations, "that if you were a cost-effect guy and wanted to look at the manpower programs of this country, it's not something you'd want to get into today."

Blake was responding to a question about Western Electric's Newark Shop once a high-visibility training center for the unemployed and unemployable. "The shop still exists," says Blake. "It performed the function for which it was designed: to employ, teach, and put to work in the mainstream.

"But today we'd wonder if we couldn't do that job better — and we have. For example, we have consolidated operations in Newark in a new office complex, rather than upstate New York or southern New Jersey."

Even more important to Western Electric is the progress of the program for which it won an award in 1969: the use of the company's vast purchasing power to encourage the development of minority businesses as suppliers. The program, which had begun informally in the late 1960s, was formalized in 1971. Last year, the company numbered almost 500 minority suppliers on its vendors' list, double the number in 1971, and it did $13-million business with them, compared with $5-million the year before.

The development of minority business as a viable economic goal is also the task of the Colorado Economic Development Assn., one of last year's winners. CEDA was founded to offer management and marketing advice — and to help get loans — for small minority-owned businesses, and it has had a string of successes since 1969.

Still, CEDA has made some changes. For one thing, it broke off its supportive services into 12 separate companies — accounting, loan packaging, venture capital, and so on. Employees own 49% of their companies and CEDA owns 51%. CEDA supplies office overhead at no charge.

The other change is an emphasis on helping bigger businesses. "We put a construction company into a business a year and a half ago," says (CEDA) founder Edward Lucero. "They did $1.7-million in the past year with $275,000 pretax profit. We could have put together three $500,000 companies, but they wouldn't have made a profit."

27 The Hazards of Corporate Responsibility

Gilbert Burck

Every Friday evening, Walter Fackler, professor of economics at the University of Chicago's Graduate School of Business, has been addressing a class of seventy-five high-ranking executives on the problems of public policy and corporate social responsibility. A more appropriate and exigent activity these days is hard to imagine. Fackler says he has never seen businessmen so confused and defensive. The doctrine that business has responsibilities "beyond business," which began to gather momentum a dozen or so years ago, is still picking up steam. Never before has the U.S. business establishment been confronted with such a bewildering variety of animadversion, such a Vanity Fair of conflicting demands and prescriptions. A detailed inventory of the "social" demands being made on business would fill several volumes; reconciling the numerous and conflicting prescriptions would baffle a synod of Solomons.

Perhaps because businessmen are so defensive, they themselves

Reprinted from the June 1973 issue of *Fortune Magazine*, pp. 114–117, by special permission; © 1973 Time Inc.

have not done much talking back to those who are making all the demands. When businessmen essay to discuss their role in society these days, they all too often sound like young ladies fifty years ago talking about sex. They cough and clear their throats and come up with moralistic platitudes. The back talk has come principally from economists — notably from some, like Milton Friedman and Henry Manne, who have generally been identified with the classical school. These "strict constructionists" argue that business serves society best when it minds its business well, and that it should take part in social activities only to the extent that these are necessary to its own well-being.

Fackler himself manages to sound like a strict constructionist much of the time. The great, the dominant, the indispensable *social* role of business, he tells his executive students, is a familiar one. In this most uncertain world, their prime job is to evaluate risks wisely, to allocate the nation's resources prudently, and to use them with optimum efficiency. Business fulfills its real social role by striving endlessly to take in more money than it pays out, or, as some of its critics would put the case, by lusting incessantly after the Almighty Dollar.

Arrayed on the other side of the argument are the social-responsibility advocates — those who want an enlarged social role for industry. For all the immense variety of their prescriptions, these advocates agree on one general proposition: business ought to accept social responsibilities *that go beyond the requirements of the law*. In addition to mere compliance with the law, say the advocates, business should actively initiate measures to abate pollution, to expand minority rights, and in general to be an exemplary citizen, and should cheerfully accept all the costs associated with this good citizenship.

Suppressing the Controversy

Many of the most vocal social-responsibility advocates, including those affiliated with one or another band of Nader's raiders, tend to extreme forms of self-righteousness. Their proposals are often couched in rather general terms; they imply that the justice of their ideas is self-evident and that only a moral delinquent, or a businessman consumed by greed, could resist them. The notion that some schemes for implementing the proposals might actually be controversial, or that there might be serious questions of equity involved in asking corporate executives to tackle social problems with money belonging to other people (i.e., their stockholders) — these thoughts often seem to be suppressed in the advocates' minds.

But there is also a more sophisticated version of the social-responsibility proposition. According to this version, corporate executives who are strict constructionists at heart, and who harbor powerful lusts for Almighty Dollars, might nevertheless conclude that an activist social posture was good for their companies. They might decide, in other words, that social activism was good public relations. They might agree with Paul Samuelson, the Nobel laureate, who takes a simple view of the new demands on corporations. "A large corporation these days," he says, "not only may engage in social responsibility; it had damn well better try do do so."

A similarly pragmatic view of the matter has been propounded by Professor Neil Jacoby of the Graduate School of Management at the University of California, Los Angeles. Jacoby has been a dean of the school, a member of the Council of Economic Advisers under Eisenhower, a fellow of the Center for the Study of Democratic Institutions, and a member of the Pay Board. His forthcoming book, *Corporate Power and Social Responsibility,* describes corporate social involvement as a fact of life. "I don't really ask companies to do a single thing that isn't profitable," Jacoby remarked recently. "But political forces are just as real as market forces, and business must respond to them, which means it often must be content with optimizing and not maximizing immediate profits."

Corporations Do It Better

Professor Henry Wallich of Yale has also advanced a rather sophisticated case for corporate social responsibility. Writing in *Fortune* last year (Books & Ideas, March, 1972), Wallich made the point that corporations can perform some social activities better than can government; and in undertaking to do more than the law requires, they are shifting activities from the public to the private sector. When one corporation undertakes social obligations not borne by its competitors, it would, of course, be at a disadvantage. Therefore, Wallich proposes, companies in an industry should be allowed to work together toward social goals without fear of antitrust action.

Some serious economists regard the social-responsibility movement as a harbinger of major changes in the business environment. Professor George Steiner of the U.C.L.A. Graduate School of Management, for instance, believes the movement implies "a new area of voluntarism" that will change large corporations' basic operating style. Generally speaking, Steiner says, the old authoritarian way of running a company will give way to permissive and statesmanlike methods; the single-minded entrepreneur will be succeeded by the broad-gauge "renaissance" manager. Centralized decision making will be accompanied, if not largely superseded, by decision making in small groups. Financial accounting will be augmented by human-resources accounting, and the "social" costs of production will be increasingly internalized.

Inevitably, government and business planning will complement each other. "We are," says Steiner prophetically, "in the process of redefining capitalism."

How Supreme Life Got the Business

A few companies are beginning to act as if they believe Steiner. One is Standard Oil Co. (Indiana), which is spending about $40 million a year on pollution control — far more than it legally has to. It also boasts a long list of other social achievements, including efforts on behalf of Chicago's schools and a determined program to hire and promote minority employees and to help minority suppliers and businessmen. Recently, for example, Standard arranged with Chicago's Supreme Life Insurance Co. of America, a company owned by blacks, to insure two plants of its Amoco chemical subsidiary in California. Standard's policy is to use not only qualified but "qualifiable" minority suppliers — i.e., it helps some to qualify.

The company's director of public affairs these days is Phillip Drotning, author of three books on the black movement in the U.S., and an advocate of a high level of corporate involvement. If Drotning has his way — and so far he has been backed by top management — the promotion of executives will depend not only on their cost and profit records but on their approach to social objectives. Managers will be supplied with the information they need to evaluate the social consequences of their decisions, and they will plan strategies that benefit both the company and society. "The heads of the company," says Drotning, "will exercise leadership among their peers in the broad business community and the public at large, to generate support for the far-reaching, long-range changes in social policy that must occur."

The goals of Chicago's CNA Financial Corp., an insurance-centered company with revenues of $1.6 billion, are pretty ambitious too. Last year the company spent close to $660,000 on dozens of selected social projects, compelled its insurance subsidiaries to demand that their clients take "corrective action" on a variety of pollution problems, and insisted on a 30 percent minority representation among the workers erecting its new headquarters building.

CNA's vice president in charge of social policy is a former social-agency administrator named David Christensen, who argues that companies typically go through several phases in the perception of their social responsibilities. First there is the "do-good" phase, in which the company builds libraries with its name on them — but goes right on dumping waste in the lake. Later comes a more systematic effort to coordinate public relations and corporate involvement in, say, urban affairs. Finally the company gets to the phase of genuine corporate responsibility, in which it is concerned less with public relations than with developing responsible ways to improve society. Conscience money is no longer needed, because the company doesn't have a bad conscience.

Nobody Talks about Cost

Christensen says that CNA is just now entering the third phase. To guide it in this period he has helped the company develop an elaborate manual on corporate responsibility — a document that details just how CNA proposes to involve all its executives in social goals, and how they in turn should involve their charges. The whole opus has a somewhat evangelical tone, suggesting the marching orders for an all-out war on the devil. What it all will cost and who will finally pay for it are matters nobody seems to talk about. Presumably, however, CNA can afford it. That is to say, CNA, unlike many less opulent and more price-competitive companies, can absorb the costs — i.e., reduce the profits of its shareholders.

Given the natural inclination of managers to demand records and evaluations, it is not surprising that many businessmen who are interested in being socially responsible are also interested in what is known as the "social audit." Just as a conventional audit sums up a company's financial performance, a social audit would describe its social performance. Hundreds of articles, pamphlets, and books have already been written about the social audit, scores of workshops and seminars have been held to discuss it, and some sizable companies are experimenting with ways to implement the idea.

So far, it is fair to say, little has come of the effort. The problem, says Professor S. Prakash Sethi of the University of California at Berkeley, is that nobody has yet drawn up an objective definition of socially responsible behavior; hence nobody has succeeded in measuring it consistently. And who, in any case, would certify that the accounting was accurate? Professor Raymond Bauer of the Harvard Graduate School of Business Administration says, "We still need to learn how to get on the learning curve."

The social-audit concept has been scoffed at even by some of the most ardent advocates of corporate social responsibility. Milton Moskowitz, a financial columnist who edits a crusading biweekly sheet called *Business & Society,* derides the social-audit concept as "nonsense, redemption through mathematics, and useful to companies only as a laundry list." F. Thomas Juster, until recently a senior economist at the National Bureau of Economic Research, has been exploring social and economic measurement. "Given the state of the art," says Juster, "we're all kidding ourselves if we think we can measure [social] output. One reason is that real outputs are very long range. . . . We can't measure that, not now . . . probably can't measure it in ten years."

One of the most insistent of all recent efforts to develop a social audit was presented in the Winter 1972–73 issue of the quarterly *Business and Society Review,* in an article by David Linowes, a partner in the accounting firm of Laventhol Krekstein Horwath & Horwath. Linowes, who likes to be alluded to as the father of socioeconomic accounting, presents a model of a social audit. The model differentiates, logically, between mandatory and voluntary corporate outlays, and proposes to put dollar figures on the employee time, the facilities, the training, etc., that a company voluntarily invests in social areas. Linowes anticipates that *Fortune*'s 500 list will someday include a corporate responsibility rating. In the same issue of the review, however, six friendly critics who were asked to comment on Linowes' suggestions raise a host of substantive and technical objections. As one puts it, Linowes tries "to shoehorn . . . into the framework of the orthodox income statement model" what are essentially nonfiscal data containing highly subjective determinations.

Meanwhile, the social-audit enthusiasts seem determined to find a way of making the thing work. A host of consultants who specialize in advising companies on the art and mystery of carrying out their responsibilities to society have got behind the idea of the social audit. "Anytime there is money to be made in some area requiring newly developed expertise," says Ralph Lewis, editor of the *Harvard Business Review,* "a new breed of consultants seems to arise." Several serious enterprises are also showing interest in the social-responsibility audit. Abt Associates Inc., a contract research organization, publishes an annual report accompanied by its version of a social audit. Meanwhile, imaginative newspapermen are setting themselves up as experts, and social audits seem to be giving the public-relations profession a new lease on life.

The Great Social Increment

All this may sound highly laudable at best and harmless enough at worst. But in some circumstances it might be very harmful indeed. It could very well threaten the phenomenon known as rising productivity.

Perhaps because most people are so used to the phrase, they often forget what a stupendous phenomenon it describes. Last year American business produced more than $900 billion worth of goods and services, more than two-thirds of which were accounted for by corporations. Owing in large part to the corporations' striving to make money, national productivity rose by 4 percent. (Corporations earned some $88 billion before taxes, $41 billion of which was taxed away for government and other social needs.)

That 4 percent figure means that business turned out roughly $36 billion *more* of goods and services than it would have if it had maintained only the productivity level of the year before. This great social increment, fluctuating from year to year but expanding at an average of about 3 percent a year, is the very foundation of the nation's way of life; these gains afford the only basis on which a better society can be built. Rising productivity alone made possible the first eight-hour day more than eighty years ago, just as rising productivity has more recently brought higher real pay, shorter hours, and larger fringe benefits. And rising productivity alone will enable the U.S. to achieve without inordinate sacrifice the benefits that the advocates of social responsibility are now demanding.

This is so important a matter that it deserves to be viewed from another perspective. Suppose productivity ceased to rise, or that it even fell a little. Unless more people worked longer, the average living standard would then remain constant or decline. The costs associated with cleaner air, training for minorities, and other socially desirable programs would increase the total price of other things by precisely the amount of those costs. Every benefit would be offset by a sacrifice. If productivity did not rise, one man's gain would be another man's loss.

It's the Consumer Who Pays

Productivity, however, rises only when a business manages to innovate successfully and when it manages to cut costs, either by using fewer resources to make a product or by turning out a better product with the same resources. As the man in charge of costs, the businessman is the agent of what might be called the "consumer at large." When the businessman wastes resources on a bad risk, it is this consumer who principally pays (although the stockholders are presumably losers too). When he reduces his costs or innovates successfully, it is the consumer who benefits.

And so, precisely because the businessman's drive for profitability is identical with his drive for lower costs, his profit is a pretty good measure of social welfare. Suppose two companies make similar products and sell them at about the same price. Company A nets $10 million, but Company B nets twice as much because it is run by a tough crew of hardheaded, no-nonsense, endlessly striving managers motivated by abundant bonuses — the kind of men corporate critics often like to describe as s.o.b.'s. To an individual consumer, the two companies might seem to offer little choice. But so far as society at large is concerned, Company B has done a much better job, because it has used $10 million less of our resources, i.e., raw material and manpower, in doing the same job. So, obviously, the s.o.b.'s have been better for society than easygoing and irresolute managers would have been. As the Lord remarked of Faust, "He who strives endlessly, him we can redeem."

It is just possible, then, that the U.S. could use more endless strivers, redeemed or not. The advocates of corporate social responsibility, indeed, seem to have overlooked what may be the real case against U.S. business: it may be using too many resources for what it turns out. Suppose, at all events, that U.S. corporations had managed to turn out that 1972 volume for 2 percent less than they actually spent. The incremental profit would have amounted to $11 billion, enough to eliminate, over the year, practically all pollution. "If the responsibility buffs really want to promote national welfare," one strict constructionist observed recently, "they should be complaining that companies aren't making *enough* money."

And so it seems reasonable to ask what effect the businessman's increasing preoccupation with those other social "responsibilities" will have on his endless striving to elevate productivity. Thirty-one years ago the late Joseph Schumpeter predicted that, as corporations grew bigger, businessmen would cease to behave like aggressive entrepreneurs, and would degenerate into mere bureaucrats. Schumpeter's prediction hasn't come true, but some now worry that it may. They fear that the new emphasis on Good Works will sicken the businessman o'er with the pale cast of thought, vitiate his drive to innovate and cut costs, and gradually convert him and his fellows into the kind of bureaucrats that infest so many marble halls of government.

Our Socially Responsible Monopolists

These are the kinds of considerations that bother Milton Friedman when he contemplates the contentions in favor of social responsibility. Friedman likes to dramatize his position by making the superficially shocking statement that the businessman's *only* social responsibility is to increase profits. He is against the acceptance of social responsibilities, because it implicitly expresses the socialist view that political, and not market, considerations should govern the allocation of resources, and over the long run this means reduced efficiency. What's more, Friedman says, "no businessman has money to spend on social responsibility unless he has monopoly power. Any businessman engaged in social responsibility ought to be immediately slapped with an antitrust suit."

In the same vein, Professor Harold Demsetz of U.C.L.A. insists that the word "responsibility" is being misused: "The only responsibility of businessmen or anyone else is to obey the laws of the land, no more, no less." If our society wants business to set up day-care centers for employees' children, for example, then it should pass a law to that effect, so that the burden will be shared by all business enterprises.

The problem of sharing that burden is one that most social-responsibility advocates seem not to have thought through. One trouble with leaving good deeds up to individual executives is that not all of their companies are equally prosperous. Now that the Kaiser empire is in trouble, for example, Edgar Kaiser is taking a hard line on demands for "responsibility" in his companies. "Not to husband resources," Kaiser says with considerable feeling, "would be social irresponsibility of the highest order." Hard-pressed companies obviously cannot undertake the social programs supported by companies with strong market power, such as utilities (whose regulated rates are based on costs). And healthily profitable companies like Standard of Indiana and CNA obviously have a great advantage over companies that are constantly battling to stay in the black.

Even companies that have the resources to undertake socially responsible projects do not necessarily possess the skills to solve most complex social problems. "The job of the public and government," says F. Thomas Juster, "is to tell business what the appropriate social objectives are; they shouldn't want business messing around with its own set of social objectives." Professor Paul Heyne of Southern Methodist University, a strict constructionist, argues that the economic system is not a playground in which businessmen should be exercising their own preferences. "Any economic system," he explains, "ought to be a social mechanism for picking up the preferences of everyone, matching these against available resources, and obtaining from what we have a maximum of what we want. The market is a mechanism of almost incredible effectiveness in the accomplishment of this task. The market works effectively because those who have command over resources continually reallocate them in response to the signals provided by relative prices. The businessman who wants to behave in a socially responsible way must depend heavily, overwhelmingly, on this information."

Just Like Embezzlement

Probably no economist has given more thought to corporate social responsibility than Henry Manne, professor of law at the University of Rochester, who began writing about the subject a dozen years ago. He observed that most companies maintained enough reserves to meet unforeseen contingencies and to offset unintended mistakes, and so could *temporarily* spend some money on social activities that raise costs without raising revenues or income. So far as consumers and employees are concerned, Manne has observed, somewhat caustically, this spending is indistinguishable in its effects from simple inefficiency or outright embezzlement.

Manne believes that the whole concept of corporate responsibility suits government officials and intellectuals — particuarly intellectuals who deride and even hate the idea of a free market. It also goes down just fine with bloviating businessmen who don't mind casting themselves as members of the divine elect. Of course, businessmen often interpret "socially responsible" policies as long-term profit maximization, i.e., "in the long run we make more money by spending to be good citizens now." Manne doesn't object to this line of reasoning so long as the spending really does maximize profits in the long run — and helps the firms survive in a free market. He says, however, that voluntary corporate altruism has never made a significant dent in any but insignificant problems. Manne has developed his own economic model of corporate responsibility — the first of its kind — and reports that it can accommodate a little, but not much, corporate giving; he finds it impossible to justify a model of substantial corporate social action.

Above all, Manne avers, any such action will result in more government controls. It implies that business and government should work together to promote social progress. "Corporate social responsibility, a doctrine offered by many as a scheme to popularize and protect free enterprise," Manne concludes, "can succeed only if the free market is abandoned in favor of government controls. The game isn't worth the candle."

There seem to have been some cases in which "socially responsible" behavior has actually hampered business operations. California's Bank of America, upset and moved by radicals' demonstrations against it, went in some time ago for being socially responsible in a big way. It appointed an executive vice president, G. Robert Truex Jr., as custodian of social policy, and he is now dabbling with a social audit. The bank also set aside no less than $200 million for low-interest loans that would help to provide housing for minority-group members and other underprivileged persons.

But the bank has found itself in a dilemma. The 2,500 loan officers in its thousand California branches pride themselves on knowing the credit-worthiness of people in their areas. Now many of these officers have been asked to lend money to people who had no conventional credit standing at all — indeed, they were being asked to *persuade* people to borrow. How, in these circumstances, do you preserve the loan officers' morale and esprit? The Bank of America is wrestling with that problem.

Some proponents of increased corporate responsibility have given high marks to Levi Strauss & Co. of San Francisco, maker of the famous Levi's and other informal apparel. As its many admirers note, the company contributes 3 percent of its net after taxes to carefully chosen social programs, does a lot of hiring from among disadvantaged minority groups, helps finance minority suppliers, and has established day-care centers for employees' children. At the same time, the company has done well. It has expanded sales from $8 million in 1946 to more than $504 million last year, and net income from $700,000 to $25 million.

Getting Their Money's Worth

But Levi Strauss is obviously getting a lot for that 3 percent. It does business in an intensely liberal city and has a market in which tastes are heavily influenced by young people. And so, whatever its top executives believe in their heart of hearts, their social-responsibility outlays would appear to be rather effective public relations. So far as an outsider can determine, these outlays cost no more than would conventional high-pressure public relations in a different kind of company.

Many of the costs associated with social responsibility, such as minority training and aid, are often marginal, out of proportion to all the time and talent that have gone into arguing about them. Behaving responsibly often means no more or less than acting humanely, treating employees and customers with consideration, avoiding ineptitudes and blunders, cultivating a sharp eye for the important little things, and knowing how to spend where the returns are high. In this sense, responsibility can accomplish a lot with relatively small cost.

But many other expenses of behaving in a socially acceptable way, such as the cost of meeting the escalating demands of the consumer advocates, will not come cheap, and might easily get out of hand. Heavy social involvements can also cost a company dear in terms of managerial talent. And so the impact of the corporate-responsibility movement on companies that must husband their resources, on the endlessly striving cost cutters, indeed on competition itself, is not yet clear. Americans can only hope that bussinessmen will retain enough of the old Adam Smith in them to keep productivity rising.

B The Professional Responsibilities of Management

28 Can Business Afford to Ignore Social Responsibilities?

Keith Davis

Few persons would deny that there are significant changes taking place in social, political, economic, and other aspects of modern culture. Some of these changes businessmen may want and others they may dislike, but in either instance the changes do exist and must be faced. As our culture changes, it is appropriate — even mandatory — that businessmen re-examine their role and the functions of business in society. One area undergoing extensive re-examination is the responsibility businessmen have to society in making business decisions. These are the questions that are being asked:

> Why do businessmen have social responsibilties, if in fact they do?

> How does a businessman know in what directions his social responsibilities lie?

> If businessmen fail to accept social responsibilities incumbent upon them, what consequences may be expected?

It is my purpose in this article to discuss these questions in a very fundamental way. Without looking at specific company practices and without insisting upon a particular program of action, I wish to discuss three basic ideas which must underlie all of our thinking about social responsibility, regardless of what choices we eventually make. The first two ideas are constant and enduring, no matter what social changes occur. The third is more directly related to social changes today, but I believe it is just as fundamental as the others.

Social responsibility is a nebulous idea and, hence, is defined in various ways. It is used here within a management context to refer to *businessmen's decisions and actions taken for reasons at least partially beyond the firm's direct economic or technical interest.*[1] Thus, social responsibility has two rather different faces. On the one hand, businessmen recognize that since they are managing an economic unit in society, they have a broad obligation to the community with regard to economic developments affecting the public welfare (such as full employment, inflation, and maintenance of competition). A quite different type of social responsibility is, on the other hand, a businessman's obligation to nurture and develop human values (such as morale, cooperation, motivation, and self-realization in work). These human values cannot be measured on an economic value scale. Accordingly, the term "social responsibility" refers to both socio-economic and socio-human obligations to others. Popular usage often omits or underplays the socio-human side, but I shall suggest later in this article that it deserves more emphasis.

Note that the importance of social responsibility in this context derives from the fact that it affects a businessman's decisions and consequently his actions toward others. Social responsibility has applied in any situation if it *influences* a businessman's decision even partially. It is not necessary that a decision be based wholly on one's attitude of social responsibility in order to qualify. For example, when a businessman decides to raise or lower prices, he is normally making an economic decision; but if the management of a leading automobile firm decided not to raise prices because of possible effects on inflation, social responsibility would be involved. As a matter of fact, *rarely* would social responsibility be the exclusive reason for a decision.

While it is true that only businessmen (rather than businesses *per se*) make socially responsible decisions, they decide in terms of the objectives and policies of their business institution, which over a period of time acquires social power in its own right. Thus each business institution and the entire business system eventually come to stand for certain

---

[1] Some socially responsible business decisions by a long, complicated process of reasoning can be "justified" as having a good chance of bringing long-run economic gain to the firm and thus paying it back for its socially responsible outlook. This long-run economic gain is often merely rationalization of decisions made for non-economic reasons, and in any case the connection is so problematical that some social responsibility is bound to be present also. An example is a decision to retain a very old employee even though his productivity is low.

socially responsible beliefs and actions. But in the last analysis it is always the businessman who makes the decision. The business institution can only give him a cultural framework, policy guidance, and a special interest.

Responsibility Goes with Power

Most persons agree that businessmen today have considerable social power. Their counsel is sought by government and community. What they say and do influences their community. This type of influence is *social power*. It comes to businessmen because they are leaders, are intelligent men of affairs, and speak for the important institution we call business. They speak for free enterprise, for or against right-to-work policies, for or against their local school bond election, and so on, *in their roles as businessmen*. When they speak and act as citizens only, and those involved recognize this fact, then whatever social power businessmen possess is that of a citizen and is beyond the bounds of this discussion. In practice, however, it is often difficult to distinguish between these two roles, thereby further complicating the situation.

To the extent that businessmen or any other group have social power, the lessons of history suggest that their social responsibility should be equated with it. Stated in the form of a general relationship, it can be said that *social responsibilities of businessmen need to be commensurate with their social power*. Though this idea is deceptively simple on its face, it is in reality rather complicated and is often overlooked by discussants of social responsibility. On the one hand, it is argued that business is business and anything which smacks of social responsibility is out of bounds (i.e., keep the power but accept no responsibility). On the other, some would have business assume responsibilities as sort of a social godfather, looking after widows, orphans, water conservation, or any other social need, simply because business has large economic resources. Both positions are equally false.

The idea that responsibility and power go hand in hand appears to be as old as civilization itself. Wherever one looks in ancient and medieval history — Palestine, Britain — men were concerned with balancing power and responsibility. Men, being somewhat less than perfect, have often failed to achieve this balance, but they generally sought it as a necessary antecedent to justice. This idea appears to have its origins in logic. It is essentially a matter of balancing one side of an equation with the other.

The idea of co-equal power and responsibility is no stranger to business either. For example, one of the tenets of scientific management is that authority and responsibility should be balanced in such a way that each employee and manager is made responsible to the extent of his authority, and vice-versa.[2] Although this tenet refers to relationships *within* the firm, it seems that it would apply as well to the larger society outside the firm. As a matter of fact, businessmen have been one of the strongest proponents of co-equal social power and responsibility, particularly in their references to labor unions.

Based upon the evidence, it appears that both business leaders and the public accept the idea of co-equal power and responsibility. Although businessmen accept the logic of this idea, their problem is learning to respect and apply it when making decisions. Granted that there are no pat answers, they still need some guides, else each shall take off in a different direction. At this point, the idea already stated continues to offer help. If "social responsibilities of businessmen need to be commensurate with their social power," then, in a general way, *in the specific operating areas* where there is power, responsibility should also reside. Let us take an example:

> Company "A" is the only major employer in a small town. It is considering moving its entire plant out of the area. Company "B" is considering moving its plant of the same size out of a large city where it is one of many employers. It would seem that, other things being equal, Company "A" should give more weight to social responsibilities to the community when considering its move.

Even accepting the greater responsibility of Company "A," and some would not go this far, we still do not know how much greater nor in what way Company "A" should let its decision be amended, if at all. Thus the principle of co-equal power and responsibility can at best serve only as a rough guide, but a real one. For example:

> Do businessmen by their industrial engineering decisions have the power to affect worker's feeling of accomplishment and self-fulfillment on the job? If so, there is roughly a co-equal responsibility.

> Do businessmen have power as businessmen to influence unemployment? To the extent that is so, is there not also social responsibility?

> Do businessmen have power to determine the honesty of advertising? To the degree that they do, is there also social responsibility?

One matter of significance is that the conditions causing power are both internal and external to the firm. In the example of advertising honesty, power is derived primarily internally from the authority struc-

---

[2] Harold Koontz and Cyril O'Donnell, *Principles of Management,* Second Edition, McGraw-Hill Book Company, New York, 1959, p. 95.

ture of the firm and management's knowledge of product characteristics. In the case of Company "A" described earlier, much of its social power is derived from the external fact that it is the only employer in a small town. Each case is situational, requiring reappraisal of power-responsibility relationships each time a major decision is made.

There are, of course, other viewpoints concerning the extent of business social responsibility, and most of them offer a much easier path for businessmen than the one I have been describing. Levitt, in a powerful attack on social responsibility of businessmen, points out that if business assumes a large measure of social responsibility for employee welfare it will lead to a sort of neo-feudalism with all its paternalistic and autocratic ills. The result would be socially less desirable than in the days before businessmen were concerned with social responsibility.[3] Selekman, in an important new analysis, suggests that attention to social responsibility will undermine the main objective of all business, which is to provide economic goods and services to society.[4] A collapse of business' basic economic objectives would indeed be a catastrophe. Certainly the primary economic objectives of business must come first, else business will lose its reason for existence. Selekman's solution is a form of constitutionalism in which the responsibility of the business, other than its economic goals, is to administer its affairs with justice according to a constitutional framework mutually established by all groups involved. These criticisms and others raise questions about putting much social responsibility into business' kit of tools, a fact which leads directly to the second fundamental point of this discussion.

Less Responsibility Leads to Less Power

Certainly, if social responsibilities could be avoided or kept to insignificant size in the total scheme of business, a weighty, difficult burden would be raised from businessmen's shoulders. Business progress would be a primrose path compared to the path of thorns which responsibilities entail. But what are the consequences of responsibility avoidance? If power and responsibility are to be relatively equal, *then the avoidance of social responsibility leads to gradual erosion of social power*. To the extent that businessmen do not accept social-responsibility opportunities as they arise, other groups will step in to assume these responsibilities. Historically, government and labor have been most active in the role of diluting business power, and probably they will

---

[3] Theodore Levitt, "The Danger of Social Responsibility," *Harvard Business Review*, September–October, 1958, pp. 41–50.

[4] Benjamin M. Selekman, *A Moral Philosophy for Business*, McGraw-Hill Book Company, New York, 1959, especially chapter 27.

continue to be the principal challenging groups.[5] I am not proposing that this *should* happen, but on basis of the evidence it appears that this will tend to happen to the extent that businessmen do not keep their social responsibilities approximately equal with their social power. In this same vein Howard R. Bowen, in his study of business social responsibilities, concluded, "And it is becoming increasingly obvious that a freedom of choice and delegation of power such as businessmen exercise, would hardly be permitted to continue without some assumption of social responsibility." [6]

Admiral Ben Moreell, Chairman of the Board, Jones and Laughlin Steel Corporation, put this idea more dramatically:

> I am convinced that unless we do [accept social responsibilities], the vacuum created by our willingness will be filled by those who would take us down the road to complete statism and inevitable moral and social collapse.[7]

History supports these viewpoints. Under the protection of common law, employers during the nineteenth century gave minor attention to worker safety. Early in the twentieth century, in the face of pressure from safety and workmen's compensation laws, employers genuinely accepted responsibility for safety. Since then there have been very few restrictions on business power in this area, because business in general has been acting responsibly. At the opposite extreme, business in the first quarter of this century remained callous about technological and market layoff. As a result, business lost some of its power to government, which administers unemployment compensation, and to unions, which restrict it by means of tight seniority clauses, supplemental unemployment benefits (SUB), and other means. *Now business finds itself in the position of paying unemployment costs it originally denied responsibility for, but having less control than when it did not pay!*

A current problem of social responsibility is gainful employment for older workers. The plight of workers in the over-45 age bracket is well known. In spite of public pronouncements of interest in them and in spite of their general employability, many of them find job opportuni-

---

[5] For government's role, see George A. Steiner, *Government's Role in Economic Life,* McGraw-Hill Book Company, New York, 1953 and Wayne L. McNaughton and Joseph Lazar, *Industrial Relations and The Government,* McGraw-Hill Book Company, New York, 1954. For labor's role, see Neil W. Chamberlain, *Collective Bargaining,* McGraw-Hill Book Company, New York, 1951 and John A. Fitch, *Social Responsibilities of Organized Labor,* Harper and Brothers, New York, 1957.

[6] Howard R. Bowen, *Social Responsibilities of the Businessman,* Harper and Brothers, New York, 1953, p. 4.

[7] Admiral Ben Moreell, "The Role of American Business in Social Progress," Indiana State Chamber of Commerce, Indianapolis, 1956, p. 20.

ties quite limited or even nonexistent. I have said elsewhere that "unless management . . . makes reasonable provision for employing older persons out of work, laws will be passed prohibiting employment discrimination against older workers." [8] Just as a glacier grinds slowly along, the responsibility-power equation gradually, but surely, finds its balance.

In line with the foregoing analysis, Levitt's proposal of "business for business' sake" loses some of its glamor, because it means substantial loss of business power. Historian Arnold J. Toynbee predicts this result when he speaks of business managers being part "of a new world civil service," not necessarily working for government, but working under such stability and elaborate rules both from within and without that they form a relatively powerless bureaucracy similar to the civil service.[9]

It is unlikely that businessmen will concede their social power so easily, and I for one do not want them to do so. Businessmen are our most capable core of organization builders and innovators. We need them. In spite of pessimistic views, businessmen during the next fifty years probably will have substantial freedom of choice regarding what social responsibilities they will take and how far they will go. As current holders of social power, they can act responsibly to hold this power if they wish to do so. If their philosophy is positive (i.e., *for* something, rather than against almost any change) they can take the intiative as instruments of social change related to business. They will then be managers in the true sense of shaping the future, rather than plaintive victims of a more restrictive environment. The choice *is* theirs.

Non-Economic Values in Business

Early in this discussion I distinguished two types of social responsibilities. One was socio-economic responsibility for general economic welfare. The other was socio-human and referred to responsibility for preserving and developing human values. Let us now further discuss this distinction as it relates to a third idea underlying the entire problem of social responsibility.

There is general consensus that the "economic man" is dead if, indeed, he ever did exist. Men at work, as customers, and as citizens of a plant community do expect more than straight economic considerations in dealing with business. Since man is more than an economic automaton computing market values, what will be the role of business in serving his other needs? My third basic idea is that *continued vitality of business depends upon its vigorous acceptance of socio-human*

---

[8] Keith Davis, *Human Relations in Business,* McGraw-Hill Book Company, New York, 1957, p. 415.
[9] Arnold J. Toynbee, "Thinking Ahead," *Harvard Business Review,* September–October, 1958, p. 168.

responsibilities along with socio-economic responsibilities. A number of people accept the general idea of social responsibility, but they argue that business is wholly an economic institution and, therefore, its responsibilities are limited only to economic aspects of general public welfare. Following this line of reasoning, businessmen might be concerned with economic costs of unemployment, but not with the loss of human dignity and the social disorganization that accompany it. They would be concerned with making work productive in order to better serve society's economic needs but not with making it meaningful in a way that provided worker fulfillment.

The idea of confining social responsibility within economic limits fails on several counts. In the first place, it is hardly possible to separate economic aspects of life from its other values. Business deals with a *whole* man in a *whole* social structure, and all aspects of this situation are interrelated. It is agreed that the economic functions of business are primary and the non-economic are secondary, but the non-economic do exist. Second, even if economic aspects of life could be wholly separated out, the general public does not seem to want business confined only to economics. They also have human expectations of business. Third, businessmen currently have socio-human power; hence, if they ignore responsibility in this area, they will be inviting further loss of power. On three counts, then, it appears unwise to equate social responsibility with economic public welfare.

As a matter of fact, it is not a question of "Will these non-economic values be admitted to the decision matrix?" but "To what extent will they be admitted?" Regardless of professions to the contrary, businessmen today are influenced by other than technical-economic values when making decisions. Businessmen are human like all the rest of us. They do have emotions and social value judgments. It is foolish to contend that they, like a machine and unlike other human beings, respond only to economic and technical data.

Businessmen in making decisions typically apply three separate value systems, along with overriding ethical-moral considerations. These are:

Technical — Based upon physical facts and scientific logic.

Economic — Based upon market values determined by consumers.

Human — Based upon social-psychological needs other than economic consumption needs. This value system often goes by the term "human relations."

In many business decisions all three of these value systems exert some weight upon the final decision. Because man is human this aspect of his life cannot be ignored by any institution that deals with him.

But there are dangers in generalizations which are too sweeping, such as, "Business is responsible for human values in general." What is needed is a concept which marks business as an instrument *for specific human goals* (along with technical-economic ones) in the life of man and his society — something which gives direction and hope to the climb of mankind from the depths of the Stone Age to the great potential which his Creator has given him. This kind of concept does not come easily but it must come eventually. By giving people motivation, social goals, and work fulfillment, business might over the long pull be termed a "movement" in the same way that history refers to the labor movement.

Certainly some major efforts at being explicit have been made recently. Theodore V. Houser, writing from the point of view of big business, stated five specific areas of social responsibility, ranging from employees to government.[10] Selekman's idea of constitutional justice was discussed earlier.[11] Crawford Greenewalt emphasized the importance of individual creativity and stated, "The important thing is that we bring into play the full potential of all men whatever their station." [12] And there are many others. For my own use I have summed these ideas into a single manageable phrase, as follows: *To fulfill the human dignity, creativity, and potential of free men.*[13] This can be businessmen's long-run guide to socially responsible action in each situation they face. The term "fulfill" is used because business cannot award goals such as human dignity. It can only develop the proper climate for their growth. The term "man" is used becuse unless *man* is free, men cannot be free. Other institutions and groups will also be interested in this goal. Businessmen are not wholly responsible here, but only partially so, approximately to the extent of their social power.

An Important Choice Ahead

The subject of social responsibility places business at an important crossroads in its history. Which way it will go is not known, but in any event social responsibility will tend to equate with social power, which means that avoidance of responsibilities as they develop will lead to loss of business power. Some hard thinking is needed so that the right

---

[10] Theodor V. Houser, *Big Business and Human Values,* McGraw-Hill Book Company, New York, 1957.

[11] Selekman (see note 4), p. 7.

[12] Crawford H. Greenewalt, *The Uncommon Man: The Individual in the Organization,* McGraw-Hill Book Company, New York, 1959.

[13] One analyst has put this point even more strongly: "The making of goods is incidental and subordinate to the making of men." Raphael Demos, "Business and the Good Society," in Edward C. Bursk, Ed., *Business and Religion,* Harper and Brothers, New York, 1959, p. 190.

course can be charted. This is not the time for pat slogans, clichés, and wheezes. Clearly, economic functions of business are primary, but this does not negate the existence of non-economic functions and responsibilities. The price of social freedom is its responsible exercise.

Because society is changing, evidence suggests that the continued vigor of business depends upon its forthright acceptance of further socio-human responsibilities. In spite of protestations of impending corporate feudalism and dilution of economic objectives, the trend in this direction is already apparent. Some of the more fruitful avenues of interest are: making work meaningful, developing persons to their fullest potential, preservation of creativity and freedom, and fulfillment of human dignity.

In summary, the *first* social responsibility of businessmen is to find workable solutions regarding the nature and extent of their own social responsibilities.

We can be confident that modern business leadership does have the capacity to deal with questions of social responsibility. Although the next fifty years will bring major social change, business should perform effectively in this instability because it is geared for change. Typically, during the last century it has had an unstable economic environment; yet it has learned to live and prosper therein. It can do the same during a period of social reevaluation by developing flexible responses to the needs of society. But if it does not do so, it will use up its capital in human and spiritual values, which is a sure way to go socially bankrupt.

29 Business Management: A Profession?

Howard R. Bowen

Walter Rauschenbusch, the great architect of the "social gospel," once wrote:

> Business life is the unregenerate section of our social order. If by some magic it could be plucked out of our total social life in all its raw selfishness, and isolated on an island, unmitigated by any other factors of our life, that island would immediately become the object of a great foreign mission crusade for all Christendom.[1]

That such words could be written by a responsible religious leader only forty years ago attests to the great progress in the mores and conduct of American business since the era of the "muckrakers." Whatever may be the faults and inadequacies of business today, words so extreme as these no longer fit. Business has unquestionably become more humane and more responsible than it was a generation ago.

At the very time Rauschenbusch was writing, the eminent jurist, Louis D. Brandeis, saw the possibilities of professionalism in business:

> . . . success in business must mean something very different from mere money-making. In business the able man ordinarily earns a larger income than one less able. So does the able man in the recognized professions — in law, medicine or engineering; and even in those professions more remote from money-making like the ministry, teaching or social work. The world's demand for efficiency is so great and the supply so small, that the price of efficiency is high in every field of human activity.
>
> The recognized professions, however, definitely reject the size of the financial return as the measure of success. They select as their test, excellence of performance in the broadest sense — and include, among other things, advance in the particular occupation and service to the community. These are the basis of all worthy reputations in the recognized professions. In them a

Reprinted with permission from the American Academy of Political and Social Science, *The Annals,* January 1955, pp. 112–117.
[1] *Christianizing the Social Order* (New York: The Macmillan Company, 1914), p. 156.

large income is the ordinary incident of success; but he who exaggerates the value of the incident is apt to fail of real success.

To the business of to-day a similar test must be applied. True, in business the earning of profit is something more than an incident of success. It is an essential condition of success; because the continued absence of profit itself spells failure. But while loss spells failure, large profits do not connote success. Success must be sought in business also in excellence of performance; and in business, excellence of performance manifests itself, among other things, in the advancing of methods and processes; in the improvement of products; in more perfect organization, eliminating friction as well as waste; in bettering the condition of the workingmen, developing their faculties and promoting their happiness; and in the establishment of right relations with customers and with the community.[2]

This paper deals with two questions, both suggested by Brandeis' eloquent words: (1) Is business management in fact becoming a profession? and (2) Should business management take on the attributes of a profession? There are many who answer one or both of these questions in the negative. My conclusion is that both questions can be answered affirmatively — that business management is gradually assuming some of the marks of a profession and that this tendency is on the whole desirable.[3] But before taking up these questions directly, it is well to consider just what is meant by the word "profession."

A full-fledged profession is a vocation in which the following conditions exist: (1) pursuit of the vocation demands that practitioners acquire an intellectually based technique; (2) practitioners assume a relationship of responsibility toward clients; (3) practitioners are organized into responsible associations which set standards for admission to practice and exert control over the actions of their members through codes of ethics.[4] In most professions, the social control exerted by the association is reinforced by public licensing and supervision. Among the traditional professions in which these conditions are most fully realized are theology, law, and medicine. Later additions are, among others, dentistry, veterinary medicine, engineering, architecture, teaching, and accounting.

---

[2] *Business — A Profession* (Boston: Small, Maynard & Company, cop. 1914 and 1925), pp. 3–5.

[3] This paper is based in part on my book *Social Responsibilities of the Businessman*, Harper & Brothers, New York, 1953.

[4] Cf. Paul Meadows, "Professional Behavior and Industrial Society," *Journal of Business*, July 1946, p. 150. See also A. M. Carr-Saunders and P. A. Wilson, *The Professions*, Oxford University Press, London, 1933; R. H. Tawney, *The Acquisitive Society*, Harcourt, Brace and Company, New York, 1920, pp. 91–122; Talcott Parsons, "The Professions and the Social Structure," *Social Forces*, May 1939, pp. 457–467.

With these criteria in mind, let us now consider the extent to which the conditions of professionalism are fulfilled in present business management.

Intellectually Based Technique

The art of management has increasingly become a subject for study and research by disciplined and disinterested investigators and scholars. The early work in this field is associated with the name of Frederick W. Taylor, who made pathbreaking studies of efficiency, especially in the art of cutting metals. Taylor's most important contribution, however, was not the particular results of his studies but his approach. He showed that the problems of business might be studied with [the] same objectivity, the same rigor, and many of the same methods as are common in the laboratories of physical sciences.

In time, many more investigators applied themselves to the problems of business, and their interests were eventually broadened to include not only productive techniques in the factory and offices but also problems of sales, advertising, finance, records, accounting, inventory control, quality control, employee selection and training, job analysis, worker morale, incentives, collective bargaining, public relations, and administrative organization. The effect of these studies, as they have accumulated from the modest beginnings of a half-century ago, is to persuade businessmen: (1) that there are efficient and inefficient ways not only of cutting metals but also of meeting problems of business relations; (2) that efficient methods are less costly and therefore more profitable than bad methods; and (3) that the efficient ways may be more easily and surely discovered through the proven methods of painstaking experiment and disinterested observation than through following rules of thumb or uninformed prejudice.

As a result of the development of an intellectually based technique, the practice of management is becoming an art for which one must prepare himself through education and experience. The education need not be formal education; yet increasing numbers of younger men are preparing themselves for managerial roles by study in schools of business, and more and more junior executives are studying for positions of greater responsibility by attendance at the many institutes, night classes, and company training programs now being provided. In short, there is a more or less systematic body of knowledge which one must acquire before one is qualified to fill a managerial position in a large corporation. This is not to say that one may learn to become a successful manager by reading books any more than one can become a great physician by reading books. In both cases, certain personal qualities and long years of experience are required. Nevertheless, formal knowledge is a practical necessity.

Responsibility to Clients

Business is sharply distinguished from the traditional professions in the nature of its clientele and in the character of its relationships to that clientele.

In the traditional professions, the clients are primarily the persons or groups who are served by the practitioners — they are the "customers." And professional ethics are concerned primarily with the relationships between the practitioners and the customers. But the clients of business, that is, the persons who are affected by business operations and for whom business is therefore responsible, include not only customers but also stockholders, workers, suppliers, citizens of the communities in which business is conducted, and, in our interdependent world, the public at large. Responsibility toward all those persons whose lives are touched by business operations.[5] In this sense, the concept of professionalism as applied to business is even broader and more inclusive than as applied to medicine or law or theology.

In most of the traditional professions, the human relationships involved are distinctively *personal* relationships. They are primarily the relationships of individual practitioners to clients who are known face to face. But in business — particularly in the large corporation — the "practitioner" is a *group* of persons who jointly constitute "management" and who are collectively responsible for the conduct of the enterprise. And the clients, often, are known only vaguely and impersonally as "stockholders," the "market," "organized labor," the "public," and so forth.[6]

Because the clientele of business is so diffuse and ramified and distant, and because business relationships are so impersonal, it is much more difficult for businessmen, as compared with members of the traditional professions, to perceive their responsibilities and to respond to them. It is one thing for a physician to realize and accept his responsibilities toward a patient whom he knows as a fellow human being; and it is quite another thing for a business management to understand that its decisions may affect the lives of flesh-and-blood human beings and to act accordingly. Our whole ethical tradition is more immediately serviceable for direct interpersonal relationships than for the kind of impersonal and distant human relationships which are common to business. This means, on the one hand that it is unusually difficult for

---

[5] This is, of course, not an absolute distinction. Practitioners of the traditional professions have responsibilities to the community—the physician for public health, the lawyer for justice, and so forth. Yet the emphasis in professional ethics is upon the relationship of the practitioner to the person served.

[6] Again this distinction is not absolute in a day of giant law firms and great medical clinics.

businessmen to acquire professional attitudes and practices, and on the other hand that businessmen deserve great credit for the substantial progress already achieved.

Management as a balance wheel

There is no doubt of an increasing acceptance among businessmen of important obligations toward their diverse clients. The concept of "stewardship" is, of course, an old one, and many businessmen have been thinking in this direction. Especially within the past few years, large numbers of business leaders have publicly acknowledged and actively preached the doctrine that they are servants of society and that management merely in the interests (narrowly defined) of stockholders is not the sole end of their duties.[7]

The following are two examples (many more might be supplied) of statements by leading businessmen in which they acknowledge their role as trustees:

> Today, most managements, in fact, operate as trustees in recognition of the claims of employees, investors, consumers, and government. The task is to keep these forces in balance and to see that each gets a fair share of industry's rewards.[8]

> It is becoming clear that in our modern society top management has the opportunity — in fact, I should say the duty — to act as a balance wheel in relation to three groups of interests — the interests of owners, of employees, and of the public, all of whom have a stake in the output of industry. Management can best represent the interests' of ownership by acting fairly and wisely with respect to the claims of employees and the public as well. It is a difficult but vital role. It seems to me only too obvious that the very survival of private enterprise requires that private enterprise act to maintain a productive and equitable relation among these three elements: the individual's right to, and the social necessity for, profits; the economic and human aspirations of all workers; and the public's demand for an abudance of goods at low cost. The alternative is plainly intensified industrial conflict followed by increased government regulation forced by an impatient public.[9]

---

[7] In an earlier issue of *The Annals,* I tried to show in some detail the growing sense of social responsibility on the part of businessmen: "How Public Spirited Is American Business?" *The Annals,* 280 (March 1952), 82–89.

[8] Clarence Francis, Chairman of General Foods Corporation, address at the annual conference of the Harvard Business School Alumni Association, June 12, 1948.

[9] F. W. Pierce, Director of Standard Oil Company of New Jersey, address before the Cincinnati Chapter of the Society for the Advancement of Management, December 6, 1945.

One must not, of course, exaggerate the extent to which businessmen and their corporations have disavowed their selfish impulses
and turned their thoughts to the social welfare. And the progress that
has occurred has been achieved primarily as a result of changes in the
social climate of opinion, attitudes, and values within which business
functions. Nevertheless, businessmen have made great progress in their
responsiveness to their obligations to society.

Professional Associations

The luxuriant growth of trade associations, better business
bureaus, chambers of commerce, and service clubs suggests that business
is in the process of developing professional associations analogous to
those in the traditional professions. These businessmen's associations
do not presume to enforce standards of competence for entry into the
practice of business management or to regulate the conduct of their
members. But they are at least marginally concerned with formulating
codes of ethics and with promoting consultation among businessmen
on problems of mutual concern. In the past the orientation of these
associations has often been toward the narrow interests of members, and
the attitudes of association officials have frequently surpassed those of
member businessmen in their reactionariness. Nevertheless, such associations have on the whole broadened the vision of members by focusing
attention on the problems of the industry, business at large, or the
community, as well as of the single enterprise.

Businessmen's associations have also been useful in providing
the sense of group consciousness which is so essential a basis for ethical
behavior.

How To Control Business

We have now considered professionalism in business in terms
of three criteria: (1) intellectually based technique, (2) responsibility
toward clients, and (3) professional organization. With reference to
each of these criteria, it can be said quite definitely that business has
been moving in the direction of professionalism. Business management
is clearly becoming a learned art for which the practitioner must prepare himself through education and experience. Businessmen are steadily
becoming more conscious of the manifold consequences of their actions
and more concerned about their social responsibilities. And business
organizations are becoming increasingly interested in the ethical aspects
of business operations. But it can be said with equal definiteness that
business has by no means reached the advanced state of professionalism

attained by, for example, the medical profession. And it seems most unlikely that it will (or should) ever attain that degree of professionalism.

The concept of "profession" implies, essentially, a particular form of *control* over the conduct of the practitioner. This control is through voluntary codes which have been formulated by his peers with primary concern for the public interest and which are enforced by these same peers. Professionalism means peer-group responsibility for the conduct of the individual practitioner of the learned arts. When we speak of professional conduct, we refer to actions of a practitioner which are consistent with the accepted code of his peer group. Professionalism is, in other words, a form of social control over the behavior of individuals. When we speak of professionalism with reference to business, we are in fact concerned about the question, How should business be controlled? and, Is professionalism a feasible or desirable method of control over business?

There is no doubt that business must be subjected to some form of social control. Men cannot safely be turned loose in pursuit of self-interest without some method of ensuring that their behavior will be comfortable to the general welfare. In general, there are three types of control available for the purpose: (1) competition, (2) governmental regulation, and (3) professionalism.

The advocates of laissez faire proposed that detailed governmental control over business decisions should be minimized, and that the control, instead, should take the form of widespread and relentless competition. (The early proponents of laissez faire lived too early to consider professionalism as a form of control.) Later, when it became apparent that extreme laissez faire afforded insufficient control over business to prevent certain abuses or undesirable conditions, other forms of social control were advocated. One of these was governmental regulation. Extreme socialists proposed that this should be virtually the sole form of control. Another alternative was professionalism, or voluntary control under the aegis of a peer group to define social responsibilities and enforce "ethical" behavior.

There are few responsible persons in the United States today who believe that any one of the three forms of social control can be relied upon exclusively. There are few remaining advocates of extreme laissez faire, even fewer socialists, and almost no proponents of complete self-regulation by business.

Americans have strong faith in competition as a regulator of business conduct, yet they doubt its usefulness as a sole form of control. They feel that government — in the form of policemen, judges, and regulatory commissions — is useful in curbing the selfishness of men and directing their activities into socially desirable channels. At the same time, they are skeptical of the socialist model of all-pervasive governmental regulation. Americans feel that there is a place for professionalism or self-regulation, yet they do not have confidence in the wisdom and restraint of private businessmen to regulate themselves without external control.

The kind of economy we are evolving is a mixed economy in which control by competition, by governmental regulation, and by self-regulation are combined. Honest men differ as to the most desirable proportions of these three types of control, and when specific problems arise they differ as to which type of remedy is preferable. But they are generally agreed that some combination of the three is essential.

Significance of professionalism

The importance of professionalism (or voluntary regulation) for business is that it offers a type of control that is intermediate between competition and governmental regulation. In so far as businessmen can learn to perceive the social consequences of their actions and voluntarily act in terms of the social interest, the abuses of laissez faire and the dangers of excessive governmental regulation may both be avoided. In this respect, tendencies toward professionalism in business may be regarded as wholesome.

At the same time, it would be naïve and dangerous to assume that voluntary regulation could or should largely supplant competition and governmental regulation in the control of our economic life. Business is different from the traditional professions in the degree to which control through competition is possible or desirable. In the case of medicine, for example, control is achieved primarily through professional self-regulation supplemented by governmental regulation, and competition is obviously unsuitable as a major form of control. For business, on the other hand, competition is a workable form of control which, though it cannot be relied upon exclusively, is more efficient than either professionalism or government. Under these circumstances, business is unlikely ever to become a full-fledged profession, nor is such a development desirable. For professionalism in business is not without danger. The apparatus of organizations and codes that is characteristic of professionalism could easily become a mask for monopoly. The tendency toward professionalism in business may be regarded as socially desirable only if it becomes a means of lessening the need for governmental control — not if it becomes a device for stifling competition.

Cases

Grafton

Grafton, a small town of about one thousand people, was located in the northwest corner of one of the northern United States. Its development began about 1922 with the discovery of several oilfields in the vicinity, and the subsequent need for facilities for refining and marketing the oil. Newton Oils, a major oil company chose Grafton for the site of a refinery with a total daily output of 1500 barrels.

Newton Oils did a great deal for the town during the following years. New homes were built for the employees and schools and churches were erected. Water works, installed outside of town by the oil company, provided water for both refinery and the town of Grafton. As the oil industry expanded and the number of oilwells in the district increased, Grafton boomed. To meet the problem of overcrowded schools, centralization took place over a radius of ten miles. In 1948, residents of the town voted for a new high school costing $750,000 and an elementary school costing over $100,000. Along with this, the establishment of a fire department and the installation of sewer facilities necessitated the expansion of the water supply. To pay for these, the town and district were bonded; that is, they pledged themselves to pay town and district taxes based on yearly assessments until all debts were paid.

Suddenly, in 1957, Newton Oils announced its intention to shut down their refinery in Grafton and to move its production to a more central location. Employees were to be included in the move — slightly more than one-half the total tax-paying population.

Grafton was faced with disaster. Of the money owed for the expanded facilities, little more than $260,000 had been paid, leaving $500,000 owing on the high school and $90,000 on the elementary school. Eleven percent of the total school taxes and more for the public utilities had been paid by Newton Oils. A number of homes owned and built by the oil company were to be moved, thus resulting in a direct loss in assessment. Businessmen in Grafton estimated that school taxes alone would increase 30 percent as a result of the loss of revenue from the refinery, and other town taxes would also balloon. Added to these problems, was the danger that many other people would also leave Grafton — the merchants and others who depended on the refinery for their livelihood. A final crisis arose when the company gave no indication as to what was to be done with the water works, leaving the residents to wonder if these, too, would be removed, or whether they would be able to buy the machinery and pipes from the company, in either case burdening themselves with additional expenses.

In addition to the grave problems facing the town as a whole, individual groups were also affected. One of the churches had begun a much-needed expansion program. Now, with the advancing possibility of a ghost town, there was no need for the huge church which had been built. Members of one of the local service clubs had solicited funds and even begun construction on a modern swimming pool designed to serve the town of Grafton and the surrounding district. They realized that this would never be needed after the departure of Newton Oils. The quality of the education received by the children would experience a sharp decline, as the town would no longer be able to support the salaries of the present teachers, and also because it seemed illogical that good teachers would want to teach in a town which resembled a ghost town.

To defend itself, the company stated its main reason for leaving. Since it was at the northern end of its area of distribution, high freight rates to the markets had to be paid on all refined products. It had thus become economically necessary to move the refinery to a more central location.

The Viking Air Compressor Company, Inc.

As he left the president's office George Ames wondered what he ought to do. His impulse was to resign, but he knew that could be a costly blot on his employment record. Moreover, there was the possibility that he was seeing things in a distorted way, that he might later regret leaving Viking before he really knew all the facts bearing on his position and its future. He decided to wait for another week before making up his mind, and in the meantime he made an appointment with Professor Farnsworth of the Amos Tuck School of Business Administration at Dartmouth College to get his advice. Mr. Ames had received his MBA degree from the Tuck School the previous June.

The Viking Air Compressor Company was founded in Bradley, Connecticut, in 1908 by Nels Larsen, an inventor and engineer who left the Westinghouse Electric Company to start his own organization. Mr. Larsen had both a successful design for a new type of air compressor and a talent for management. He led Viking to steadily increasing successes in the air compressor industry. In 1971 Viking held a steady 25 percent of the air compressor business in the United States, with total annual sales of $180 million. Mr. John T. Larsen, grandson of the founder, was chairman of the board and chief executive officer. Three other descendants of the founder were officers of the company, and the rest of the management team had been developed from Viking employees who rose through the ranks. The ownership of Viking was substantially in the Larsen family hands.

In March 1971 Mr. Oscar Stewart, vice president for personnel administration of Viking, visited the Amos Tuck School to talk with MBA candidates interested in a new position to be created in the Viking structure the following June. Mr. Stewart explained to Dean Robert Y. Kimball, Tuck's director of placement, that Viking had never hired MBA's directly from business schools but wanted to experiment in 1971 with this method of bringing fresh ideas and new techniques into the firm.

Reprinted by the courtesy of Dr. John W. Hennessey, Jr., The Amos Tuck School of Business Administration, Dartmouth College. Copyright © 1972. This case has been disguised where feasible to permit its use for instructional purposes.

The corporate officers had decided, according to Mr. Stewart, to begin to test the effectiveness of the recruitment of MBA's by hiring a business school graduate to become director of public affairs, with the assignment of coordinating the relationships between Viking and outside agencies seeking financial contributions from the company.

As Mr. Stewart described the job to the students he interviewed at Tuck in March 1971, it would contain such tasks as (1) proposing to the Board of Directors the best criteria to use in deciding how to make corporate gifts to charitable organizations of all kinds; (2) supplying the chief officers of the company with information about the participation of Viking employees in public service activities; (3) recommending future strategy for Viking in the employment of women and members of minority groups; and (4) serving as secretary to the newly formed Committee on Corporate Responsibility, which consisted of five members of the Board of Directors.

George Ames accepted the post of director of public affairs at Viking. He had been chosen by Vice President Stewart as the most promising of the five attractive Tuck applicants for the new position. Mr. Ames reported for work on July 1, 1971, after a short vacation and immediately plunged into the difficult task of gathering information about his new assignment. Mr. Stewart told him that his primary task would be to work with the board's Committee on Corporate Responsibility, mainly to propose new policy guidelines to the board at its September 10 meeting. Mr. Stewart added that there were two other areas of high priority: (1) the corporation's attitude toward public service of employees, and (2) developing criteria for corporate philanthropic giving.

As Vice President Stewart explained to George in early July, the Committee on Corporate Responsibility was created at the January meeting of the Viking Board of Directors after unanimous endorsement of the suggestion made by Dr. Thomas A. Barr, pastor of the local Congregational Church and one of the four outside members of the twelve-man board. Reverend Barr's major support for his recommendation was the observation that the General Motors Corporation had taken a similar step, under some pressure, and that corporate responsibility was an idea whose time had come on the American scene. In response to the question, what will such a committee do, Reverend Barr replied that there need be no hurry in defining the detailed responsibilities of the committee and that, furthermore, there could not possibly be any harm or drawbacks in setting it up as soon as possible. He added that the public relations value of such a gesture should not be underestimated. In establishing the Committee on Corporate Responsibility, the board voted to require the first progress report from the committee in September 1971.

The Committee on Corporate Responsibility met following the

February meeting of the Board of Directors and decided to delay any definitive action until an executive secretary could be hired. Vice President Stewart was asked to keep this post in mind as he interviewed MBA graduates of several of the leading business schools, and so he did.

George Ames met with the chairman of the Committee on Responsibility at a luncheon on July 21, 1971, arranged by Vice President Stewart. The committee chairman was Mr. Paul Merrow, one of the most respected lawyers in northern Connecticut and the son of one of the first board members of Viking when the company was incorporated in the 1920's. Mr. Merrow expressed his pleasure that George Ames was working on the corporate responsibility question and asked him to prepare a report that might be reviewed by the committee just prior to the September board meeting. What he wanted, he explained to Mr. Ames, was an analysis of the three or four possible approaches to corporate responsibility the Directors ought to consider. Merrow asked for a listing of the pros and cons of these various approaches. He said that Mr. Ames should consider this very much like an assignment in a course at the Tuck School. He would be performing a task that none of the board members had the time or academic background to do and thus he would substantially improve the decision making of the Board of Directors.

Mr. Merrow concluded the luncheon by saying that he would like Mr. Ames to proceed on his own during the summer but that he would be glad to confer with him in early September. Mr. Merrow explained that he was leaving the next day for a legal conference in Europe and would be on an extended vacation until September 6. He said that he had "the proxies" of the other committee members and that they would prefer not to get involved in working on committee tasks until after the September board meeting.

George Ames worked assiduously during August reading all the articles and books he could find in the area of corporate responsibility, including the background of developments in the General Motors situation. He decided not to talk about this particular assignment with other officers of Viking, primarily because of Mr. Merrow's injunction that the committee itself would prefer not to engage in substantive talk about the issues until the September board meeting. George feared he would do more harm than good by talking before he knew his subject well.

In early September John Larsen asked George to see him, and the following conversation took place:

John Larsen: I've asked you to see me this morning and tell me what progress you have been making in developing background materials for the work of the Committee on Corporate Responsibility.

Mr. Merrow told me he had asked you to do some digging and that you would have a brief report to make at the September 10 meeting of the board. I know Mr. Merrow hoped he would be back from Europe in time to talk with you before the board meeting, but it now appears he will be lucky to make the meeting at all. He expects to arrive in town about noon on the 10th.

George Ames: Mr. Larsen, I appreciate the opportunity I have been given to help Viking by developing recommendations about possible strategies for the company to follow in the area of corporate responsibility. Mr. Merrow told me I ought to develop alternative proposals for recommendations to the board, and I have as recently as yesterday finally been able to narrow the field so that I can make four recommendations with confidence.

I realize the board may prefer to consider them one at a time, at different meetings. But I would like to tell you about all four so that you will know what my report will contain.

I have decided that the most important issue in the area of corporate responsibility is equal opportunity hiring. I have been able to develop statistics from the personnel records, which show that Viking is rather far behind most major national corporations in the percentage of blacks and women now employed. And although I am sure conscientious efforts have been made by all officers to remedy this, I cannot stress too strongly how much of a time bomb the present situation is. There will be wide ramifications if we do not improve our record.

The second item of priority which I see is the development of corporate sanctions for public service activities of employees. I believe the company should grant paid leaves of absence for employees who wish to accept public service posts. At present we have done that only for two vice presidents who have been in charge of the Northern Connecticut United Fund. In each case the man was lent to the charitable organization for two full weeks. What I have in mind is a much wider program which would grant employees leaves of absence to work in poverty programs in urban ghettos or in VISTA projects in Connecticut or neighboring states.

It seems to me a third priority is to develop a committee of consumers who will monitor the safety features and other quality items having to do with our products. If we do not do this we will have Ralph Nader breathing down our necks, as has already happened in the automotive industry and some others.

Finally, I strongly recommend that we close our sales contact in Capetown, South Africa, and establish policies that will avoid our being embarrassed as a corporation by discriminatory or dictatorial policies of foreign governments which become critically important political and social issues here in this country.

I feel sure these are great issues of our times, and I hope the board will be willing to debate them at the September 10 meeting. I know I could learn a great deal in my position if such a debate could take place.

Mr. Larsen: Young man, I want to congratulate you on how articulately you have told me about some of the things you have learned in the MBA program at the Tuck School. I envy fellows of your generation who go through MBA programs because you get an opportunity to think about policy problems at a much earlier age than my generation ever did. Indeed, my only complaint is that the business schools go too far to educate young men to think they know how to run a company long before they have enough real experience to be even a first-line supervisor.

Now I think you have your assignment all backwards as secretary to the Committee on Corporate Responsibility, and I will tell you why I think that. The committee hasn't even met yet, and your remarks make it sound as if you have written the final report. Worse than that, it sounds like the final report of the Committee on Corporate Responsibility of the General Motors Company, not Viking. Everybody knows we've done as good a job as we can to hire blacks and women. There just aren't many such people in the work force in our part of Connecticut who could fit our talent standards, and we are going to follow our historical policy of nondiscrimination as we hire the best people to do Viking jobs. We owe it to our stockholders to make a profit, and if we don't do that, we don't have the right to do anything else.

Your remarks on public service activities for our employees are equally off target. The first obligation of our employees is to give a fair day's work for a fair day's pay. All public service activities are extracurricular activities, and that's the way they must be. In order for us to sponsor public service on company time, we would have to discriminate between good and bad activities. And that would get us into partisan politics and preoccupy all of our executive time. How would the company have done if I had been a part-time chief executive officer in the last five years? That is a preposterous idea! At the same time, by working harder on my regular job I have been able some evenings and some weekends to work in fund-raising activities for the Boy Scouts, YMCA, and heaven knows how many other charitable organizations. I would expect every employee to do the same and not to expect the corporation to subsidize activities in their roles as private citizens. As far as public service is concerned, "live and let live" should be our corporate motto. If we encourage public service activities and include them as part of our compensation and promotion system, we will be bogged down in a fantastic collection of information about private lives which will lead to chaos. Even the most superficial examination of this question should have led you to see the problems with the route your theory took you.

As far as the safety of our products and other demands

consumers might make, that's all done through the marketplace, as you will come to understand. If our projects were not safe or durable, they wouldn't sell. You could have found this out had you talked with our production and marketing people, as you certainly should have done by now. It's our responsibility to decide after careful market research what the air compressor needs of America are and will be in the future. We don't need a special panel of bleeding hearts to lead us along paths where we are already expert.

As for our selling operations in South Africa, I'm afraid you just don't know what you are talking about. As long as there is no plank of American foreign policy or federal law that tells corporations where they can and where they can't sell their products, American businesses must depend on the free market system. President Nixon is talking about opening the trade doors to mainland China. Do you think for one moment the practices of the Chinese government are any less nefarious in some respects than the practices of the South African government? Of course not. And yet you would probably urge me in your liberal way to establish a selling office in Peking just to go along with the new liberal ideas of our president, and I call that kind of pragmatism ridiculous.

Come to think of it, how could you miss this opportunity to lecture the board on our responsibilities for pollution control and our obligations to get out of the military-industrial complex by cancelling all of our air compressor contracts with the federal government!

Young man, you have shown yourself to be a wooly-minded theoretician and I want to tell you that bluntly now so that you will not think me hypocritical at any later point. I will tell the Committee on Corporate Responsibility that you have not had time to prepare your first briefing of the Board of Directors, and then I want to have a meeting with you and the chairman of the Corporate Responsibility Committee on Monday morning, September 20.

That's all I have time for now. I'll see you later.

Bibliography

Adizes, I., and J. F. Weston. "Comparative Models of Social Responsibility." *Academy of Management Journal,* 16 (March 1973), 112–128.

"Analysts Weigh Significance of Corporate Social Responsibility." *Trusts and Estates,* 110 (September 1971), 756–757.

Burck, Gilbert. "The Hazards of Corporate Social Responsibility." *Fortune,* June 1973, pp. 114–117ff.

Davis, Keith. "Case For and Against Business Assumption of Social Responsibilities." *Academy of Management Journal,* June 1973, pp. 312–322.

Eilbirt, H. "Corporate Responsibility Officer." *Business Horizons* 16 (February 1973), 45–51.

Gertenberg, R. C. "Corporate Responsiveness and Profitability." *Conference Board Record,* 9 (November 1972), 51–53.

"Is Management a Profession?" *Industry Week,* February 19, 1973, pp. 40–44.

Kinard, J. L. "About this Business of Social Responsibility." *Personnel Journal* 53 (November 1974), 825–828.

Novick, D. "Cost-Benefit Analysis and Social Responsibility." *Business Horizons,* 16 (October 1973), 63–72.

" 'Social Issues Aren't Responsibility of Business,' Ritchie Tells Communicators." *Advertising Age,* September 28, 1970, p. 60.

Votaw, D. "Genius Becomes Rare: A Comment on the Doctrine of Social Responsibility." *California Management Review,* 15 (Winter 1972), 25–31; (Spring 1973), 5–19.

Part Eight
Business-Society Goals, Policies, and Ethics

Conflicts of goals between business and society pervade all of the issues treated in this book. For this reason we need to look at a comprehensive statement of national social goals and to appraise both the conflicts between business and national priorities, and the changing developments for each set of goals.

A. Business and National Social Goals

The article "Business and Society: Contemporary Issues and National Goals" [30] provides an overview of the potential range of social responsibilities that the business person may assume in the future. But first let us review some of the fundamentals of business-society relationships. The business person is concerned with a great variety of interest groups. Because of the diversity and scope of these publics, business must take a more encompassing view of society and attempt to develop not only a public relations image, but also an operating business philosophy that will more effectively relate business to society. This philosophy should result from a comparative analysis of business and national social goals so that any potential conflicts may be reconciled. For example, if the primary national goal is the maximum development of the individual, a primary concern of business should be the individual manager-employee relationship as a reflection of the aggregate relationship of business to society. If business is to provide the type of leadership that will maximize the achievement of individual and group goals in society, managers must delineate their rights and duties to society. They must then develop a business-society philosophy with a positively stated code of ethics that will serve as a guideline for the attainment of such goals as well as the resolution of any controversy.

The National Goals Research Staff has provided an updating of the national goals for the 1970s in a report entitled "Toward Balanced Growth: Quantity with Quality." This report recommends policy priorities as models for achieving balanced mixes of quantity and quality in the future. In particular, the report aimed for a new humanism for U.S. society with a shift of goals toward the broad areas of service, knowledge, and social change. It is noteworthy that it emphasizes broad policy guidelines versus specific goal determination as a means of achieving better mixes, and better balances in the mixes, of goals in the decade of the 1970s.

While the magnitude of business-society problems may require a redefinition of the role of business in U.S. society, there are also many problems that require specific business policy formulations. George Steiner considers these in the article "Social Policies for Business" [31]. By defining social responsibilities in the form of corporate social policies he reports that business can insure its participation in the redrafting of a "social contract," rather than letting other groups and institutions in society determine policy without the representation of business. This may result in altered expectations of what we have known as managerial capitalism, but it will also be a step forward in insuring a future balance between business and society in the resolution of the many conflicts between them.

Not since the 1930s has there been such severe public disfavor announced through protests against business. A review of the problems underlying these protests in the 1970s reveals a substantial list of conflicts between business and society. These have been refined to a list of ten by the Committee for Economic Development as follows: economic growth and efficiency, education, employment and training, civil rights and equal opportunity, urban renewal and development, pollution abatement, conservation and recreation, culture and the arts, medical care, and government. With these ten category guidelines, business can more readily approach the most important problems, especially in its policy review and formulation process.

Society is expecting much more from corporations than in the past, to the point that even the "quality of life" in the U.S. will become the business of business. It is in the business person's best interest to meet those expectations. Therefore, business must participate in drafting new rules for its conduct. The fear of growing social expectations pushing business too far, too fast, is perhaps the greatest impetus for business to become actively involved in the process of policy formulation. George Steiner suggests a variety of ideas for consideration in forming policy.

An example of goals conflicts is presented in the Fisher Manufacturing Company case. While these conflicts are internal ones in a particular organization, they nevertheless affect the management, the employees, and also the community in which they operate. Autocratic and arbitrary determination of goals on the part of corporate management has caused this extensive range of conflicts. In this case, the goals of the president, emphasizing new products and manufacturing processes over profitable product expansion, so seriously conflict with the management staff that the survival of the corporation is challenged by other managers. The extreme diversity of goals in this case are illustrative of internal business goals conflicts, and suggest that externally defined goals would tend to conflict even more with internal goals, having a more significant effect on the firm, and the community in which it operates.

B. Business Ethics

Business ethics have been a concern and problem for the business person throughout the twentieth century. Many of these problems were subsumed under the social responsibility concept, especially in the fifties and sixties. The explosion of environmental problems in the seventies tended to provide an umbrella for all business problems in conflict with the environment and society.

A new trend in business ethics is reported in "Stiffer Rules for Business Ethics" [32]. The public is concerned with stricter ethical standards, especially in this post-Watergate age. There is an innumerable array of ethical problems that develop in the so-called "gray" areas — those aspects of conduct that are not obviously right or wrong. Society rewards business for achieving economic goals, but provides strong legal sanctions if it uses clearly unethical practices in the process. As a result of the free competitive system the business person must reconcile a variety of pressures and temptations to act in ways that may not be illegal but may be questionable ethically.

The *Business Week* article cites over twenty ethical problem areas, including such major ones as misleading reporting to the public, failure to control the unethical behavior of employees, misuse of management consultants, and also the misuse of lawyers or CPAs. Another major category of ethical problems in business is the relationship of business and government. This includes the use of congressional assistance, if not influence, and the types and amounts of personal campaign contributions. Income tax declarations too often fall into the ethical gray area, especially donations, travel and entertainment expenses, and tax shelters. Ethical difficulties also arise from problems with the Securities and Exchange Commission's rules against "inside information." A review of these ethical problems indicates increasing pressures from society to prescribe more explicit rules against unethical practices. *Business Week* has also included in this article guidelines for dealing with the following eight ethical problem areas: incomplete disclosure, the corrupt boss, the corrupt subordinate, the inadvertent remark, the purified idea, the passive director, the expense account vacation, and the stock option trap. These guidelines provide not only a delineation of the trend toward stiffer rules for business ethics, but also a version of a "social audit" of performance in these potentially unethical areas.

The article "Are New Business Ethics Beyond Reality?" [33] presents a different perspective of business ethics problems. The constant evolution of U.S. social mores, and the concomitant changing definition of unethical business practices, present dynamic problems that do not lend themselves to rigid rules. The *Industry Week* article examines whether business should comply only with civil laws, or should also comply with moral laws. Milton Friedman, the noted University of Chicago economist, has stated that business serves society best by concentrating on what it does best — doing business (exclusively). Many economists, management theorists, and practitioners agree with Friedman that the primary if not exclusive purpose of business is profit, and that in pursuing profit business will best serve the public through the most efficient utilization of resources in a free-market economy. This perspective emphasizes the major responsibilities of the business person to the stockholder, and to profit making. But there are other spokespeople who believe that the youth of modern society will not accept this. Due to the massive power of business, it can easily act unjustly with individuals and groups, can pollute if not destroy the environment, and produce and sell unnecessary products.

Business usually cannot direct its actions toward profits exclusively, but must follow a pattern of responsible moral actions. The article recommends that the business community become more sensitive to ethical issues, especially in view of the increasing interest of the general public. The authors also suggest that the level of ethical behavior may well be correlated with the level of profits in what might be called the ability-to-pay concept. In summary, it appears that business must face moral as well as economic limitations on its decisions and behavior.

Business has a unique opportunity to perform a leadership role through its position of power and influence. While *Industry Week* does not suggest that social issues should take precedence over profits, it does suggest that business is moving toward greater moral responsibility in response to its critics. It further suggests that this will be an evolutionary process. As such, both business and the public must mutually adjust to each step in improving the ethical climate. The article makes a final point that society should also provide guidelines for ethical behavior in the form of incentives, to either accelerate or prohibit certain practices. In this way society would insure that the responsibility for ethical behavior would fall equally on all business managers and organizations. In short, business cannot do it alone.

The Anatomy of a Price Fixing Conspiracy case confronts us with the realistic pressures of a competitive economy. Within such an economy there is no easy and automatic resolution of conflict to be achieved by simple formulas. The case points out the inherent complexities of any free society and, in particular, those conflict areas in the economic realm. It is highly probable that these problems are often created as much by distrust and lack of understanding of motives and actions of individuals and groups in our society, as by actual unethical intent.

Another major point to consider in our discussion of business ethics is the recommendation of Professor Robert W. Austin of Harvard University in his writings on "A Positive Code of Ethics," quoted in *Business Week,* June 17, 1961. Professor Austin appealed not only for a code of ethics but also for a positively oriented one. He believes that a listing of "Shalt Nots" is incapable of meeting managerial needs and must be supplanted by a positive code that fulfills the professional requirements of management with a commitment to social responsibilities. I would suggest that such a positive statement might well be in the form of a delineation of business goals that are parallel and consistent with national goals. These might be readily constructed from the substantive content of the social audits now under consideration today.

A Business and National-Social Goals

30 Business and Society: Contemporary Issues and National Goals

William T. Greenwood

Issues of conflict have arisen between business and society because of outside pressures from individuals and groups. Most *conspicuous* among pressure groups are labor and government. The constant increase in the number and variety of these issues reveals the urgent necessity for resolving them in some systematic and comprehensive manner.

But labor and government are not the only pressure groups interested in the objectives and practices of business. The contemporary scene has produced many other group and individual pressures. This fact is supported by business literature in the decade of the fifties. A survey of business periodicals between 1950 and 1963 reveal over 1,000 articles discussing these issues external to the firm. In the majority of these discussions, pro and con positions were presented treating these controversial topics, and the balance of other approaches constituted new trends of thought and action for the businessman. The issue-topics discussed most frequently in the business periodical literature of the past decade are grouped and classified in Table 1. It will be noted that the problems of business size, freedom, competition, profits, profit-sharing, anti-trust actions, and the legitimacy of free-enterprise capitalism have been treated as major issues of the day in spite of the many debates and dissertations on these same issues in prior decades and, in some cases, centuries of time.

The public relations function of business has undergone revolutionary changes in this period. New trends creating corporate images provide systematic guides and controls in coping with external pressures on the firm. This trend developed in response to influences designed to

Table 1 Comparison of Contemporary Business and Society Issues with National Goals

Contemporary Issues

I. Our Free Enterprise Society
A. Capitalism and Freedom
B. Business, Competition, and Government
C. The Role of Profits

II. Business and Its Publics
A. Public Relations and the Corporate Image
B. The Political Role of the Businessman
C. The Problem of Business Giving

III. Business and the Individual in Society
A. Human Relations and Leadership
B. For Business: Conformity or Individualism

IV. Labor-Management Relationships
A. Labor Relations and Collective Bargaining

B. Management's Employment Responsibilities
C. Fair Employment Practices

V. Ethics, Religion, and Business
A. Ethical Aspects of Business Practice
B. Business and Religion

VI. Trends Toward a Philosophy of Management
A. Management Rights
B. Business Objectives
C. Management Philosophy

VII. Social Responsibilities of Business
A. The Social Responsibility Concept
B. Professional Responsibilities of Power Groups
C. Responsibilities of the Future

National Goals

I. Goals at Home
1. The Individual
2. Equality
3. The Democratic Process
4. Education
5. The Arts and Sciences
6. The Democratic Economy
7. Economic Growth
8. Technological Change

9. Agriculture
10. Living Conditions
11. Health and Welfare

II. Goals Abroad
12. Helping to Build an Open and Peaceful World
13. The Defense of the Free World
14. Disarmament
15. The United Nations

National Goals Essays

I. American Fundamentals
1. The Individual
2. The Democratic Process

II. Goals at Home
3. National Goals in Education
4. A Great Age for Science
5. The Quality of American Culture
6. An Effective and Democratic Organization of the Economy
7. High Employment and Growth in the American Economy
8. Technological Change

9. Farm Policy for the Sixties
10. Framework for an Urban Society
11. Meeting Human Needs

III. The Role of Government
12. The Federal System
13. The Public Service

IV. The World We Seek
14. The United States Role in the World
15. Foreign Economic Policy and Objectives
16. A Look Further Ahead

The American Assembly *Goals for Americans,* The Report of the President's Commission on National Goals and Chapters Submitted for the Consideration of the Commission (New York: Prentice-Hall, 1960), p. 4. Reprinted with permission from Prentice-Hall.

guide the political activities and charitable functions of business. The human relations problems of the businessman have been dominant in the period following World War II, especially in delineating problems and developing methods for their resolution in the period of the fifties. The conflict between the individual employee, the firm, and traditional management practices is now waged over the necessity for organizing work around people as opposed to the traditional pattern of people around work.

Other problems of participative versus autocratic leadership and individual versus conformity practices have assumed a position of prominence in the literature. Labor-management issues have been reduced from an infinite variety of problems to fundamental underlying issues relating to the success of our collective bargaining system, management's assumption of employment opportunity responsibilities, and external pressures for consideration of fair-employment practices as opposed to arbitrary managerial decisions. These issues have motivated the search for new labor-management relationships to provide harmony and peace in achieving economic and social objectives in society.

Common to the afore-mentioned problems of business with individuals and groups in society have been the questions of morality and ethics in business-management practices. Business has been increasingly buffeted by criticisms for its failure to meet the moral-ethical-religious needs of our society and the apparent lack of reconciliation of business goals and philosophies with those of individuals and groups in society. The new developments in all of these areas have created a cumulative pressure for the business firm to reconcile these conflicts in some uniform and consistent way. These pressures have evolved into increasing demands for business creeds and philosophies by which the issues can be resolved. Diverse and unclassified business and management philosophies of the past have contributed little toward a universally applicable systematic approach. Attrition of management prerogatives and rights has demanded a redefinition of conflicting rights. Business objectives have often been exclusive, creating new pressures from outside groups whose objectives come into serious conflict with those of business.

These developments have culminated in the expression of expectations for management in the form of social responsibilities. While yet in the debatable or issue stage, increasing demands have been made for business to equate its powers with social responsibilties in our society. As business managers are forced to take on the role of professional men, their responsibilities will have to be defined in order to provide uniform ethical standards that can be enforced by the profession.

The traditional goals and practices of the businessman are finally challenged for their limited scope in developing solutions for the economic problems of our age. Business objectives and policies not only fail to assess the international ramifications of our domestic economic issues, but, in many cases, are seriously detrimental to total economic development. Humanitarian, philosophical, religious, and foreign policy problems confront the businessman because his objectives and practices frequently come into conflict with societal goals.

Resolution of these many issues of the 1950's and 1960's is the dominant challenge to business today. The evolution of these issues indicates the need for an over-all solution which must come from a systematic and comprehensive set of values, a philosophy that will define universally acceptable objectives which, in turn, can be manifested in specific responsibilities for business managers. Such a set of objectives and values might have as its first consideration the Goals for Americans defined by President Eisenhower's Commission on National Goals for the 1960's. A comparison of these goals with the issues of the 1950's as found in the survey of business literature for that period are outlined in Table 1.

Fifteen national goals are concisely defined for Americans, eleven for domestic problems and four for foreign issues. The goals are supplemented and amplified in sixteen essays on the relevant points of each. A significant correlation may be noted between the issues of the 1950's and the goals of the 1960's. Because of this correlation, the goals provide an initial means of formulating a more universally applicable structure of business goals, philosophies, and creeds. These national goals will be discussed in the sequential structure of the contemporary issues of business and society.

Our Free Enterprise Society

Among the issues facing business and society during the 50's, the one relating to our free enterprise society is the most fundamental of all. Laissez-faire capitalism is defended on one hand as necessary to maintain political freedoms, achieve our national economic goals, and as a dependable trustee for society by assumption of its professional responsibilities. At the same time, its critics deplore the overprivileged position of management resulting in the loss of social and political values in our democracy. These losses have resulted from the existence and use of excessive power of large business firms and conflicting objectives and practices inherent in the competitive process. The increase in frequency and types of these conflicts relating to our free enterprise society is indicative of underlying issues which have not yet been resolved. For example, the basic concepts of freedom and capitalism or free enterprise have meant different things to different people. These concepts have taken on different meanings at different points of time in the evolution of our capitalistic system, and the failure of business management to understand and to adapt to these changes has further complicated the issue. These problems have been compounded by the increasing role of government at federal, state, and local levels. It is also contended that the underlying cause of the entry of government into these areas of business activity has been the failure of business to develop either the ability or the willingness to resolve them. This failure to meet business responsibilities has created a vacuum into which government and labor have entered to assume these responsibilities to society.

The resolution of these problems may be enhanced by a consideration of the correlated national goals. In this instance, Goal No. 3, The Democratic Process, suggests that the:

> degree of effective liberty available to its people should be the ultimate test for any nation. Democracy is the only means so far devised by which a nation can meet this test.[1]

This plea for maximum use of the democratic process provides a guide for business in avoiding the pursuit of objectives and methods that may take the form of rugged individualism and greedy (or unethical) laissez-faire capitalism. These types of business practices have historically led to social-government controls.

Government's regulation of business during the fifties manifests the continuation of increasing social controls. Whether this is due predominantly to irresponsible business practices or excessive government zeal and bureaucratic growth is a moot question. Both business and government should be alerted to their mutual responsibilities. Business must openly recognize and cooperate with legitimate external interest groups and:

> Government participation in the economy should be limited to those instances where it is essential to the national interest and where private individuals or organizations cannot adequately meet the needs.[2]

On the other hand, business must recognize that capitalism is only one of many functions and value-goals of our democratic society. It must realize that:

> The Bill of Rights was not designed for corporations; free enterprise is only one fruit of liberty, not its root. Property and business exist for the benefit of individuals and have no inherent rights.[3]

This quotation from Essay No. 1, The Individual, succinctly states the essential relationship of business to the individual and society. A reconsideration of the fundamental concepts defining the relative positions of business and other individuals and groups in society must therefore start with an analysis of the original meaning of these terms.

---

[1] *Goals for Americans,* Prentice-Hall, New York, 1960, p. 4.
[2] *Ibid.,* p. 9.
[3] *Ibid.,* p. 52.

The inherent complexity of many of the goals of society sometimes leads to positions that appear contradictory. For example, Goal No. 7, Economic Growth, provides directives for the businessman, by saying that:

> The economy should grow at the maximum rate consistent with primary dependence upon free enterprise and the avoidance of market inflation.[4]

Conflicting with these goals are pressures for corporate taxation, government regulations, and policy directives affecting existing concentrations of power under the anti-trust laws. The goal of economic growth also embraces the objective of full employment through the determination of unacceptable unemployment levels ranging between 3.4 and 6 per cent.

Business has much to gain from these national goals in its search for support of its own growth goals. Desirable tax programs, increased depreciation allowances, and minimum interference in the free-market mechanism by governmental activity are sought by both business and the President's Commission. This is qualified to some extent by approval of governmental action where serious imbalances and inequities are incurred in the maximum economic growth quest. Dr. Clark Kerr in his Essay No. 6, An Effective and Democratic Organization of the Economy, states that:

> Governmental action cannot, of course, be called upon to redress all imbalances which are bound to occur from time to time in a dynamic economy. It should be reserved for cases where the imbalance of power is serious and continuing.[5]

Dr. Kerr also desires that:

> The role of government should be restricted to clear cases of national interests which cannot be served by private means, and the government should withdraw whenever its participation is no longer essential — when the particular public need no longer exists or when it can be adequately met by private economic activity.[6]

The latter idea of withdrawal has yet to be successfully voiced by the business community or considered in a general way by government or society. This, therefore, offers an area of potential significance as business attempts to achieve both its economic and social goals in society.

In its maintenance of a free enterprise society, business can greatly enhance the increased freedom of activity in the economic realm by changing its attitude toward the legitimate co-existence of business

---

[4] *Ibid.*, p. 10.
[5] *Ibid.*, p. 154.
[6] *Ibid.*, p. 160.

and government. While much is gained through the exercise of counter-vailing power, especially by the dominant groups in our society, an admission by business that many government controls and services need not be reserved to the private sector of the economy would be a helpful starting point. Dr. James P. Dixon, Jr., states this position in Essay No. 11, Meeting Human Needs, when he says:

> Society as a whole has two functions. It can develop ways by which people can meet their own needs more readily and fruit-fully, and it can develop ways by which society as a whole can meet needs that would otherwise be unmet. There are individ-uals who will meet their own needs, and others who cannot.[7]

Business, contrary to the position advocated in this quotation, has generally taken the position that government intervention in meeting social needs in the economic realm is undesirable. When the statements of Dr. Kerr and Dr. Dixon are combined, the legitimacy and desirability of government involvement should be better understood and also advo-cated by business leaders in our society. In this form of cooperation and collaboration with other groups in society, business not only can more successfully achieve its goals, but also can reduce animosity held by many groups toward the historical business image of arbitrary power decisions.

Another issue of increasing interest to both the businessman and the President's Commission is the role of profits in our society. Nothing could be more fundamental to the businessman in terms of our free enterprise society than the profit motive. On the other hand, an increas-ing number of new issues have developed in the past decade concerning the proper role of profits and their rightful distribution. Economic growth goals desire levels of reinvested profits which often negate other claims made upon them, notably those of the stockholder, society via government taxation, and recent labor union claims. More basic than this, profits as the primary incentive and regulator of our economic system have been de-emphasized in recent theory and practice. Theories of satisfactory returns and workable competition have supplanted the classical theory of profit maximization. Many theorists and business managers have voiced alarm at this transition with claims that under-utilization of economic resources must result. Continuing arguments have been maintained by both sides. This contemporary issue is considered in Goal No. 7, Economic Growth, when it is advocated that:

> Public policies, particularly an overhaul of the tax system, in-cluding depreciation allowances, should seek to improve the cli-mate for new investment and the balancing of investment with consumption. We should give attention to policies favoring com-

---

[7] *Ibid.*, p. 249.

pletely new ventures which involve a high degree of risk and growth potential.[8]

New perspectives toward profits are difficult to conceive by the businessman. A further study of this concept within the framework of all national goals may help to illuminate the many facets of the problem and clarify the action that may be taken toward its resolution.

In addition to the changing role of profits in our society, profit-sharing claims have also established a beachhead on the collective bargaining scene. While the rights of labor to share in profits has not been resolved, precedents have been set recently in the American Motors-United Auto Workers contract and in the Kaiser Steel Fontana Plant contract in California. The question of consumer and society interests in profits is also being increasingly voiced today. Added to this is the variety of humanitarian, philosophical, theological, and foreign policy claims for participation by underdeveloped countries in our economic bounties. Both theoretically and pragmatically, the problem has been compounded for the businessman. If business is to reconcile these conflicts, it must first understand the nature of the democratic society within which it operates. The relative priority of the conflicting claims between business and other groups and individuals in society will ultimately be decided through democratic procedures. As Dr. Kerr says in Essay No. 6:

> The problem becomes one of balance, as is always true of the operation of a pluralistic society such as our own. The public objectives which we may select for our economy must be weighted against their cost in the area of individual rights.[9]

Business and Its Publics

Business has historically shown a high degree of personal interest in its public relations functions. These functions have in the past been related particularly to the consumer groups with whom business dealt. In recent years, other groups have increased in size and numbers and have brought pressures of opposition to the goals and objectives sought by business. The broad institutional groups of labor and federal, state, and local governments have been most important in this respect. In dealing with an increasing variety of social and institutional groups, business has been forced to develop a many-faceted image to represent its goals and operating practices to each of them.

In performing the public relations function in the past, business has often been condemned by society for unethical practices that

---

[8] *Ibid.*, p. 10.
[9] *Ibid.*, p. 159.

approach manipulation; and society has sought in many cases to bring counteracting pressures. One aspect of this relationship of business to society is considered by Mr. August Heckscher in Essay No. 5, The Quality of American Culture, wherein he states:

> An industrial civilization, brought to the highest point of development, has still to prove that it can nourish and sustain a rich, cultural life. In the case of the United States, it is evident that cultural attainments have not kept pace with improvements in other fields. . . . The ethic of the contemporary economic system emphasizes consumption, with 'happiness' and 'comfort' as the objectives to be sought. The end product seems to be a great mass prepared to listen long hours to the worst of TV or radio and to make our newsstands — with their diet of mediocrity — what they are.[10]

In his concluding remarks, Mr. Heckscher questions the advances of materialism, the type of materialism promoted by business in its public relations programs. He is concerned with the exclusive interest in economic satisfactions and implies responsibility for the considerations of a way of life that will emphasize more the qualities and ideals of our humanity. The degree to which business public relations influence public opinion toward values of a low order to the detriment of higher cultural goals may confront business leadership with new responsibilities in the future. These admonitions of Mr. Heckscher should direct us to the ideals and values that affect our society, particularly insofar as business influences them. It would appear that if business is to be successful in dealing with its many publics, it probably will have to consider them in some hierarchical sequence. For example, it could classify them by (a) size — international, national, industry, state, community, etc., (b) special interests — consumers, suppliers, employees, government, related firms, etc.; and (c) philosophies, ideals and values — religious, cultural, economic, political, etc. Based upon these classifications, business could then consider when and where its exclusive pursuit of the profit objective may come into serious conflicts with other societal goals.

The point of greatest conflict for most firms in handling public relations problems is at the community level. Given the highest degree of interdependence between business firms and communities, the pressures upon business and the variety and degree of activities in which business is involved in the community and political life become most significant. Also, the expectations of society for business leadership and support are manifold in these communities. In Goal No. 10, Living Conditions, these expectations are pronounced for the need of private leadership to aid in procuring improved community services and renewal

---

[10] *Ibid.*, p. 127.

programs. Community interest in industrial development and location are the order of the day and the degree of social and community dependence on industrial and economic growth can only increase these expectations in the future. Goal No. 10 supports this need with a plea for greater industry-municipal cooperation in experimenting with new ideas and programs for community development. This call for business leadership is further emphasized in Essay No. 10, Framework for An Urban Society, wherein it is stated that:

> The goals and means for metropolitan progress include all the proposals in earlier sections, but the key instruments may be outlined: 1. Stronger civic, business, and political leadership at the metropolitan level, willing to accept the need for innovation.[11]

The increasing number of business-society issues found in the business literature testify to the increasing demands being made upon businessmen. With this wave of externally created problems, business is faced with the necessity of making the most delicate decisions as to which claims and groups are both legitimate and deserving of business support. The legitimacy of the activities of these interest groups in our society is established for us by Mr. Rossiter in Essay No. 2, The Democratic Process, wherein he says:

> This leads us naturally to consider the thousands of interest groups, no less fondly as pressure groups or lobbies, and more fondly as civic groups, that form one of the continuing wonders of American life. Whatever we call these groups, we are aware that they swing a sizable amount of persuasive power over the men who make and execute policy in all governments in all parts of the land, and that the democratic process would be very different without them. They do not have a high standing in the mythology of American democracy. Indeed, they are often represented as the worst enemies of democracy. Yet they are natural products of an open, plural, energetic society, serving effectively to institutionalize two of our most precious liberties: freedom of association, and the right of petition. They, like the parties, can be no better, no more honest, no more broad-minded than the men who direct or support them. Laws that seek to regulate them can reach only a small way; most hopes for cleansing their methods and raising their sights begin and end with educating the active citizenry.
>   The one large objection that we might keep in view as we strive to make the interest groups a healthier feature of American democracy is to give them a broader, more democratic character to the influence they exert. The serious doubts we have about these groups arise out of contemplation of their purposes

---

[11] *Ibid.*, p. 243.

as well as of their methods. Too many of them have too much energy to burn, money to spend, and thus influence to peddle in behalf of highly special and selfish interests. What the democratic process needs is the strengthening of existing organizations (and perhaps creation of new ones) that are broad rather than narrow in scope, general rather than paticular in interest, public rather than private in operation.[12]

If the businessman is given this fuller perspective of the legitimacy, and even the necessity, of these conflicting interest and pressure groups, he should be better able to adapt himself to his environment and resolve these conflicts with opposing interest groups.

Of the number of increasing roles assumed by the businessman in society today, his role as a political leader in the community is probably the most controversial. Specific political activities are prohibited the businessman by law, such as contributions to particular political organizations. On the other hand, business is compelled with a high degree of responsibility to represent the legitimate interests of its stockholders, business, industry, and free-enterprise system. Conflicting with these responsibilities are claims made by opposing power, pressure, and interest groups. Beyond protecting his own individual interests, he also assumes a leadership role, particularly in the community in which he operates. This leadership role often takes the form of active public service as has been exemplified for us by many business leaders assuming these roles at great personal sacrifice, the best example being the position of Secretary of Defense in our national government. This participation by businessmen is not only desirable for business as an institution in society, but also contributes to an ideal representation, a goal advocated by Mr. Wallace S. Sayre in Essay No. 13, The Public Service. Mr. Sayre's concern includes a fair share of our nation's skills and talents at all levels of government.

One of the most significant claims of the various pressure and interest groups is for contributions to a variety of community, charitable, and philanthropic causes. Unfortunately, business has yet to formulate an effective philosophy and policies for systematically handling these requests, and in most cases adapts itself to the relative degrees of pressure and influence forced upon it. One area of increasing demand is the appeal for funds for education, particulary private higher education, in our society. In addition to these private requests, Goal No. 4, Education, recommends that

> Greater resources — private, corporate, municipal, state, and federal — must be mobilized. A higher proportion of the gross national product must be devoted to educational purposes. This

---

[12] *Ibid.*, p. 71.

is at once an investment in the individual, in the democratic process, in the growth of the economy, and in the stature of the United States.[13]

It is further stated that not only should greater proportions be devoted to this purpose, but that for business these contributions should be doubled by the year 1970. (Essay No. 3, National Goals in Education, by John W. Gardner.)

A consideration of these goals and essays offers the individual businessman an opportunity to gain a wider perspective of his public relations problems and to more effectively relate himself to these publics. By anticipating the expectations of the pressure-interest groups in the future, business is forewarned and should be able to accomplish a more effective job of public relations by relating its objectives to broad national goals, particularly those strongly advocated by the most significant groups in society.

Business and the Individual in Society

Interest in the relationship of business to the individual in society has shown a dramatic increase since the end of World War II. This interest has been primarily in the consideration of human relations problems, types of managerial leadership, and the effects of these two activities on the controversial position of individualism and conformity within business organizations. These problems have caused a debate over ends and means within the business firm and economic system in ascertaining the sources and limits of managerial rights and responsibilities as they operate toward business or individual goals. The President's Commission on National Goals puts the position of the individual in context in the introduction to its report when it states:

> The paramount goal of the United States was set long ago. It is to guard the rights of the individual, to insure his development, and to enlarge his opportunity. It is set forth in the Declaration of Independence drafted by Thomas Jefferson and adopted by the Continental Congress on July 4, 1776. The goals we here identify are within the framework of the original plan and are calculated to bring to fruition the dreams of the men who laid the foundation of this country.[14]

The human relations problem is also considered in Essay No. 11, Meeting Human Needs, by Dr. James P. Dixon, Jr.:

> We have a strong desire to help persons in need. We believe that the individual is central to our society, that the principal asset of

---

[13] *Ibid.,* p. 6.
[14] *Ibid.,* p. 1.

human society is human life itself, and that society must therefore help to protect the lives and interests of every individual. . . .

At the same time, deep conviction that the individual and his
productivity are basic to our free society makes us reluctant to
meet human needs in a fashion which might reduce individual
initiative and self-reliance.[15]

If management perceives the individual as does the Commission
on National Goals, that is, central and primary to our whole society, it
is highly questionable whether improper human relations practices
would be as likely to occur. In fact, it is questionable whether the findings of recent behavioral science studies relevant to leadership and
conflicts between the individual and business organizations would have
been necessary to bring these problems to the attention of business
managers. Instead, those problems which seriously conflict with the basic
aims and goals of the individual in our society would have been detected
and resolved at much earlier dates. A philosophical consideration of the
rights of the individual within the full context of society including the
free enterprise system should mitigate the tensions and conflicts now
researched in such great detail by these behavioral scientists.

The broad view of business-individual-society relations is considered in Goal No. 6, The Democratic Economy, by emphasizing freedom for individuals in the economic realm. A high priority is implicitly
assigned to this goal when the responsibility for adaptation is placed on
our economic system in making necessary adjustments to the needs of
our political system. The relative importance of political and individual
as opposed to economic rights is elaborated on by Mr. Henry M.
Wriston in Essay No. 1, The Individual:

The economic argument is not primary, but it is exceedingly
strong. Endless talk of the need for capital and machinery ob-
scures the far more vital need for brains. To promote economic
growth, it is necessary to think not only in terms of what the
federal government can do or what private capital can do, not
merely in terms of law and regulation and investment. Far more
vital is the development and exploitation of the innate capacities
of people to the fullest degree. The most severe limitations upon
the expansion of the economy are deficiency and rigidity in the
skills of the work force.[16]

The effect of this interpretation is to add a new dimension to the role of
business leadership in a democratic society. This position has also been
increasingly taken in recent business literature wherein the preferable
types of managerial leadership are discussed. Mr. Wriston on this subject decries the pattern of centralized autocratic leadership and recom-

---

[15] *Ibid.,* p. 249.
[16] *Ibid.,* pp. 53, 54.

mends instead a more democratic distribution of management decision making and leadership. These considerations of the type of leadership that management must adopt in the individual firm and in the total economic system should provide strong guides toward the elimination of autocratic types of leadership: leadership in which arbitrary decisions result in inequitable effects on individuals within the organization. The whole question of leadership relates to the problem of conformity and the opposing degree of individualism sought by personalities within business organizations. Given the image of the organization man and the research findings of behavioral scientists revealing serious conflicts between the individual and the organizational structure-authority system, business is hard-pressed to reconcile these two opposing goals in a balanced and mutually satisfactory way. The question is, what is the acceptable degree of conformity necessary within a business organization to meet its goals and policies, as opposed to the social and political mandate for the highest degree of individualism? As Mr. Wriston says in Essay No. 1:

> A business corporation may become so bureaucratized that only an 'organization man' can survive. Corporate policy may oppose taking 'controversial' positions on public questions or actively participating in a political party, particularly one not favored by the management. In dozens of intangible ways it may restrict freedom. All sorts of devices, even including 'benefits,' may reduce the mobility of the individual, and virtually tie him to his place of occupation. The tendency of every organization to eat up its members is perennial and must be fought every step of the way.[17]

It is noteworthy to recognize that Goal No. 1, At Home, as established by the President's Commission is "The Individual." This goal initially states that:

> The status of the individual must remain our primary concern. All our institutions — political, social, and economic — must further enhance the dignity of the citizen, promote the maximum development of his capabilities, stimulate their responsible exercise, and widen the range and effectiveness of opportunities for individual choice.[18]

If business is to effectively synthesize and apply the findings of the behavioral scientists to human relations problems within the business organization, it must also consider the correlation of these findings with the goals defined for our nation and the philosophical principles underlying them. Given the mandate from society for an efficient utilization of the economic responsibility for allocation of resources in a free

---

[17] *Ibid.*, p. 52.
[18] *Ibid.*, p. 3.

society, business must meet this mandate through efficient and effective operations in meeting both the needs of individual firms and the ever-changing needs of our pluralistic society. This means that while the problems of democratic participation of the individuals in the economic sphere are severely limited in terms of their frequent incompatibility with the achievement of the prime mandate of economic and efficient production goals, there must nevertheless be the overriding consideration of the individual and the democratic process in the daily routine of business operations. One of the best means of adopting objectives and policies that will reduce the conflicts between the individual and the organization is to relate the organization to broader national, social, and individual goals whereby a higher degree of harmony and equitable balance of these goals can be achieved by the various competing claimants.

Labor-Management Relationships

The best-known conflict area of business and society is that of labor-management relationships. With the legislatively established institutions of union recognition and collective bargaining, labor and management are engaged in a continuous power struggle for the achievement of their respective goals. Today this problem has taken on a new emphasis because of strikes, featherbedding practices, and the relative inability of labor and management to resolve their differences without serious adverse effects on society. The emergence of government as a final arbitrator through increasing legislation and regulations raises the serious question of the maintenance of the desired freedom in the resolution of these conflicts. Goal No. 6, The Democratic Economy, recommends that:

> Collective bargaining between the representatives of workers and employers should continue as the nation's chief method for determining wages and working conditions.
>
> Conferences among management, union leaders, and representatives of the public can contribute to mutual understanding of problems that affect the welfare of the economy as a whole.
>
> Corporations and labor unions must limit the influence they exert on the private lives of their members. Unions must continue to develop adequate grievance procedures and greater opportunities for legitimate opposition. Professional organizations and trade associations should conduct their affairs on a democratic basis.[19]

Collective bargaining agreements have affected the competitive position of American business abroad, a fact which has been cited

---

[19] *Ibid.,* p. 9.

repeatedly in our daily press. The effect of these agreements on total national growth is also cited in the concluding notes for the national goals. In order to avoid these undesirable effects, business must develop a broader perspective of the collective bargaining process — a societal perspective. This perspective reveals initially a high degree of interrelationships between these groups. This interrelationship in turn can be interpreted as interdependencies between the institutional forces of business, labor, government, and society. It makes all the more pressing the consideration of the need for governmental participation, mediation, and, if necessary, arbitration to resolve these conflicts which seriously affect the national interests. At the same time, the overriding consideration of resolving these conflicts freely rather than arbitrarily by some governmental body evoked the following statement by Dr. Clark Kerr in Essay No. 6, An Effective and Democratic Organization of the Economy:

> In the area of national emergency strikes, the government might enter earlier into potentially difficult situations and play a more aggressive role in making settlement proposals, but collective bargaining still works best when it is left to the parties. Compulsory arbitration leads automatically to wage-fixing, as in Australia. And the Australian situation also indicates that it is very difficult, in a democracy, to make such arbitration really compulsory. There are several alternative courses to compulsory arbitration, including different degrees of mediation and a fact-finding and voluntary arbitration. Experience has shown that it is better to have several such courses of action available to be chosen in accordance with the situation, rather than to rely on a single rigid course of action. The greater use of independent third parties to assist in collective bargaining, for example, has been helpful in several instances when major changes and rules and arrangements were involved.[20]

Foremost among labor-management issues today is the problem of job security, levels of unemployment, and, implicitly, the employment responsibilities of our economy in general and of individual firms in particular. With the present rate of technological advance, displacements of personnel, persistent levels of unemployment, and the view of business from the trustee concept of serving society in providing employment opportunities, serious consideration must be forthcoming for achieving these goals of job security in the present and in the future. Dr. Clark Kerr in Essay No. 6 explains this in these terms:

> A concept of public responsibility for the effectiveness of the economic organization was gradually taking shape. This concept received perhaps its most conscious and formal recognition in the Employment Act of 1946. The act set forth "the continuing

---

[20] *Ibid.*, p. 161.

policy and responsibility of the federal government" as follows: "to coordinate and utilize all its plans, functions and resources for the purpose of creating and maintaining in a manner calculated to foster and promote free competitive enterprise and the general welfare, conditions under which there will be afforded useful employment opportunities, including self-employment, for those able, willing and seeking work, and to promote maximum employment, production and purchasing power." [21]

Other statements are made in the national goals essays supporting this position. For example, Dr. James P. Dixon, Jr. points out the fact that unemployment insurance is not the answer to the problem, but rather, more jobs (Essay No. 11, Meeting Human Needs). Also in Essay No. 8, Technological Change, Mr. Thomas J. Watson, Jr. indicates an increasing acceptance of responsibility for full employment by the American businessman.

The causes of unemployment are difficult to enumerate and assess, and the variety of corrective actions which can be taken too easily allow for shifting of the responsibility. The effects of the problem resulting from technological developments and persistent unemployment levels in particular industries and regions of our country emphasize a shifting downward of the responsibility from the national levels to particular industries, areas, and individual firms. A hope for the future may be contained in the remarks of Mr. Warren Weaver in Essay No. 4, A Great Age for Science, when he says:

> An energetic development of science is absolutely essential to the continuing flow of new knowledge which leads to new inventions, new materials, new procedures, new industries, new opportunities for employment, and, in total, to a sound and vigorous economy. . . .
>
> Rather spectacular evidence may be found by observing that the rapidly developing portion of our economy — one could even say the fast-moving stocks on the exchange — are those based upon relatively new scientific advances, such as in solid state physics, (transistors, etc.), electronics, computors, and automation, etc. [22]

The consideration of these national goals should help to provide some guidelines and portents of the future for management in meeting these increasing employment responsibilities.

Another contemporary problem of labor-management relationships has been created by the efforts of unions and governmental bodies to offset management's arbitrary decisions affecting individual personnel. When these arbibtrary decisions take on the form of discrmination

---

[21] *Ibid.*, p. 158.
[22] *Ibid.*, pp. 112, 113.

in terms of race, color, creed, and other nonessential reasons, grievances often blossom into widespread movements resulting in such activities as governmental legislation for fair employment-practices commissions. As stated in Goal No. 2. Equality:

> Vestiges of religious prejudice, handicaps to women, and, most important, discrimination on the basis of race must be recognized as morally wrong, economically wasteful, and in many respects dangerous. In this decade we must sharply lower these last stubborn barriers. . . .
> Respect for the individual means respect for every individual. Every man and woman must have equal rights before the law, and an equal opportunity to vote and hold office, to be educated, to get a job, and to be promoted when qualified, to buy a home, to participate fully in community affairs. These goals, which are at the core of our system, must be achieved by action at all levels.[23]

This responsibility harks back to the type of managerial leadership employed to develop and utilize human potentials to the fullest. A failure to maximize this potential not only affects individuals and minority groups, but also is a waste of manpower resources and skills needed for productivity goals (Goal No. 5, The Arts and Sciences). Dr. Clark Kerr also emphasizes the importance of failing to provide the "equality of opportunity" through discriminatory practices because of its negative effects on the basic nature of the economic process. Mr. George Meany of the AFL-CIO expresses his disappointment at the failure of the President's Commission to support a national fair employment-practices law which would complement state and local laws of the same type. These citations not only serve to establish goals for the businessman, but also establish the fact that they can be best achieved within the traditions of our free enterprise society through responsible and perfectly legitimate management and governmental actions. They establish specific goals for the consideration of the businessman and enhance the reasonable expectations that these goals may be achieved with due regard for freedom of all group and individuals operating within our capitalistic system.

Ethics, Religion and Business

Business has in recent years been condemned for unethical practices such as price-fixing, sweetheart contracts, business espionage, and particularly for misleading and untruthful public relations practices. The role of business in our free-enterprise society has even been cited in some cases as a moral failure. Some go further and say that it is

---

[23] *Ibid.*, pp. 3, 4.

inherently in contradiction to the religious, ethical, and moral principles of our society. From all of these contentions, one fact is made clear: business faces the problem of developing an ethic compatible and operative with the many ethics in society. Given the community ethic, the Judaeo-Christian ethic, the Ten Commandments, and the Golden Rule, many tenets are found common to all of these, but there is never-theless extreme difficulty in making applications of their principles in specific business conflict situations. Goal No. 2, Equality, emphasizes the moral wrong involved in religious and racial prejudice, for example, and for other arbitrary practices that create serious inequities for indi-viduals and groups in our society.

The question of ethics for business, or any other group in so-ciety, readily evolves into a question of its identification with a given religion or set of values. Since religions are the major value-forming institutions in our society, any set of values to be used for the determina-tion of right and wrong moral actions will probably find some identifica-tion with particular religious ethics. While businessmen face the difficulty of relating business to religious principles, it is nevertheless recom-mended that they draw upon this framework in order to establish their own individual ethics that will provide guides for their contacts with the many groups in society. The businessman has been challenged in the literature to effectively relate the meaning and significance of work to spiritual principles in order to enhance the dignity and self-fulfillment of the men involved in the enterprise. This is further supported by Essay No. 1, The Individual, wherein Henry M. Wriston says:

> This goal touches the foundations of democracy. From the first it was realized that popular government required an educated citizenry. The declaration in the Northwest Ordinance of 1787 is classic: "Religion, morality, and knowledge being necessary to good government and the happiness of mankind, schools and the means of education shall forever be encouraged." What was necessary then is doubly essential today.[24]

In the concluding remarks on the National Goals, it is stated that:

> The very deepest goals for Americans relate to the spiritual health of our people. The right of every individual to seek God in the well springs of truth, each in his own way, is infinitely precious. . . .
>
> Our faith is that man lives, not by bread alone, but by self-respect, by regard for other men, by convictions of right and wrong, by strong religious faith.[25]

---

[24] *Ibid.,* p. 53.
[25] *Ibid.,* pp. 22, 23.

In order to effectively relate the goals, policies, and operations of a business enterprise to those higher values held by our society, the businessman must first reach the conviction of Mr. Wriston that:

> Dignity does not derive from a man's economic situation, nor from his vocation. It does not require a white-collar job or any other status symbol. It rests exclusively upon the lively faith that individuals are beings of infinite value.[26]

Business is therefore pressed to re-examine its goals, policies, and operations in light of existing ethical and religious values in our society. This should include consideration of those components of a value system that results from the conviction that:

> The humanities, the social sciences, and the natural sciences, all are essential for a rounded, cultural life. Literature and history are vital to understanding, the capacity to feel and communicate, to a sense of values.[27]

Given the relationship between the objectives and goals of business and the broader objectives and goals emphasized in our present-day society, business is provided with the means of establishing a more comprehensive code of ethics with which it can contribute to the development of a profession for its managers. In turn, this profession can develop and implement a philosophy which will be comprehensive enough to effectively relate the whole system of business to the broader system of society.

Trends toward a Philosophy of Management

The persistently increasing number of issues and conflicts between business and society has been attributed to the many individual and group interests that relate significantly to business. By identifying the most important value-goals of these groups and individuals, the seriousness of these conflicts is indicated by their ethical and religious implications. The great variety of, and degree of differences between, these issues requires the formulation of a comprehensive approach with a more universal application, a new philosophy for business-management and society. This philosophy will serve to reconcile the conflicts of rights, identify and relate the respective objectives, and, in the process of its formulation, identify those factors integral to a philosophy for business management. It will serve as a framework for the professionalization of business managers, and will provide a type of professional leadership that can give a positive orientation to the consideration of these problems.

---

[26] *Ibid.*, p. 49.
[27] *Ibid.*, p. 8.

Most areas of conflict, when reduced to their essential features, relate to the rights of the individuals and groups concerned. Business has historically regarded its prerogatives as exclusive and unilateral. The exercise of the private property right by business is certainly a legitimate right to be protected by our society. On the other hand, these rights come into increasing conflict, particuarly with the institutional power group of labor. With the significant attrition of traditional management prerogatives through the collective bargaining process, management is now hard pressed to arrest this trend by a well-reasoned and documented statement of its necessary and legitimate rights.

The opposition of labor and other groups in society to the arbitrary use of managerial prerogatives is supported in Goal No. 3, The Democratic Process, wherein it is stated that:

> Private interest groups exemplify the rights of assembly and petition. Thus, the functioning of pressure groups of many kinds has become a part of our democratic process. Special interest groups must operate legitimately. The program of any particular group can be opposed most effectively by the formation of a counter group. There is need for more which represent broader interests such as consumers and taxpayers.[28]

To put the issue into a fuller context, Mr. Wriston in Essay No. 1, The Individual, states that:

> Each person has both particular and general interests, individual wants and social needs. When the general interest is over accentuated, freedom declines and may disappear; first controls, then paternalism supervene. On the other hand, if individual interests utterly neglect social needs, anarchy is the end result. The consequence of either extreme is loss of liberty.[29]

The rights of management, labor, and all individuals and groups in society find their legal source in the Constitution of the United States, but prerequisite to its adoption was the promise of a Bill of Rights to protect the individual. This Bill of Rights amplified in principle form the basic rights of life, liberty, and the pursuit of happiness initially considered in the Declaration of Independence. If management is to delineate its rights, particuarly on those issue areas wherein their rights come into conflict with those of labor or other individuals or groups in society, it must go back to these basic documents to establish a priority of rights. Quite often the rights with which management is most concerned are those that have been traditionally regarded as managerial prerogatives over time, in light of the accepted objectives sought by the business firm. In this respect, the dependability and applicability of these

---

[28] *Ibid.*, p. 5.
[29] *Ibid.*, p. 48.

rights will relate to the legitimacy of the objectives which they seek to achieve.

There is probably no greater or more significant point of conflict between business and society than the debate over the purpose and objectives of business itself. Classical economic theory advocating profit maximization comes into conflict with the new concept of economics emphasizing social responsibility and satisfactory profits. A study of business in America reveals a tremendous variety of goals sought by business firms and a pattern of both similarities and differences in terms of the priority of these goals. Unquestionably, the goal of profits has been paramount in most cases. On the other hand, the new philosophy is quoted by an increasing number of writers relegating profits to a satisfactory level in order to achieve a more equitable allocation of earnings to other individuals and groups in society. It is precisely at this point that the National Goals defined by the President's Commission appear to have their greatest application as an aid in the resolution of business-society conflicts. If business will relate the goals which it has traditionally sought to these national goals, the opportunity will be created for achieving maximum collaboration and equity with society. This should result in some redefinition of their goals and respective priorities on the part of business managers. Dr. Clark Kerr provides an interrelationship of these goals in Essay No. 6 when he says:

> In today's world, our economic system must continue to serve the individual directly by providing opportunities for his material well being and advancement. But this alone is not enough. Our economy must also serve the individual indirectly by enabling the nation to meet such challenges as the maintenance of an adequate, diversified, enormously expensive defense system; the acceptance of broad responsibility in the area of international cooperation, including especially assistance to under-developed countries; the maintenance and expansion of an educational system far greater in scope and quality than ever before envisioned, to meet the demands of the modern world; the provision of public services required by rapid and extensive urbanization and by rising standards regarding the minimum requirements of life in a civilized community — in short, the whole range of endeavors suggested throughout this volume as essential steps toward the continuing fulfillment of our basic national purpose.[30]

The effects of not working for these public as well as individual business goals are also described by Dr. Kerr when he says:

> The present economic process, developed over the decades after so much discussion, is geared to maximizing the freedom of individuals and private groups to make their own decisions. But

---

[30] *Ibid.*, p. 150.

these decisions have yielded depressions in earlier years and in recent years constant inflation, not stability; moderate rates of growth, not forced draft advances; strikes, not uniform industrial peace; additional durable consumer goods more readily than a new school, a new park, a new concert hall; an apparent sense of purposelessness, instead of visible public objectives.[31]

To make business goals both legitimate and more meaningful, they can be related to these other goals in society, giving mutual achievement and satisfaction to the groups and individuals concerned. For example, Thomas J. Watson, Jr., recommends in Essay No. 8, Technological Change, three basic national goals in the technological area.

> Technological change should be used to improve men's lives. . . . Technological change should be encouraged to meet our own increasing industrial needs, to stimulate our social and economic progress, and to face successfully the long-term challenge of international communism. Technological knowledge should be shared so that people throughout the world, particularly in the under-developed nation countries, may improve their lives and benefit from up-to-date technology.[32]

A study in depth relating business and national goals can contribute also to the formulation of a philosophy which will have a mutuality of application to individuals, groups, and business in our society. Looking at perhaps the most fundamental conflict between business and society, that of the individual exercise of the private property right as opposed to individual and group liberties in our society, we detect a significant trend of judiciary decisions and executive policy statements supporting liberty when these rights come into conflict. But with the variety of goals and conflicts in our society, Messrs. Stein, and Denison, in Essay No. 7, High Employment and Growth in the American Economy, explain that:

> There is a limit to the number of goals that the American people or any people can pursue, the number of crusades they can engage in. There is a limit to our supply of leadership for "pointing the way" and to the supply of attention and followership. In this sense, any goals proposed at the expense of others that are or might have been advanced, and the cost of elevating accelerated economic growth to the front rank of goals is that something else is deprived of that position. . . .
>
> There may be value in having a "national goal" aside from the benefits of achieving any particular goal and almost without regard to what the goal is. The goal may be inspiring, give "point" to life, and serve as a common bond holding the society

---

[31] *Ibid.*, p. 158.
[32] *Ibid.*, p. 196.

together. This may be a benefit even though at the present stage of history a psychological need would be better served by a goal less materialistic and less parochial than the growth of the American economy.[33]

In the discussion of business-society issues and conflicts today, the end result most often sought is a recommendation for the definition and acceptance of greater social responsibilities on the part of the businessman. Therefore, the definition and implementation of a comprehensive philosophy for business management to effectively relate itself to its society will inherently contain a definition of business rights and duties, the latter now referred to as social responsibilities.

Social Responsibilities of Business

While discussion of social responsibilities for business managers has increased tremendously in the literature and at the dinner table in our society, the concept nevertheless remains a very controversial one. One point of view would reassign to business the economic function with profit orientation as its sole goal. Classical economic theory claims that the maximum allocation of resources, and therefore maximum benefit to society, will be achieved by following this goal exclusively. A resolution of this debate might be enhanced by recommendations made by the President's Commission on National Goals. For example, Dr. Clark Kerr in Essay No. 6, says:

> Industrialization has brought the individual rich benefits in health, material goods, and the leisure and means important to individual fulfillment. But it has also created large and powerful private organizations whose influence over the individual gives rise to new and often subtle questions of democratic procedure. And it has made individuals increasingly interdependent in many spheres. The economic success or failure of an individual or a private group today may depend upon or may affect many others. The complexities and costs of many desirable projects are completely beyond the scope of private individuals. Industrialization is resulting in new concepts of public responsibility and of public endeavors.[34]

The axiom that responsibility must always equal the degree of power in our society also finds application to this issue. Mr. Clinton Rossiter, in Essay No. 2, The Democratic Process, says:

> This fact of power puts a new strain on all Americans, but especially on those who hold public responsibilities. . . . the men to whom we assign control of our finances, public services, and

---

[33] *Ibid.*, p. 190.
[34] *Ibid.*, p. 150.

schools, of our factories, fields, and facilities of transportation. They, too, hold far too much power over the lives of other men to be exempted from the growing demand for decision-makers and administrators who are first of all mature and prudent. What we might call the "imperative of responsibility" must pervade and stiffen the whole spirit of democracy.[35]

Control of power, individuals, and groups in society has been provided in our democratic system by the development of checks and balances within the political system. Business power has been checked particularly by organized labor, but much more so by social controls at all levels of government. Dr. Clark Kerr warns against failures of existing checks and balances to control collusion of these power centers, for example, business and labor in the collective bargaining process. Collusion has also been found between institutional power groups, as well as within them. The effects of these practices have been to pass on to society the unnecessary, often illegal, and certainly unethical costs that defeat the achievements of our free enterprise society; the most efficient allocation and utilization of resources.

If business management is to professionalize its role in society, it must formulate in great detail its social responsibilities. This is particularly applicable to those areas where large degrees of power and interdependence exist between industries, business firms, individuals, and groups in the local or even international community. Commitment on the part of professionalized management groups to the achievement of corporate, economic *and* broader national goals of our society-economy should and can enhance business' position in both the short and long run. Relating business to society, particularly from the standpoint of the public relations function, has typically been to consider those societies upon whom business depends, such as customers, stockholders, and employees. Of late there has been an increasing trend toward recognizing other publics because of increasing degrees of interdependent relationships with supplier firms, service industries, etc. This trend, in many instances, has reached the point where giant corporations have assumed responsibilities not normally considered within the bailiwick of traditional business functions. This has applied, for example, in situations where either extensive international operations or degrees of monopolistic control over skills and capital resources affecting other nations in the world made the assumption of these responsibilities both desirable and, in some instances, necessary.

It is significant to note that a recent consensus of fifty of the world's top thinkers revealed an almost unanimous conclusion that the prime problem facing America in the next twenty years is that of assist-

---

[35] *Ibid.,* p. 76.

ing the under-developed nations to emerge as free, strong, democratic societies. They also cited the national problems of inflation and full employment.[36] There is a comparable priority assigned in the goals cited by the President's Commission wherein 4 of the 15 goals established for Americans for the decade of the 1960's relate to activities abroad. These goals provide for assisting the under-developed countries, defending the free world, achieving disarmament, and supporting the United Nations. In the introduction to these "goals abroad" it is stated:

> The basic foreign policy of the United States should be the preservation of its own independence and free institutions. Our position before the world should be neither defensive nor belligerent. We should cooperate with the nations whose ideals and interests are in harmony with ours. We should seek to mitigate tensions, and search for acceptable areas of accommodation with opponents. The safe-guarded reduction of armaments is an essential goal.[37]

The types of assistance recommended by the Commission reveal an overwhelming emphasis upon trade rather than aid. Starting with the premise that a free-world economy will also be the healthiest economy, appeals are made for systematic tariff reductions to preserve a vital national economy (Goal No. 12, Helping to Build an Open and Peaceful World). These actions would be accompanied by similar support from other healthy free-world nations for the purpose of creating strong and free nation-economies in the under-developed countries.

Mr. John J. McCloy in Essay No. 15, Foreign Economic Policy and Objectives, establishes the primary principle upon which these international goals are based. Since our country has been the dominant world exporter of industrial goods and since we depend significantly upon critical materials and other goods as the major world importer, an inherent economic interdependency has been created. This interdependency is increasing rather than decreasing, and, therefore, a philosophy of mutual rights and duties in the international political economy is required to regulate these relationships. This interdependency between our country and other nations in the world, politically, economically, etc., creates a uniformity of interests and goals that can be best understood through the common denominator of all human beings and societies throughout the world. The difficulty for the businessman is in establishing the relative degree of legitimate interdependency when claims are made upon business for support and in the resolution of conflicts that are occurring increasingly between business and other groups. In support of this basic common denominator, Mr. McCloy tells us that:

---

[36] "The Next Twenty Years," *Fortune,* January 1958, pp. 110–111, 188–191.

[37] *Goals for Americans, op. cit.,* p. 15.

At the same time there is in the American character a broad streak of humanitarianism, an instinct of generosity toward those who are less fortunate. If for no other reason than that it is in keeping with our ingrained habits and values, we are bound to come to the aid of peoples in the less-developed lands.[38]

Mr. McCloy refers us to some specific actions and considerations when he explains the relationship and justification for economic assistance to the less-developed lands. He says:

In the highly industrialized states, economic advance is so rapid that the standard of living may rise 100 per cent within a generation. The tendency therefore is for the gap in living standards between the industrialized and the under-developed regions to widen rather than narrow. . . .

The United States, with the highest standard of living ever attained by mankind, cannot safely shirk a leading role in making available to the economically under-developed nations the benefits of the industrial and technological revolutions. In the interests of its own peace and progress it must assume a heavy burden, for it cannot hope to prosper in isolation. Its goals must be the creation of a world order compatible with American traditions as well as with American interests in security, one in which all nations will have a reasonable opportunity for economic progress and social well-being.[39]

American interests in security referred to by Mr. McCloy are made evident by the dominant expenditures in the U.S. national budget — appropriations for national defense. The twentieth century has negated the concept of isolationism. It is economically and militarily unfeasible and also immoral, according to most moral and religious ethics in American society. Therefore Goal No. 13, The Defense of the Free World, develops our responsibilities in the world order by making recommendations for counter-measures to meet the Soviet and Communist China threats. This goal asks for continuing support for military alliances and also for programs that may ultimately achieve independence for countries now subject to communist influence and domination.

If the variety and significance of goals already cited to this point have not convinced the individual businessman, Goal No. 14 on Disarmament should be considered. This goal contends that:

Since a major nuclear war would be a world catastrophe, the limitation and control of nuclear armament is imperative. Disarmament should be our ultimate goal. It cannot be attained without eliminating the sources of distrust and fear among nations. Hence, our immediate task must be the step-by-step ad-

---

[38] *Ibid.,* p. 343.
[39] *Ibid.,* p. 317.

vance toward control of nuclear weapons and their means of delivery, with effective international inspection.[40]

Concomitant with the achievement of disarmament is the support of the organization through which its accomplishment must come. Goal No. 15, The United Nations, recommends that:

> A key goal in the pursuit of a vigorous and effective United States foreign policy is the preservation and strengthening of the United Nations. Over the next decade, it will be under tremendous strain. However, it remains the chief instrument available for building a genuine community of nations.[41]

While it may not be expected that all of these national goals will be achieved simultaneously or to the degree which is believed desirable by the President's Commission, it is nevertheless inconceivable to move in any direction other than toward their achievement. The greatest contribution of the national goals may rest in their consideration by the United States businessman in order to see in total perspective the many conflicting values, goals, interests, and pressures that are legitimately sought by individuals and groups in the American and world societies. In summary, the individual businessman must widen his perspective in considering his goals and practices in a free enterprise society. This perspective must include a recognition of the many goal-seeking groups and individuals in society. It will require assessments of the legitimacy of the increasing interdependency of business with these groups and individuals. Finally, it must seek through involvement with all groups and individuals a national consensus on the goals most important to our society as a whole. In this way a statement of national goals can be translated into a positive philosophy and ethic to which a professional commitment can be made.

---

[40] *Ibid.,* p. 19.
[41] *Ibid.,* p. 20.

31   Social Policies for Business

George A. Steiner

We are witnessing today an important paradox. On the one
hand business is being roundly attacked and condemned, not only as
an institution but also for specific actions. David Rockefeller puts it
this way: "It is scarcely an exaggeration to say that right now American
business is facing its most severe public disfavor since the 1930s. We are
assailed for demeaning the worker, deceiving the consumer, destroying
the environment and disillusioning the younger generation." [1] Yet at no
time in our history has business been a greater beneficial force in society.
At no time in our history have businessmen thought more about the
consequences of their actions.

The underlying cause of this paradox is that there are important
changes taking place in what the public expects business to do. So far,
business is responding to these new demands without major problems.
Most observers predict however, that in the future the demands which
the public will place on business to do things in the social area not
traditionally assumed by business will accelerate. If this takes place without very careful consideration of the consequences, the results could be
catastrophic for business and the community.

Unfortunately, the forces at work are moving without a clear
understanding of or agreement upon what responsibilities business has or
should assume in the social area. It is about time that we tried to get
specific about underlying policies which should govern businesses' assumption of social responsibilities. It is also time to develop concrete
policies and actions which may be used by an individual company in its
pursuit of social responsibilities.

This paper is an effort to establish these concrete guides. Before
getting to them, however, a background analysis is presented of changing
attitudes toward, and definitions of business social responsibilities.

© 1972 by The Regents of the University of California. Reprinted from
California Management Review, Vol. XV, No. 2, pp. 17–24 by permission
of The Regents.
[1] David Rockefeller, address to the Advertising Council, reported in the
Los Angeles Times, January 3, 1971.

Changing Views of Business Social Responsibilities

Much has been written about business social responsibilities which need not be reiterated. It is useful to make a few comments, however, about changing views of business social responsibilities.

Under the classical operation of the private enterprise system, society's basic demands upon business were to produce goods and services efficiently. That was just about the one and only social responsibility expected of business. This view has been reaffirmed by Milton Friedman, a respected economist, in the following well-known statement: ". . . there is one and only one social responsibility of business — to use its resources and engage in activities designed to increase its profits so long as it stays within the rules of the game, which is to say, engages in open and free competition, without deception or fraud. . . . Few trends could so thoroughly undermine the very foundations of our free society as the acceptance by corporate officials of a social responsibility other than to make as much money for their stockholders as possible." [2] This view of managerial responsibility is strongly held today by many people in and out of business.

There is a growing rejection of this concept of corporate managerial responsibility, however, both in and out of business. It is felt that to hold firmly to such restricted concepts of corporate responsibility, especially by managers in the large companies, would not be in the best interests of either company stockholders or the public. Paul Samuelson, another highly respected economist, implies this when he says: "A large corporation these days not only may engage in social responsibilities, it had damn well better try to do so." [3]

That business has social responsibilities which may be assumed even though there is a drain on short-range profits and even though there may be no clear connection with current social action and long-range profits is a growing idea. Although there is no consensus about this, it represents a significantly different attitude about management's responsibilities than the classical view. Is a business justified in the pursuit of social responsibilities which reduce "net" profits? Fletcher Byrom, Chairman of the Board of Koppers Company, Inc., answers this way: ". . . you can't continue a business without profit, but profits are not the be-all and end-all of the corporation . . . if it does not at the same time serve the needs of society, then the corporation as an

---

[2] Milton Friedman, *Capitalism and Freedom,* University of Chicago Press, Chicago, 1962, p. 133.
[3] Paul A. Samuelson, "Love That Corporation," *Mountain Bell Magazine* (Mountain Bell Telephone Company, Spring 1971), p. 24.

instrumentality of accomplishment will surely perish, and deserves to perish." [4] Here is a recognition that corporations exist because society wishes them to fulfill a purpose and when the social purpose changes, so will the activities of corporations.

Edward N. Cole, the President of General Motors Corporation, makes clearer guidelines for company action in response to social needs: "The big challenge to American business — as I see it — is to carefully evaluate the constantly changing expressions of public and national goals. Then we must modify our own objectives and programs to meet — as far as possible within the realm of economic and technological feasibility — the new demands of the society we serve." [5]

Insofar as business is concerned, especially large business, the debate about whether business has social responsibilities was ended for all practical purposes by the Committee for Economic Development report on *Social Responsibilities of Business Corporations,* issued in June 1971. This group of prominent business leaders concluded as follows: ". . . it is in the 'enlightened self-interest' of corporations to promote the public welfare in a positive way." [6] On the next page the CED said: "Indeed, the corporate interest broadly defined by management can support involvement in helping to solve virtually any social problem, because people who have a good environment, education, and opportunity make better employees, customers, and neighbors for business than those who are poor, ignorant, and oppressed." [7]

The Social Contract and Social Responsibilities

At any one time in any society there is a set of generally accepted relationships, obligations and duties between the major institutions and the people. Philosophers and political theorists have called this set of common understandings "the social contract." Throughout the industrialized nations of the world, and particularly in this country, many of the provisions which affect business in the social contract are now under scrutiny and/or are being rewritten.

Of particular concern in this paper are the social responsibilities of business. They are a major part of today's social contract. Some of the changes in the social contract arising from new attitudes toward business social responsibilities are coming into clearer focus. Unfortu-

---

[4] Fletcher Byrom, quoted in *Koppers Foundation* (Koppers Company, Inc.), p. 2.

[5] Edward N. Cole, "Management Priorities for the 1970s," *Michigan Business Review,* July 1970, p. 1.

[6] Committee for Economic Development, *Social Responsibilities of Business Corporations,* CED, New York, June 1971, p. 27.

[7] *Ibid.,* p. 28.

nately, however, the major dimensions of the new relationships for which there should be a general consensus are very fuzzy.

What are social responsibilities of business?

Social responsibilities may be considered from three points of view: conceptual, internal vs. external, and impact on profits. They are closely interrelated and not mutually exclusive.

Conceptually, social responsibilities may refer to "the businessman's decisions and actions taken for reasons at least partially beyond the firm's direct economic or technical interest." [8] A somewhat broader view says they are obligations to "pursue those policies, to make those decisions, or to follow those lines of action which are desirable in terms of the objectives and values of our society." [9] Perhaps an even wider dimension is the following: "By 'social responsibility' we mean intelligent and objective concern for the welfare of society that restrains individual and corporate behavior from ultimately destructive activities, no matter how immediately profitable, and leads in the direction of positive contributions to human betterment, variously as the latter may be defined." [10] Fundamentally, these definitions say that actions taken by a business which in some degree help society to achieve one or more of its objectives are socially responsible actions.

Business responsibilities can be classified into those which are internal in or external to a business. *Internal* social responsibilities, for instance, are concerned with assuring due process, justice, equality and morality in employee selection, training, promotion, and firing; or, they may relate to improving worker environment. *External* social responsibilities refer to actions to hire hard-core unemployed, rebuild ghetto housing, improve the balance of payments, ease racial tensions, stimulate minority entrepreneurship, and so on. Additional specific responsibilities will be illustrated later.

Social responsibilities may be classified in terms of their impact on profits. A company, in my judgment, may take socially responsible actions which serve to improve short-range profits. For instance, a company may install a machine to replace one which is hazardous to workers. In doing so it may also set forth new rules concerning worker bonuses and promotion which result in higher productivity while at the same time erasing injustices.

The impact on profits may be diffuse and unclear. For instance,

---

[8] Keith Davis, "Can Business Afford To Ignore Social Responsibilities?" *California Management Review,* Spring 1960, p. 70.

[9] Howard R. Bowen, *Social Responsibilities of the Businessman,* Harper & Brothers, New York, 1953, p. 6.

[10] Kenneth Andrews, *The Concept of Corporate Strategy,* Dow Jones-Irwin, Inc., Homewood, Illinois, 1971, p. 120.

giving or increasing scholarships to children of employees may reduce short-range profits. The program may be justified, however, on the grounds that employee loyalty will strengthen and result in greater profits. Also, hiring educated children of employees may bring new profitable talent to the company. Such programs may be justified also on the grounds that the company believes society needs better educated people and that somehow the net result will be to the advantage of the company. This latter justification can be selfish or altruistic. Of course, actions can be taken which clearly reduce profits (installing expensive antipollution devices, for example).

Usually, businessmen will not take actions which will reduce both short- and long-range profits. They may be willing to take an action that reduces short-range profits if they believe that it will somehow increase long-range profits. It may not always be easy, however, to draw a creditable relationship between a current action and the impact on long-range profits. Hence, rationalization of specific actions which cut short-range profits on the grounds that long-range profits will be expanded may lack conviction. Cleaning up a ghetto may improve the climate for business generally but if one company does it the long-range impact on profits of that company may be unclear.

Several conclusions can be drawn from these views. The assumption of social responsibility does not necessarily mean a reduction of either short- or long-range profits, or both. Also, many of the requirements for socially responsible action are identical with what used to be called business integrity, acting ethically, or being good corporate citizens. Today's demands for socially responsible actions, however, go well beyond these traditional expectations.

A list of socially responsible actions

There is no generally accepted list of business social responsibilities against which an individual company can appraise its actions. The CED in the report referred to above listed ten major categories: economic growth and efficiency, education, employment and training, civil rights and equal opportunity, urban renewal and development, pollution abatement, conservation and recreation, culture and the arts, medical care, and government.[11] Under each there were listed specific actions. For example, under economic growth and efficiency were the following:

Increasing productivity in the private sector of the economy.

Improving the innovativeness and performance of busines management.

---

[11] CED, *op. cit.*, pp. 37–40.

Enhancing competition.

Cooperating with the government in developing more effective measures to control inflation and achieve high levels of employment.

Supporting fiscal and monetary policies for steady economic growth.

Helping the post-Vietnam conversion of the economy.

Under urban renewal and development were:

Leadership and financial support for city and regional planning and development.

Building or improving low-income housing.

Building shopping centers, new communities, new cities.

Improving transportation systems.

Neither the major headings nor the subheadings are, of course, complete. The above classification does indicate, however, a rather broad range of possible social activities of business.

What is behind business acceptance of the idea that it has social responsibilities?

To accept the idea of social responsibilities much beyond the classical view is contrary to traditional typical business thinking. Why, then, do more and more businessmen accept the idea?

First, society is expecting more of its corporations. There is no consensus about precisely what the societal demand is, but it is growing, intensifying, and deepening. A few of the major underlying causes are: Business is a major, although not the only, cause of environmental pollution and as conditions worsen greater demands are made for business to clean up the mess it has created. One must not underestimate, also, the extent to which pressures for business to take socially responsible actions have grown out of dissatisfactions with a variety of business practices. "Consumerism" is not a fad based on a myth. Also, the ability of business to solve problems is an important reason why people want it to do things historically not requested of it. Society simply wants business to help it solve some of its major social problems.

Ironically, the great success of business is an additional reason for the new demands made upon it. For the first time in the history of the world a very large and densely populated nation has for all practical purposes solved the economic problem. This means that, despite the pockets of poverty which exist in this country, a major portion of the population has access to acceptable levels of economic goods and services. Material wants are satisfied for most people; man, whose total wants are insatiable, now desires an improvement in the quality of life. People expect their business institutions to help them do this.

Peter Drucker sees this new aspect of the social contract as follows: ". . . the new demand is . . . a demand that business and businessmen make concern for society central to the conduct of business itself. It is a demand that the quality of life become the business of business. The traditional approach asks: How can we arrange the making of cars (or of shoes) so as not to impinge on social values and beliefs, on individuals and their freedom, and on the good society altogether? The new demand is for business to make social values and beliefs, create freedom for the individual, and altogether produce the good society." [12]

The shift is dramatically illustrated in the ways in which communities view belching smokestacks. A short time ago black smoke from the chimney of an industrial plant was viewed with rejoicing because it provided much needed jobs and material well-being. Now, it is condemned because it pollutes the air.

Second, businessmen feel it is in their enlightened self-interest to assume social responsibilities. The CED states above that healthy communities provide a better climate for strong and profitable business than disintegrating communities. Arjay Miller, former President of Ford Motor Company and now the dean of a business school, adds a new dimension in these words: "Under current conditions, management cannot effectively discharge its long-run responsibilities to shareholders unless it also behaves responsibly toward employees, customers, government, education and the public at large. The ability of a corporation to protect and enhance the stockholder's equity depends crucially upon the prosperity, goodwill and confidence of the larger community. Acceptance of a large measure of responsibility toward the community is therefore good business as well as good citizenship." [13]

Third, more and more business leaders understand that if business does not act the government will. The public is demanding more socially responsible performance from business. If business does not respond appropriately the results can be disastrous to business and to society. One consequence would be the increasing growth of restrictive governmental laws. This could result in so much interference in business decision-making as to erode the productivity of business.

This does not, of course, imply that the government will not increase laws which will be designed to force business to take more

---

[12] Peter Drucker, ed., *Preparing Tomorrow's Business Leaders Today,* Prentice-Hall, Inc., Englewood Cliffs, New Jersey, 1969, p. 77.
[13] Arjay Miller, "New Roles for the Campus and the Corporation," *Michigan Business Review,* November 1966, pp. 2–3.

socially responsible actions. That clearly is the trend of the future. Rather, the statement means that the more business responds to societal interests the less pressure will be placed on government to step in.

For the sake of business, as well as society generally, businessmen must participate in the drafting of new rules for business conduct. "There can be no greater danger," writes Melvin Anshen, "than to permit the new rules to be formulated by either the small group of critics armed only with malevolence toward the existing system or the much larger group sincerely motivated by concern for ameliorating social ills but grossly handicapped by their ignorance of the techniques and dynamism of private enterprise." [14] But business will not be allowed to participate in rule-making if it offers its services only after its stubborn resistance to change has been overcome by public pressure.

There are, of course, many other reasons why business leaders not only accept but desire to assume social responsibilities. They are citizens and want to take actions which will help society solve its problems. They wish to act ethically and justly. They also see that social activities may have both short- and long-term payoffs in profitability.

Corporations have now assumed social responsibilities to a degree far beyond that of only a few years ago. But in the aggregate it has not constituted anything like a major operational shift. There is no doubt, however, that some social critics would have business assume social obligations far beyond what could be considered reasonable in the context of a private enterprise system. Some of the rhetoric of business leaders, while probably not intending to do so, propounds action beyond appropriate boundaries. We should have no fear, however, that present-day business managers will go overboard in their assumption of social responsibilities. We should fear accelerating social expectations which push business too far and too fast in assuming responsibilities.

Rising expectations for a better life for more people are desirable; but if they become excessive they can thwart achieving the very objectives which are sought. Our amazingly productive economic machine has taught us that we can have virtually any volume of an economic good we want, but we cannot have every economic good that everyone wants — we still have poverty, inequitable distribution of income, massive economic needs in building cities, and so on. We need an increasingly efficient economic machine to reduce effectively these problems. If the demands of the new humanism are excessive, however, resources can be diverted and the business institution deployed in such a way as to lessen our ability to reduce and eliminate these economic and social problems.

The question of what elements to put into a social contract

---

[14] Melvin Anshen, "Changing the Social Contract: A Role for Business," *Columbia Journal of World Business,* November–December 1970, p. 12.

which will determine and limit businesses' assumption of social obligations must obviously be faced. In the following section are advanced a few rules which, it is hoped, will stimulate debate and further refinement.

Socially Responsible Actions in the New Social Contract

We are groping our way in drafting social responsibility rules for business in the new social contract. There is no consensus. We are in need of an acceptable theory upon which to draw up the new guidelines. Whatever is eventually developed, however, is not likely to provide the simple and easy-to-follow prescription of the classical profit maximization standard.

1. There is no formula. Each business is left with the problem of determining for itself whether it has social responsibilities and how much shall be accepted. However, the first social responsibility of a firm is to think carefully about its social responsibilities.

2. Business is still predominantly an economic institution rather than one established to meet non-economic objectives of society. Society still has great dependence upon business to perform efficiently its economic job, and will continue to measure performance basically upon the established economic standards. Individual monetary profit is still accepted as the central motivator. Will and Ariel Durant confirm the value of this policy when, in looking back at the long history of civilizations they studied, they concluded: "The experience of the past leaves little doubt that every economic system must sooner or later rely upon some form of the profit motive to stir individuals and groups to productivity. Substitutes like slavery, police supervision, or ideological enthusiasm prove too unproductive, too expensive, or too transient."[15]

3. It is legitimate today for a company to do things in the social realm which are not directly related to either short- or long-range profits.

4. Whereas in the past a company might focus its attention solely on its economic function and be subject to little or no censure if its actions had adverse impacts on the quality of life of individuals, today's society requires that a company consider and limit, if it can, adverse impacts of its actions on the lives and well-being of individuals. Laws will be passed to prescribe

---

[15] Will and Ariel Durant, *The Lessons of History,* Simon and Shuster, New York, 1968, p. 54.

business responsibility. Where laws are not clear, and where legal standards are not established, impacts of business actions on individuals should be considered and respected in the decision-making process.

5. It is the duty of business today to anticipate potentially serious impacts of its actions on individuals and prevent undesirable results.

6. The larger a company becomes the greater are its social responsibilities and the more society takes an interest in what it does.

7. Each business has responsibilities in some way commensurate with its powers.

8. Social responsibilities will vary with individual companies.

9. No one should expect a business voluntarily to jeopardize its ability to attract stockholder investment, to survive in the competitive arena, and to grow. The survival and growth of an individual business are social responsibilities of that business.

10. The assumption of social responsibilities should not erode competition among companies at home or abroad.

11. Business should be asked to assume only those social responsibilities for which it has unique capabilities of fulfilling. Other institutions, such as government, should assume social responsibilities for which they are uniquely capable. Government, as well as other institutions, can and should help business to discharge its social responsibilities.

12. Business today should seek to internalize its external costs. In the past, businesses were excused from bearing such costs of production as air and water pollution, scarring hillsides in the search of coal, and defacing natural beauty. Society held the economic output of business to be of the highest priority. Today, priorities are shifting to expect business to bear its social costs.

Many of these criteria are vague and mean different things to different people. The extent to which they prescribe as well as limit businesses' assumption of social responsibilities depends upon further definition. These guides can, however, provide a basis for an individual company to develop policies and to take specific actions in light of today's changing social contract.

Suggested Policies

The following is not meant to be a complete list from which a company might select policies. Like the above listing, it is only illustrative. Each item should be prefaced by: "It is the policy of this company"

1. . . . to think carefully about implementing and act to implement socially responsible policies.
2. . . . to make full use of tax deductibility laws through contributions, when profit margins permit.
3. . . . to bear the social costs attendant upon its operations when it is possible to do so without jeopardizing its competitive or financial position.
4. . . . to concentrate action programs on limited objectives. No company can take significant action in every area of social responsibility. It can achieve more if it selects areas in which to concentrate its efforts.
5. . . . to concentrate action programs on areas strategically related to the present and prospective economic functions of the business.
6. . . . to begin action programs close at home before spreading out or acting in far distant regions.
7. . . . to deal first with what appears to the company to be the most urgent areas of concern.
8. . . . to facilitate employee actions which can be taken as individuals rather than as representatives of the company.
9. . . . to search for product and service opportunities to permit our company, and others, to make profits while at the same time advancing the social interests; but not all social actions should be taken solely for profit.
10. . . . to take actions in the name of social responsibilities but not at the expense of that required level of profits needed to maintain the economic strength desired by top management. Actions taken in the name of social responsibility should enhance the economic strength of the company and/or the business community. The overall mission of the company is two-pronged, as follows:

   To set forth and achieve corporate objectives which meet specified social challenges ranging from product quality to the "quality of life" requirements, both internally and externally.

   To increase the company's earnings per share at a rate required to meet share-owner/profit expectations *and* these new requirements.

11. . . . to take socially responsive actions on a continuous basis, rather than ad hoc, one at a time, or for a short duration.
12. . . . to examine carefully before proceeding the socially responsive needs which the company wishes to address, the contributions which the company can make, the risks involved for

the company, and the potential benefits to both the company and society.

13. . . . to avoid excessive publicity campaigns about socially responsible actions of the company.

Policies in Functional Areas

These company-wide policies can be used to develop subpolicies in selecting functional areas. To illustrate, in the marketing area subpolicies might be set forth as follows:[16]

Advertising will avoid statements which take advantage of unsophisticated buyers (such as children and the less educated), shall avoid exploiting emotions, and shall be honest.

Products in the company's product line will not be injurious to users and will achieve the highest possible quality and service for the price.

Research and development will be oriented, to the greatest extent possible, to produce products which are non-pollutants.

Specific Company Actions

Policies lead to actions. A few specific actions which each company might consider taking are:

1. Establish responsibility within the company for defining the company's social responsibilities.
2. Make a social audit of the company.[17] This refers to an analysis and/or evaluation of the social, as contrasted with the economic, performance of the company. There is no consensus about what a social audit is or how a company should go about doing it. More companies, however, are or are thinking about making one. (The social audit can be done in #1, or a separate individual or group can be asked to do it.)
3. Review the basic policy of the company for assuming social responsibilities. (This can be done in #1, #2, or separately.)
4. Define specific corporate objectives in specific areas of social responsibilities, and set forth concrete strategies and plans to achieve them. (In this process, examine carefully costs and problems for each major action and company capabilities.)

---

[16] George Schwartz, "Marketing: The Societal Concept," *University of Washington Business Review,* Autumn 1971, pp. 31–38.

[17] George A. Steiner, "Should Business Adopt the Social Audit?" *The Conference Board Record,* May 1972, pp. 7–10.

5. Establish policies and procedures for the contributions of a philanthropic nature made by the company.
6. Lay out policies and plans to stimulate socially responsible actions by individuals in the company.
7. Revise the measurement and reward system to make sure that managers set goals in terms of both social and economic ends, and develop rewards to reflect accomplishment in both.
8. Develop cost/benefit analyses which are appropriate for different levels of decision-making and which will serve to improve decision-making in the area of social responsibilities.

Conclusion

There is today a growing demand for adding to the social responsibilities of business. It is not at all likely that in the immediate years ahead this will lessen. Businessmen may not like it but they should try to understand it in order better to manage their companies in the face of it.

Today's managers generally have a good capability in adapting to changing economic and technical environmental forces. They have not had much experience in adjusting their decision-making processes and their companies to rapidly changing and accelerating social expectations about the new business role in society. Perfecting this managerial capability constitutes a major requirement for the future for at least two reasons.

First, it is in the best interests of business and the community for managers to participate in redrafting the social contract. Their contributions to the process may prevent society from making excessive and impossible demands on business which would prevent it from achieving the objectives society seeks.

Second, the present and prospective demands on business will importantly change the thinking and practice of managers, especially in the large companies. Indeed, it seems no exaggeration to say that the net result will be a redefinition of managerial capitalism. For business and society to remain strong in and after this process it is important that business managers continue to be aware of their significant social roles in society.

Most social responsibilities which business will be expected to assume, over and beyond those at the present time, will be legislated by government. But there will be a widening band assumed by managers, especially of larger corporations, reflecting rising social expectations. The best interests of business and of society will be served if we can maintain an appropriate balance between the two. We need acceptable policies to assure this balance.

B   Business Ethics

---

32   Stiffer Rules for Business Ethics

Business Week

Bribing a purchasing agent to buy your product is illegal, and cheating on your tax return can send you to jail. But what about inadvertently leaking inside information about your company? Or how much pressure can you put on a government official? When is a subordinate merely being ambitiously aggressive, and when is he being flat-out dishonest?

The public wants stricter ethical standards from the men who run its government and its economy in this age of Watergate and of corporate responsibility. But what is ethical and what is not? Some acts are simply dishonest; some can be read either way. What looks ethical at first glance may not look that way in hindsight. What was acceptable yesterday may be out-of-bounds today.

There is a fine line between propriety and impropriety, and it is finer for the executive then for most because of the conflicting pressures that beset him. Society rewards him for performance, but penalizes him savagely if he is unethical in achieving that performance. The pressure to achieve is so intense that the temptation to cut a corner can be overwhelming; the reaction to a man caught cutting a corner, however, can be just as overwhelming.

"All the laws in the world won't prevent unethical conduct," says Richard L. Kattel, president of Citizens & Southern National Bank of Atlanta. "It's a matter of personal integrity." Adds Kenneth

---

Andrews, a Harvard Business School professor who is also a director of Xerox Corp. and other companies: "If it's black and white, and a man has normal courage and security, he'll say no. It's in the gray areas that a businessman may more likely founder."

Balancing Act

The gray areas come up every day — where the law is not clear, where the ground rules are not hard, where the line between right and wrong is almost imperceptibly fine. How is the executive to deal with them? There are no final answers — only advice from other men who face the same problem.

First, there is the general advice — the self-searching "Watergate TV test," for instance, dreamed up by Arjay Miller, the former president of Ford Motor Co., who is now dean of Stanford University's business school. "Ask yourself," says Miller, "would I feel comfortable in reporting my action on TV?" If not, there is more searching in store.

If you get caught in a gray area, says Andrews of Harvard, talk it out. "Ventilate the problem," he says. "Get divergent views."

Sidney Davidson, dean of the University of Chicago School of Business, urges executives to avoid trouble by taking time to determine "the real purpose of the company." Every company exists to make money, says Davidson, but there are limits on how far it can go. Get the corporate purpose fixed in mind, he says, and make certain your fellow executives understand it.

A bit of common sense comes from Thomas J. Barlow, president of Anderson, Clayton & Co., a Houston-based food company. Says Barlow: "Anytime you see somebody making big talk about how much money can be made in a deal, scrutinize him carefully, because there is usually something in all that smoke that deserves scrutiny."

Common Pitfalls

A gray-area ethical conflict can pop up almost anywhere in your business, but some areas are particularly treacherous.

Reporting problems are probably the most common of all — not lying outright in reporting to the public, but stretching things just a bit. The director of accounting and auditing standards at a Big Eight accounting firm explains one common trap. Often, he says, an executive will latch onto a rosy forecast from a middle manager — a sky-high sales forecast, for instance, or a very low cost estimate — and pass it on to the investment community as the company's "best estimate." Investors are misled, and the company may face trouble with the Securities

& Exchange Commission or shareholders. "It's a common disease of overoptimism among executives," says the CPA.

Another reporting trap is simply leaving out a significant fact. Earlier this month the SEC charged Avis, Inc., with sending "false and misleading" reports to shareholders. The company failed to disclose that roughly 70% of its earnings for the first quarter of 1973 had arisen from sales of cars instead of from rentals and leases. In the first quarter of 1972, only about 25% of earnings had come from car sales. This, said the SEC, misled investors.

Where do you draw the line? Suppose the difference in earnings had been 40% against 35%, instead of 70% vs. 25%. Would the SEC have deemed this five-point spread a "material fact" that had to be disclosed? There is no hard answer. If you must err, it may be better to say too much.

Closing One Eye

Another pitfall is the failure to clamp down on the unethical conduct of a subordinate. It is easy enough for the manager to argue that the subordinate is, after all, meeting bottom-line profit requirements. "This is a variation of 'team pressure'," says a Cincinnati machine tool manufacturer. "But if you let one thing get past you this year, next year the guy will pull something twice as bad."

A tragic example of this pitfall is the case of Walter J. Rauscher, a former executive vice-president of American Airlines who was sentenced to jail this month. He had been involved in a supplier kickback scheme that was instigated by a subordinate. "He is a decent man," says an American Airlines official who has known Rauscher for years. "He was drawn into the trouble by a subordinate who was an SOB."

It is always difficult for the top men in a company to know how much pressure to put on the men beneath them. "The top manager has a duty not to push so hard that middle managers are pushed to unethical compromise," says Charles F. Luce, chairman of Consolidated Edison Co. in New York, the nation's largest electrical utility. Other chief executives agree, in principle. "I think the doing is harder than the saying," comments the machine tool president. "The ethical question comes in," he adds, "when you push somebody hard and they do wrong — and you sit back and wash your hands of it."

The reverse of this — failing to oppose the domination of an unethical boss — has gotten many honest second-line executives into trouble, often because of a misguided sense of loyalty. "But failing to say 'no' to a corrupt boss can be the product of fear, as well," notes Mayo J. Thompson, a Texas corporation lawyer who became a member of the

Federal Trade Commission in 1973. "I've seen too many cases in business," he adds, "where people caved in to a dominating and strong man."

Consultants' Role

An executive can get into trouble by "using" a management consultant, notes Albert McDonald, the managing director of McKinsey & Co., the management consultants.

"Often when the stakes are high — say a major acquisition — we're called in purely for an impartial opinion," explains McDonald. "But there are times when bad faith exists — when the top man knows he will benefit personally from the expansion. He wants us to help bolster his viewpoint."

The consultant soon realizes that the executive is seeking protection. "Ethics is surely involved," says McDonald, "when the project is marginal, and he still shows great enthusiasm for it."

A specialist in executive compensation insists that some managers use poor ethical judgment in pushing for "perks" that may be hard to justify.

This compensation specialist thinks that the executive treads a dangerous line in pushing too hard for such extras as company cars and free use of city apartments — especially when they are for personal, not business, use. That can raise problems with board members, shareholders and even with the Internal Revenue Service.

Two-Way Deal

Businessmen are warned against testing doubtful schemes on their lawyers or CPAs. "The businessman does a double-think," says a New Jersey lawyer whose clients include several large companies. "He'll try to slip something by — inflating a crucial report, say — and if the lawyer or CPA lets it pass, he'll feel that somehow the idea has been purified."

Businessmen can expect to face a stiffer attitude from both lawyers and CPAs, since both professions have been shaken recently by well-publicized legal actions. The National Student Marketing Corp. case, which brought a string of indictments ending last year, involved false and misleading financial reports. The SEC complaint named, among others, one of Wall Street's most prestigious law firms, White & Case. On the accountants' side, the SEC last month censured Touche Ross & Co., a Big Eight firm, in connection with a San Diego securities fraud complaint against U.S. Financial, Inc., and others. This month Peat, Marwick, Mitchell & Co., another Big Eight member, was named a co-defendant in an SEC fraud complaint involving Republic National Life Insurance Co.

The mood of the accountants is summed up by a prominent CPA in New York: "The ethical standard is on both sides. The auditor has a duty to investigate, but the businessman has a primary duty to report fairly."

Loose talk can cause trouble. White & Case partner Orison S. Marden, who was trial lawyer in the landmark Texas Gulf Sulphur case, in the late 1960s, warns: "On the golf course or at the bridge table, a man may disclose information about his company and not realize that what he is saying is 'inside information' that might confront him later on in a courtroom."

You can land in hot water in dealing with your stock options in ways other than borrowing from the company at a bargain interest rate. Take the case, cited by a New York securities lawyer, of the executive who owns 3,000 shares of his company's stock and holds an option to buy 3,000 more. The option price is 10 and current market is 30. He sells 1,000 shares at 30 and buys 3,000 at 10. "The trouble is," says the lawyer, "he has an illegal profit — within the SEC's six-month insider trading rule."

No Excuse

In today's climate, just sitting quiet and not asking questions can pose dangers for the executive. The 1968 BarChris decision held outside directors personally liable for the transgressions of a company. Lawyers now are quick to warn outside directors that ignoring what goes on within the company can mean trouble. Even if the director did not know, he still can be held liable because he should have known.

Even the age-old game of padding the expense account draws fire from Justice Potter Stewart of the Supreme Court. "A lesser thing, like expense account chiseling, can undermine a man in time," he says. "It makes him prone to something more serious later on."

From Congress to City Council

The booby traps in everyday lobbying

"In dealing with government," warns Supreme Court Justice Potter Stewart, "businessmen tend to be far too cynical. Too often they want a 'fixer'." That could not have been more apparent than during the Agnew and Watergate dramas this past year. Top corporations and corporate executives got into hot water for illegal contributions to Presidential campaigns, while corrupt politics at the local level led to the resignation of Spiro Agnew.

More than almost any other group in society, businessmen deal with government frequently and on every level, from Congress and the regulatory agencies in Washington to the home-town city council and zoning board. The ethical booby traps in all this are many — and sometimes scary.

You have every right, of course, to present your views — and present them forcefully — to elected and appointed officials. You can write, phone, or make a personal visit. But there is a line between what is reasonable and proper and what is not, and every businessman must learn how to draw that line.

Proper examples If you think you have a legitimate beef, do not be afraid to lean on your congressman. He is your representative in Washington and can often help. A St. Joseph (Mo.) company recently faced closing for lack of fuel. It appealed to Senator Thomas F. Eagleton for help — and got it. Eagleton's office bypassed the Federal Energy Office, called a major oil company directly, and got the fuel. And when some Delaware chemical companies thought they were getting less oil than they were entitled to, their state's senators jointly called an unofficial hearing to get all company information and then presented it to energy czar William Simon. Both approaches were direct, open, and entirely proper.

Representative Charles E. Bennett (D-Fla.) a longtime champion of setting stiff ethical standards for Congress, thinks you should go all out for legislation you support. Says Bennett: "Be vigorous. Pound the table for it even if the new law would make money for you. This is proper if you believe in it. What's wrong is to mislead as to your own personal interest."

Dealing with contract questions or with regulatory agencies is more ticklish. Seeking a congressman's direct help on a contract is out. Generally, he will do no more than request a "status report" or try to speed a dragging decision. But if you feel victimized — denied a contract even though you were low bidder, for example — your congressman might ask the General Accounting Office to look into it. That is standard procedure in Washington.

Do not hesitate to seek guidance in determining how to deal with a situation. If you are inexperienced in the ways of Washington, your industry's trade association can give you some pointers. The local lobbyist can often be a goldmine of information — telling you who to see, and who not to see.

For the most part, a congressman will help a businessman from home without expecting direct favors in return. "But," says one veteran on Capitol Hill, "you'd be naive to think that a politician isn't more inclined to go out of his way for someone who helps him."

One way of helping him, of course, is with a personal campaign contribution — made in the normal way, and on the record. Offering one at the time you seek a favor, or even hinting of one in the future, is more than heavy-handed — it comes close to bribery.

Says Bennett: "Don't be confused by rationalizations such as 'others are doing it' — they're just garbage and make no difference."

Easy does it The facts of life in post-Watergate Washington are that a moderate personal campaign contribution — made at the next election — might well be in order. Only if private giving is banned by law, will this change.

As to other gifts, the rule holds: "If you can eat it or drink it at one sitting, it's O.K." But birthday cigars, Christmas bottles, and such, have mostly faded from the picture. The topsy-turvy of political ethics is shown by the honorariums offered to congressmen when they make speeches — which are accepted by most. The range of fees is $300 to as high as $3,000.

Pretty much the same rules hold at the state and local government levels, with some important variations. One marked difference in working with state legislators is that you are almost forced by the surroundings to personalize your dealings. "The legislator has little staff or office space," notes Representative Thomas F. Railsbach (R-Ill.), who has had wide state and local government experience. "What you have to do is take your man to lunch and talk quietly. This is quite proper."

Railsbach and other professional politicians feel that there is no great difference in the basic attitudes at the state level. A smart businessman, says Railsbach, will be "low key and noncoercive. Don't bluster because you are in your own state."

On state-level campaign contributions, one veteran political worker says: "Stay away from anything that smacks of a trade-off. Do it once, and you'll do it forever, and it will get more costly." Even if you are tempted to go along, the price of "going along" can dent the pocketbook.

Fight city hall On the local level, the businessman-government official relationship is even more personal — and often more treacherous — than at the state capital. The pressure to go along with the system can be intense, and staying above it can be hard. But, Ambrose Lindhorst, a Cincinnati lawyer who spent 20 years in local politics, warns that condoning — "or suffering" — is the wrong way to deal with it. "Businessmen faced with kickbacks should get off their duffs and take action to clean things up at city hall," says Lindhorst. He argues that once you start making payoffs to policemen, building inspectors, and others, at "the curbstone level," you will be in for trouble. Once started, the practice never ends.

The thing to do in such a situation, says Lindhorst, is to try as strongly as you can to work with other businessmen to "flatten" graft. "If you 'go along,' you become responsible — you ask for it," he says.

Another problem is that dealings at the local government level can take you into contact with personal friends. You may have an old school chum or a country club crony who also happens to be the mayor, or a councilman, or a member of the zoning board. The question is how to proceed when your situation brings you in contact with the man. How close is too close? "There is nothing wrong with inviting your friend to lunch and presenting your problem," says Lindhorst, "as long as your position is legally sound and there is nothing clandestine about it."

The Nixon tax case?

No year to trifle with the IRS

The income tax form presents the businessman with one of the most agonizing ethical dilemmas he ever has to face. No matter how honest he sees himself, there is always the temptation to reach to the limit — and maybe a little beyond. And the way in which President Nixon has handled his taxes makes the dilemma all the more acute this year.

"The system of voluntary compliance is fragile at any time," says Sheldon S. Cohen, former Commissioner of Internal Revenue and now a Washington tax lawyer. "It won't crack, but it has been shaken."

The danger in 1974 is that even the businessman who normally files a perfectly straightforward return may try to stretch the rules this time — taking an overblown charitable deduction, perhaps, or listing some borderline travel and entertainment expenses. Yet, by all reports, the Nixon situation will make the IRS even tougher than usual this year. And even an innocent mistake on your return can mean an audit, and sometimes a penalty.

An audit can be time-consuming and infuriating. A penalty will cost you money, usually 6% of your total tax due, though IRS can also decide to audit your returns for the previous three years and penalties can pile up. The IRS seldom brings tax fraud charges in "gray-area" cases, but it can happen. At the least, that can mean some unfavorable newspaper publicity. Note: if you think you have erred on your 1973 tax return — and it is in the mail — you still have the option to file an amended, corrected return that will take you off the hook.

Tax lawyers and advisers tick off three major areas where gray-area conflicts are likely to arise:

Donations This is what tripped up Dr. Armand Hammer, chairman of Occidental Petroleum Corp., earlier this month. He ran into well-publicized trouble with the IRS over deductions for donations of art works to charity. You can usually escape trouble if you have the work in question valued by two reputable appraisers. But other charitable deduction problems are getting more attention. Backdating a document proving a donation to charity is obviously one. Here the donor usually moves the date back across the Dec. 31 dateline, thus getting advantage of the deduction in the previous year.

"Too many advisers and clients bend the truth to do this," notes Cohen. " 'Past intention' is used to justify it but it's flirting with fraud."

Travel and entertainment Here, the IRS seems to be paying most attention to the combination business-pleasure trip. "This is one of those gray cases where a little leeway is O.K., but there's been horrendous chiseling," says Michael Graetz, a former tax lawyer at the Treasury who is now teaching at the University of Virginia law school.

He cites the case of a businessman who takes his wife along on a business trip to the Caribbean. The question: Can the wife's costs be deducted?

"Say he pays $60 a night for a double room," says Graetz. "But the single rate is $40. He should deduct the $40, not the $60, and he knows it." There are federal appeals court cases, he explains, including *Disney* (1969). In that case, Roy Disney, Walt Disney's brother, convinced the court that his wife's expenses were deductible because she had assisted him in displaying a "family image" which was essential to his business.

"But a case like this," Graetz says, "is ammunition for the chiselers."

Shelters Too many pitchmen have pushed too hard on tax shelters. IRS Commissioner Donald C. Alexander promised a crackdown last November, and some tax men believe it is now due.

Be especially careful about any shelter that offers an exceptionally big front-end deduction. An important Tax Court case, *Schultz* (1968), involving up-front deductions in a whiskey shelter, shows that reaching too far on these deductions can spell trouble. And the definition of "reaching too far" may be broadened. In a cattle feeding deal, for example, writing off a huge feed bill at the start riles the IRS, and you might have to go to court to fight for the deduction.

Meanwhile, tax men are steering clients around other pitfalls. Here are some of current interest:

> Fees for tax and investment advice are deductible. Fees for general legal work are not. Some businessmen have been hit by the IRS for writing off a personal lawyer's charge for both.

> Foreign bank accouts can cause trouble, warns Cohen. "Somebody says to a man at lunch, 'set up a Swiss account, everybody's doing it.' " Cohen explains. "He sets it up, and a year later is prosecuted for not reporting this on his 1040. The IRS has ways of picking up this sort of thing," he says.

Interest paid on a loan to buy tax-exempt bonds is nondeductible. But income from tax-exempts is not shown on the 1040, so the interest deduction sometimes gets put on the form. Courts try hard, though, to protect the nondeduction rule. In a recent federal appellate court case, *Mariorenzi* (1974), the owner of some tax-exempts borrowed money from a bank. The court said that since he could have sold some of the bonds to raise money, part of the loan interest was not deductible.

Lopsided real estate valuations can create problems for taxpayers. An investor will buy a building with land and place too much valuation on the building in relation to the land to pick up a bigger depreciation writeoff. But the IRS often unearths these cases.

One of the most common traps is to follow the advice of a less than reputable tax man. Says David Kentoff, a tax lawyer with the Washington firm of Arnold & Porter: "You can't rid yourself of responsibility when you hire a tax man to do things you can't bring yourself to do."

The SEC on "Insiders"

When not to use "inside information"

A businessman can make money from what he knows, and in years past many did — using inside information to make a killing in the market. But the rules about who is an insider and what constitutes inside information have been tightened in a series of cases, from Texas Gulf Sulphur to a Liggett & Myers case last year that helped define "public" information.

The hazard is that the new rules have not been drawn finely enough yet to follow without risking trouble.

You can get some idea of how "insider" is being defined these days by looking at the sort of people who have gotten into trouble.

Directors and top executives are clearly insiders. Department heads are too if they are privy to information not available to the general investing public. That holds true for lower-echelon people as well, such as the TGS geologist who talked about his company's Canadian mineral strike. And most experts believe that the definition of an insider will be extended still further. For example, you might get into trouble with the SEC by trading the stock of another company on the basis of information gained from it during merger negotiations. Other potential targets include longtime customers and suppliers of a company.

Be close-mouthed The definition of what is inside information remains very fuzzy, and lawyers are telling clients to keep mum about company business outside the company. A good rule-of-thumb: Might a reasonable person make an investment decision based on the information that you provided?

You can be tagged a "tipee" and get in trouble simply by using material inside information gained from others. If you have a good reason to believe that what you have learned is no more than "street gossip," you are probably free to act as you choose. Otherwise, wait until the information has become public before acting — especially if you know that the original source of the information was himself an insider.

Even the definition of "public" is being broadened. The SEC insists that the public has not been adequately informed if the information in question has gone to just a few security analysts or is contained in a press release with limited distribution. For information to be public, it must be widely disseminated, and investors must have had adequate time to act upon it.

Do not expect early help from the SEC in the form of guidelines. Some have been promised, but the SEC will not say when.

Business Ethics: Guidelines for Eight Gray Areas

1. The incomplete disclosure

Provide more information rather than less, even if it goes beyond what the Securities & Exchange Commission and other agencies require. Put yourself in the investor's place and ask, "What do I want to know?" The SEC keeps requiring fuller disclosure, and failure to disclose can bring a suit.

2. The corrupt boss

Many middle managers have gotten into serious trouble — and a few have wound up in jail — by caving in to a boss who cared more about ends than means. Speak up as soon as you are faced with an ethical problem; you may set things straight. "If you can't, get out," says a Xerox director.

3. The corrupt subordinate

As a senior man, don't worry about rocking the boat, just get rid of him. A tolerant, "nice guy" attitude can put both of you in trouble. And his misdeeds can infect his co-workers.

4. The inadvertent remark

Think twice about what you tell anyone about your business — at lunch, in the locker room, over the bridge table. A chance remark might get you nailed for leaking company secrets. And the law about passing "inside information" is vague. You could wind up in a courtroom.

5. The "purified" idea

You can usually find a lawyer or a CPA who will endorse a questionable idea or plan — especially if you phrase it just the right way. Just remember, the plan is still questionable and it can get you in trouble.

6. The passive director

Whether you are an inside or an outside director, don't just sit back silent and rubber-stamp management. You can be sued, and the courts take a hard line nowadays on director liability. "Speak up or drop out," says one man who has served on 11 boards.

7. The expense-account vacation

Go easy on tax deductions for combination business-pleasure trips. Deduct for your wife only if she is actually involved in your business. This is a hot item with the IRS now.

8. The stock option trap

Beware of "fast" option transactions — buying and selling your company's stock within the six-month trading rule period for insiders. More businessmen are getting tripped up on this one.

33 Are New Business Ethics beyond Reality?

Industry Week

Not too long ago, it would have been easy to write a story on business ethics.

You'd have started with a big picture of Schultz the butcher with 13 oz of hamburger and 3 oz of thumb on the scale, and then you'd throw in a few comments on the importance of absolute honesty in the basic buyer-seller relationship.

Next you'd add some warnings about what unethical practices can lead to, and then you'd finish strong with about three paragraphs saying something vague like, "while some unethical practices still exist, businessmen on the whole can be proud of their record in the area of ethics."

And then you'd take off your Puritan hip boots.

Fortunately, a story on ethics isn't so easy today. As our society evolves, it is constantly changing its definition of ethical business practices. Business is playing a larger role in our lives every day, and people just won't buy that old line anymore that what's good for business is good for America. In short, ethics have gone beyond the buyer-seller stage. The qusetion is, how far beyond?

Although there are many ideas as to just what "ethical" should mean to a businessman today, most of them seem to fit into two broad categories — and the ethics argument boils down to: Should business comply only with civil laws which often lag society's evolving mores, or should it comply with moral laws?

Both sides of the argument have impressive lists of supporters. The noted economist Milton Friedman has often said that business can serve society best by concentrating on what it does best — doing business.

On the other side, many argue that business is too omnipresent in society to deny its moral and social responsibility.

But what is this social and moral responsibility? This is the ethical issue of 1971. As Dr. Frederick W. Dow, Hayes-Healy professor

Reprinted with permission from *Industry Week,* January 11, 1971, pp. 51–54.

of marketing at the University of Notre Dame's College of Business Administration, Notre Dame, Ind., asks: Should legality and profitability be the only factors a businessman considers prior to an action, or should he consider whether the action is morally right or wrong?

Profit's the Thing!

"Business has no public responsibilities beyond conducting itself within legal restraints. Its sole purpose is to make a profit for its stockholders or owners. That's how it can best serve the public," argues Robert V. Horton, assistant professor of economics at Purdue University, Lafayette, Ind., and a former general partner at Goldman, Sachs & Co., one of New York's major investment firms.

Prof. Horton admits business plays a huge role in our society, but argues that "even with all its intrusions into our lives, it still serves us best by making a profit."

As an example, he cites what happened to a shoe manufacturer that at one time was the largest in the nation.

"This firm was a model of good corporate citizenship. It built parks in cities where it had plants, established many special programs for employees, and tried to look out for the communities' best interests — and remember this was back in the 1920s.

"For example, the market for work shoes began to decline — but work shoes used more leather than regular shoes, and cutting work shoe production would have hurt the leather suppliers in plant communities. So, rather than hurt part of the communities, the firm continued producing work shoes at the same rate. It evidently hoped to capture a larger share of the work shoe market, but it didn't," he explains.

After a few more similar decisions without regard for the question of profitability, the bottom fell out. "The firm had to lay off half its workforce. The result? Thousands of people out of work, towns' economies dead, and the firm nearly ruined. Even today it hasn't recovered. It's still little more than an also-ran in the shoe industry."

As Prof. Horton asks, didn't this firm's failure to make profitability the vital factor in its decisions cause far more damage to its communities than it could ever have overcome by its public consciousness?

"You can argue that this firm went too far, but who can say what's too far? You say only help good causes, but who can say what's a good cause? You say deviate from the profit motive only within reason, but what's within reason?

"Your stockholders gave you one job — making money for them. Who the hell can give you the right to stray from that task? Forget the monkey business and do what you do best. Make money. You'll make your greatest contribution to society by building a strong business that promises regular employment," he urges.

Youth Won't Buy It

But however correct this approach might be, its a good bet the public won't buy it. The younger generation especially is looking to business to solve many problems, problems many of them feel business created.

As Notre Dame's Dr. Dow explains, "Business has the wealth generating responsibility in our society, but in producing this wealth it can deal unjustly with individuals and groups, can contaminate our air and streams, can produce and sell unnecessary products, and can drown us in solid wastes."

This omnipresence of business and the growing concentration of industrial power gives the individual manager a great leverage in his actions, leverage that changes the manager's ethical responsibilities.

"Executives acting in their corporate roles have a more binding moral responsibility to carefully measure the effects of their actions than they do when they act as ordinary citizens," Dr. Dow explains. They can't just follow the profit motive, because "the insulation of the executive from the results of his action makes it easy for him to avoid the 'pricks of conscience' that could result from direct contact with the harmed individual or group."

A Positive Reaction

Has business reacted to this growing responsibility? "I believe the business community has realized the general public has become more sensitive to the issue of ethics and business has reacted positively," says Dr. John A. Hornaday, chairman, Management Div., Babson College, Babson Park, Mass. "Business has become more aware of its obligations to the community and its obligation to set standards," he adds.

But if business is accepting this moral obligation, it brings up Prof. Horton's question — how far should it go?

"The sensitivity of a corporation's social consciousness is not unrelated to its current level of profitmaking," explains Richard J. Nelson, assistant vice president, public affairs, Inland Steel Co., Chicago.

"If your profit level is good, your stockholders are far more tolerant of doing things in the social area. However, if you start to skip dividends, they begin to ask you some very tough questions.

"Like many large firms, we gauge our participation in commu-

nity affairs in terms of profits and total resources. For example, our Inland Steel-Ryerson Foundation is funded according to our profit level."

But does the foundation approach of setting aside part of your
earnings to meet social obligations answer the demand? Can the corporate mind deal with these problems? As Mr. Nelson points out, long-
accepted attitudes can hinder the corporation.

"A few years ago, more than half of our foundation's funds
went to help colleges and universities," he explains, "but we decided
we'd try to do more to ease urban problems. We re-examined our funding to see if we could put additional dollars into some high-risk urban
programs."

The foundation found the money, and began looking for ways
to use it — but this caused an unexpected problem. "By their nature,
investments in social action programs are high-risk projects. Despite
our intentions, we found there's still an emotional block in business
against high-risk investments. They just don't seem to fit in with the
businessman's traditional role of trustee of stockholders' funds."

Although Inland went ahead with the urban programs, its experience points out one problem that foundations encounter.

If the foundation approach isn't enough, the next step is taking
the social and ethical implications for every business decision into account. However, here you run directly into profitability. What takes
precedence?

"The private enterprise system has one goal — operating the
resource conversion process as efficiently as possible because resources
are limited," notes Notre Dame's Dr. Dow. However, he adds that the
term "resources" has moral as well as economic parameters.

"Businessmen today have an outstanding opportunity to be on
the cutting edge of moral change. The institutional leverage we spoke of
earlier — it should be looked upon in a morally positive fashion," he
explains.

Inland's Mr. Nelson agrees that corporate leverage can be
an important tool for social change. "If a young executive finds that his
social goals and those of his firm coincide, he's got one strong base to
operate from. If a businessman is moving for change, he can speak out
far more authoritatively than someone who has the stereotyped image of
a do-gooder."

However, both Dr. Dow and Mr. Nelson stop short of saying
social issues should take precedence.

"Business must go beyond the pure economics of any issue, but
we have no right to ask it to solve the social ills of the world," explains
Dr. Dow, "I believe there's a great deal of misunderstanding of the role
private enterprise plays in our society. People argue that if business
only had proper ethics we'd solve all our problems. This simply isn't
so."

Babson College's Dr. Hornaday agrees, noting that while business is becoming more sensitive to moral and ethical issues, "the general population is actually becoming less ethical. For example, consider the growing problems of shoplifting and employee thefts, the decrease in personal reliability, the laxity in meeting contract obligations. I honestly believe personal ethics are on the decline."

The Next Move

It may be true that business is moving toward greater moral responsibility, but is it moving quickly enough to suit its many vocal critics? It seems we're hearing angry voices damning the private enterprise system every day.

"Advances in business ethics are achieved through long periods of tension, painful confrontation, turmoil, and protest," notes Dr. Dow. "In the process of long, turbulent, and painful moral change the first step begins when a previously accepted practice arouses misgivings among sensitive observers who are usually small in number and relatively powerless."

Such was the case, he notes, with child labor. At one time it was considered proper — it was merely a business agreement between parents and company. Those who questioned the practice were laughed at. It took years before society decided that child labor was wrong.

His point: eventually business and public both adjust. For the future, Dr. Dow is "optimistic on the continuing evolution of an improving ethical climate in private industry in the U.S. . . . the generation coming into power today has a strong commitment to ameliorating social injustice and a great concern with the impact of institutions on individuals in society."

But that still hasn't answered the question of profitability, and Dr. Dow doesn't think business alone can answer that question. "Society must decide that there are certain issues so important right now that we must direct a greater percentage of our resources to them. It must see to it that the burden of social and ethical responsibility falls prohibit certain practices. Through sanctions and incentives, society must see to it that the burden of social and ethical responsibility falls evenly on all.

"Business can't do it alone. Business must never forget that its primary role is the effective conversion of resources."

Cases

Fisher Manufacturing Company

In the early spring of 1964, The Fisher Manufacturing Company appeared to be on the verge of greatly increasing its sales and scope of operations. Since its organization by Mr. Leonard Fisher in 1955, the company realized profits from the manufacture and sale of wood-plastic building panels. In 1958, for instance, a profit of approximately $25,000 was earned, in addition to the approximately $15,000 drawings for that year by Mr. Fisher.

Since 1958 reported profits were not as substantial because much time and between $75,000 and $100,000 of funds were applied to research and development, and were considered expense items. Nevertheless, profits were shown in every year except 1961, when a loss of approximately $12,000 was incurred. This was in the midst of the development of the largest portion of the new products and manufacturing processes. During this period much of Mr. Fisher's time was devoted to research and development. The erstwhile profitable lines which were the basis of the 1955–58 substantial profits were not emphasized, but rather attention was centered on the development of the new products

---

Reprinted with permission from Hargrove, Harrison and Swearingen, *Business Policy Cases with Behavioral Science Implications* (Rev. Ed., Homewood, Illinois: Richard D. Irwin, Inc.).

This case was prepared by Professor Herbert G. Hicks of Louisiana State University, a member of the Southern Case Writers Association, as a basis for class discussion. Southern Case Writers cases are not intended as examples of correct or incorrect administrative or technical practices. All names have been disguised.

and new manufacturing processes. During the fiscal year ended June 30, 1963, the firm showed a profit of $17,500, in addiiton to officers' salaries.

On July 1, 1963, the company moved from the small southern town in which it was located to a larger town, in Mississippi, of nearly 40,000 population. To accommodate this greatly expanded scope of operations, the company was financially reorganized in October 1, 1963. At this time, the old stock was retired, and a new issue of 400,000 shares of $1 par value was authorized. Leonard Fisher was given $200,000 par value of the new stock in exchange for his old stock. It was anticipated that the $200,000 net capital that was authorized would help the firm in realizing growth due to its position of having new products, new and efficient manufacturing processes, a new plant, a new qualified plant manager, and some of the best knowledge and experience in its field.

The Organization and the Officers

An organization chart of the company (Exhibit A) shows the formal relationships which existed as of January 1, 1964, in accord with the established procedures in the company.

According to company literature, the president was the chief executive officer in the company and had final and complete authority and responsibility for all the operations. However, each manager was to make all practicable decisions in his area because of a policy of decentralized authority. Performance was to be measured primarily by pre-set goals and with data provided in systematic ways.

The officers were:

Leonard Fisher, founder of the company, Chairman of the Board, and President, age 45, was born near Baton Rouge, Louisiana. After completing high school in Baton Rouge, he worked in various construction jobs in Baton Rouge and New Orleans, with most of this work in the area of insulation. From 1941 to 1945, he served in the United States Army and rose to the rank of Sergeant in Armored Maintenance. During his last year in the Army, Mr. Fisher was in charge of a twelve man truck maintenance crew.

Leaving the Army in late 1945, Mr. Fisher entered his uncle's hardware and building supply business in central Louisiana. By 1946, his uncle had allowed him to buy into the business, which was experiencing rapid growth in the post-war boom. Although this business enjoyed considerable success and growth, Mr. Fisher decided in 1954 to start his own business for the manufacture of wood-plastic building panels, in which he had become interested as the answer to the demand for sturdy, durable panels that could be easily installed and would give

Exhibit A Organization

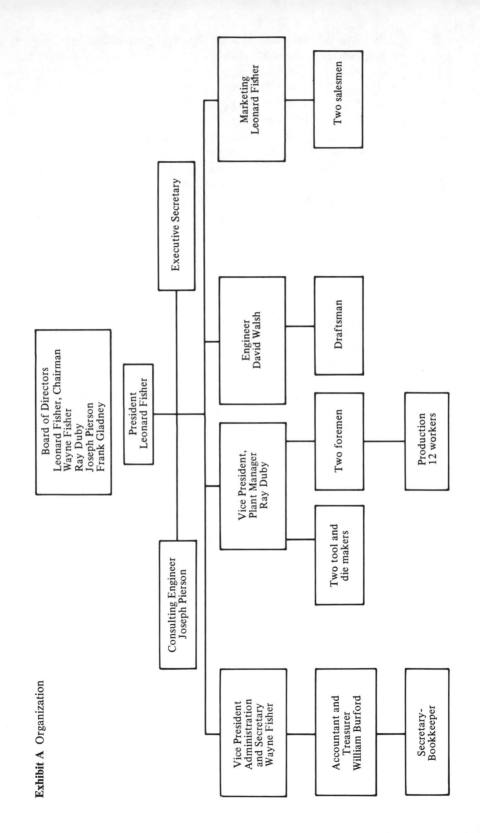

good insulation performance. These panels were made by a technique which combined wood shavings and plastic materials in a molding process to produce panels of varying sizes and widths.

After completing arrangements for his new business, The Fisher Manufacturing Company, Mr. Fisher took the approximately $45,000 which he had accumulated during his association with his uncle and started the new venture. Under Mr. Fisher's careful and constant supervision, the company has grown to its present size. Although not trained formally, Mr. Fisher is recognized as one of the foremost authorities in the nation in insulation panel technology and applications. He has exhibited a high level of proficiency in all areas of the industry. His acceptance as an expert in the industry is reflected in the officer capacities which he holds in two national organizations and the number of addresses he has made to professional groups and other interested parties.

Throughout the growth of the company, Mr. Fisher has personally designed, engineered, and supervised the production of a wide range of the wood-plastic panels and related products.

Wayne Fisher, age 32, Leonard's younger brother, was the Vice-President of Administration and Secretary of the company, a position he had held since joining the firm in the fall of 1959. In this position, Wayne was in charge of personnel, planning and policy, accounting, motivation and incentives, and finance. Leonard's idea was to groom his younger brother to take over the presidency within the next four years, so that he, Leonard, might become a "super salesman" for the company and not be bothered with administrative details, although he would still retain his position as Chairman of the Board.

After graduating from Baton Rouge High School, Wayne attended Louisiana State University, where he received an undergraduate degree in mechanical engineering in 1954. After working for several months as a design engineer for a St. Louis firm, he entered the United States Air Force as an engineering officer. While in the Air Force he supervised up to 175 employees and was in charge of a power plant and other equipment worth approximately $18,000,000.

Resigning from the Air Force in 1957, Wayne entered Graduate School at The University of Texas, where he was awarded a Master in Business Administration degree in August of 1959. While in school in Austin, Wayne was employed part-time at The Balcones Research Center, working on government projects.

Ray Duby, Vice-President and Plant Manager, was 29 years old and a native of Natchez, Mississippi. He indicated in his resume that he had attended several different courses in production management, taught in high school and at one of the small Mississippi state colleges. He had also attended several management seminars held at Mississippi State University.

Prior to joining The Fisher Manufacturing Company in the spring of 1963, Ray was employed by Johnson & Johnson, Inc., a metal working firm located in New Orleans. With this company he was promoted from line foreman to plant superintendent, and was offered the position of plant manager when he advised his superiors of his plans to resign and join Fisher because he felt that his opportunities were greater there. At Johnson & Johnson Ray had up to 125 men under his supervision, and he was in full charge of all production facilities, buildings, and equipment. He had eight years of training in production cost control and budgetary controls. He also had considerable experience in the engineering of products, and was in charge of tooling and die programs at Johnson & Johnson.

The following quotation is from Ray Duby's resume which he sent to Leonard Fisher and the other company officers in early 1963.

In the future, I plan to actively try and work myself out of my present position. I expect to set a good example for my subordinates to do the same, and thus have a rapidly growing organization which will stay ahead of any competition.

My *ultimate goal is — the Presidency!*

Joseph Pierson, age 54, was a Director and Consulting Engineer for Fisher Manufacturing Company. After receiving his mechanical engineering degree from M.I.T. in Boston, Mr. Pierson was affiliated with several companies in engineering design capacities; then he took a position with Boeing Aircraft in 1942. At Boeing, he was instrumental in designing several significant contributions to the war effort. He ended his career in the aircraft field as an assistant plant superintendent.

After the war he acquired and directed an electric motor manufacturing plant in New Orleans. Since that time he has expanded and consolidated his operations to include multiple line electrical equipment. Although he still maintains an interest in his business complex, the major part of his time for the next few years will be spent in helping to increase production at Fisher. In his words, "Fisher Manufacturing Company has the greatest potential of any company with which I have ever been affiliated."

David Walsh, Production Engineer for the company, was 39 years old and a native of the town in which the plant is located. He graduated from high school in 1943 and entered one of the small state universities where he studied electrical engineering for two years. Interrupting his education to serve in the United States Navy for two years, he returned to finish his degree in electrical engineering. After graduating, he was employed by an oil company and eventually advanced to a position of heading up an oil exploration crew. This job carried him to many foreign countries and gave him experience in hiring, maintenance of equipment, purchasing and promoting good foreign relations. In

1959, he left the oil company to be with his family more. His next job as a research engineer with a national manufacturer of windows, doors, and curtain walls carried him to the West Coast and the Middle West operations of the company. He left this company in the fall of 1963 to join Fisher Manufacturing Company because "I felt my new employer had greater growth capacity than the company I was presently with."

William Burford, Accountant and Treasurer, was 32 years of age and a native of Little Rock, Arkansas. After graduating from the University of Arkansas with a Bachelor's degree in Accounting in 1954, he went to work for a national accounting firm in their Dallas office, and was subsequently transferred to their New Orleans office in 1957. In 1960 he joined Fisher Manufacturing Company as their accountant because of the great potential which he felt existed for the company. A statement in his resume read, "I feel that my past experience will be an asset to the company in many ways, and that both Fisher and I will be able to grow and mature together."

Frank Gladney, a Board member and old friend of Leonard Fisher, had purchased some of the stock of the company when it was organized in 1954. Although he gave advice to the company on occasions about finances, his role in the company was largely passive.

Other employees in the company were:

Sam Clark   assembler
William Cooper   semiautomatic mold
David Cross   die maker
Joe Panzica   assembler
Rick Harrison   semiautomatic mold
Joe Burke   carpenter
Tom Patterson   material control
Gil Thrasher   toolmaker
Sherman Anderson   assembler
Ronald Peacock   foreman
Mike Williams   salesman
Jerry Smith   draftsman
Holt Kelley   welder
Bill Davidson   chemical mixer
Manuel Jordan   semiautomatic mold
George Mason   salesman
Curtis Hatcher   assembler
Paul Davis   foreman
Martha Roberts   executive secretary
Sarah Edwards   secretary-bookkeeper

Cooper, Anderson, and Jordan were Negroes and had been with the company longer than those in other positions.

The Products

The Fisher Manufacturing Company originally produced insulation panels for refrigerated storage units. These panels were made by a patented process, purchased by Leonard Fisher in 1953, that combined wood shavings and plastic foam. However, since 1960 the company had been pushing for expansion into nonrefrigerated building applications, which would include prefabricated convenience stores and service stations. Further, applications of the panels to interior curtain walls were being vigorously investigated. Even though these products constituted a lucrative market, Leonard Fisher has constantly stressed that the company must continue to innovate in order to continue to grow. Therefore, he states that the product line will include anything that the company is able to produce profitably, for to restrict the product line would restrict innovation and opportunity and lead to an early decline in sales when the competition in the present lines becomes intense. The prospectus of the company, as written by Wayne Fisher, stated:

> A policy of the Company is to be market oriented. The functions of both marketing and production are to satisfy customer needs. More specifically, the function of marketing is not merely to sell what the production function can produce. Both production and marketing are to view themselves in the partnership of creating customer satisfactions.

The major products of the company fell into the classes described below.

Non-refrigerated boxes

Non-refrigerated boxes made from wood-plastic panels were a product that had such excellent insulation qualities that they could replace, for instance, refrigerated trucks used in the distribution of frozen food. The frozen items could simply be placed in the boxes in the morning, and without refrigeration they would stay frozen all day.

The company enjoyed a competitive advantage because of its pioneer production of the panels for the refrigeration industry. Estimated sales were:

Fiscal Year Ended June 30	Amount
1964	600 boxes at $75 = $ 45,000
1965	2,000 boxes at $75 = $150,000
1966	3,000 boxes at $75 = $225,000

Wood-plastic architectural building panels

These panels were the key to the Company's growth and profits because they were used in some form or another in every one of the Company's products. Because of the cost, insulating, and structural advantage over competing products, the situation was generally one where superior products to those presently on the market could be offered at lower prices than present products commanded.

The Company had invested very heavily in research, development, and engineering and had developed a manufacturing process superior and less costly than any other known process.

Present production capacity for these panels by the Company was easily 5,000,000 sq. ft. of panels per year. If pushed, the present facilities could produce 8,000,000 sq. ft. per year. With the investment of an additional ten thousand dollars, production could be increased to 15,000,000 sq. ft. per year.

Productive capacity for these panels appears virtually unlimited. Moreover, since this was a new product, the Company had not yet been able to find the demand limits of the market. Fisher executives strongly felt that in the areas of cold storage plants, refrigerated room and boxes, non-refrigerated boxes, prefabricated buildings and interior curtain walls, the product the Company had was superior to competing products and could be sold at lower than competitive prices at a profit.

However, the company could not make accurate estimates of the size of the market for these panels, but it was Leonard's opinion that the market was tremendously large. Very conservatively, he estimated that sales of panels, in addition to those used in their other products described above, would be:

Fiscal Year Ended June 30	Amount
1964	72,000 sq. ft. × $1.00 = $ 72,000
1965	240,000 sq. ft. × $1.00 = $240,000
1966	360,000 sq. ft. × $1.00 = $360,000

After returning from a mid-winter vacation-business trip to Trinidad, Leonard started pushing the idea that the company should use its knowledge and product resources to set up an outlet for its panels in the West Indies. He suggested to a Board meeting that since supermarkets were just beginning to develop in the Islands and since low cost, sturdy housing was also in demand, the company could find a profitable and extensive market for its products there. In order to acquaint the local businessman with the advantages of the panels, he wanted to set up a mango juice processing plant made out of the panels as a model of their various uses. Further, he said the plant itself would be profitable since there would be a ready market for the juice in the States. The Board decided not to take any definite action on Leonard's latest proposal, but to keep the possibilities in mind.

Pre-fabricated stores and service stations

As another end use of the panels, the Company was in a position to supply pre-fabricated stores and service stations. Like the panel sales, the size of this market was indeterminate, but it estimated from experience in this area that sales would be:

Fiscal Year
Ended June 30   Amount
  1964   20 stores @ \$15,000 = \$300,000
  1965   40 stores @ \$15,000 = \$600,000
  1966   60 stores @ \$15,000 = \$900,000

The Company felt that the construction of convenience and grocery stores would provide a means of capitalizing on some knowledge of store lay-out, design, and merchandising in the grocery field. Leonard Fisher was recognized as an authority in all these areas. He had twice addressed the Southern Association of Convenience Stores on these topics. Further, Wayne Fisher had extensive training in this area while in graduate school.

Incidents at Fisher Manufacturing Company

The following incidents took place during the month of March 1964. Because many of the workmen had appeared uneasy with Leonard in an office which had a window looking directly into the plant area, Leonard had moved to an office in a Motor Hotel two blocks from the plant. During March, Leonard traveled on company business a great deal; consequently, with Leonard out of town and in line with Wayne's recent innovation of stressing the need for written communication instead of spoken (he had given out pads with the words DON'T SAY IT — WRITE IT! at the top), several memos appeared which might normally not be written.

Incident
INTER-OFFICE CORRESPONDENCE   March 3, 1964
To: Leonard
By: Wayne

The following quote was interesting to me:

> The test of a good manager is not how good he is at bossing, but how little bossing he has to do because of the training of his men and the organization of their work.

Incident
INTER-OFFICE CORRESPONDENCE   March 3, 1964
To: Ray
Subject: Panel Costs
By: Wayne

Please get me labor costs for our standard wall panels in the following quantities per month:

100
150
200
250

INTER-OFFICE CORRESPONDENCE   March 5, 1964

To: Ray

Subject: When foremen are sick

By: Leonard

I thought I made it clear that if a foreman is out for some reason that Cooper, Anderson, or Jordan are not to take over. Those niggers may be able to operate that complex machinery OK, but it just wouldn't look right or be right for them to operate people. With me going out of town tomorrow I don't want this to happen again.

Incident

William Burford entered Wayne's office late in the afternoon on March 10, and the following conversation took place.

Fisher: Hi, Bill, what's on your mind?

Burford: I've got those revised cost statements you wanted. The projections were really off. If Ray doesn't come a little closer, we're going to have to revise all our projections, 'cause it doesn't look like we'll hit anywhere near the sales level we need.

Fisher: Yea, I know that things aren't going exactly to plan, but with a little bit of luck the adjustments won't be too significant. Besides, we can't do any juggling until Leonard gets back next week.

Burford: True, but we've got another problem that's going to have to be solved right now.

Fisher: How's that?

Burford: Well, Martha (Martha Roberts, executive secretary) called her lawyer this afternoon. She blew up when I asked her to clear her desk. You remember Leonard got on a "clean the office up" campaign before he left, and I finally got around to saying something to her. She said that if the company was too cheap to hire a janitor then she wasn't going to do that. And that not only was she not doing the work of an executive secretary, but that she had not seen any executives around this place.

Fisher: What did you do?

Burford: I told her that we would try to work something out, but I heard her call some lawyer anyway after I left the office.

Fisher: What do you think we should do?

Burford: I don't know. There's really not enough work to keep Martha busy all the time, but I hate to see her leave because Leonard will put Cynthia (Leonard's wife) in there and she'll be just like a spy when he's not around.

Fisher: Now, Bill, you know that Cynthia won't be purposefully spying on anyone if she comes in.

Burford: Hell, if I don't! Leonard's been complaining about Martha for a month now, and she's a damned good secretary regardless of what he says. Besides, now that he's exiled over at the motel he just wants someone here that'll tell him everything that happens.

Incident

Martha called in on March 10 and said that she would not be returning to work, and asked that her final check be mailed to her.

Incident

An excerpt from an Air Mail, Special Delivery letter to Wayne from Leonard at a manufacturers' conference in Chicago, dated March 10 and received March 11.

> . . . so in the light of the ideas and encouragement I've picked up here, I think that we should move up the time schedule for you to take over the operations and let me concentrate on selling. I think I can begin to build a really top-notch force right away. I showed some of our material to a salesman from Alcoa, and he said we had the hottest building material in the country and he would like to talk to us about joining up. And he wasn't the only one that's showed such enthusiasm.

Incident

INTER-OFFICE CORRESPONDENCE   March 13, 1964
To: Bill Burford
Subject: Source and Application of Funds Statements
By: Wayne

I have not yet received the statements which you promised to have in my office by today at noon. I had planned to work on them over the weekend. Perhaps it has been delayed in getting to me, if so please disregard the following.

I believe it is important that you keep your promises or at least let the other person know in advance that you can't.

Incident

The following letter was written to Leonard on March 16. Carbon copies were sent to all members of the Board.

> Dear Mr. Fisher:
> This is to inform you of my resignation as accountant-office manager of your company.

I am truly sorry to bring this up at a time when we are just getting operations under control, but I feel that public accounting is more promising and suited for me.

I believe that we are able to say that the worst part is over and my resigning now will not affect operations.

I have gained valuable experience with this company during the short while employed, and want to personally congratulate all the men and yourself for the fine efforts and patience extended during this re-organization.

I hope that my resignation will not hinder our relations as professional men, but instead, improve them.

If ever I may be of assistance to you or any employee of your firm, you can be assured that the matter will receive my immediate attention.

Yours very truly,
s/William Burford

Incident

INTER-OFFICE CORRESPONDENCE   March 19, 1964
To: Leonard
Subject: Bond Issue
By: Wayne

A bond issue for us might be a good idea. I have done most of the work already and will discuss it in detail at your house Sunday. I would estimate the cost of a $250,000 issue as follows:

$ 400	Printing
300	Filing fee
500	Selling costs
$1200	

Of course, I do not think it would be wise for you to spend too much time selling these if you could better spend your time on sales.

INTER-OFFICE CORRESPONDENCE   March 20, 1964
To: Leonard
Subject: Ideas to discuss as soon as we can
By: Wayne

I feel that the following ideas are helpful in the present stage of the development of *our* organization. It seems to me that a thing that we need in the organization is more discipline (not necessarily punishment, now, discipline). And discipline to do the following things:

1. Planning. Set up goals and objectives *in advance* and *stick* to them. (Unless there are very compelling reasons to change.)

2. Controlling. Comparing what *does* happen with what was *supposed to happen according to the plan*. Obviously, no real control can be done without good planning in the first place.

Incident

On the afternoon of March 20 Wayne went in the plant area to talk to Ray about getting more realistic cost estimates on panels. The conversation eventually got around to the company as a whole.

Duby: Frankly, Wayne, I don't think anyone pays any attention to what I say around here. I'm not paying my own way and Leonard won't sit down and talk things over with me. If things don't improve, then I'm going to leave this mess.

Fisher: Ray, it's not all that bad. We're just going through some growing pains that all businesses have to experience when they move from small to large scale operations.

Duby: That may be true, but why in the hell won't Leonard let me run the plant like I want to? After all, he hired me to make decisions, and now when he's around he tries to run the whole show. We're on an eternal merry-go-round; we're not moving, not making sales. Every time we get a new product all lined up, it's off on some tangent and the really good ideas are left by the wayside.

Fisher: OK, simmer down, Ray. Things may not be going very smoothly right now, but a lot of the trouble between you and Leonard can be traced to you. You're competitive with him too much — after all, this just adds fuel to any smoldering fires. And of course he's defensive about this company's operations, he did start the company you know.

Duby: Well, you're right of course, but if things don't cool down, then Leonard's going to have a heartattack or something, and I'm going to get out of here but fast.

Fisher: I promise I'll try to talk to Leonard about all this tension as soon as we get all the other matters taken care of. A lot has piled up while he's been away.

Incident

Going through his desk late on the night of March 21 after returning from his business trip, Leonard found the following on top of a stack of correspondence.

To: Leonard
By: Wayne

I sincerely hope that we'll be able to sit down Sunday and work something out definitely about several problems.

On Sunday, after discussing Leonard's trip and some minor company problems, Wayne and Leonard had a long discussion about all the recent developments in the company. The following are excerpts from the conversation.

Leonard: Well, it just seems like Duby's not panning out as we expected. I think he really sold us a bill of goods, and we believed that he'd produce a helluva lot better than he did. Don't you agree?

Wayne: Yes, but I don't think Ray's to blame alone. We've had an awful lot of tension and disruption in the plant recently, although he really has messed us up on those estimates about the panels.

Leonard: Right! I'm going to call him in Monday and find out what his excuse is. I have several people in mind that I know can do his job, and probably all of them can do it better than him! In fact, the more I think about it, the more I know we can get along a lot better without Ray Duby.

Wayne: Leonard, at least promise you'll give him a chance to explain. After all, several of his mistakes can be traced to your not bothering to write out a communication and then expecting him to remember a lot of details.

Leonard: My failure to write everything out is beside the point. Besides you know I hate to write things out because of my poor grammar and spelling. After all, I can't have the employees thinking I'm an illiterate. You stick to the memos, Little Brother, and I'll stick to making the big decisions and pushing those sales up.

Leonard: I'm sold on the idea that we're about to really get moving, and we'll pass up a golden opportunity if we don't go through with that idea of mine about setting up an operation in Trinidad. I want you to go down there with me as soon as we can get a new plant manager and get him squared away.

Wayne: I thought we had decided not to do anything about that right now, until we sort of get firmed up in some other areas.

Leonard: No, I'm sure this is the best thing right now. The other areas will take care of themselves. We just can't make the mistake of not taking advantage of all those sales waiting for us down there.

Wayne: Leonard, don't you think we're jumping around too much? We just get going with one product, in one area, and then before things are really running smoothly, we jump into something else. There's a lot more to being a success than making sales, you know.

Leonard: Hell, Wayne, if you can sell enough, you can cover up any managerial mistakes you make along the way — you don't have to go to college to know that. I want those sales. That's what'll make us a big company.

Wayne: That may be your idea, but mine is different; and if we don't get some organization and cooperation here, then I'm pulling out. You might have built this company into what it is today, but you damn sure will never get any further with the attitude you have now. And I don't want to worry with it and then have the lid blow off in my face — and that's exactly where we're headed!

Incident

INTER-OFFICE CORRESPONDENCE   March 24, 1964
To: Mr. Ray Duby
Subject: Resignation
By: Leonard Fisher, President

After our talk yesterday, I'm sure the best thing for you to do is to resign. Your failure to follow orders and the general mess in the plant and the poor estimates all show that you would be better off somewhere else, and we would too.

I expect you to turn your resignation letter in to Wayne by noon tomorrow. He'll give you a check for one weeks work. Good luck in finding a new job.

INTER-OFFICE CORRESPONDENCE   March 24, 1964
To: Wayne
Subject: Duby's Resignation
By: Leonard

Ray will never work out no better than he has. I told him to resign by noon Wednesday. Give him a check for one weeks wages. Better place an ad in the New Orleans paper for a new man. I'll interview applicants when I get back in town Friday. Sorry I won't be here until then, but am sure you can work things out OK.

Balance Sheet—December 31, 1963

	Assets		
Current Assets:			
Cash on Hand and in Bank			$ 2,075.91
Accounts Receivable		$ 50,620.01	
Less: Allowance for Doubtful			
Accounts		5,010.13	45,609.88

Notes Receivable		1,451.73	
Inventories		83,071.07	
Prepaid Insurance		1,250.32	
Deposits on Notes Receivable			
Discounted		13,604.38	
Total Current Assets			$147,063.29

Other Assets:
Telephone & Utility Deposits			$ 227.50

Fixed Assets:
Land		$ 10,000.00	
Building	$ 97,114.61		
Machinery and Equipment	77,990.14		
Automobiles and Trucks	14,015.19		
Furniture and Fixtures	5,121.61		
Total Depreciable Assets	$194,241.55		
Accumulated Depreciation	29,881.97	164,359.58	
Total Fixed Assets			$174,359.58

Intangible Assets:
Goodwill			$ 82,184.16
Total Assets			$403,834.53

Liabilities and Stockholders' Equity

Current Liabilities:
Accounts Payable		$ 28,525.98	
Mortgage Payable — Sherman Building Co.		15,000.00	
Federal Income Taxes Payable		2,742.20	
Accrued Payroll and Other Taxes		3,056.37	
Accrued Payroll		1,149.13	
Accrued Expenses — Other		726.41	
Reserve for Warranty on Panels		7,072.75	
Long-Term Liabilities:			$ 58,272.84
Mortgage Payable — Townson Building Assn.			$ 69,028.74
Total Liabilities			$127,301.58

Stockholders' Equity:
Capital Stock (Note)		$273,100.00	
Surplus Arising from Re-evaluation of			
Fixed Assets		14,142.88	
Retained Earnings (Deficit)		(10,709.93)	
Total Stockholders' Equity			$276,532.95
Total Liabilities and Stockholders' Equity			$403,834.53

Source: Fisher Manufacturing Company.

Statement of Income (Loss)
for the Six Month Period Ended December 31, 1963

Income:
Sales	$264,367.15	
Less: Sales Returns and Allowances	5,599.23	
Net Sales		$258,767.92
Cost of Sales		$233,175.08
Gross Profit on Sales		$ 25,592.84

Operating Expenses:		
Factory Selling Expenses	$ 10,392.74	
Factory General Expenses	12,624.64	
Operating Expenses	30,722.73	
Total Operating Expenses		$ 53,740.11
Net Loss from Operations		($ 28,147.27)
Other Income:		
Discounts Earned	$ 2,781.10	
Interest and Carrying Charges	2,108.41	
Miscellaneous	221.94	
Total Other Income		$ 5,111.45
Net Loss before Other Deductions		($ 23,035.82)
Other Deductions:		
Interest		$ 2,536.95
Net Loss for the Period		($ 25,572.77)

Source: Fisher Manufacturing Company.

Projected Statement of Income for the Year Ended June 30, 1964
(At June 30, 1963)

		Amounts		Percent to Sales
Sales			$838,000.00	100.00%
Cost of Goods Sold:				
Direct Material		$603,600.00		72.01%
Direct Labor		38,100.00		4.56%
Factory Overhead:				
Indirect Labor	$16,850.00			
Overtime Premium	10,700.00			
Factory Supplies	11,800.00			
Utilities	1,600.00			
Repair and Upkeep	3,700.00			
Employee Benefits	2,350.00			
Supervision	400.00			
Rent	7,900.00			
Engineering	5,500.00			
Depreciation	8,600.00			
Insurance	2,400.00			
Payroll Taxes	4,250.00			
Superintendent	13,000.00			
Miscellaneous	1,750.00	90,800.00		10.85%
Total Cost of Goods Sold			732,500.00	87.42%
Gross Profit on Sales			105,500.00	12.85%
Selling Expenses:				
Salesmen's Salaries & Commissions		$ 34,400.00		
Depreciation		300.00		
Insurance		825.00		
Payroll Taxes		625.00		
Salesmens' Traveling Expenses		6,275.00		

Advertising	1,175.00	
Rent	700.00	
Stationery and Printing	175.00	
Telephone	5,600.00	
Delivery Expense	1,500.00	
Miscellaneous	425.00	
Total Selling Expenses	52,000.00	6.20%
Net Profit on Sales	53,500.00	6.38%

General and Adminstrative Expenses:

Salaries	19,000.00	
Depreciation	300.00	
Insurance	425.00	
Payroll Taxes	1,150.00	
Travel and Entertainment	375.00	
Telephone	1,800.00	
Rent	375.00	
Utilities	100.00	
Repair and Upkeep	400.00	
Employee Benefits	350.00	
Engineering	625.00	
Experiments	375.00	
Professional Fees	8,500.00	
Stationery and Printing	1,025.00	
Miscellaneous	1,000.00	
Total General and Administrative Expenses	35,800.00	4.27%
Net Income from Operations	17,700.00	2.11%

Other Income:

Discounts Earned	9,000.00	1.07%
Net Income before Other Deductions	26,700.00	3.18%

Other Deductions:

Administrative Services	1,200.00	
Interest	4,500.00	
Total Other Deductions	5,700.00	.68%
Net Income for the Year	$21,000.00	2.50%

Source: Fisher Manufacturing Company.

Projected Income Statements for Fiscal Years Ending June 30
(Thousands of Dollars)
(At June 30, 1963)

	1964	1965	1966	1967
Sales	$838	$3,000	$4,500	$5,500
Cost of Goods Sold (80%)	670	2,400	3,600	4,400
Gross Profit on Sales (25%)	168	600	900	1,100
Selling Expense (7.5%)	63	225	338	412
Net Profit on Sales (12.5%)	105	375	562	688
Gen. and Adm. Expense (2.5%)	21	75	112	138
	84	300	450	550

Less Expense for New Plant	61	—	—	—
Net Income before Taxes	24	300	450	550
Taxes	12	150	225	275
Net Profit after Taxes	$ 12	$ 150	$ 225	$ 275

Source: Fisher Manufacturing Company.

The Anatomy of a Price-Fixing Conspiracy

This is the case history of a price-fixing conspiracy. It took place in a small industry in a middle-sized town, but it has the same characteristics as conspiracies recently uncovered and made public that operated nationally and in major industries.

It is not worth notice simply because it operated in violation of the law, or because it is unusual. Federal antitrust enforcers acknowledge that conspiracies of this type probably function in dozens of industries and dozens of cities around the nation. Antitrust agents simply are not equipped to uncover them. Price-fixing conspiracies, after all, are conducted in secret.

But this case is noteworthy because price-fixing is a subject not often openly discussed. There is little understanding about what a price conspiracy is, even less about what goes into the start of a "fix" and what factors lead to its demise. This story is presented with the thought that better understanding of what makes otherwise honest businessmen take part in an illegal activity will benefit both the business community and the government agencies that watch out for such things.

Reprinted from the September 8, 1962 issue of *Business Week*, pp. 72–73, by special permission. Copyright © 1961 by McGraw-Hill, Inc.

Setting the Scene

The industry involved here is ready-mixed concrete; the area, a medium-sized industrial city where construction has boomed for the last 15 years. The conspiracy is not operating now, but many of the factors that led up to its inception are appearing again. It could start up any day.

As it happens, the ready-mix industry is vulnerable to price-fixing. It is essentially a local business; trucks can haul wet concrete within a radius of only 15 miles or so. It is a retail business — ready-mix producers, like supermarkets, set prices largely by what competition is charging. It is an easy industry to enter. A smart operator with a good credit line can set up a "portable" plant for only a few thousand dollars.

In the city where this story takes place there are more than a dozen competitors now. They have the typical small-business weakness of inadequate accounting facilities. Producers usually don't really know how much it costs them to sell, mix, and haul a yard of concrete, so prices often have no relation to costs.

High Overhead

It is an industry with high overhead costs. A truck fleet must be maintained to meet peak demand, and trucks cost up to $24,000 each. Volume is subject to extreme seasonal fluctuations. There is little business in winter, and in summer a couple of days of rain can transform a highly profitable week into a dismal one. It takes as much manpower to run a plant waiting for the weather to break, or waiting for contractors to get jobs ready to pour, as it does to man a plant operating full-tilt for a 15-hour day.

It is an industry of many small companies — this town's largest ready-mix producer grosses under $1-million a year. Producers and their principal customers, the contractors, are often good friends. Each producer knows what big jobs his competitors have.

Sighting a competitor's truck heading in the direction of one of his own big jobs causes momentary panic in a producer, and he'll give chase to find out where the truck is going. Contractors can be prima donnas and, almost on whim, cancel a big order from one producer and give it to another, with two quick phone calls.

The Fix

Ready-mix producers in this town decided late in 1959 to "stabilize" their prices at $14.50 a yard. The "fix was on" for about 18 months. Last year, distrust among competitors led to its breakdown.

The price, even while fixed, was not unreasonable; in some areas, concrete regularly sells for $16 or $17 a yard. But the factors that led up to the conspiracy, and to its end, make a fascinating story.

Postwar Experience

Prior to World War II, this town had only a couple of producers, and only one of them, Smith, had a sizable operation. In those days, ready-mix was not as popular as it is now but each producer had a good business.

The postwar building boom made ready-mix more popular. In the late 1940s, producer Jones set up a sizable plant. There still was plenty of business for the first producer; indeed, contractors had to schedule pouring weeks ahead. If it happened to rain on your day, tough luck — get in line again.

Big contractors avoided this bottleneck by setting up their own concrete plants and buying transit-mix trucks. New competitors moved in, too.

By the mid-1950s, the building boom had slacked off. The independents were scratching for business. The contractor-owned producers, finding themselves with excess capacity, also were bidding for outside jobs. Since their overhead was at least partially absorbed by the larger contracting business, they could afford to go in with low prices. Prices weakened and, by the time the 1958 recession hit, nobody was making any profit.

Trade Group Action

For some years, producers had sponsored a local trade association that served as a clearing house for credit ratings and worked on quality control. As prices plummeted, producers began to wonder if they could gain price stability through the association. All those who showed up for an association meeting in the fall of 1959 were disgruntled about prices, and when one of the small producers suggested it might be time to "stabilize," they were ready.

They all knew that Smith, still the largest, would have to agree before the fix could work. They quickly hit on $14.50 because that was the price that had been "stabilized" in a nearby metropolitan area. Then, over drinks in a hotel room, they haggled for more than five hours how to do it, how to enforce it, how to avoid going to jail.

Ethical Qualms

The thought of price-fixing went against the grain for most of the participants, though there was some debate as to whether such an agreement was legal or not. They concluded that it was not. But prices were weakening by the day, and their practical decision, somewhat over-dramatized, was that they'd rather go to jail than starve. There was no effort to hit upon a system of bid rotations, because this practice was viewed as an out-and-out illegality.

"It was sort of like the difference between getting a ticket for parking and a ticket for speeding," says one.

It was probably this reluctance that eventually led to the end of the fix.

Administering Prices

The new price became effective in a couple of weeks. Jobs already contracted for were protected; each producer drew up a list of these protected jobs that was put in a sealed envelope and filed, to guard against later accusations of price-cutting.

A three-man "enforcement" committee also was appointed, but for the first several months it had little work to do. The association met weekly and reviewed "I know where I can get it cheaper" complaints from contractors. There were few charges of claim-jumping among producers themselves and, for the first year or so, the enforcement committee conducted only a couple of investigations into the alleged price-cutting. Producers were building trust among themselves, and the fix was, in fact, working well. Prices were "stabilized."

In practice, the committee could do little to enforce the price, as became obvious when the fix started to fall apart. Enforcement was based on personal relationships. If a rumor got about that a price had been cut, the suspected offender got a phone call from a member of the committee, who suggested that he stop. Says one participant: "I reckon everybody had some deals going, but they were all kept pretty quiet."

One producer, invited to lunch by a committee member, was charged with cutting his price on a big job. He had the foresight to bring with him his purchase order, proving he had not.

The Falling-Out

After more than a year, Smith claimed he was losing jobs. He accused his smaller competitors of "chiseling." Maybe they were, maybe not; at any rate, they had become more aggressive and were selling harder.

There was no doubt that "deals" were worked out. A producer with excavating equipment, for example, would hold the price on concrete but give a lower bid for excavation work. Concrete forms, which contractors usually must rent or buy, were thrown in free. Discounts were offered on other supplies.

But there were two effective pressures against admitting to price-cutting: (1) producers did not want to be known as "chiselers," and (2) of course, they wanted to hold the $14.50 price.

During a long, ill-tempered lunch, Smith accused Jones of cutting prices and stealing a big job. Jones denied it. Smith made a similar accusation against another smaller producer, and this producer showed a purchase order proving he did not cut. Smith accused him of giving a kickback.

Smith was not the only dissatisfied producer; by this time there was a good deal of distrust among the group. Smith was angry, but he had been considering the situation coolly, too. He finally said he was "sick of the way you all are fooling around," and announced an across-the-board cut of 50¢ a yard. Without anyone saying so, everybody knew there was no longer any price agreement. Prices dipped to close to $13.75.

Back to Free Enterprise

Business so far in 1962 has been worse than last year, and producers are making less, or losing more. Producer Jones says his profit-and-loss sheet looks worse than in 1961, when his before-tax profit was $1,250. Jones figures that when he sells concrete at $12.50 a yard, he's just covering expenses and not paying overhead, to say nothing of making a profit. He's making some sales at $12.50 right now, although maybe a slightly greater proportion of his sales now are at a higher price than last year after the price break.

For the last year or so, the association has continued to function, but not as a price-fixing vehicle. Lately, though, there has been some talk about this.

Jones' only objection to a new fix is that it probably won't work any better now than it did before. Establishment of a system of bid rotation or a central collection agency would be the only way to make it work, he feels. But he thinks producers simply would not consider rotating bids. And if a central collection agency was set up, it would mean no "deals."

Says Jones: "The only reason it worked for as long as it did before is because everybody had their deals going."

But things are tough. "Probably half of us are hanging on from day to day," says Jones. "And the more jobs you sell at $12, the worse it gets. I suppose the only way out of this fussin' is for some of the bigger men to buy up some of the smaller ones and either put them out of business or run them part-time."

Bibliography

Andrews, K. R. "Can the Best Corporations Be Made Moral?" *Harvard Business Review,* 51 (May 1973), 57–64.

Brock, B. "Place of Competition among National Goals," *Conference Board Record,* 8 (November 1971), 6–13.

Buchan, P. B. "Corporate Risk Policies," *Management Advisor,* 10 (September 1973), 45–51.

"Church and Office Bridge a Gap." *Business Week,* September 26, 1970, p. 52.

Duerr, M., and F. F. Randall. "Special Goals for Private Business: An International Survey." *Conference Board Record,* 8 (March 1971), 27–30.

Fuller, R. M. "Business Ethics: Present and Future." *Personnel Administration,* 34 (September 1971), 48–55.

Goodman, C. S., and C. M. Crawford. "Young Executives: A Source of New Ethics?" *Personnel Journal,* March 1974, pp. 180–187.

Guth, W. D. "Strategies for Research in Policy Formulation." *Journal of Business,* 46 (October 1973), 499–511.

Hayes, D. A. "Management Goals in a Crisis Society." *Michigan Business Review,* 22 (November 1970), 7–11.

"Most Americans Believe Business Has a Social Conscience, Opinion Research Study Shows." *Advertising Age,* August 31, 1970, p. 42.

Palmer, H. B. "New Imperatives for Tomorrow's Policy Makers." *Conference Board Record,* 7 (January 1970), 68–72.

Tosi, H. L., et al. "Setting Goals in Management by Objectives." *California Management Review,* 12 (Summer 1970), 70–78.

Part Nine
Public Relations and the Corporate Image

As business operates in a free enterprise economy, it forms interdependent relationships with specific groups. In terms of society at large, the general public is the regulator of the system and of the individual firms composing it. The actions of business people individually and collectively are constantly appraised by society and by the various institutions operating within it. Good community relations have always been important to business, and for the larger business firm, the community may well become the state, the nation, or even the international community.

Business deals with many publics, and in these relationships often "wears many hats." That is, business tends to assume a different posture toward various interest groups while developing a coherent public image that reflects its objectives and policies. The publics to whom business most frequently addresses itself are its stockholders, customers, related business firms with whom it deals, employees, influential interest groups, and government agencies at the local, state, and national level. In dealing with these various publics business must perform a vast array of voluntary tasks, such as giving financial assistance and managerial leadership to civic drives and programs.

A. The Corporate Image

Business is concerned with a variety of interest and pressure groups in society because of their influence upon the environment in which the corporation must operate. In order to deal effectively with these groups business has attempted to develop a complex and integrated corporate image. This image provides a means of maintaining uniformity and consistency in those basic company practices and policies that affect the success of the firm in the eyes of its publics. In "The Corporate Image in Public Relations" [34] Richard Eells advocates the development of a multi-faceted corporate image that would relate the corporation to its social environment while simultaneously serving corporate objectives. This would entail the assignment of priorities to corporate goals and the formulation of policies to insure their achievement. To accomplish this task, management must identify and establish a hierarchy of important — or "key" — publics and determine the variety of roles, interests, and pressures they represent. The function of defining the corporate image then becomes a process of formulating policies and statements that effectively interrelate corporate objectives and key publics.

Public relations experts often advise that the corporate image represent the philosophy, character, and personality of the corporation. By-and-large the real image of the corporation will be determined by its standard business practices, not by official speeches, or published statements on company policy. However, this does not diminish the value of company policies to the process of decision making. Company policies, when used as a guide, provide managerial control over actions and decisions made by individuals within each department throughout the organization.

The article "How Business Faces a Hostile Climate" [35] supports the importance of public relations policies in the development of a corporate image. Business has encountered an increasing number of protest groups, in the seventies. These encounters have revealed a variety of credibility gaps that have prompted business to search for an identity that can be reconciled with its publics. The article recommends that policy be substituted for publicity as a means of solving the corporate image problem. A climate of mistrust has developed in the educated public and as a result, business has lost face with many institutional groups in society. And business has very often become the scapegoat or target for this discontent. While many of the tactics of these publics may seem unfair, there are nevertheless many legitimate complaints that must be resolved. In spite of large, sophisticated public relations departments the company stands or falls on what it does rather than what it says. With recent debates over environmental problems, public relations has become engaged in a war of press releases that in itself is very dangerous.

It is significant to note that *Business Week* strongly urges less talk and more action, and that policies are the first step in determining what these actions will be. The article advises businesses to reform their tarnished images and to direct actions with policy guidelines in the development of an image that can stand the credibility tests of society. A final point, which may serve as a starting point in the redefinition of the corporate image, may be the concept of "social rent" proposed by Coca Cola's chairman, J. Paul Austin. He contends that his company is dedicated to paying a social rent in meeting its responsibilities to society. If business does not give social responsibility and public acceptability adequate consideration, Austin contends that sooner or later there may not be any business to operate.

The Heartland Gas Company case presents a composite of the various publics to whom a company may respond. In this case, a public utility relates its overall company objectives to the programs and activities of each department, and each component to its various publics. This case illustrates the necessity of formulating corporate policies to insure consistent action among departments in order to create an integrated corporate image.

B. Corporate Philanthropy

Today's community organizations frequently enlist the support and expertise of business managers. Business people often volunteer their services in support of community projects. As an integral part of the community, business management has a legitimate place in defining and supporting community goals. They also have a unique contribution to make to community projects by providing managerial know-how and experienced leadership.

Community needs are articulated in an ever-increasing number of ways. Among the traditional appeals made to business by the community are requests for financial contributions to public and private programs relating to community welfare. Community solicitation for funds is increasing as the number of sponsoring organizations and programs grow. While the legality of corporate philanthropy has already been resolved in court, the question of business giving or philanthropy as an advisable corporate act is nevertheless debatable. Corporate managers must establish criteria for selecting recipients, the determination of appropriate amounts and types of gifts, and the relationship of corporate giving to overall corporate objectives and policies.

In "A Philosophy for Corporate Giving" [36] Richard Eells contends that corporate giving must be directly related to corporate objectives. He argues that responsible managers must provide a sound rationale for donative management, following a "prudential" theory of corporate giving. He rejects the concept that corporate giving be based solely on philanthropic principles and argues that good business practice — or prudential decision making — guide managers in their donative policies. By relating financial contributions to the long-term goals and profits of the business, business can then more effectively justify these contributions to stockholders. Eells recommends that managers consider each donative proposal in light of specific company objectives.

While the corporate giving function of business philanthropy is perhaps the major one performed by business today, business is also undertaking other types of philanthropic activities. This is especially true in the seventies where the increasing demands for business involvement in social problems has resulted in experimentation on the part of business. The article "The Role of Philanthropy in Social Progress" [37] considers the significant philanthropic role of business in its total sense. Dana Creel reviews the history of philanthropy over centuries, identifying its primary function as that of rendering service and altering institutions by individual participation from the private sector of our society. He acknowledges the necessary interplay of the public and the private sector in a pluralistic society, but also recognizes the increasing number of responsibilities taken over by the private sector in recent years.

In the United States the basic services of health, education, and welfare were originally the primary responsibility of philanthropic funds, and it was not until following World War II that the public sector became engaged in these activities more significantly than the private sector. Mr. Creel is particularly concerned that the 1969 Tax Reform Act would reduce the incentives for philanthropic giving and increase restrictions on the private sector, especially the foundations. He suggests that our social problems are so complex that government, corporations, and philanthropic organizations especially foundations, must all cooperate in attacking the problems because of their increased scope and complexity. He also hopes that the corporation will provide leadership roles as it has in the past, not only in the corporate giving function, but also in its role of resolving social issues and influencing social institutions. He would envision greater cooperation in the future between government, business, and philanthropy in dealing with social problems, and is hopeful of a recent trend toward governmental activities at the local and state levels of government.

The concept of corporate philanthropy identifies the responsibility of business for both carrying its fair share of the financial burden in the form of corporate giving and performing leadership roles in resolving social problems. The participation of business with government and foundations, can help to maintain a balance between the private and public sectors in a free society. If this balance is not maintained, freedoms must certainly erode.

The Hanley Engineering Corporation case provides a specific example of the practical problems involved in corporate donative decision making. A manager must consider the relationship of a community adult education program to the long-range goals of the corporation as well as the influence of a personal friend conducting the fund drive. The priority of different public appeals made to the corporation for donations and the ability of the corporation to commit itself to future donations are also factors that the manager must carefully weigh in the decision to support the drive. These questions require an explicit and complete corporate policy that can be applied to all community appeals. If a policy is not formulated, the company will be subject to inconsistencies in making donative decisions in the future.

In conclusion, the variety of requests and demands from many publics require business to define corporate policies for handling these demands consistently and equitably over time. These policies represent the many facets of the corporate personality, character, and philosophy. In fact, the basic set of policy statements of most corporations serve as their philosophies. These policies will provide the means of recognizing the many publics and evaluating the significance of their claims in relation to corporate objectives.

A   The Corporate Image

34   The Corporate Image in Public Relations
Richard Eells

Despite huge dollar outlays for corporate public relations, many public-relations programs designed to serve long-range corporate goals fall far short of the mark. Usually the basic reason is that corporate managers tend to think of public relations as a peripheral matter — rather than a major function of management. They do this because they fail to understand that the way in which a corporation relates itsef to society is vital to its existence.

The recognition of public relations as a major *function* of management, along with such well-established functions as engineering, manufacturing marketing, and finance, is fairly recent. As a unique kind of work, public relations has become specialized both as to personnel and as to major staff and operating units. In the past, unlike specialists in other functions, public-relations specialists often have had no exclusive claim on the kind of work they performed. Today their responsibilities cover specific areas which have begun to be defined by a special literature and special skill and techniques.

Broad Concept of Public Relations

The purpose of this article is to examine certain problems which the public-relations function poses for management and to suggest approaches to their resolution. Basic to this discussion is a broad concept of public relations. From the viewpoint of the board and executive management, who must conduct the corporation's affairs as more than just a profitable business operation, a broad concept of public relationships is indispensable. The institutional character of the concern, its long-range goals, its essential role in the society that nourishes it, its contributions to many different groups which, in turn, contribute to its welfare — all these are compelling for thoughtful inquiry into the public-relations function of the twentieth-century American corporation.

By public relations I mean the communication of the corporate image to key groups, both inside and outside the corporation, for two purposes: (1) to relate the corporation to its social environs, and (2) to serve the corporate objectives. This is much more than publicity through the press, radio, and television, although this is certainly a valid, if limited purpose in itself. This broad definition of public relations has many implications, of course; but two in particular have special significance for the subsequent discussion.

The first is that in order to "relate the corporation to its social environs," public-relations work must be reciprocal. A company should listen as much as it talks — perhaps more so. When the company limits itself to *sending* messages, it is engaging in but one phase of the communication process.[1] For communication means also that messages are received and responded to, and that the responses get back to the original sender, who adjusts further messages in light of these responses. Moreover, this listening needs to be continuous and systematic since both the audience responses and the media are constantly changing as a result of social and technological dynamics.

Even though a company can demonstrate a near-total recall of its messages through opinion surveys, it may not be getting its true message across. Moreover, aside from the practical necessity of knowing how its specific messages have been received, the corporation's image of itself as a social institution depends in large part upon two-way communication, as will be shown later in this paper. For the time being, however, suffice it to say that it is an egregious error on the part of

---

1 See James G. Miller, "Toward a General Theory for the Behavioral Sciences," in L. D. White (ed.), *The State of the Social Sciences,* University of Chicago Press, Chicago, 1956, pp. 29–65, on the "diffusion function" and "information transfer"; Colin Cherry, " 'Communication Theory' — and Human Behavior," in Ayer, Haldane, *et al., Studies in Communication,* Martin Secker & Warburg, London, 1955, pp. 45–67; B. L. Smith, H. D. Lasswell and R. D. Casey, *Propaganda, Communication and Public Opinion: A Comprehensive Reference Guide,* Princeton University Press, Princeton, 1946, with four essays on the science of mass communication; and Warren Weaver, "Recent Contributions to the Mathematical Theory of Communication," in C. E. Shannon and W. Weaver, *The Mathematical Theory of Communication,* University of Illinois Press, Urbana, Illinois, 1949.

management to assume that it is "adequate" communication to achieve the apparent conversion of the listener.

The second implication is that a company's public-relations program must do more than relate the organization to its social environs; it must serve the corporate objectives. In order to do this, management must define the corporation's own broad economic and political goals as concretely as possible. Thus, a broad concept of public relations must unfold in a two-step process:

1. Identifying the *real* corporate goals in their order of priority; and
2. Translating these goals into effective policies and programs that will communicate and relate the corporation to the Greater Society in terms of these goals.

Without these two steps, taken sequentially, public-relations work will inevitably continue to be either haphazard, or in accordance with preconceived personal notions of corporate public-relations managers, or of external public-relations agencies.

There are many possible ways of stating a company's objectives.[2] When well done, the objectives will take into account all the major groups of people — or "publics" — with which a company carries on relations, and the major purposes of its relationships with those publics.

Public-relations and executive managers should keep in mind, however, that the published objectives of a company will never reflect all of the goals and values of the corporation as an institution nor of its management as human beings. For example, the goals of influence and strength are never explicitly mentioned objectives. These, however, are objectives of every going concern as basic as are wealth, well-being, skill, enlightenment, respect, rectitude, and affection. (This list of goals, incidentally, is representative of the goals that men hold universally, though of course with considerable variation in priority from person to person, place to place, and from one point of time to another.)

For every business organization, then, a key purpose should be to translate corporate goals into realistic public-relations policies that successfully project the desired corporate image to all the company's publics.

Defining the Corporate Image

One major problem in projecting a favorable and consistent corporate image is the difficulty corporate managers themselves have in perceiving the corporation in terms of twentieth-century social beliefs,

---

[2] See Stewart Thompson, *Management Creeds and Philosophies,* American Management Association, New York, 1958.

expectations, and promises. Thus the image they themselves have and the image they project is anything but clear and meaningful. Frequently the managers' inability to see themselves and their company as people on the outside see them, compounds the difficulty.

Each manager sees his corporation in terms of his own "operational code," which includes his system of values (i.e., what he wants, what he believes is good, and what he wants to achieve). More importantly for his view of the corporation, his code includes how he sees the world in which his company operates. Unfortunately, as Herbert Simon points out, "The limit of human understanding of complex social structures leads human beings to construct simplified maps (i.e., theories or models) of the social system in which they are acting, and to behave as though the maps were the reality." [3]

The complex social structure, of which one's company is a part, cannot be seen or felt directly in all of its implications; the manager must rely upon inherited maps, and theories. From these, the manager forms his own image of the corporation as a social institution. Some of the maps, and thus the corporate image in the managerial mind, are exceedingly realistic and usable for short excursions into the immediate corporate environment and for specific functional tasks, such as marketing a product or recruiting equity capital. For the wider-ranging journeys which public relations entails, the maps may be disastrously misleading. Long-term planning for the company and assessment of the social, political, and economic trends of the human environment require models different from those managers are likely to have at their disposal.

For example, the notion that the "proper" relationship between the corporation and its socio-political environment is one of laissez-faire, as defined in classical economics, has long persisted. Such models have permeated the literature which businessmen were taught to respect in their college courses. Today, these models are probably more widely accepted among corporate executives than the more recent and more realistic models proposed by contemporary economic theorists who deal with changed conditions, both in public and in business administration.

Many policy-makers have inherited and try to apply time-bound concepts not only of the nation-state and of public government, but also of private enterprise itself. This makes for unrealistic and often inconsistent perception of the corporation on management's part; and, since the policies of management affect the public's image of the corporation, it is not surprising to find that the corporate image held by the corporation's key publics may also be confused. Their image of business is confused because it mirrors inconsistencies in the minds and behavior of the men who manage the business enterprise.

For example, the attitude "no other world but our company"

---

[3] Herbert A. Simon, "Comments on the Theory of Organization," *American Political Science Review,* Vol. 46, No. 4, December, 1952, p. 1135.

may lead to *company policies* opposed to *national policies* of tariff abatement, even though such national policies may make for firmer alliances with countries oriented toward the West and nations still uncommitted in the world struggle. In the same vein of internal inconsistencies, there are those who claim that the sole and exclusive purpose of the corporation is economic, so that management is apparently obliged to maximize profits to the exclusion of all other considerations. Some managers, however, who take this position with great zeal will exhibit equal zeal in undertaking defense contracts that yield little or no profit to the company on the ground that such is the duty of a good corporate citizen. These apparent inconsistencies can be solved, but not without a philosophy of business on which to formulate a realistic theory of public relations.

This emphasis on the necessity for management to be aware of its social role and of the publics' view of that role should not be construed to mean that all companies are duty-bound to identify with larger spheres of interest — community-wide, national, or international. On the contrary, in a system such as ours, in which diversity is regarded as a necessary condition of a free society, a business corporation, no matter how large, cannot permit its image to become frayed at the edges and fused with the image of society as a whole.

The business corporation must maintain a distinct individuality, a high degree of integrity, and great flexibility in order to withstand the constant pressures on its growth which, if unrelieved, so frequently and so easily lead to state intervention and finally, state control. Accurate knowledge and realism in evaluating the goals, aspirations, needs, and activities of others outside the corporate "island" are consistent with a forthright stand in favor of corporate self-interest and indeed are essential to managements' realistic perception of the corporate image. Diffuse and equivocal policy-making arises in part from lack of such knowledge.

If management is to project an image that is unique, timely, internally consistent, and meaningful to the publics at which it is directed, it must itself have such an image.

In short, management's own image of the corporation must rest ultimately on an accurate and penetrating analysis of the corporate environment. Thus the two-way communication mentioned earlier is important not only for testing the effectiveness of specific public-relations programs, but also for formulating the basic corporate image which guides policy.

Publics Shape the Corporate Environment

The large corporation has many publics with which communication must be maintained. To identify these publics and determine their characteristics is important to management for two reasons: (1) the publics shape the corporation's attitudes and dynamics which should affect management's own image of the corporation; and (2) in order to project this image effectively, once management has defined it, corporations must know the predictions of the groups with which they maintain relations. Selecting the publics is an important element of public-relations policy. Too narrow a view of corporate interests in the complex environment may impair the effectiveness of public-relations programs by unduly limiting the publics. Yet, some lines must be drawn. Occasionally there may be a tendency to exclude certain publics for budgetary reasons with the plausible argument that those excluded are too remote from the affairs of business. Or there may be confusion as to the meaningful categories of publics for public relations as distinguished from other kinds of functional work within the organization as a whole.

There are three possible approaches which management can take in trying to pinpoint its publics. The *first* would be to identify and separate internal and external publics or groups. The *second* would be to identify the publics or groups by the roles individuals play in their life situations. The *third* would be to identify the publics or groups by their direct or indirect contributions to the corporation and their claims upon it.

If we classify publics by the first method (internal and external groups), certain difficulties arise. In our classification scheme we would include such typical groups as employees, unions, management, customers, share owners, suppliers, competitors, distributors, dealers, and so on — groupings that obviously bear directly on the nature of the enterprise. Obviously, the membership of some of these groups overlap. For example, employees are members of the internal company "team," but they are also members of an external organization that bargains collectively with management. As the latter, they may sometimes be identified in the minds of some managers with an adversary interest, but, as employees, elaborate efforts are made to identify them with "the company." Does their union constitute a public for the purpose of public-relations work? And how is this kind of work to be integrated with "union relations"?

Special problems with wide social implications and with very immediate implications for public-relations programs arise when employees are regarded as a part of the formal organization of the company. It has been argued that the company's demands upon them, as a part of the formal organization, may be quite out of line with their needs as well-integrated and healthy persons, as individuals.[4] The formal

---

[4] See Chris Argyris, *Personality and Organization*, Harper, New York, 1957, p. 233.

organization itself, as well as directive leadership by management (as distinguished from "democratic leadership"), tight management controls, and "human-relations" programs are said to be devices that managers use to heighten the employees' feeling that they are part of the "team" in order to increase their productivity.

In its relations with unions, on the other hand, management hardly seeks identity of interests, at least not in the same sense. It will seek a common ground for determining policies as to wage structures, working conditions, benefits, and the like; but it will resist attempts on the part of a union to encroach upon "management prerogatives" and thus to identify itself with the company as an institution.

To some extent, the second approach (identifying publics by listing roles that people play), is an improvement on simply separating internal and external publics. An inventory of publics by this method would include people in their roles as: members of the national community; citizens, voters, and constituents; customers, share owners, employees, and suppliers; members of the press; members of educational groups; leaders and members of religious groups; members of governmental agencies; members of industry and trade organizations; members of service organizations; members of professional and scientific societies; members of fraternal, cultural, and ethnic associations.

This listing makes the assumption that a company may have a relationship with the same individual in various ways, through the various roles he plays in his life situations. Every person plays many roles and each of these roles carries with it definite attitudes, beliefs, customs, codes, manners, aspirations. In order to communicate successfully with its publics by reaching people in their various roles, a company must acquire a working knowledge of the characteristics of these roles. To be able "to listen" to people, as well as "to speak" to them through media, a corporation must direct its antennae in a number of directions. Role listing provides a clue to these directions.

The third approach identifies the publics in terms of their contributions to and claims on the enterprise. Many directly or indirectly contribute their effort, time and substance to the establishment and growth of the corporation. For this reason, many lay claim to the fruits of its productivity.

Four general categories of *direct* contributor-claimants can be identified, and these are almost universally recognized as such in current thought about the modern business corporation. They consist of the corporation's security holders, its customers, its employees, and its suppliers. Each of these groups expects the corporation to meet specific kinds of responsibilities and each, in turn owes specific duties.

Four *indirect* claimant groups can be identified: competitors in the business community; local communities; the general public; and governments (local, state, and federal).

This third approach to defining publics has great merit because it is the only one which permits management to identify and evaluate specific contributions and claims made by the various groups. By such identification and evaluation, management can sharpen its perception of its responsibilities to these various publics. Once corporate social responsibility has been established, it becomes integral to the goals of the corporation, thus taking on more tangible meaning for those who must portray the corporate image in terms of corporate goals.

In practice, an eclectic approach — taking the best from all three approaches to fit existing company organization — would probably be the most effective way for companies generally to identify their various publics and thus to modify and supplement the "social maps" which in such large measure affect management's own images of their companies.

Coordination of "Communicating-Activities"

Another important aspect of relating the corporation to its social environment is that relationships with key publics are maintained in countless ways other than through publicity releases from the public-relations department. Thus, if the corporate image in the public eye is not to be confused and contradictory, all those activities which establish relationships with any group must be coordinated. So extensive and complex are the relationships of a corporation with publics that a more nearly accurate term (if we exclude relationships with groups of people within the corporation) would be "external relations" — one variation of the term that nation-states use to distinguish problems of foreign policy from those of domestic policy. Why would it not be wise for the large corporation to have a "Department of External Affairs" which would be responsible for all activities establishing relationships with the outside?

The idea is tempting. But it overlooks the hard fact that external relations are infinitely varied, complex, and comprehensive. They involve marketing, supply, legal relations, financial relations, and a host of others. To merge all of these functional kinds of external relations into a single organizational unit is manifestly impossible. Nation-states are not able to do it, as witness the corps of attachés in foreign embassies — each of the attachés being responsible not to the foreign office but to some other department of the home government. One might add that, in this age of pressure toward people-to-people contacts across international frontiers, the attempt by governmens to funnel all such contacts through state departments and foreign offices becomes increasingly impracticable.

Foreign policy, the cynics say, is the art of influencing other nations to your own nation's ends. Corporation public-relations policy, by analogy, could be said to be the art of influencing external groups of interest to corporate ends.

Neither the policies of states nor those of corporations may be so cynical as all this, but the instruments of policy remain the same and they do exhibit striking similarities. The instruments of foreign policy include arms, economic measures, diplomacy (negotiation and agreement), and communication through mass media and other channels (government-to-people). The instruments of corporation policy — in its external relations with various groups in the environment — include legal measures, economic measures, negotiation and agreement, and communication through mass media and other channels (corporation-to-people). The application of all these instruments contributes to the corporate image held by the world outside.

To get an overview of the entire range of external relations of the corporation (on which there is practically no literature today) would require a systematic survey of all the ways in which particular companies use all these instruments. Such a survey would undoubtedly show that some companies make inadequate use of some of these instruments and that few indeed coordinate their application with singleness of purpose. This coordination is a top-management responsibility and can be called the "relations" function in its broadest sense.

But the question arises whether top management is properly equipped to undertake this coordination. Usually it is not, for top management often lacks the information necessary for it to adjust its own corporate image to the needs and wants of its social environment and to see the cause-and-effect relationships between that environment and the instruments of policy. It is not sufficient to insist, as is often done, that the necessary staff exists, but is distributed among various departments and committees. It is undoubtedly true that every specialized department has its own antennae out to the pertinent environmental forces that affect its particular kind of work. What is often lacking, however, is a synthesis. Even in the larger corporation there is no systematic effort made to synthesize public-relations "intelligence" with all corporate activities. Such a synthesis would present a unified picture to executive management of the *changing role of the company as seen from the outside.* After the synthesis, the next step would be a follow-up to determine whether the appropriate policy decisions had been made throughout the company. Instead, there is usually a mass of unrelated reports on external relations of all sorts that are circulated to many desks at various times. The mass of reports is never processed as a whole or acted upon as a whole, nor indeed is it ever intended to be acted upon as a whole.

This problem is not peculiar to the corporation. The intelligence operations of governments also appear to fail notoriously in the critical act of integrating the necessary information needed by policy-makers at top-executive and legislative levels. Continuous failure to solve this problem for any nation could mean a national disaster. Failure to solve it in the corporation could have a direct bearing upon its survival as an institution.

Where, then, do the public-relations specialists fit into this broad concept of public relations? Public-relations specialists should properly be the specialists on communication as a potent instrument in all aspects of corporate policy, and not just specialists in the use of mass media. As specialists, their task should be both to counsel executive management in the work of coordinating all the relationships which the corporation has with various publics and to advise company specialists (in marketing, finance, legal work, manufacturing, etc.) on adjusting to the corporate environment in the interest of advancing such types of work.

In order to accomplish these tasks, public-relations specialists should be knowledgeable in:

1. The identity and characteristics of all the key publics toward which company messages are to be directed and from which messages are to be received.
2. The content and purpose of these messages, with special attention to the things that should be said and done in public view by persons and components acting on behalf of the company.
3. The corporate image, not only as it appears in the minds of the key publics toward which company messages are directed and from which messages are received, but also as it operates upon the minds of company personnel in their decision making in all kinds of external relations.
4. The most effective media or channels to be used for communicating with the key publics, not excluding the possible effect of unintended messages sent out from the company in the form of activities that are not usually considered to be public-relations work.
5. The effects of outwardly directed messages upon these key publics, measured not only in terms of their verbal responses, their opinions and attitudes, but also their actions with respect to matters of concern to all decision makers in every kind of functional work throughout the company.[5]

---

[5] The literature of this field is growing rapidly, as indicated in the bibliographical works: Smith, Lasswell and Casey, (note (1) above) and Bruce Lannes Smith and Chitra Smith, *International Communication and Political Opinion: A Guide to the Literature,* Princeton University Press, Princeton, 1956. A concise diagrammatic statement of the elements in the communication process by W. Phillips Davison and Alexander L. George is available in "An Outline for the Study of International Political Com-

Since some decisions in public relations obviously deal with highly technical matters (e.g., choice of media, content analysis, etc.) there is always danger that public relations, for this reason, will be regarded as peripheral to the central issues of business policy. This is far from the truth. The choice of key publics, for instance, may profoundly affect the growth and even the survival of the corporation. To cite a single illustration: to exclude government officials from a list of key publics could be a vital error, especially in an age of mounting governmental regulation of business at every level of public government.

Because the "fit" of the corporation into the prevailing social norms depends upon managerial decisions in all functional fields and not just upon the activities of the public-relations department, a corollary function of public-relations departments, then, would be to keep a watchful eye upon relationships of the entire organization with the public. The specialists would alert the entire organization to public-sensed deviations from standards of performance set by general company objectives. Feedback of opinion polling may be highly useful in developing a new set of premises for future policy decisions in various functional areas. It may be used also, of course, for policy-making in public-relations work with respect to informational output, or "selling" the company.

Some may object that this is too comprehensive a function to require of the public-relations specialist. Perhaps this is asking too much because of the way public-relations work is sometimes organized and staffed, and, especially, in view of the relatively subordinate role the public-relations specialist plays in the operation of many firms. But the answer is simple. The function is of vital importance to the large corporation. If one prefers to attach the public-relations label only to those who perform the more modest role of proclaiming the virtues of the company, then another name must be found for this broader function.

To summarize briefly, then, in order to communicate a meaningful image of the corporation to its key publics, somewhere in the organization someone must perform the broad "intelligence" function of sensing the social climate in which the corporation operates. This is necessary both to management's defining a realistic corporate image and to the effective communication of that image. The success of the projection of that image depends also on how well management is able to coordinate company activities that produce an image in the public eye as a by-product with the specific public-relations function which has as its major goal the projection of the corporate image.

munication," in Wilbur Schramm (ed.), *The Process and Effects of Mass Communication,* University of Illinois Press, Urbana, 1954, pp. 433–443, applying the general principles expounded by Schramm in his article on "How Communication Works" in the same volume, pp. 3–26.

Once executive management appreciates this broader view of public relations as an aspect of communication and as an instrument of corporate policy, many of the current public-relations practices and programs of corporations may well be headed for the junk-pile.

35 How Business Faces a Hostile Climate

Business Week

"Businessmen have been treated like folk heroes," says Ralph E. Ablon, chief executive officer of Ogden Corp. "The public thought of them as Horatio Alger characters when they didn't deserve it. Now people are finding out that businessmen have somewhat clay-like feet, and are basically in the business of looking out for themselves and are doing it rather well."

The fall from grace that Ablon so accurately describes has been swift and painful. Only five years ago, more than half the population thought of business with high or moderate approval. Today, according to polls taken by Opinion Research Corp., a clear-cut majority of 60% holds business in low esteem. Such findings are echoed by other pollsters and confirmed in soundings by the American Management Assn. itself. In a research study published at the end of last month, the AMA reported that nearly two out of three industrial companies feel they have serious corporate image problems.

In the face of such sudden, and sometimes passionate, unpopularity, business has been searching desperately for the proper way to react. Its first impulse was to deny heatedly the charges made against it, but it soon discovered that charges make more headlines than denials. A prime example was International Telephone & Telegraph Corp.'s assertion that it had not plotted to interfere with the seating of a new Chilean president.

Next, business often tried to paper over the cracks that had so rudely been exposed with a thin coating of public relations. But this, too, has failed to bring back the good old days of universal respect for business.

Now a number of thoughtful business leaders have begun to face up to the fact that policy, not publicity, may hold the key to their predicament. To test their thesis, they are taking steps to meet their critics more than halfway — by setting up consumer panels, for instance, or sponsoring community services.

Climate of Mistrust

None of this would have happened without the realization that business is operating in a new climate. "There was a feeling in the past that if we ran our business well, that was our only function," says John H. Filer, 47-year-old chief executive of the $4-billion Aetna Life & Casualty Co. "Never mind trying to have an impact on our society. Even today you have a broad spectrum of opinion. Milton Friedman says, 'Stick to your business and run it as efficiently and profitably as you can and others will take care of the social, community, and institutional problems.' I happen to think that you have to do both." Filer also says that the problem of business is performance, not image.

There is virtual unanimity among businessmen about the origins of their new affliction. "I think the problem of mistrust of business is that an increasingly more sophisticated and better-educated public is losing faith in all institutions," says Frank G. Harrington, vice-president for public responsibilities at INA Corp., the Philadelphia-based holding company with interests in insurance and real estate. "Things that used to be sacrosanct — like faith in the courts, or a degree from Yale or Harvard, or a clerical collar — are under attack. Our system is not working as well as we would like. The people want a better world and are dissatisfied with what their leaders are doing to get it," he adds.

Executive Resentment

Business has been a natural target of this discontent because the public sees it as part of the power structure. And modern communications have helped to increase its malaise. "We're living in an age when the big, broad gencralization receives a lot more attention than the definitive fact-finding answer," says H. Walton Cloke, vice-president for public relations and advertising for North American Rockwell

Corp. "It's easy to say that corporations pollute, for instance, and hang a tag on them. The individual doesn't have to prove anything. That kind of generalization gets a lot more attention than the detailed reply that industry gives."

Many businessmen share Cloke's resentment at what they see as unfair attacks. They feel that business has done well by America. "I keep saying that a basic good that Tenneco performs is meeting its payroll," says Nelson W. Freeman, chairman and president of the broadly based industrial company which has headquarters in Houston. "We help nearly 65,000 employees around the world earn a livelihood for themselves and their families. Their good work helps our company turn out the best products we can in the service of millions of customers. We buy from thousands of other companies, which in turn help their employees earn a living. And we pay dividends to a quarter of a million shareholders whose investment makes all this possible."

But in an age of product recalls, cost overruns, and antitrust consent decrees, the argument that business automatically benefits others — employees, customers, suppliers, and shareholders — has lost its popularity. Richard Kattel, president of Citizens & Southern National Bank in Atlanta, is nearer the mainstream when he says: "The anti-big business mood is partly our fault. I think big business has a tendency to stick its head in the ground in terms of public opinion."

Misguided

Businessmen's traditional path to influencing public opinion has been through public relations. When a crisis arose, or an executive felt it was time to let the public know something, he ordered his P.R. department to produce a press release, hoping the important newspapers and magazines would print the release exactly as it was written. Too often, the executive did not understand that almost no newspaper or magazine operates that way. The press prefers to report its own story. Some public relations men, who should have understood this, did not, or were unwilling to warn management about what would happen. Instead, P.R. men thought like management men instead of putting themselves into the shoes of editors.

In some cases, the P.R. man is actually part of the advertising or sales staff, so his prime interest is in selling products, rather than in interpreting the company's position on important social and political matters. At Bucyrus-Erie Co., a $184-million heavy equipment manufacturer, for example, the P.R. director's chief responsibility is sales promotions, and he reports to the sales department. Company President Eugene Berg believes his union and his employees are Bucyrus-Erie's main public.

Most large companies maintain separate P.R. departments,

though there is now a healthy wariness about what they can be expected to accomplish. "Public relations must get our story across, but we stand or fall on what we do," says Francis M. Barnes, senior vice-president at Crown Zellerbach Corp., a paper and timber products company based in San Francisco, which maintains a P.R. staff of eight. Barnes believes that the environmental area is particularly prone to become "a war of press releases." Eli Black, chairman of United Brands Co., is equally cautious. "Public relations, as an end to itself, is dangerous. P.R. as a constructive tool for telling a story — if there is a story to be told — is effective."

T. J. Barlow, president of Anderson, Clayton & Co., a Houston-based food and agricultural products company which has a P.R. staff of four, says: "We don't blow our horn because we just don't believe in it. We use public relations when we have something important to say." Summing up, Theodore H. Mecke, Jr., vice-president for public affairs for Ford Motor Co., points out that pure image-building is not worth the effort. "You can't do one thing and have an image of doing something else," he says. "The public perceives accurately and a company's standing reflects its actions, policies, and products."

Less Talk, More Action

Policies, in fact, are now where the action is. Many companies, especially those in the consumer goods field, are finding that the only deterrent to criticism is to meet it by changing company practices. Some corporations have gone to extraordinary lengths along these lines.

In Philadelphia, Strawbridge & Clothier, a nine-unit department store chain, has set up a series of consumer advisory boards drawn from the ranks of ordinary shoppers. Approximately every two months, a group of 12 to 15 consumers meets at the branch stores to discuss S&C's performance and make suggestions. So far, the sessions have led the company to establish Time For Tots centers in the stores at which mothers can leave their children for an hour while they shop. In response to complaints that S&C was not involved enough with the community, the company has also begun offering eight-week courses in no less than 110 subjects — ranging from gourmet cooking to karate — at a cost of $15 each. Curiously enough, S&C feels that the one trouble with the boards is that they have not been sufficiently critical.

On a similar plane, Kenneth Monfort, 44-year-old president of Monfort of Colorado, Inc., a $200-million meat processor and distributor, has appointed a Committee for the '70's to bring in outside views on his company's performance as a corporate citizen. Eight people are in the group, including a lawyer, a black, and a woman. They are paid $100 a day for expenses and have access to top company officials. To date, their suggestions have ranged from telling the company it ought to use its expertise to help smaller operators in the food chain to painting slaughterhouse walls a brighter color. The committee will meet this fall to render a final report.

Monfort himself has already decided to carry out one desirable change. He is moving his huge and pungent cattle feedlots out of range of Greeley, Colo., at a cost of $5-million. In the long run, this may free the present site for lucrative real estate development, but for now, he is acting altruistically and without community pressure. "We could sure use the $5-million somewhere else," he says, "but it was a case of realizing that the odor was getting less and less acceptable year by year."

Similarly, Boston Gas Co., the public utility branch of Eastern Gas & Fuel Associates, recently commissioned artist Corita Kent to design a painting that now covers a huge gas tank.

People Conscious

The impersonal face of modern business is much to blame for the public's jaundiced view, and one company that has taken that to heart is Aetna Life. "We used to use form letters and credit reports much more extensively than we do today," says Aetna's Filer. "But I think the public clearly wants more responsiveness from the corporations. We've spent a great deal of time and money trying to avoid rubbing the fur of individual policyholders or claimants the wrong way."

At INA, another major insurer, there is also a commitment to making the company more responsive. It has a program to rehabilitate accident victims whose cases were considered hopeless. "It's a matter of looking at people with a claim not as adversaries, but as people who are suffering. We try to build their bodies and their lives, and we've had some pretty spectacular results," says Frank Harrington, who will shortly move from running corporate affairs to a new post in charge of human relations. Fortuitously, Harrington says INA's rehabilitation efforts have actually netted the company a profit because it has helped some claimants who were thought to be totally disabled to get back to work.

Reforming an Image

One of the broadest based programs to rebuild an image with new policies is that of United Brands, which in 1969 took over United Fruit Co., the company that made the phrase "banana republic" almost an obscenity. United Fruit's ruthless exploitation of Central America so incensed the public that long after it had begun making progressive reforms its recruiters were thrown off campuses, its New York piers were bombed, and it was threatened with boycotts. At first the company tried to ignore the fuss. During the turbulent 1960s, it featured a film called *Treasure of the Tropics,* which was full of syrupy music, happy natives, and perfect bananas, but this only increased its unpopularity.

By 1969, when United Brands took it over, United Fruit was deep into extensive reform. It had built better housing for workers, raised wages, disposed of company stores, and let local farmers share some of the profits it was reaping from their countries. But the old image stuck. To help dispel it, United Fruit earmarked $25,000 for another film. The result was *Yanqui Go Home,* a brutally candid company history which ends by saying that United Fruit still has a long way to go, but at least it has made a start. "Most P.R. guys hate it because it's too frank," says Thomas McCann, a Boston consultant who handles United Fruit's P.R. "But the payoff is that people are viewing our company in light of current events rather than past history."

As further proof of its reform, United Fruit signed its first contract with Cesar Chavez' United Farm Workers when the union struck the company's extensive lettuce fields in the West. "This cost us our management. They quit because they didn't agree," says Chairman Black. "It was a very unpopular stand with the industry."

Reaching the Public

To get the news of such good deeds to the media, most companies prefer to use inside P.R. departments rather than outside agencies, even though the agencies may have wider experience and greater expertise. Banker Richard Kattel feels this makes sense because "no one on the outside can really understand the flavor and style and philosophy and commitment that this bank has without growing up in it and living in it a while." Eastern Gas & Fuel Associates President Eli Goldston says that an executive considering P.R. has a simple choice: "It's a traditional make or buy decision, and you perform a great disservice if you buy rather than make. An outside firm can only transmit outside, it can't transmit inward — and the most important function is input."

Despite these disclaimers, executives do turn to some of the country's 1,700 P.R. agencies when they need special counsel. A manufacturer in the East may want advice on setting up a plant in the South, a Midwest retailer may need help in attracting interest from Wall Street, a diversified company with many U.S. branches may decide it is time to cash in on the growing European Common Market.

Thus, Ford Motor used the P.R. department of Grey Advertising, Inc., in its recent Ford Listens Better print and broadcast campaigns, in which consumers were invited to write or call Ford's new customer service division. North American Rockwell called in Burson-

Marsteller to help its sales efforts in Western Europe because they do not yet justify setting up an inhouse facility. Banker Kattel took on New York City's Ruder & Finn when the Justice Dept. began an antitrust action over C&E's proposed merger with some smaller banks. "We needed some outside feeling on how to approach [the problem] to get the customers and stockholders to join with us in an effort to combat what Justice was saying," Kattel explains.

Social Rent

Whether they opt for internal P.R., external P.R., or a combination, a growing number of businessmen appear to think that such cosmetics are only skin deep. To help them win back the public's admiration, they are devoting more energy to finding out what the public wants.

Coca-Cola Co., for example, has jointed half a dozen other companies in commissioning a long-term survey by the Yankelovitch organization to discover how people view U.S. society and whether business can help supply their needs. Says Coke's chairman, J. Paul Austin: "This company is dedicated to paying its social rent." Elsewhere in Atlanta, Harold J. Brockey, chairman of Rich's department store, is paying for a shorter study that will look at public attitudes toward his company. At North American Rockwell, P.R. Vice-President Cloke is using an outside firm to collate all clippings and photos that mention the company to find out what they mean for NAR. In Dallas, John W. Johnson, vice-president for advertising and public relations for LTV Corp., is thinking about ways to get the business message across in universities. "Enormous influence is wielded by professors, and I think business has dropped the ball for a long time in not maintaining close relationships with campuses," Johnson says.

If these studies are translated into action, there could be a new *rapprochement* between business and the public, even though the rift today looks depressingly deep. Some businessmen, such as Colorado's Monfort, take an optimistic view. "A person with a social conscience can make a greater contribution by being in business today than in the academic field or in labor," he enthuses. "The challenge is probably even as great as being in government itself." A far larger proportion of businessmen probably share the pragmatic view of insurance man Filer, who says: "You must operate your business with public acceptability, or sooner or later you aren't going to have any business to operate."

B Corporate Philanthropy

36 A Philosophy for Corporate Giving

Richard Eells

Why do we need a rationale for corporate giving? A rationale is presumably a reasoned argument, and argument — it has been said — is a discussion that has two sides and no end. Heated argument, moreover, is something the other fellow starts. Why not avoid it all in the case of corporate giving, simply by going ahead with the giving and stopping all the argument?

The trouble is that corporate giving involves the exercise of a legal corporate power — the donative power — by directors and executive managers who are responsible for their acts, including the act of corporate giving. Individual philanthropists may be able to reject debate about their case for giving. Responsible managers are expected to explain their use of this power. The corporate donor may be an artificial person, but these managers are the real persons who decide who gets what from a corporation's funds, and they must be ready with reasons for a donative decision. The reasons constitute a rationale that is more than an explanation.

As we look back over the past decade, I think it is possible to chalk up some progress toward the development of a sound rationale for corporate giving. Today, we have a corpus of juristic rationale that pretty well settles the old argument about the donative power. For legal purposes in most jurisdictions in the United States, corporate managers do not have to show a "direct benefit" to the donor company to justify

Reprinted with permission from *The Conference Board Record,* January 1968, pp. 14–18. © The Conference Board 1968.

a corporate gift. In some jurisdictions, the door is in fact open to corporate philanthropy in the best sense of that term. As one lawyer put it:

> In the name of social need and institutional responsibility, the remnants of greed have been swept aside and the law has proclaimed that the business corporation may love humanity. Indeed, it may express its love in a most practical way — with dollars.

I do not mean to imply that the legal argument is entirely settled. Corporate counsel must always be consulted for an acceptable rationale of corporate giving as well as for specific donative programs. But in general, the donative power in corporations is well established. There are, of course, other legal questions besides corporate power to make donations, and one in particular should be noted. The famous 5% clause represents a long-standing policy of the national government that corporate giving is to be encouraged through the offer of deductions in the corporate income tax. In practice, this amounts to a 1% clause since corporations have never come through with much more than this small part of their pretax income. It had been hoped that they would do far more to aid philanthropic giving in this country. Think what it would mean if they were to do this. In 1964, the total of 5% would have come to something like $3.15 billion. Corporate pretax income that year was reported to be $63,059,000,000. Properly distributed, such an amount could aid impressively in meeting some of this nation's most serious domestic problems.

The original and continuing grounds for this Federal tax policy in favor of corporate giving have always had an important influence on the rational of corporate giving. A company is certainly justified in insisting that the corporate sector is expected to do its part in the nation's total philanthropic effort. Stockholders can be shown that the tax-deductible gift is a relatively inexpensive way to achieve some business objectives. This is not, of course, a strong element in the rationale. If corporate gifts are a good thing, the "tax bargin" does not enhance their essential wisdom and virtue. The more important argument from the stockholders' point of view is that a corporate gift affects their equity favorably — or at least not adversely.

While these juristic developments have not been the most important developments during the past decade, since most of the legal aspects of corporate giving rationale were settled in 1957, the steps taken by legislatures and courts did open the way to the most important development in the decade past.

Professional donative management has now become the order of the day in leading companies. The whole activity of corporate giving has now become an accepted part of good corporate management. The donative decision, as we are now coming to appreciate more and more, is part and parcel of the whole decision process in managing a business. It ought to be considered in that context. (Corporate giving, in other words, is now properly regarded as one of the functional kinds of work that managers do on behalf of a corporation as a business unit.) If the donative decision is an integral part of the managerial decision process in business corporations, then one must expect a rationale for corporate giving that measures up to the reasoning used for all good management practice. One of the things we expect in reasoned management is the use of observation and induction as much as possible and intuition as little as possible.

A professional attitude toward donative work has become more and more evident in recent years. This observation applies to medium-sized as well as large companies, even to some that are relatively small. Expertise is sought and insisted upon to an extent that was not generally observable ten years ago. There are specific assignments of personnel to the donative task, and this fact alone has had a lot to do with progress toward sound rationale. Assignment of the donative task to specialized company managerial or staff components is not rare. And there are, of course, the company-sponsored foundations. Altogether, there has been a rather formidable growth of professionalism in this field that is without parallel in any other country.

Volume of giving is another factor of significance to be noted during the past decade. But there has not been any great upward trend. In fact, corporate giving has been of quite modest proportions for a nation that is more prosperous than any other, is presumably the leader of the free West against the oppressive East of communism, and is expected to practice in the world arena what Professor George Liska has called "the international politics of primacy." [1]

The actual figures for corporate giving are in dispute and cannot be stated with certainty. The officially reported amount for 1964 was $729 million, but it is arguable that business giving came to a good deal more than that. Total private giving in the United States for all causes in 1966 probably came to $13.6 billion. Reported and direct corporate giving was probably 6% of that, or over $800 million. To be nearer the mark, one must add certain undisclosed and indirect non-cash corporate contributions such as gifts-in-kind, the lending of company personnel, and all the relevant administrative and other internal expense in disaster relief, and good will expenditures for charitable local causes in the course of business. If this were done, business donors would then stand higher among those who are often classified as the major philanthropic donors. Individuals' gifts for religion always overshadow all the

---

[1] George Liska, *Imperial America: The International Politics of Primacy,* The Johns Hopkins Press, Baltimore, 1967.

rest. But if these individual donors for religious purposes are set to one side it is probable that corporations and company-sponsored foundations provide from a fourth to a third of the remaining national philanthropic outlay.

A notable change during the past decade has been the *shift in corporate giving from traditional toward new fields*. There was a shift toward higher education a few years ago, and now there seems to be one toward cultural fields, notably the arts. Interpretation of the facts about this shift (admittedly we all need a better empirical basis for these judgments, but statistical methods are improving) leads to varying results. We may or may not be headed toward a basic shift in fields of corporate support. But there may turn out to have been, in retrospect, another kind of basic shift — one away from fields that draw more and more public support. Federal support of the arts is a case in point. Will the rationale of corporate giving, in view of the new national foundations in the arts and the humanities, now weaken on the necessity for strong private-sector support of these fields by corporations? My own view is that public support of the arts, now begun at last and on a most modest scale, should in no way disparage the corporate effort to strengthen this vital aspect of the corporate milieu.

But it is too soon to tell what the effect will be. One thing does seem fairly certain. The waxing and waning of public support in given fields — such as the arts, education, housing, the attack on poverty, and so on — may have a decided effect on both the trends and the rationale of corporate giving. Unless business giving is guided by wisdom, the effect could be disastrous in the vital field of education. We are headed toward the necessity of massive public financial support of the universities, for example, and here both corporate and governmental (especially Federal) support will be indispensable. The tendency to rest the case for corporate support on an attempt to prevent Federal support must therefore be resisted.

All of these major events and trends of the past decade point to the necessity of a thorough review of the whole philosophy of corporate giving.

The "Prudential" Theory of Corporate Giving

During the past decade, there have been two different approaches to this philosophy of corporate giving. Some say that the real motivation for corporate giving is and should be entirely philanthropic — done, that is to say, for the love of mankind alone, and completely as a public service. Others say that corporation giving is a matter of straight business expediency and therefore a completely self-regarding act. There are variations of these extreme positions, as well as modified views in between. There is a good deal of truth in some of these positions, but probably the whole truth in none of them.

The prudential basis of the donative rationale has always appealed to me as the most reliable one in the long run. By the prudential theory I mean that managerial reasoning for *good donative decision-making has to do with good business practice far more than with philanthropy*. Corporate giving should not, I think, be governed mainly by philanthropic principles but rather by the principles of prudent corporate management. Managers should certainly take every deduction that the law allows for gifts made from corporate funds, but these gifts are justifiable mainly because there are good reasons for such expenditures in the pursuit of a company's business objectives. The business objectives of corporations must not, of course, be narrowly limited to profit-maximization alone.

There are similarities between this theory and a general theory of prudential investment of corporate assets. Long-term benefits from wise investment — say in research and development — are certainly within the range of good and rational business practice by responsible corporate managers. Yet this term "prudential" as applied to corporate giving has been questioned on the ground that it calls up antiquated economic theory. To base corporate giving on prudential grounds, it has been argued, is to elevate the pursuit of corporate gain erroneously to the level of noble action in the public interest, much as the conventional wisdom in economics had seen the wondrous work of the invisible hand in an economy of shopkeepers.

This allegation of wrong-headed economics as the basis for a prudential theory of corporate giving is of course misdirected. A prudential theory of corporate giving is not rooted in an economics of corporate selfishness. It must be conceded, furthermore, that there is a substantial corpus of legal reasoning to substantiate managerial donative action on straight philanthropic grounds. We should all welcome this happy development. This legal reasoning can very well form a part of the rationale of corporate giving. But not the most important part. For corporate giving, which I believe to be far below what it ought to be both in dollar amounts and the things supported, ought to stand logically on its own feet. It needs to be justified in its own terms as an appropriate *corporate* function, and should not merely follow in the tail of public policy.

From this point of view, the most significant addresses of the rationale of corporate giving are the most influential sectors of the business community itself, and not public officialdom. Congress may possibly change its mind on the 5% clause. Legislators and judges might some day renege on their presently liberal views of corporate powers. But whatever happens in those quarters, corporate directors and managers must hold on to a prudential position and not let themselves back down one inch from their own businesslike reasons for extensive corporate support programs.

The prudential position, as I view it, makes no extreme claim for corporate support policy that is narrowly self-regarding, or for procedures that require a showing of probable pecuniary benefits from every corporate gift regardless of the public interest. It was never intended, when the 5% clause was introduced 30 years ago, that businessmen would forsake the profit motive and turn themselves into philanthropists. Nor was it intended, on the other hand, that they should get deductions only if they blinded themselves to any possibility of benefits. It was assumed that public interest and corporate benefit were simulanteous and reasonable ends of donative policy in corporations for profit.

There is today a rising demand for support from the private sector for urgently needed social measures in the public interest, many of which cannot be fully supported by public governments. For example, neither public support nor private investment alone can turn the trick in meeting educational needs or the needs of our cities. In a fundamental sense, the prudential theory of corporate giving necessarily merges corporate interest with public interest in a basic conception of the modern corporation and its role in our free society. There is no necessary conflict in principle between the pursuit of long-term returns to a company as a business institution in a free society, and the pursuit of public interest. "Benefit" to a company under a modern reading of the old common-law rule certainly does not exclude concurrent and long-term returns shared by business institutions generally and the environing society.

One of the most important benefits of wise business giving is the strength it lends to free institutions in the corporate environment. It seems now to be widely recognized that this is so, and I doubt that this was so ten years ago. Corporate donors are well prepared to counter the charge that we have what collectivists call a "riot of pluralism" in the American capitalistic system. Rationalizaiton of a nation's economy that merges public and private sectors completely, so that the private sector disappears, carries with it a threat of statism that has to be guarded against. For this reason, corporate giving has correctly been justified as a preventive measure, aiding the vital private institutions of our society to survive and prosper. The principle has, of course, wide application — in education, in the arts, in the sciences, in social services, in recreation, and in many other humane fields. The pluralist principle urges dispersal rather than concentration of decision centers and insists upon private-sector as well as a public-sector attack on social problems. Corporate giving on these grounds can now be brought under a rule of prudential action that yields benefits to a company through its social milieu.

As business has come to be regarded as a profession and the corporation as a major social institution of our time, there is also a strong trend toward the idea that corporate "social responsibility" demands corporate giving. It is sometimes said that this responsibility theory competes with the view of corporate giving on prudential grounds.

The prudential approach requires those who do donative work to begin with the company's purposes, its aims as a business, and to consider each donative proposal as a means toward one or more of these ends. Corporate giving can sometimes be shown to be a very good, often the very best, way to achieve a company's *business* objectives. Nor must it for one moment be conceded that this linkage necessarily means pursuit of corporate self-interest at the expense of public interest. Both can be served.

But under the responsibility theory of corporate giving, one is likely to begin with completely exterior considerations — with reference, for example, to those on the outside to which a company presumably owes responsibilities — and then to seek a linkage of logic with company interests, if indeed any such linkage is sought at all. It is quite appropriate to begin and end the logical process with reference to the external institutions in foundation philanthropy. But not, I think, in the donative work by a company component. (A foundation is a non-business entity.)

So far as donative work by a company component is concerned, the objection is sometimes made that in linking company interests with donative effects one runs the danger of losing tax and other advantages because the philanthropic motive in all its purity is said to be absent. But I see no harm in the linkage between business purpose and donative efforts as long as there is no quid-pro-quo transaction. What is given must be a gift with no strings attached; but that does not preclude giving for firm-related purposes. An automobile manufacturer can reasonably support research on highway safety. Who could properly question a company's support of local community funds merely because its employees may benefit thereby, or a local art center because business today has got to offer a rich cultural environment if it hopes to recruit and hold able employees?

I hope no one will think that the prudential approach rules out very long-range and incommensurable benefits. On the contrary, I believe that corporate giving has been on the cautious side in the past. I think that the goals of the future should be quite far-out. In fact, some long-headed managers of corporate donative work today are already reaching very far out indeed, and properly so, for donative objectives that would hardly have been regarded as company-related at all just a few years ago.

Support of the arts is a case in point. A new corporate ecology has taken hold in the business community; I mean by this that there is emerging a new science of the corporation as an institution within its milieu, and even a technology of application that seeks the right balance in what Professor Boulding has referred to as the ecosystem of our highly organized society. Now it is beginning to be understood that the goals of giving and the goals of business converge at novel and distant points. As Dr. Frank Stanton, President of CBS, put it recently in remarks before the Arts Council in Columbus, Ohio:

> We are all becoming parts of each other's world, and business is learning, along with every other sector of society — it may be slowly, but I believe surely — that it is not an island unto itself and that it both nourishes and is nourished by all those other activities that give any society character, richness, variety and meaning.

Dr. Stanton pointed to the recent history of the support of higher eduction by business as sufficient evidence of its "broadened horizons and increased awarenesses." As to the arts, he asked whether they were not "ultimately the meeting ground where liberal education and progressive business come together." For it is "the aim of a liberal education to give significance and nourishment to the individual human life," and it is "the arts, especially, that remind men of their humanity and of the sustaining values of our culture." So the first place to worry about American life losing its vitality of individualism, he thought, was in the arts. "If this happens, no liberal education will save our kind of society, and no business enterprise will long endure in what is left of it."

This, I think, is a succinct statement of the prudential theory of corporate giving. I do not believe that it is a crass rationale of expediency. Nor is it one that lays an inescapable duty on companies to give. Every company must decide for itself whether and how to do that. But I do think that with a good corporate ecology to stand on, and with good organization and procedure within every company or able outside consultants to look after donative work, the probability of a sound expansion of effort in this field is good.

During the past decade, we have moved toward that goal. I believe that during the next one — say by 1980 — we shall see some very hard-headed giving (prudent, prudential, or responsible, as you please) that will move into radically new areas that we do not anticipate today. It will be done because business and other leaders of our society will find it both good and necessary: good for society, good for the corporate donor, and necessary to both.

37   The Role of Philanthropy in Social Progress

Dana Creel

There is considerable controversy over the proposition that philanthropy should have anything to do with social change — much less social progress. And those of us in the foundation field who have gone through the hearings before the House Ways and Means Committee and the Senate Finance Committee and are now faced with the 1969 Tax Reform Act are fully aware of it.

The controversy seems baffling and incomprehensible, except from the viewpoint of those who simply do not understand the history of philanthropy — or those who would turn back the clock, or hold to the *status quo* for reasons of self-interest, or just plain fear of the future.

For I see philanthropy as the handmaiden of change. Like any instrument of power — the right to vote for instance — it can be used frivolously or for retrogressive ends just as readily as for progressive goals. No matter how it is used, it is an instrument for change. Change, however, is not necessarily progress, and only the wisdom with which philanthropy is applied determines that the result of changes constitutes progress.

The history of philanthropy over the years gives it an essential and undeniable right to be engaged in the business of social progress, to play a role which I believe to be essential and critical to the future of the nation and the quality of our lives in the years ahead.

Philanthropy, the word, by derivation means love of mankind. It has, however, much broader connotations. It means nothing less than private, voluntary action employed by individuals, singularly or in groups, as an instrument for changing and improving their environment — social, economic, and physical. In this light, philanthropy is a primary means by which people render service or alter the institutions of society to make them more responsive to their own needs and the needs of others. Obviously, the democratic processes of government may also serve these ends, although such processes are not as directly responsive nor as flexible as voluntary action.

Reprinted with permission from *The Conference Board Record,* June 1970, pp. 9–22. © The Conference Board 1970.

It is from the interplay of the two sectors that this nation has become a pluralistic society. Indeed, if this country has a genius, it is the creation and maintenance of a productive, flexible, cooperative pluralism which, when it is functioning properly, can produce maximum progress for all elements and interests.

We sometimes think of philanthropy as being uniquely American. This is not the case. What is unique is the extent and manner in which it has been woven into the texture of this country. Its early beginnings go back to the Hebrews and Greeks, and the concept of alms to the poor and suffering. Later, the Romans expanded it to enrichment of the life of the community as a whole.

Christianity added the concept of duty — the duty to give for the atonement of sins, and, rather naturally, the church became a major instrumentality to receive and distribute philanthropic funds. Eventually in England the church became the principal custodian of charitable funds to the point that the secular authorities felt challenged. In fact, in the 12th century somewhere between a third and a half of the wealth of the country was under ecclesiastical control.

The outcome in England was a prolonged struggle between the church and state, which ended with the confiscation of church properties in the 16th century. There followed a revolutionary shift from religious preoccupation to secular needs, with growing philanthropic concern for the poor and suffering and the development of remedial institutions, such as hospitals and schools.

American Backgrounds

This was the background for the attitudes that were current in the early days of this country. Our government was predominantly concerned with the problems of security and the maintenance of an internal order in which the private sector could function effectively. This left even such basic services as health, education, and welfare the responsibility of philanthropic funds, supported by the strong sense of moral or religious duty to help one's fellow man and the hardheaded recognition that by helping others one can help oneself. Thus private philanthropy, until the later part of the 19th century, was the principal means for establishing and supporting schools, colleges, hospitals, and the relief of the poor, the aged, and the disabled.

Philanthropy was not only the creator of such institutions as Harvard, Williams, Amherst, Mount Holyoke, Cornell and Johns Hopkins, it was also the main source of their continuing support. Not until after the Civil War did the government, through the establishment of the Institution of Land Grant Colleges, become a really active participant in the field of higher education. Only in the latter part of the 19th century were public schools established in a number of states, and it was well into the 20th century before public assistance was extended in any significant degree to the fields of health and welfare.[1]

Even in the mid-1930's, privately supported institutions in the field of education, health, and welfare were carrying the long share, and it was not until after World War II that the government really began to expand its activities into practically every area that had traditionally been the primary responsibility of philanthropy.

There has since been an increasing tendency to turn to the government. By 1969 governmenal funds accounted for 50% of the total expenditure for hospital costs. Of the 51,500,000 children in schools this year [1970] (from kindergarten through twelfth grade), the Office of Education estimates that 45,800,000 are in public schools, against 5,700,000 in private schools. Indeed, there has been comparable expansion of government activity in almost every area except religion. In some, such as relief, the government has, to all intents and purposes, assumed the entire burden.

The fact that governmental programs have overshadowed the voluntary sector in size and scope does not mean the importance of the private sector has decreased, however. In my opinion it is more needed than ever, but there I become pessimistic. To preserve it, we must provide not only funds but, even more importantly, thoughtful and dedicated leadership, for the private, voluntary sector is in financial crisis. For example, with the exception of a few of the very strongest, our private colleges will be facing all but insurmountable financial problems in the next few years.

What with inflation and increased demands for service, the private institutions are not receiving sufficient leadership or financial support to continue what I think is their clear role — one of flexible and quick response to new and urgent problems, the development of new and untried techniques and solutions, dealing with issues and needs that are not politically feasible for government participation, supplementing and also competing with government in order to provide meaningful choices of programs, and conducting impartial testing, measuring, and evaluating of government and private programs.

Without this kind of strong voluntary action which has so far had a major role in shaping our lives, we will have a very different kind of society from that of the past. It will be one in which personal initia-

---

[1] A congressional committee investigating foundations in 1915 said, "Two groups of foundations, namely the Rockefeller and Carnegie Foundations together, have funds amounting to at least $250 million, yielding an annual revenue of at least $13,500,000, which is twice as great as the appropriations of the Federal government for similar purposes, namely education and social service."

tive and responsibility will be surrendered more and more to an all-encompassing government.

It is true, of course, that the private, voluntary sector has grown over the years, and much has been made of this growth, but it is not proportionate to the growth of other sectors of our economy, and it has been woefully insufficient to meet the needs of private institutions. Growth that does not keep pace is really falling behind, and I think the extent of what is happening and what it portends is not fully understood.

Current Prospects

The 1969 Tax Reform Act is an exceedingly complicated legislation. Its various provisions, taken as a whole, reduce the incentives for philanthropic giving and restrict the use of philanthropic funds. Its underlying philosophy reflects the notion that, since the creation and continuation of foundations is encouraged and made possible through tax incentives, they represent in part, funds that would otherwise have been paid to the government in taxes. Foundation activities should therefore, it is argued, be subject to governmental regulation on matters of substantive program as well as administration. The implications of this philosophy do not stop with the foundations, but apply to the whole private, voluntary sector, and run counter to the freedom of traditional action accorded the private sector.

Another aspect of the Act causing some concern is the provision prohibiting foundations from activities which influence the legislative process or the decisions and actions of governmental officials. The implications of this are far reaching. No one knows what this may mean at this stage of "big government" with Federal, state and local programs reaching into practically every area of activity.

Front-line, innovative activity in the past was almost wholly in the private sector. Today government is on the forward edge of programs involving social change — areas which have become increasingly controversial and highly political.

If foundations should be broadly restricted by law from engaging in the activities which have become controversial or involved in politics, the forward edges of social change could become prohibited grounds, with foundations forced to withdraw from the action and concentrate on politically non-sensitive areas.

This is, indeed, a frightening prospect, for there are fewer and fewer areas in which one can grow without stepping on the omnipresent toes of government. The problems of the urban city, for instance, encompass many of the most vital and pressing problems of our society. To enter into these problems is to go into a veritable thicket of governmental programs and political sensitivity.

The implications do not stop with private foundations. They apply to the whole private, voluntary sector, and top Treasury officials have confirmed this by saying that, as soon as the Treasury has gained experience in dealing with private foundations under the present legislation, there is every intention to extend similar regulatory or supervisory measures to the broader field of voluntary organizations — schools, churches, welfare organizations, etc.

This is a thought to conjure with. Ironically, this cutting away of philanthropic muscle comes at a time when private citizens and organizations are being called upon for increased participation in the solution of the critical social problems that confront us. The general role of philanthropy may remain constant, but its concerns and activities must vary with the needs and problems of the times.

Our problems are monumental — extensive urban blight, population pressures, racial and social conflict with various forms of polarization, the fragmentation of our population, widening rebellion on the part of youth and minorities against the Establishment. To compound these problems there is a general loss of any basic and unifying consensus of values. This presents the paradox of a traditional and moralistic society without morals. Even more crucial is a prevailing sense of loss of dignity and of the impotence of individuals to be effective in changing existing institutions in any significant way or rapidly enough.

The problems are before us, and appear to be societal and of a different nature and magnitude from those of even the recent past. We have developed great facility for dealing with specifics, but we are only at the threshold of learning how to deal with broad, societal problems, and these are the problems of today and tomorrow.

It is encouraging that government, corporations, and philanthropy, particularly foundations, are all seeking to develop approaches to these problems. To reach the best solution, they must be tackled by all, each in his way. So I take great hope from the growing awareness of industrial leaders that corporations, large and small, will have a responsibility to seeking solutions to these broad problems, not only in their day-to-day operations but also in their philanthropic programs. They now total about $1 billion a year, with every indication that this amount will increase substantially in the future.

But dollars alone are not the whole answer. Much more important is how the dollars are applied. Thoughtful leadership will be the key to whether the private, voluntary sector is to continue to have a consequential role in the future of America, whether we will maintain a pluralistic approach in developing solutions from which we can determine those that will best shape our society.

There have been great changes in the Sixties, but the wind of change will reach tornado proportions in the Seventies. The great question is whether change can be effected rapidly enough and in an orderly way to avoid a breakdown in the social and economic fabric of the country. In order to determine and achieve solutions to problems demanding action, massive programs will be required, and they will take time. And time can be bought only if beginnings can be made quickly enough to convince those who desperately care that progress can be made through orderly change in existing institutions and in a way that accords a sense of human dignity and power to the individual to exert an influence on matters which affect his daily life. This is a task that requires full cooperation between government, commerce and industry, and philanthropy — both corporate and private.

The newest, fastest-growing entrant into the field is corporate philanthropy. Corporations have the opportunity to see that a much greater proportion of their philanthropic activity is directed to problem-solving. Industry, too, in its operations as well as its philanthropic programs, is becoming more concerned with social community problems and its responsibility to participate in their solutions.

I have found in the last few years an exciting trend toward local control of both governmental and private activities which encourages individual initiatives. There is a growing disenchantment with rigid, centralized, national programs. Voluntary agencies also are becoming more sensitive to the desires and leadership of the communities or constituencies which they seek to serve.

The ultimate goal of government, business, industry and the voluntary, private sector should be to give new force to this trend, which I call pluralism, in which the individual has a choice and a part to play in this task.

Cases

The Heartland Gas Company

The Organization

The Heartland Gas Company is a privately owned gas utility company. The company's operating area embraces approximately two-thirds of one state and includes retail distribution of natural gas to over five hundred communities. It has over 800,000 retail customers. In addition, it serves approximately 300,000 customers indirectly through wholesale sale of gas to thirty-one other utility companies in adjoining areas. The annual sales volume exceeds 300 billion cubic feet.

Heartland is an integrated gas company. The distribution function described above is but one phase of the total operation. The company has production, storage, and transmission operations which rival the distribution phase in importance. They operate approximately 1800 producing wells, purchase gas from about 3800 other local producing wells which are independently owned, operate about 1500 storage wells and thirty-three compressor stations. These facilities are all connected into a complex piping system which ultimately delivers the gas to the consumer. The company has approximately 17,200 linear miles of pipeline in its system. The total plant investment is approximately $360,000,000.

The production, storage, and transmission phases of this company are very important from the standpoint of assuring an adequate

Reprinted by the courtesy of Dr. Richard T. Rudduck, Professor of Management, and Dean K. Seizert, M.B.A., The University of Toledo.

supply to the ultimate consumer, and it is conceded that the conduct of employees in these departments have a bearing upon public relations but its over-all effect is minor when compared with the effect of the distribution department. This is due to the fact that the distribution department is responsible for all company functions after the gas has been delivered to the "city gate" or central measuring and pressure regulating station on the outskirts of any community the company serves. Assuming an adequate supply is made available to this point, this analysis will be limited to the organization of the distribution department and the relationship of various functions to the over-all public relations activity.

The Heartland Gas Company is organized on a line and staff principle. Top management consists of a board of directors, a president, a vice president and general manager, a secretary, a treasurer, a vice president in charge of engineering and planning, a vice president in charge of production and storage, a vice president in charge of distribution, a vice president in charge of rates and regulation, a vice president in charge of transmission, and a vice president in charge of wholesale. The organization chart in Exhibit 1 illustrates the top management's line of authority. It also shows the administrative level of such specialized functions as director of information, director of employee relations, and the manager of purchasing and stores.

The distribution department is organized under the vice president in charge of distribution on a line and staff basis. He has a staff in the headquarters office which are experts in each of the distribution functions. These include a service manager, a plant manager, an office manager, a business promotion manager, and an industrial sales manager. The operating area of the company is divided into six districts with each district's operations administered by a district manager. The district manager also reports to the vice president, distribution.

The organizational chart in Exhibit 2 shows the line of authority of the company's "middle management."

The management of each district is separated into five major functions under the district manager in a manner similar to that under the vice-president, distribution. In most cases, the district covers such a large geographical area that it is necessary for the area to be further sub-divided into divisions with a division manager in charge of operations in several communities. The division managers also report to the district manager.

The division managers are responsible for all functions within their area and have local managers working directly for them. On a local level, the manager is in charge of all operations. The separate functions of service and plant are sometimes consolidated if the community is relatively small so that the individual responsible for plant operations may also be responsible for services. In some cases, the office function is handled directly by the local manager. The business promotion

Exhibit 1 Organization Chart

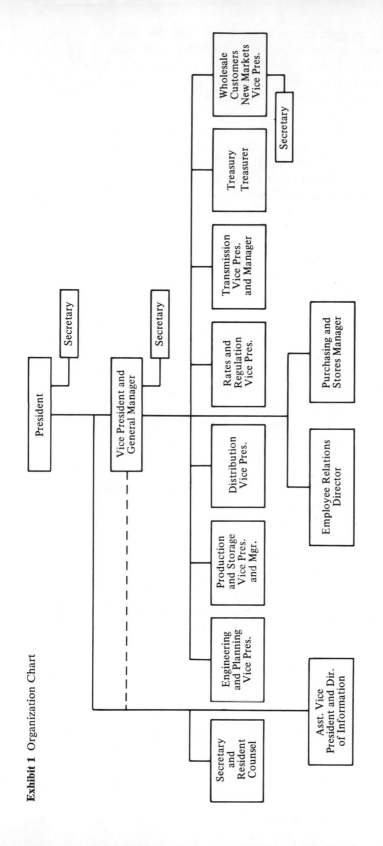

Exhibit 2 Organization Chart

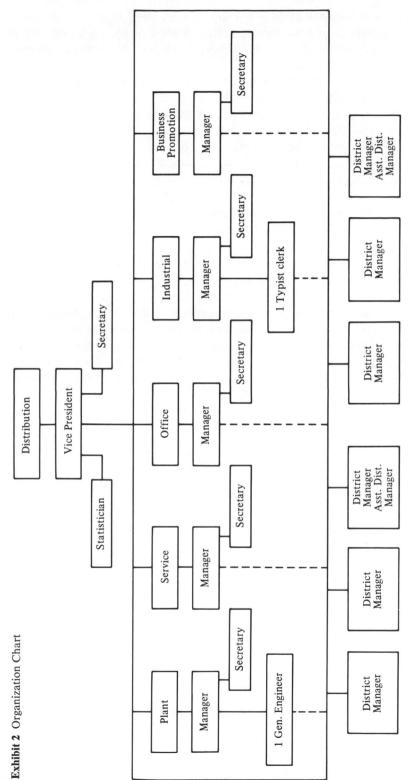

activities are not delegated below the division level. In most cases, there is a business promotion representative in each division who reports to his counterpart in the district office. Industrial department activities remain at the district level.

To simplify the organization chart, the writer has chosen a consolidated district structure without a division manager level for illustration purposes. Exhibit 3 shows the line of authority in such a district operation.

Because public relations, good or bad, stems from the words and deeds of district personnel dealing directly with the customer, it is advisable to examine the district structure in greater detail.

The district manager

The district manager is responsible for the over-all conduct of the company's affairs within his operating area. He is the man who must administer top management's broad policies at the point where the customer and the company get together. Harold Young, a partner in the investment firm of Eastman, Dillon, Union Securities & Company, pointed out in an article on utility management that, "A district manager can 'make or break' a company at the grass-roots level." [1]

From a standpoint of public relations as well as operations, the district manager is the central figure. Although Young's article was devoted to the utility business district manager in general, his description of the district manager's public relations function is very appropriate for this specific company.[2]

> The District Manager, so far as most of the customers are concerned, is the man out front. If something goes wrong, the average customer does not think of the President, the General Manager, or any other of the "big brass." He thinks of the District Manager and makes a beeline for his office or gets him quickly on the telephone. Hence, the man who sits behind the District Manager's desk must have patience, tact, and a super-abundance of ability to get along with people. He must be prepared always to present and defend the case of the company and still send a customer away with ruffled feathers smoothed.
>
> However, it would be unfair to paint a picture of a District Manager as a glorified fireman who goes into action when something is wrong. The situation is quite the contrary, and because a good District Manager is always on the job, the task of hearing and settling complaints is often pretty well minimized. One of the big success secrets is that the District Manager, if he is worth his salt, is an integral part of the area for which he is responsi-

---

[1] Harold H. Young, *The District Manager — Unsung Hero, Public Utilities Fortnightly,* Washington, D.C., Oct. 22, 1953, p. 4.
[2] *Ibid.*

ble. His position in the community, or communities he serves, is usually an outstanding one. It is rare to find a District Manager who is not only a good citizen but also a reasonably prominent one.

The district manager is expected to take an active interest in community affairs. It is extremely desirable that he become well acquainted with other business leaders and civic officials. These contacts are very valuable in the never-ending job of "keeping a finger on the public pulse." The job of keeping informed requires an awareness and sensitivity which are best cultivated with the willing assistance of people who feel they know the manager well enough to offer criticism and information regarding public attitudes. The district manager in each of Heartland's distribution districts is expected to belong to the Rotary Club in the district headquarters town. He is expected to belong to a country club and join in other local club activities which offer opportunities to meet people and cultivate friends for himself and the company.

Everyone agrees that the public relations responsibility is of prime importance in the public utility field but so are the many basic operating functions which are the essential foundation upon which the public relations program is built. The district manager has many responsibilities, therefore it is important that all phases of the job be kept in their true perspective to avoid too much emphasis being placed on one phase at the expense of another.

The Heartland Gas Company's district organization is designed to serve as a balance wheel in this respect. Each of the major functions is supervised by a member of the district manager's staff. It is the department head's duty to keep him advised if a problem arises or if changing conditions make it apparent that a problem will result if a present operating procedure is continued. This element in the operation of each department cannot be neglected. Each department head must maintain vigilance and a genuine interest in public relations as well as his routine operating functions if the program is to be successful. The district manager or a higher managerial level make the ultimate decision to change policies and procedure, but the department head must operate each department in an efficient, productive manner. It might be said that, with the district manager's guidance, the department heads are accountable for keeping the company moving forward and the conduct of its employees.

The service department

The service manager is in charge of meter service, appliance service, customer's service records, and the telephone contact personnel who answer all routine customer inquiries or complaints. In metropolitan areas, these assignments are carried out by personnel with specific

Exhibit 3 Consolidated District Structure

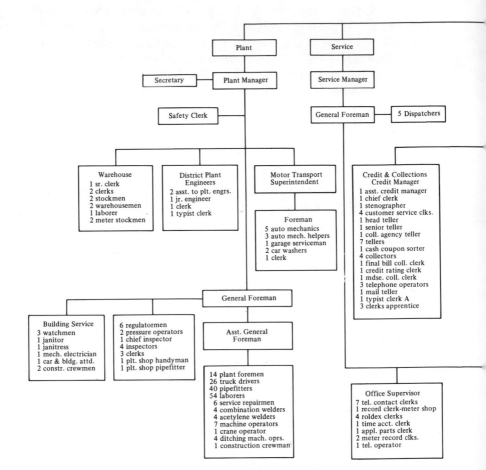

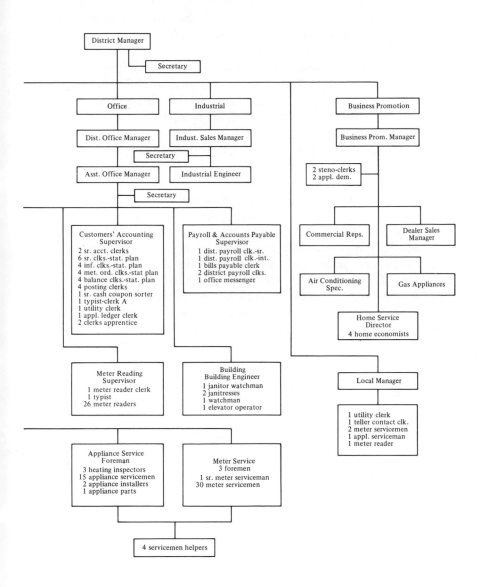

District Manager
Secretary

Office
Dist. Office Manager
Secretary
Asst. Office Manager
Secretary

Industrial
Indust. Sales Manager
Industrial Engineer

Business Promotion
Business Prom. Manager
2 steno-clerks
2 appl. dem.

Customers' Accounting
Supervisor
2 sr. acct. clerks
6 sr. clks.-stat. plan
4 inf. clks.-stat. plan
4 met. ord. clks.-stat plan
4 balance clks.-stat. plan
4 posting clerks
1 sr. cash coupon sorter
1 typist-clerk A
1 utility clerk
1 appl. ledger clerk
2 clerks apprentice

Payroll & Accounts Payable
Supervisor
1 dist. payroll clk.-sr.
1 dist. payroll clk.-int.
1 bills payable clerk
2 district payroll clks.
1 office messenger

Commercial Reps.

Dealer Sales
Manager

Air Conditioning
Spec.

Gas Appliances

Home Service
Director
4 home economists

Meter Reading
Supervisor
1 meter reader clerk
1 typist
26 meter readers

Building
Building Engineer
1 janitor watchman
2 janitresses
1 watchman
1 elevator operator

Local Manager

1 utility clerk
1 teller contact clk.
2 meter servicemen
1 appl. serviceman
1 meter reader

Appliance Service
Foreman
3 heating inspectors
15 appliance servicemen
2 appliance installers
1 appliance parts

Meter Service
3 foremen
1 sr. meter serviceman
30 meter servicemen

4 servicemen helpers

job classifications, whereas in small communities, the various service functions may be performed by one or two individuals who capably handle all types of service orders. In a metropolitan area, the work is divided among meter servicemen, appliance servicemen, heating specialists, installation men, and helpers. A radio dispatching system is used with a group of dispatchers communicating with the service trucks when necessary throughout the work shift.

The service manager is assisted by a general foreman. The supervisory staff is then broken down to the foremen level with foremen in charge of meter service and appliance service. In addition to the service foreman reporting to the general foreman, he has an office manager who directly supervises the keeping of customer service records and the personnel answering customer telephone calls.

The service department plays a very important roll in public relations. Exclusive of bill payments, the serviceman and the telephone contact men are the only contact the average customer has with the company except for a possible contact with a meter reader.

The training the servicemen receive to quickly and efficiently adjust or install appliances is a continuous process. As new models and design changes are introduced, the men must be schooled in the proper adjustment of the appliance. This is done by the service manager keeping informed of all changes and arranging for factory representatives to explain and demonstrate. The serviceman's attitude as well as skill has a bearing on the impression he leaves with a customer. For this reason, all personnel in this department must be reminded frequently of their key position in the over-all public relations program of the company.

The plant department

The plant manager is in charge of all distribution piping and construction. In addition to the construction and plant operations, he is in charge of plant engineering, warehousing, motor transport, and building services. In a typical district, each of these functions is supervised by an individual who reports directly to the plant manager.

Construction is supervised by a general foreman who is aided by several assistant general foremen. The assistant general foremen each have a specific branch of construction work to supervise. One is in charge of maintenance and repair, two for line extensions, one for service connections, and one for pressure regulation. The crew foremen who directly supervise the construction crews report to the assistant general foreman. This line type organization is very successful in fixing responsibility and avoids having too many people reporting to one individual for him to perform effectively. It also keeps the general foreman and the plant manager from becoming too involved in rather insignificant details and allows them to devote their time and thought to the over-all planning and administration of the construction program.

Efficient construction crews providing gas service by extending piping to new customers when it is required with a minimum of inconvenience and delay can very favorably impress the public. Opinions are also based upon the general conduct of the construction personnel in their daily work assignments. Foremen must constantly strive to reduce inefficiencies and waste to gain public respect. This problem is not peculiar to utilities, however, it is more apparent to the public because all work is carried on under the public's eyes whereas private industry is not under such close scrutiny. It is also important that they remain "housekeeping" conscious on the job and leave open construction areas well barricaded and lighted to protect the public.

Plant engineering works very closely with the construction department. It is their duty to design and plan new plant facilities and piping to keep abreast of a constantly increasing market. As new housing developments are erected and new factories are built, it is necessary to expand the existing piping system. This department is supervised by the senior engineer who has several distribution engineers, assistant distribution engineers, corrosion engineers, and a clerical supervisor under his leadership. Besides planning plant construction, they prepare all necessary paper work and maintain records of pipe locations, pressures and other pertinent information to operate an extensive distribution system properly. Distribution planning affects the adequacy of the supply to the customer, therefore, it is a vital factor in the opinion each customer has of the company.

Warehousing is controlled by a supervisor who has a senior clerk, and several clerks, stockmen and warehousemen working for him. This department maintains an inventory of construction material as well as appliances, appliance parts and meters for use by all operating departments. The maintenance of an adequate supply of tools and material is a very important factor in the successful completion of a construction project or the prompt servicing of customers' appliances. From this standpoint, the manner in which this department's affairs are conducted has a bearing on public relations.

The motor transport department is headed by a superintendent who is assisted by a foreman on each of the two work shifts. The foremen supervise the activities of the auto mechanics, auto mechanics helpers, garage servicemen, car washers and clerical personnel. Motor transport is responsible for the maintenance and repair of all company vehicles and general tools. In addition to the repair of cars and trucks, the mechanics must be well versed in the servicing of all types of internal combustion engines, compressors, and heavy duty construction equipment such as tractors, cranes, bulldozers, and side booms. The general appearance of the company's rolling stock has a bearing on public opinion. If cars and trucks are allowed to remain in service with dented fenders or are always dirty, it can create a bad impression. The same impression can be created by having to tow heavy equipment back to the garage through heavy traffic because it cannot be started at the job site. The company is aware of these possibilities and has a scheduled service and preventative maintenance program. They also strive to keep the equipment free of dents, well painted, and frequently washed for appearance sake.

The building services section reports directly to the construction department's general foreman. This group is composed of building watchmen, janitors and building maintenance personnel. The security and maintenance of company property is the responsibility of this group. Naturally, the appearance and cleanliness of company buildings is important from a public relations standpoint.

The commercial department

The office manager is in charge of meter reading, customer's accounting, credit and collections, payroll and accounts payable, and a building services section. Each of these specific departments within the commercial department is supervised by individuals who report directly to the office manager.

The meter reading department's supervisor is in charge of the reading of customers' meters each month. Meter reading must be conducted in a business-like, well mannered fashion to avoid criticism of the action of employees on customers' premises. The supervisor must thoroughly train new meter readers so their actions will be a credit to the company. The accuracy of the readings they obtain is also of major consequence. The customer expects to be properly billed each month. Billing errors resulting from incorrect readings are very irritating to the customer and reduce his confidence in the company. These reasons illustrate the importance of a public relations consciousness in this group.

The customer's accounting department prepares the customers' bills each month based upon the meter readings provided by the meter reading department. This is principally a clerical operation which has become highly automated in recent years, through the use of IBM billing equipment. The meter reading is recorded on a card with a special pencil by the meter reader. This card is then introduced directly into the IBM equipment which senses the reading at the beginning of the billing period, the reading at the end of the billing period, calculates the consumption and the amount of money owed by the customer, and finally records the consumption and dollar amount on the bill. This equipment has substantially reduced the human errors which occasionally caused incorrect bills in the past. The installation of this system resulted in both time and labor savings. Needless to say, it also had a very desirable effect upon public relations by insuring greater accuracy.

The credit and collection department is headed by the credit manager who is assisted by an Assistant Credit Manager and a head teller. The Credit Manager is in charge of the collection of bills. This entails the supervision of the tellers, numerous clerical employees and collectors. The credit department is also in a key public relations position because of its direct customer contact activities. The average customer that pays his bill over the company's counter expects prompt courteous treatment. Some come direclty to the company's offices to apply for service or to request adjustment of appliances. In this case, they are greeted and their needs cared for by members of the credit department staff. In some cases, they are there to request an extension of time in the payment of bills. Regardless of the reason for their visit, it is very important that they leave completely satisfied and favorably impressed.

The payroll and accounts payable department performs the internal functions of paying bills incurred by the company and dispensing the company payroll. They also maintain employee records for life insurance, hospitalization and other employee benefits. The prompt payment of invoices received has a favorable effect upon suppliers' relations which is another factor in the over-all public relations program.

The business promotion department

The business promotion manager is in charge of most of the company's promotional activities within the district. His chief function is to elevate the position of gas in relation to all competitive fuels and forms of energy. Although the company does not merchandise appliances directly to the public, they do have an extensive program established to facilitate their sale through other sources. The ultimate objective is to increase the acceptance of gas equipment by the public and subsequently increase the consumption level. The business promotion department personnel are separated into specific branches of the activity in metropolitan areas to provide expert assistance to home builders, appliance dealers and heating and air conditioning contractors. In districts that are widespread, it becomes necessary for one business promotion representative in each division of the district to provide this specialized service in all phases of promotional activity. To provide a better understanding of the various activities, the writer has chosen to examine each specific function as a separate job and point out its public relations significance.

Dealer sales activities are those cooperative activities which pertain directly to appliance dealers and are under the direction of a Dealer Sales Manager. The dealers vary in size from the small independent appliance merchant to the large national chain department stores. The company encourages them to promote the sale of gas appliances through sales campaigns and increased advertising. The assistance given to dealers takes many forms. If a dealer has a special promotional event planned, the company's dealer sales manager will gladly arrange for the home service department to have a home economist present to demonstrate gas appliances and explain the virtues of gas cookery. The dealer sales manager will also enter into cooperative newspaper advertising of gas appliances in conjunction with the event. In this case, the company will pay a portion of the advertising expense. Special floor display material, window displays, or point of sale displays may be furnished by the company. During special sales campaigns, the dealer sales manager may also offer special sales inducements to the appliance salesmen in each store. This usually is in the form of a small bonus paid by the company and gives each salesman an opportunity to supplement his normal commission on an appliance sale. It is expected that he will emphasize the sales features of the gas equipment under these circumstances in an effort to influence his prospect toward a gas equipment purchase because he will benefit more by its sale.

All of the cooperation given to appliance dealers is intended to improve the company's relations with this group and to increase gas appliance sales. Naturally, the owner of such a business is receptive because he is able to increase his advertising coverage, improve the quality of his displays, and offer special attractions to customers. In addition, his salesmen are grateful for the extra compensation resulting from sales. As a further sales aid, the company cooperates with dealers by offering free adjustment service on new appliances sold by him.

One other important public relations function performed by the dealer sales manager is his placement of gas appliances in the public schools. Under this program, the company provides the most modern gas ranges and refrigerators available for use in the high school and grade school home economics departments. This equipment is replaced every two years at no charge to the schools. This is done to acquaint future homemakers with gas cookery and to maintain a desirable relationship with the school system.

The home service department is a segment of business promotion which deals directly with the homemaker. This department is composed of several home economists who conduct demonstrations, explain new equipment and advise customers on the latest cooking and baking techniques.

One phase of this department's work is tied directly to the sale of appliances through dealers. After a gas appliance is sold, the dealer advises the home service department who sends a representative to the home to demonstrate the operation of the appliance to the lady of the house.

Group demonstrations are conducted for various women's club groups, girl scouts, boy scouts and others. These demonstrations offer an excellent opportunity to show off new equipment innovations as well as teach the younger groups to cook on gas.

The department also works directly with the schools to provide future homemakers with information about gas equipment and its proper use and care.

The home economists working in this department can have a very desirable effect upon future business because they devote much of their time to working with young people who will be tomorrow's customers. This program not only affects the opinion of those directly involved but also that of their friends and families.

Builder sales activities are conducted to increase the number of gas appliances installed in new homes. Gas advisors work directly with building contractors who are involved in new home construction. To this market the company does merchandise equipment. The dealer can buy appliances for installation in new homes at a rather attractive price. In addition to the sale of appliances, the Gas advisors are responsible for the development of several promotions each year with various builders. The object is to get gas appliances featured in homes that are open for public inspection. Each year the company features a "House of Enchantment" which is an all-gas equipped home complete with gas actuated air conditioning. The house is promoted jointly by the builder, the furniture dealer that has decorated and furnished the house, and the company. The house usually offers many intriguing features and is highly publicized. During the period it is open for public inspection, it is visited by thousands of people interested in new homes. This offers an ideal way to show the latest gas equipment to an interested public.

From a public relations standpoint, the builder sales program affects both the builder and the customer public. If a closer relationship with a builder results in his installing gas equipment in speculative homes rather than competitive equipment, the desired result has been achieved. He will do so only if he is convinced that the equipment he buys will make that house easier to sell than it otherwise would be. The program is designed to favorably impress the public by displaying to them the modernity of gas appliances and thus increase their acceptance.

The field of residential air conditioning is handled by an air conditioning specialist. It is his duty to work with heating and air conditioning dealers, architects and customers in the promotion of residential and small commercial air conditioning. In most cases, this involves direct customer contact to interest them in air conditioning and then designing an appropriate system. The air conditioning specialist must be well versed in the application of residential heating and air conditioning equipment and duct layout techniques.

The company is dedicated to the sale of high quality air

conditioning systems. They are not interested in competing in the low-priced, low quality air conditioning market. It is felt that a high equipment standard must be maintained, and the quality of service must be higher than that offered by competitive air conditioning if the acceptance of gas actuated air conditioning is to improve. For this reason, the air conditioning specialist must be qualified to select equipment which will capably fill the needs as well as design a system which will give the customer complete satisfaction.

Although this function affects a relatively small number of customers and contractors in the trade directly, their reaction to the results has definite public relations significance. The best recommendation a product can get is the testimonial of a satisfied customer.

Commercial sales activities are directed toward another segment of the company's business. This phase of promotion is confined to commercial customers, restaurant equipment dealers, plumbers and large volume space heating contractors. Primarily this phase is a combination of cooperation directly with the customer and his contractor. Because of the size of most commercial projects, the company's commercial representative frequently becomes involved early in the planning stage through inquiries made by an architect, a contractor, or perhaps, the owner, into the availability of gas for the intended uses. In most cases, the size of the project is large enough that the planner realizes that some preliminary checking must be done to assure an adequate source. This is true whether the project requires gas for space heating only or if a quantity of gas is to be used for processing, such as would be found in a restaurant, bakery or laundry. It is the commercial representative's job to see that gas is used wherever practical in such instances. He will work directly with the planner to advise him of any specific requirements or aid in the planning by advising him of the size of gas lines to be installed, the meter location, size and piping details, or help in determining the proper type of equipment to install. In addition to serving the planners of new projects, he also must contact existing customers to determine their future needs and aid them in the correction of any service problems they may have. Direct customer contact through follow-up and canvassing is a very important element of success in this portion of the business. For this reason, the personnel selected for this assignment must be well grounded in gas application fundamentals as well as have the desirable characteristics of a good salesman. The advice he gives must be accurate or the company's public relations will suffer. The assistance and recommendations rendered may result in the expenditure of large sums of money. If his judgment has been poor, the consequence can be disastrous to the company's prestige in the eyes of the parties affected.

The commercial representative works directly with school boards, their administrative staffs, church councils, and municipal officials, as well as individual owners of commercial enterprises. For this reason, he is a key figure in our relations with the community public as well as the customer public. He is active in outside organizations such as the local restaurant association, the Chamber of Commerce, or perhaps technical groups such as the National Association of Power Engineers. Contacts made at meetings can be helpful because they are made on a semi-social basis. This allows the commercial representative to become better acquainted with the people he is dealing with. In turn, it allows them to know him better which can be good or bad depending upon his "words and deeds" under these circumstances. It is hoped that to know him better means that they will increase their respect for his judgment and call him whenever a fuel application problem arises. His conduct may influence a school board's decision to use gas or a competitive fuel in a new school, or it may lead a consulting engineer to recommend another fuel for a large project. For these reasons, the company must select qualified people for this job. The impact on public relations as a result of selecting the wrong man can be very severe.

The industrial department

The industrial sales manager is in charge of four principle functions: industrial development, the promotion and retention of industrial processing loads, the promotion of large volume air conditioning, and the promotion of gas in competitive large volume space heating situations. Depending upon the district's size and the number of accounts to be handled, the industrial sales manager may be assisted by one or more industrial engineers and industrial representatives. To qualify for a position in this department, the candidate must be a graduate engineer with a desirable personality. He must be aggressive and display a "sales outlook." Because of the technical nature of the work and the importance of contacts made, the management, by necessity, is very selective in the placement of personnel in this department. In each district, the industrial department operates on the district level rather than assigning individuals to the divisions. In widespread districts, this is modified by locating the industrial engineers in strategic locations in the district and making them responsible for a given area, but they still report to the industrial sales manager and remain a part of the district organization.

In the field of industrial development, the industrial department actively encourages new industries to settle in the area. This activity is not confined to merely contacting prospective industries but includes many other facets although this contact is an important part of the program. In addition, the industrial department cooperates with all other local agencies interested in industrial development. This is done through membership in the local Chamber of Commerce Industrial Development Committee, attendance at seminars and clinics devoted to industrial development which are sponsored by state organizations, co-operation with local governmental agencies such as planning commissions, and with other companies and organizations who are working with prospects. The company also engages in some national advertising directed to industries interested in expanding or relocating. This advertising outlines the many desirable features of the company's operating area. They also prepare brochures for direct mailing to prospects. The over-all program is a comprehensive system to help the economic growth of the communities the company serves.

From a community relations standpoint, the industrial development program is very important and should have very desirable results. The company benefits not only through the addition of a new industry but through the many desirable side effects created through increased employment in the community. Every new industrial plant not only creates jobs within the plant but also generates the increased buying power which supports many additional commercial businesses which are responsible for services. This also strengthens the banking interests and the general prosperity of the community.

The promotion and retention of industrial process loads is also an important phase of the industrial department's business. Many industries require large volumes of gas as an integral part of their conversion of raw materials into finished products. The proper application of heat requires the maximum flexibility possible combined with precise control methods. In many cases, the properties of gas have made it an indispensable tool. The industrial department personnel must be experts in the field of heat application in order to serve as consultants to industry as specific utilization problems arise. The assistance they offer their customers in the solution of such problems helps increase the acceptance of gas as a product. To further qualify industrial engineers for this type of work, the company sends them to the Institute of Gas Technology at the Illinois Institute of Technology where they receive an extensive concentrated course on gas utilization. The company realizes that there are occasions when the selection of a competitive fuel is the most practical solution to a problem. In this case, the company representative frankly advises the customer that the competitive fuel is the best choice. Although this does not sell gas for this particular process, it does earn the respect of the customer because he feels he has received an unbiased, honest answer. He will more quickly accept the representative's judgment when the next heat applicable problem comes up.

To be effective in this job, the department personnel must keep up to date with technological changes in all phases of fuel utilization. In addition to the numerous applications of gas to form heat for such operations as forging, heat treating, baking, drying, metal melting, glass melting, and many others, the representative must be familiar with processes which require gas as a raw material. Practically all modern heat treating techniques employ the use of a protective atmosphere prepared from natural gas or ammonia. Natural gas is also being used as a raw material in the petrochemical industry to provide the hydro-carbons which ultimately become synthetic fibers, fertilizer or some other wondrous product. The industrial department's goal is to be recognized by its customers as being technically qualified to answer all of their questions concerning processes requiring heat. This is a valuable sales tool as well as a favorable public relations factor.

Along with the service rendered directly to the customer, one should consider the effect of having satisfactorily completed the proposed project. The assistance rendered in the creation of new processes within an existing industry has the same desirable effects as the establishment of a new industry.

The promotion of the use of gas actuated large volume air conditioning is another function performed by the industrial department. Large volume air conditioning to the Heartland Gas Company means an installation requiring twenty-five tons of capacity or more. This criteria establishes the size project that will be handled by industrial department personnel instead of the air conditioning specialist of the business promotion department. This is the logical point in sizes to change the sales responsibility, because residential style and size equipment is normally used for smaller tonnage jobs and the smallest commercial type equipment available is in a twenty-five ton size. Buildings large enough to require twenty-five tons of air conditioning capacity or more are normally designed by an architect rather than from private plans. This is the reason the program entails scheduled contacts with local architects, mechanical engineering consultants, and installing contractors as well as calling on prospective owners. Because this field is highly competitive, the relationship cultivated with the architects and consultants has a definite bearing upon the success of the program.

Industrial department personnel help the architect and consultant by sizing and laying out the necessary gas piping and meter setting for them as well as providing them with complete information regarding the availability of gas for the project. Due to the fact that the use of gas for air conditioning is not a widely accepted practice, it is necessary for the industrial department personnel to try to educate the architect and consultant by providing him with information concerning the types of equipment available, the sizes, and the advantages of each type. In many cases, this also leads to the preparation of an owning and operating cost analysis for his use in comparing gas equipment with competitive equipment. The gas industry is hopeful that as architects and others interested in specifying air conditioning equipment become familiar with what is available and realize that dependable equipment is obtainable from several manufacturers, they will specify gas equipment. Until 1959, the gas industry had a very limited amount of equipment available for large tonnage systems. Until that time, only one manufacturer made an absorption air conditioning machine larger than fifty tons capacity. Since that time, two other prominent manufacturers with fine reputations in the air conditioning field have entered the absorption market. This has changed the attitude of many architects and consultants concerning absorption equipment because they had always been hesitant about specifying equipment available through only one manufacturer. As a result, the contact job performed by the industrial department has become more rewarding.

From a public relations standpoint, this phase of industrial department business is significant because of the influence this relatively small group of architects and engineers has over the customer who is investing in a new building. If product acceptance can be obtained through large volume air conditioning, the residential market will also become more penetrable.

Competitive large volume space heating is the fourth facet of industrial department responsibility. Space heating has always been a competitive market due to the difference in price of various fuels. In each case, an evaluation must be made of the facts other than the direct fuel costs. Large volume space heating normally involves the use of industrial type space heaters or steam generators depending upon the building design and the use to which it will be put. Many installations can be as adequately heated by one fuel as another. Many times the selection of fuel is based upon the degree of refinement of the system, the ease of control, the amount of maintenance required and the dependability of the fuel source. Industrial department personnel are qualified to evaluate all of the factors to be considered and to prepare a complete owning and operating cost study for consideration by the prospective building owner before his final decision is reached.

It is the company's policy to present a completely factual cost study without favoring gas except where the facts justify it. Some companies do not follow this policy and attempt to deceive the prospect by presenting him with a series of half-truths which favor their fuel or equipment. A utility company cannot afford to practice deceit. It would have the worst possible public relations effect. The company feels that it must maintain the highest possible integrity in competitive situations if it is to preserve its respected corporate image in the community.

The company reviews its program

It can be seen from the description of the company organization that each department has a public relations obligation. Periodically, it is necessary to review the current standing to be certain that the public relations program is being effectively handled. For this reason, the management occasionally analyzes its position to see if changes are required to implement further improvement.

The current review and many of the pertinent facts disclosed therein are described to point out the necessity for developing a dynamic program which receives a reappraisal at frequent time intervals.

Performance review

During the course of a day, the Heartland Gas Company switchboard handles eight hundred fifty telephone calls from customers. The calls primarily pertain to service requests and inquiries concerning all phases of the business. Normally all calls of this nature are channeled into the telephone contact section of the service department. Eight men are assigned to receive calls of this nature and to answer the customers' questions. In the past ten years, the telephone contact section has been progressively expanded from a complement of four employees to the number now on the job. These additional employees were added because of the increased number of calls which were being handled daily. To a degree, this was brought about by the addition of approximately 3000 new customers to the lines each year. The average number of telephone calls handled per man per day was eighty in 1950. The number of calls received per customer per year was 0.91 in 1950. The year end tabulations for 1960 revealed that the average number of calls handled per man per day was ninety-five and the number of calls per customer per year was 1.42.

This increased telephone activity causes overloads in the system at times during peak hours. The company is aware that such an increase could cause problems and wants to completely evaluate the condition. To determine what could be done to correct this situation, the company requested the telephone company to conduct a survey over a prolonged period and to make their recommendations. After the telephone company had carefully checked the number of calls being placed into the company daily for six weeks and had monitored calls to each department, the following recommendations were made:

1. Reduce the amount of time spent on each call.
2. Answer the telephones more promptly.
3. Increase the number of people available to take calls during peak periods.
4. Increase the number of trunk lines into the company to accommodate more calls simultaneously.
5. Attempt to improve the personnel's telephone answering technique.

The company is constantly striving to improve its telephone service to customers because they realize the importance of this vital customer contact. After receiving the results of the telephone company's survey and its recommendations, the management decided to make a more thorough evaluation of the system to ascertain where changes should be inaugurated to make further improvements. To do this, calls were monitored to determine how well the contacts were being handled from the standpoint of information given to the customer and how delays occur which tie up the switchboard.

The supervisor in charge of the telephone contact section relayed the following cases to point out how public relations problems can develop from the use and abuse of a telephone.

Mr. Smith's lost meter Mr. Smith, a customer, called to advise the company that he had recently purchased a different home and planned to move in three days. He requested that the service to his existing home be terminated on Friday and service be established at his new address the same day. The telephone contact man wrote down both addresses and asked Mr. Smith to hold the telephone while he checked the records. After a considerable lapse of time, the telephone contact man returned to the telephone and advised the customer that service could be terminated at the present address on Friday but there would be some delay in receiving service at the new house because the records showed that no gas was installed there. He further explained that the customer would have to install a gas pipe to the property line and the company would have to make a connection to its main before the meter could be installed. The customer told the employee that he was certain that a gas meter was in the basement of the new home. The employee responded by telling the customer that he must be mistaken.

Mr. Smith said he would check and call back. He then drove over to the new house, went into the basement and found a gas meter installed. Mr. Smith again called the telephone contact man and told him there was a meter in the basement. The telephone contact man told him there couldn't be because there was no record of such an installation in the service files. To convince him, Mr. Smith resorted to saying, "If you want me to, I'll bring the meter down and put it on your desk to prove it." Service was established in his name on Friday as he originally requested.

To further complicate the company's relationship with this customer, he didn't get a bill for the first three months at the new location. One day he was home for lunch and happened to see a gas company meter reader leave the house next door. When the meter reader started to pass his house without stopping, Mr. Smith called to him and asked why his meter was not being read. The meter reader told him that there wasn't any gas service in the house so he always passed it by. Mr. Smith straightened out this problem by leading the meter reader into his basement and showing him the meter. Since that time, the records for the Smith account have been brought up to date and no further difficulty has occurred.

Mr. Jones' high bill Another customer, Mr. Jones, called to inquire about the amount of his gas bill. He explained that the current bill represented the largest gas bill he has ever received, yet the weather during the month was no more severe than previously and he had made no changes which would affect his consumption. The telephone contact man in this case politely asked Mr. Jones to wait until he could check the Accounting Department records. While Mr. Jones held one line, the telephone contact man then used a second line to call the accounting department for information concerning the account. After some delay obtaining the necessary information, he returned to the call from Mr. Jones and advised him that the records showed that a meter reading had been taken and the bill was not an estimate. He further explained that because of the size of the bill, he would gladly issue a service order to have a second reading taken to confirm the bill. Mr. Jones was pleased with the treatment he received from the courteous contact man but was disgruntled over having to wait several minutes to receive satisfaction.

Mr. Thomas' new house Mr. Thomas, a prospective customer, had recently been transferred here by his company and had just purchased a new home from a local builder and wished to get gas service as quickly as possible because he wanted to start heating the home to dry it thoroughly before moving his family from another city. His first impression of the company was created by receiving a "busy" signal when he called. His second was created when, after getting the company operator and stating what he wanted, the lines into the telephone contact section were busy. After waiting for a line to be available, the telephone rang numerous times before it was answered. Mr. Thomas then explained that he wanted to apply for service for a newly constructed home. He waited while the telephone contact man checked the service records to see if a service connection had previously been made in the name of the builder. He was then advised that because no connection had been made, he would have to talk with the engineering department. Mr. Thomas' call was then transferred to the engineering department where he was informed that they would mail him the necessary application for him to fill out and mail back. When the completed application was returned, the connection would be made as quickly as possible; however, he should anticipate about a two-week delay because of a backlog of such applications. Mr. Thomas explained the urgency of his request and was given special consideration so that he could avoid moving his family into a hotel until the work was completed.

Cases of these types were uncovered as a result of the section's supervisor monitoring calls. The supervisor quickly added that bad contacts do not occur very often when the total number of calls handled daily are considered. The cases described are not typical contacts but are examples of extremes. A great percentage of all telephone calls are expeditiously carried to a quick, concise conclusion to both parties' complete satisfaction.

Simultaneously, the management conducted a survey of customer's opinions of the quality of service offered by servicemen in their homes to see if this area contributed to the higher number of telephone calls received. The service manager relayed several calls which were brought to his attention which had interesting public relations results.

Mrs. James' new range Mrs. James was delighted with her recent purchase of a new gas range from her appliance dealer. The dealer explained at the time of her purchase that the Gas Company would gladly adjust the range after it was installed if she would call and advise the company when she wished service. Mrs. James had the new range delivered and installed, then called to have it adjusted. Arrangements were made for a serviceman to visit her home the following day. When the serviceman arrived, Mrs. James asked him how he liked her new range. He promptly told her that he didn't like it and that she should have purchased a different make which would give her better results and fewer maintenance problems. The serviceman adjusted the equipment without further comment. The mechanical part of his job was perfect but he left a different impression with Mrs. James. Mrs. James called the appliance dealer and accused him of selling inferior merchandise. After hearing the story, the dealer called the gas company and "commented" on the serviceman's "diplomacy."

The politician's pride One serviceman was called to the home of a customer to calibrate an oven the day after a local election. The serviceman arrived in apparent poor spirits. He was polite to the lady of the house and performed as a model employee as he lit the oven and started to check the thermostat. Then the lady of the house made the mistake of asking him what he thought of the election results. The serviceman then gave her his very complete opinion of the persons that had won the election including a description of the last horses they stole. He didn't know that the lady's husband was the campaign manager of one of the successful candidates.

Mr. Richards' faulty furnace Mr. Richards called the gas company one morning to report that he had detected an odor of gas in his basement and wished to have it checked. Within a half hour, a serviceman was at Mr. Richards' home to investigate for leakage. Instead of greeting the customer with "good morning" when he opened the door, the serviceman's comment was, "You picked a fine day to have a gas leak." He then proceeded to shut the gas off to test the customer's lines to determine whether or not they were pressure tight. When Mr. Richards asked him what he was doing, his only reply was "I'm checking for leaks." After putting air pressure on the piping, he told the customer that the automatic valve on the furnace was defective and that a plumber would have to replace it before service could be restored. When asked how long it would take to get him back after repairs were made, he merely said, "I don't know." Fortunately, a plumber did replace the defective valve early in the same afternoon and Mr. Richards did get service restored the same day — by a different serviceman.

The first serviceman did a very efficient job of handling the mechanical part of his job; however, the customer was less impressed by his mechanical ability than by his "bed-side manners."

The service manager maintains a training schedule which keeps all service employees acquainted with all technical developments in appliances. They are thoroughly schooled in the latest changes so they will be equipped with the "know how" to do a complete and efficient job of servicing on the customer's premises.

In order to measure the opinion of the commercial segment of the business, they, too, were surveyed. This survey included both customers and the tradesmen and professionals most frequently involved in large projects.

The business promotion manager interviewed architects, consulting engineers and piping contractors specializing in large commercial work. His conclusions were as follows:

> Our main problem is trying to educate the people interested in bidding large jobs so they will understand our requirements. It seems that every time a large shopping center or other commercial job is being constructed, the commercial representative has to go over every small detail with the bidders. If we don't do this, the owner doesn't get two bids back on the same basis. When this happens, the owner is unable to evaluate the bids. Usually the contract is then awarded on the basis of price only. Later, the owner is subjected to extras which cost more than he anticipated.
>
> This problem is frequently caused by the architect's lack of detail in his specifications. He leaves it up to each bidder to work out his own details with the gas company or bid the job without any instruction. Because of this common practice, we are occasionally accused of being inconsistent in our requirements. There may be some foundation for this accusation because each job may have five or six contractors submitting bids. When they inquire about the details, perhaps they talk to different people in the department. Of course, many times there is more than one way to do the job; therefore, they may get

slightly different information. Contractors also claim that we are too slow in providing the information at times so they don't wait but bid without our recommendations.

When such problems occur and the installation is improper, it becomes necessary for the contractor to change the installation to conform with the company's specifications. If any additional expenses are incurred, the contractor passes this additional cost on to the customer. The customer feels that this charge which increases the cost of his total project is unnecessary and usually holds the gas company responsible instead of his architect, the consulting engineer or the installing contractor.

The company also decided to review its relationship with the community. In this case, in reviewing the record, they found that the company was held in reasonably high regard by both local government and the community agencies. The local press has reacted favorably to the publicity releases offered by the company and has not opposed the company in rate applications or any other company function requiring public support. In all, the company's relationship could be considered favorable.

After reviewing the problems revealed by the close check on customer telephone contacts, by the survey of service performance, the interviews conducted in the commercial field, and the general community attitude, it was decided action was warranted to improve its public relations in all phases of its business.

Hanley Engineering Corporation

Byron Dobie, a 1959 graduate of the Amos Tuck School, was administrative assistant to Mr. Lincoln Lashton, President of Hanley Engineering Corporation. Byron had joined the training program of Hanley in June 1959 and was appointed Mr. Lashton's administrative aide in August 1960.

The Hanley Engineering Corporation was located in Pittsburgh, Pennsylvania, where it was founded in 1878. The Company provided engineering services of various kinds and had gradually built a national reputation for excellence in its consultations on such large construction jobs as bridges, dams, and hydroelectric installations. Nearly all of the executives of Hanley had engineering or technical degrees from university engineering schools. The stock of the Hanley Corporation was publicly subscribed; forty per cent of it was held by the family of George Hanley, the company's founder.

On September 19, 1960 the following conversation took place between Mr. Lashton and Byron Dobie.

Mr. Lashton: Byron, in the morning mail I got a letter which I want you to read. It raises an issue that I plan to put on the agenda of the October meeting of the Executive Committee. I want you to write a memorandum to me in preparation for that meeting. But first read the letter.

[Byron read the letter, attached here as Exhibit 1.]

Byron: Mr. Stokely is a personal friend of yours, isn't he, Mr. Lashton?

Mr. Lashton: Yes, we've been rather close friends for more than twenty-five years. I'm sure you know Stokely as one of the most respected men in Pittsburgh. He is practically Mr. Public Service, and he has done immeasurable good for Pittsburgh. Also, of course, we do a lot of work with Pioneer.

Byron: What kind of memo do you want me to put together?

Mr. Lashton: Our executive committee meeting is October

14th. I want to discuss Stokely's letter at that time, and prior to the meeting I will circulate his letter and some material on the activities of the Fund for Adult Education.

What I want you to do is this: give me by noon on October 8th a memo telling me what issues you think are involved for Hanley in considering our proper reaction to Mr. Stokely's letter. Also, I want you to include a brief discussion of your personal definition of "liberal education" and what relevance this concept has to the operation of Hanley Engineering Corporation.

Your memo will be a help to me. I may not agree with it and I'll tell you if I don't. I'm not going to talk with you about it at all because I want your views undistorted by my predispositions. I know you can't possibly make any recommendations and I don't want you to. But you can give me a comprehensive idea of the issues which are involved in thinking about what decision the executive committee must make.

Byron: Will you show my memo to other people?

Mr. Lashton: Probably not. I'll have to see it before I decide that. It is primarily for my own use in preparing for the executive committee meeting.

(End of dialogue)

Exhibit 1

Office of the President
Pioneer Steel Corporation
Pittsburgh, Pennsylvania
September 16, 1960

Mr. Lincoln R. Lashton, President
Hanley Engineering Corporation
Carnegie Building
411 Federal Street
Pittsburgh 3, Pennsylvania

Dear Lincoln:

As you know I am serving on the Board of Directors of the Fund for Adult Education. The Fund was established by the Ford Foundation in 1951 as an independent organization to advance and improve "that part of the educational process which begins when formal schooling is finished." The Directors of the Fund defined "its special task as that of supporting programs of liberal adult education which will contribute to the development of mature, wise, and responsible citizens who can participate intelligently in a free society." For the period 1951 through 1961, the Fund received from the Ford Foundation a total of $47,400,000.

The Fund has supported the development and offering of a wide variety of formal and informal programs of liberal adult education through institutions of higher learning; national organizations; fellowship awards and special training programs; public understanding; fact-finding, research, and evaluation; and educational television. The impact of these programs has been broad, and the Board has felt special gratification at the response to these efforts on the part of the business community.

At the end of 1961 the Fund's financial backing from The Ford Foundation will come to an end, and we are making plans to replace Ford support with that of a wide variety of institutions and persons interested in continuing liberal education for adults.

My own special interest is to develop support from my colleagues in Pittsburgh industry to provide a financial cornerstone, as it were, for the contributions other sectors of the Greater Pittsburgh community will want to make. As I told you recently, Lincoln, we see the promise of substantial rewards to our metropolis in such projects as expanding the power and influence of WPEX, our educational TV channel, giving grants to the local universities to offer programs and conduct experiments in the adult education field, and sponsoring public colloquia to promote liberal education among adults.

It is time for us to be concrete. I am asking the presidents of one hundred prominent business organizations in Pittsburgh to provide the leadership we need, by declaring what types and amounts of contribution they will make on behalf of their companies for the continuing support of this vital program. I think you agree, Lincoln, that we need to act; and the sooner the better.

The initial meeting of our group of one hundred Pittsburgh presidents will be on Thursday, October 20th, at 12:00 noon in the Duquesne Room at the University Club. At that time, I would like to discuss detailed plans with you, propose a $200,000 annual budget, and ask you each for (1) your reactions to the whole program and (2) what amount of support your company is prepared to give, in terms both of financial aid and executive time.

Please call me, Lincoln, if there are any questions you would like to discuss before October 20th.

Cordially,
James T. Stokely
President

Bibliography

Baker, H. G. "Identity and Social Responsibility Policies: Six Large Corporations Examined." *Business Horizons,* 16 (April 1973), 23–28.

Crumbley, D. L. "Finalized Regulations Show that Philanthropy Can Still Be Rewarding." *Taxes* 51 (April 1973), 227–234.

Dreyfus, Patricia. "Corporate Identity: A Critical Assessment." *Management Review,* June 1970, pp. 12–16.

Dunne, E. "How To Discover Your Company's Reputation." *Management Review,* August 1974, pp. 52–54.

Goodman, S. J. "Raising the Image of Business." *Stores,* March 1974, p. 11.

Harris, L. "Public Credibility of American Business." *Conference Board Record,* 10 (March 1973), 33–38.

"Industry Needs To Tell It's Story; But Do the Media Treat It Fairly?" *Industry Week,* January 8, 1973, pp. 60–63.

Mertes, J. E. "Genesis of the Corporate Image." *Michigan State University Business Topics,* 19 (Winter 1971), 35–46.

Moran, J. "Using PR Strategy to Project A New Corporate Image and Help Increase Sales." *Public Relations Journal,* 30 (October 1974), 20–21.

"Negative Business Image Draws Worldwide Concern." *Business Week,* September 13, 1971, pp. 13–14ff.

Ross, D. N. "Business Confronts Itself at the Credibility Gap." *Conference Board Record,* 10 (July 1973), 24–27.

Ross, I. "View from Stewart Mott's Penthouse." *Fortune,* 89 (March 1974), 134–140.

Schwartz, R. A. "Corporate Philanthropic Contributions." *Journal of Finance,* 23 (June 1968), 479–497.

Wojtusiak, J. "In Support of the Arts, Companies Know What They Like." *Conference Board Record,* 7 (January 1970), 62–65.

Part Ten
Appraising Future Business-Society Responsibilities

A. Business-Society Issues

An historical analysis of the changes and trends in business and society over the past twenty-five years is the subject of the selection "Comparative Analysis of Business-Society Issues Over Three Decades" [38]. This analysis notes that a number of issues increased considerably in the sixties over the fifties, but more significantly, the number and severity of issues in the early seventies exceeded both previous decades. Most dramatic among the changes have been issues that have gone full cycle: from appeals for government-business separation, to advocacy of government-business partnerships, to a return to protests against government bailouts of business and support of greater government-business separation. One such issue is the influence of environmental constraints and problems. Another issue that has experienced full-cycle development is that of participative management. From pleas for participation in the 1950s, business shifted to situational applications in the 1960s but returned to a very strong participative trend in the 1970s, not only to obtain more effective management leadership styles, but also to meet the significant attitudinal changes in participation expectations of protest groups. A third issue affected by full-cycle development involved conflicts between business and religion. Religion had rather significant concerns about business in the fifties, shifting to virtually no concerns in the sixties, and returning to concerns in the form of organized religious action groups focused against business in the seventies. These developments indicate the short-run dynamics of the conflicts between business and society in a democratic society and economy.

The radical confrontations of many groups against business in the 1970s have been most significant among recent trends. In the past, groups made many appeals and pleas, but mostly in verbal and written form. In the 1970s organized action has been the pattern. In order to meet these vigilant moves on the part of many groups in society, business must somehow formulate a philosophy that will allow it to deal with protest in rigorous and specific terms of management's rights and responsibilities. This will likely evolve through a more professional stand on the part of management, through the active formulation of corporate policies that will provide action guidelines leading to a more credible corporate image, and, hopefully, through a positive code of ethics. The latest and most comprehensive mandate to the individual in business is that in the future his or her position must be that of a leader and not a follower in reconciling these business-society issues. This will include a more statesmanlike posture by which business will not only resolve conflicts, but will also promote its legitimate interests.

The most recent change in social responsibility trends is discussed in the selection "Social Responsibility Fades as a Matter of Corporate Concern" [39]. The *Wall Street Journal* carried this message, reporting on the cancellation of programs concerned with social responsibility. The article contends that we do not hear as much about the subject now because social concerns belonged to the era of the sixties when companies were rich. This dramatic shift is of course a realistic one, and apparently due to the economic pressures for business survival and the maintenance of full employment. It appears that business and society priorities will be reordered, until such a time that the economic health of our economy allows for greater flexibility in pursuing socially responsible programs. This does not mean that socially irresponsible actions on the part of management, to the detriment of society, will be tolerated. The history of issues in business and society includes lessons from the depression of the 1930s. Even when business may have the power to engage in arbitrary, irreponsible acts in the short run, it can no longer do so without serious repercussions from society.

The article "The Future of Capitalism" [40] relates the future of these issues to the total economic system. We have already explored the economic problems of inflation, unemployment, and recession, and the long-run costs of economic growth earlier in this book, and now Robert L. Heilbroner considers noneconomic issues for the system. He believes that historical projections of the success or failure of capitalism appear to have both been refuted. Capitalism has not collapsed, as predicted by the Marxists, but neither has it continued to survive and grow in utopian terms. Heilbroner contends that capitalism faces two challenges that may destroy it and will certainly alter its existence: one is the result of technological growth and the other is the result of affluence. We have already recognized the threat of pollution as a result of technological growth. Heilbroner also sees in technology the power to effect considerable social change as a result of breakthroughs in medicine and psychology, for example. The problems that have developed from affluence concern the shift in the attitude toward work. To work is no longer an imperative for survival, and Heilbroner believes that this passivity holds serious implications for social harmony as well as future productivity and growth.

Heilbroner questions the ability of capitalism to effectively meet these challenges alone.

The social responsibility problems faced by business in the future therefore include elements of understanding social and political values, behavior patterns, and their trends. Economic success no longer guarantees social harmony, and the problems of the byproducts of economic growth and affluence are rapidly increasing. Do we now face a subordination of the economic system to the oncoming social and political goals of our society, a complete reversal of the past century? The problems of capitalism can no longer be resolved by the self-correcting mechanisms of the system, and the political superstructure is taking over a system to which it had been historically subordinated. If the need for social control continues because of inherent failures of the system, Heilbroner questions the viability of capitalism, the private property right, and the market system. Therefore management must address itself to extremely complex sociopolitical problems. It appears that the future reconciliation of business-society issues will require the sophistication of a management philosopher, and a combined and systematic effort on the part of U.S. business managers to forecast, analyze, and formulate business policies for all major issues. Eventually these policies may be synthesized into a management philosophy that can direct all managers in resolving the business-social-political problems of the future.

B. Appraising Social Responsibilities: The Social Audit

Over the past twenty-five years there have been repeated appeals for some accounting on the part of business for the degree to which it meets its responsibilities to society. As far back as 1953 the concept of a social audit for the corporation was advocated by Howard R. Bowen in a study he made for the Federal Council of Churches entitled *Social Responsibilities of the Businessman*. Now, the corporate social audit is one of the most consistently treated topics. In the article "What Is A Corporate Social Audit?" [41] Professors Bauer and Fenn spell out for us the development of the pressures for the social audit and their opinions on the content of the first stage of such an audit. They first refer to the audit as a systematic assessment and report of company activities with social impact. These activities to a great extent have resulted from external pressures brought to bear on business as well as a company's own forecasting of future social needs.

The authors raise many questions concerning the concept of the corporate social audit. For example, what cost measures will be used to determine success or failure, where will the data be acquired, and what will be the accuracy of this information? Since the social audit is in the early stages of development the authors contend that it is not likely that a perfect instrument will be developed soon. Instead they recommend what they call a "process audit," which would identify the major social programs of a corporation, define the program goals in meaningful terms, provide a rationale for the purposes of these goals, and describe what is being done at the present time on the programs that have been formulated. They recommend that in the early stage of audit development it is most important to recognize social auditing as a process. They also believe that a flexible audit instrument would be more appropriate for the assessment of service programs.

The selection "Components of A Social Audit of the Corporation" [42] provides another approach, in which the content of the audit is a delineation of those business-society conflicts that have been debated in the business periodical literature over the past twenty-five years. The issues that have prevailed in that time, including the recent wave of environmental problems in the seventies, provide a sequential "factor content" for a social audit of the corporation that includes the following: free enterprise system issues, protest group pressures, organization-individual conflicts, labor-management relations, ethical problems, social responsibilities, formulation of business-society goals and philosophies, public relations policies, social action programs, and forecasts and plans for future business-society conflicts. Within these ten major categories, fifty strategic conflict rating factors have been defined, weighted, and applied under a 10,000-point rating system. This system is an appraisal of the "percentage of industry potential achieved" by individual firms in the performance of social functions of business. The selection includes an example of this social audit system. The general content of the fifty factors of the audit and the variable weights applied to each factor in the audit allow application of a social audit to different industries and different size organizations.

In developing the social audit we made the significant finding that policy formulation and written policy guides are imperative for business actions in a socially responsible fashion. Unless the policies are written and effectively applied, they may again assume the public relations role of image making, which too often becomes inconsistent with corporate practices. Another major finding was that without the specific delegation and designation of corporate organizational responsibility, it is likely that policies and programs will not be applied over time. If specific corporate responsibility is assigned to individuals and departments, social programs will be far more significantly achieved.

In conclusion, the diversity and changes in the types and amounts of public expectations are so dynamic that they require business to systematically approach the social responsibility function in the future. While at present we may note a radical shift in the concern for social responsibilities, we have only to review the lessons of the depression of the 1930s to realize that some mistakes should not be repeated. This means that socially responsible actions should not be relegated to the research closet. It seems incumbent as a final note to business, that in a recession, the lessons learned from the depression of the thirties should be immediately applied.

A   Business-Society Issues

38   Comparative Analysis of Business-Society Issues over Three Decades

William T. Greenwood

Significant changes appear to have been made in the issue-conflicts between business and society in the decades of the fifties, sixties, and seventies. These issue-conflicts have been measured by the frequency and significance of their treatment in the business periodical literature since 1950.

The starting point for the appraisal of these issue-conflict trends is a compilation of those issues of the 1950's in the first edition of *Issues in Business and Society.*[1] To avoid an excessively long bibliography, it is recommended that this book be checked for individual bibliographical citations. The issues of the 50's are abstracted as follows:

I. Our Free Enterprise Society
   A. Capitalism and freedom — A background of the evolutionary stages of capitalism and an evaluation of the economic freedom of the businessman in free enterprise and his conflicts with the freedoms of other individuals and groups in society.
   B. Business, Competition, and Government — The problems of the power of big business, and concern with the increase in federal controls over business such as antitrust, etc.

Reprinted with permission from *Management Theory, Research and Practice — The Search for Unity,* Southern Management Association Proceedings, Mississippi State University, 1972, pp. 170–178.

[1] W. T. Greenwood, *Issues in Business and Society,* Houghton Mifflin, Boston, 1964.

C. The Role of Profits — The limitations of profit maximization, and concern with the benefits and problems of profit sharing, especially as an ethical right.

II. Business and Its Publics

  A. Public Relations and the Corporate Image — Ethical problems of false corporate images in business relations with multiple groups and objectives.

  B. The Political Role of the Businessman — The debate of the legitimacy and responsibility of the businessman to engage in politics, and his role in encouraging and/or coercing subordinate participation.

  C. The Problem of Business Giving — The pros and cons of the responsibility and the right of corporate philanthropy in legal terms, and in terms of the directness to which the contributions relate to corporate objectives.

III. Business and the Individual in Society

  A. Human Relations and Leadership — Evaluation of the need for human relations in handling employees, and especially of the participative style of management versus "keep them happy" fad perspective.

  B. Conformity or Individualism in Business — A consideration of the extremes of rugged individualism in business, emphasizing freedom of the individual and his creative and innovative contributions versus excessive and arbitrary organizational conformity.

IV. Labor-Management Relationships

  A. Labor Relations and Collective Bargaining — A critique of the collective bargaining process as it contributes to inflation as opposed to the increased effectiveness of professional labor relations on the part of both labor and management.

  B. Management's Employment Responsibilities — The responsibility of business and the Federal government for maintaining full employment, and a consideration of an extensive range of alternative means of achieving this under competitive conditions.

  C. Fair Employment Practices — Pro and con arguments on fair employment practices commission legislation throughout the United States.

V. Ethics, Religion, and Business

  A. Ethical Aspects of Business Practice — Arguments for the ethical responsibility of the businessman versus his productive economic responsibility, and of the potential need and development of a code of ethics for the businessman.

  B. Business and Religion — Examination of the "inherent conflicts" between business and religion, and the potential responsibility of business to provide means of relating work goals and individual religious goals in the job.

VI. Trends toward a Philosophy of Management
A. Management Rights — The rights and prerogatives of management, especially as they relate to labor-management relationships, and a philosophical evaluation of the nature and derivation of management's legitimate rights.
B. Business Objectives — A delineation of the business objectives required for survival, and an evaluation of the many business objectives under differing cultural conditions.
C. Management Philosophy — A comparison of the need for a business philosophy of individualism versus government controls, and arguments against excessive individualism in managerial philosophies.

VII. Social Responsibilities in Business
A. The Social Responsibility Concept — The historical evolution of the social responsibility concept, and arguments against social responsibility for management because of the inherent dangers working against the free enterprise system.
B. Professional Responsibilities of Power Groups — Appraisal of the social responsibility level required to be commensurate with the degree of managerial power in both large organizations and in small organizations in terms of "socio-human power." Evaluation of the feasibility and desirability of management becoming a profession.
C. Responsibilities of the Future — A survey of business-management projections for the next twenty years emphasizing the problems of inflation, unemployment, and underdeveloped nations of the world. A comparative analysis of all business-society issues of the 1950's with the national goals delineated for the U. S. at the end of this decade.

The business-society conflict-issues of the decade of the 1950's provides us with a basic framework from which we can examine the trends of these issues and conflicts into the future. In particular, they represent the "proximate" problems faced by the operating manager today versus the more remote and perhaps academic ones that have been treated in the literature in the past decades and centuries. It is particularly interesting to note that the majority of the conflicts can be related directly to the national goals formulated for America in the late 1950's and the social responsibilities inherent in these goals. It therefore appears that the basic starting point of the evaluation of business-management goals and responsibilities to society can best be considered by a review of our national goals at a given point of time. This will not be all inclusive; nevertheless it is probably the most comprehensive perspective illustrating actual and potential goals-conflicts between business and society.

Business-Society Issues Trends: 1950's and 1960's

The broad classifications of business-society issues appear to have remained the same, while many of the individual issues have changed considerably. In general a majority of the issues have remained in the forefront of the literature, illustrating the fact that many of these issues are perennial conflicts of the institutional power groups in society: business, labor unions, and the individuals in American society. Because of the freedoms protected for both the individuals and institutional groups in society, it is only to be expected that conflicts will prevail, and the hope and expectation would be that they be minimized, or reconciled in more equitable terms over time.

I. The free enterprise society issue now finds a revolutionary point of view. Historically business has been adamantly opposed to governmental intervention and regulation of business in a free society and economy. Because of the extensiveness of business-government problems, the recommendation has now been made that government and business seek a partnership relationship in an attempt to resolve these problems, versus the opposing positions held in the past.[2] The long standing critiques of profit maximization are opposed in the 1960's in a more detailed rationale for the justification of profits for both business and society.

II. Business and its public's sector include new contributions for the corporate image process in the public relations functions. A more professional approach is now taken in the development of "constructive" images, including a movement from the defensive position of unethical images to an emphasis on the positive development of the many image facets of the corporation. Also in this sector the issue of corporate giving is raised to a more professional level under a "prudential" theory of business giving. The issue of the political role of the businessman dropped from the scene in this decade, but time will tell whether or not it may recur as a major responsibility of the businessman. These new developments represent significant progress in the degree of evaluation and sophistication in the articulation of business' role in society. And it is these kinds of developments that will inherently lead toward more professional management in their reasoning and articulating their legitimate social rights and responsibilities.

---

[2] W. T. Greenwood, "A Changing Balance of Power: New Partnership of Government and Business," *Business Week,* July 17, 1965, pp. 85–106.

III. A new development in the sixties was the business-youth conflict to the business-individual sector. The apparent rejection of business by a growing segment of the youth in America, especially the university student, constituted a new issue for business which may be with us for some time to come.[3] The human relations problems dropped from the scene, but were actually reconsidered in the leadership style of participative management. A significant breakthrough appears to have been made in the leadership style issue in that the state of the art reached the point of refuting any one style as being best, making the decision for the leadership style most appropriate to the situation.[4]

These trends provide a breakthrough in the issue of leadership theory after years of research and debate, and the new problem of youth-business conflicts presents totally new perspectives of conformity versus individualism considered in the decade of the 1950's. The youth revolution then appears to have brought a new level of concern to business that affects them both internally and externally as they attempt to work more effectively with the individual in society.

IV. Labor-management relationships found significantly new developments. The collective bargaining problem was extended to include the unemployment-inflation tradeoff issue [5] and the right to work issue was re-emphasized in this decade.[6] The unemployment-inflation tradeoff problem presented management with a higher level of responsibility in attempting to make collective bargaining work more effectively, and also to meet the employment responsibilities of business and government. This means that management in the second decade of business-society issues must take a higher perspective of the problems as they are treated in the aggregate for the whole of America's economy and society. This is especially true for widespread unemployment levels [7] and prevailing inflation.

V. The ethics, business, and religion sector appears to have received little attention during this decade. But this probably suggests that the ethical perspectives of business responsibilities were treated in

---

[3] Duncan Norton-Taylor, "The Private World of the Class of '66," *Fortune,* February 1966, pp. 128–132, 166, 168, 170, 172.

[4] Robert C. Albrook, "Participative Management: Time for a Second Look," *Fortune,* May 1967, pp. 166–170, 197, 198, 200.

[5] Robert C. Albrook, "GOP Is Thrown a Price-Job Curve," *Business Week,* March 22, 1969, pp. 60, 62, 64.

[6] Clair M. Cook and William Jones Fannin, "The Battle Over 14(b)," *The Christian Century,* July 28, 1965, pp. 937–940.

[7] Ad Hoc Committee on the Triple Revolution, "Machines Do It Better than Humans: An Assessment of a Workless Society and Proposals for Action," *Advertising Age,* April 6, 1964, pp. 121–122, 124, 126.

more detail and in a more accepting fashion as business-management particular social responsibilities rather than addressing them from the viewpoint of their ethical practices.

VI. The philosophy of management received little change in the decade of the sixties, and what occurred was a qualitative versus a quantitative change. The theory and philosophy that defend the rights and prerogatives of management were severely restricted in the decade of the fifties, but in the decade of the 1960's, a delineation of the responsibilities of management to effectively control organizations in terms of survival and growth appears to have articulated at a much higher level the legitimate rights and duties of management in relation to society.

VII. The social responsibility topic was not debated as much as treated under new issues, presented in the following new section.

VIII. The new social responsibility issues were so extensive that they have been included in the 1960's under the heading of business-environment issues. In particular, the growing urban problems have led to a second proposal that government and business join hands in a partnership to more effectively attack these problems.[8] Pollution abatement has become a nationwide problem, and how to deal with it remains to be seen in terms of its complexity, and in terms of the different organizations and groups that may share this responsibility with business.[9] The so-called community responsibilities of management have been extended from the local and national communities to the international scene especially by the multinational firms.[10] Once again the recommendation is made that a government-business partnership be developed in order to have participation of business in foreign policy determination affecting these multinational firms.[11] One issue-conflict came and left the scene within the decade of the sixties, that of cigarette advertising. Governmental legislation provided a "social control" resolution of the problem, especially insofar as any voluntary management social responsibility was involved.

The future social responsibilities of management have been expanded to the point that not only the role of a professional manager will

---

[8] Ad Hoc Committee on the Triple Revolution, "Business and the Urban Crisis," *Business Week,* February 3, 1968, pp. 57–72.

[9] National Industrial Conference Board, "Pollution Abatement in Industry: Policies and Practices," *Conference Board Record,* December 1966, pp. 35–38.

[10] Henry H. Fowler, "National Interests and Multinational Business," *California Management Review,* Vol. VIII, No. 1 (Fall 1965), 3–12.

[11] Theodore J. Gordon, "The Environment and Corporate Change," *Conference Board Record,* June 1967, pp. 40–44.

be required to resolve these issues, but now the role of business statesmen is proposed to meet the responsibilities of the future. This is also
reflected in the changing perspectives of national goals in which the
President's Commission reevaluated the goals in terms of a balanced
growth of the American economy and its components, with an emphasis
upon quality as well as quantity of both business and life for individuals
and groups in American society.[12] This implictly carries with it a higher
level of social responsibility for the businessman, perhaps in the terms
of the business statesmen of the future.

In general the decade of the 1960's brought a revolutionary
change from government-business perennial opposition and conflict to
the recommendation that a partnership be established in order to jointly
resolve problems beyond the scope of each. Fortunately, the professional
development of management theory provided excellent articulations of
business-society issues, paving the way for a more professional level of
management practice and perhaps business statesmanship in the future.
Therefore the decade of the sixties constituted a major step forward for
management in incorporating in its theory the social responsibility concept and philosophy.

Business-Society Issues: 1960's into the Seventies

I. The free enterprise society enters the decade of the 1970's
with a new variety of issues. In almost a full circle swing from business
versus government into the government-business partnership, we now find
protests against governmental involvement in bailing out large firms in
distress except in those instances where there is a high degree of national interest.[13] Already the government-business partnership raises
questions as to where the line can be drawn between government and
private enterprises, and the ideology of free enterprise is contested in
terms of its applicability in the international community.

Profits are reevaluated as strategic forces in the economy and
in terms of their contributions to the pollution problem.[14] The relation
of the profit motive to the social problems emerging in this decade is
considered, with at least one perspective that the two will dovetail.[15]
Profit-sharing remains an issue of concern in both the aspects of the
right to profits in collective bargaining and also the motivation and

---

12 National Goals Research Staff, *Toward Balanced Growth: Quantity
with Quality,* U.S. Government Printing Office, Washington, D.C., 1970.
13 National Goals Research Staff, "Managers Oppose Bail-Outs — Except in the National Interest," *Industry Week,* August 2, 1971, pp. 40–41.
14 National Goals Research Staff, "Pollution and the Profit Motive,"
Business Week, April 11, 1970, p. 82.
15 National Goals Research Staff, "Profit Motive, Social Problems Will
Dove-Tail," *Industry Week,* March 23, 1970, pp. 12–13.

productivity of profits in profit-sharing programs. In summary, the questions raised concerning the free enterprise system in the early stages of this decade should make this issue an increasingly active one in the coming years.

II. Business and its publics, in the performance of the public relation function of the corporation, face immediate conflicts. Environmental problems have developed public relations crises, and increasing criticism toward business projects a militant decade of the seventies. The public expectations of business, especially in the areas of social involvement and ecology, may force business into an identity crisis in assessing its role in society.[16] And last, but not least, the reemergence of the consumer voice appears so strident as to require new lines of communication to minimize the level of this overt conflict.[17] Corporate giving is reviewed not so much in terms of philanthropy, but in terms of the responsible role it should play in social progress.[18] Again, the number and variety of issues portend a much more active and professionally sophisticated involvement in the public relations function.

III. Business and the individual in society issues have been more significant in number and intensity in the past two years than in the prior decade of the 1960's. For example, concern with more participative management has perhaps brought about a reshift to this as the "ideal" style of management, especially in terms of the claims of the rights of the individuals to participate more effectively in the organization.[19] The old concept of industrial democracy, or management of the organization by all of its members, apparently has been reactivated under the concept of corporate democracy.[20] It is contended that decentralization may evolve into a worker's management, and that with the growing protest of the individual worker and consumer, the corporation may be the next institution to fall.[21] The problem of business and youth remains an active one, with more comprehensive perspectives searching for understanding on the part of both groups.

---

[16] National Goals Research Staff, "Companies Face an Identity Crisis," *Business Week,* February 20, 1971, pp. 52–55.

[17] E. B. Weiss, "Hot Lines to Industry Will Help Consumers Keep Cool," *Advertising Age,* May 31, 1971, p. 36.

[18] D. Creel, "Role of Philanthropy in Social Progress," *Conference Board Record,* 7 (June 1970), 9–12.

[19] D. Creel, "Symposium: Workers Participation in Management: An International Comparison," *Industrial Relations,* 9 (February 1970), 117–214.

[20] D. W. Ewing, "Who Wants Corporate Democracy?", *Harvard Business Review,* 49 (September 1971), 12–14.

[21] A. G. Athos, "Is the Corporation Next To Fall," *Harvard Business Review,* 48 (January 1970), 49–61.

IV. Labor-management relations remain much the same in terms of collective bargaining and full employment, but the right to work issue remains very much alive in the decade of the 1970's,[22] while the civil rights-fair employment practices increases with a major new emphasis. The problem of fair employment practices for the Negro increasingly is taking its toll in terms of its effect on the overall corporate image. But more significantly, Title VII of the Fair Employment Act has become overwhelmingly active from women's liberation movements contesting discrimination in employment for women, unequal pay, lack of managerial opportunities, and lack of opportunity for entry of black women into business organizations.[23] It appears that the problems of continuing inflation and widespread protest against unfair employment practices will force management into more creative efforts to resolve these problems, and also to protect their corporate image against widespread criticism.

V. Ethics, religion and business present new problems, and the ressurection of an old issue. The new approach is contained in the perspective of ethical problems for the business manager with increased consideration of his ethical activities in terms of a social conscience on social issues, and a professional perspective in his utilizing marketing research to determine attitudes toward business ethics at this time.[24] In a sense the resurrection of the religion-business issue was more significantly active in the 1950's, but is relatively dormant in the 1960's. A repeated emphasis is found on the responsibility of management to provide a means of bridging the gap between work and God, including the new concept of a religious manager.[25] The new developments in this area will require heightened sensitivity of management to develop a keener perception of the ethical impact of its business practices, and the ethical expectations on the part of the consumer and individual in society. This may well entail a reevaluation of potential business-religion conflicts.

VI. Business-management philosophies receive widespread and severe challenges in the early stages of this decade. Business is once again contested to consider partnership rights of other parties in the

---

[22] A. G. Athos, "Stroking Up a Drive for Right-To-Walk," *Business Week,* March 14, 1970, pp. 28–29.

[23] A. G. Athos, "Women's Lib; Marching as to War," *Economist,* March 6, 1971, p. 30.

[24] R. M. Fulmer, "Business Ethics: Present and Future," *Personnel Administration,* 34 (September 1971), 48–55.

[25] J. Senger, "Religious Manager," *Academy of Management Journal,* 13 (June 1970), 179–186.

management of the firm.[26] The social crises emerging in the seventies are asking that management redefine its goals, determine their hierarchy, and consider them in an international as well as national context. These objectives, rights, and implicit responsibilities are asking for a changing management philosophy, one that will provide a new ideology for managerial leadership and for resolving business-society conflicts, both at home and abroad.[27] And it is in the realm of the formulation of a corporate creed, philosophy, or ideology that management may well make its breakthrough in the decade of the seventies by not only evaluating all of its business-society conflicts, but integrating them into a business-management philosophy, with universal application.[28]

VII. The social responsibility concept debate continues, but the preponderance of views favor the concept. In particular, pressures are being voiced for a higher degree of involvement on the part of business in helping social ills, reducing pollution and serving the consumer.[29] These are treated in their particulars in the next section.

VIII. Business and its environment, in both the present and the future, find immediate and changing challenges in radical confrontations or revolutions in the public expectations on business.[30] With a call for self-renewal, business is expected to exercise far greater leadership in achieving social change and meeting social needs. In particular business is asked to develop a broader concept of the environment including ecology and the total environment.[31] Pollution, urban, and consumer problems receive widespread concern, but again the major challenge is in a broad and enlightened leadership for meeting social change. The future will require this kind of leadership, with an imperative for developing policies for meeting the social crises of the present and the future.[32]

A review of the changes in business-society issues over these decades seems to find an awakening to the issues in the fifties, strong

---

26 K. R. Robinson, "Partnership with Management: Absurdity or Necessity," *Labor Gazette*, 71 (May 1971), 299–307.

27 G. C. Lodge, "Top Priority: Renovating Our Ideology," *Harvard Business Review*, 48 (September 1970), 43–55.

28 G. A. Steiner, "Changing Managerial Philosophies," *Business Horizons*, 14 (June 1971), 5–10.

29 Moskowitz, "Companies Must Take Social Duties Seriously," *Advertising Age*, September 27, 1971, p. 86.

30 H. Ford, "Revolution in Public Expectations," *Public Relations Journal*, 26 (October 1970), 16–18.

31 F. A. Lindsay, "Management and the Total Environment," *Columbia Journal of World Business*, 5 (January 1970), 18–25.

32 H. B. Palmer, "New Imperatives for Tomorrow's Policy-Makers," *Conference Board Record*, 7 (January 1970), 68–72.

voices and even demands for business meeting its social responsibilities in the sixties, and in the seventies, calls for, and cites examples of, actions to force business to respond. Some conflict-issues appear to have gone full cycle: Government-Business separation, to partnership, to protests against government bailouts of business; participative management pleas, to situational applications, to a participative trend; concern with business-religion conflicts, to no concern in the sixties, and a concern plus leveraged actions against business in the seventies.[33] These full cycle examples vividly portray the short-run dynamics of the many perennial conflicts between business and society in a "free" democratic society and economy.

Radical confrontations by many groups in society now will force management to action, versus protests or inactions of the past. Business must develop broader perspectives on these issues and become more articulate in the use of philosophical concepts underlying the rights and responsibilities. In short, it must professionalize to the extent of positively conceived policies, corporate images and a philosophy that will relate the goals and functions of business with those of society. Finally, this philosophy must be implemented with aggressive leadership and statesmanlike negotiations in order to defend and promote the rights and responsibilities of business as a legitimate "interest" group in society.

[33] H. B. Palmer, "Social Activists Stir Up the Annual Meeting," *Business Week,* April 1, 1972, pp. 48–49.

39 Social Responsibility Fades as a Matter of Corporate Concern

The Wall Street Journal

"A lot of attention to social issues is being postponed while immediate survival issues are being addressed," says Clark Abt, president of Abt Associates, a Cambridge, Mass., consulting firm specializing in social issues. One indicator: Abt was forced to cancel a two-day seminar later this month on "The Social Performance of American Business during the Next Decade." It had room for 100 executives, found no more than 10 would come.

American Management Association eliminates briefings on social issues from this year's schedule for lack of interest. Its latest such meeting in October drew 13 people. Says Jack O'Dwyer, who publishes a weekly newsletter on the public relations field, "You don't hear much about social responsibility now. That belonged in the 1960's when companies were rich."

Sign of the times: *Business & Society,* a $75-a-year newsletter started on the West Coast in 1968 to keep companies informed about social issues, formally closes up shop.

40 The Future of Capitalism

Robert L. Heilbroner

Was ever a generation so uncertain about its destiny as our own? It seems to me that our foresight is indeed clouded in a way that sets us off from previous generations, at least those of fairly recent times. The cloudiness is not the result of our sheer ignorance — that is more or less a constant throughout history. It results rather from our knowledge. Not because we know too little, but precisely because we have learned too much, it has become singularly difficult to answer with assurance the question: Does capitalism have a future?

Anyone who presumes to discuss the outlook for capitalism, that is, must face the following disconcerting fact: The two most cogent predictions with regard to the future of capitalism have both been tried and found wanting. The first of these — never, perhaps, dominant within the Western world — has always provided a powerful current of thought for those who opposed capitalism. This is the theory, basically Marxian in origin, that capitalism is an inherently *self-destructive social order*.

I need hardly say that history has not confirmed the seemingly irrefutable "logic" of this apocalyptic view of capitalism. Capitalism teetered in the United States and England, but it did not collapse; and with the exception of Russia, wherever capitalism underwent violent change, as in Germany and Italy, the direction of the movement was to the Right, not to the Left. Even more disconcerting to the believer in the Marxian drama, when the storm of fascism had passed, capitalism re-emerged in excellent economic health, as witness the post-World War II histories of West Germany and Japan.

What happened to disconfirm the Marxian prognosis of the future of capitalism? Here we begin to encounter those new elements in our knowledge that make present-day prediction so difficult. The first such element is the realization that the industrial working class is not revolutionary in its temper.

Why did the doctrine of the inevitability of class war fail?

From *World*, September 12, 1972, pp. 27–30. Reprinted by permission of Saturday Review, 1972. Copyright Saturday Review.

The reasons are many. Primary, of course, is that the economic system did not collapse, so that the pressures of economic misery so vividly described by Marx were slowly alleviated. Next in importance is that the combined economic and technological pressures of an expansive capitalism did not serve to swell, but rather contracted, the numbers of the proletariat, opening the way for many to join the ranks of white-collar workers. As a result, the political temper and social outlook of the working class became progressively less "proletarian" and progressively more "bourgeois" — destroying as a further consequence the unity and discipline that Marx had expected of his revolutionary class. And not least in this array of causes must be placed the disillusion that gradually attached itself to the idea of socialism, as the harsh realities of Stalinism brought an end to the hope that the end of capitalism would usher in an instant transition to a new, classless society.

The second of the now-disproven predictions — this one far more widely believed in among Western societies — is the opposite of the first: namely, that some form of capitalism — call it ameliorative, or welfare, capitalism — could continue to sustain and extend its hegemony.

What do I mean when I say this has been disproven? Certainly not that capitalism is incapable of continuing its impressive record of economic growth. Certainly not that capitalism cannot improve the distribution of income, or its provision of social services. What I have in mind is something much more fundamentally shaking, especially for those who hope that the future can be discerned with clarity by projecting the economic trends of the present. *It is that economic success does not guarantee social harmony.*

Of all the elements of knowledge gained in the past generation I can think of none so radically challenging for the social theorist. Let me present as an instance the case of the United States. Had anyone in the 1930s been told that the U.S. Gross National Product in the early 1970s would surpass a trillion dollars — effectively *doubling* the real per capita income within the lifespan of the majority of the population then alive — I am sure he would have felt safe in predicting an era of unprecedented social peace and goodwill.

Yet that enormous economic change has taken place and social harmony has not resulted. Economic growth, in other words, did not prove the great solvent for social difficulties. The economic transformation from the conditions of the 1930s to those of the 1970s has not lessened the potential for racial disturbance, has not headed off the explosion of juvenile disorders, the widespread decay in urban amenities, or a serious deterioration in national morale. Indeed, growth has brought new problems, environmental and other. Nor has such an experience been confined to the United States. Unprecedented growth in France and Germany has not prevented violent outbreaks of dissatisfaction in those countries, particularly among the young. Nor have Sweden or England or the Netherlands — all countries in which real living standards have vastly improved and in which special efforts have been made to lessen the economic and social distance between classes — been spared a share of the expression of profound social discontents.

This inability of a "successful" capitalism to guarantee social harmony adds more than another neutral element of knowledge to our present uncertainty with regard to the future. I think it is fair to say that among the new evidences of social unrest — the drug culture, the cry for participatory democracy, the alienation of students, the new sexual morality, the retreat to the life of the commune — none is congenial with or supportive of those attitudes and behavior patterns on which capitalism has traditionally rested. It is possible, in other words, that we stand at the threshold of an era in which deep-seated changes in lifeways will undermine capitalism in a manner as fatal as the most dramatic proletarian revolution might do, although perhaps less rapidly or romantically.

Yet the fact that we cannot discern the road ahead does not mean that we are hopelessly lost. On the contrary, because we are forced to stop, we are in a position to do something that the motorist cannot — examine the ground beneath us and perhaps derive some better idea of the geology of the region in which we find ourselves. Now, the composition of this ground, which we will call "capitalism," is considerably different from the idea of it that underlay both the pessimistic and optimistic conceptions of the country through which we thought we were traveling. For in both the Marxian and the "liberal" views of capitalism — divergent as they might be otherwise — there was an important common belief. In both schools of thought, capitalism was formerly described as an economic system in which the means of production were privately owned and the marketplace regulated the main currents of economic activity. But that was not the important thing: *both the apocalyptic and the ameliorative views of capitalism saw the economic machinery of the system as dominant, and the political and social accoutrements as subordinate.*

To begin with, then, let us recognize that both views erected stereotypes of capitalism which ignored important aspects of reality. The Marxian concept of governments being "the executive committee of the bourgeoisie" failed to take into account the very wide latitude that, from the early nineteenth century, government was capable of applying to its task of attending to the interests of the economic ruling classes. And on the other side of the ideological divide, those who believed that the inherent economic tendencies of the system should be allowed to work themselves out with a minimum of political interference closed their eyes to the fact that the governing institutions have always intervened to maintain capitalism as a system in good working order — now stepping in to promote economic activity, now curbing excessive competition, now establishing certain social standards of safety and well-being.

Moreover it is also clear as we look back over the history of capitalism, in particular since World War I, that the range and depth of government penetration into the economic process have undergone a slow, uneven, but in the end, decisive increase.

This fact has two important effects on our thinking. The first is that the rise of the political "superstructure" to a position of much greater equality with — indeed, perhaps superiority to — the economic base leads to ever greater uncertainty in our predictions. For whatever our belief as to the outcome of the economic mechanism of capitalism — whether, again, it be conceived as self-destructive or ameliorative — our ability to project a trajectory for that economic mechanism weakens when the economic machinery no longer works "by itself" but is continuously subject to political direction. Second and equally clear, the "politicization" of capitalism opens all predictions to the vagaries of the political process, or of social currents such as the changes in life-style to which I earlier referred — aspects of the social system with respect to which we possess no predictive capabilities whatsoever.

Yet with the disappearance of the old stereotypes of capitalism comes an awareness of other aspects of the system that may yet enable us to see some little distance into the surrounding gloom.

For instance, despite the persistence of private ownership of the means of production and the market, the system we call "capitalism" turns out in fact to be a *family of systems* capable of a very great variation in political and social (not to mention economic) performance: witness the guaranteed lifetime employment offered by the big Japanese corporations, and on the other hand, the near-indentured labor of the Union of South Africa; the highly developed welfare system of the United States; the *"dolce vita"* of Italy and the Calvinist atmosphere of Germany; the effective government of three language groups in Switzerland, and the extreme difficulties encountered in governing two language groups in Canada.

In the face of such a spectrum of political and social structures, it should be clear that it is no longer possible to declare with assurance what constitutes the "pure" model of capitalism. This is certainly not to say that this broad spectrum of capitalist societies does not display common problems or face similar challenges. But if social prognosis is to offer more than a mere wishful projection, it cannot predict how such problems and challenges will be met by arguing in terms of a stereotyped "capitalism" that never quite existed.

What, therefore, *do* capitalist societies have in common? I imagine that you think I will now recite a familiar list of ailments: inflation, unemployment, foreign exchange difficulties, competition, and the like. But the truth is I see little that can be forecast with regard to this so-standard range of capitalist ills other than that we will cope with them with about the same mixed results of success and failure as we now experience.

Instead, I wish to turn to quite a different set of problems: namely, the deleterious side effects of certain kinds of economic growth. We have all been aware for some time of the specific dangers posed by pollution-generating output. What we are only now becoming aware of is the possibility that pollution may pose a problem of such dire implications that only a global ceiling on production will assure our very survival.

We do not yet know whether drastic production limitations will in fact be imperative; that depends largely on our ability to develop technologies that will permit the detoxification of certain effluents, the recycling of scarce materials, the efficient use of low-grade minerals, etc. But it seems highly probable that within the lifetime of the present generation a degree of social control will have to be exercised over the level and composition of production that far exceeds anything now known in any capitalist country. Whether the basic institutions of the capitalist mechanism — private ownership of resources and plants, and the reliance on the market as a main instrument of allocation — would survive such a severe constraint is at least problematical.

But there is a second problem — of equal gravity and of perhaps more certain advent. This is the challenge of rising affluence. Economic well-being, however little it speaks to the question of social harmony and content, assuredly *does* bring one consequence: the ability of those who enjoy some degree of affluence to withstand the pressures which underlie the smooth operations of all capitalist and (although less publicized) all socialist systems. For, given the fact that most labor is still monotonous and unrewarding, there is only one answer to the question: "Why do men work?" It is: "Because they have to."

But as the general level of affluence rises, there is a corresponding slow decline in the brute necessity of a search for employment at any price or any place. Already in the United States we see the coexistence of large numbers of "unemployed" youths and unfilled jobs of menial kinds which in a former age would have been quickly filled, or the parallel rise of unemployment among women and unfilled opportunities for domestic labor.

It is no doubt a considerable triumph for a society to reach a level of general affluence at which the unemployed person no longer has to accept gratefully whatever dispensations the market makes available. But we must not hide from ourselves the price of this social victory. That price, very simply, is a vastly increased risk of social breakdown. The extreme vulnerability of all urbanized environments to work stoppages leaves us exposed to potential catastrophes whose foretaste has been felt in the United States (and elsewhere) when strikes of garbagemen have left city populations exposed to disease, strikes of teachers have allowed outbursts of juvenile misbehavior, strikes of air controllers have paralyzed transportation systems.

Societies have, of course, always been vulnerable to work stoppages if they lasted very long. But in the past, two factors militated against a real test of society's vulnerability. One was the concentration of the work force in the industrial sectors, where the effect of strikes — for example in steel or coal — was cushioned by the presence of inventories on which the public could subsist for a considerable time. And the second was the general poverty of most workers, which greatly hampered their staying power when on strike.

In the urbanized, increasingly affluent setting of today and tomorrow, these safeguards have been greatly weakened. No inventories can be accumulated of the vital social services that sustain city life. Meanwhile the staying power of the work force has been very greatly increased. What then will provide the social discipline once exerted by the harsh pressure of necessity? We do not know. Appeals to conscience and to patriotism, the bribe of ever-higher wages, the intervention of public agencies, the use of troops, the outright militarization of labor are all more than mere possibilities — they have already been used on more than one occasion. I cannot predict which measures will be used in the future by which nations, or what damage will be done to civil liberties or to the union movement as a result. I can only state that as industrial societies move to ever higher levels of affluence, the economic pressures of the marketplace can no longer be counted on to provide its necessary labor as a matter of course.

Thus a consideration of the problems now facing the family of capitalisms brings one to a curious new perspective. More and more of the kinds of problems to which we find capitalism exposed reach over to affect socialism as well — by which I mean reach over to affect that family of societies that rests on an economic base of public ownership and planning.

Two such problems stand preeminently to the fore. One has to do with the common technologies that are used by all industrial societies, capitalist or socialist. By this I do not mean that there is one and only one way of making steel, electric power, or cloth. A considerable variation in production techniques can be observed from one country to the next. Yet in all industrialized countries, these processes have one characteristic in common — they are organized to achieve a more or less continuous flow of outputs. This in turn requires that there be a continuous flow of inputs, usually applied in the sequential form of mass production, as each commodity is gradually transformed from its original to its final state. Unlike the choice that seems to be available in the institutions of government, in social welfare practices, in life-style in general, when it comes to economic life, mature capitalism and mature socialism are both forced to use production "styles" whose resemblances to one another far outweigh their differences.

This observation is perhaps commonplace. But from it follow consequences of considerable importance. For the presence of a common style of production imposes a common "style" of social organization. The presence of huge units of production, each requiring internal order and external coordination with other huge units (or with final consumers), brings to all industrial societies a common scaffolding of control-mechanisms that surrounds the central structure of production itself. This scaffolding, visible as the ministries, the planning agencies, the corporate headquarters, the regulatory commissions of capitalist and socialist economies, constitutes the *economic bureaucracy* that is the counterpart of industrial production itself.

No doubt there is a vast deal of difference between the bureaucracy of a central planning board and that of a cartel or a conglomerate corporation. But one resemblance nevertheless seems crucial; *it is that the industrial process imposes on all who come into contact with it, labor and management alike, a necessity to coordinate efforts in ways that must be specified by an industrial bureaucracy.* I do not claim that industrial production cannot eventually be decentralized, democratized, personalized — only that efforts to achieve these ends will have to overcome the "imperatives" of mass production, and that this struggle will be no easier for socialist societies than for capitalist ones.

Another problem is the increasing necessity to establish effective social controls over the generation and application of science and technology in daily life. We are all aware that we have entered a new era of technological capability of which nuclear energy is only the most spectacular example. Genetic engineering, human transplants, the postponement of death, the conditioning of behavior through electrodes implanted in the brain — all these are either actualities or near-term possibilities for medical science. No less extraordinary are new developments or possibilities in the technology of personal surveillance, of weather-control, and still other areas.

What marks all technological change to some degree, marks these developments to an exaggerated degree. That is their capacity to work large-scale social change, often in directions that we distrust or fear. To control the effects of these technologies, perhaps to inhibit or forbid their application, will therefore become a major challenge — perhaps *the* major challenge — for governments of all advanced nations in the future, socialists no less than capitalists.

From what I have said it must be clear that I believe we can dimly discern something about the terrain over which *all* industrial societies will have to make their way. To be sure, this is a "prediction" of a very different kind from that which would tell us the turns and twists of the road on which any particular industrial society will travel. It is one thing to see the obstacles of technology or industrial organization, or the difficulties of ecology or affluence, and quite another to make the guess — for it can only be a guess — that Sweden will succeed and the United States fail, or vice versa; or that the family of socialist nations will surmount the obstacles, while the family of capitalist nations will not.

Capitalism throughout the world is still saddled with the obsolete privileges of inherited wealth, with the dubious force of acquisitiveness as a source of social morale, and with the problems of reconciling powerful vested interests with needed social policies. On the other hand, however, most advanced capitalist governments enjoy some experience with parliamentary forms of government and some subscription to civil rights and liberties. Thereby they provide themselves with channels that may facilitate the necessary restructuring of their economic institutions, and that may serve as safeguards against the abuse of political control.

On the socialist side, we find an array of nations that have the advantage of a socio-economic system stripped of the mystique of the private "ownership" of the means of production and the presumed legitimacy of the uncontrolled workings of the market. On the negative side is the cumbersomeness of their present planning mechanisms, their failure to develop incentives superior to those of capitalism, and above all their still rudimentary realization of political freedom.

One last word. Throughout the globe, a long period of acquiescence before the fates is coming to an end. The passivity of the general run of men is waning. Where there was resignation there is now impatience. Where there was acceptance there is now the demand for control.

The end of acquiescence poses challenges to all societies, but perhaps in particular to those in which the silent operation of the marketplace has traditionally given rise to the illusion that society requires no controls. Thus I believe the ultimate challenge to the institutions, motivations, political structures, lifeways, and ideologies of capitalist nations is whether they can accommodate themselves to the requirements of a society in which an attitude of "social fatalism" is being replaced by one of social purpose. If this pronouncement is too imprecise for those who like their prophecies clearcut, at least it may offer consolation to those who see in such a vision the necessary stimulus to fight for the eventual attainment of a good society, be it capitalist or socialist.

B Appraising Social Responsibilities: The Social Audit

41 What *Is* a Corporate Social Audit?

Raymond A. Bauer
Dan H. Fenn, Jr.

Once the murky notion of the social responsibility of business began to take on popular appeal and specific shape, it was inevitable that public pressure would begin to build for some sort of business accountability in the social sphere. After all, if society really believes that corporations should broaden their concept of their own function to include social responsibility, articulate members of society are going to demonstrate and implement that belief by demanding some kind of accounting of corporate performance in noneconomic areas.

This demand that corporations be socially accountable has been augmented by a growing realization among businessmen that corporate social programs have been haphazard in their growth, poorly aimed and weakly coordinated, and little known or understood — even within a given corporation. Further, if specific programs are hazy and obscure, the notion of "total social impact" has proved almost completely opaque, not just to businessmen, but to society as a whole. Thus it should surprise no one that the pressure for and talk about a formal "social audit," in some way analogous to a financial audit, have increased measurably in recent months, both within and outside companies.

The social audit is indeed a relatively new development; it has only a thin history prior to the 1970's. It first appeared on the scene when the accepted definition of "corporate social responsibility" was no longer being formulated primarily by businessmen, but rather by social activists who had reason to capitalize on a general suspicion of all "establishment" institutions, including business. What the term means is commensurately vague, and there is precious little agreement on how such an audit ought to be conducted.

In the pages that follow, we present a description and analysis of some of the problems encountered by those who are attempting to perform social audits and outline an approach that appears to us to be viable. We term this approach the "first-step audit." It is designed to provide data that are immediately useful for corporate executives; it is also designed to put the whole effort toward social accounting on an upward learning curve by combining descriptive information with quantitative measures in a meaningful way. Hopefully, the first-step audit will be helpful to businessmen who are trying to resolve such questions as: "What activities should I be auditing? What measures should I use? And what standards of performance should I use to calibrate my record?"

Some readers will say that what we are proposing is not an *audit* at all, but rather a form of social *report*. So be it; but we cannot see that the question of terminology has much significance at this point. The loose usage of the word "audit" has characterized discussions of corporate social audits and is sanctioned neither by dictionaries nor the accounting profession. An audit means the independent attestation of facts by some outside party, but it is clear to us that independent attestation is a step that still lies far down the road. The first-step audit we shall describe will prove, we believe, a useful way station.

For the purposes of this discussion, we shall take "social audit" to mean: *a commitment to systematic assessment of and reporting on some meaningful, definable domain of a company's activities that have social impact.* This definition is a fairly disciplined one, and one that will allow the activities now carried on under the social-audit banner to be included in a more embracing form, with independent attestation, at a later date.

Sources of Pressure

As we have said, there are powerful forces loose in the land that are demanding some kind of social audit:

Authors' note: Our thinking on the issue of the social audit is reported here in condensed form. Readers who wish further information about our work on social auditing and the process-audit concept may consult *The Corporate Social Audit* by Raymond A. Bauer and Dan H. Fenn, Jr., The Russell Sage Foundation, New York, 1972.

1. Executives generally desire to acquire both an individual and a corporate image of social responsibility, one that harmonizes with a public concern which they (and we) do not believe is going to subside.
2. Businessmen, like everyone else, are caught up in the changing mores and priorities of the society and are concerned today about matters which only a few years ago did not worry them. The level of this concern should not be underestimated. Pollution, the disadvantaged and minorities, clarity and directness in advertising — issues like these have moved rapidly onto (and higher and higher on) the agendas of corporate executives.
3. Another influence is commercial. A number of consultants, sensing the possibility of a new source of business and inherently curious about the whole complex area, are trying to develop ways of performing social audits.
4. Then there is the stimulus of the outside "auditors" — the Naders, the Council on Economic Priorities, the new mutual funds, the recently established journal called *Business and Society Review,* minority groups, ecologists, and so forth, all of whom have a stake in making public almost anything that a company may want to hide. Obviously, such stimuli encourage management to present their cases in ways they think accurate and proper; but, perhaps even more important, managements want to know what is in store for their companies if they are attacked. This second motivation has obtained in some of the companies with which we are acquainted, where managements actually do not (or did not) know what or how well they were doing, although they may have had some suspicions.
5. Nonprofit organizations such as churches and educational institutions have spurred the idea of social auditing. Urged by their constituents to establish a "social portfolio," to sanitize their holding of paper from companies adjudged irresponsible, or to influence the policies of those in which they have investments, these organizations have been seeking (usually with painful unsuccess) to establish some way of determining if Company X is or is not socially responsible.
6. Investment houses which, for a variety of reasons, are establishing funds specializing in "clean" securities are also generating interest. These houses face the problem of identifying companies that both act responsibly and promise to be good long-term gainers. This is not a simple matter: it begs a gaggle of questions turning on what is "good social performance."
7. The social activists themselves have an obvious stake in some kind of measurements. If they expect to have significant impact

on corporate behavior, they need some yardsticks to use in advising the general public of the social health of this or that company.

Confusion of Methods

It is precisely this broad spectrum of pressures for social auditing that causes much of the confusion. Everybody is talking about the social audit, but scarcely anyone agrees with anyone else as to exactly what it is, and no two organizations are doing it quite the same way. To illustrate:

> In one company, the chief executive assigned the task of designing a social audit procedure to his public affairs group. This group, naturally enough, was primarily interested in increasing the company's role in community affairs and consequently designed an audit that would demonstrate a close linkage between social programs and long-range profitability.
>
> Another CEO [chief executive officer] wanted to satisfy his own conscience that his company was, indeed, behaving responsibly. Inevitably, the issues and norms selected for the audit were those which were important to him personally, and the nature and precision of the data generated were determined by how much he needed to know to sleep at night.
>
> One president wanted to make sure that his corporation's social programs were producing the maximum benefit to society for the investment being made. He focused the auditing effort on making an inventory of what the company was doing and evaluating the usefulness of each program vis-à-vis others in which the company might engage. Hence his audit was designed to answer such questions as this: "Should we be working with the public schools in town instead of sponsoring low-income housing?"
>
> The relevant question for a church or an educational institution is this: "Which companies are doing well in ways that are of particular concern to our constituency?" If a constituency is upset about apartheid, or antipersonnel weapons, or pollution, the only questions the audit must answer — within the bounds of financial prudence — are whether or not any companies represented in the institution's portfolio are viewed by the constituency as socially responsible on this particular range of points; and, correspondingly, the audit will be designed to pro-

vide just the data that show whether the criteria are in fact being met.

Consider the social activist who seeks to force corporations to halt activities that have (as he thinks) antisocial effects, and who also seeks to enlist them in the effort to improve the world around them. Here, again, the task is different, and the audit will be different. The activist will select the issues that strike him as being especially significant and collect enough data to convince himself and the general public, which is the ultimate source of his influence, that improper things are being done.

The consulting firm interested in helping clients with the auditing problem obviously wants to develop a version of the social audit which is financially and professionally feasible and applicable for as wide a variety of clients as possible. Its non-individualistic approach is bound to conflict and contrast with those of other auditors.

The company that is seeking either a good image or protection against attack will select those areas for investigation that, in its judgment, will satisfy the public it is trying to impress (which may, incidentally, include its own employees). Since the audit data must be made public, the company will probably need to make investigations and disclosures that are very extensive — extensive enough to convince an audience that is growing ever more skeptical of corporate pronouncements. Its audit is bound to be company-specific, by virtue of the nature and depth of the data required.

In short, many purposes and programs are currently crowding and jostling under the umbrella of the social audit. Nevertheless, the full vision continues to be that, in the future, companies shall report their social performance with the same regularity and the same appearance of precision with which they now report their financial performance.

The question to be asked is whether the audit can ever be developed to a state that will satisfy that austere vision.

The Vision vs. Experience

In the past few months, we have investigated a number of organizations that are engaged in one or another kind of social auditing. We have talked with consulting firms and looked at their efforts. We have met with and, in some cases, worked with companies in many different industries that are taking bites at the apple. We have been associated with several of the social action groups. We have studied some of the investment houses. And we have now reached the point, we feel, where we can define five significant difficulties imbedded in this auditing process.

1. How do we decide what to audit?

As the social auditor enters the thicket of implementation, the first bramble bush he will meet is the question of what to audit. What are the areas of social responsibility, anyway? As we have surveyed current practice, we have found almost as many answers as there are auditors.

Pollution and the hiring and promotion of minorities (including women) receive a roughly consistent priority, but after that things are fairly wide open. Some auditors virtually ignore corporate giving and community programs; others include them. Quite a few stress consumerist issues of various kinds; others go heavy on munitions manufacturing, or investments in South Africa or Portugal. Still others focus on employee well-being — fringe benefits, promotion opportunities, safety, and so forth.

The choice is not easy to make. When he comes to decide whether to include a specific factor, the auditor inevitably realizes the full complexity of some of these issues. For many, Polaroid's involvement in South Africa was a simple matter, but the company did not find it so. Finally, after a strenuous internal debate, the company came to the conclusion that it would better satisfy its social responsibility in the long run, even in the eyes of the groups pressing for withdrawal, by remaining in that unhappy land than by leaving it.

Equally, some of the components of social responsibility are as vague as they are complex. For example, how does the auditor grapple with a subject like "quality of work?" This term can — and does — mean everything from the adequacy of fringe benefits to the degree of employee participation in corporate decisions. Executives in one company found to their surprise that employees felt it was socially irresponsible for management to demand of them as much time and effort as the corporate mission required. Clearly, quality of work is too imprecise a quantity to be taken for granted.

Defining the *relevant parts* of social responsibility creates further difficulties. For some, a social audit is adequate if it simply examines the community activities in which a corporation is engaged. For others, this is ducking the issue: the relevant point, they feel, is the impact a company is having on society because of the business it is in or the way in which it is conducting that business. An insurance company might ask itself, for example, what good it does to audit its investment in low-income housing and minority enterprises but ignore its redlining policies in the ghettos? Similarly, one might argue that a change in the traditional hiring practices of a company is going to have a far greater beneficial effect on a community than all the gifts it makes to the Community Fund.

Finally, the definitions of corporate social responsibility are still evolving. If one takes the recent past as a basis for prediction, he would have to guess that expectations will rise, that standards of performance will be hoisted, that new and unforeseen issues will be introduced, and that some of today's causes will become less relevant. Thus, in 1973, good labor relations is no longer much of an issue; similarly, if pollution laws are strengthened and enforced, pollution control may not be worth auditing in the future. Social responsibility is a moving target, and this fact greatly complicates the choice of what to audit.

Roughly, the decision as to what to audit has to be determined in one of two ways. Either the top corporate executives, on the basis of their interests and their perceptions of the concerns of their constituents, must make the choices, or some kind of survey of the relevant constituencies must be conducted. A good case can be made for either approach; it is largely a question of what purpose a company has determined for the audit.

2. What are the measures?

Once a company has defined the areas it wants to audit, it must decide how to measure its performance.

One obvious way is by cost — what it spends in each area. But even if a company selects only a narrow definition of social responsibility and focuses just on the costs of its so-called social programs (for example, English-language programs or housing rehabilitation), how does it determine what the true costs of such activities are? How does it measure the executive time that goes into them? How does it assign overhead to them? How does it assess the opportunity costs involved?

Furthermore, cost by itself is an inadequate measure, since the main question the company will want to answer about each activity is, "Was it a success?" The difficulty in answering this question is that such corporate activities can ordinarily be measured only in terms of such intermediate effects as the number of people who have received a given type of service — say, the number of community residents whose apartments have been rehabilitated. Few social programs can satisfactorily document what the delivery of these services did for the people who received them.

In addition, these activities are extremely expensive to evaluate, and it is doubtful whether any company would find it feasible to make frequent evaluations of its total contributions

A compounding difficulty here is that the answer to the question, even if one gets it, may be valueless. If a company ascertains the number of high school students who use the computer it has donated, what has it really learned? Probably, not very much.

3. What constitutes success?

Thus we come to the problem of defining what constitutes success — that is, of defining the appropriate norms against which a company should measure. Even if a company can make a sound selection of items to audit and can develop some satisfactory measure for its performance on these items, how will it know when it has done a job right? How good is good?

Government standards (if they exist) may fill part of the need here, but most of us would feel that such standards are minimums for performance, not norms for judging success. Furthermore, in many areas such as pollution and minority hiring, there is so much variation of factors from industry to industry in the problems with which companies are confronted that one probably needs separate performance norms for each. Sometimes this is possible; more often it is not; but even when it is, it is rarely adequate. One would not expect Con Ed's records for hiring and promoting Puerto Ricans to look like those of PG&E. Specialized norms mean tougher comparisons in measurement.

In an effort to cut through such problems some people have suggested that the effectiveness of a company's program in meeting a social issue is the norm that should be used. We have already referred to the difficulty of evaluating social programs and the even greater difficulty of comparing the ones selected with others which could have been undertaken.

There is also another difficulty with this approach. The success of a program for training the hard-core unemployed, for example, can be measured in terms of numbers completing the course, being hired, and being retained in the job. But if an observer tries to go the next step and judge whether a particular company's hard-core training program solved or even significantly contributed to the solution of a social problem, the verdict may well be dismal, simply because any one company's contribution is unlikely to solve a problem unless it is a very large company in a very small community.

4. Where are the data?

Next we should mention the difficulty of collecting data in this area. It is expensive and time consuming for a large, complex company to collect adequate data about its social programs, much less determine which of its activities have a social impact and thus should be studied. Quite frequently, outside auditors have difficulty getting at the kind of information they need. Even inside auditors may run into real problems. For example, one company with only minimal manufacturing operations but extensive retailing ones decided to hire a group of students to check on what it assumed were the few locations where it could be polluting. It very quickly became apparent that the job was truly immense, because the company was disposing of solid wastes in literally hundreds of company locations. The group could only sample, not study, the company's pollution programs.

Another reason for this difficulty is stubborn internal resistance. Even if the CEO wants a social audit, he is likely to encounter foot dragging, if not outright opposition, within his own family. In conglomerates in particular, division managers resent what they perceive as an intrusion into "their" private files.

Also, managers do not seem to care much for morale surveys to see what the people they supervise think of the company and its record in social performance. Others disagree philosophically with the whole social-responsibility idea; some even say that if the boss wants to fool around with it at his level and work with the Boy's Club somewhere, okay — but he had better keep his liberal do-goodism out of operations. This kind of controversy has forced more than one CEO to back off and scale down his internal audit from what he had intended.

In one company, the headquarters staff started to audit the condition of the employees because they thought it would be the easiest way to cut their teeth before they began to audit other matters. Believing that equal employment was well accepted in the company, both as the law of the land and the right thing to do, they sent people to check records in one of the divisions.

The division head, however, flatly refused to let them look at the files; and when he finally did consent to open the drawers as a result of a topside order, he continued to be as uncooperative as possible within the terms of the directive he had received. At this point, the company began to reconsider the whole social-audit idea.

5. How accurate can we be?

Unfortunately, there has been an inordinate amount of loose talk about the social audit, much of it in responsible journals or in responsible places. For example, Thomas Oliphant, writing in *The Boston Globe,* said: "Almost all of this data exists right now on some corporate executive's desk. What is lacking is the decision to put it all together and release it to the public in a manner modeled roughly after financial accounting standards to ensure a maximum of information and a bare minimum of public relations."[1] To that statement, and the many similar ones being made today, we reply," Nonsense."

But, unfortunately, it is worse than nonsense. The twin myths that such a thing as a social audit exists and that financial audits are hard and precise have misled some businessmen into trying to create a report on their social performance which has the same precision and accuracy they attribute to the balance sheet.

---

[1] "The New Accounting: Profit, Loss and Society," May 1971.

The fact is that we are not yet at the point where such an audit is possible, and we may never get there — indeed, we may never have to. The social audit, even when we have learned how to do one that is credible internally and externally, may look nothing like a financial audit at all. We are only on the edge of the thicket, and what we really need is not a man with *the* answer, but a number of men with the courage to try to frame *an* answer — to experiment, to learn about how to measure and report on social performance, and to pass what they learn along to the rest of us.

The Abt experiment Only one of the companies we studied, Abt Associates, had completed anything that could meaningfully be called a social audit.

The Abt audit of its own activities is a public document included in the firm's annual report. It is an effort to represent, in purely dollar terms, the company's social assets and liabilities — in other words, its social impact. This represents a diligent and ingenious pioneering work, especially on the part of the president, Dr. Clark Abt, who spearheaded the effort. However, considering the novelty of this effort, it is no surprise that the firm's accountants did not give it their official sanction.

There are various reasons why we think that this format is *not* the one most likely to be adopted by large, complex companies:

> It does not appear to respond to the currently perceived needs of the executives of such organizations nor to the realities of their situations, as we understand them. For example, the Abt audit is organized around the total social impact of the company rather than around an assessment of its social programs. While this approach has great conceptual attractiveness, it is not particularly well adapted to the needs which are expressed by the executives with whom we are familiar, whose concerns, objectives, and aspirations for an audit are far more limited than Dr. Abt's.

> Abt Associates is a relatively small consulting firm. The total social impact of a large complex company is not nearly so amenable to this kind of financial summary.

> The goal of the Abt audit, once again, is to render social performance in dollar terms in balance sheet form. Thus it does not disclose (it may even hide) the firm's performance in social programs in which its executives are interested. For example, a company could be spending large amounts of money inefficiently, on pollution control or hard-core training, on giving substantial sums to irrelevant charities. And, indeed, in

the course of conducting his audit, Abt found out some unwelcome facts about his organization and changed policy accordingly. But the actual rendering of his findings into balance sheet form was, in our view, a superfluous technical exercise. Our sense is that few companies are interested in supporting this last step of technical virtuosity *if the information can meaningfully be presented in other ways.*

Abt's audit is designed for external reporting. However, most executives are interested at this time in internal reporting for internal assessment. The prospect of external reporting exacerbates the already considerable anxiety of such executives.

Finally, the Abt form of a social audit is so abstract and complicated that we find few, if any, executives (never mind laymen) who claim to understand it as an overall entity — nor do we feel we can explain it as a totality.

We do, however, encourage the reader to consult the Abt annual report to form an independent judgment. We may well be too sharply critical; and, indeed, we have a personal bias to which we must confess. We feel that the attempt to reduce social performance to dollar terms is perverse. While monetary measurs are of great utility in many contexts, this utility is, finally, limited; we feel there is likely to be fatal error in employing the dollar measures as exhaustive representations of social phenomena.

Our judgment is not so negative with respect to proposals for auditing the dollar *costs* of social contributions, although we are respectful of both the difficulties and the tricky judgmental questions imbedded in such calculating. Mainly we are skeptical of the availability and possibility of rendering the social *consequences* — whether positive or negative — in dollar terms.

All in all, given the complexities and complications of doing a social audit, given the various forms which an audit might take, and given the varying uses to which it might be put, we judge it a mistake to specify at this time just what its final form should or will be. Instead, we believe that the task of management for the immediate future is to get on the learning curve.

This is best accomplished by tackling the auditing problem in a way that is sufficiently modest to be attainable, yet of sufficient scope to have both some utility and some value as a base for more ambitious versions of the social audit. The first steps toward a social audit also should be defined with an eye toward the organizational conflicts that a social audit can bring about.

Hints for Getting Started

Thus our first suggestion is that the audit be initially designed for internal purposes only — that is, for aiding in the decision making process and for helping officers assess the company's social performance, both with a view to its vulnerabilities and to changes that management may want to make in its activities. Such a course offers dual benefits.

For one thing, it relieves the anxieties of those corporate officers who fear the embarrassment of disclosure, enabling the company to make corrections with a certain amount of privacy if it chooses to do so. Equally, it allows officers to take what guidance they can from data and judgments that may be too imprecise to present to the public, and it bypasses their natural fears that their professional and financial future may be adversely affected.

We make this suggestion — that the first effort to a social audit be aimed at internal decision making — in full recognition that the audit is likely to be reported to the public sooner or later. We only propose that there be no initial *commitment* to publication of the first-round audit, so that this learning experience can be entered into with a minimum of anxiety and a minimum of demand for technical elegance.

We also suggest that a company first focus on its programs rather than on its social impact. There are three strong practical reasons for this recommendation. Two of them are those we just cited for aiming the audit at internal decision making: the magnitude of the task and executive anxiety. The task of considering, measuring, and evaluating all the impacts of a large, complex company on society boggles the mind; it also seems very threatening to anxious executives, since the results of such an analysis may strike at the very core of the business. A deodorant manufacturer might become a stench in its own nostrils.

The third reason is the sheer difficulty of defining the limits of social impact, which is surely a conceptual haymaker, as terms go.

Again we recognize the limitations and counterarguments to what we are proposing. For many industries, one could argue that a company's social activities are merely cosmetics that conceal the impact of its regular business activities. There is little reason for crediting a drug company, say, with an excellent domestic employment policy without investigating its promotion policies and labeling practices in other countries. This counterargument concludes that the auditor's concern must be global. Nonetheless, we advise early simplification for the sake of avoiding endless debates that might well take on the color of theological disputes.

We also recognize that when a company is examining its social programs, it may also want to look at its regular business activities as a separate, parallel effort, especially if either its internal or external constituencies are demanding such an examination or are likely to do so.

For example, one bank is looking at the impact of its lending policies, realizing that these are related to the social audit it is undertaking; but the bank is not at this stage considering the policy investigation as part of the audit. Similarly, even where public pressure encourages or forces a company to look at one or more of its regular business activities — for example, munitions manufacturing, construction in Vietnam, or doing business in South Africa — such examinations ought to be handled separately from the initial audit.

If companies accept these two suggestions — focusing only on internal use and social program evaluation — life will be much simpler, but still complicated enough to be interesting. The audit will have a "meaningful, definable domain," as our statement suggests it must, but the domain will still be virgin wilderness.

We must point out, however, that a compromise is available which some companies may prefer to adopt. A company may feel it imperative to define those constituencies to which its actions are most relevant — employees, customers, stockholders, "the community," and so on — and survey these constituencies to determine for which aspects of social performance they hold the company responsible and what their expectations are.

This procedure would establish a "definable domain" for social auditing in a quite different fashion from the path we have recommended; but it has one defensive advantage worth mentioning, namely, public attitudes. Its disadvantage may be that it probably does not provide as valuable a learning experience as our more orderly first step does for the company that plans to build toward a more complete audit. Hence, on balance, we believe that concentration on social programs as the "defined domain" is the preferable route.

Inventory and cost

Assuming a company decides to review its social programs first, its next step should be to compile an inventory of its explicitly social programs. For almost every company, this list will include the currently popular issues of pollution control, minority and female hiring, and promotion practices. Let us say that it will also include corporate giving. From there on, the nature of the list is likely to vary with the corporation in question, and it will not always be easy to decide what ought to be included and what ought to be excluded, or why.

A typical instance of such a difficulty is whether to include executive participation in community affairs when the executives contribute their own time. Our advice is to exclude any item from the list that is not the result of an explicit corporate policy involving a meaningful level of resource commitment. We also advise companies to exclude any item that causes substantial argument. (Of course, a company would do well to keep a list of rejected items, for future perspective.)

There will be other kinds of difficulty as well. In some instances, management may discover that there is no central source of information on everything the company is doing in the social area; hence compiling the list may take more effort than one would expect or accept.

Once the inventory has been reduced to those socially motivated activities to which the company has clearly made a commitment and which it accepts as "social programs," management can begin to assemble the costs and performance data associated with them, to get a picture of the extent of the company's commitment to each one and to social programs as a whole.

The first area is the matter of costs. Generally, there will be less difficulty in getting the direct costs of each activity than in ascertaining the true costs, which is quite a different matter, as we have already pointed out. These true costs should include allocated overhead and opportunity costs as well, wherever the resources might have been put to different use. A company's ability to get such true costs readily will depend on how the relevant items are represented in its accounting system, what system it is using to measure work, and the like. One should also realize that even if the basic data are available, special allocation conventions may be required.

Since considerable expense and effort are required, the auditors and management should make an explicit decision as to whether they deem it worthwhile to establish the true costs of social activities, whether they are willing to go with a rough estimate, or whether they will be content with knowing only the direct costs.

Our sense is that the public at large is not likely to be interested in the true costs of a company's social activities. Even though the true costs would represent a more accurate picture of the company's level of effort, they are likely to be perceived as padded figures.

However, for *management* decision making, true cost will be important. If it proves difficult to get true costs in the first audit attempt, and a decision is made to forgo this information, this circumstance should signal the need for establishing mechanisms for assessing true costs in the future. It is highly probable that there is no thoroughly satisfactory way to do this at present, although Professors Neil Churchill and John Shank are currently researching this problem at the Harvard Business School.

The second area of quantitative measurement is performance data. The place to start is still readily available statistical data that show the level of effort expended and measure the output. For example, how many hard-core unemployed have been trained, or apartments renovated, or children served in a day-care center? It is true, as we have pointed out, that pulling together such material may be difficult. It is also true that this kind of material does not necessarily show, in and of itself, the *effectiveness* of the programs.

Perhaps the assistance extended to minority businesses has in fact done more harm than good in that the funds generated ultimately are spent outside the inner city, or the failures have served to discourage people from starting ventures instead of encouraging them to do so. But we shall return to this difficult matter of norms and social benefits in a moment. Suffice to say at this point that there are some figures that can be obtained, and that they do constitute legitimate data for a social audit.

Here again, we would opt for a kind of "creaming" approach. Rather than spending inordinate amounts of time either in determining what figures should be collected or which should be included, we would urge that the most obvious and easily ascertainable be the ones that are reported. It is too early in the state of the art to try to squeeze out the last, ultimate figure or to fight through the finest kind of judgments as to what should be in or out.

Ethics of public reporting These first two steps of an audit will give a picture of the extent and nature of the company's social programs and of the resources committed thereto. The display of just these two sets of information will be of help to many managements in assessing their social performance. These sets of information could also be the basis for reporting to the public, should management choose to do so.

It may be argued that reporting data such as these is very little different than what is being done for public relations purposes by many companies in their annual reports or in special publications. We grant this. But we see nothing wrong in a company's communicating the extent and nature of its social activities and the magnitude of effort behind those activities, provided the coverage is complete and the reporting honest.

Such an audit would at least reveal the extent of the company's concern. One of us recently conducted a study of the reaction of Bostonians to the efforts Boston business was making to help the community, and we were struck by the fact that success or failure, or even quantity of effort, is outweighed in people's minds by evidence that companies or individuals actually are concerned and are doing something about it. Businessmen are not expected to solve the problems of the city, nor are they expected to be successful in every venture they undertake. However, they are expected to take the problems seriously.

Thus an honest and straightforward public reporting of what a company is doing, accompanied by the figures that are available, seems to us to be perfectly appropriate if public reporting is the name of the game.

Questions of measures and norms

We know a fair number of companies that have taken one or both of these first two steps — inventorying activities and assessing costs. Some have done it as part of a social audit activity; others, for the more straightforward reason that management wanted to know what the company was doing. None found that this was a trivial effort, and a number found that the mere assemblage of information as to what the company was doing was already of value to management.

However, we doubt that managers who take the concept of a social audit seriously will want to stop at this point. They will want to make an assessment of how well they are doing in their various social activities. Since this seems to us to be an inevitable direction for the social audit, we would encourage this step — but with moderation, because assessing performance is beset with grave difficulties. Assessment in the first audit should be limited to only several of the most important activities.

Here, we must distinguish between cases where true measures of performance are available and cases where they are not (we shall discuss the second of these possibilities when we describe the process audit).

Now a true performance measure is a measure of the ultimate result that an activity is intended to accomplish. We have already identified the two types of program areas for which performance measures are most likely to be available — pollution and employment. Some of these performance measures may be the fallout of the "easily available" data which are noted at the inventory stage, but such data are bound to be incomplete; a company is very likely to have data available on emissions into the air and water, for example, but it is not equally likely to know about its contribution to solid waste. Personnel records, too, will vary with respect to the availability of information about the employment of minorities.

Norms, also, are required, and once again the picture is cloudy and uneven. There are laws of various kinds by which to judge one's levels of emissions into air and water, but not for emissions of solid waste. Nor are there likely to be industrywide norms of performance unless the industry in question has been studied by the Council for Economic Priorities or some similar organization.

Some commentators suggest that one should judge pollution performance by what is technologically feasible, and this may work out in some cases; however, cost/benefit trade-offs are only too likely to crop up. Again, companies can get industry norms for the employment status of minorities from the Equal Employment Opportunities Commission, but these industrywide norms may have to be adjusted to the idiosyncracies of the communities in which a company's installations are located.

However, while it may be possible to get adequate performance measures and norms for some of a company's social programs, for others it will be difficult to the point of virtual impossibility. The results of a community development program, for example, perhaps will not be clear until sometime in the future, and a particular company's contributions to these developments will be hard to isolate even then. Again, management might be satisfied with judging a program for training the hard-core unemployed by the number of candidates who graduate from the program and secure employment, but management might also view these numbers as only intermediate measures of the long-term effects which it regards as crucial.

Wherever the auditing team and management feel that there are no adequate performance measurs of a social program — and this is likly to be true of almost all service programs — we advocate a *process* audit, which we shall now describe. We have not yet seen such a process audit completed. What we propose takes as its model such innovative efforts of the accounting profession as the management audit.[2]

The Process Audit

The first step in a process audit should be an assessment of the circumstances under which each social program being audited came into being. (We consciously avoid saying "the reason" for the program, since in many instances the circumstance is likely to be less rational than the term "reason" implies.) While this search into origins may at first glance look like navel gazing, it is likely to be crucial for informed future decision making. A company that does not know how it gets into things is likely to get into things it does not want to do.

The second step is to explicate the goals of the program — that is, to produce a statement of what it is intended to accomplish.

The third is to spell out the rationale behind the activity. A company should specify what it proposes to do to attain the goals, and why it thinks this set of actions will achieve them.

The final step in the process audit is to describe what is actually being done as opposed to what the rationale says ought to be done. We assume that this description will include any relevant quantitative measures, such as numbers and types of persons served, and any available intermediate measures of performance, such as proportions of defaults on loans.

The goal of such a process audit is to assemble the information that will make it possible for a person to intelligently assess the program, to decide whether he agrees with its goals, to decide whether the

---

2 See Olin C. Snellgrave, "The Management: Organizational Guidance System," *Management Review,* March 1972, pp. 41–45.

rationale is appropriate to the goals, and to judge whether the actual implementation promises to attain those goals satisfactorily.

Process audits are most likely to be appropriate for service programs, which are notoriously hard to evaluate but around which considerable amounts of expertise develop. Thus appropriate norms for process audits are likely to be standards of best practice. Where it seems in order, then, a process audit might be conducted in part by one or another expert in the area, especially since companies vary considerably in their relevant in-house capabilities.

Even where the purpose of the adult is just to clarify internal decision making, a company may want to bring in an outside expert to help define the relevant factors to assess and to make the final evaluation of a program. When such expertise is brought to bear, management can better judge whether it is satisfied with present activities, whether it wants one or another changed and improved, and whether it wants to shift its efforts among activities.

Once all the above information is assembled for management scrutiny, and possibly for presentation to the public (an option always open to management), we would regard the first round of a social audit to be completed. It seems likely that the public will be uninterested in the first step of the process audit we have proposed — namely, the circumstances under which the company undertook the activity (though there may be instances where this is relevant). However, the remaining steps develop information that would be helpful and acceptable to the public in its evaluation of the company's performance.

There are many ways in which an initial process will be incomplete and imperfect, compared with what a company might aspire to later. It may be bulky and cumbersome. The format will be unstandardized. Only a portion of the company's social impact will be assessed. And of that which is assessed, only the most important activities will be given any treatment beyond bare identification, description, and specification of costs. Further, such technical problems as assessment of true costs and performance measurement will be handled in a fairly rough and ready manner.

But the show will be on the road. Management will be in a considerably better position to make decisions and take actions. It will also know whether it wants to report to the public at this stage; and if it does, it will have a respectable report from which to work. Furthermore:

The foundations for future auditing will have been laid.

The nucleus of an auditing team will have been trained.

The controller will have had his first taste of the problem of assessing the true costs of social programs.

Management will have a realistic basis for estimating what an audit costs and is worth.

Hopefully, the fears of corporate executives will be surfaced and assuaged.

To the extent that management thinks it desirable, it can build expanded ambitions into future audits.

The very fact that management has undertaken an honest, systematic effort will be a plus.

The reader will note that we have said nothing about the relationship between responsibility and profitability. This is intentional. We have specifically excluded from our version of a first audit any attempt to assess the contribution of social activities to the profitability of a company. We believe that this exercise is possible only in the case of a minority of such activities, and that the attempt to complete this exercise, while having a certain appeal to technical virtuosity, is likely to divert attention from the more straightforward objectives we have proposed — namely, management information and public reporting.

The future needs

We close on the question of whether a company can carry out such an audit on itself. As the reader would expect, there is not a yes-or-no answer to this question. It is better to rephrase the question and ask whether the company can benefit from outside help. In fact, at present, there is not much outside help to turn to. Only a few consultants have had any experience in social auditing, and the experience of even those few is limited.

Our conclusion is that a certain amount of outside help can be useful both as a source of discipline and direction, and as a spur to keep the audit moving. Most companies have had trouble on these scores. Outsiders can also supply technical help on such matters as assembling true costs, preparing information for distribution to management and the public, and the process audit.

Eventually, we assume, if the social audit develops viably, the accounting profession will be centrally involved, both in setting up systems to gather data and in attesting to the truth of the data for the purpose of improving its credibility. This is already a matter of considerable interest in the accounting profession, but at this point everyone in the race is standing on the same starting line. The most important task now is to start running. Only in that way will we learn what the track is really like.

42 Components of a Social Audit of the Corporation

William T. Greenwood

Business and society issues-conflicts have continually increased through the decades of the 1950s, 1960s and especially in the 1970s. As early as 1953 a social audit of the corporation was recommended as a periodic examination to evaluate corporate performance from a social viewpoint by Howard R. Bowden.[1] This was one of seven major recommendations made by Bowen to increase the effectiveness of social responsibility by business managers and was directed toward the appraisal of company policies, to be made by independent, outside experts. In the same decade a social audit of the enterprise was called for by Fred H. Blum for application to a company with the intent of finding out how well the satisfaction of basic human needs of employees was being achieved.[2] He emphasized the need for unity and integrity of the organization in providing meaningful work and more democratic controls over the workers. His social audit focused attention on people, with human values as cost items, and made these human values central to the organization.

In the decade of the sixties another call was made for the measurement of the social performance of business by Theodore J. Kreps.[3] He sought to identify the irresponsible actions of business that should be substituted with social responsibility measurements of the social performance of business. Using a basic economic orientation, he evaluated different types of business, industrial, economic, and public policies in an attempt to measure the social performance of business. But it was not until the decade of the seventies that a large number of calls were made, not only for a social audit, but for its immediate application, with the implicit and explicit threat that if these audits were not performed periodically by measurement, some external group would impose them upon business.

In 1971 a plea was made for a double audit of business, both

---

[1] Howard R. Bowen, *Social Responsibilities of the Businessman*, Harper Bros., New York, 1953.
[2] Fred H. Blum, "Social Audit of the Enterprise," *Harvard Business Review*, March–April 1958, pp. 77–86.
[3] T. J. Kreps, "Measurement of the Social Performance of Business," *Annals of the American Academy*, September 1962, pp. 20–31.

fiscal and social.[4] It emphasized the fact that profits should never be the sole function or goal of business. At this time the president of Arthur D. Little, Inc. made the prediction that business cannot persuade the public that it has been a good corporate citizen without the use of some kind of social audit. He also predicted that business would soon have to submit to such an instrument.

In the fall of 1971 a series of front-page articles in the *Wall Street Journal* examined a number of the social problems of business. One article in these stories dramatically made the point that while "social accounting" did not yet exist, business was anxious to present in objective terms what benefits their enterprises did contribute to society. Since profit and loss statements do not presently allow for social performance measurements, it was predicted by a senior vice president and comptroller of the Bank of America that within three to five years annual reports will be required to include data on a company's social outlays. Some authorities suggested complete "social audits" of business by outside consultants within a decade.[5] With references to the review of internal corporate policies and corporate social policies, the stage appeared to be set for business to either develop a social audit and apply it to themselves, or have it applied to external social groups or institutions in the immediate future.

Specific areas of corporate responsibility were cited in legislative hearings by Senator Patman to curb corporate wrongdoings.[6] These included conflicts of interest by directors and management, standards for representation on boards of directors, corporate disclosure requirements, etc. By this time the question of whether or not business should adopt a social audit was under serious debate in the literature, and while no significant consensus had been achieved, trends seemed irreversible toward the development and application of such an instrument. Even if such a social audit or evaluation of social performance of the business was to be developed, many questions remain as to what it would do, how it would be developed, by whom it would be applied, etc. One request has been made for an immediate annual evaluation of a socio-economic operating statement of the firm which would include the organization's relations with people, relations with its environment, and relations with its product.[7] But the major concern seems to be with developing such an instrument and applying it immediately.

---

[4] B. L. Masse, "Next Step for Business: Social Audit," *America,* April 3, 1971.

[5] B. L. Masse, "Puzzled Businessmen Ponder New Methods of Measuring Success," *Wall Street Journal,* December 9, 1971, pp. 1 and 25.

[6] B. L. Masse, "Patmans Panel May Hold Hearings Soon on Ways to Curb Corporate Wrongdoing," *Wall Street Journal,* January 3, 1972.

[7] David F. Linowes, "Let's Get on with the Social Audit: A Specific Proposal, *Business and Society Review/Innovation,* 4 (Winter 1973–73) 39–42.

Components of a Social Audit

The components of a social audit of the corporation are outlined in the Appendix. In this audit, those business and society issue-conflicts that have prevailed over the past three decades of time, and especially those that have received the greatest attention in the seventies provide the sequential "factor content" for a social audit. Fifty factor issues are included in the audit, and structured in a descending order in which they might be logically appraised and redefined in an annual social audit of the corporation. They are briefly described in the following paragraphs.

Issue-conflicts of the free enterprise system include problems of management rights and duties, profit and social goals, and other broad issues affecting the total economic system.[8] Corporate policies defined for these problems provide general guidelines for corporate practice and programs in response to protest movements and groups, especially in the present decade.[9] The perennial problems of "organization person" practices and nonconformist individuals and groups require management leadership styles and corporate policies to enhance the development and utilization of individual human and organization potentials.[10] This extends readily into labor-management relations practices and policies that should tend to improve these relations in both the long and shortrun.[11]

Many ethical problems of the past have prevailed throughout the twentieth century. Even today specific unethical practices are so widespread as to require particular corporate policies, if not written codes of ethics.[12] At the heart of ethical and unethical practices is the fundamental question of management's acceptance or rejection of the social responsibility concept, and the organizational responsibility assignment to insure the continued "management" of corporate social policies.[13] When all ethical and social responsibility problems are seen in complete array, the need for their inclusion in the definition of corporate goals and policies, if not their summary treatment in corporate

[8] David F. Linowes, "Profit Motive, Social Problems Will Dove-Tail," *Industry Week,* March 23, 1970, pp. 12–13.

[9] H. Ford, "Revolution in Public Expectations," *Public Relations Journal,* 26 (October 1970), 16–18.

[10] H. Ford, "Symposium: Workers Participation in Management: An International Comparison," *Industrial Relations,* (February, 1970), 117–214.

[11] D. W. Ewing, "Who Wants Corporate Democracy?" *Harvard Business Review,* 49 (September 1971), 12–14.

[12] R. M. Fulmer, "Business Ethics: Present and Future," *Personnel Administration,* 34 (September 1971), 48–55.

[13] Moskowitz, "Companies Must Take Social Duties Seriously," *Advertising Age,* September 27, 1971, p. 86.

creeds or philosophies, is readily seen.[14] When overall corporate policies are related to strategic corporate practices, including those basic comparative-competitive advantages of the corporation, they may then be compiled in an integrated corporate image for public relations guidelines in the corporation.[15] The implementation of overall corporate public relations policies must not be accomplished by translating them into action, or into "process" programs, as in corporate involvement in social action "community" programs.[16] Since the "community" may be local, state, regional, national, and/or international, this may well encompass the majority of corporate social responsibilities.

The increasing trend of business and society issue-conflicts, especially in the present decade, indicate that future conflicts must be forecasted and "managed" if business is to minimize these conflicts in the future.[17] Therefore corporate long-range planning must include corporate responsibility assignments to provide the boards of directors with decision information on future business-society problems.

Social Audit Rating System

The sequential "factor content," as described in the prior paragraphs, contain those business and society issue-conflicts treated most significantly, most frequently, and most recently in the business periodical literature of the past twenty-five years. These strategic issue-conflict rating factors are compiled under ten headings in the audit, and applied under a 10,000-point rating system in the appraisal of the "percent of industry and corporate *potential* achieved" by individual firms in the performance of the social (responsibilities) functions of business. The system provides ten alternative ratings of 0, 10, 20, 30–100 "percent of industry and corporate potential." For each of the fifty social "factors" in the audit, the corporation may estimate the degree of percent to which it has achieved its potential in relation to its own past performance, and in relation to the degree to which major firms within its industry have established practices. Since all of the fifty factors may not apply to any one corporation, or some factors may be significantly different in their proportionate importance to the firm, a provision is made for weighting each of the question areas. For example, the *average* weight of a total of a possible 1,000 points is assigned to each of the

[14] G. A. Steiner, "Changing Managerial Philosophies," *Business Horizons*, 14 (June 1971), 5–10.

[15] G. A. Steiner, "Companies Face an Identity Crisis," *Business Week*, February 20, 1971, pp. 52–55.

[16] G. A. Steiner, "Pollution and the Profit Motive," *Business Week*, April 11, 1970, p. 82.

[17] H. B. Palmer, "New Imperatives for Tomorrow's Policy-Makers," *Conference Board Record*, 7 (January 1970), 68–72.

ten categories. But this 1,000 may be changed from 0 to 2,000 or 4,000, with the provision that the total points will equal 10,000 points. As the weighting may be varied for each of the ten major sections, so may the weightings be varied for each of the five questions found in the ten sections. This provides a flexibility for assigning the proportionate importance of each of the factors to each individual corporation. The 10,000-point summary provides a total that is readily translated into a percentage of "the extent to which the corporation has achieved a *reasonable* potential of its present day social responsibilities of the firm and of its industry."

Two major findings evolved from the research in the development of this audit[:] (1) the necessity of specific organizational responsibility assignments for each of the major sectors to insure that performance will be measured, and that individuals will be held accountable within the corporation for their performance versus public relations window dressing[;] and (2) corporate social policies will be defined in detail, and implemented as a means of insuring company-wide consistency in the handling of future issue-conflicts of the corporation.

Other Perspectives on the Social Audit

Alternatives to the social audit include human asset accounting, developed by Rensis Likert in the mesurement of social contributions, and also a social balance sheet as developed by Abt Associates, delineating social assets available to the organization, and also the social commitments, obligations, and equity.[18] It does not appear that the state of this art has been developed to the point that it would have widespread application to a majority of corporations. Others have recommended that the corporate social audit include an inventory of corporate activities with social impact, explaining how they were developed, providing informal evaluation of those in progress, and assessing ways in which social programs may be meshed with objectives of the firm and society. Bauer and Fenn have cited this, and also their skepticism concerning the conversion of these social activities to dollars on the balance sheet, and instead emphasize what they call "process audits," which will delineate what is being done, and how it is being done in formal programs in the corporation versus measurements of their accomplishment.[19] In effect, they say that the state of the art is in such an early stage, that we are still in the learning process and therefore should focus our programs on a "process audit" resulting

---

[18] H. B. Palmer, "A New Twist to People Accounting," *Business Week,* October 21, 1972, p. 67.

[19] H. B. Palmer, "The First Attempts At a Corporate Social Audit," *Business Week,* September 23, 1972, pp. 88–92.

from explicit corporate policies. Other audits now available include "An Audit of Corporate Social Responsibility" by Social Research, Inc., which attempts to assess corporate accomplishment against society's current expectations.[20] This includes a statement of public beliefs about the value of corporate actions and attempts to delineate units of "social values."

The social audit of the corporation in Appendix I hopefully provides the first step of a comprehensive audit approach, enabling the firm to systematically evaluate the major contemporary business and society issues-conflicts and to also arrive at some quantitative or percentage assessment of their actual versus potential performance. It is intended that the audit will provide a control guide agains the potential polarity of "no performance" or activity on the part of the corporation, or some significant deviation or exception from past corporate or present industry practices, perhaps in control limit terms of 10 to 20 percent variations.

---

[20] H. B. Palmer, "Audit Now Available To Measure Corporate Social Responsibility," *The Marketing News,* March 15, 1972, pp. 1 and 4.

Bibliography

Blau, J. "True Meaning of Capitalism." *Commercial and Financial Chronicle,* September 2, 1974, p. 4.

———. "Can Capitalism Survive." *Time,* July 14, 1975, pp. 52–64.

Cole, Edward N. "Management Priorities for the 1970's." *Michigan Business Review,* 22 (July 1970), 1–6.

Corson, J. J. "The Great-What-Is-It: The Social Audit." *Nation's Business,* 60 (July 1972), 54–56.

———. "First Attempts At a Social Audit." *Business Week,* September 23, 1972, pp. 88–89.

Gordon, T. J. "America's Social Crisis: Future Perspectives." *Conference Board Record,* 8 (July 1971), 33–35.

Humble, J. "Getting Ready for the Social Responsibility Audit," *Director,* February 1973, pp. 176–180.

Lindsay, F. A. "Management and the Total Environment." *Columbia Journal of World Business,* 5 (January 1970), 19–25.

Linowes, D. F. "Approach to Socio-Economic Accounting." *Conference Board Record,* 9 (November 1972), 58–61.

MacNamee, H. "Business Leadership in Social Change." *Conference Board Record,* 8 (July 1971), 25–32.

———. "New Group Offers Data on World Environment." *Industry Week,* December 2, 1974, p. 26ff.

Reed, William K. "Our Future Business Environment." *Conference Board Record,* 7 (June 1970), 57–61.

Steiner, George. "Should Business Adopt the Social Audit?" *Conference Board Record,* 9 (May 1972), 7–10.

Appendix

A Social Audit of the Corporation

I. The Free Enterprise System: Promotion, Defense, and Preservation by Socially Responsible Management	Rating		Weight		Total
To What Extent:					
have management rights and responsibilities been excessively restrictive, and have they also been defined, communicated, and reviewed for the organization?	3	×	20	=	60
have long-run profit and social goals been integrated in line with legitimate protests from society?	4	×	20	=	80
do corporate policies prevent corporate practices leading to antitrust violations and other governmental regulations?	6	×	20	=	120
are profits and productivity gains shared equitably with shareholders, management, labor, consumers, and society?	5	×	20	=	100
are natural resources appreciably used, and excess waste and depletion avoided through corporate policies?	8	×	20	=	160
				Total	520

II. Responses to Protest Movements and Groups	Rating		Weight		Total
To What Extent:					
do corporate policies provide for systematic handling of consumer complaints with designated organizational responsibility and as agenda items at executive committee meetings?	4	×	20	=	80

are policy guidelines in writing concerning product information, quality, warranties, and so forth.	6	× 16	=	96
are advertising policies modified in response to consumer complaints concerning truth in advertising, inoffensive statements, and so on.	5	× 12	=	60
are the protests of youths and minorities responded to with specific policy interpretations, definitions, or revisions?	4	× 14	=	56
are cost reductions partially shared with consumer groups via price decreases?	2	× 18	=	36
			Total	328

III. Organization, Management, Group, and Individual Conflicts

Rating   Weight   Total

To What Extent:

is the potential of each person evaluated, developed, and utilized to the benefit of *both* the organization and the individual?

is the organizational structure modified to provide meaningful work experiences to satisfy basic human needs, as well as the efficiency and control goals of organization?

is an organizational climate development that fosters creative-innovative contributions rather than unnecessary conformity and "organization men"?

is a management leadership style applied to organization, group, and individual needs according to the particular situation?

are procedures for "appeals systems" (or organizational justice) made available to all employees to better resolve organizational conflicts?

IV. More Effective Labor-Management Relations

Rating   Weight   Total

To What Extent:

is collective bargaining (Wagner-National Labor Relations Act of 1935) understood and recognized as the "law of the land," and as a legitimate individual need and right in seeking a balance of power in employer-employee relations?

do labor and management recognize their joint responsibility to society and the potential results of collective bargaining, such as inflation?

are specific policies defined for guiding all corporate managers in improving labor-management relations and curbing antiunion attitudes and practices?

do corporate policies ensure "fair employment practices" in line with the Civil Rights Act provisions for minorities (race, age, sex, creed, and color) for equal job opportunities, wages, promotions, management opportunities, and so on?

is a job security policy formulated to provide for transfers, retraining, and new technologies, automated operations, and so on?

V. Ethical Problems — Prevention and Control	Rating	Weight	Total

To What Extent:

have corporate policies been defined to resolve "conflict of interest" problems?

does a written code of ethics provide guidelines against unethical practices, and also provide positive ethical guidelines and goals for management decisions?

have corporate policies and practices been checked against U.S. Senate (Patman) hearings and legislative proposal "topics" (see *Wall Street Journal,* January 3, 1972, for example)?

have problems of price fixing, monopolistic practices, and noncompliance with requirements of federal agencies been avoided or minimized by specific corporate policies?

are moral and ethical practices of the corporation systematically and periodically evaluated, with assigned responsibility within the organization?

VI. Social Responsibilities — Recognition and Acceptance	Rating	Weight	Total

To What Extent:

is the social responsibility concept accepted and implemented in your corporation?

do social responsibility policies provide some check and balance against misuse of power of superiors over subordinates?

are social costs passed on to the consumer or shared equitably by all groups with vested interests (stockholders, employees, consumers, and society)?

has specific responsibility been assigned to an individual for administration of corporate social policies?

have you in the past engaged in some form of annual "social audit" for appraising the degree to which social responsibilities of the firm are met?

VII. Corporate Planning: Goals, Policies, Creeds,   **Rating**   **Weight**   **Total**
and Philosophies

> *To What Extent:*

do corporate goals and policies include "professional management" responsibilities to society?

does the Board of Directors or Executive Committee assign priorities for corporate and social goals and policies?

are the legitimate interests and complaints of stockholders, employees, consumers, suppliers, and society included in the corporate planning process?

has a corporate creed or philosophy been written and communicated to reconcile corporate and national social goal conflicts?

are short- and long-run profit maximization goal conflicts reconciled by balanced mixes of corporate and social goals?

VIII. Corporate Public Relations Policy   **Rating**   **Weight**   **Total**
Guidelines

> *To What Extent:*

have you developed a positive rather than negative "social image" of the corporation in view of current antibusiness social protests?

are business-public conflicts prevented by the identification and integration of corporate strategic goals with the goals of the many interest and pressure groups?

are public relations releases made of business "position statements" in response to social protests?

do you encourage individual employee participation in political activities rather than exert corporate influence on particular positions?

are there written policies pertaining to corporate gifts for social needs (for example, monetary contributions of up to 5 percent of net profits and nonmonetary contributions like advising minority business people and providing release time for employee participation in urban programs.)

IX. Corporate Involvement in Social Action   **Rating**   **Weight**   **Total**
Programs

> *To What Extent:*

is your participation in local community programs provided for in written corporate policies?

is your corporation involved in major urban problem-solving programs (for example, urban renewal, low-cost housing, minority enterprises)?

does your corporation participate in the solving of state, regional, industry, national, and international "community problems"?

have you defined new policies and initiated new programs to minimize corporate damage to the ecological environment resulting from air and water pollution, trash and waste disposal and so forth?

do research and development programs include estimates of social costs such as pollution, resulting from new technologies, processes, products, and packagings, and are provisions made for product redesign and waste recycling to minimize these problems where applicable?

X. Future Responsibilities, Plans, and Programs	**Rating**	**Weight**	**Total**

To What Extent:

does corporate long-range planning and forecasting include projections of future business-society conflicts?

are plans being made for cooperation with governmental units (federal, state, and local) to better resolve conflicts in the future?

are specific organizational responsibilities assigned to ensure corporate participation and leadership in programs to resolve business-society conflicts in the future?

do corporate long-range plans and policies provide more flexible means of adapting to changing social pressures and issues?

are long-range corporate goals and policies reevaluated in order to be better reconciled with national social goals of the future (for example, a greater emphasis on the quality of life rather than growth)?